The Greenwood encyclopedia
of folktales and fairy tales /

THE GREENWOOD ENCYCLOPEDIA OF FOLKTALES AND FAIRY TALES

ADVISORY BOARD MEMBERS

THE GREENWOOD ENCYCLOPEDIA OF FOLKTALES AND FAIRY TALES

Volume 3: Q–Z

Edited by
Donald Haase

GREENWOOD PRESS
Westport, Connecticut · London

Library of Congress Cataloging-in-Publication Data

The Greenwood encyclopedia of folktales and fairy tales / edited by Donald Haase.
    p. cm.
  Includes bibliographical references and index.
  ISBN-13: 978-0-313-33441-2 ((set) : alk. paper)
  ISBN-13: 978-0-313-33442-9 ((vol. 1) : alk. paper)
  ISBN-13: 978-0-313-33443-6 ((vol. 2) : alk. paper)
  ISBN-13: 978-0-313-33444-3 ((vol. 3) : alk. paper)
  1. Folklore—Encyclopedias. 2. Tales—Encyclopedias. 3. Fairy
tales—Encyclopedias. I. Haase, Donald.
  GR74.G73 2008
  398.203—dc22   2007031698

British Library Cataloguing in Publication Data is available.

Library of Congress Catalog Card Number: 2007031698

ISBN-13: 978-0-313-33441-2 (set)
       978-0-313-33442-9 (vol. 1)
       978-0-313-33443-6 (vol. 2)
       978-0-313-33444-3 (vol. 3)

First published in 2008

Greenwood Press, 88 Post Road West, Westport, CT 06881
An imprint of Greenwood Publishing Group, Inc.
www.greenwood.com

Printed in the United States of America

∞™

The paper used in this book complies with the
Permanent Paper Standard issued by the National
Information Standards Organization (Z39.48–1984).

10 9 8 7 6 5 4 3 2 1

CONTENTS

LIST OF ENTRIES

Volume 2: G–P

Q

Queen

Queens appear in many different folktales and serve in diverse roles. In most cases, queens fall into one of three categories: protagonist, serving as the focus of action; antagonist and villain, acting against the hero in some way; or secondary figure, such as a helper figure, who assists the hero in the background, often acting in complicity with a **king** character. The queen's role and significance are informed by her royal status, which conveys not only a high social status but also authority and power.

Because of the social status and power associated with being queen, folktales and fairy tales frequently describe a character's ascent to queenship to depict an individual's development or rise to power. This key aspect of queenship is expressed by Vladimir **Propp**'s thirty-first **function**: The Hero Marries and Ascends to the Throne. Although Propp's label for this function refers to a male protagonist (hero), fairy tales also end with the heroine marrying into royalty or being upgraded from **princess** to queen. For example, in Jacob and Wilhelm **Grimm**'s "Rumpelstiltskin" (ATU 500, The Name of the Supernatural Helper) a poor miller's daughter—assisted initially by a **magic helper**—ascends from her low social status to become queen. In the Grimms' version of ATU 440 (The **Frog King** or Iron Henry), a young princess, who is a mere child at the beginning, by the end of the tale has married a young king, implicitly becoming his queen. In terms of its significance, achieving the status of queen can, on the one hand, be interpreted as the lower class's expression of political wish fulfillment (according to **sociohistorical approaches**) or, on the other hand, as symbolic of an individual's having reached a new stage of maturation or psychological development (according to **psychological approaches**).

In her role as protagonist, the queen is often in peril, for royal status frequently brings with it a degree of danger. In an example of the **tale type** The Clever Girl and the King (ATU 875B), the story of **Sheherazade** from the *Arabian Nights*, a king kills each of the women he marries until one tricks him into delaying her execution by telling stories. In tales such as "Rumpelstiltskin" (ATU 500), a woman has an impossible task placed before her. When she succeeds with the aid of a supernatural helper, she becomes queen but is also put in peril of losing her firstborn child until she finds a way to trick the helper.

Peril also comes to protagonist queens in the form of false accusations. The figure of the wrongly accused queen demonstrates her significant relation to virtue. In tales identified as

Our Lady's Child (ATU 710), a queen is accused of infanticide. In those belonging to the type known as The Prince Whose Wishes Always Come True (ATU 652), the queen is accused of eating her own son. In the Crescentia tale type (ATU 712), an empress is accused of adultery and murder. The queen's association with virtue is also underlined when her virtue is tested. In tales related to the type Griselda (ATU 887), a king tests the virtue of his queen by pretending to kill her sons and marry her daughter. Like many protagonist queens, she remains virtuous and is rewarded in the end.

There are other types of protagonist queens. Some versions of ATU 451, The Maiden Who Seeks Her **Brothers**, feature a protagonist who is a queen. In certain versions of ATU 514, The Shift of Sex, a queen pretends that her daughter is actually her son. Tale type ATU 459, The Make-Believe Son (Daughter), features a queen who, when cast out, invents a child from nothing to reconcile with her kingly husband. Finally, in ATU 460A, The Journey to God (Fortune), a ruler asks why the kingdom cannot be enlarged by war. The answer to the riddle is that the ruler is a queen who should instead expand her realm through **marriage**.

While many queens in folktales are protagonists and a focus of virtue, queens appear just as regularly as villains and embodiments of evil. One way of distinguishing villainous queens is to consider the target of their villainy. Some evil queens target their kings. The King and the Lamia (ATU 411) and The Magic Bird-Heart (ATU 567) are tale types that feature kings marrying unwisely, in the first case to an evil snake woman and in the second to a woman who steals the magic with which the king ascended the throne. In The Unfaithful Queen (ATU 871A), a queen cheats on her husband and subsequently kills him.

Some villainous queens target their own children or stepchildren. One of the most infamous of these appears in tales of **Snow White** (ATU 709), in which an evil queen targets her beautiful daughter out of jealousy of her beauty. The queen in Walt **Disney**'s animated version of *Snow White and the Seven Dwarfs* (1937) has become in popular consciousness a dominant visual embodiment of this villainous character. However, the jealous queen in tales of Snow White is far from alone. In tales of the type known as The Son of the King and the Son of the Smith (ATU 920), a queen commands the **death** of her son when he calls her a whore. In The Princess Who Murdered Her Child (ATU 781), a queen kills her own offspring, but her crime is revealed by a bird. The Goldener tale type (ATU 314) portrays a queen who wants to kill the **prince**, in some versions her son, and in others her stepson. In tales of the type Born from Fruit (Fish) (ATU 705A), a queen mutilates her daughter-in-law and disguises herself to sleep with her own son. Perhaps the most gruesome type is ATU 462, The Outcast Queens and the **Ogress** Queen. In this tale, a king with multiple wives casts them out and blinds them, and the blinded queens resort to eating their own children, all except the youngest.

Some queens fit the villainous model not due to specific malfeasance but based on their antagonistic role in the story. In versions of the Princess on the Pea (ATU 704), the queen tests possible brides for her son the prince by placing a pea underneath many mattresses. In A Young Woman Disguised as a Man Is Wooed by the Queen (ATU 514**), the queen is not so much a direct villain but an obstacle to heroine's plans.

Sometimes a queen in a story is neither protagonist nor antagonist, but simply part of the tale. These queens can be important to the plot of the story, as in Oedipus (ATU 931) or Gregory on the Stone (ATU 933), where the protagonist marries his **mother**, the queen. However, in these cases, the queen is neither protagonist nor antagonist, neither heroine nor villain. In The Princess in the Coffin (ATU 307), a childless royal couple makes a tragically misinterpreted wish. **Sleeping Beauty** (ATU 410) similarly features a royal couple whose folly leads to the suffering of the protagonist. Peau d'Asne (ATU 510B) revolves around a queen who requires that her husband remarry only a woman with certain physical characteristics. While these queens are implicated in the suffering of the protagonist, they are not directly villainous.

Queens also play a significant role in **literary fairy tale**s, **fantasy**, and other modern forms of fairy tale. For example, Victorian-era literary fairy tales by British authors often depicted queens to engage questions of **gender**, female power, and other contemporary political issues. Queens, both evil and benevolent, figure in works of authors of fairy tales and fantasy, from Hans Christian **Andersen**'s Snow Queen ("Sneedronningen," 1844) and Lewis **Carroll**'s Queen of Hearts (*Alice's Adventures in Wonderland*, 1865) to C. S. **Lewis**'s White Witch (Queen of Narnia) and the queens that populate **film and video** from Disney's *Snow White* to its antithesis *Shrek*. The queen's survival as a recognizable figure in contemporary fairy tales attests to the character's continuing importance as a cultural symbol. *See also* False Bride; Politics.

Further Readings: Brown, Eric C. "The Influence of Queen Victoria on England's Literary Fairy Tale." *Marvels & Tales* 13 (1999): 31–51; Lesko, Leonard H. "Three Late Egyptian Stories Reconsidered." *Egyptological Studies in Honor of Richard A. Parker Presented on the Occasion of His 78th Birthday, December 10, 1983.* Edited by Leonard H. Lesko. Hanover, NH: University Press of New England for Brown University Press, 1986. 98–103; Okanlawon, Tunde. "Royalty in the Oral Literature of the Niger Delta." *International Folklore Review: Folklore Studies from Overseas* 7 (1990): 8–9.

B. Grantham Aldred

R

Race and Ethnicity

Neither race nor ethnicity can be easily defined. In contemporary scholarly discourse, both are generally seen as social constructions rather than physical realities. Race is considered the adaptation of physical markers of body type to symbolize social conflict and social hierarchy, and ethnicity is viewed as the adaptation of broader markers of culture to do the same work. Their historical definitions have often given them a greater material reality. They have, in the past, been theorized as real qualitative differences between groups of people—definite hierarchies of civilization, savagery, and barbarism that have justified white European domination. The concepts are often underutilized in contemporary scholarship on fairy tales and folktales, but their prominence in culture at large has lent them an important role in understanding both the content of folk narrative and the way in which it has been used.

Because these concepts are so visible, the United States is an obvious locale for studying race and ethnicity in folk narrative. Folk narrative collections have had a significant presence in discussions of race in the United States, both commenting on and helping to create some of the dominant currents in race thinking. In the nineteenth century, white authors and folklore **collectors** like Joel Chandler **Harris**, J. A. Macon, and even Alcée Fortier, who published extensively in the *Journal of American Folklore*, made use of African American folk narratives to reinforce race-based perceptions of blacks as lazy and superstitious, or to generate race-based fantasies of a black population not only forgiving for prior slavery but also amicable toward their supposed white betters and eager to be dominated once more. By the second decade of the twentieth century, African American authors and collectors such as Zora Neale **Hurston** used folk narrative and its materials for the purposes of empowerment rather than degradation. Hurston and others sought to demonstrate the richness of African American culture and folklore and to emphasize its resilience in the face of oppression.

In more recent times, folk narrative has been no less present in discussions of these two notions. In literature, African American writers like Toni Morrison and Alice **Walker**, as well as Native American writers such as Leslie Marmon **Silko** and N. Scott **Momaday**, have utilized folktale **motif**s in their writing, in part to demonstrate continuity and identity with their racial or ethnic heritages. In *The **Woman Warrior*** (1976), Maxine Hong Kingston does much the same thing, discussing the Chinese American immigrant experience through the lens of Chinese folktale motifs. In a more scholarly vein, anthropologists and folklorists such as Barre Toelken and Dell Hymes have begun to examine the relationship between folk narrative and Native American culture, exploring the significance of narrative **performance** in individual and group identity, while as early as 1960, Roger Abrahams, Bruce Jackson, John Szwed, and others did similar work with the culture of urban blacks.

But these issues are not present only in the United States. In Europe, too, race and ethnicity have historically claimed a centrality in the study of folktales and fairy tales. On the continent, the same Herderian nationalist impulses that spurred folklore research in Germany, Scandinavia, and Finland—impulses central to the creation of the **historic-geographic method** and folklore collections from those of Elias Lönnrot and Evald **Tang Kristensen** to those of Jacob and Wilhelm **Grimm**—also provided the theoretical basis for institutionalized racism like that of National Socialism. In England, many of the scholars engaged in the study of folk narrative were also at the vanguard of racism and ethnocentricity. E. B. Tylor and Andrew **Lang** were proponents of a unilinear evolutionary theory that divided the world into civilization, savagery, and barbarism, with white male Europeans at the top of that hierarchy, and **peasant**s, **women**, and dark-skinned, exotic "others" at the bottom. Friedrich Max **Müller**, meanwhile, argued for a historical understanding of **myth** that was inseparable from his racially segregated, Aryan-centric schema for the world.

These issues are prominent, too, in the actual content of European folk narrative. In Estonian folktales and **legend**s, the **devil** is often portrayed as a German nobleman. Likewise, Scandinavian folk narratives often accuse the Finns and the Sami of witchcraft. As early as the fourteenth century, literary adaptations of folktales such as Geoffrey **Chaucer**'s "Prioress's Tale" have painted Jews as an evil and mysterious ethnic other—as murderers of children or, as in the case of William **Shakespeare**'s *The Merchant of Venice*, heartless usurers—while for nearly as long, similar narratives have portrayed the Roma as dirty **thieves**. Racial and ethnic tensions do travel two ways however, and the Roma, in turn, have often depicted the white European majority as dirty and easily duped, while the Jews, though less frequently, have done more or less the same.

Race and ethnicity are commonly perceived as solely matters of skin tone and physiognomy. Even in the most progressive scholarly and popular sources, discussions begin and end with issues of black and white. And while such an understanding of these issues is seemingly warranted looking just at the North American case, understandings of these two concepts both in European folktales and in historical thinking about them demonstrate the degree to which it is inaccurate. Racism may in fact manifest itself across gradients of skin tone, as in the United States, but just as often, it is as much a matter of what is signified as what does the signifying—as much a matter of hierarchies of class and power as of outward appearances.
See also African American Tales; Anti-Semitism; Nationalism; Native American Tales; Négritude, Créolité, and Folktale.

Further Readings: Jackson, Bruce, ed. *The Negro and his Folklore in Nineteenth-Century Periodicals.* Austin: American Folklore Society and University of Texas Press, 1967; Omi, Michael, and Howard Winant. *Racial Formation in the United States: From the 1960s to the 1990s.* New York: Routledge, 1994; Szwed, John F., and Roger D. Abrahams. *Afro-American Folk Culture: An Annotated Bibliography.* New York: Basic Books, 1978.

Adam Zolkover

Rackham, Arthur (1867–1939)

During the golden age of children's books launched by Lewis **Carroll**'s *Alice's Adventures in Wonderland* (1865), the British illustrator Arthur Rackham fashioned images both spritely and haunting for fairy tales and **fantasy** literature. "I thought he was one of the goblins out of Grimms' Fairy Tales," Rackham's nephew recalled in reminiscences about his famous uncle. Rackham used himself as a model for many of the whimsical creatures that inhabit his illustrated books, and the uncanny resemblance between him and his creations was often noted.

Known for his "wide and elfish grin," Rackham grew up in a respectable, middle-class Victorian family. As a child, he showed a talent for drawing and would smuggle paper and pencil into bed. On the recommendation of a physician, the sixteen-year-old Rackham left school to take a six-month sea voyage, journeying to Australia in 1893 with family friends and returning in good health. Convinced that his real calling was at the easel, he entered the Lambeth School of Art but was obliged to spend 1885 to 1892 working in an insurance office. He left the insurance business to become a full-time graphic journalist at the *Westminster Budget*, where his "Sketches from Life" received critical and popular acclaim.

In 1900, Rackham was invited to illustrate *The Fairy Tales of the Brothers Grimm*, a volume for which he felt "more affection" than for his many other works. By 1905, when he published an edition of *Rip Van Winkle*, his reputation as the Edwardian era's most prominent illustrator was firmly established. Rackham was in great demand and was invited to illustrate J. M. **Barrie**'s *Peter Pan in Kensington Garden* of 1906 (Barrie believed that he had "shed glory" on the work) and Lewis Carroll's *Alice's Adventures in Wonderland* of 1907. He endorsed the importance of fantasy in books for children and affirmed the "educative power of imaginative, fantastic, and playful pictures and writings for children in their most impressionable years." For Rackham, illustrations also conveyed the pleasures of the text, communicating the "sense of delight or emotion aroused by the accompanying passage of literature."

Rackham's projects included illustrations for adult readers as well. His illustrated versions of Richard Wagner's *Ring of the Nibelung* (1910–11) and William **Shakespeare**'s *A Midsummer Night's Dream* (1908) ranked among his greatest critical and commercial successes. In 1927, he sailed to New York, where his works were on exhibit and met with an enthusiastic reception. In his last years, he completed the illustrations for Kenneth Grahame's *Wind in the Willows* (1940), a work to which he had a powerful sentimental attachment.

Rackham illustrated nearly ninety volumes. Influenced by Albrecht Dürer, George **Cruikshank**, John Tenniel, and Aubrey Beardsley, he is best known for his sure sense of line, his mastery of the three-color process with its muted hues, and the creation of a mysterious world filled with gnomes, nymphs, giants, elves, sea serpents, and fairies in intricate landscapes of gnarled branches, foaming waves, sinuous vines, and anthropomorphized trees. A firm believer in the partnership between author and illustrator, he endorsed the notion that illustrations can take an interpretive turn, giving an "independent view of the author's subject." Rackham exercised a strong influence on future generations of illustrators, most notably the Walt **Disney** studios, whose feature film of *Snow White* contains scenes clearly inspired by his style. Rackham died of cancer in 1939, just a few weeks after he had put the final touches on *The Wind in the Willows*. His last drawing presents a scene in which Mole and Rat are loading their rowboat for a picnic. *See also* Art; Children's Literature; Illustration.

Further Readings: Hamilton, James. *Arthur Rackham: A Life with Illustration.* London: Pavilion, 1990; Hudson, Derek. *Arthur Rackham: His Life and Work.* London: Heinemann, 1960.

Maria Tatar

Racó, Jordi des. *See* Alcover, Antoni Maria

Ranke, Kurt (1908–1985)

Kurt Ranke was a German folklorist and folktale scholar whose most enduring contributions to the study of folk narrative were largely organizational in nature. In 1958, while a professor of *Volkskunde* (**folklore**) at the University of Kiel, he established *Fabula: Journal of Folktale Studies.* The first international conference focusing exclusively on the folktale was organized by Ranke in 1959 and led to the founding of the International Society for Folk Narrative Research. Ranke served as its first president as well as editor-in-chief of the German-language *Enzyklopädie des Märchens* (*Encyclopedia of the Folktale*), which he established following his move to the University of Göttingen.

Ranke worked primarily in the areas of the folktale and genre theory. He was a student of Walter **Anderson,** and his dissertation—published in 1934 as *Die zwei Brüder* (*The Two Brothers*) and written in the tradition of the **historic-geographic method**—traced the "normal" or most typical form of ATU 303, The **Twins** or Blood **Brothers**, to western Europe, most probably France. In addition to two edited collections, a three-volume collection of folktales from Schleswig-Holstein, and *Folktales of Germany*, published in Richard M. **Dorson**'s Folktales of the World series, Ranke authored more than eighty entries for the *Enzyklopädie* as well as articles on *einfache Formen* (**simple forms**) and the continuity between oral and literary traditions.

Further Reading: "History and Scope of the EM." *Enzyklopädie des Märchens.* http://wwwuser.gwdg.de/~enzmaer/vorstellung-engl.html.

Mary Beth Stein

Raud, Eno (1928–1996)

The Estonian author of **children's literature** Eno Raud is one of Estonia's most translated writers. Among his earlier works, Raud published several adaptations of **folktale**s and **legend**s, including *Kaval-Ants ja Vanapagan* (*Crafty Hans and Old Devil,* 1958), a story about the Estonian giant hero *Suur Tõll* (*Toell the Great,* 1959), and *Kalevipoeg* (1961), a prose retelling of Friedrich Reinhold **Kreutzwald**'s **epic** poem.

One of his best-known works, *Sipsik* (1962, sequel 1970; translated into English as *Raggie,* 1992), is a story about a small girl, her brother, and their rag doll, which comes to life. Raggie helps to gauge the boundary between what is allowed and what is not and to make the child's dreams come true—appearing on television and traveling into space. *Raggie* also helps the reader to see the world from both the child's and the adult's perspective and treats **childhood**'s problems in a warm and delicate manner.

The *Naksitrallid* tetralogy (1972; translated into English as *Three Jolly Fellows,* 1982–85) describes the adventures of the three dwarfish men: Muff, Halfshoe, and Mossbeard. Their journeys in a red car take the reader from the realm of the everyday to the world of contemporary fairy tales, through which different problems in life (such as brotherhood, fame, and vanity) and people's relationship with nature are explored. An animated cartoon based on the books was released in 1984 (see **Animation**).

In addition to his children's books, Raud is also popular for his adventure books for young people. His works are characterized by gentle humor, which often involves wordplay, and the exciting intertwining of contemporary reality and fantastic events. *See also* Estonian Tales.

Further Reading: Jaaksoo, Andres. *A Guide to Estonian Children's Literature '85.* Tallinn: Eesti Raamat, 1985. 55–59

Risto Järv

The Red Shoes (1948)

Directed by Michael Powell and Emeric Pressburger, the British film *The Red Shoes* offers two interlinked **adaptation**s of the Hans Christian **Andersen** story of that name ("De røde sko," 1845). The original is a harsh nineteenth-century Christian **parable** about sin (a girl named Karen gives in to the temptation to wear red **shoe**s to church for her confirmation), followed eventually by penitence (she persuades an executioner to cut off her feet as the only way of getting free of the nonstop dancing shoes) and then redemption (she flies on a sunbeam to heaven, where the red shoes are forgiven).

At the film's heart is a fourteen-minute cine-ballet which follows the outlines of the Andersen original, retaining the church and the community as the moral forces opposed to waywardness, and the girl's ceaseless dance through fields, forests, graveyards, and city streets as the central action. For the purpose of dramatizing this conflict, the shoemaker is the **devil** in disguise, giving the shoes magic powers so that they attract the girl and jump onto her feet as if of their own volition. Opposing him is a non-Andersen character, the boy, representing love; he tries to warn and rescue her, but fails. The only Andersen element completely missing is the foot-chopping.

At the same time, the cine-ballet contains shots that do not aspire to be Andersen: they are created within the mind of the dancer, Vicky. In an offstage prelude, Vicky and composer/conductor Julian have long been bickering over a question of musical tempo, but just before the first performance, they realize they are in love. At one point in the ballet, Vicky sees Julian leave his podium, climb onto the stage, and become her partner; at another, she feels that she is a flower swaying in the wind, a cloud drifting in the sky—exactly as Julian had promised when she feared she would be earthbound. A third perception gives her a glimpse of the future, when an image of the shoemaker/devil turns into an image of the impresario Lermontov, who is demanding total artistic dedication from her. Then, to her relief, Lermontov's image is replaced by that of Julian, offering her an alternative future.

This is indeed how the offstage narrative develops. A parallel with the Andersen story is suggested by Lermontov defining ballet as his religion, and Karen's inability to break free from the red shoes is presented as an example of single-minded commitment to art. For a while, Vicky escapes her dilemma by marrying Julian and leaving the company; but Lermontov and her ballet shoes lure her back. In the climactic scenes, she is bandied between Julian, offering love, and Lermontov, offering greatness. In a confused frenzy, she rushes from the room, apparently to go onstage to dance, but the red shoes take over and make her jump in front of an express train. Her dying words to Julian—"Take off the red shoes"—invoke her gestures in the final scene of the ballet, while the **blood** on her legs is a nod toward Andersen and the executioner. *See also* Colors; Dance; Film and Video.

Further Readings: Christie, Ian, and Andrew Moor, eds. *The Cinema of Michael Powell: International Perspectives on an English Film-Maker.* London: BFI Publishing, 2005; Lazar, David, ed. *Michael Powell Interviews.* Jackson: University of Mississippi Press, 2003; Powell, Michael. *A Life in the Movies: An Autobiography.* London: Heinemann, 1986.

Terry Staples

Rego, Paula (1935–)

Paula Rego is a Portuguese painter who studied in London at the Slade School of Art from 1952 to 1956. She has lived and worked in Britain since 1976, the year in which she received a grant from the Calouste Gulbenkian Foundation to do research on fairy tales. Rego has illustrated several works dealing with fairy tales, including *Contos populares* (*Folktales*, 1974–75) and *Nursery Rhymes* (1989). Rego also has drawn on fairy tales in several series of artworks based on Sir James Matthew **Barrie**'s *Peter Pan* (1992), the story of "**Snow White**" (1995), and Carlo **Collodi**'s *Pinocchio* (1995–96). Although she explores the tradition of **storytelling**, her images are never a direct illustration of the stories to which they refer. Instead her images constitute an allusion or metaphor, a parodic subverting of the original. Rego depicts personal conflicts, **family** relations, **childhood**, the dynamics of love, social conditioning, the **politics** of power, **violence**, **gender** relations, female identity, and sexuality (as in *Dog Woman*, 1994, and the *Abortion* series, 1999).

Rego's influences range from well-known artists such as Jean Dubuffet, Pablo Picasso, and James Gillray, to Walt **Disney**'s films (for example, in her *Dancing Ostriches* series, 1995), **opera**, and fairy tales. In 1990, she became the first Associate Artist of the National Gallery in London. Rego's most recent paintings continue to explore ideas of femininity and challenge institutionalized values and moral codes, as seen in *The Pillowman* (2004), which derived from Martin McDonagh's play of that same name about a writer whose dark fairy tales cause him to be suspected of murdering children. *See also* Art; Illustration.

Further Readings: Coldwell, Paul. "Paula Rego—Printmaker." *The Saatchi Gallery.* http://www.saatchi-gallery.co.uk/artists/paula_rego_about.htm; Rego, Paula. Interview with Marina Warner. BBC Four. October 21, 1988. http://www.bbc.co.uk/bbcfour/audiointerviews/profilepages/regop1.shtml.

Ana Raquel Fernandes

Reiniger, Lotte (1899–1981)

German silhouette artist, animator, and director Lotte Reiniger is famed for her pioneering animated feature film *Die Abenteuer des Prinzen Achmed* (*The Adventures of Prince Achmed*), completed in 1926. Living in Berlin, Lotte as a teenager loved the films of French filmmaker Georges **Méliès** and German director Paul Wegener (who is known for *Der Golem*, 1914). While studying drama at the Theaterschule of Max Reinhardt, her talent for making silhouette portraits soon led to her supplying the animated wooden rats for Wegener's *Der Rattenfänger von Hameln* (*The Pied Piper of Hamelin*, 1918). In the experimental

A still from the 1926 German film *The Adventures of Prince Achmed / Die Abenteuer des Prinzen Achmed*. [Image Entertainment/Photofest]

animated studio at the Institut für Kulturforschung (Institute for Cultural Studies) she met her future creative partner and husband, Carl Koch, whom she married in 1921.

Fairy-tale themes are evident in some of Reiniger's first short silhouette films, such as *Der fliegende Koffer* (*The Flying Trunk*, 1921), based on the tale by Hans Christian **Andersen**, and *Aschenputtel* (***Cinderella***, 1922) and *Dornröschen* (***Sleeping Beauty*** 1922), both based on tales from the Brothers **Grimm**. From 1923 to 1925, Reiniger produced the ninety-minute silhouette feature *Die Abenteuer des Prinzen Achmed*, with a plot that is largely a pastiche of stories from the ***Arabian Nights***. Anticipating, in terms of technique, Walt **Disney**'s ***Snow White*** *and the Seven Dwarfs* (1937) by more than a decade, Reiniger devised the first multiplane camera for certain effects. With the rise of Nazi Germany, Reiniger and Koch decided to emigrate, but only in 1949 were they able to settle permanently in London.

Prince Achmed begins with an African **sorcerer** conjuring a mechanical flying horse, a character reminiscent of the tale of "Prince Ahmed and the Fairy Peri Banu" from the *Arabian Nights*. When the sorcerer's request to marry Prince Achmed's sister, Dinarzade, is declined, he tricks Achmed into mounting the mechanical horse. Before Achmed understands the horse's mechanism, he reaches the islands of Wak-Wak. Here, he secretly watches beautiful **fairy** Pari Banu bathing, steals her feather cloak, and thus forces her to follow him (a **motif** derived from the *Arabian Nights*' tale "Hasan of Basra"). The evil sorcerer soon abducts Pari Banu and sells her to the emperor of China. Meanwhile, Achmed is held prisoner on top of the fire mountain, where he gains the support of a **witch** who is the sorcerer's intimate enemy. When searching for Pari Banu, Achmed meets **Aladdin**, who tells him his tale and informs him of his love for Dinarzade. The story culminates in a magic fight between the witch and the sorcerer, in which each of them subsequently transforms into various ferocious animals (a scene reminiscent of **tale type** ATU 325, The Magician and His Pupil). In the end, the evil sorcerer is eliminated, and all are reunited and return home.

Some of the shorts Reiniger produced in later years also deal with fairy-tale themes, mostly derived from the collection of the Brothers Grimm, such as *Die goldene Gans* (*The Goose That Laid Golden Eggs*, 1944), *Snow White and Rose Red* (1953), *The Three Wishes* (1953), *The Gallant Little Tailor* (1954), *The Sleeping Beauty* (1954), *The Frog Prince* (1954), *Cinderella* (1955), and *Hansel and Gretel* (1955). **See also** Animation; *Arabian Nights* Films; Film and Video; Silent Films and Fairy Tales.

Further Readings: Crafton, Donald. *Before Mickey: The Animated Film, 1898–1928.* Chicago: University of Chicago Press, 1993; Happ, Alfred. *Lotte Reiniger, 1899–1981: Schöpferin einer neuen Silhouetten-kunst.* Tübingen: Kulturamt, 2004.

Ulrich Marzolph

Religious Tale

Narratives that include characters such as God, the **devil**, Jesus Christ, the Virgin Mary, and various saints have been called "religious tales." Many religious tales illustrate Christian doctrines and teach moral lessons, such as those tales in which God or Christ visits people incognito, rewarding some for hospitality and punishing those who are unkind. Other religious tales seem more playful, even profane. Some offer humorous commentary on the **Bible**, such as the tale about God's creating Eve from the tail of a monkey, a dog, or some other animal who had stolen Adam's rib (ATU 798, Woman Created from Monkey's Tail).

Religious **legend**s and religious tales belong together, but the latter tend to be multi-episodic and more entertaining, whereas the former focus on a single or just a few events and express serious belief, as in legends about the devil's punishing immoral behavior and taking sinners to hell. Religious tales are found not only in Christian cultures but also belong to Jewish, Islamic, Hindu, and Buddhist **folklore** and to the traditions of other religions. Prominent religious tales include Buddhist **Jātaka**s, which tell about the previous lives of Gautama Buddha, who practiced moral behavior and selfless generosity for ages until he attained enlightenment. Jātakas have been addressed to the laity as didactic examples of how to move on toward better incarnations and ultimate liberation. *See also* Didactic Tale; Exemplum, Exempla; Myth; Punishment and Reward; Saint's Legend.

Further Reading: Bray, Dorothy Ann. *A List of Motifs in the Lives of Early Irish Saints.* Helsinki: Academia Scientiarum Fennica, 1992.

Ülo Valk

Reward. *See* Punishment and Reward

Reynard the Fox

Reynard the Fox is the **trickster** hero of works known as "beast epics" from northern and western Europe. Reynard is first known to appear in the mock-**epic** *Ysengrimus* written by Nivardus between 1148 and 1149 in Ghent. Ysengrimus the **wolf** is repeatedly tricked by Reinardus. The character reappeared in the 1170s in the *Roman de Renart*, a series of narrative poems with the same characters, including Chanticleer the Rooster and Tibert the **Cat**. This anonymous series of works is often divided into "branches," including the most famous Branch I, also known as "Le plaid" or "Reynard's Trial," in which Reynard is tried for crimes against the animal kingdom and eventually escapes **punishment** through trickery.

The next appearance of Reynard was in Alsace, in Heinrich der Glichsaere's 1191 work *Reinhart Fuchs*, an adaptation of the *Roman de Renart* with additional original work. More versions followed, including texts in English, Swedish, and Latin.

Scholars have viewed the Reynard stories as social satire, with early versions being critical of the Roman Catholic church. Over the years, Reynard has reappeared in popular culture. Russian-born composer Igor Stravinsky used the tale in a ballet commonly known under its French title, *Renard: Histoire burlesque chantée et jouée* (*The Fox: Burlesque Tale Sung and Played*, composed in 1916 and first staged in 1922). Drawing on Johann Wolfgang von **Goethe**'s *Reineke Fuchs* (1794), Irene and Władysław Starewicz made *Le roman de Renard*, an early French stop-action **animation** that premiered in 1937 in Berlin with a German soundtrack. An animated version was also made in Holland in 1943, based on Robert van Genechten's anti-Semitic children's story *Van den vos Reynaerde* (1937). In the twenty-first century, Reynard the Fox has made his appearance in the **graphic novel** series Fables (2002–) by Bill Willingham. One interesting societal effect of Reynard is that in the French language, the archaic word *goupil* was replaced by the modern *renard*, or fox. ***See also*** Anti-Semitism; Fable; Kreutzwald, Friedrich Reinhold.

Further Reading: Varty, Kenneth, ed. *Reynard the Fox: Social Engagement and Cultural Metamorphoses in the Beast Epic from the Middle Ages to the Present*. New York: Berghahn Books, 2000.

B. Grantham Aldred

Richter, Ludwig (1803–1884)

Ludwig Richter (born Adrian Ludwig Richter) was a German artist of the later Romantic period who was enormously popular during his lifetime, primarily for his **illustration**s in numerous collections of fairy tales. He learned the art of engraving as a child in his father's workshop. Over the course of his career, Richter produced a vast portfolio of etchings, intricate woodcuts, and landscape paintings. His landscapes were so well regarded that he was appointed professor of landscape painting at the Dresden Academy of Art in 1836. However, it was Richter's fairy-tale illustrations that captured the popular imagination and made him famous among the general public in his time. His illustrations for *Ludwig **Bechstein**'s Märchenbuch* (*Ludwig Bechstein's Fairy-Tale Book*, 1853) and an 1842 edition of Johann Karl August **Musäus**'s *Volksmärchen der Deutschen* (*Folktales of the Germans*) are two of the best-known collections. He also produced illustrations for Hans Christian **Andersen**'s individual fairy tales, although not for the more famous collections. Many of his illustrations were later co-opted for various editions of the **Grimm**s' fairy tales and have thus endured as a classic and recognized style for fairy-tale illustration. Indeed, Richter was one of several illustrators who influenced Walt **Disney**'s visual concept in his early fairy-tale **film**s.

His accomplished etchings and woodcuts, often rendered in a benignly humorous manner, depict a utopian vision of Germany's history, a bucolic view of the countryside, and an idyllic observation of the populace. These characteristics encompass the popular sentiments of nineteenth-century Germany as it imagined an idealized, unified country, and mark Richter as one of the era's most representative artists. ***See also*** Art.

Further Readings: Demisch, Heinz. *Ludwig Richter, 1803–1884: Eine Revision*. Berlin: Mann, 2003; Hand, Joachim Neidhardt. *Ludwig Richter*. Vienna: A. Schroll, 1969.

Louise Speed

Riddle

The riddle is an oral form that plays a part in social interactions, whether in local folk contests or in literature. A contest of wits and knowledge is at the heart of riddle-work, which is often tied to cultural **initiation** rites and can occur in either a playful setting (as with the joke-riddle or riddling session) or a serious one (as with the neck-riddle, found in ATU 927, Out-Riddling the Judge, wherein a condemned man saves his own neck by posing a riddle that the executioner cannot solve). The so-called true-riddle poses an enigmatic question, often joining seemingly disparate elements through some sort of wordplay ("red all over" becomes "read all over"). In some tales, the riddle mirrors the story's plot, which turns on what solving a riddle either gains or loses a character. The linguistic cleverness in riddling is analogous to the cunning or magic that in many tales allows a person or thing to be transformed into another (a **peasant** girl turns into a **princess**; a frog becomes a **prince**). In many early forms of the riddle, disparate elements point either to bawdy meanings or to sexual taboos, themes also explored in many tales (for eaxample, the "riddle" of one man being both **father** and husband). Many folktales also directly involve riddles, linking riddle-work with the contest or impossible-test **motifs**, or presenting a clever character specializing in solving riddles. *See also* Jest and Joke.

Further Readings: Abrahams, Roger D., and Alan Dundes. "Riddles." *Folklore and Folklife: An Introduction.* Edited by Richard M. Dorson. Chicago: University of Chicago Press, 1972. 130–43; Lau, Kimberly J. "Structure, Society, and Symbolism: Toward a Holistic Interpretation of Fairy Tales." *Western Folklore* 55 (1996): 233–43; Taylor, Archer, ed. *English Riddles from Oral Tradition.* Berkeley: University of California Press, 1951.

Lori Schroeder Haslem

Rimsky-Korsakov, Nikolai (1844–1908)

Nikolai Rimsky-Korsakov undoubtedly belongs to those artists who create their own world, in his case, a musical and often magical one, inhabited by puppets and mythical figures. Born in Tikhvin, not far from St. Petersburg, Rimsky-Korsakov grew up playing the piano and listening to the church bells from the Tikhvin monastery. While studying at the College of Naval Cadets in St. Petersburg, Rimsky-Korsakov often visited the **opera**, where he became very fond of Mikhail **Glinka**'s work. His first composition to gain recognition was the "musical picture" *Sadko* (1867), which he completed after a two-year voyage around the world as a sailor. Based on a *bylina*, or folk **epic**, from Novgorod, the story tells about a minstrel and rich merchant, Sadko, who is thrown overboard from his ship because the Sea King wants him to play at court. The music causes a terrible storm, and Sadko is rescued by St. Nicholas. *Sadko* was later transformed into an opera.

Antar, a symphony from 1867, elaborates Oriental **motifs**. The popularity of Oriental subjects and the ***Arabian Nights*** in Russia is furthermore exemplified by the symphonic suite ***Sheherazade*** (1888). Among Rimsky-Korsakov's later works are several operas with motifs from Russian and Ukrainian folktale and fairy-tale traditions. In *Maiskaya noch'* (*May Night*, 1878), the son of the local mayor desires to marry the village beauty against the will of his **father**. He is assisted by the Queen of the Water Nymphs, who wishes to reward him for helping her out with her stepmother, and so he is allowed to marry the girl he adores. The story is based on a tale by Nikolai Gogol, who is also the author of "Noch' pered Rozhdestvom" ("The Night before Christmas," 1832), which became an opera in 1894. As in *May Night*, mythological characters intervene in the action. The hero is a blacksmith who wins his bride by flying to St. Petersburg on the back of the **devil** and gets her the slippers of the Empress Catherine. *Skazka o tsare Saltane* (*The Tale of Tsar Saltan*, 1899–1900) is based on one of Aleksandr **Pushkin**'s most beloved fairy tales. While the tsar is away at war, a son, **Prince** Gvidon, is born to him. In their envy, the two malicious **sisters** of his wife send the tsar a message that she has given **birth** to a monster. The tsar orders both **mother** and child to be thrown into the sea in a barrel. Gvidon grows miraculously, the barrel lands on an island, and when Gvidon rescues a swan from a kite, she turns out to be a **princess**. She helps him to create a new kingdom, and finally the reunion of the tsar and his **family** may take place. *Zolotoi petushok* (*The Golden Cockerel*, 1907) was Rimsky-Korsakov's last opera. Once again, a fairy tale by Pushkin served as the source. Because of its critical portrayal of the tsar, the opera was banned by the censors; however, it was staged in 1909, one year after the death of the composer. *See also* Music; Tchaikovsky, Pyotr Il'ich.

Further Readings: Abraham, Gerald. *Studies in Russian Music.* Freeport, NY: Books for Libraries Press, 1968; Seaman, Gerald R. *Nikolai Andreevich Rimsky-Korsakov: A Guide to Research.* New York: Garland, 1988.

Janina Orlov

Ritchie, Anne Thackeray (1837–1919)

During a prolific career that spanned nearly sixty years, the English author Anne Thackeray Ritchie wrote in a wide variety of genres. In addition to several collections of essays, short stories, and fairy tales, she produced five well-received **novel**s: *The Story of Elizabeth* (1863), *The Village on the Cliff* (1867), *Old Kensington* (1873), *Miss Angel* (1875), and *Mrs. Dymond* (1885). Ritchie also wrote biographical works and memoirs, including the individual introductions to the complete works of her father/mentor, William Makepeace **Thackeray**, and studies of other writers: *Madame de Sévigné* (1881), *A Book of Sibyls: Mrs. Barbauld, Mrs. Opie, Miss Edgeworth, Miss Austen* (1883), and *Records of Tennyson, Ruskin and Robert and Elizabeth Browning* (1892). Although well known and popular during her lifetime, most of Ritchie's works are out of print today and not easily accessible to readers.

In her fairy-tale writings, Ritchie revised such tales as "**Cinderella**," "Jack and the Beanstalk," "**Little Red Riding Hood**," and "**Sleeping Beauty**." Published in two volumes as *Five Old Friends and a Young **Prince*** (1868) and *Bluebeard's Keys and Other Stories* (1874), her revisions have distinctive features in common: a staging of the **storytelling** situation; contemporary settings replete with descriptions of local customs and conduct; ingenious alterations of magical elements into realistic ones; and restrained but explicit criticism of pretentiousness, materialism, and the restricted situation of **women** in Victorian society. Her fairy tales simultaneously convey a "soft" romantic picture of Victorian domestic life and mirror some of its harsher social realities. *See also* English Tales.

Further Readings: Gérin, Winifred. *Anne Thackeray Ritchie: A Biography.* Oxford: Oxford University Press, 1981; MacKay, Carol Hanbery. *Creative Negativity: Four Victorian Exemplars of the Female Quest.* Stanford, CA: Stanford University Press, 2001.

Shuli Barzilai

Rite of Passage. *See* Initiation

Robber. *See* Thief

Rodari, Gianni (1920–1980)

One of the most original twentieth-century Italian pedagogues and writers for children, Italian author Gianni Rodari has been widely translated abroad. Stressing the importance of

storytelling as a playful activity and a route to recovering the **oral tradition**, Rodari believed in the power of the written word as an educational and liberating force. In *La grammatica della fantasia: Introduzione all'arte di inventare storie* (*The Grammar of Fantasy: An Introduction to the Art of Inventing Stories*, 1973), Rodari asserts that words can effect emancipation only when they are in the hands of each person equally: "I hope that this small book can be useful for all those people who believe it necessary for the imagination to have a place in education . . . and for all those who know the liberating value of the word. 'Every possible use of words should be made available to every single person'—this seems to me to be a good motto with a democratic sound. Not because everyone should be an artist, but because no one should be a slave" (Zipes, 3). Recipient in 1970 of the prestigious Hans Christian **Andersen** Award, Rodari was acclaimed worldwide as a "pied piper" of the imaginative life, an author who introduced children to **fantasy** with techniques for inventing stories and learning from make-believe.

Before publishing such masterpieces as *Favole al telefono* (*Fairy Tales over the Phone*, 1962), *Il libro degli errori* (*The Book of Mistakes*, 1964), and *The Grammar of Fantasy*, Rodari worked at the end of World War II as a political journalist for the Communist Party's paper *L'Unità*, where he composed essays for children. Appointed by the party in 1950 to edit the children's weekly *Il pioniere*, Rodari began to dedicate himself wholly to **children's literature** when he had written sufficient material to publish a collection of nursery rhymes. His first book, *Il libro della filastrocche* (*The Book of Rhymes*, 1950), contains comic rhymes previously published in *L'Unità* and *Vie nuove*. His second book, *Il romanzo di Cipollino* (*The Novel of Cipollino*, 1951), features the tyrant **prince** Cipollino, who had appeared before in the pages of *Il pioniere*.

A former educator, Rodari underscored the power of stories as fundamental educational tools; thus, he participated in the 1960s in the Educational Cooperation Movement and advanced teaching reforms in Italy. This period also marked the beginning of Rodari's collaboration with the prestigious Italian editorial house Einaudi and the diffusion and popularity of his works abroad. *Filastrocche in cielo e in terra* (*Nursery Rhymes in Heaven and on Earth*, 1960) made manifest Rodari's focus on renewing children's literature with linguistic and fantastical elements. *Fairy Tales over the Phone*, short stories told by Signor Bianchi, a traveling salesman, to his daughter each evening on the phone, includes plays on words and classic fairy tales in disguise. Themes plucked from reality address social injustice and human tragedy. Infused, however, with Rodari's signature humor, the stories rise to a surrealistic plane. There is, for instance, the lone violet that blooms at the North Pole, melts the polar ice cap by sheer will, and sacrifices its precious life so that flowers, houses, and children can one day populate the frozen land. Another tale tells of a **soldier**'s son who, covered by the blanket of his dead **father**, falls asleep to a **fairy**'s story while she weaves a blanket big enough to cover every poor, cold child in the world.

The Book of Errors offers rhymes and tales about such characters as Professor Grammaticus to highlight the grammar and spelling mistakes made by children (in red) and the social injustices committed by adults (in blue). "Often errors aren't found in words," Rodari urges, "but in things; it is necessary to correct dictation, but necessary above all things to correct the world." *La torta in cielo* (*A Pie in the Sky*, 1966), *Venti storie piú una* (*Twenty Stories Plus One*, 1969), and *Tante storie per giocare* (*Many Stories for Play*, 1971) followed before Rodari gained recognition in the United States with the publication of *The Grammar of Fantasy*.

In his classic handbook for teachers and parents, Rodari presents a series of techniques to invent tales for children and invite them to collaborate in the creative process. He espouses the "Fantastic Binomial," the act of making a connection between two unrelated words to create a story; the "Fantastic Hypothesis," a story that begins with the question, "What would happen if . . ."; and the "Lapsus," a creative error made in a story that opens the door to a new tale. Rodari also promotes the use of familiar fairy tales by recasting and combining classic stories (**Cinderella** marries **Bluebeard**; Pinocchio becomes a pupil of **Snow White**), inverting a classic tale (**Little Red Riding Hood** is naughty; the **wolf** is recast as hero), and scripting an original epilogue (such as what happens after Cinderella marries the prince).

For Rodari, fairy tales educate the mind as the site of all potential hypotheses about life; tales present the magic key to enter reality via diverse paths, helping children study the world by offering the images with which to critique it. In "Le vecchie fiabe sono da buttar via? Pro e contro il gatto con gli stivali" ("Should Old Fairy Tales Be Thrown Away? Pros and Cons of **Puss in Boots**"), Rodari pronounces fairy tales as the first material for constructing our personalities and our vision of the world. By judging the actions and reactions of fairy-tale characters, children can both delight in the pleasure of fantasy and question human morality, subsequently forming their own ideas of justice. *See also* Childhood and Children; Italian Tales; Pedagogy.

Further Readings: Poesio, Carla, and Pino Boero. "Gianni Rodari: An Appreciation." *Phaedrus* (1981): 20–21; Rodari, Gianni. "Le vecchie fiabe sono da buttar via? Pro e contro il gatto con gli stivali." *Il Giornale dei Genitori* December 1971: 11; Zagni, Patrizia. *Rodari*. Florence: La Nuova Italia, 1975; Zipes, Jack, trans. *The Grammar of Fantasy: An Introduction to the Art of Inventing Stories.* By Gianni Rodari. New York: Teachers and Writers Collaborative, 1996.

Gina M. Miele

Róheim, Géza (1891–1953)

Géza Róheim was a Hungarian folklorist who applied psychological theories, especially those of Sigmund **Freud**, to worldwide **folklore**, including folktales and fairy tales. Róheim is one of the few scholars with folkloristic training to also undergo psychoanalysis and incorporate those insights into his research. A polyglot, Róheim analyzed published folk narrative texts and also did **fieldwork** (notably in aboriginal Australia). Róheim's comparative scope and innovative interpretations ensure his importance in the study of folk narrative.

A prolific writer, Róheim contested and elaborated on various approaches to folktales and fairy tales in many of his essays. In "Psychoanalysis and the Folktale" (1922), Róheim argued for the existence of wish fulfillment in folktales, especially wishes of a sexual nature. Unlike many who applied psychological frameworks to folklore, Róheim recognized the manifold existence and variation inherent to folklore, and he frequently used multiple versions of a tale. For instance, Róheim analyzed international **variant**s of ATU 333, Little Red Riding Hood, in his essay "Fairy Tale and Dream" (1953). He concluded that the tale's protagonists—the girl, her (grand)mother, and the wolf—are in fact the same sleeping person, folded within womb and stomach, all representing the dreamer. Róheim not only linked the latent symbols in dreams and tales, but also contended that folk narratives originate in dreams—a provocative hypothesis, like much of his work. *See also* Psychological Approaches.

Further Reading: Róheim, Géza. *Fire in the Dragon and Other Psychoanalytic Essays on Folklore.* Edited by Alan Dundes. Princeton, NJ: Princeton University Press, 1992.

Jeana Jorgensen

Röhrich, Lutz (1922–2006)

The German folklorist Lutz Röhrich is internationally renowned for his writings on folk songs, **ballad**s, **folktale**s, **proverbs**, **riddle**s, and **joke**s. Röhrich's major contribution to folktale studies came with his very first book, *Märchen und Wirklichkeit* (*Folktales and Reality*, 1956), in which he argued that the point is not to look for reality in the folktale but to study the relationship of the folktale to reality. From this perspective, he showed that the relationship of folk narratives to reality keeps changing over time and history. For example, heroic **legend**s are narratives in which people's belief changes over time, and that in turn changes the nature of their existence and status in society.

With Röhrich's theory comes the realization that the meaning of the folktale lies in the way it is perceived and interpreted, and that folktales have been used by different ideologues to usher in their own thoughts and ideas. This insight helps to clarify, for example, the way in which **folklore** was (ab)used by the Nazis in Germany during the 1930s. Röhrich is responsible in a significant way for reestablishing the discipline of *Volkskunde* (ethnology or folklore studies) in post–World War II Germany, where the Nazi association with folklore had caused popular resistence to the concept and the idea itself.

At the time of his death in 2006, Röhrich was professor emeritus at the University of Freiburg, where he had inspired many generations of folklore scholars. He also served as the director of the Deutsches Volksliedarchiv (German Folksong **Archives**). *See also* Socio-historical Approaches.

Further Reading: Röhrich, Lutz. *Folktales and Reality*. Translated by Peter Tokofsky. Bloomington: Indiana University Press, 1991.

Sadhana Naithani

Le roi et l'oiseau (*The King and Mister Bird*) (1980)

This French animated feature film directed by Paul Grimault originally had a connection with Hans Christian **Andersen**'s tale "Hyrdinden og skorstensfeieren" ("The Shepherdess and the Chimney Sweep," 1845). However, over three decades it turned into something quite different.

Poet Jacques Prévert and animator Paul Grimault met during the German occupation of France, and decided to collaborate on a film project when France regained freedom. Prévert went on to write *Les enfants du paradis* (*Children of Paradise*, 1945) and Grimault to direct a short film, *La flûte magique* (*The Magic Flute*, 1946), derived from Wolfgang Amadeus Mozart's **opera**; then they worked together on *Le petit soldat* (1947), a ten-minute version of Andersen's "Den standhaftige tinsoldat" ("The Steadfast Tin Soldier," 1838), sharing first prize with Walt **Disney**'s *Melody Time* at the 1947 Venice Film Festival.

Upon this success, they decided to animate "The Shepherdess and the Chimney Sweep," a tale about two china figurines who fall in love and decide to elope. However, in the process of turning a ten-minute story into an eighty-minute film, everything in the original was dropped but the title and the two protagonists. The action was to take place in Tachycardia, where the despotic **king**, who looks like Hitler and acts like Stalin, tolerates no opposition. When the king falls in love with a shepherdess in a painting on his palace wall, he determines to marry her and eradicate the sweep; but they are saved by a witty freedom-loving bird, who alone can combat the king's power.

However, Grimault was forced to leave this project halfway through, because after three years, the producer insisted on faster progress. Finished off by other hands and disavowed by both Prévert and Grimault, the sixty-three-minute *La bergère et le ramoneur* (*The Shepherdess and the Chimney Sweep*) was released in 1952. It too won a prize at Venice, but performed poorly in cinemas. In the United States, an English-dubbed version, *The Curious Adventures of Mr. Wonderbird,* was given **television** screenings in slots aimed at children.

Grimault and Prévert moved on, but did not forget their broken dream. Then in 1967, Grimault managed to reacquire the 1952 film. He discarded all alien footage and worked with Prévert to update the screenplay for the 1970s, making it tougher and less sentimental. The characters of the king and the bird, and their ideological conflict, were expanded and sharpened; the pursuit and capture of the fleeing lovers became simply illustrations of the king's power. A giant robot used by the king to wreak destruction similarly exemplifies screenplay changes. In the climax of the 1952 film, the robot loses its power, and the liberated people start a new society; but in the closing shots of the second version, the robot, still fully functioning, frees a baby bird and then smashes its cage. The message was that technology can be used for good or for ill, but it cannot be disinvented.

In 1977, just as animation work was to start, Prévert died. The film was finally completed under its new title two years later, and Grimault dedicated it to Prévert, declaring it to be the film they had been striving for. Thus, a tale about a shepherdess who finds freedom too frightening, and prefers to go back to confinement, led in stages to the creation of a film **fable** that asserts the opposite: life without freedom is no life at all. *See also* Animation; Film and Video.

Further Readings: Le roi et l'oiseau. Directed by Paul Grimault. 1980. DVD. Studio Canal, 2004; Pagliano, Jean-Pierre. *Paul Grimault.* Paris: Dreamland, 1996.

Terry Staples

Rossetti, Christina Georgina (1830–1894)

English poet Christina Rossetti wrote "Goblin Market," a narrative poem noted for its vivid descriptions and intense, possibly sexual, depictions of love. Rossetti also created several fantastic tales in verse and prose, including *The **Prince**'s Progress* (1866) and *Speaking Likenesses* (1874). However, "Goblin Market," first published in *Goblin Market and Other Poems* (1862), remains her best-known tale.

"Goblin Market" tells of two **sisters**, Laura and Lizzie. Each evening in summer, the maidens hear the calls of goblin fruit vendors. Lizzie avoids the goblins as evil, but Laura decides to visit them and sees exotic beings with traits of both humans and animals. She is amazed by the variety of fruit they sell, all ripe at the same time. Laura complains she has no money, whereupon the goblins request a curl of her **hair**. Laura weeps but yields to the goblins' demand, and then gorges herself. Later, she craves more fruit, but no longer can see or hear the goblins. She weakens and ages rapidly. To save Laura, Lizzie goes to buy fruit from the goblins, but gives them a silver penny rather than her hair. The goblins will not let Lizzie leave with the fruit. When she refuses to eat with them and demands her money back, they attack her and try to force fruit into her mouth. She shuts her mouth until the goblins return her coin and flee. Her face dripping with juice, Lizzie returns to Laura. While kissing Lizzie, Laura consumes the juice and suffers greatly throughout the night.

The goblins' spell is broken, and Laura is restored. The poem ends with the adult Laura telling both her children and Lizzie's about their experiences.

Critical interpretations of "Goblin Market" vary greatly. The goblins are seen as metaphors for **sexuality**, danger, or sin. Lizzie's passive resistance to the goblins' attack is compared to both rape and the passion of Christ. The fruit is related to the forbidden fruit in Genesis as well as to other supernatural fruits, such as the pomegranate eaten by Proserpina. Scholars find many other parallels to folk traditions, including the goblins' glamour when the maidens first approach, the influence silver has upon them, and the timelessness of their existence (neither sister knows the time after their goblin encounters).

Since the age of the sisters is vague, they are discussed variously as youth or adults. They seem to be girls in Rossetti's text, yet Dante Gabriel Rossetti's illustrations show relatively mature **women**. Since many passages may seem to suggest sexual feeling, the maidens are sometimes seen as only symbolically sisters but actually lovers, or else as women victimized by **men**. (It has often been pointed out that Rossetti was working with young prostitutes when she wrote the poem.) The poem appeals to many readers by evoking the imagination while eluding efforts to assign it specific meanings. *See also* Art; Childhood and Children; Food; Violence.

Further Reading: Rossetti, Christina G. *The Complete Poems of Christina Rossetti*. Edited by R. W. Crump and Betty S. Flowers. London: Penguin, 2001.

Paul James Buczkowski

Rowling, J. K. (1965–)

The modern-day success story of the Harry Potter **novel**s, the children's fantasies about a young wizard at a magical school, has made British writer J. K. Rowling—the pen name of Joanne Rowling—a household name. The publication of *Harry Potter and the Sorcerer's Stone* in 1997 initiated the Harry Potter phenomenon, a publishing success story and popular cultural force that has also sparked a resurgence in the success of children's fantasy literature as a genre. While the Harry Potter books are clearly magical **fable**s that partake of fairy tale's structure and simplicity, they are also complex generic fabrications, owing as much to modern **fantasy**, **myth**, **film** and the old-fashioned school story as they do to fairy tale or folklore. Indeed, the most folkloric aspect of the series may well be the media's adoption of Rowling herself as a classic **Cinderella** narrative in her rise from impoverished single-motherhood to become one of the wealthiest women in Britain. The Harry Potter phenomenon is significant particularly because it partially represents both a marketing coup and a particularly apposite response to a generation reared on **television** and geared toward easy reading. While the books have arguably inspired children to rediscover literature, they are considerably less complex and accomplished than many other classics of children's fantasy and, like classic fairy tale, have a reactionary tendency toward racism and sexism that is somewhat disturbingly uncritical.

Harry Potter himself is something of an inverted Cinderella figure, the despised and marginalized member of an uncaring **family** who is revealed, instead, to have a dazzling destiny and power relating to something very close to a christening curse. Nonetheless, his magical abilities and clearly defined destiny are clichés, not of fairy tale, but of the modern fantasy romance, which has a characteristic interest in heroes who are inherently magical, rather than fairy tale's focus on ordinary protagonists faced with the magical. The impulse of the stories is to normalize magic with a nostalgic, 1950s sense of the mundane, very different from fairy tale's sense of wonder. Harry's adventures often resemble the initiatory scenarios of fairy tale, the protagonist faced with a series of tests or quests that entail **magic object**s—the Mirror of Erised, the sword of Griffindor, and the invisibility cloak—and encounters with monstrous creatures or **magic helper**s. Even the magic helpers, however, are either straightforwardly mythic (such as hippogriffs, centaurs, and Fawkes the phoenix), or, as with teachers or house **elves**, operate as a debased echo of modern fantasy in the post-**Tolkien** mode. Perhaps the most interesting folkloric aspect of the series has only recently been revealed, with the plot's development in *Harry Potter and the Half-Blood Prince* (2005): the black enchanter Voldemort is, in fact, that classic fairy-tale creature, the **sorcerer** with his heart, or in this case soul, hidden in a magic object. The denouement of the series with the seventh book, *Harry Potter and the Deathly Hallows* (2007), entails Harry finding and destroying Voldemort's hidden life. *See also* Children's Literature; Harry Potter Films.

Further Readings: Anatol, Giselle Liza, ed. *Reading Harry Potter: Critical Essays.* Westport, CT: Praeger Publishers, 2003; Whited, Lana A., ed. *The Ivory Tower and Harry Potter: Perspectives on a Literary Phenomenon.* Columbia: University of Missouri Press, 2002.

Jessica Tiffin

Rudbeck, Erik. *See* Salmelainen, Eero

Rumi, Jalal al-Din (1207–1273)

Born in the city of Balkh in present-day northern Afghanistan, Jalal al-Din Rumi is usually known as Moulânâ (Our Lord; Turkish Mevlânâ) in the East and is renowned as the major mystical poet of Persian literature.

Rumi's father, the theologian and preacher Baha' al-Din Sultan al-'ulama' Valad, left Balkh with his family around the year 1212 after a dispute with the local ruler. They went on a pilgrimage to Mecca via Iran and eventually took residence in the Anatolian city of Konya around the year 1228. Rumi studied Islamic theology and mysticism with various teachers, traveled to the Syrian cities of Aleppo and Damascus and probably also met the famous theosophic scholar Ibn al-'Arabi (died 1240). He spent the major part of his later life in Konya, where he practiced as a famous scholar and mystical teacher. After his death, Rumi's disciples, particularly his son Sultan Valad, developed his mystical teachings into the foundations of the Mevlevi order of dervishes that still exists today. This order is widely known as the "dancing dervishes" (or "whirling dervishes") for its ecstatic dancing performances in white robes. Rumi's mystical teachings have, against the backdrop of a popular neomysticism, engendered a downright "Rumi-mania," particularly in the United States in the twentieth century.

Rumi's teaching is closely linked with his understanding of (Islamic) mysticism, in which his longing for unity with the supreme God is expressed in terms of carnal love. He was initiated into this branch of knowledge by the wandering dervish Shams al-Din from Tabriz, to whom he felt deeply inclined. When Shams al-Din was murdered by his jealous disciples in 1247, Rumi's love and remorse were channeled into poetry and an excessive inclination to music and dance. His major work is a poem of roughly 26,000 verses known as *Masnavi-ye ma'navi*, whose title may be translated as "Poem Concerned with the Inner Qualities of Being."

According to tradition, Rumi's *Masnavi* was dictated spontaneously to one of his intimates in fulfilling the request of his disciples to explain the essence of Islamic mysticism in simpler terms than those of previous mystics. A major part of Rumi's teaching went by way of exemplary stories, a device widely popular in Oriental teaching that had already been employed by his predecessors Sana'i (died 1131) and 'Attar (died 1221). As a result, the *Masnavi* contains hundreds of stories, many of which belong to the common stock of tales widely known in both East and West. Still widely read and taught today, the *Masnavi* is responsible for the popularity of many a folktale in the Islamic world. Meanwhile, Rumi never told the tales for sheer entertainment, but always employed them to teach his mystical understanding of the world, even in such obscene tales as the one about the sexual intercourse of the lady and her maid with a mule. ***See also*** Iranian Tales; South Asian Tales.

Further Readings: Lewis, Franklin D. *Rumi: Past and Present, East and West; The Life, Teaching and Poetry of Jalâl al-Din Rumi.* Oxford: Oneworld, 2000; Marzolph, Ulrich. "Popular Narratives in Galâloddin Rumi's Masnavi." *The Arabist* 12–14 (1995): 275–87; Schimmel, Annemarie. *The Triumphal Sun: A Study of the Works of Jalâloddin Rumi.* 2nd edition. London: East-West Publications, 1980.

Ulrich Marzolph

Rushdie, Salman (1947–)

Salman Rushdie is an Indian-born British novelist and essayist whose writing incorporates elements of **postmodernism**, postcolonialism, and **magical realism**. Part of the generation of post-independence writers, Rushdie emphasizes the ambiguity of modern nationhood and selfhood and reworks traditional European and Oriental(ist) **folk** traditions and fantasy to a heightened sense of this **hybridity** or "mongrelization." Rushdie's work evokes strong reactions, most notably the infamous *fatwa* issued after the release of his *Satanic Verses* (1989), which was held to be blasphemous against the teachings of Islam; but additionally, his themes are overtly critical of political and social wrongs, and his use of language and form destabilizing.

Rushdie's work is an ingenious hybrid of East and West, interweaving strands of divergent histories, **motif**s, and languages into new, often incongruous and incompatible patterns. Using the worlds of **fantasy** that he creates and the metaphorical language he borrows and reworks, along with an English grammar and syntax that is filtered through an Indian sensibility, Rushdie finds a platform to explore, criticize, and reflect on the present-day consequences of colonialism, postcolonialism, migration, globalization, displacement, and the power inherent in language and the spoken and written word. Attempting to center the marginalized hybrid, or migrant position, Rushdie necessarily turns to magical realism to temporarily reconcile the separate realities of worlds in collision. The fantastical worlds he creates, familiar and yet foreign, and slightly askew to the real world, are the perfect platform from which to decenter autocratic versions of reality, reveal the insanity of the real world, and yet, simultaneously, to

Salman Rushdie at the Guardian Hay Festival at Hay on Wye in Powys, Wales, 2006. [Getty Images]

disallow any authoritative claims on alternatives to that reality. Rushdie finds utility in both fairy-tale and folktale material because not only does its familiarity provide a basis from which to reinvent, but it also is a well-understood mirror for reality, even if that mirror is fractured and fragmented and sometimes reassembled in apparently disorienting ways. All of Rushdie's **novel**s incorporate magical realism, but *Midnight's Children* (1981), *Shame* (1983), *Satanic Verses*, and *Haroun and the Sea of Stories* (1990) are those in which he assembles fairy-tale themes most emphatically and effectively.

Although his first novel, *Grimus* (1975), contains these elements, it is generally considered a beginning foray and not representative of his best work. With *Midnight's Children*, however, winner of the 1980 Booker Prize, Rushdie developed a powerful style. Part autobiographical, part allegorical, part **frame narrative**, part historical, and part fantasy, it is a long, intricately interwoven tale of the world of post-independence and post-partition India and Pakistan, seen through the life of the main character and narrator, Saleem, and all of the other remarkable 1,001 children born on August 15, 1947—the moment of India's independence. The **birth**s and lives of midnight's children are an allegory for the birth of India, and the thwarted promise it (they) offered. Not only are the 1,001 midnight's children evocative of the *Thousand and One Nights* (**Arabian Nights**) and all of their magic and potential, but the narrator himself, negotiating back and forth between frames, is a reference not only to the most famous embedded-in-the-story-and-yet-outside-of-it-narrator, **Sheherazade**, but also to Rushdie's own position in the story and outside of it, writing from a position of exile. Rushdie comments on this in the introduction to his collection of essays *Imaginary Homelands* (1991), in which he acknowledges that Saleem is suspect in his narration because of his fallible memory and fragmentary vision, but argues that "the broken mirror may actually be as valuable as the one which is supposedly unflawed." Thus Rushdie defines his novels as inherently political, providing alternative readings to events recounted in official histories. This fragmentariness also places Rushdie's work within a larger contemporary literary context: the modern **novel**, which seeks to undermine the authority of the Enlightenment; the postmodernist project, in which he, along with the likes of Angela **Carter**, experiments with fairy-tale themes; and the magical realism of Günter **Grass**, whose *Die Blechtrommel* (*The Tin Drum*, 1959) served as an inspiration to Rushdie's *Midnight's Children*.

Shame (1983) follows a similarly fantastical and semiautobiographical strain, picking up the time line roughly where *Midnight's Children* left off—the 1970s—but shifting the location to Pakistan, although Rushdie stressed he was writing about not only the "real" Pakistan. The central stories follow the lives and families of General Raza Hyder and Iskander Harappa (based on the careers of President General Mohammed Zia ul-Haq and Prime Minister Zulfikar Ali Bhutto). As in *Midnight's Children*, however, these are intersected by many other stories, all melting into one another and yet casting all claims on centrality into doubt. One of these is the occasional appearance of the narrator, an outsider whose authority is self-consciously questioned and questionable.

The theme of shame and national disgrace that stems from absolutism, corrupted power, and violence runs through *Shame* but is deflected and incorporated in Sufiya Zinobia, the retarded and rejected daughter of Raza Hyder. At birth, Sufiya blushes for the shame of the nation that is literalized, projected, and played out on the bodies of **women** through the generalized shame of their sex. Rushdie upends the "**Beauty and the Beast**" theme and locates both—beauty and the beast—within Sufiya. Although she is initially a beautiful if vacuous child, the beast of shame is impossible to contain, and it emerges and wreaks an inverted vengeance on those imposing the terms of dishonor—wrenching the heads off **men** and eviscerating them through their truncated torsos. Sufiya is a multilayered fantasy creature through whom Rushdie refers to a mélange of fairy-tale creatures to disorient the reader, suggesting the familiar in order to destabilize.

Whereas in his previous novels Rushdie locates his critique of religion within the context of political corruption, in *The Satanic Verses* he takes it head on, ridiculing Muslim absolutism. His implication that the Qur'an is a story, folklore, not only relativizes the Qur'an, it also suggests its fallibility, and that of Mohammed. This act of apostasy prompted the Ayatollah Khomeini, then leader of Iran, to issue the *fatwa* calling for the murder of Rushdie and the immediate martyrdom of his executioner. In an instance of the absurdity of real-word events surpassing that of imaginative fantasy, the *fatwa* not only resulted in Rusdie's exile and his going into hiding, but also in widespread book banning, demonstrations, and deaths, including those of the Japanese and Turkish translators of the book.

The events following the *fatwa* resulted in Rushdie's only "children's book," and the book most redolent with fairy-tale references—*Haroun and the Sea of Stories*. In *Haroun*, Rushdie seeks to reach out to his estranged son, but also tackles the imbricated relationship of language and power made poignant and literal in his personal plight. *Haroun and the Sea of Stories* is a treatise on the nature of language, **storytelling**, and narrative. The two main characters, Haroun and his father Rashid, evoke one of the recurrent personalities in the stories of the *Thousand and One Nights*—**Harun al-Rashid**. Rashid is a famous storyteller who loses his ability because the evil tyrant Khattam-Shud ("Completely Finished") has cut off his supply to the stream of stories and thereby silenced him. Khattam-Shud rules over a dark, silent country. In his tyranny he seeks to eliminate all stories, which he sees as unruly and threatening. Haroun must take Rashid to the Sea of Stories (referring to the eleventh-century work of Somadeva) to recover his father's storytelling, and thus follows a well-trod heroic quest. Along the way he is aided by three fantastic companions, putting to mind Dorothy's companions in *The Wizard of Oz*. *Haroun* is not only an impassioned argument against tyranny and in support of freedom of speech; it also posits a link between nation and narration. Moreover, it is a discussion about the nature of narrative formation itself. It argues against contained narratives, whether in the name of national purity or in folkloristic, indexical terms, and, through the mixing of genres and multinational themes, suggests the multivocal and hybrid nature of narrative.

In subsequent works, Rushdie has continued approaching contemporary issues through magical realism in discussing the complicated interconnectedness of the East and the West. However, he has ventured more into fantasy and is less reliant on familiar fairy-tale themes: *East, West* (1994) is a collection of short stories; in *The Moor's Last Sigh* (1995), the setting is again contemporary Bombay, but the main characters are Portuguese settlers; *The Ground Beneath Her Feet* (1999) delves into the international world of rock music and superstardom; and in *Fury* (2001), Rushdie moves across the Atlantic to situate his novel in the experiences of an ageing Indian expatriate living in New York at the fin de siècle. In his most recent novel to date, *Shalimar the Clown* (2005), Rushdie's conventional novel, in which the lives of apparently disparate characters are linked across great distances and entire generations, is set against the backdrop of international terrorism, personal passions, and the messy, contested region of Kashmir—famed in Orientalist lore and a contemporary unresolved consequence of the partition, and, ultimately, the ineptitude of the British Raj. *See also* Colonialism.

Further Reading: Justyna Deszcz. *Rushdie in Wonderland: Fairytaleness in Salman Rushdie's Fiction.* Frankfurt a.M.: Main: Peter Lang, 2004.

JoAnn Conrad

Ruskin, John (1819–1900)

John Ruskin contended that his exposure to "fairy legends" as a small boy affected his lifelong career as Victorian England's foremost aesthetic and cultural critic. In "Fairy Land" (1883), two lectures on illustrators such as Kate Greenaway and Helen Allingham, he questioned "his early training" as a believer in the marvelous: "scenes of California and the Rocky Mountains," he now maintained, might well be more "wonderful" than any imaginary landscape in the *Arabian Nights*.

Still, try as he might, the early impact made by the 1823 volume of **Grimm** fairy tales translated by Edgar **Taylor** and illustrated by George **Cruikshank** was hard to exorcise. By 1841, Ruskin had finished *The King of the Golden River*, the first Victorian **literary fairy tale** for children; it appeared in 1851, with fine **illustration**s by Richard Doyle. Although Ruskin disparaged this effort ("a fairly good imitation of Grimm and Charles **Dickens**, with some true Alpine feeling of my own"), its success prompted writers such as George **MacDonald,** Lewis **Carroll,** and Jean **Ingelow** to market their own tales of wonder. Ruskin upheld the "purity" of fairy-tale classics in 1868 upon reissuing the Taylor/Cruikshank volume with a prefatory essay in which he argued that, if kept intact, such tales could act as cultural bulwarks "against the glacial cold of science." William Makepeace **Thackeray**'s deliberately impure *The Rose and the Ring* (1854) had already challenged that notion, as would Juliana Horatia **Ewing** in her *Old-Fashioned Fairy Tales* of 1882. *See also* English Tales.

Further Reading: Knoepflmacher, U. C. "Resisting Growth: Ruskin's *King of the Golden River.*" *Ventures into Childland: Victorians, Fairy Tales, and Femininity.* Chicago: Chicago University Press, 1998. 36–72.

U. C. Knoepflmacher

Russian Tales

The Russian folktale tradition is one of the richest in Europe, especially in terms of the diversity of identifiable **tale type**s. According to the comparative index of East Slavic tale types—*Sravnitel'ny ukazatel syuzhetov* (abbreviated SUS)—the total number of Russian tale types exceeds 1,233, which is the largest known among European traditions with the exception of Ukrainian (which has some 1,339 types). Russian tales fall into the usual range of categories, including **animal tale**s, **wonder tale**s (both magical and heroic), **legendary tale**s, tales of everyday life (*bytovye*), tales of the clever **fool**, and more than 500 varieties of **anecdote**s. A special category of tales—the *zavetnye skazki* ("forbidden tales")—includes those whose publication was prohibited by tsarist and later Soviet censorship. These include **bawdy tale**s on erotic themes as well as tales deemed satirical of the **clergy**. Special collections of such tales by Aleksandr **Afanas'ev** and Nikolai Onchukov have been published in Russia only since the fall of the Soviet Union in 1989. **Archives** are believed to contain more such tales and offer the prospect of new research.

The roots of Russian **folklore** are in some regards unique in the context of European folklore. Although Russian tales share in the general Indo-European heritage, some of their most

"Ruslan and Lyudmila" illustrated by Theodore Nadejen in *Tales and Legends of Old Russia* by Ida Zeitlin (New York: George H. Doran Company, 1926), p. 186. [Courtesy of the Eloise Ramsey Collection of Literature for Young People, University Libraries, Wayne State University]

archaic features show an affinity with the eastern Indo-Iranian branch, to which Slavic linguistically belongs. This is especially true of the animal tales and the wonder tales, which make up a significant portion of the Russian corpus. Moreover, some of the Russian—and Ukrainian and Belarusian—tale types are unique to these three related peoples, including The **Wolf** and the **Pig** (SUS 106*), The Birds' Tsar Kuk (SUS 221B*), Nikita the Tanner (SUS 3002), and A Drunkard Enters Paradise (SUS 800*).

Although it is clear that literary tales from the fifteenth century onward reflect the **oral tradition**, actual collections of oral tales exist only since the eighteenth century. These were heavily redacted in accordance with contemporary literary practice. In the Romantic era, writers such as Aleksandr **Pushkin** and Nikolai Gogol made extensive use of folkloric tradition in their writing, but it was in the latter half of the nineteenth century that the first great collections were produced. Chief among these are Aleksandr Afanas'ev's *Narodnye russkie skazki* (*Russian Folktales*, 1855–1863; also translated as *Russian Fairy Tales*) and Ivan Khudyakov's collection of 1860–62. At the beginning of the twentieth century, important collections were issued by Nikolai Onchukov, Dmitry Sadovnikov, Aleksei Smirnov, Boris and Yuri Sokolov, and D. K. Zelenin. During the Soviet era, **fieldwork** produced many important collections, especially those by Mark Azadovskii, Dmitry Balashov, N. K. Mitropol'skaya, A. I. Nikiforov, and F. V. Tumilevich. **Collecting** continues sporadically today both in the White Sea region and in the more remote areas of eastern Siberia.

Twentieth-century Russian scholars gave special prominence to the folktale as **performance**. A particularly important and influential example of this is the work of Azadovskii, whose 1926 study of the illiterate storyteller Natalia Vinokurova from the Upper Lena district of Siberia demonstrated the importance of the **context** and performance of **storytelling** long before these became focal points for American folklorists in the 1960s. Azadovskii's study, first published in German as *Eine sibirische Märchenerzählerin,* was translated into English as *A Siberian Tale Teller* in 1974 and remains a classic. This emphasis on the storyteller resulted in collections of the folktales of A. D. Lomtev, Abram Novopol'tsev, Magai (Egor Sorokovikov), Fillip Gospodarev, A. N. Korol'kova, M. M. Korguev, and others.

Eighteenth-century collections of folktales reflect the taste and editorial practices of the times. They were published in the stylized literary language without regard to a narrator's own style or local dialect. The provenance of the majority of these tales is not recorded and is thus unknown. Afanas'ev and Khudyakov, working in the mid-nineteenth century, were more careful to record the origins of their tales, and, in the case of the former, to publish them in the original dialect or language (Ukrainian or Belarusian) when it differed from Russian. However, both compilers edited their texts to a degree that cannot be determined today. Only in the twentieth century have folklorists been careful to record features of the original language, including rhymes and rhythms that are an element of many oral tales. Yet even now, the language of published tales closely approximates that of the standard Russian language, especially with regard to substandard lexicon. Special features common to many tales include a preamble intended to get the audience's attention and a closing statement such as "I was there, I drank wine and beer. It ran over my moustaches and none got into my mouth." Here, the audience is expected to provide compensation (beer, vodka, or even money) for the entertainment.

No new animal tale types have been found in Russian for many years. They survive outside academic collections in editions for children, often lavishly illustrated. Of the approximately 120 types of animal tales in the Russian repertoire, the most popular involve the fox, wolf, and bear, sometimes in conjunction with a **peasant** or domestic animals. The fox is invariably clever; the wolf is stupid, cruel, and greedy, and the bear bumbling and stupid but in the end lovable. Russian animal tales show some resemblance to those in the Sanskrit *Panchatantra* but almost none to early western European collections. Russian scholars are nearly unanimous in tracing the tales of wild animals to extremely archaic notions of totemism, some of which survived in the Russian countryside into the nineteenth century.

Following Vladimir **Propp**, Russian scholars have traced the roots of wonder tales to ancient **myth** and associated rites of **initiation.** They were apparently told by **men** exclusively to adolescent boys until the late eighteenth century; this practice survived among the fishermen of the remote White Sea area and the fur trappers operating along the great North Russian rivers until well into the twentieth century. References to **women** as narrators appear only at the very end of the eighteenth century. Even after World War II, these tales were still widely regarded by many as having a magic function, which controlled the time of day, the season, and the locale for the narration. The vast majority of these tales are centered on an adolescent boy, usually named Ivan, who is bound to succeed against overwhelming odds. The tales invariably begin in a situation where the would-be hero is apparently doomed: he is an orphan, the third son destined to inherit nothing, or disadvantaged by some unattractive physical feature. If he is not kidnapped, an external force may summon him to action, and he sets out into the unknown. He will usually enter a dense wood, where he encounters some physical monster or other threatening force that will generally end up helping him to conquer his fear. Often the threat in the wood will come from the Russian **witch Baba Yaga**, whose repulsive physical features and abode tie her to the land of the dead. In many such tales, Ivan will escape from the witch and travel to a mythical tsardom, where he will encounter a serpent, a giant, or some other evil that is guarding a treasure or a captive tsarevna (the daughter of a tsar). The hero's conquest is invariably followed by his return, but never to his own home: Ivan's elevated or altered status takes him to court, where he is married to the tsarevna and inherits a portion of the tsardom. There are comparatively fewer tales wherein female characters play an important role. This may be for historical reasons, both reflecting Russian society and the folkloric tradition. It is worth noting that in more recent tales, the role of women is greatly expanded.

Russian **legend**s consist of two basic types: those based on topics taken from the Judeo-Christian tradition, including the apocrypha and saints' lives (**saint's legend**); and those fictitious tales centered on an historical person or event. Favorite themes encompass Christ and his apostles, and popular Russian saints such as Il'ya, Nikolai, and Georgy, and their interaction with impoverished Russian peasants. A popular beginning is "In the days when Christ still walked about Rus." Legends also tell of Ivan the Terrible, Peter the Great, or an outstanding popular figure such as Sten'ka Razin, but they do not generally focus on other historical characters. Afanas'ev prepared the first collection of legends by 1859, although the censorship of the time forbade their actual publication until 1913. Afanas'ev was particularly attracted to tales that reflected what he regarded as ancient myths. Thus, in one such legend, a peasant and his wife decide to frighten the Savior. They hide under a field rake, and the peasant begins roaring like a bear while his wife cuckoos. God curses them, turning them into these very creatures forever. Another tale tells the story of the cursing of sparrows. While the swallows attempt to lead the Jews away from Christ's hiding place, the sparrows' peeping leads them to Him and thus to His crucifixion. Hence, sparrows may not be used for human food. Russian **religious tale**s are highly moralistic, while tales about the tsars and others reflect popular beliefs about a good tsar or rebel who is close to his people. These are distinguished from political anecdotes that were primarily told by the educated class and may be characterized by their contemporary contents.

Russian tales of everyday life are also known as stories of love and life or as **novella**s. They represent a late stage in the development of the Russian folktale and are primarily present in collections of the later nineteenth and twentieth centuries. Reflective of life in the countryside, they are centered on knavery and trickery—especially the interactions between peasants and landlords, merchants, and government officials—or on courtships. Reflecting changes in Russian society, the role of merchants is prominent in many of the tales belonging to this category, and women often play the role of antagonist to unscrupulous but witless men. Tales of love are invariably sad, wistful, and focused on unfulfilled desire. Many of the tales of love and life end violently in beheadings, hangings, murders, or maimings. There are virtually none with "happy endings." Among the more peculiar are those on the theme Why They Stopped Killing the Old Folks (Haney 6: nos. 645–47). In one such tale, a **soldier** convinces **Death** to go into a sack and take no more souls. Soon, however, the aged and infirm beg for the release that Death brings. When the soldier himself falls into a cellar, however, he too longs for Death, who then comes when let out of the sack to release all those who long for her. During the Soviet era, scholars were obliged to interpret these tales as reflective of the class struggle against landlords, priests, and other oppressors, and so described them in this way. Since the death of Stalin in 1953, most Russian scholars have referred to them as tales of "everyday life," while admitting that it is the general background of the tale that represents peasant or merchant reality and not the tale's plot. In the period just before the fall of the Soviet Union, scholars pointed to the satirical nature of such stories. Since 1989, scholars have published new collections of these tales, and some have begun using the term "Russian popular novellas" to describe this genre.

Tales of clever fools are known in the Aarne-Thompson-Uther classification system as "Tales of the Stupid **Ogre** (Giant, Devil)." In Russian tales of this kind, the protagonist is the village fool who easily outwits his opponents, the priest with his wife, or the imp and his grandfather, the devil. One characteristic of these stories is the ease with which narrators have combined several tale types into one narrative, thus creating a single tale that may involve the attempts of the priest to deceive his worker, his efforts to be rid of the worker by sending him to the devil, and then the devil or imp's attempts to outwit the worker or fool. Without exception, the devil loses the contests, as does the priest, who may also end up losing his life or his wife to the fool.

Throughout the nineteenth and early twentieth centuries, Russian scholars followed approaches to the study of folktales dominant in western Europe. Thus, Afanas'ev and Fyodor Buslaev, as representatives of the mythological school, focused on interpreting the tales as remnants of ancient myths (see **Mythological Approaches**). On the other hand, in the aftermath of the reforms of the 1850s, social democrats and populists emphasized directly collecting the tales of the Russian people to show the deplorable conditions of the peasantry. Their efforts brought many new tales and collections of tales to the attention of scholars. So did the work of Dmitry Zelenin, Nikolai Onchukov, and scholars who represent a third, ethnographic approach to the study of the tales (see **Ethnographic Approaches**). In 1915, the brothers Iu. M. and B. M. Sokolov published their two-volume collection of tales from the White Lake area; this—alongside the collections of Afanas'ev and Onchukov—is considered the greatest collecting achievement of the prerevolutionary era. Collecting continued after the revolutions of 1917, resulting in the important work by Azadovskii and others in recording the repertoires of several outstanding contemporary narrators. Aleksandr Veselovsky and N. P. Andreev were adherents to the **historic-geographic method** and **comparative method**. In 1929, Andreev, following Antti **Aarne**'s scheme for categorizing folk narratives, produced the first guide to tale types in Russian. More recent Russian work is connected with Propp and his followers. Propp's *Morfologiya skazki* (*Morphology of the Folktale*, 1928) and *Istoricheskie korni volshebnoi skazki* (*Historical Roots of the Wondertale*, 1946) have been especially influential in the study of the fairy or wonder tale. The syntactic approach of Propp's morphology and the Russians' predilection for tracing the history of folktales continue to exercise influence even recently, as can be seen in the writings of Elena Novik, Irina Razumova, and Elena Shastina.

Many Russian artists, musicians, writers, and filmmakers show the influence of folktales and fairy tales in their work. Drawing on both folk sources and **literary fairy tale**s, composers such as Nikolai **Rimsky-Korsakov** and Pyotr Il'ich **Tchaikovsky** have produced **music** for fairy-tale **opera**, **theater**, and **dance**, and are especially well known internationally. Russian artists such as Ivan **Bilibin** and Viktor Vasnetsov have made important contributions to the art of fairy-tale **illustration**. Since the nineteenth century, Russian writers have produced many interesting **adaptation**s of traditional narratives and original literary tales, including authors such as Kornei **Chukovsky**, Pyotr **Ershov**, Ivan Krylov, Samuil Marshak, Aleksandr **Pushkin**, Mikhail Saltykov-Shchedrin, and Lev **Tolstoy**. Fairy-tale scholarship and **children's literature** studies have begun devoting more attention to these and other writers, especially in light of their sociopolitical significance. Folklore, folktales, and fairy tales also play a significant role in Russian **film**—for example, in the work of Aleksandr Rou—which, like the Russian literary tradition, deserves more attention from scholars of fairy-tale studies. *See also* Slavic Tales; Soviet Fairy-Tale Films.

Further Readings: Afanasyev, Aleksandr. *Russian Secret Tales: Bawdy Folktales of Old Russia.* Baltimore: Genealogical Publishing Co., 1998; Azadovskii, Mark. *A Siberian Tale Teller.* Translated by James R. Dow. Austin: University of Texas, 1974; Balina, Marina, Helena Goscilo, and Mark Lipovetsky, eds. *Politicizing Magic: An Anthology of Russian and Soviet Fairy Tales.* Evanston, IL: Northwestern University Press, 2005; Barag, L. G., et al. *Sravnitel'ny ukazatel syuzhetov: Vostochnoslavyanskaya skazka.* Leningrad: Nauka, 1979; Becker, Richarda. *Die weibliche Initiation im ostslawischen Zaubermärchen.* Berlin: Otto Harrassowitz, 1990; Guterman, Norbert, trans. *Russian Fairy Tales: From the Collections of Aleksandr Afanas'ev.* New York: Pantheon, 1945; Haney, Jack V., ed. *The Complete Russian Folktale.* 7 volumes. Armonk, NY: M. E. Sharpe, 1999–2006; Ivanits, Linda. J. *Russian Folk Belief.* Armonk, New York: M. E. Sharpe, 1989; Johns, Andreas. *Baba Yaga: The Ambiguous Mother and Witch of the Russian Folktale.* New York: Peter Lang, 2004; Propp, Vladimir. *Morphology of the Folktale.* Translated by Laurence Scott. Revised and edited by Louis A. Wagner. 2nd edition. 1968. Austin: University of Texas Press, 1996; ———. *Theory and History of Folklore.* Translated by Ariadna Y. Martin and Richard P. Martin. Minneapolis: University of Minnesota Press, 1984.

Jack V. Haney

S

S., Svend Otto (1916–1996)

As a prolific Danish illustrator of fairy tales, Svend Otto S. has been described as a Scandinavian naturalist often creating a certain magical timelessness in his realist, yet artistically interpreted, style. Nature is often foregrounded, and Svend Otto S. is known for doing meticulous research on the landscapes he used to illustrate the mindscapes of the fairy tales. The interplay between text and **illustration** is always based on a deep obligation to the tale.

Awarded the Hans Christian Andersen Medal in 1978, Svend Otto S. set out with a picture book version of "The Ugly Duckling" in 1940 and kept returning to the universes of Hans Christian **Andersen**, Jacob and Wilhelm **Grimm**, Peter Christen **Asbjørnsen**, and Jørgen **Moe**. In *Børnenes H. C. Andersen* (1972; translated as *Hans Andersen Fairy Tales*, 1985), Svend Otto S. illustrates sixteen of Andersen's best-known tales in a style responding to Andersen's use of characteristic details, often catching the feature of dual address in the rendering of atmosphere. Many illustrations of Grimms' tales focus on landscape and nature as a foil to humans and animals, and the trolls of Asbjørnsen and Moe's tales often resemble age-old natural growths. The weather in all its forms takes on a special role in Svend Otto S.'s universe, including more than fifty picture book retellings. ***See also*** Scandinavian Tales.

Further Reading: Kirsten Bystrup. *De tegner for børn: Portrætter af 12 danske bønebogsillustratorer.* Copenhagen: DBC, 1994.

Helene Høyrup

Saga

A saga is purportedly a historical narrative, written mainly in Iceland from the twelfth century onward but dealing largely with the period before and around the Icelandic acceptance of Christianity (1000 CE). Sagas contain a great deal of valuable material about the **oral tradition** and folk belief in early northern Europe, especially the northern Germanic area, and provide some of the earliest examples of folktale **motif**s from these parts.

Allegedly historical, sagas traditionally fall into the following groups: *riddarasögur* (romances) and *heilagramannasögur* (sagas of saints), which are essentially loose translations of French and English medieval chivalric romances and foreign hagiographic **legend**s; *biskupasögur* (sagas of Icelandic bishops); *konungasögur* (kings' sagas), which deal principally with Norwegian **king**s; *Íslendingasögur* (sagas of Icelanders), which tell of the first settlers of Iceland from the late ninth century; *samtímasögur* (contemporary sagas of thirteenth-century Iceland); and *fornaldarsögur* (sagas of ancient times), which deal with the legendary past of Scandinavia. The *biskupasögur, konungasögur, Íslendingasögur, samtímasögur,* and *fornaldarsögur* are all, to a greater or lesser extent, based on material that has existed in the Nordic oral tradition for some centuries. This material ranges from individual motifs to longer personal narratives, **memorate**s, belief legends (of ghosts, trolls, dreams, *fylgjur* or spirit doubles, **elves**, water-horses, **changeling**s, mermen, and more), and even early fairy tales (especially in the *fornaldarsögur*). These works testify to the early cultural contacts that existed not only between the Nordic and the Germanic countries but also between the Icelanders and the medieval Irish and Scots. *See also* Middle Ages; Religious Tale; Saint's Legend; Scandinavian Tales.

Further Reading: Jónas Kristjánsson. *Eddas and Sagas: Iceland's Medieval Literature.* Translated by Peter Foote. Reykjavík: Hið íslenska bókmenntafélag, 1988.

Terry Gunnell

Saint's Legend

While the term "**legend**" originally referred to the story of the life of a saint, and in some contexts still is understood in that narrow way (as with the German cognate *Legende*), folkorists use "saint's legend" to designate tales told about Christian saints. Martyrs were venerated from the beginnings of Christianity in the hope that the faithful might participate in the saint's inherent power and mercy. Hagiography, or the writing of a saint's biography, emerged as an identifiable genre as early as the fifth century CE. Reading about the exemplary quality of a saint's life linked its audience to the godhead through an unbroken chain. Typology, which linked the particular saint with biblical figures who functioned as types or exemplars, was a central device for establishing both a recognizable religious context for the saint and a chain of spiritual impact. Saintliness is chiefly evidenced by the emulation of Christ's example: rejection of family, abandonment of possessions, mortification of the body, fasting and constant prayer, and often violent **death** at the hands of persecutors. A text presented as the "Life" of a saint is apt to include fantastic **legend**s associated with the saint's suffering and death. The purpose of connecting readers to Christ through the saint is to enjoin the audience to emulate such behavior, not in the arena of heroic suffering, but in the humbler temptations and vicissitudes of everyday life, and to model how the saint is able to intercede on their behalf.

Saint's legends were widely read throughout the **Middle Ages** and Renaissance, and remain popular reading material in the modern era. The most famous collection is the *Legenda aurea* (*The Golden Legend*), compiled by Jacobus de Voragine around 1260 CE. In the modern era, Donald Attwater's 1956 revision of Alban Butler's *Lives of the Saints* (1756–59) remains the premier work, and marks a shift in emphasis from heroic suffering to love and compassion for fellow human beings. *See also* Bible, Bible Tale; Religious Tale.

Further Readings: Altman, Charles. "Two Types of Opposition and the Structure of Latin Saints' Lives." *Medievalia et Humanistica* 6 (1975): 1–11; Hock, Ronald F., J. Bradley Chance, and Judith Perkins. *Ancient Fiction and Early Christian Narrative.* Atlanta: Scholars Press, 1998; Wogan-Browne, Jocelyn. *Saints Lives and Women's Literary Culture.* New York: Oxford University Press, 2001.

John Stephens

Salmelainen, Eero (1830–1867)

Famous for his excellent four-volume edition of Finnish folktales and fairy tales, the first of its kind ever published in Finland, Eero Salmelainen (pseudonym of Erik Rudbeck) stands out as one of the main figures in developing the language of Finnish literature. Born into a Swedish speaking family but influenced by contemporary fennomanic ideology, promoted by his teacher, professor and senator J. V. Snellman, Salmelainen, like many of his contemporaries, changed his Swedish name into a Finnish one. Studies in philosophy and languages at Alexander University in Helsinki took him to Russia and St. Petersburg. On his return to Finland, he joined the Finnish Literary Society, which had published the Finnish national epic *Kalevala*. At twenty years of age, Salmelainen became editor of the publication *Suomen kansan satuja ja tarinoita* (*The **Märchen** and **Legends** of the Finnish People*). The first volume appeared in 1852, the fourth and last in 1866. Encouraged by an enthusiastic reception, in 1856 Salmelainen began working on his thesis, "Om Finnarnes folkdikt i obunden berättande form" ("On Finnish Folk Poetry in Free Narrative Form"), which unfortunately became a disaster for the promising young scholar. Accusations of plagiarism were made, and although they were clearly unjustified, his work was nevertheless rejected, which affected the rest of his life. As a secondary-school teacher, Salmelainen still found the time to publish articles on religious and folkloric issues. He also edited two journals for children and young adults. His reader *Pääskysen pakinat* (*Tales of a Swallow*), published in 1857, became very popular. *See also* Finnish Tales.

Further Reading: Bowman, James Cloyd, and Margery Williams Bianco. *Tales from a Finnish Tupa.* From a translation by Aili Kolehmainen. Chicago: A. Whitman, 1964.

Janina Orlov

Salomone-Marino, Salvatore (1847–1916)

Sicilian folklorist and practicing physician Salvatore Salomone-Marino was a longtime friend and collaborator of fellow Sicilian folklorist Giuseppe **Pitrè**. Born in the Borgetto province of Palermo, Sicily, he studied medicine and surgery at the University of Palermo, where he graduated in 1873. In 1876, he became head physician at Palermo's Ospedale Civico, and by 1887 was chair of Special Medical Pathology at the University of Messina, in Sicily. With Pitrè, Salomone-Marino cofounded and coedited the first major Italian **folklore** journal, *Archivio per lo studio delle tradizioni popolari* (*Archives for the Study of Popular Traditions*), which was published in twenty-four volumes from 1882 until 1906. In 1884, Salomone-Marino was one of the founding members of the Italian Folklore Society. He was also an active member of numerous academies and societies, including the Royal Academy of Science and Arts in Palermo, the Royal Academy of Medical Science of Palermo, and the Sicilian Society for the History of the Country.

Salomone-Marino published many studies on medicine, history, and literature, as well as on folklore. Frequent topics of his folklore writings include Sicilian folk songs, **poetry**, and **legend**s, including *Canti popolari siciliani* (*Sicilian Folk Songs*, 1867) and *Leggende popolari siciliane in poesia* (*Sicilian Folk Legends in Poetry*, 1880). Salomone-Marino's most enduring work is *Costumi ed usanze dei contadini di Sicilia* (*Customs and Habits of the Sicilian Peasants*, 1897). *See also* Italian Tales.

Further Reading: Cocchiara, Giuseppe. *Storia degli studi delle tradizioni popolari in Italia.* Palermo: G. B. Palumbo Editore, 1947.

Linda J. Lee

Salon

The seventeenth-century literary salon in France is the birthplace of the *conte de fées*. Although Charles **Perrault** and other **men** attended and helped establish this literary genre, the salons were primarily a site for female interaction and literary invention. The tales **women** produced reflected their position in society, their response to canonical and male-dominated forms, and their visions of social interaction. Women throughout Europe continued to use the salon to comment on their social status and sometimes to produce fairy tales.

The literary salons developed during the seventeenth-century French **gender** and culture wars. Italy and the French court had seen salons, but the Marquise de Rambouillet's Parisian *chamber bleue* in the 1630s created the space where highly educated aristocratic women, the *précieuses*, gathered to discuss contemporary intellectual and literary disputes. With the founding of the all-male academies (the *Académie Française* in 1634 and the *Académie des Sciences* in 1666), women became increasingly marginalized socially and politically. Intellectual debates focused on gender roles in cultural production, and the academies began to define who would pursue knowledge and how. In the famous Quarrel of the Ancients and the Moderns, begun in 1687, the "ancients" championed Greco-Roman literary models and disdained magic in serious literature; the "moderns" praised models from French **folklore** and medieval, courtly tradition. Perrault was one of the leading voices and writers for the moderns, with his "Griselidis" ("Griselda," 1691) one of the first public salvos.

In 1690—seven years before Perrault's more famous *Histoires ou contes du temps passé* (*Stories or Tales of Times Past*, 1697) and a year before "Griselda"—Marie-Catherine d'**Aulnoy** interjected her first *conte de fées*, "L'île de la félicité" ("The Island of Happiness"), into a **novel**. This tale was followed in 1697 by her four-volume *Les contes des fées* (*Tales of the Fairies*), contemporaneous with Perrault's now canonical work, and a year later by a second four-volume collection. As a sign of their popularity, all forty-eight of d'Aulnoy's tales (and those of other *conteuses*—female fairy-tale authors) were included in the monumental *Le cabinet des fées* (*The Fairies' Cabinet*, 1785–89) and were soon available in **translation** across Europe.

Following de Rambouillet's example, aristocratic women in the France of Louis XIV had begun to resist their social, political, and intellectual alienation. The *salonnières* created an autonomous public forum—in private—for recitation, theatrical performance, and **storytelling**; they turned to the fairy tale precisely because it occupied a marginal, indefinite space between oral, popular culture and elite literary traditions and allowed for formal and thematic experimentation and sociopolitical criticism.

On a formal level, the *salonnières'* tales paid homage to manners and etiquette, spontaneity in speech and lambent conversational ability. The style of their written tales suggested an oral source, with frequent formulaic requests for telling and effusive praise for a tale well told. Although they professed their stories were from the common **folk**, the *conteuses* distanced themselves from the nursemaids and peasant women male *conteurs* like Perrault conjured. In the salons, they were sibyls and **fairies**, and the iconography of their frontispieces clearly situated them in a lettered, educated milieu. Many of their tales drew on the earlier literary traditions of Giambattista **Basile** and Giovan Francesco **Straparola**.

On a thematic level, the *salonnières* focused on their social and biological realities. Tales were frequently a kind of self-portrait; while male prescriptive literature celebrated arranged **marriage**s, motherhood, and homebound females, the *conteuses* and their heroines became undomesticated. Expectant **mother**s and childbirth often took center stage: more than half of d'Aulnoy's tales refer to pregnancy; one-quarter of her tales and one-third of Henriette-Julie de Castelnau, Comtesse de **Murat**'s depict an infertile royal couple helped by a fairy. Heroines may have children out of wedlock or with animal sires; newborns might be animals or monsters, or transformed into them.

Men and women wrote *contes de fées*—thirteen of the **French tales** published between 1690 and 1700 consist of men's and women's versions of the same story—but female authors dominated. Seven *conteuses* authored two-thirds of the tales published between 1690 and 1715. Besides d'Aulnoy and de Murat, the most important include Catherine **Bernard**, Charlotte-Rose de Caumont de **La Force**, and Perrault's niece, Marie-Jeanne **Lhéritier de Villandon**.

Many formal and thematic aspects of these tales resonated in other women's works across national and linguistic borders—de La Force's treatment of older literary texts, for example, anticipated those Benedikte **Naubert** later used in Germany. The salon model also continued to serve women in other countries, most notably Germany. Between 1780 and 1848, *salonnières* such as Bettina von **Arnim** and Amalie von **Helvig** hosted gatherings in Berlin patterned on those in Paris.

One of the most interesting Berlin salons was the *Kaffeterkreis* (coffee circle), founded in 1843 by daughters of Berlin's intellectual elite. Just as the French *salonnières* had responded with fairy tales to the debate of the Ancients and the Moderns, the von Arnim daughters and their friends responded to the emerging canonical tales as the first generation acculturated by the tales of the Brothers **Grimm**, the Romantics, and Hans Christian **Andersen**. Consciously drawing on the *salonnière* tradition, and with a strong desire for intellectual and social equality, the girls of the *Kaffeterkreis* wrote tales that questioned their assigned gender roles and the fairy-tale wedding as the route to happiness and fulfillment. In an extension of the private sphere into a self-made public, they performed fairy-tale plays with strong female images like **Mother Holle**, Lorely, **Undine,** and Melusine.

The tales of the *salonnières* did not exert an influence on canonical forms but demonstrably on other women. These tales and their authors received long-overdue critical attention by feminists in the later twentieth century. ***See also*** Birth; Feminism; Infertility.

Further Readings: Canepa, Nancy C., ed. *Out of the Woods: The Origins of the Literary Fairy Tale in Italy and France*. Detroit: Wayne State University Press, 1997; Jarvis, Shawn C. "Trivial Pursuit? Women Deconstructing the Grimmian Model in the *Kaffeterkreis*." *The Reception of Grimms' Fairy Tales: Responses, Reactions, Revisions*. Edited by Donald Haase. Detroit: Wayne State University Press, 1993. 102–26.

Shawn C. Jarvis

Sand, George (1804–1876)

The feminist-Romantic novelist and prolific writer George Sand (pseudonym of Amandine-Aurore-Lucile Dudevant, née Dupin) wrote more than sixty novels and memoirs and corresponded with other important writers of her time, among them Gustave Flaubert. Sand included references to **folklore** and **storytelling** in **novel**s like *François le champi* (*Francis the Waif*, 1847), *La petite Fadette* (*Little Fadette*, 1849), and *La mare au diable* (*The Devil's Pool*, 1846), as well as in her Bildungsromane (novels of development), such as *Consuelo* (1842) and *Les maîtres sonneurs* (*The Bagpipers*, 1853). In these novels, most of the characters have fairy and folk characteristics. They are depicted with weaknesses, both physical or moral; and, as in many tales, at the end they become heroes or heroines by acquiring skills that set them positively apart. They either become masters of an art—in most cases, music—or spiritual guides. In *La petite Fadette*, for instance, the heroine, at first ugly, mean, and scary due to some unexplained magical happenings around her, by the end of the narration turns out to embody all of the positive attributes imaginable.

Sand's interest in the fairy tale was due primarily to the influence of her region of origin, Le Berry. A distinct feature of this area is the blend of Catholicism and local folklore and fairy lore. Dating from the **Middle Ages**, these ancestral beliefs led the local peasants and craftsmen, among whom Sand grew up, to refer to **fairies** (*les fadets*) in their evening story-telling and daily lives. Thus, Sand's stories include a blend of realism linked to the countryside and of fairy lore grounded in local beliefs. Sand reproduces the orality of the tale tradition, opening her novels with storytellers who narrate the plot as extradiegetic narrators.

In her memoirs, *Histoire de ma vie* (*The Story of My Life*, 1855), Sand further acknowledges being influenced by her readings of tales by Charles **Perrault** and Marie-Catherine d'**Aulnoy**. Her stories also were influenced by E. T. A. **Hoffmann**'s idealistic approach to nature. Her later works include a collection of tales, *Contes d'une grand-mère* (*Tales of a Grandmother*, 1872), which she wrote for her two grandchildren. These stories have an educational purpose, conveying the message that anybody can overcome their foibles and become a stronger person by means of persistence and a belief in nature's gifts. Tales from this collection include "Le nuage rose" ("The Pink Cloud"), "Les ailes de courage" ("Wings of Courage"), "Le géant Yéous" ("Yeous the Giant"), "Le chêne parlant" ("The Talking Oak Tree"), and "La fée poussière" ("The Fairy Dust"). For Sand, the greatest magic comes from nature, which in turn participates in the identity quest of the young heroes and heroines. ***See also*** Faerie and Fairy Lore; French Tales.

Further Readings: Capasso, Ruth Carver. "Traduction libre: Science in *Les Contes d'une Grand-mère*." *George Sand Studies* 16 (1997): 57–68; Didier, Béatrice. "George Sand et les structures du conte populaire." *George Sand.* Edited by Simone Vierne. Paris: CDU/SEDES, 1983. 101–14.

Caroline Jumel

Sandburg, Carl (1878–1967)

Twice awarded the Pulitzer Prize for poetry and for biography, American author Carl Sandburg also wrote *Rootabaga Stories* (1922), a collection of fairy tales inspired by questions from his young daughters. Later came *Rootabaga Pigeons* (1923), *Rootabaga Country* (1929), and *Potato Face* (1930). Born into meager economic circumstances to working-class parents, Sandburg read the fairy tales of writers such as Hans Christian **Andersen**, but believed that European-generated fairy tales were too centered on royalty to speak to American **childhood** experience, especially in the 1920s prairie lands.

Having traveled across the prairie as a hobo, Sandburg wrote tales featuring railroads that zigzag among whimsically named small towns, encountering such figures as **pig**s wearing bibs and tutelary deities as corn **fairies**. In the largest town, the Village of Liver-and-Onions, skyscrapers converse and even decide to have a child. Many of Sandburg's tales have a clear **moral** message about being true to one's character or valuing unique personality traits, but, perhaps most distinctively, the tales revel in the very sounds of language, playing often with nonsense or onomatopoeic words and with allegorical names like Eeta Peeca Pie, Slipfoot, and Gimme the Ax. Sandburg's tales engage in a gently mocking **fantasy** of everyday life, centering on such momentous events as the wedding of a rag doll and broom handle or the elaborate social interactions of umbrellas and straw hats. *See also* North American Tales.

Further Readings: Callahan, North. *Carl Sandburg: His Life and Works*. University Park: Pennsylvania State University Press, 1987; Niven, Penelope. *Carl Sandburg: A Biography*. New York: Scribner, 1991.

Lori Schroeder Haslem

Sarnelli, Pompeo (1649–1724)

The writer and Bishop Pompeo Sarnelli was born in Bari, Italy. In 1674, he edited the first edition of Giambattista **Basile**'s *Lo cunto de li cunti* (*The Tale of Tales*) to carry the alternate name of *Pentamerone* on the frontispiece, and in 1684, he published his own *Posilicheata* (*An Outing to Posillipo*) under the pseudonym of Masillo Reppone de Gnanopoli. The latter consists of five fairy tales told in Neapolitan dialect and embedded in a realistic **frame narrative** in which peasant **women** entertain guests at the end of a country banquet by telling tales. It is the only other seventeenth-century Italian collection of fairy tales besides Basile's *The Tale of Tales*. Both the overall structure and style owe much to Basile's model. Sarnelli fuses, for example, elements from learned and folk cultures, and opts for an abundance of metaphor. The tales themselves—"La pieta ricompensata" ("Mercy Recompensed"), "La serva fedele" ("The Faithful Servant"), "L'ingannatrice ingannata" ("The Deceiver Deceived"), "La gallinella" ("The Young Hen"), and "La testa e la coda" ("The Head and the Tale")—contain common folkloric **motif**s, such as kindness rewarded, magical resurrection from **death**, **fairies**' curses, the cruel **mother**-in-law, false messages, and helping animals. The tales do not appear to be derived directly from oral folktales, but were probably adapted by Sarnelli from already mediated versions of popular tales in circulation. Unlike Basile's opus, *An Outing to Posillipo* has met with little critical acclaim. *See also* Italian Tales.

Further Reading: Malato, Enrico, ed. and introd. *Posilicheata*. By Pompeo Sarnelli. Rome: Gabriele e Mariateresa Benincasa, 1986.

Nancy Canepa

Scandinavian Tales

Situated on the periphery of Europe, the Scandinavian countries' traditional folktales and fairy tales reflect societies that were late to be Christianized and late to lose their rural, agrarian identities. In these societies, oral narrative was an integral part of life for centuries. Folkloristic **motif**s and survivals of oral culture are evident in the great Eddic poems and the magnificent Icelandic **saga**s, which were first written down in the thirteenth century, as well as in **king**'s sagas and the mythical-heroic sagas.

Similar pagan religious backgrounds, common customs and beliefs, and essentially a common language give Scandinavian tales a recognizable character. Strictly speaking, Scandinavia includes the countries on the Scandinavian peninsula, but this overview is a linguistic one and will encompass the countries of Denmark (with the Faeroes), Iceland, Norway, Sweden, and Swedish Finland. **Finnish tales** are excluded here, except for tales from the Swedish-speaking part of Finland, because Finnish, unlike the others, is not a Germanic language. The following overview should not be considered exhaustive.

Denmark and the Faeroe Islands

As in many European countries, the publication of the **Grimm** brothers' *Kinder- und Hausmärchen* (*Children's and Household Tales*, 1812–15) was a stimulus for the collection of folktales; but even before the Grimms, there was great interest in Denmark in the folk **ballad**. *It hundrede vdvaalde danske viser* (*One Hundred Selected Danish Ballads*), collected by Anders Sørenssøn Vedel, was published in 1591 and was the first printed collection of ballads in Europe. It became tremendously popular in Peder Syv's 1695 edition. Syv added another 100 songs and published his edition as *200 Viser om Konger oc Kemper oc andre* (*200 Ballads about Kings and Heroes and Others*). This edition was constantly being reprinted and was as popular in Norway (united with Denmark at this time) as it was in Denmark. *Udvalgte danske viser fra Middelalderen* (*Selected Danish Ballads of the Middle Ages*, 1812–14) was published by several **collectors** shortly after the Grimms' *Altdänische Heldenlieder, Balladen und Märchen* (*Ancient Danish Hero Songs, Lays, and Tales*) appeared in 1811.

Following the example of the Grimms' *Deutsche Sagen* (*German Legends*, 1816–18), the librarian Just Mathias Thiele published *Danske folkesagn* (*Danish Folk Legends*, 1818–23). Thiele compiled **legend**s from a variety of sources and edited the material. In 1823, Mathias Winther published *Danske folkeeventyr* (*Danish Folktales*), a collection that was translated into English in 1989. The ballad collector Svend **Grundtvig** released *Gamle danske minder i folkemunde* (*Old Danish Lore in Oral Tradition*, 1854–61) and *Danske folkeeventyr* (*Danish Folktales*) in 1876 and 1878, and also collected legends between 1839 and 1883 that were not published until 1944. But the most prolific Danish collector was undoubtedly Evald **Tang Kristensen**, who compiled an enormous amount of folk material from Jutland and published nearly eighty books during his lifetime. Tang Kristensen was unusual in that he also collected information about some of his **informant**s and the circumstances of performance. Bengt **Holbek**'s influential *Interpretation of Fairy Tales: Danish Folklore in a European Perspective* (1987) is based primarily on data from Tang Kristensen's collection. Not to be overlooked in any review of Danish folk narrative is the contribution of Axel Olrik, who was one of the key figures in the establishment of folkloristics as an international academic discipline. His article from 1908, "Episke love i folkdigtningen" ("The Epic Laws of Folk Narrative"), is one of the classics of **folklore** research.

In 1816, Adam **Oehlenschläger** published *Eventyr af forskjellige digtere* (*Fairy Tales from Several Writers*), an influential collection of translated **literary fairy tale**s from Johann Karl August **Musäus**, Ludwig **Tieck**, the painter Philipp Otto Runge, Friedrich de la Motte **Fouqué**, and the Brothers Grimm. When Jørgen **Moe** read these stories, he wrote admiringly of them to Peter Christen **Asbjørnsen**, with the caveat, "But of course, they're not Norwegian!" Bernhard Severin Ingemann published *Eventyr og fortællinger* (*Fairy Tales and Stories*) in 1820. The story "Moster Maria" ("Aunt Maria") features the **Bluebeard** motif, and "Sphinxen" ("The Sphinx") was inspired by E. T. A. **Hoffmann**.

The giant of the Danish literary fairy tale is, of course, Hans Christian **Andersen**. Andersen published 156 tales in four collections from 1835 to 1872, and although Danish folktales provided the kernel for some of the stories, both in written form and from his childhood memories, Andersen read widely and was influenced as much by numerous literary sources, including Hoffmann and the other German Romantics, as well as Charles **Dickens**, Jonathan Swift, Giovan Francesco **Straparola** in J. Chr. Riise's 1818 translation, and many others.

From his childhood he was familiar with the *Thousand and One Nights* (or the **Arabian Nights**) in Antoine **Galland**'s French edition of 1704–17, and the **Aladdin** motif is evident in one of his first fairy tales, "Fyrtøjet" ("The Tinderbox"). Andersen has been called the father of the modern fairy tale, and many of his successors in the genre have engaged in intertextual conversations with his classic creations (see **Intertextuality**). There have also been many adaptations and, in some cases, the original Andersen story can scarcely be recognized at all, such as in the **Walt Disney Company**'s **film** interpretation of "Den lille havfrue" ("The Little Mermaid").

Although Andersen overshadows all other Danish fairy-tale writers, there have been others who wrote within the genre, although often with a twist. Carl **Ewald** was a prolific fairy-tale author who wrote many volumes of tales with a realism that precluded a happy ending. By 1900, he was the most significant Danish fairy-tale writer in Europe after Andersen. Holger Drachmann published a fairy-tale comedy *Det var engang* (*Once upon a Time*) in 1885. Viggo Stuckenberg's 1899 collection of stories, *Vejbred* (*The Plantain*), includes entertaining fairy tales such as "Kongens datter" ("The King's Daughter"), in which a troll who has stolen a **princess** is relieved when she's rescued by a poor tailor's son. She had rearranged the possessions in his cave so that he couldn't find anything! In the twentieth century, Karen Blixen, writing as Isak Dinesen, utilized fairy-tale motifs in several of her complex stories, as in "The Pearl" from *Winter's Tales* (1942); and it has been said that everything Tove Ditlevsen wrote was a version of a fairy tale. Villy Sørensen wrote modern absurd and grotesque fairy tales and **parable**s with an ironic twist in collections such as *Ufarlige historier* (*Harmless Tales*, 1955) and many others. Knud Holten's *Med hjertet i livet* (*My Heart Leaps Up*, 1972) is a modern fairy tale set in a science-fiction setting. Bjarne Reuter, who sometimes blends reality with fantasy, has retold old tales in his *Rottefængeren fra Hameln* (*The Rat Catcher of Hameln*, 1976) and *Drengen der ikke kunne blive bange* (*The Boy Who Felt No Fear*, 1978). His fantasy novel, *Shamran*, 1985, is reminiscent of Astrid **Lindgren**'s *Bröderna lejonhjärta* (*The Brothers Lionheart*, 1973).

The number of **fantasy** tales in Danish increased during the 1980s and 1990s and continue to be popular, perhaps because of the success of the Harry Potter stories. Louis Jensen's *Den frygtelige hånd* (*The Terrible Hand*, 2001) is a metatext which refers to Hoffmann and Grimm (see **Metafiction**). Recently, Bent Haller's *Mig og fanden–En fortælling om et eventyr* (*Me and the Devil: A Tale of a Fairy Tale*, 2002) is a pastiche of Hans Christian Andersen fairy tales in which the protagonist breaks with the genre in the end by refusing to marry the princess.

Of course, Andersen's stories also inspired Danish artists such as Lorenz Frølich, Hans Kristian Tegner, and Kay **Nielsen**. There is a long tradition of excellence in Danish children's picture-book **illustration**. Jens Sigsgaard's *Palle alene i verden* (*Palle Alone in the World*, 1942), about a boy who wakes up to find that he is alone in the world, is a fairy tale illustrated by Arne Ungermann. Among many other artists of note who have illustrated fairy tales are Svend Otto **S.** and Ib Spang Olsen. In general, it can be said that Denmark is most innovative in the genre of children's picture books rather than in the modern fairy-tale genre.

In the Faeroe Islands, best known today for its tradition of ballad dancing, one of the first collectors of folktales was Johan Hendrik Schröter, who was largely responsible for the publication of one of the early Faeroese ballad collections. The first to publish traditional stories in the Faeroese language was Venceslaus Ulricus Hammershaimb, who worked to establish a written Faeroese language. The first texts published by Hammershaimb appeared in a

Danish journal in 1846. Additional stories appeared in *Antiquarisk Tidsskrift* (*Antiquarian Journal*, 1849–51). In 1891, he published *Færösk anthologi* (*Faeroese Anthology*), which contained texts in varying genres. Another early collector was Jakob Jakobsen, who collaborated with Hammershaimb on the anthology and who published *Faeröske folkesagn og æventyr* (*Faeroese Folk Legends and Tales*) in 1889–1901. Many Faeroese legends deal with early residents of the Faeroe Islands and are quite reminiscent of the Icelandic *þættir* (short stories). Stories about the legendary Peder Arrheboe were used as the basis for Jørgen-Frantz Jacobsen's novel *Barbara* (1939), published in Danish. Hans Andrias Djurhuus was a Faeroese writer who wrote fairy tales, as well as poetry, songs, and longer prose texts. Hans Jakob Jacobsen, who wrote as Heðin Brú and is considered the most important Faeroese writer of his generation, published the standard Faeroese fairy tale collection, *Ævintýr I–VI*, in six volumes between 1959 and 1974.

Iceland

If Danish fairy-tale writers are overshadowed by Hans Christian Andersen on the world stage, a similar phenomenon is true of Icelandic folktales and legends. The long shadow of the splendid medieval sagas casts everything else into the shade. But Iceland's early literacy and the stable nature of the Icelandic language led to an ongoing symbiotic relationship between the written and the oral. The first collector of folktales in Iceland was Árni Magnússon, and the work of the Grimms inspired collectors in Iceland as elsewhere. In 1852, Jón Árnason and Magnús Grimson published a small edition, *Íslenzk æfintýri* (*Icelandic Folktales*). Most of the texts were contributed by contacts the two collectors had around the country. They were encouraged by the German scholar Konrad Maurer, who published a collection of Icelandic legends in 1860. Two large volumes of folktales, *Íslenzkar þjóðsögur og æfintýri* (*Icelandic Folk Legends and Tales*), were published in 1862–64 by Árnason. From 1895 to 1965, a revival of **collecting** resulted in the publication of more than fifty collections of folktales and legends. A comprehensive collection is the sixteen volume *Íslenzkar jóðsögur og–sagnir* (*Icelandic Folktales and Legends*, 1922–58). There are many affinities between Icelandic tales and the corpus of European folktales, but the Icelandic stories are often firmly localized.

Much of modern Icelandic literature is dominated by lyric poetry and realistic prose, but there are some contemporary writers who have used folkloristic motifs in a creative, postmodern way. There is also a strong tradition of fantasy in Icelandic **children's literature**. Most recently, a new generation of children's writers have found inspiration in folkloristic motifs.

Norway

The folktale and fairy-tale collections collected and published in 1841–44 by Jørgen Moe and Peter Christen Asbjørnsen in Norway are probably the Scandinavian tales that are best known outside of Scandinavia, having appeared in numerous **translation**s and **adaptation**s. Part of the appeal is undoubtedly due to the many fine illustrations over the years by artists such as Erik Werenskiold and Theodor **Kittelsen**, among others. Moe and Asbjørnsen made a conscious effort to recreate the oral narrative style in their renditions and also were concerned with giving the tales a uniquely Norwegian flavor, particularly by using specifically

Norwegian language terms and syntax, since the written language of Norway at the time was Danish. The first small collection of *Norske folkeeventyr* (*Norwegian Folktales*) appeared in 1841, and subsequent tales were published in each of the following three years. Jacob Grimm himself declared that the Norwegian folktales were superior to all other folktale collections, a point of view that undoubtedly had much to do with Moe and Asbjørnsen's method. Asbjørnsen and Moe redacted the oral narratives they collected to the best of their ability as "a good storyteller would tell them." Most of the tales in *Norwegian Folktales* were collected in eastern Norway, and many were **wonder tale**s, **fable**s, and humorous **anecdote**s. Asbjørnsen independently published two volumes of legendary material, *Norske huldreeventyr og folkesagn* (*Norwegian Fairy Tales and Folk Legends*) in 1845 and 1848, which he encapsulated within **frame narrative**s. Asbjørnsen continued to collect and revise the folktale and legend collections until his death, and his work to incorporate more and more contemporary Norwegian language usage was continued by Jørgen Moe's son, Moltke Moe, a folklorist in his own right. Most modern editions of the Norwegian tales blend stories from the two collections indiscriminately.

While Moe and Asbjørnsen are the best-known collectors, they were neither the first, nor the most prolific. Andreas Faye had published a collection of legends, *Norske sagn* (*Norwegian Legends*) in 1833, which was changed to *Norske folke-sagn* in the second edition of 1844 to reflect the growing interest in the "**folk**." Many of the many collections of folktales published in Norwegian are regional in scope. Andris Eivindson Vang collected and published folktales and legends from Valdres (1850 and 1870), and Johan E. C. Nielsen published legends from Hallingdal in 1868. Johannes Skar published eight volumes of folk traditions from Setesdal, *Gamalt or Setesdal* (*Old Traditions from Setesdal*, 1903–16), but the most-prolific collector was undoubtedly the Telemark collector and scholar Rikard Berge, an important figure in Norwegian folklore research. Berge was careful in annotating information about sources and **informant**s. Titles of his work include *Norske eventyr og sagn* (*Norwegian Folktales and Legends*, 1909–13) in collaboration with Sophus Bugge, *Norske folkeeventyr* (*Norwegian Folktales*, 1914), and *Norsk sogukunst* (*The Art of Norwegian Folk Narrative*, 1924). Collecting of all types of traditional material continued throughout most of the twentieth century with regional collections from many parts of the country. Many of these were published by the Norwegian Folklore Society. Of importance to the field of folktale scholarship was the pioneering work of Reidar Thoralf Christiansen, who constructed a type index of Norwegian fairy tales and a type index for migratory legends, and Knut Liestøl, whose scholarly emphasis was the historical legend. In 1984, Ørnulf Hodne published *The Types of the Norwegian Folktale* with more inclusive records and according to the Aarne-Thompson system of classifying **tale type**s.

Much of mid- and late-nineteenth-century Norwegian literature was produced in a period of realism and naturalism, but in 1891 and 1892, Jonas Lie, one of the "big four" in Norwegian literature, published two volumes of literary fairy tales, *Trold* (*Trolls*). The stories are filled with fantasy and symbolism and a lyric visionary mysticism. A blending of realism with fairy tale and **myth** is characteristic of *Østenfor sol, vestenfor maane og bagom Babylons taarn* (*East of the Sun, West of the Moon, and behind the Tower of Babylon*, 1905). In *Flaggermus-vinger* (*Batwings*, 1895), Hans E. Kinck published a classic of Norwegian neo-Romanticism. The stories are colorful and filled with both humor and tragedy. Several of Tryggve Andersen's short stories are built on folk beliefs, such as the story "Veteranen" ("The Veteran") included in *Gamle folk og andre fortællinger* (*Old Folks and Other Stories*,

1904), in which an old man becomes convinced that he is doomed because his daughter sees his *vardøger*, a premonitory sight or sound of a person before his actual arrival. The gifted novelist Olav Dunn published *Blind-Anders* (*Blind Anders*) in 1924, in which a character from his monumental series of novels about the people of Juvik tells fairy tales and local legends. A talented writer who blended folktales with the literary fairy tale and who is almost unknown outside of Scandinavia was Regine Normann. Her novel *Eiler Hundevart*, 1916, follows a fairy-tale pattern. In *Eventyr* (*Fairy Tales*, 1925) and *Nye eventyr* (*New Fairy Tales*, 1926), she retold fairy tales of northern Norway to great effect. Normann also published two collections of legendary material in a short-story format, *Nordlandsnatt* (*Nordland's Night*, 1927) and *Det gråner mot høst* (*Autumn Is Dawning*, 1930). The Norwegian writer André Bjerke was reputed to have said that he could only think of three twentieth-century writers who had been able to create real fairy tales: Rudyard Kipling, Selma **Lagerlöf**, and Regine Normann.

In general, it can be said that much of Norwegian literature throughout the twentieth century was realistic and that the literary fairy tale was not prevalent. Folklore and legend often were incorporated in the many multivolume historical novels, but often merely to give local color to regional descriptions. Symbolism became important at mid-century, but it was usually fused with realism, rather than fantasy. One exception from this realistic norm is the religious existentialist Alfred Hauge. His *Vegen til det døde paradiset* (*The Road to the Dead Paradise*, 1951) is an allegory of a religious quest set in the time of the plague.

It can be said that there is no strong literary fairy tale tradition in Norway. It is possible that the overarching popularity and classic status of Asbjørnsen and Moe's folktale collection have had the same affect on Norwegian literary tales as Andersen has had on the Danish. It has been said that the famous Norwegian folktales have such a firm form that everyone knows what a real fairy tale is supposed to sound like, and that has made it difficult to create literary tales that are both original and national. Although realism prevails even in Norwegian children's literature, there are important exceptions. It is quite common for Norwegian authors to write for both children and adults. Nils Johan Rud published realistic novels for adults, and in much of his work for children, although fantasy prevails, his sense of social justice is evident. Some of the stories from two early collections of fairy tales, *Skougumslottet* (*Skougum Castle*, 1931) and *Tusser og troll og andre eventyr* (*Sprites and Trolls and Other Fairy Tales*, 1934), were revised and reprinted along with new ones in *I eventyrskog* (*In the Fairy-Tale Forest*, 1955). A children's classic that has been translated into many languages is *Trollkrittet* (*The Magic Chalk*, 1948) by Zinken Hopp, in which a little boy uses a magic chalk that gives life to whatever he draws, including a gate into the world of the fairy tale. Vigdis Rojahn both wrote about and drew the little troll-like creatures who populate books such as *Bustus* (1950) and several others. Perhaps the best-known figure internationally is Alf **Prøysen**, whose children's fairy tales about a woman who can become the size of a teaspoon are popular worldwide. *Gumman som blev liten som en tesked* (*Little Old Mrs. Pepperpot*) first appeared in a Swedish edition in 1956. Three other Mrs. Pepperpot collections followed. Another innovator in the use of fairy-tale elements is Thorbjørn Egner, whose *Karius og Baktus* (*Carius and Bactus*, 1949) is a classic. Fairy tales about animals are the subject of *Klatremus og de andre dyrene i Hakkebakkeskogen* (*Climbing-Mouse and Other Animals in Hakkebakk Wood*, 1953). In *Folk og røvere i Kardemomme By* (*The Singing Town*, 1955), Egner combined music and text with his own drawings to create a fantasy town where the most important virtue is kindness. In 1953, Ebba Haslund published *Frøken*

Askeladd (*Miss Ash-Lad*). Most of the book relates an *Alice in Wonderland*-like dream of the young heroine.

In some of his books in the late 1960s, and in *Gutten som fant kirkesølvet* (*The Boy Who Found the Church Silver*, 1970), Reidar Brodtkorb combined fairy tale and the realities of daily life with social criticism. As in Denmark, the 1980s was a time of magic realism in Norwegian children's literature, with an emphasis on fantasy novels and science fiction. The work of Tor Åge Bringsværd continues this tradition. Tormod Haugen blends fantasy with realism in many of his works and borrows motifs from the Norwegian folktale tradition as well as international children's literature. He won the prestigious Hans Christian Andersen Award in 1990, and his works reflect his interest in the contemporary problems of young people. In the novels of Jostein **Gaarder,** fairy-tale motifs take a postmodern twist as Gaarder often weaves story within complex story (see **Postmodernism**). Most recently, *Appelsinpiken* (*The Orange Girl*, 2003) has been called a fairy tale for adults.

There is a wide range among modern Norwegian picture books, with some writers and illustrators turning fairy-tale motifs on their heads. Fam **Ekman**'s *Skoen* (*The Shoe*, 2001) is a **Cinderella** tale with a twist and a surprise ending. Fairy-tale motifs and animal fables are central to Ekman's authorship, and her books are collector's items for their unique illustrations.

Sweden

The influence of the Grimms was also felt in Sweden. In addition to three volumes of folk songs published by Arvid August Afzelius and Erik Gustaf Geijer, Gunnar Olof Hyltén-Cavallius and George Stephens collected texts in the 1830s and 1840s. These became the basis of *Svenska folksagor och äfventyr* (*Swedish Folktales and Fairy Tales*, 1844–49). This early collection never achieved the popularity of the Norwegian tales, perhaps because Hyltén-Cavallius retold the tales in a deliberately archaic language. In 1882, Herman Hofberg published a collection of Swedish legends, *Svenska folksägner* (*Swedish Folk Legends*). As in Norway, there were many regional collectors, and there was great interest in collecting tales from the various provinces in their distinctive dialects. An important series of volumes of folktale and legend collections, *Svenska sagor och sägner* (*Swedish Folktales and Legends*), was published between 1937 and 1961 by Gustav Adolfs Akademien. The contemporary folklorist Bengt af Klingberg has written many books on Swedish folklore, including *Svenska sagor och sägner* (*Swedish Folktales and Legends*, 1972).

A Swedish *Aesop* appeared in 1603, translated by Nicolaus Balk from a German fable collection composed by Nathan Chytraeus in the 1570s; and *Reyncke Fosz* (**Reynard the Fox**) appeared in 1621, translated by Sigfrid Aron Forsius from a Low German edition. Bengt Lidner wrote a book of fables, but these were mostly translations from German and French. A genre that arose with Romanticism was the fairy-tale play; within this genre lies Per Daniel Amadeus Atterbom's *Lycksalighetens ö* (*The Isle of Bliss*, 1824–27), which is considered his major work, and which may have been one source of inspiration for Hans Christian **Andersen**'s story "Paradisets Have" ("The Garden of Eden," 1839). Carl Jonas Love Almquist utilized fairy tale and myth for satirical purposes. His satirical fairy tale *Ormus och Ariman* (*Ormazd and Ahriman*) was published in 1839. Thekla Knös, a contemporary of Almquist, wrote fairy tales and works in other genres. One of the early Swedish literary fairy tales was *Lille Viggs äfventyr på julafton* (*Little Viggs' Adventure on Christmas Eve*, 1875) by Viktor Rydberg, which was illustrated by Jenny **Nyström**, a pioneer in Swedish fairy-tale illustration. There are two cynical fairy tales in Hjalmar Söderberg's first collection of short stories, *Historietter* (*Short Stories*, 1898): "Sotarfrun" ("The Chimneysweep's Wife") and "Sann historia" ("True Story"). This collection has been called an ancestor of 1951 Nobel Prize winner Pär **Lagerkvist**'s *Onda sagor* (*Evil Tales*, 1924), a collection of stories that give the folktale pattern a modernist twist. Best known today as a playwright, August **Strindberg** published *Sagor* (*Tales*, 1903), in which his experimental use of the folktale and fairy tale imitates Andersen. It has been said that the grotesque characterizations in his *Svarta fanor* (*Black Banners*, 1907) gives the work the quality of an evil fairy tale.

Fairy tales flourished in the neo-Romanticism of late nineteenth-early twentieth century Sweden. Some of the most important writers include the Danish-born Helena **Nyblom**, who began writing fairy tales after her conversion to Catholicism in 1895. Her first fairy-tale collection for children was *Der var en gang, aeventyr for smaa og store* (*Once upon a Time, Fairy Tales for Young and Old*, 1897). Many of her tales are still eminently readable, with a clear feminist element (see **Feminist Tales**). Other fairy-tale authors of the period include Anna Maria Roos and Anna Wahlenberg. Among picture book writers, Elsa **Beskow** began contributing to the children's magazine *Jultomten* (*The Christmas Brownie*) in 1894. Her breakthrough work was *Puttes äfventyr i blåbärsskogen* (*Peter in Blueberry Land*, 1901). Other favorites still being read include *Tomtebobarnen* (*Children of the Forest*, 1910) and *Tant Grön, Tant Brun och Tant Gredelin* (*Aunt Green, Aunt Brown and Aunt Lavender*, 1918). John Bauer, whose gentle troll images never seem frightening, illustrated books for both Wahlenberg and Helena Nyblom. He contributed to the annual Christmas book *Bland tomtar och troll* (*Among Elves and Trolls*) beginning in 1907. Gustaf Tenggren also established a name for himself as an artist by drawing for this annual before he emigrated to America.

With *Nils Holgerssons underbara resa genom Sverige* (*The Wonderful Adventures of Nils*, 1906–7), the 1909 winner of the Nobel Prize in Literature, Selma Lagerlöf, created a fairy-tale classic. The lazy and naughty Nils, who is transformed to the size of a **Tom Thumb**, must redeem himself by good deeds as he travels over Sweden on the back of the wild goose. Commissioned as a geography textbook, the work was most influential outside of Sweden, and is still being read and enjoyed all over the world. Lagerlöf utilized folkloristic material in much of her work, particularly the legend, as in *Gösta Berlings saga* (*The Story of Gösta Berling*, 1891), although she also could use fairy-tale motifs to great effect. *En herrgårdssägen* (*The Tale of a Manor*, 1899) is a story with a **Beauty-and-the-Beast** motif, and Lagerlöf also used the evil stepmother motif in several texts. She cultivated a storytelling style that is reminiscent of oral narrative, and her use of folkloristic motifs from her childhood was tremendously influential both in Sweden and abroad.

The great innovator in Swedish children's literature and in the genre of the literary fairy tale was Astrid Lindgren. Her most famous creation is, of course, Pippi Longstocking, who played havoc with the established girls' book heroine in *Pippi Längstrump* (1945) and the two sequels from 1946 and 1948; but it is in the heroic quest novels such as *Mio, min Mio* (*Mio, My Son*, 1954) and *Bröderna lejonhjärta* (*The Brothers Lionheart*, 1973) that Lindgren revitalized the fairy-tale genre. The heroes Mio and Rusky are characters with whom young readers can identify, rather than superheroic stereotypes. They are little and lonely and afraid, and yet are able to conquer their fear and accomplish their goals. Lindgren's last great fairy-tale novel is *Ronia rövardotter* (*Ronia, the Robber's Daughter*, 1981) with a strong female heroine. Lindgren also revitalized the **tall tale** in her three books about the incorrigible Emil, whose pranks are the talk of the town, and fairy-tale motifs as well as intertextual references are present in much of her oeuvre (see **Intertextuality**).

The dominant genre in Swedish literature in the 1950s was poetry, and in the 1960s, much of the literature in Sweden engaged in political debate and social criticism. However, during this decade, Maria **Gripe** published several excellent fairy-tale **novel**s, including *Glasblåsarns barn* (*The Glassblower's Children*, 1964) and the experimental *Landet Utanför* (*The Land Beyond*, 1967). Questions of identity are central to her work, and the influence of Hans Christian Andersen is evident in her use of several motifs. Among her more than forty books are popular series about Josephine and Hugo, Elvis Karlsson, and Lotten. Her prolific career has spanned five decades.

While literature for youth often deals with problems in a realistic narrative, Scandinavian picture books are innovative, sometimes counterconventional, and often full of fantasy. In recent years, the Swedish picture-book genre has been flourishing, as in the rest of Scandinavia, and some of the best works have been translated into other languages. One of the internationally best-known writers and illustrators is Sven Nordqvist, whose imaginative Findus and Pettson stories, beginning with *Pannkakstårtan* (*The Birthday Cake*, 1984), are those with which a child can identify. The little **cat** Findus and his master Pettson's adventures always end happily, and Nordqvist's detailed illustrations are enjoyed by both children and adults. Among the many talented modern writers and illustrators is Pija Lindenbaum, whose provocative and humorous *Else-Marie och småpapporna* (*Else-Marie and the Seven Fathers*) was published in 1990.

Swedish Finland

The publication of the **Kalevala** by Elias Lönnrot in 1835 was the impetus for folklore collection in Finland, but the focus was on Finnish-language poetry and folk songs. The first important promoter of the collection of Swedish folklore in Finland was J. O. I. Rancken. A large amount of Swedish-speaking Finland's folk tradition has been published in the multi-volume *Finlands svenska folkdiktning* (*Finland's Swedish Folk Literature*, 1917–). The contribution of Finnish scholars to folklore research has been monumental, including the development of the **historic-geographic method** of folktale analysis, and Antti **Aarne**'s index of tale types, first published in 1910.

Zacharias **Topelius** is often considered the originator of Swedish-language literary fairy tales. He published *Sagor* (*Fairy Tales*) in 1847 and the eight-part series *Läsning för barn* (*Stories for Children*) between 1865 and 1896. His work was greatly influenced by Hans Christian Andersen. The best-known Finno-Swedish writer of fairy tales is undoubtedly Tove **Jansson**. The little Moomintrolls who live in the Moomin Valley are known and loved around the world by both children and adults. A gifted artist, Jansson studied art in Stockholm, Helsinki, and Paris. The first Moomin book, *Småtrollen och den stora översvämningen* (*The Little Trolls and the Great Flood*) was published in 1945, with eight more to follow, the last in 1970. Tove Jansson was the recipient of many awards, including the Nils Holgersson Plaque in 1953 and the Hans Christian Andersen Award in 1966.

Fantasy and fairy tale have had a great impact on Finnish children's literature. Contributing to innovations within this genre is the Finno-Swedish author Irmelin Sandman Lilius, whose work may be described as an amalgamation of fairy tale, myth, and fantasy. Sandman Lilius' protagonists are often young girls who leave home and experience adventures, as in *Enhörningen* (*The Unicorn*, 1962) and *Morgenlandet* (*The Land of Tomorrow*, 1967).

The Nordic countries have contributed individual geniuses of great originality who have influenced the development of the fairy-tale genre far beyond the borders of their nations. Even so, the tradition that began when the enormously influential Georg Brandes urged Scandinavian writers to debate the problems of their time is still prevalent in the various national literatures, and realism dominates. Perhaps living on the northern periphery, with its extremes of light and darkness, gives Scandinavians a worldview in which reality is almost fantasy enough. *See also* Theater.

Further Readings: Beyer, Harald, and Edvard Beyer. *Norsk litteratur historie*. Oslo: H. Aschehoug, 1978; Borum, Poul. *Danish Literature*. Copenhagen: Det Danske Selskap, 1979; Hagemann, Sonja. *Barnelitteratur i Norge, 1914–1970*. Oslo: H. Aschehoug, 1974; Holbek, Bengt. *Interpretation of Fairy Tales: Danish Folklore in a European Perspective*. Helsinki: Academia Scientiarum Fennica, 1987; Kvideland, Reimund. "The Collecting and Study of Tales in Scandinavia." *A Companion to the Fairy Tale*. Edited by Hilda Ellis Davidson and Anna Chaudhri. Cambridge: D. S. Brewer, 2003; Kvideland, Reimund, and Henning K. Sehmsdorf, eds. *All the World's Reward: Folktales Told by Five Scandinavian Storytellers*. Seattle: University of Washington Press, 1999; ———, eds. *Scandinavian Folk Belief and Legend*. Minneapolis: University of Minnesota Press, 1988; *Nordic Literature 2003*. Nordic Literature and Library Committee. Copenhagen. http://www.nordic-literature.org/2003/; Thompson, Stith. *The Folktale*. 1946. Berkeley: University of California Press, 1977; Warme, Lars G., ed. *A History of Swedish Literature*. Lincoln: University of Nebraska Press, 1996.

Marte Hult

Schami, Rafik (1946–)

Rafik Schami (a pseudonym that means "friend from Damascus") is a writer and storyteller of Syrian origin who lives in Germany and writes in German. Born Suheil Fadél in an Aramaic-Christian enclave outside Damascus, Schami left Syria in 1971, partly for political reasons, to study chemistry in Heidelberg. After receiving his doctorate, he worked as a chemist in German industry until 1982, when he became a freelance writer. Throughout his life, he has been active as a storyteller (in Arabic, *hakawati*) and as a writer of stories based on oral and written Arabic traditions. His first German collections include tales of the life of *Gastarbeiter* (unskilled guest workers) in Germany. He was also active in establishing a literary series, Südwind (1980–85), and an organization, PoLiKunst (1980–87), that promoted the work of contemporary German writers who were born elsewhere. He has twice received the Adelbert von **Chamisso** Prize for foreigners writing in German, among many other honors.

From 1981 to 1996, Schami gave 1,290 public readings, more than **Sheherezade**, as he says himself. Since then, he has concentrated on his writing, though the techniques and strategies of oral narrative still play an important role in his work. In stories like "Die Wunderlampe" ("The Magic Lamp") from his collection *Der erste Ritt durchs Nadelsöhr* (*The First Ride Through the Eye of the Needle*, 1985), he takes an important **motif** from Arabic **legend**, the genie who lives in an oil lamp, and turns it into a political **parable** of human greed and lust for power: the king wants to use the genie's powers to conquer the lands of gold, oil, and copper. The mad multiplication of lamps and genies finally leads to the overthrow of the **king**, the disappearance of the genies, and the apparent liberation of the people.

In his linked collection *Erzähler der Nacht* (*Storytellers of the Night*, 1989; translated as *Damascus Nights*, 1993), Schami revives the digressive, embedded tale-telling strategies of the **Arabian Nights**. The illiterate old coachman and storyteller Salim, who has told stories night after night in his house in Damascus in the politically troubled 1960s, is suddenly and mysteriously unable to speak. In each chapter, one of his circle of male friends tells a story about his own past in an attempt to find the secret of Salim's silence and bring back his voice. The last storyteller, surprisingly enough a woman, returns us to the tradition of She-herezade and brings Salim back into the **storytelling** world. His final dream, about a demon, is also a dream about storytelling as communication. In a telling metaphor, he compares words to flowers that can bloom only in a listener's ear. In this book and others, like the related *Eine Hand voller Sterne* (*A Handful of Stars*, 1987), Schami emphasizes the importance of the interaction of teller and audience, even in written forms.

Further Readings: Amin, Magda. "Stories, Stories, Stories: Rafik Schami's *Erzähler der Nacht*." *Alif: Journal of Comparative Poetics* 20 (2000): 211–33; Schami, Rafik. "The Magic Lamp." Translated by Alfred L. Cobbs. *Marvels & Tales* 16 (2002): 84–99.

Elizabeth Wanning Harries

Schenda, Rudolf (1930–2000)

Rudolf Schenda documented the power of the printed page to conserve popular narratives in sixteenth- to twentieth-century European popular literature and culture, providing in *Volk ohne Buch* (*People without Books*, 1970), *Die Lesestoffe der kleinen Leute* (*The Reading Material of Ordinary People*, 1976), and *Vom Mund zu Ohr* (*From Mouth to Ear*, 1993) scores of examples of stories printed largely unchanged over centuries. Schenda argued that print underlay oral tellings of European fairy tales and that a conception of **fairy tale**s (as modern scholars understand the subject) existed only from the late eighteenth century onward.

In Schenda's view, print initiated **oral tradition**s. He showed that cheaply printed Italian "Bertoldo" tales revived material from the **Bible** and distributed it among ordinary people throughout southern Europe. Schenda repeatedly found that if printed stories existed within a mixed society of literates and illiterates, those stories soon found their way to illiterates.

In the early 1980s, Schenda formulated foundational questions about fairy tales: Were they ancient traditions or modern creations? What is/was fairy tales' relationship to orality? Are they a form of oral communication or a form of printed reading material? How do print and oral forms relate to one other historically? Who produces fairy tales, who tells them, and who consumes them, both now and in the past?

Schenda's questioning of Romantic theories of an ancient and unbroken oral tradition and of lower-class origins of folk narrative suggested radically different mechanisms for the creation and dissemination of folk narrative, and profoundly altered how a new generation of European folk-narrative scholars viewed the subject. Skeptical about psychoanalytic and pedagogic reverence for fairy tales, he saw such veneration of the genre as a denial of the lower classes' actual psychosocial requirements and ordinary people's real oral communications. Schenda wished to rehistoricize fairy tales; reintegrate them into their cultural environment; revive the texts psychosocially; study people's access to and use of books and print, illiterates' literary knowledge, and the print sources of their tales; and revise assumptions about late medieval and early modern scholarly authors' folkloristic knowledge. Schenda believed that, from at least the 1100s onward, rising levels of literacy enriched oral culture with additions from antique, Arabic, and Celtic literatures while simultaneously displacing orality as a separate and independent entity. He therefore criticized the belief that classic French fairy-tale authors had taken their tales from the **folk** and denied that German fairy tales had been transmitted orally, positing instead millions of fairy-tale texts as tradition bearers. European folklorists, Schenda noted, view the "common man" as a humble country ploughman or shepherd, whereas social historians understand the common man as more educated and more literately participatory in society, proof of which he saw in the numerous visual representations of girls and women buying books and pamphlets from colporteurs (peddlers of books).

Further Readings: Bottigheimer, Ruth B. "Rudolf Schenda and Folk Narrative." *Europeæa* 3.1 (1997): 123–32; Messerli, Alfred. "Cheap Prints and Visual Medias." *Europeæa* 3.1 (1997): 133–40; Schenda, Rudolf. "Semiliterate and Semi-Oral Processes." Translated by Ruth B. Bottigheimer. *Marvels & Tales* 21 (2007): 127–40; ———. "Telling Tales—Spreading Tales: Change in the Communicative Forms of a Popular Genre." Translated by Ruth B. Bottigheimer. *Fairy Tales and Society: Illusion, Allusion, and Paradigm.* Edited by Ruth B. Bottigheimer. Philadelphia: University of Pennsylvania Press, 1986. 75–94; Rubini, Luise. "Bio-Bibliographical Notes." *Europeæa* 3.1 (1997): 141–55.

Ruth B. Bottigheimer

Schwind, Moritz von (1804–1871)

Nineteenth-century Austrian painter and illustrator Moritz von Schwind is one of the most representative artists of the later Romantic period in Germany and is best known for his oil paintings, watercolors, and woodcuts of fairy-tale themes. Born and educated in Vienna, Schwind moved to Munich in 1828, where he became particularly well known for his pictorial contributions to the *Münchner Bilderbogen* (*Munich Broadsides*), a series of single-sheet publications of illustrated stories. A true product of his time, Schwind was fascinated with the Romantic interest in the revival of German folktales and fairy tales, and many of his paintings retold these stories in pictorial cycles. One of his better-known works in this format is *Das Märchen vom Aschenbrödel* (*The Fairy Tale of* **Cinderella**, 1854), painted in four main panels with smaller **illustration**s surrounding each. Schwind's classical, realistic style is characteristic of the

A scene from Mortiz von Schwind's broadside version of "The Juniper Tree." From *Moritz von Schwinds fröhliche Romantik* by Ernst Wilhelm Bredt (München: Hugo Schmidt Verlag, 1917).

Romantic era, as is the idealized world of medieval chivalry in which he imagined most of his fairy-tale characters and settings. A close friend and contemporary of Franz Schubert, Schwind also was passionate about **music,** and musical themes can be seen throughout his work.

In 1864, Schwind was commissioned to paint a series of frescoes in the foyer of the Vienna State Opera House, and he chose as his theme Wolfgang Amadeus Mozart's *Die Zauberflöte* (*The Magic Flute*). These frescoes are still extant, and the space is known as the "Schwind Foyer." Other frescoes by Schwind can be seen in both the Munich Residential Palace and the Hohenschwangau Castle. However, it was his renditions of fairy tales in the *Munich Broadsheets* that established his fame and popularity during his lifetime. *See also* Art.

Further Reading: Kalkschmidt, Eugen. *Moritz von Schwind, der Mann und das Werk.* Munich: F. Bruckmann, 1943.

Louise Speed

Scieszka, Jon (1954–)

The highly popular American children's author Jon Scieszka had a profound influence on picture books from the end of the 1980s to the beginning of the 1990s with his innovative stories inspired by folktales and fairy tales. His close collaboration with the illustrator Lane Smith resulted in several groundbreaking picture books. Their first, *The True Story of the 3 Little Pigs!* (1989), as told to Scieszka by A. Wolf, offers a funny, alternate account of the familiar events, told from the **wolf**'s perspective. In 1991, Scieszka published *The Frog Prince Continued* (1991), illustrated by Steve Johnson, a tongue-in-cheek sequel that expands, but also distorts, this famous fairy tale. Scieszka is no doubt best known as the author of *The Stinky Cheese Man and Other Fairly Stupid Tales* (1992), illustrated by Smith and designed by Molly Leach, a hugely successful picture book that was named an Honor Book in the 1993 Caldecott Medal awards. In this hilarious **parody** of well-known fairy tales, Scieszka and Smith poke fun at the codes and conventions of the genre. Their irreverent collage of folktale and fairy-tale fragments resulted in a postmodern picturebook that appeals to adults as well as children. *See also* Postmodernism.

Further Reading: McGillis, Roderick. "'Ages All': Readers, Texts, and Intertexts in *The Stinky Cheese Man and Other Fairly Stupid Tales.*" *Transcending Boundaries: Writing for a Dual Audience of Children and Adults.* Edited by Sandra L. Beckett. New York: Garland, 1999. 111–26.

Sandra L. Beckett

The Secret of Roan Inish (1994)

The Secret of Roan Inish, written and directed by John Sayles, is a lyrical film about the persistence and value of folk belief and tradition. Adapted from Rosalie Fry's novel *The Secret of the Ron Mor Skerry* (1957), the film relocates the setting from Scotland to Ireland and expands the original story by interweaving the selkie story of Celtic folktale with other folktale **motif**s (the feral child, the mysterious journey, and the return to an abandoned home) and with various folk beliefs, skills, and traditions. Through this expansion, the film explores relationships between a sense of place and identity in postwar coastal Ireland as seen through the lens of mid-1990s postmodern culture.

The core selkie story relates how a fisherman accidentally sees a selkie maiden in her human form and steals her skin, without which she is unable to return to the sea. He thus gains power over her and compels her to marry him. After some years, her skin is finally found, usually by one of her human children, and she leaves her husband and children and returns to the sea. *The Secret of Roan Inish* is about the descendants of such a selkie, living now as a dispersed and dispossessed people. On the day, economic circumstances forced them to leave their island home on tiny Roan Inish (in Gaelic, "island of the seals"); a baby, Jamie, was washed out to sea in his cradle and presumed to have drowned. At the beginning of the film, his ten-year-old sister, Fiona, is sent after the death of her **mother** to live with her grandparents in a fishing village in sight of Roan Inish. She soon learns the **legend** that the **family** has selkie blood, visible in her dark-haired relatives, and then accidentally discovers that Jamie is still alive and is being cared for by the seals. Fiona grasps that the seals are keeping Jamie to make the family move back to the island, to perpetuate the link between selkies and humans, and she persuades her teenage cousin Eamon to help her secretly restore the dilapidated cottages and gardens. Once the island is reinhabited, Jamie is restored. A great part of the film's persuasive effectiveness is the use of evocative camera work (by Haskell Wexler) to underpin a realistic narrative mode.

The selkie story hinges on the strength of the bond between the selkie and the sea, but in the film, this bond is put into the service of the larger suggestion that to be free and have a sense of agency within contemporary society is to be possessed of and by a place, its history, and traditions. Hence, Fiona learns through her interactions with family and place the importance of tradition and a sense of belonging. While the figure of the captured selkie woman embodies the connections among displacement, dispossession, and loss of identity, the inevitability of her return to the sea imbues tradition with a fatalistic sense of loss. Fiona, however, discovers that the mythic element in her heritage also can be empowering, as she works to change her family's fate for the better. *See also* Celtic Tales; Film and Video; Mermaid.

Further Readings: Selby, Emily F., and Deborah P. Dixon. "Between Worlds: Considering Celtic Feminine Identities in *The Secret of Roan Inish.*" *Gender, Place and Culture: A Journal of Feminist Geography* 5.1 (1998): 5–28; Thomson, David. *The People of the Sea: A Journey in Search of the Seal Legend.* Washington, D.C.: Counterpoint, 2000.

John Stephens

Ségur, Sophie, Comtesse de (1799–1874)

The French children's author known as the Comtesse de Ségur was born Sophie Rostopchine, the daughter of a Russian count. Sophie spent most of her childhood on her family's huge estate at Voronono, and in Moscow, where her father became governor in 1812 under Tsar Alexander I. In 1816, Count Rostopchine fell into disgrace, and his family fled to France. Less than three years later, Sophie married Count Eugene de Ségur, who largely let her raise their eight children by herself at his Norman country estate, Les Nouettes.

Ségur was almost sixty when she began her literary career. Before turning to more realistic children's novels, she wrote two original fairy tales, "Histoire de Blondine" ("The Story of Blondine") and "Le bon petit Henri" ("Good Little Henry"), which Louis Hachette published in the magazine *La semaine des enfants* (*The Children's Weekly*, 1857). Three more fairy tales followed: "Histoire de la Princesse Rosette" ("The Story of Princess Rosette"), "La petite souris grise" ("The Little Gray Mouse"), and "Ourson." These tales formed the collection *Nouveau contes de fées* (*New Fairy Tales*), published with **illustration**s by

Gustave **Doré** in 1857. Ségur's rich tales all feature children who must overcome not only wicked enemies but their own human flaws to live happy and loving lives. The stories were reprinted in 1917 as part of the famous series of illustrated children's books, the Bibliothèque Rose. This edition of Ségur's tales provided the source for the cutout illustrations lining one of artist Joseph Cornell's famous boxes, the appropriately named *Nouveaux contes de feés*. **See also** Children's Literature; French Tales.

Further Reading: Brown, Penny. "Gustave Doré's Magical Realism: The *Nouveaux contes de fée*s of the Comtesse de Ségur." *Modern Language Review* 95 (2000): 964–77.

Elizabeth Wanning Harries

Seki Keigo (1899–1990)

Seki Keigo, along with **Yanagita** Kunio, pioneered folktale research in Japan. Seki studied philosophy at Toyo University, where he served as librarian at the university library. From 1950 to 1958, Seki published *Nihon mukashibanashi shūsei* (*Collection of Japanese Folktales*), a six-volume work in which he classified **Japanese tales** into three groups following the system used by Antti **Aarne** and Stith **Thompson** in *The Types of the Folktale* (1928; second revision, 1961): animal tales, ordinary folktales, and humorous tales. Personally dissatisfied with the **tale-type** numbers he had developed, Seki created a new catalogue, "Nihon mukashibanashi no kata" ("Types of Japanese Folktales"), which he published at the end of the last volume of *Nihon mukashibanashi shūsei*. However, the initial tale-type numbers had already become so popular that the new catalogue could not catch on. As a consequence, contemporary folklorists still use Seki's original tale-type numbers.

Seki's main research interest was the origin of Japanese folktales and the ways in which Japanese tales were imported from other countries. The result of his research was *Nihon no mukashibanashi: Hikaku kenkyū josetsu* (*Folktale: An Introduction to the Comparative Study of the Folktale*, 1977), in which Seki was able to demonstrate that many folktales with allegedly Japanese origins actually must have been imported from China, India, and the Near East. Using his knowledge of German, he translated Kaarle Krohn's *Die folkloristische Arbeitsmethode* (*Folklore Methodology*, 1926) and Aarne's *Vergleichende Märchenforschung* (*Comparative Studies of Folklore*, 1908) into Japanese. In 1977, Seki founded Nihon Koshobungei Gakkai—the Japanese Society for Folk Literature—and served as the organization's first president. Seki's influence on Japanese folktale studies has been significant and continues to generate important comparative research.

Further Readings: Seki Keigo. *Folktales of Japan*. Translated by Robert J. Adams. Chicago: University of Chicago Press, 1963; ———. "Types of Japanese Folktales." *Asian Folklore Studies* 35 (1966): 1–220.

Toshio Ozawa

Sendak, Maurice (1928–)

Separations and returns—so prominent in the fantasies and fairy tales he would write, illustrate, and stage throughout his artistic career—were already featured in emotionally charged Hebrew **legend**s that little Murray (Maurice) Sendak and his older two siblings first heard from their inventive immigrant father during their Brooklyn childhood. A tale in which a little boy encounters the huge angelic shapes of Abraham and Sarah before his parents can recover his frozen body seems to have held a special significance for the sickly but resilient child whom the adult artist has resolutely kept alive.

Scenes from "**Little Red Riding Hood**," "**Hansel and Gretel**," "**Aladdin**," and "Pinocchio" were among the toy prototypes—designed by Jack Sendak but decorated by Maurice—that the brothers vainly hoped F. A. O. Schwarz's Manhattan store might mass-produce in 1948. Soon, however, Maurice, who had already made life-size figures of **Snow White** and the Seven Dwarfs for a show window, was hired to work on the toy shop's window displays. The store's book department stocked major illustrators he could study—George **Cruikshank**, Walter **Crane**, Wilhelm Busch, and Ralph Caldecott. It was there that Sendak met the children's book editor Ursula Nordstrom. Impressed by the young man's drawings, she contracted him to illustrate three Harper books. Of these, Ruth Krauss's successful *A Hole Is to Dig* (1952) made him, as he put it, "an official person."

Maurice Sendak, "Oh how the poor little sister did grieve," from *Juniper Tree and Other Tales from the Grimms* (New York: Farrar, Straus and Giroux 1973, p. 165). [Copyright © 1973 by Maurice Sendak. Reproduced by permission of Maurice Sendak.]

The first two picture books for which Sendak wrote his own text, *Kenny's Window* (1956) and *Very Far Away* (1957), anticipated *Where the Wild Things Are* (1963) by featuring an escape. Like Kenny and Martin, or like Mickey (*In the Night Kitchen*, 1970) and Jennie in *Higglety, Pigglety, Pop!* (1967), Max defiantly sails into a **fantasy** world of his own making. In a book in which the verbal text is steadily subordinated to—and eventually displaced by—the graphics that carry the story, the first two **illustration**s suggest that the boy in a **wolf** suit is an incipient artist. In *Where the Wild Things Are*, Max builds a private children's space for his imaginings and has already produced a rudimentary sketch of a toothy Wild Thing. His **mother** may see him as a miscreant, but Max's "mischief" is as nourishing as the hot **food** he finds at his journey's end.

Although critics initially repudiated the "terrible" Wild Things as improper for children, Max's monsters were quickly accepted as playful agents for self-mastery. Sendak helped his cause in "Balsa Wood and Fairy Tales" (1964), a polemical essay published a year after the book's appearance. He contrasted the rigidity of perfectionists who insisted on a "so-called healthy or suitable literature for children" to the elasticity of creative children. The frightening "tangle of life" depicted by "the brothers **Grimm** and Mr. H. C. **Andersen**," Sendak argued, was dissolved into "fantasy, which upsets the delicate insides of children less than it does the adults." Although he had yet to illustrate the Grimms, Sendak had by then memorably interpreted a wide array of nineteenth-century **literary fairy tale**s: Andersen's *Seven Tales* (1959), Wilhelm **Hauff**'s *Dwarf Long-Nose* (1960), Clemens **Brentano**'s *The Tale of Gockel, Hinkel, and Gackeliah* (1961), and *Schoolmaster Whackwell's*

Wonderful Songs (1962), as well as Frank Stockton's *The Griffin and the Minor Canon* (1963) and *The Bee-Man of Orn* (1964). Sendak then turned to three writers he prized: the Victorian allegorist George **MacDonald** and two contemporaries, the Yiddish fabulist Isaac Bashevis **Singer** and the poet Randall **Jarrell**.

Sendak's intricate crosshatched drawings for MacDonald's *The Golden Key* (1967), Singer's *Zlateh the Goat* (1966), and Jarrell's posthumously published *Fly By Night* (1976) rely on old photographs to inject personal associations. Thus, for instance, the features of the girl Tangle, so eerily clasped by forest branches, is derived from Lewis **Carroll**'s photograph of MacDonald's daughter Irene. Again, portraits of Sendak's relatives slain in the Holocaust and of his own mother find their way into complicated compositions for the Singer and Jarrell texts. Still, in their teasing mixtures of levity and gravity, the drawings for MacDonald's *The Light Princess* (1969) or the characterless "decorations" for Jarrell's *The Animal Family* (1965) are hardly less exquisite.

Yet Sendak's visual interpretation of fairy tales surely reached its high point in the drawings he provided for Jarrell's and Lore Segal's translations in the two-volume *The Juniper Tree and Other Tales from the Grimms* (1973). His rendering of the **witch**, Gretel, and a huge German shepherd who looms above a barely visible Hansel forms a quadrangle that is topped by a Sendakian full moon. Whereas the roundness of a huge pot in the forefront clashes with the rectangular lamp held by the witch, the tiny moon encourages the viewer to circle the rigid square formed by animal/boy/girl/woman. The composition's angularity thus dissolves into a curvilinear flow. "Reading" such pictures as complements to the narratives in *The Juniper Tree* requires a decoding not needed in a children's book such as *King Grisly-Beard: A Tale from the Brothers Grimm* (1973), in which Sendak returns to the comic-book mode of *In the Night Kitchen*. He later reverted to this cartoonish mode, sometimes incongruously so, in picturebooks that attempt to confront cultural nightmares such as homelessness and AIDS (*We Are All in the Dumps with Jack and Guy*, 1993) or the fate of the **opera**-performing Terezin children who were killed at Auschwitz (*Brundibar*, 2003).

A better antidote for such anxieties is the more lyrical, pastel-hued mode that Sendak deploys in texts such as *Outside Over There* (1981) and *Dear Mili: An Old Tale by Wilhelm Grimm* (1988), both of which depict a girl's journey into a dangerous alternate reality. That these two picture books about vulnerable female wanderers should feature Mozart as an icon seems apt. Sendak likes to stress that young Pamina is saved from **death** by three genies who are cast as boys in *The Magic Flute*, the opera for which he devised elaborate sets and costumes just before he led Ida into a netherworld. In *Dear Mili*, wedged between stagecraft for two more Mozart operas (*The Goose from Cairo*, 1986, and *Idomeneo*, 1989), Sendak faithfully follows the Christian legend that Wilhelm Grimm had sent to console a grieving girl. But by having Mozart, himself a shortlived wunderkind, direct an orchestra of martyred Jewish children, he also injects a new reconciliation. Mozart's ghostly child ensemble is placed in the background of a two-page drawing that shows the girl protagonist innocently playing with her guardian angel among graves with Hebrew inscriptions, while, in the foreground, St. Joseph tends the immense blooms of his flower garden. This rendering of a pastoral limbo aligns the older Germano-Austrian culture Sendak admires with his tortured consciousness of the Nazi's child victims. It also gives a new twist to the biblical legend he had heard from his father. ***See also*** Childhood and Children; Children's Literature.

Further Readings: Kushner, Tony. *The Art of Maurice Sendak: 1980 to the Present.* New York: Harry N. Abrams, 2003; Lanes, Selma. *The Art of Maurice Sendak.* New York: Harry N. Abrams, 1980; Sendak, Maurice. *Caldecott & Co.: Notes on Books & Pictures.* New York: Farrar, Straus, and Giroux, 1988.

U. C. Knoepflmacher

Sex, Sexuality

Few themes are more central to folktales and fairy tales than sex and sexuality. Still, these two notions do not have the same status, and it is useful to distinguish between them, even if they are interconnected in obvious and important ways. Sex, as the explicit depiction of sexual activity, is perhaps not as prominent as sexuality, the (conscious and unconscious) manifestations of human beings' erotic dispositions. Defined thusly, sex is limited to a specific corpus (for instance, erotic jokes and stories in **folklore** and pornographic fairy tales) or to occasional allusions in well-known, otherwise seemingly innocent folktales and fairy tales. Sexuality, however, is represented far more commonly, as it is in all art forms of all times and cultures. As a fundamental component of human existence, sexuality necessarily occupies a privileged place among folktale and fairy-tale themes. For many if not most readers, love and **marriage**, especially in the best-known stories (or promoted as such by the mass market), are the sine qua non of folktales and fairy tales. Not matter how stereotypical, this linkage has brought to the fore just how much the themes of love and marriage rely on and perpetuate conceptions of sexuality and, if only implicitly, of sex. Of course, these conceptions have come under intense scrutiny over the past thirty years, with focus on the expectations instilled in young readers and particularly in young girls. But beyond clarifying the profound influence folktales and fairy tales have had, feminist critiques, coupled with feminist rewritings, have highlighted the multiple ways that sexuality and **gender** are interconnected and the highly efficient use folktales and fairy tales have made of those interconnections. One has only to think of the commonplace reference to the fairy-tale **prince** and **princess** or to the "happily ever after" ending in everyday speech to grasp the genre's influence on cultural preconceptions of gender and sexuality. Granted, such preconceptions are often evoked only to be dismissed, and, besides, they are only one part of the reality of folktales and fairy tales. Yet, the fact that they continue to flourish proves that the genre's association with sex and sexuality is deeply rooted.

But no matter how entrenched, the broad cultural clichés about fairy-tale sexuality are predictably disconnected from the historical realities of the genre. While there are certainly folktales and fairy tales that conform to these clichés (with such things as quests to rescue a princess, or a happy ending with a marriage, among others), representations of sexuality in the varieties of folktale and fairy tale across time and in different regions of the world cannot be summarized by any single or simplistic account. Accordingly, what follows will not give a comprehensive overview of the topic in all folktale and fairy-tale traditions, but will instead focus on some its salient features in the history of western European fairy tales and their critical reception.

The very first literary fairy tales accentuate sex and sexuality in ways that would probably surprise many readers today. Borrowing from the Italian **novella** tradition that developed from Giovanni **Boccaccio**, among others, Giovan Francesco **Straparola**'s *Le piacevoli notti* (*The Pleasant Nights*, 1550–53) contain many sexually suggestive comments, allusions, jokes, and episodes. In the first **fable** of the second night, a prince born in a **pig**'s form, after killing his first two wives, is married to a maiden who readily accepts him into the marriage bed even though he is covered with mud, whereupon he kisses her "on the face and neck and bosom and shoulders with his tongue, and she [is] not backward in returning his caresses." All in all, however, frank sexual description such as this follows the fairly widespread Renaissance tradition of bawdy humor, which does not prevent Straparola from presenting "**moral**s" for his tales. Nearly a century later, Giambattista **Basile**'s *Lo cunto de li cunti overo lo trattenemiemto pe peccerille* (*The Tale of Tales, or Entertainment for Little Ones*, 1634–36), also known as the *Pentamerone*, continued to make frequent use of sexual allusion, although couched in the period's mannerist prose style that made liberal use of metaphor and allegory. As was the case with Straparola before him, Basile's nonchalant humor frequently makes light of what we would today consider to be sexual aggression. For instance, in "Sole, Luna e Talia ("Sun, Moon, and Talia," his version of the story better known as "**Sleeping Beauty**"), Basile describes in a matter-of-fact tone how a king finds Talia sleeping in a tower and, "feeling his blood course hotly through his veins ... carried her to a bed, whereon he gathered the first fruits of love." Compared with Straparola, though, Basile's descriptions are more restrained due to his use of euphemism. Charles **Perrault**, in late seventeenth-century France, took this vein even further, suppressing almost all bawdy allusions but including occasional asides to what savvy readers understand to be sexual activity. In one version of "Sleeping Beauty," for example, Perrault's narrator explains, seemingly innocently, that after being awakened by the prince, Sleeping Beauty stayed awake all night with him since she was not tired, "having slept for one hundred years." Not unlike his Italian predecessors, Perrault displayed a penchant for misogynist humor, especially in his morals, recycling *gaulois* commonplace about the excesses of **women**'s sexuality. Wry humor is not unknown to the many women who were writing fairy tales at the same time as Perrault, although on the whole it was less common. In its stead, writers such as Marie-Catherine d'**Aulnoy**, Charlotte-Rose de Caumont de **La Force**, and Henriette-Julie de Castelnau, Comtesse de **Murat** are perhaps most noteworthy for reworking the chivalric love plot from the **novel**s, **opera**s, and plays of their day and thereby often exploring new paths for female desire.

The eighteenth-century "vogue" of **literary fairy tale**s in France took the genre in many different directions. At one extreme were the first tales written explicitly and exclusively for children by Jeanne-Marie **Leprince de Beaumont** and which emphasized the dangers for girls of sexual immorality (albeit in elliptical fashion). At the other extreme were a series of tales, authored by Jean-François de Bastide, Claude-Prosper de Crébillon, and Claude-Henri de Voisenon, among others, which parodied the conventions of the genre to present erotic *double entendre*. Also important was Antoine **Galland**'s **translation/adaptation** of the *Arabian Nights—Les milles et une nuits* (*Thousand and One Nights*, 1704–17) and the many imitations it inspired. Although rarely explicit in their depiction of sex, "Oriental" tales did promote many of the clichés of an exoticized sexuality that were to become current in other genres and art forms: harems, betrayal, and jealousy, for example.

When, in the nineteenth century, production of literary fairy tales shifted principally to Germany and England, the mores of the period had a profound influence on the representation of sexuality. In their *Kinder- und Hausmärchen* (*Children's and Household Tales*, 1812–15), the Brothers **Grimm** assiduously eliminated references to premarital sex, **incest**, or even pregnancy that appeared in the versions of their **informant**s or in other published sources. At the same time, they did not hesitate to amplify physical **violence**, especially to drive home various "moral" lessons. For the Grimms, as for many others before and after them, explicit signs of bodily sexuality were taboo, but physical violence was not. This paradox is also valid for the tales of Hans Christian **Andersen**, although his heroes and heroines are often beset by longings which, if not explicitly sexual, have been interpreted as such. His frequent tragic endings give a dystopic cast to his (implicit or metaphorical) depiction of sexuality—for example, the unrequited desire in "Den lille havfrue ("The Little **Mermaid**," 1837). If nineteenth-century English fairy tales often eschew romantic plots in favor of heavy-handed didactic moralism, some writers, notably Oscar **Wilde**, revel in a sensuousness that can easily have sexual overtones. On occasion, his stories seem to portray unconventional situations with erotic implications, as the love between the male swallow and the hero in "The Happy Prince" (1888) suggests. Where writing leaves sexuality implicit, beginning especially in the nineteenth century, book **illustration** often makes it explicit. Many of the now-famous drawings and engravings of fairy tales by Walter **Crane**, Gustave **Doré**, and Arthur **Rackham**, among many others, bring out the erotic energy of the stories through bodily gestures, line of sight, or **clothing**. (For instance, Doré's engraving of Little Red Riding Hood, made even more famous as the cover of Bruno **Bettelheim**'s *The Uses of Enchantment* [1976], foregrounds the ambivalent modesty of the heroine next to the voracious desire of the **wolf**.)

Sexuality is given a wide array of portrayals in twentieth-century fairy tales. Beyond the continued production of "classic" tales for children, without doubt the most important development was the appearance of the **Walt Disney Company**'s fairy-tale film, which reshaped cultural expectations for the genre. As feminists in particular pointed out, Disney's versions have had a particularly negative influence on girls, encouraging them to link their self-worth to finding a "perfect" mate and instilling in them a passive femininity. Concomitant with their effect on gender roles, the Disney versions necessarily influenced conceptions of sexuality, albeit in more subtle and implicit ways. For girls, the overriding message is not to actively pursue one's own desires but rather to expect a fairy-tale prince to bring everlasting bliss. And although the influence on boys is not often considered, Disney's portrayal of male gender and sex roles is no less deleterious, creating as it does expectations that are just as impossible as those for girls. To be sure, recent films such as *Aladdin* (1992) and *Beauty and the Beast* (1991) seek to revamp the respective gender roles of both the heroine and hero; and yet, the underlying logic governing expectations for sexuality remains unchanged.

Although less popular than Disney's versions, other fairy tales for children have attempted to provide very different models of gender and sexuality. Such is certainly the case with **feminist tales** by Jeanne Desy, Jay Williams, and Jane **Yolen** (for instance) that present resolutely active heroines who refuse the traditionally passive model and instead follow a course of action of their own choosing. By privileging the heroines' own desires, whether sexual or not, these tales at the very least endorse an active exploration of feminine sexuality. Such is certainly the case in Jay Williams' "Petronella" (1973), whose eponymous heroine sets out on a quest to find a prince only to discover in the end that she prefers a lowly enchanter, turning down the offer of marriage from Prince Ferdinand.

Similar to children's tales, twentieth-century fairy tales for adults present diverse approaches to sexuality. At the turn of the century, "decadent" writers in France such as Anatole France, Jean Lorrain, and Catulle Mendès frequently used the fairy tale to intermingle eroticism and violence, notably through the femme fatale. During the second half of the century, numerous writers, notably in English-speaking countries, used fairy tales to address sexuality in straightforward ways. Most prominent have been rewritings that reflect on feminine sexuality confronted by male oppression. In the fairy-tale poems of Anne **Sexton**, sexual violence against women receives striking and often disturbing treatment. Although in very different stylistic veins, Margaret **Atwood** and Robert **Coover** have likewise focused on the connections between violence and sexuality; but where Atwood has tended to concentrate on the fate of her heroines, Coover has reflected on the hardships of desire itself. However, it is arguably Angela **Carter** who made the most extensive use of the fairy tale to explore and to reconceive preconceptions about sex and sexuality. In her collection *The Bloody Chamber* (1979), especially, Carter at once gives a powerful critique of female victimhood and explores various forms of feminine sexual subjectivity, often against the backdrop of a mysterious setting. Several of her heroines refuse to allow "beastly" desire to become the sole province of **men** and adopt it for themselves. Through her reworkings of fairy-tale material, Carter not only makes explicit the charged erotic relationships in well-known tales but also rethinks the very premise of traditional fairy-tale sexuality. An equally profound but very different rethinking of sexuality occurs in the recent phenomenon of **gay and lesbian tales**, most of which are addressed to adult readers. Emma **Donoghue** and Peter Cashorali, among others, endeavor to rewrite the heterosexual love plot so central to the fairy-tale tradition. So doing, they show the consequences that the lack of fairy-tale depictions of same-sex desire and the heterosexist usage of traditional fairy-tale love plots have had on gays and lesbians. Most of all, of course, they aim to create tales that portray a variety of same-sex relationships, in a range of settings from the contemporary to the archaic.

The understanding of sex and sexuality in folktales and fairy tales has been profoundly shaped by two fields of study in particular: psychology and **feminism**. It is well known that Sigmund **Freud**, the founder of modern psychology, argued that fairy-tale elements are often found in dreams or other unconscious material and that these elements are symbols for sexual trauma of various sorts. But Freud's concern was not to analyze fairy tales per se. Instead, several of his followers, among them Franz Riklin, Herbert Silberer, and Ernest Jones, developed his intuition that fairy tales express sexual desires in symbolic form and reveal the consequences of sexual repression. Even more influential was Otto Rank's work, which studied mythological and fairy-tale heroes using the Freudian notions of the Oedipus complex and the family romance. **Psychological approaches** to fairy tales based on the theories of Carl Gustav **Jung** have garnered a wide following, especially within studies by Hedwig von Beit, Joseph Campbell, and Marie-Louise von **Franz**. Departing as it does from the Freudian model, this perspective does not foreground sexuality, even though it stresses the male and female "**archetype**s" (animus and anima, respectively) found in fairy tales. Explicit analysis of sex and sexuality is much more prominent in Bruno Bettelheim's popular yet controversial study, which claimed that fairy tales depict unconscious struggles, allowing children to face their anxieties (especially those connected with the oedipal complex and sibling rivalry) on their way to adulthood. Going a step further than earlier Freudian critics, he also insisted that, in both representation and reception, fairy tales undo the repression of sex and change it into something "beautiful."

The extent to which the genre can be interpreted as optimistically as Bettelheim claimed is one of the crucial topics of concern for feminist fairy-tale criticism. Beginning with the debate between Allison Lurie and Marcia Lieberman in the early 1970s, a body of scholarship has emerged to consider how fairy tales have served—and may continue to serve—the cause of women's liberation, conceived broadly. Although this work has concentrated on gender, and specifically on the representation of women and its effects on girls, it has done much to elucidate the dynamics of sexuality in the genre, if only indirectly. For instance, an early topic of debate was the role fairy tales play in developing notions of "romance." While some critics, such as Lieberman, Andrea Dworkin, and Susan Brownmiller, condemned certain fairy tales for disguising and perpetuating male oppression (even in its most physical form, such as rape), others, such as Karen Rowe and Madonna Kolbenschlag, stressed that the genre, if reconceived, could be used to effect change in women's experience. As fairy-tale criticism has developed over the past twenty years and has considered in increasing detail the genre's various historical and social contexts of production, the importance of feminist approaches has likewise grown, with the rediscovery of women-authored fairy tales and investigations into constructions of gender from numerous perspectives.

Still, to date, much remains to be done, by building on feminist work and exploring yet other avenues. Studies of "**Little Red Riding Hood**" by Catherine Orenstein and Jack **Zipes,** of the Grimms' tales and "**Bluebeard**" by Maria Tatar, and of postmodern fairy tales by Christina Bacchilega show how multifaceted and rewarding the study of sex and sexuality can be. By and large, however, scholars are only beginning to bring to bear the insights from the emerging fields of sexuality studies and queer studies. As they do, it will become clear once again just how central folktales and fairy tales are as expressions of individual and social existence. *See also* Bawdy Tale; Childhood and Children; Erotic Tales; Fabliau, Fabliaux; Jest and Joke; Trauma and Therapy.

Further Readings: Bacchilega, Christina. *Postmodern Fairy Tales: Gender and Narrative Strategies.* Philadelphia: University of Pennsylvania Press, 1997; Bettleheim, Bruno. *The Uses of Enchantment: The Meaning and Importance of Fairy Tales.* New York: Knopf, 1976; Orenstein, Catherine. *Little Red Riding Hood Uncloaked: Sex, Morality, and the Evolution of the Fairy Tale.* New York: Basic Books, 2002; Röhrich, Lutz. "Erotik, Sexualität." *Enzyklopädie des Märchens.* Edited by Kurt Ranke et al. Volume 4. Berlin: Walter de Gruyter, 1984. 234–78; Tatar, Maria. *The Hard Facts of the Grimms' Fairy Tales.* Princeton, NJ: Princeton University Press, 1987; ———. *Secrets beyond the Door: The Story of Bluebeard and His Wives.* Princeton, NJ: Princeton University Press, 2004; Zipes, Jack, ed. *The Trials and Tribulations of Little Red Riding Hood.* 2nd edition. New York: Routledge, 1993.

Lewis C. Seifert

Sexton, Anne (1928–1974)

Anne Sexton, an important American poet, is perhaps best known for her revisions of fairy tales. In her volume *Transformations* (1971), she surrounded tales retold from the Brothers **Grimm** with her own sardonic, often personal commentary. Her work has inspired generations of **women** writers to reimagine tales and to comment on them.

Sexton came to **poetry** the hard way. Though she lived in affluent Boston suburbs all of her life, she herself was never comfortable there. While a student at Garland Junior College, she eloped at nineteen with Alfred (Kayo) Sexton. She became severely depressed after the birth of each of her two daughters. As she said in a 1968 interview, "I was trying my damnedest to lead a conventional life, for that was how I was brought up, and it was what my husband wanted of me. But one can't build little white picket fences to keep the nightmares out." She was hospitalized intermittently after her frequent suicide attempts; her therapist, Dr. Martin Orne, suggested that she write poetry. She joined several writing groups in the Boston area, where she met Robert Lowell, Sylvia Plath, and her lifelong friend Maxine

Kumin. Her first volume of poetry, *To Bedlam and Part Way Back* (1960), won her wide recognition, and she continued to publish regularly throughout the rest of her short, troubled life. Her 1966 volume *Live or Die* won the 1967 Pulitzer Prize in poetry. She committed suicide in 1974, the same day she finished correcting the proofs for her posthumous volume *The Awful Rowing toward God* (1975).

Transformations includes poems based on seventeen of the Grimms' tales, from the very well-known ("**Snow White**," "Rapunzel," "Red Riding Hood") to the more obscure ("The White Snake," "The Little Peasant," "The Maiden without Hands"). Sexton chose to begin with a version of the tale "The Golden Key," which the Grimms placed last (as number 200) in later editions of their collection. In her version, "The Gold Key," she introduces herself as the speaker: "a middle-aged witch, me." (Throughout her writing career, Sexton tended to identify herself as a **witch** or "Dame Sexton," and always began her readings with her poem "Her Kind," which stresses this identification.) Though she said that "The Gold Key" did not have the "zest" of the others, it introduces both the icy, demythologizing narrative voice and the pop-art theme that run throughout the volume. In this poem, Sexton seems to be alluding to contemporary sculpture such as Claes Oldenberg's blown-up baseball bats; her work on the tales, too, depends on the isolation and exaggeration of everyday situations and objects. Like the boy in the opening poem, she is waiting for the "Presto!" that will transform them.

Throughout *Transformations*, Sexton emphasizes the psychological horrors of her own middle-class life. In "Red Riding Hood," for example, she emphasizes the terrible gap between ordinary experiences and her reactions to them. As Kurt Vonnegut says in his introduction to the volume, "she domesticates my terror," but at the same time, she reveals the terror behind the domestic world of the 1950s and 1960s.

Sexton structures most of her retellings of the Grimms' tales in the same way. She gives them a prologue, often intensely personal, linking them to problems in contemporary life; then she retells the tale with her own surprising adjectives and grotesque images; then she ends with a brief coda that replaces and questions the traditional "happily ever after" ending. In the final poem, "Briar Rose" (based on **Sleeping Beauty**), for example, she begins with a journey back into her **childhood**, possibly in therapy; retells the story while stressing her **father**'s role and the **princess**'s fear of sleep after her awakening; and then, in the longest coda in the volume, sketches her own nightmarish life as a "trance girl" who cannot forget her father's abuse, real or imagined. The ending also returns for a moment to the opening poem ("Presto! / She's out of prison"), though in fact it is a prison she can never really leave. The personal, autobiographical frame she creates forces her readers to reread the tales in the context of contemporary experience, and to look for darker, often Freudian subtexts.

Sexton's life and work have always been controversial. Critics have disagreed about the ways she represented women's lives, some claiming her as an early feminist, others seeing her work as detailing the dilemmas of an intelligent housewife without suggesting any solutions. Some think that she simply repeats what she calls "that story" of the rise from rags to riches in her poem "**Cinderella**"; others believe that her version of the tale reveals and criticizes the bland conformity of the traditional ending. Critics have also disagreed about whether to place her with other so-called confessional poets such as Robert Lowell and Sylvia Plath. Diane Middlebrook's 1991 biography raised ethical questions about the use of Sexton's therapists' notes and tapes as a biographical source.

Transformations was itself transformed into a chamber **opera** or "entertainment" by the composer Conrad Susa in 1973, in collaboration with Sexton. Set in a mental hospital, the opera's mixture of musical styles and textures, from Gustav Mahler to the foxtrot and tango, captures the flavors of ten of Sexton's poems; it has often been performed, primarily in the United States. Sexton's volume has also continued to influence writers who want to question the behavior the Grimms' tales seem to prescribe for women, from Olga **Broumas** in *Beginning with O* (1977) to Emma **Donoghue** in her volume of linked stories *Kissing the Witch* (1997), among many others. *See also* Adaptation; Feminism; Feminist Tales; Little Red Riding Hood; Trauma and Therapy.

Further Readings: George, Diana Hume. *Oedipus Anne: The Poetry of Anne Sexton.* Urbana: University of Illinois Press, 1987; Middlebrook, Diane Wood. *Anne Sexton: A Biography.* Boston: Houghton Mifflin, 1991; Sexton, Linda Gray, and Lois Ames, eds. *Anne Sexton: A Self-Portrait in Letters.* Boston: Houghton Mifflin, 1977.

Elizabeth Wanning Harries

Shakespeare, William (1564–1616)

In his comedies and tragedies, even in his history plays, the world's foremost poet-playwright, William Shakespeare, makes conspicuous use of folktale plots and characters. Virtually every Shakespeare play depends on some folktale element, from *The Comedy of Errors* (Motif K1311.1, Husband's twin brother mistaken by woman for her husband) through *Measure for Measure* (Motif P14.19, King goes in disguise at night to observe his subjects), *Henry IV, Part One* (Motif P233.8, Prodigal son returns), and *Romeo and Juliet* (Motif K1860, Deception by feigned death [sleep]), to *Hamlet* (Motif K1818.3, Disguise as madman [fool]) and *The Winter's Tale* (Motif S451, Outcast wife at last united with husband and children). These folktale elements come to him through written sources, excepting only *The Taming of the Shrew*, which dramatizes an old **joke** that Shakespeare knew orally (ATU 901).

The plot of the **tale type** known as Pound of Flesh (ATU 890), for instance, is a prominent feature of *The Merchant of Venice*. So is the three caskets **motif** (L211, Modest choice: three caskets type). Both came to Shakespeare from the popular fourteenth-century collection **Gesta Romanorum** (*Deeds of the Romans*). In the often-underrated *Cymbeline*, Shakespeare borrows from Giovanni **Boccaccio** (*Decameron* 2.9) and elsewhere the folktale plot of The Wager on the Wife's Chastity (ATU 882). *King Lear*, influenced by Plutarch, Raphael Holinshed, Michel de Montaigne, and Edmund Spenser, retells the story Love Like Salt (ATU 923; related to **Cinderella**, ATU 510A). Below the surface level, the structure of *Macbeth* has been interpreted as the posing and solving of a **riddle**. At the outset, the predictions of the Weird Sisters are incomprehensible; the solutions come later, after **blood** has been shed. By imitating and adapting the riddle-and-answer format, Shakespeare creates the formal structure of his tragedy. At a still deeper level, the *Henry IV* plays, as well as comedies such as *As You Like It*, put onstage the carnival pattern of a temporary residence in an unofficial existence, followed by a return to "real" life.

Shakespeare's **fairies** in *A Midsummer Night's Dream* derive from classical, mythological, medieval, and contemporary sources. **Puck**, the fairy closest to Celtic tradition, anticipates Ariel in *The Tempest*, which otherwise draws on fairy belief but not on fairy tale or folktale. Fairy belief also shows in the last act of *The Merry Wives of Windsor*. Modern productions of Shakespeare's comedies—*Twelfth Night, The Winter's Tale*, even the bitter *All's Well That Ends Well*—often strike viewers as having a fairy-tale quality, but not from any use of fairy-tale plots or characters. *See also* Faerie and Fairy Lore; Theater.

Further Readings: Barber, C. L. *Shakespeare's Festive Comedy: A Study of Dramatic Form and Its Relation to Social Custom.* Princeton, NJ: Princeton University Press, 1959; Briggs, Katharine M. *The Anatomy of Puck: An Examination of Fairy Beliefs among Shakespeare's Contemporaries and Successors.* London: Routledge and Kegan Paul, 1959; Dundes, Alan. " 'To Love My Father All': A Psychoanalytic Study of the Folktale Source of *King Lear.*" *Interpreting Folklore.* Bloomington: Indiana University Press, 1980. 211–22; Gorfain, Phyllis. "Riddles and Tragic Structure in *Macbeth.*" *Misssissippi Folklore Register* 10 (1976): 187–209.

Lee Haring

Shape-Shifting. *See* Transformation

Sheherazade

The name Sheherazade derives from the Persian *chehr-âzâd*, denoting a person of noble origin and/or appearance. As the narrator who tells the tales of the *Thousand and One Nights* (or the *Arabian Nights*), Sheherazade has become synonymous with creative **storytelling** as well as with **feminism** in the Islamic world.

The **frame narrative** of the *Arabian Nights* opens with King Shahriyar being so furious about his wife's sexual infidelity (and the infidelity of **women** in general) that he decides to marry a virgin every night and have her executed the next morning. When the number of suitable women has been exhausted, the vizier's daughter, Sheherazade, is determined to cure the **king**'s cruel habit. She marries him and, after consummating the **marriage**, has her sister (or, in other versions, her maid) Dunyazade ask the king's permission for Sheherazade to tell him a tale from her vast repertoire. When morning dawns, Sheherazade intentionally breaks off the tale at a dramatic point, and the curious king allows her to stay alive so as to finish the tale the next night. This continues for 1,001 nights, when Sheherazade finally shows the king the three children she has meanwhile born to him. The king repents his previous habit, and all live happily ever after.

First mentioned in Arabic sources of the tenth century, the frame tale probably indicates a lost Iranian prototype. Since the earliest preserved manuscripts of the *Arabian Nights*, dating from the fifteenth century, Sheherazade's major personal characteristics include self-consciousness,

"Scheherazadè, the heroine of the Thousand and One Nights," illustration by Edmund Dulac, from *Stories from the Arabian Nights* by Laurence Housman (New York: George H. Doran Company, n.d.), frontispiece.

courage, erudition, and cleverness. The first tales she tells deal with persons who ransom their lives by either telling a tale or by having somebody else tell a tale for their sake. This stratagem links the fate of the narrative characters to Sheherazade's own and thus implicitly works as a further factor to reform the king.

While King Shahriyar's cruel habit has been interpreted as an uninhibited exertion of male dominance, the therapeutic value of Sheherazade's tales consists of initiating him from a narcissistic self-indulgence into a true partnership based on mutual respect. In mirroring the king's dilemma in a caring and thoughtful way, Sheherazade heals him from his manic depression. Furthermore, she leads him to acknowledge (albeit unconsciously) the authority of her humanist values that are not only imperative for individual married life but for the well-being of society in general.

In Western **art**, Sheherazade has inspired innumerable **illustration**s and creative **adaptation**s of her tale in **music**, **dance**, **opera**, and **film**. Orientalist illustrations of the *Arabian Nights* often imply a lascivious seductress. Meanwhile, an important dilemma has so far largely been unnoticed: after all, the presumably male authors of the *Arabian Nights* employ a female narrator to put into action their own (male) images of a female role model before a predominantly male audience. *See also Arabian Nights* Films.

Further Readings: Attar, Samar, and Gerhard Fischer. "Promiscuity, Emancipation, Submission: The Civilizing Process and the Establishment of a Female Role Model in the Frame-Story of 1001 Nights." *Arab Studies Quarterly* 13.3–4 (1991): 1–18; Clinton, Jerome W. "Madness and Cure in the *Thousand and One Nights*." *Fairy Tales and Society: Illusion, Allusion and Paradigm*. Edited by Ruth B. Bottigheimer. Philadelphia: University of Pennsylvania Press, 1986. 35–51; Enderwitz, Susanne. "Shahrazâd Is One of Us: Practical Narrative, Theoretical Discussion, and Feminist Discourse." *Marvels & Tales* 18 (2004): 187–200; Marzolph, Ulrich, and Richard van Leeuwen, eds. *The Arabian Nights Encyclopedia*. Volume 2. Denver: ABC-CLIO, 2004. 701–02.

Ulrich Marzolph

Sherman, Delia (1951–)

President of the Interstitial Arts Foundation, Delia Sherman is an American author of **fantasy** and numerous fairy-tale retellings told from slanted perspectives. Her first **novel**, *Through a Brazen Mirror* (1989), addressed the theme of the Scottish **ballad** "The Famous Flower of Serving Men" and presented a queer reading of the source material. Four years later, her second novel, *The Porcelain Dove* (1993), won the Mythopoeic Award for Fantasy Fiction. *The Porcelain Dove* is less a strict retelling and more a thematic exploration of the time following upon the period of the ***contes de fées***. Set during the time of the French Revolution, the tale centers on the experiences of Berthe Duvet, a lady's maid. Ferociously attached to her young mistress, Berthe follows her to her new estate upon her **marriage**, only to discover that the hereditary holdings of the Duc de Malveaux include not only an estate in the south of France containing a magical chamber dedicated to the *contes* but also a curse.

More recently, Sherman has focused her work in the genre of **children's literature**. Her novel *Changeling* (2006) explores an alternate New York (called New York Between) populated by every imaginable creature out of **folklore**, fairy tales, and popular culture. The inhabitants of New York Between include not only the Wild Hunt, **mermaid**s, and **dragon**s, but also vampires, ticket-scalping ghouls, and, of course, mortal **changeling**s, all of whom struggle to observe the rules of Folk Lore. Sherman has also co-written a novel, *The Fall of the Kings* (2002), with her partner Ellen **Kushner**.

Further Readings: Attebery, Brian. "Gender, Fantasy, and the Authority of Tradition." *Journal of the Fantastic in the Arts* 7 (1996): 51–60; Pilinovsky, Helen. "Interstitial Arts: An Interview with Delia Sherman." *Journal of the Fantastic in the Arts* 15 (2004): 248–50.

Helen Pilinovsky

Shoe

In general, the term "shoe" encompasses all kinds of human footwear. In the context of fairy tales and folktales, shoes may be moccasins, slippers, ballet shoes, boots, clogs, and sandals, marvelous or otherwise. Shoes in fairy tales contribute to the action by moving, and so by extension they may be involved, for example, in dancing, escape, flight, or wandering. They are also extremely desirable, either by virtue of their elegant appearance or their magical powers (**Motif** D1065, Magic footwear). Their magic qualities usually lie in their ability to cover long distances instantly (Motif D1521.1, Seven-league boots), to make the wearer invisible (Motif D1361.38, Magic boots render invisible), or to allow the wearer to fly (Motif D1520.10, Magic transportation by shoes). Rich in symbolic qualities, shoes may be associated with social status, identity, female beauty, or **sexuality**.

One of the most famous shoes is **Cinderella**'s glass slipper, which she loses at the ball and which leads the **prince** to discover her (ATU 510A). This tale is paralleled by the legend given by Strabo of how the sight of Rhodopis's sandal filled the pharaoh Psammetichos with desire. In either case, the elegant piece of footwear that identifies its owner evokes female beauty. Cinderella's slipper, which fits her foot and hers alone, is associated with female sexuality. The motif of the bridal slipper test (Motif H36.1) is common to many of the world's cultures. The danced-out shoes (ATU 306; Motif F1015.1.1) worn by a bewitched princess are likewise associated with femininity and female sexuality but suggest a deviation in social behavior, namely the avoidance of **marriage**, that requires correction. The red shoes in Hans Christian **Andersen**'s tale of that name are also associated with deviant female social behavior in that, bewitched as they are, they wear their owner out with dancing.

Puss in Boots (ATU 545B; Motif B582.1.1) acquires a human appearance to help his master. His boots, a caricature of high social status, have contributed to the development of a charming iconography, such as that evident in Gustave **Doré**'s nineteenth-century engravings. By contrast, the marvelous boots that Tom Thumb steals from the **ogre** are an example of shoes functioning as a perfect instrument of movement (ATU 700, **Thumbling**; ATU 327B, The Brothers and the Ogre). Hermes's and Perseus's winged sandals (Motif D1065.5, Magic sandals) are a mythological counterpart to the flying shoes of fairy tales. The Youth and the Pretty Shoes (ATU 1731) is a folktale that focuses on the most desirable and tempting aspect of shoes—a quality mentioned in Jacob and Wilhelm **Grimm**'s "The **Elves** and the Shoemaker" (included under the title "Die Wichtelmänner"—"The Elves"—in the Grimms' collection).

The wearing out of iron shoes (Motifs H1125 and Q502.2), usually three pairs, is a motif common to various tales and is mostly combined with some difficult task or quest, as in The Search for the Lost Husband (ATU 425). Dancing to **death** in red-hot shoes (Motif Q414.4) figures in tales as a **punishment** for the wicked, as, for instance, in the case of **Snow White**'s stepmother (ATU 709). ***See also*** Clothing; Magic Object.

Further Readings: Cardigos, Isabelle. "The Wearing and Shedding of Enchanted Shoes." *Estudos de Literatura Oral* 5 (1999): 219–28; Rooth, Anna Birgitta. *The Cinderella Cycle.* Lund: Gleerup, 1951. 103–10.

Marilena Papachristophorou

Shrek and *Shrek II* (2001, 2004)

Directed by Andrew Adamson and Vicky Jenson, *Shrek* (2001) and its sequel *Shrek II* (2004) are contemporary animated fairy-tale films that represent something of a culmination of the self-aware, parodic use of fairy tale in modern popular narratives. Their amusing adventure plots enshrine not only a postmodern and highly self-conscious awareness of classic fairy tale but also a wry sense of contemporary popular culture. While they reference **fantasy** films of various kinds, their most important intertexts, rather than coming from Charles **Perrault** or the Brothers **Grimm**, are the fairy-tale films of Walt **Disney**. *Shrek* is based on a children's book of the same name by author William Steig (1990). While the plot is nominally faithful to the original, the illustrated picture book is a simpler story, written with irony, understatement, wordplay, and a stronger message about self-acceptance. Its slightly sketchy, untidy artwork is also considerably removed from the clean, solid shapes of the DreamWorks film.

The **animation** used by DreamWorks Animation in making *Shrek* was groundbreaking at the time and particularly favors realism of facial expression and movement. Nonetheless, the two films make use of the same parallels that rendered the Disney fairy tale so effective, the conceptual match between the bright, simplified shapes of animation and the lack of realism and uncluttered texture of fairy tale itself. *Shrek*'s effect is in its cheerful and iconoclastic inversion of classical fairy-tale **motif**s. The film includes a "**Sleeping Beauty**" element with an attendant christening curse, a **dragon**-slaying quest, and a somewhat convoluted false-suitor plot; but its central trope is an inverted "**Beauty and the Beast**," with the final **transformation** being from **princess** to monster, rather than from monster to **prince**. Other fairy-tale elements wander waywardly through the story, among them a magic **mirror**, **animal helper**s, and various references to figures from both fairy tale and children's nursery rhyme—**pigs**, **wolves**, **Snow White**, Robin Hood, the Gingerbread Man, and the Three Blind Mice. The film's tone is knowing and self-conscious, relying on audience recognition and enjoyment of fairy tale's familiarity.

A similar structure is found in *Shrek II*, but its Prince Charming, Fairy Godmother, Ugly Sister, and Frog Prince become the mechanisms by which the "happily ever after" of the first film is attacked. The true obstacle to happiness in the story is the attempt to impose an ideology that denies the validity of the contented monsters and to reassert a more conventional fairy-tale ethos. The Beauty-and-the-Beast transformation is permitted in this film, with Shrek becoming a ruggedly handsome prince; however, it is ultimately denied, repeating the pattern of the first film and restoring the conclusion that finds the monsters happy together in their ugliness. The references to contemporary popular culture are perhaps more overt in *Shrek II*, with the equation of Princess Fiona's kingdom with the glitz of Hollywood, and with a wry imposition of conventional in-law problems onto the traditional fairy-tale **marriage**.

The films are comic, entertaining, and self-aware. They effectively reference not only fairy tale but also **fantasy** film, including classics such as ***The Princess Bride*** (1987),

Ladyhawke (1985), and recent hits such as *The Matrix* (1999) and ***The Lord of the Rings*** (2000–2003). They thus situate themselves within a broader discourse of magical narrative than either the fairy tale or the folkloric. Most importantly, however, both *Shrek* films provide a sustained and irreverent attack on their inevitable point of comparison, the Disney-animated fairy tale that dominated the field throughout most of the twentieth century. Not only do the *Shrek* films visually reference Disney characters, but they also deliberately set out to deny the saccharine morality and overtly family atmosphere associated with Disney productions. Princess Fiona's transformation scene is a studied reproduction of the Beast's transformation in Disney's *Beauty and the Beast*, and Lord Farquaad's magic mirror explicitly references the one in Disney's *Snow White and the Seven Dwarfs*. Disney's tendency to use endearing animal sidekicks, however, is ruthlessly pilloried not only in the robust characters of the Donkey and **Puss in Boots**, but in Princess Fiona's duet with a bluebird, who explodes as she hits a high note. *Shrek* and its sequel deny the stilted unreality of Disney's musical format. The only character who sings is the Fairy Godmother of the second film, and her musical numbers are clearly part of her monstrous oversubscription to fairy-tale cliché. The family values of Disney are also attacked in the body humor and occasional grossness of the *Shrek* films.

The most interesting aspect of *Shrek* and *Shrek II* is thus not its **intertextuality**, but its ideology. Apart from the conscious undercutting of Disney, the film attacks fairy tale on a more general level: the conflation of the monster and hero into one figure parodies not only the structural expectations of fairy tale but its unambiguous morality and weight of cultural expectation. The initiatory and civilizing aspects of fairy-tale adventure are examined and ultimately rejected in favor of a message of individuality that also deliberately attacks the beauty **myth** of modern consumer culture. Rather like the updated fairy tales of Terry **Pratchett**, the *Shrek* films identify the fairy tale as a totalitarian discourse, one that must be resisted or overthrown for true self-definition and happiness. Lord Farquaad's excessively tidy kingdom of Duloc thus fulfils the same narrative purpose in *Shrek* as does the Fairy Godmother's industrial mass-production of magic in *Shrek II*: both elements highlight the fairy tale as an ultimately dehumanizing ideal. *See also* Children's Literature; Film and Video; Postmodernism.

Further Reading: Zipes, Jack. "The Radical Morality of Rats, Fairies, Wizards, and Ogres: Taking Children's Literature Seriously." *Breaking the Magic Spell: Radical Theories of Folk and Fairy Tales*. Revised expanded edition. Lexington: University Press of Kentucky, 2002. 206–31.

Jessica Tiffin

Shua, Ana María (1951–)

Argentine writer Ana María Shua has written more than forty books in nearly every genre: **poetry**, **novel**s, short stories, **theater**, **film**, **children's literature**, and Jewish **folklore**. Her works have received literary prizes and have been translated into several languages and published throughout the world.

Shua's exploration of the fairy-tale genre was first developed in a volume of short stories entitled *Los días de pesca* (*Fishing Days*, 1981). In it, Shua recalls a few fairy tales to which she adds a disruptive twist. Her revisionist project was later expanded in the collection of short stories *Casa de Geishas* (*House of Geishas*, 1992), particularly in the section entitled "Versiones" ("Versions"), in which she included twenty-nine texts that are rewrites of well-known fairy tales such as "**Cinderella**," "**Snow White**," and "The **Frog King**." "Versions" also includes retellings of classic **myth**s, Jewish folklore, and stories from the medieval bestiary.

Shua ultimately aims at liberating **women** from traditional patriarchal stereotypes. She does so by offering readers multiple versions of the original texts, thus forcing them to critically examine the extent to which the patterns of classical fairy tales reflect patriarchal assumptions about **gender** identity. *See also* Feminism; Feminist Tales.

Further Readings: Bilbija, Ksenija. "In Whose Own Image? Ana María Shua's Gendered Poetics of Fairy Tales." *El río de los sueños: Aproximaciones críticas a la obra de Ana María Shua.* Edited by Rhonda Dahl Buchanan. Washington, DC: Organization of American States, 2001. 205–18; Buchanan, Rhonda Dahl. "Literature's Rebellious Genre: The Short Short Story in Ana María Shua's *Casa de geishas.*" *Revista Interamericana de Bibliografía* 46.1–4 (1996): 179–92.

Carolina Fernández-Rodríguez

Shvarts, Evgeny (1897–1958)

Evgeny Shvarts is known as a Russian author of fairy tales and fairy-tale plays for both children and adults. He entered the literary scene soon after his arrival in St. Petersburg in 1921, where he got to know Kornei **Chukovsky** and was invited to join the division of **children's literature** at Gosizdat Publishers, as well as to write for the most popular children's journals at the time. He was also close to the avant-garde group Oberiu. Between 1924 and 1931, Shvarts published more than twenty books for children, including verse tales inspired by the tradition of Russian **puppet theater**, the grotesque, and **folklore**, as well as **didactic tale**s about traffic regulations and the heroic deeds of young pioneers. His play *Underwood* (1928) proved that he had found his ultimate mode of artistic expression: drama with elements of fairy tale. Several of his plays are based on tales by Hans Christian **Andersen**. *Snezhnaya koroleva* (*The Snow Queen*, 1939) and a few others address children, while *Goly korol'* (*The Naked King*, based on "The Emperor's New Clothes"), written in 1934 but published only in 1960, has a clear allegorical dimension. The satirical dimension of Shvarts's plays, which speak to the abuse of power by rulers, raised red flags with Communist censors. *Ten'* (*The Shadow*, 1940) was removed from the theater's repertoire after opening night, and *Drakon* (*The Dragon*)—probably his most widely known play—was written in 1943–44 but was not published until 1962 because of political repression. Although Shvarts also composed some fairy tales in prose, it was his achievement as a satirist who expressed his thoughts by means of fairy tale that earned him an international reputation. *See also* Russian Tales.

Further Readings: Corten, Irina H. "Evgeny Lvovich Shvarts: A Biographical Sketch." *Russian Literature Triquarterly* 16 (1979): 222–43; ———. "Evgenii L'vovich Shvarts: A Selected Bibliography." *Russian Literature Triquarterly* 16 (1979): 333–39; Corten, Irina H. "Evgenii Shvarts as a Russian Adapter of Hans Christian Andersen and Charles Perrault." *Russian Review* 37 (1978): 51–67.

Janina Orlov

Silent Films and Fairy Tales

Ever since the first motion pictures were presented to the public, fairy tales and their **motif**s have provided some of the raw materials out of which popular films are made. During the silent period, fairy-tale movies were primarily produced in the United States,

Germany, France, and Scandinavia. Of the 250 full-length pictures produced with a fairy-tale background and shown in Europe and North America between 1895 and 1975, 39 percent may be classified using the Aarne-Thompson-Uther system, that is, they are based on genuine **folktale**s or folktale motifs. Another 25 percent include folktale motifs in stories of more general character.

In most cases, the screenplays for these films were not developed from orally transmitted texts, but adapted either from printed fairy tales or from literary and musical works with folktale elements. Of all silent fairy-tale films, roughly 60 percent deal with traditional fairy tales and **legend**s; another 30 percent feature folklore motifs, characters of **folklore** origin (for example, **Till Eulenspiegel** of **tale type** ATU 1635*), or a fairy-tale setting such as the milieu of the *Arabian Nights*. Eighty percent of all films based on fairy-tales and produced up to the point when talkies took over in 1928 may be categorized by ATU types 300–1199: tales of magic, **religious tale**s, realistic tales (**novella**s), or tales of the stupid **ogre**.

Silent films were not specifically targeted at either adult or young audiences. In the conflict between films for children and films for the general public, the industry opted for the latter. It wasn't until the early 1930s that children's fairy-tale films intended for viewing in venues such as schools were produced on a greater scale.

The first German fairy-tale film was *Hänsel und Gretel* (1897, directed by Oskar Messter), an adaptation based not on the classic Grimm fairy tale but on the popular **opera** by Engelbert **Humperdinck**. The first U.S.-produced film with a folklore background was *Rip van Winkle* (1903, directed by Joseph Jefferson; composed of scenes from his famous stage success). This story was also picked up by French director and magician Georges **Méliès** in 1905, again inspired by an opera, this time by Jules Massenet's of the same year. French fairy-tale film production had begun a few years earlier with *Cendrillon* (1899, directed by Méliès). Several remakes were produced of "**Hansel and Gretel**" (six German films between 1897 and 1926), "**Cinderella**" (six films between 1907 and 1923, including three American, two German, and one French), "**Snow White**" (five films between 1907 and 1928, including three American and two German), and "**Sleeping Beauty**" (four German films between 1912 and 1929). In addition, the following fairy tales were filmed two or more times during the silent period: "**Little Red Riding Hood**" (Germany, 1910; the United States, 1911; France, 1929), and "Jack and the Beanstalk" (the United States, 1917 and 1924). It is impossible, however, to provide a complete list, since only very few fairy-tale films from the silent years have survived. As a consequence, early film history may only be reconstructed with the help of press articles, film catalogues, and lists compiled for copyright and censorship purposes.

Fairy-tale films in the silent era relied on widely known sources such as Jacob and Wilhelm **Grimm**'s *Kinder- und Hausmärchen* (*Children's and Household Tales*, 1812–15) or tales by Hans Christian **Andersen**. With regard to German films in particular, the popular fairy tales by Wilhelm **Hauff** were another noteworthy source for at least seven films between 1916 and 1930. Popular literary and musical works often served as sources for these films. In the United States, L. Frank **Baum**'s *The Wonderful Wizard of Oz* (1900) was first filmed in 1910 and again in 1925. Sir James Matthew **Barrie**'s *Peter Pan* (1904) was produced by Paramount Pictures in 1924.

Legendary characters such as Faust have been filmed many times. Twenty-six Faust films have been catalogued for the period between 1897 and 1926 alone. Half of these were of French origin, including the very first, a Pathé production of 1897 directed by Georges

Hatot. In Great Britain, Faust films appeared in 1897 and 1910. In the United States, there were seven between 1897 and 1921, one (*Bill Bumper's Bargain*, 1911) a parody of Charles Gounod's opera. Germany contributed two Faust films. The first (1910, directed by Messter), which was intended to accompany the phonograph record of a scene from Gounod's opera, was followed in 1926 by Friedrich Wilhelm Murnau's celebrated masterpiece, which reached a global audience. An Italian Faust (1909, directed by Mario Caserini) and a Danish film (*Doctor X*, 1914, directed by Robert Dinesen) complete the list.

German silent film turned the doppelgänger figure (Motif E723) into filmed legend with prominent examples such as *Der Student von Prag* (*The Student of Prague*) in its two versions of 1913 (directed by Stellan Rye) and 1926 (directed by Henrik Galeen). A version with sound appeared in 1935. The creative mind behind these productions was the influential Berlin actor Paul Wegener, who directed and appeared in several films based on fairy tales, legends, and occult stories. The best known of these—based on folklore Motif D1635, Golem—are *Der Golem* (1914, codirected by with Henrik Galeen) and *Der Golem wie er in die Welt kam* (*The Golem, How He Came into the World*, 1920). The making of *The Golem* was itself turned into a film, written, directed, and performed by Wegener in 1917 (*Der Golem und die Tänzerin* [*The Golem and the Dancer*]). Adding a mandrake demon (Motif D965.1) to the story, director Nils Chrisander produced *Alraune und der Golem* (*The Mandrake and the Golem*) in 1919, a German production under Danish direction which made use of German Romantic writer Achim von Arnim's novel *Isabella von Ägypten* (*Isabella of Egypt*, 1812). These films were built around legendary characters.

In other cases, it was the fairy-tale setting that inspired the story. For example, the milieu of the *Arabian Nights* has been used extensively, leading to the subgenre of fairy-tale adventure films set in exotic locations, beginning with *Die feindlichen Teppichhändler oder die friedensstiftende Fee* (*The Hostile Carpet Dealers and the Peace-Making Fairy*, Germany, 1908) and culminating in *The Thief of Bagdad* (the United States, 1924). **See also** Arabian Nights Films; Film and Video; Maeterlinck, Maurice; Peter Pan Films; Reiniger, Lotte; Thief of Bagdad Films.

Further Readings: Haase, Donald. "The *Arabian Nights,* Visual Culture, and Early German Cinema." *The Arabian Nights in Transnational Perspective.* Edited by Ulrich Marzolph. Detroit: Wayne State University Press, 2007. 245–60; Liptay, Fabienne: *Wunderwelten: Märchen im Film.* Remscheid: Gardez, 2004.

Willi Höfig

Silko, Leslie Marmon (1948–)

As one of the first Native American **women** writers to incorporate **Native American tales** and **myth** into her fiction, Leslie Marmon Silko has contributed to a broader understanding of indigenous **storytelling** styles, concepts, and meanings for non-Native readers. Her best-known **novel**, *Ceremony* (1977), intertwines the healing of Tayo, a young mixed-blood World War II veteran who returns to the Laguna Reservation broken by his wartime experiences in the Pacific, with the Laguna Pueblo creation myth of the first peoples to emerge from the worlds below.

Silko's 1981 *Storyteller* contains many versions of the Laguna myth of "Yellow Woman," who was kidnapped by a deity only to return home later with her twin sons (see **Twins**). One of these versions, a short story anthologized often, has a contemporary young Laguna wife wonder if the stranger who has seduced her is a Mexican cattle rustler or a mountain spirit. She also wonders if she is herself or the woman kidnapped in the old story.

Silko has stated that Pueblo tellers don't differentiate between types of tales; stories about the sacred past and about recent everyday occurrences are equally important and often blend into each other. She considers her own fiction an extension of this Pueblo perspective on story. *See also* Race and Ethnicity.

Further Reading: Silko, Leslie Marmon. "Language and Literature from a Pueblo Indian's Perspective." *English Literature: Opening Up the Canon.* Edited by Leslie A. Fiedler and Houston A. Baker. Baltimore: Johns Hopkins University Press, 1979. 54–72.

Janet L. Langlois

Simple Forms

With the 1929 publication of *Einfache Formen* (*Simple Forms*), the Dutch literary scholar André Jolles identified the **märchen**, or **fairy tale**, as one of eight simple or preliterary forms of folk narrative. The other simple forms included the **saint's legend**, **legend**, **myth**, **riddle**, proverb, *Kasus* (case or example), *Memorabile* (report), and the **joke**. *Simple Forms* presented folklorists and literary scholars with one of the first classification systems distinguishing folk narrative genres according to the characteristic attitudes animating them and giving them their specific expression.

Jolles derives his notion of the simple form from Jacob **Grimm**'s distinction between "nature poetry" (*Naturpoesie*) and "art poetry" (*Kunstpoesie*), with the simple form corresponding to Grimm's view of the spontaneously occurring nature poetry. Like Vladimir **Propp**, Jolles presents *Simple Forms* as an answer to the problem of form. In contrast to Propp, however, he does not approach form from the perspective of structure, but as a phenomenological problem. Jolles's system turns on three central concepts: *Geistesbeschäftigung* (occupation of the intellect), *Sprachgebärde* (gestures of language), and *Gestalt* (pattern). For each simple form, Jolles identifies a characteristic mental attitude which finds expression in preexisting forms of language. The starting point of his method is the "realization" of the genre in its more fully developed form. While not identical to the simple form, the realization retains the characteristic nature and expression of the genre. For example, the modern-day sports report shares the same intellectual occupation, namely *imitatio* or adoration of the saint, as found in the saint's legend of the **Middle Ages**. In the case of the märchen, the characteristic intellectual occupation is that of a "naïve morality" which seeks to overcome an immoral reality and views "the world as it should be."

Almost immediately, there were both objections to and proposals for modification of Jolles's typology. The strongest criticisms were leveled at the Romantic theory of language and antiquated terminology. Many rejected the evolutionary framework that reduced simple forms to crude precursors of high literary forms. Critics of Jolles questioned the exclusion of the **fable** as well as the inclusion of the more complex **folktale**. The Swiss fairy tale scholar, Max **Lüthi**, disputed whether one single "occupation of the intellect" could adequately account for the diverse types of folktales. Carl von Sydow and others proposed the addition of subtypes in the effort to expand Jolles' typology.

One of the most sustained and productive efforts to amend Jolles's typology was led by the German folk-narrative scholar, Kurt **Ranke**, who maintained the simple form is an archetypical form of human expression, originating in the basic responses of the human soul to the world around it. In the case of märchen, a fairy-tale-like response to the world is one that gives expression to humankind's desire for happiness and fulfillment and elevates the world to mythic and heroic dimensions.

Further Readings: Jolles, André. *Einfache Formen: Legende, Sage, Mythe, Rätsel, Spruch, Kasus, Memorabile, Märchen, Witz.* 1929. Tübingen: Max Niemeyer, 1982; Ranke, Kurt. "Einfache Formen." *Journal of the Folklore Institute* 4 (1967): 17–31.

Mary Beth Stein

Simpleton

Since a person of impaired intelligence is quite noticeable in a community, and may be bizarre in some contexts, much lore centers on the attitudes and actions of such persons, typically known in folktales as a simpletons, fools, or numskulls. The simpleton figures as a leading character in many kinds of folktales, which are usually short and have a witty punch line.

Following the classification system developed by Antti **Aarne** and Stith **Thompson,** Hans-Jörg Uther's *The Types of International Folktales* allots special sections to such narratives under the general section devoted to "Jokes and Anecdotes" (ATU 1200–1999). These include, for example, "Stories about a Fool" (ATU 1200–1349); "Stories about Married Couples" (ATU 1350–1439), which encompass foolish wives, foolish husbands, and foolish couples; "The Stupid Man" (ATU 1675–1724); and other categories of tales in which foolish characters may play a role. The focus in these narratives is usually on wrong applications of work techniques by the foolish person, or misunderstandings of ordinary things or customs. Sayings or instructions can be taken out of context by the fool, or literally when the proper import would be figurative. A numskull may, for instance, sit on eggs to hatch them in imitation of a hen, put a cow on the roof of a house to eat the grass growing there, cut the branch of a tree on which he is sitting, or burn down a house so as to rid it of fleas. He may also mistake ordinary things for ghosts, or think himself dead, be frightened by his own shadow, or mistake his reflection in water or in a **mirror** for somebody else.

One widespread folktale (ATU 1600, The Fool as Murderer) tells of a fool seeing his **brothers** murder an oppressive person and bury the body. Later, he tells the police where the corpse is, but they find a billy goat there, which has been substituted for the body by the brothers. The fool remarks that the murdered man must have had horns. Several folktales tell of a foolish husband or wife. A cuckolded man, for instance, is blindfolded by his wife so that he cannot see her lover, or believes that the lover is a speaking animal in the house, or is otherwise deceived or misled. One very popular story (ATU 1653, The Robbers under the Tree) tells of how a foolish wife detaches the door from its hinges when told to "pull it after" her, but later, when the couple sleep on the door in a tree, she is terrified on hearing some robbers congregate under the tree. In her panic, she causes the door to fall upon the robbers, who are killed by the accident, and she and her husband get their loot.

The idea that foolishness can have its advantages is of great antiquity. This also must derive from the special notice taken of a mentally retarded person due to the uniqueness of the condition. Accordingly, the foolish person can be thought of as having some special hidden abilities, in which he shares a role in folk belief with other individuals who have extraordinary lifestyles. People such as scholars, clergymen, skilled artisans, or itinerants, because of their unusual social positions, are often considered to have arcane or magical powers. Being outside of the norm for members of the community, they are in some way exotic and thus can be thought of as exceeding the normal human potential. Similarly, persons with traits that mark them out—unusual physiognomy, hair color, or general demeanor—may imagined to be special. This way of thinking extends to people with physical blemishes, especially since, in such cases, there would be an expectation that nature would somehow compensate for the handicap. Thus, for instance, individuals who are blind are often thought of as having second sight—the gift of clairvoyance, prophecy, or skill in the auditory arts such as poetry, song, or music.

In these cases, there may of course be a natural basis for the folk supposition. Special skills and unusual or colorful experiences entail particular knowledge and vocabulary, making for increased technical and social abilities and causing the **folk** to exaggerate their scope and range into the realm of mystery. People with physical blemishes will naturally learn to compensate for their handicaps to whatever extent possible, and thus show some unusual skills of alertness or even technique, becoming as a result the focus of some folk marvel.

Mental deficiency, perhaps more than anything else, makes an individual exceptional, and the attention paid to the unusual is multiplied in such a case. The deficiency is naturally puzzling to the folk, and explanations are sought for it in fanciful thinking—representing it as being the result of some misfortune or interference by otherworld forces before, during, or after the individual's **birth**. In addition, the idea that some compensation is inevitable would suggest that a hidden type of knowledge could lie at the basis of the affliction, a knowledge which might be kindled and brought into practical use given suitable treatment and circumstances. The observable fact that some types of mental deficiency entail the "idiot-savant" syndrome—extraordinary ability in terms of memory and calculation—would be seen to underline this view that a simpleton is really a brilliant person in unlikely guise. All of this is of course rendered more rational by the fact that many people of intellectual genius spend much of their time engrossed in thinking and therefore appear to be socially gauche or distanced from their fellows.

Factors such as these seem to have always given rise to a tendency to regard a mentally retarded person as a living example of paradox. In primitive religions, the shaman may be recognized as an intermediary between human society and otherworld forces through his exhibiting socially marginal characteristics and even deranged behavior. It is impressive to note how such ideas have persisted within the cultural ambit of the world's great religions. Philosophical minds, of course, have always taken account of the fact that paradox lies at the root of human existence—life and **death** are mutually dependent, good and bad fortune may be two sides of the same coin, displays of piety and unselfishness can often mask their opposites, and so on. Accordingly, the paradoxes associated with the mental state of individuals would be considered by spiritual philosophers as evidence of the true human condition. The forthright but yet incongruous nature of the fool, to which feigning and pretense is so alien, would be considered a good illustration of this truth.

In this context may be considered the apparent contradictions of social norms involved in the sayings and deeds of those such as Krishna, Gautama, and Christ, and of numerous mystics of the Hindu, Buddhist, Judaic, Christian, and Islamic traditions. Similar attitudes lay behind the reputed actions of some secular philosophers, most notably Diogenes and the Cynics. In these cases, the wise men and women were using the idea of unworldliness as a teaching device, presenting simplicity as a necessary part of meaningful living but not entailing full derogation of ordinary responsibilities. In some cases, however, the commitment could be to a more extreme and permanent renunciation of social living. Thus, for instance, the hermits or "Desert Fathers" of eastern Christianity and some of the dervishes of Islamic tradition tended to consider the deliberate choice of irrationality as a sanctifying process.

The sacred fools of various religious traditions saw themselves as jolting people into a sense of true reality by means such as surprise, contradiction, and ambiguity, thereby paralleling the antics of the clown as an entertainer. The clown deliberately garbles social distinctions, using incongruity as the basis of humor. For his part, the fool is not a fanciful phenomenon but a social one, and his antics result from the fact that he is unable to make the distinctions. Once the notion of wisdom hidden within foolishness becomes part of popular consciousness, however, the borderline between clown and fool can become blurred. In medieval entertainment, the clown in some instances undertook his profession because of mental marginality in his or her own nature, and, similarly, some sacred fools were often in practice suffering from mental affliction. Thus, in Islamic popular tradition, fools were held in high regard because their mental condition was believed to put them in special contact with the divine. In Christianity generally, and more especially in aspects of Russian Orthodoxism, the "fools of God" wandered through the countryside, supported by the populace who highly valued their piety and looked to them for advice and for blessings and cures.

In Irish popular speech, a general term used for a mentally retarded individual is *duine le Dia* ("a person with God"), and the words of such a person are thought of as very telling. Medieval Irish literature has a striking example of the holy fool in the person of Comhdhán, who was said to have been a saint and an imbecile with flashes of extraordinary brilliance. He was called "the son of two skills"—one of which was foolishness and the other wisdom. He traveled around Ireland, alternately appearing as a numskull, a prophetic saint, and an inspired poet. In his case, the contradictory qualities resulted from a fit of madness in his youth when he was disappointed in love. His condition, awkward in the extreme though it was, was considered the epitome of human achievement, and he had many pervasive powers—such as being able to walk on water, breathe underwater, and communicate with the fish and birds.

The hilarious escapades of clever fools are a source of amusement in the popular lore and sometimes in the literary traditions of many countries. Most notable are **Till Eulenspiegel** in the Netherlands, who with inane antics outwits highly accomplished social figures; and the Mulla **Nasreddin** in the Middle East, whose foolish behavior has the hidden purpose of exposing the emptiness of many social mores. *See also* Clergy; Disability; Jest and Joke.

Further Readings: Dowman, Keith. *The Divine Madman*. London: Rider, 1980; Feuerstein, Georg. *Holy Madness*. New York: Penguin Books, 1992. 3–53; Lane, Edward William *Manners and Customs of the Modern Egyptians*. London: Ward, Lock & Co, 1890. 208–15; Ó hÓgáin, Dáithí. *The Lore of Ireland*. Cork: The Collins Press, 2006. 93–96, 103–04; Thompson, Ewa M. *Understanding Russia: The Holy Fool in Russian Culture*. New York: University Press of America, 1987; Welsford, Enid. *The Fool: His Social and Literary History*. Gloucester: Peter Smith, 1966.

Dáithí Ó hÓgáin

Sindbad

Commonly labeled "the sailor," Sindbad is a merchant who narrates a series of seven fantastic travel adventures. The tales became an integral part of the *Arabian Nights* by way of their inclusion in Antoine **Galland**'s French **translation** *Les mille et une nuits* (*Thousand and One Nights*, 1704–17).

In the **frame narrative**, a poor porter named Sindbad (or, sometimes, Hindbad) in Bagdad in the days of caliph **Harun al-Rashid** rests before the house of a wealthy man. As he overhears the people inside enjoying themselves, he laments the injustice of fate, but is invited to join the party. The merchant Sindbad makes his poor namesake his boon-companion and proceeds to narrate his journeys.

Born as the son of a wealthy merchant, he squandered his inheritance and finally decided to engage in overseas trade. On his journeys, he was shipwrecked several times and mostly ended up on a lonely island or an unknown shore. After variously experiencing hardships and, sometimes, prosperity in far-off lands, he usually regained his belongings and returned home wealthier than ever before.

During the first journey, his company mistakes a resting whale for an island. On his second journey, they find the huge egg of the bird Rokhkh; bound to the bird's claw, Sindbad reaches a valley where the people collect diamonds by employing bloody carcasses. During the third journey, the company is held prisoner by a huge cannibal **ogre** from whose castle they manage to escape only by blinding him with a red-hot spit. On the fourth journey, his comrades are held prisoner by a cannibal tribe who fatten and slaughter them. Later, when his wife dies in a foreign country, he is buried in a cave together with her and survives by killing the partners of other people buried later. His fifth journey brings him to an island on which an old man forces him to be carried around; he escapes by making the old man drunk and killing him. During the sixth journey, he makes his escape from a deserted island by rafting on a subterranean river. On the seventh journey, Sindbad gains riches when an elephant shows him the secret place where elephants go to die and allows him to collect the ivory. In an alternative version, he marries a woman belonging to a tribe of demons and only returns home after an absence of twenty-seven years.

Tales similar to those of Sindbad are already known from an ancient Egyptian papyrus (c. 2000–1800 BCE). Their present version, compiled between the tenth and the thirteenth centuries, draws from various works of Arabic geographical literature and has its closest parallel in the collection of sailors' yarns compiled by the Persian captain Borzorg ibn Shahriyar in the tenth century. Some of the fantastic **motif**s have been known since Greek antiquity, such as the whale mistaken for an island, the blinding of the cannibal ogre (compare the adventure of Ulysses and Polyphemus), and the fattening of Sindbad's companions (compare the adventure of Ulysses and Circe).

Sindbad's tales mirror the spirit of a prospering class of merchants. While they demonstrate an uncompromising ethic of success, the protagonist's unscrupulous behavior is to some extent balanced by his social responsibility. In modern European cultures, Sindbad's name has become the quintessential expression of foreign travel. *See also* Arabian Nights Films; Film and Video.

Further Readings: Marzolph, Ulrich, and Richard van Leeuwen, eds. *The Arabian Nights Encyclopedia.* Volume 1. Denver: ABC-CLIO, 2004. 383–89; Molan, Peter D. "Sindbad the Sailor: A Commentary on the Ethics of Violence." *Journal of the American Oriental Society* 98 (1978): 237–47.

Ulrich Marzolph

Singer, Isaac Bashevis (1904–1991)

Isaac Bashevis Singer was a Nobel Prize-winning (1978) Polish-born writer of Yiddish in America who wrote about the folktales as well as the small town life of his childhood. Born near Warsaw, the son of a Hasidic rabbi, Singer originally studied at a rabbinical seminary. His first writing was published in 1935, the year he followed his older brother Israel Joshua Singer, also a notable writer, to America. From the United States, he explored the world of religion, superstition, and the intrusion of the modern world, originally publishing most of his work in the Yiddish-language newspaper *The Forward* (published since 1897 in New York City). His works, including novels, collections of short stories, and memoirs, have been criticized for their openness about the motivation of lust, foolishness, and human weakness in the small towns of his homeland. He first came to the attention of the English-reading public with the publication of Saul Bellow's translation of his story "Gimpel, the Fool" in *Partisan Review* in 1953.

Although he readily dealt with adult themes, he produced almost as many books for children as for adults, including *Zlateh the Goat and Other Stories* (1966, illustrated by Maurice **Sendak**, a Newberry Honor Book), *Stories for Children* (1984), *Alone in the Wild Forest* (1971, illustrated by Margot Zemach), and *The Fools of Chelm and Their History* (1973, illustrated by Uri Shulevitz). Populated by angels and demons, **peasant**s and merchants, sinners and the devout, his stories use folktale narrative to evoke a lost world.

Further Readings: Denman, Hugh, ed. *Isaac Bashevis Singer: His Work and His World*. Leiden: Brill, 2002; Noiville, Florence. *Isaac B. Singer: A Life*. Translated by Catherine Temerson. New York: Farrar, Straus & Giroux, 2006.

George Bodmer

Sisters

The female siblings in a **family**, sisters are important figures in folktales and fairy tales. They may help or hinder their siblings, while their virtues or vices are often propel the narrative. Their **birth** order and role in the family (as stepsisters, half-sisters, or biological sisters) highlight both conflict and unity within the family unit. Sisters' interactions—reflecting both functional and dysfunctional family relations—often throw into stark relief struggles for succession, inheritance, and status. Of interest is what sister tales say about **women**'s roles in the patriarchy, about female interactions, and how editorial practices impact the socialization of girls through folktales and fairy tales.

Tales often have constellations of three sisters in opposition to one another, signaled by stark contrasts between them, such as beautiful/ugly, kind/unkind, youngest/oldest, self-effacing/vain, and industrious/lazy. Other stories highlight the different treatment of biological children and stepchildren, where stepmothers advantage their own children and neglect or mistreat their stepdaughters as in ATU 431, The House in the Forest, or ATU 511, One-Eye, Two-Eyes, Three-Eyes.

Tales with preadolescent girls typically amplify the rewards and punishments for female virtue and vice in an all-female world. One typical tale type represented internationally in this category is ATU 480, **The Kind and the Unkind Girls**. There the browbeaten (step)-sister enters an underground realm and endures trials to test her readiness for "female" duties—**food** production (symbolically in the form of apple tree needing harvesting and bread needing baking) and animal husbandry (a cow needing milking). After uncomplainingly serving an otherworldly spirit, keeping house, and performing difficult tasks, she returns to the upper world and is richly rewarded for her service. When her sister follows in her footsteps, hoping to reap the same rewards, her waywardness and bad behavior are punished in equal measure. The tale foregrounds the nurturing, self-sacrificing domesticity of the worthy (step)daughter against the selfishness and slothfulness of the unworthy biological daughter.

In the case of adolescent or nubile girls, the stark contrasts between them signal their marriageability. These sisters are in competition for a mate, as in ATU 510A, **Cinderella**, or are simply jealous of their sister's good fortune, as in ATU 432, The Prince as Bird, wherein the envious sisters contrive to drive away their youngest sister's lover. Animal bridegroom stories, such as ATU 425C, **Beauty and the Beast**, and ATU 441, Hans My Hedgehog, find the youngest sister rewarded for her kindness to a suitor previously rejected by her sisters: her charity eventually leads to her disenchanting the beast into a fabulous mate.

As adults, envious sisters may try to foil their sister's happiness. Jealousy rules these tales because of one sister's good fortune, mate, or virtue. In ATU 707, The Three Golden Children, for example, the sisters boast about their ability to produce marvelous children. When the youngest sister becomes the **queen** and bears three such children, the jealous sisters steal the heirs and replace them with **changeling** animals and otherwise plot to ruin her standing with her husband by accusing their sister of **cannibalism** or sorcery.

Sometimes sisters redress injustices done to other family members—male or female. A good example is ATU 311, Rescue by the Sister. In this tale type, two sisters fall under the power of a demonic suitor, are killed when they open a **forbidden room**, and later are resuscitated by their youngest sister, who tricks the demon. In her inimitable goodness, a kind sister may refuse to punish her siblings, even when they have mistreated or betrayed her. She often shares with them her newfound wealth and good fortune and even finds them suitable spouses.

Interactions between sisters and **brothers** are quite different than with those between sisters. When interacting with brothers, sisters often must play heroic parts or engage in numerous adventures together, as in ATU 327A, **Hansel and Gretel**, where it is the resourceful sister who vanquishes the **witch** and saves her brother. In ATU 450, Little Brother and Little Sister, the hapless brother endangers them by transgressing a prohibition, is consequently turned into an animal, and must be saved through his sister's cleverness. Another is the sister's quest to save or rescue her brothers, as in ATU 451, The Maiden Who Seeks Her Brothers; after they are turned into animals by a parent's hasty wish, the sister searches for them. When she finds them, she establishes an orderly household, tends and sews for them, and then ultimately disenchants them through long suffering and extended periods of silence, which she bears ungrudgingly—even when standing on the pyre.

Affection between a sister and her brother may take a positive or negative turn. In some tales, such as ATU 403, The Black and the White Bride, the brother may serve as a matchmaker between his sister and a majestic spouse. In other tales, such as ATU 313E, The Sister's Flight, a sister may become the object of the brother's incestuous desire. Although sisters restore the family unit in most tales, some stories focus on the sister's duplicity and her attempts to kill her brother or harm her family. In ATU 315, The Faithless Sister, a very common tale internationally, the brother and sister flee some peril together. After she takes a demon lover (typically a robber, **dragon**, or **wolf**), she tries to rid herself of her brother. In this same cycle, ATU 315A, The Cannibal Sister, the voracious sister devours her family, their livestock, and their entire village before the dogs of her one surviving brother devour her.

The editorial stance of authors and illustrators affects the representation of sisters in print sources. Many scholars have suggested that **collectors** and **editors** revised their stories to socialize to girls into obedient, subservient, dutiful wives and sisters; others have studied how the **illustration**s of women in nineteenth-century collections grew increasingly negative. Collections edited by women often present a different vision of sister and sibling interactions. *See also* Incest; Punishment and Reward.

Further Readings: Cullen, Bonnie. "For Whom the Shoe Fits: *Cinderella* in the Hands of Victorian Illustrators and Writers." *Lion and the Unicorn* 27.1 (2003): 57–82; El-Shamy, Hasan. "Siblings in *Alf laylah wa-layla.*" *Marvels & Tales* 18 (2004): 170–86; Ragan, Kathleen, ed. *Fearless Girls, Wise Women, and Beloved Sisters: Heroines in Folktales from Around the World.* New York: Norton, 1998.

Shawn C. Jarvis

Slavic Tales

The Slavic peoples of eastern and southeastern Europe are subdivided according to geographical and linguistic criteria into three groups: the Eastern, Western, and Southern Slavs; their settlement areas correspond to narrative regions. Slavic folktales in general tally with common European narratives. They differ in the popularity of particular **tale type**s and figures, in their localizations, adaptations to the environment in which they are told, as well as in style and language. An important fact with regard to the manifold functions of **folklore** is that in modern times, only Russia and Poland (until 1795) had been sovereign states. The establishment or reestablishment of Slavic national states took place in the nineteenth, twentieth, and twenty-first centuries, most being successor states of the Ottoman and the Habsburg empires, and, from 1990 on, of the Soviet Union and Yugoslavia.

Interest in folklore developed at the end of the eighteenth century, first with regard to songs. In this, Johann Gottfried Herder with his special esteem for Slavic people, whom he understood to be one entity, was highly influential. Folklore—considered as a national heritage—played an important part during the so-called rebirth of Slavic people, in the process of constructing national identities and establishing modern written languages, activities that were closely linked to the Romantic movement. Systematic **collecting** and **editing** of folktales started in about the mid-nineteenth century and continued well into the twentieth century. In 1865, the Czech archivist, writer, and folklorist Karel Jaromír Erben, who sympathized with the ideas of Illyrism and Panslavism, published a representative anthology of Slavic folktales in the original languages. In the second half of the twentieth century, folklore contests and festivals were organized, partly in cooperation with academic folklorists. Nowadays, fairy tales are scarcely alive in their original functions in adult **storytelling** communities. They have become almost exclusively part of **children's literature** and remain alive as book tales in the form they were given by classical collectors and editors more than 100 years ago, but also in literary versions. Orally, they live on in popularized forms created for radio and stage recitations and in screen **adaptation**s for **film** and **television**.

Eastern Slavs

Ukrainian and Belarusian narrative traditions and research about them have been marked by political history. After the decline of the Kievan Rus (thirteenth century) the main parts of the Ukrainian and Belarusian speaking territories were affiliated with the Lithuanian and the Polish states, and with the Russian Empire since the seventeenth century, whereas Ukrainian Eastern Galicia and Bukovina belonged to the Austrian Empire. Ukraine and

Belarus are intermediate zones. Their eastern parts had links to Russian folklore, the western to Polish or Slovakian traditions. The majority of Eastern Slavs are traditionally Orthodox Christians. Canonical religious writings and apocrypha came from the Byzantines and also secular literature like the Alexander Romance. Around 1600, part of the Ukrainian Orthodox Church united with the Catholic Church, introducing western European **exempla** collections. Polemics against this union by Orthodox authors were interwoven with **legend**s about miraculous **punishment**s of the followers of Rome and desecrators of Orthodox churches or icons. From the sixteenth century until the beginning of the twentieth century, heroic **epic** poetry (*dumy*) recited to instrumental accompaniment was a significant genre of Ukrainian folklore. The repertoire of the wandering professional minstrels included reports about military exploits of the Cossacks against Turks and Poles. Later, historical, religious, sociocritical, and humorous songs were performed by blind minstrels. Since the seventeenth and eighteenth centuries, poor students from seminaries or unemployed graduate cantors, making a living as traveling semiprofessional singers and storytellers, popularized anecdotes about students and **clergy**, some of which were anticlerical. In Belarus, blind hurdy-gurdy beggars narrated **religious tale**s. Presumably, fairy tales were commonly known since it was the custom to show gratitude for hospitality by telling tales, a practice that is also confirmed within the fairy tales themselves.

Beginning in the 1840s, the first to show interest in Ukrainian folktales were the Ukrainian writer Taras H. Shevchenko and his friend, the Russian painter Lev Zhemchuzhnikov, who collected Ukrainian folktales (1856/57). Among the most important collectors in Central Ukraine were Ivan Ya. Rudchenko (1869/70), Pavlo P. Chubyns'ky (1878), the writer Borys D. Hrinchenko (1895/97), and Volodymyr Lesevych (1904), who confined his collection to the repertoire of one single teller. The most important collections from Western Ukraine are those of Osyp Rozdol's'ky (1895–1900, annotated by the writer Ivan Ya. Franko), Volodymyr O. Shukhevych (1908), and especially Volodymyr M. Hnatyuk (1897/ 98/1915). Newly collected materials have been published by Petro V. Lintur (1959–68) from Carpathian Ukraine, by Mykhailo Hyryak from Ukrainians in Eastern Slovakia (1965–78), and by Oleksandra Yu. Britsna and Inna Golovakha (2004), whose collections are limited to legends. The best-known author using Ukrainian folktales is Nikolai Gogol, who came from the Ukrainian landed gentry. His short story *Vy* (*The Vij*, 1835), for example, is a literary version of the tale type known as The Princess in the Coffin (ATU 307).

Polish scholars and authors, among them Adam Mickiewicz, were the first to kindle interest in Belarusian folklore. Antoni Józef Gliński's intensively redacted collection *Bajarz polski* (*The Polish Tale Teller*, 1853; translated as *Polish Fairy Tales*, 1920) is a case in point. Considered a typical Polish collection, it in fact contains adaptations from classical works of Russian authors such as Aleksandr **Pushkin** as well as Belarusian materials. Important collectors of Belarusian tales are Pavel V. Shein (1893), Evdokim R. Romanov (1887, 1891, 1901), Michał Federowski (1897–1903), and Alyaksandr Serzhputouski (1911, 1926).

In the Eastern Slavic catalogue of tale types by Barag et al. (known in abbreviated form as SUS), we find the following distribution of genres in individual national repertoires: a high frequency of **animal tale**s is especially characteristic of the Ukrainian repertoire, containing 336 tale types as compared to 119 in the Russian and 87 in the Belarusian repertoire. The Ukrainian material presents a slightly higher number of ordinary tales: 225 types of magic or **wonder tale**s (Russian, 225; Belarusian, 199), 132 types of **religious tale**s (Russian, 106; Belarusian, 118), 143 types of realistic tales, or **novella**s (Russian, 137;

Belarusian, 69), and 78 types concerning tales of the stupid **ogre** (Russian, 84; Belarusian, 60). As far as **anecdote**s and **joke**s are concerned, however, the Russian material exhibits more variety: 562 Russian types as compared to 425 Ukrainian and 357 Belarusian types. Tale types widespread among one of the three East Slavic people are as a rule also popular among the two others. This is true, for example, of the story of the three **brothers** conceived by magic, in which the animal son fights multiheaded **dragon**s on a bridge three times (ATU 300A, The Fight on the Bridge). A striking exception is the fairy tale The Three Oranges (ATU 408), which is known in Ukrainian variants but seems to not to exist in the Russian and Belarusian traditions.

Belarusian and Ukrainian fairy tales, told in colloquial language, contain a number of formalized expressions that are often rhymed. Introductory formulas serve to transport the audience into the fictional time and world of fairy tales. Besides the familiar, international opening "Once upon a time," a frequent formula goes: "In a certain kingdom, in a certain land there lived … "—sometimes followed in Belarusian fairy tales by the words "long, long ago, when we did not yet exist" or "when perhaps our great-grandparents were not in the world." Some Belarusian tales start with a prelude that is not connected to the tale's plot—for example, "This isn't the tale but an opening. The tale comes tomorrow after the meal, when we are filled with soft bread. And now we start our tale. In a certain kingdom …, just where we live, on the earth in front of the sky, on a plain place like on a wether, seven versts aside, once upon a time.…" The teller may introduce episodes by saying, "Speedily a tale is told, but with less speed a deed is done." Closing formulas, functioning as a transition between the fictitious and the real world, are widespread. A standard conclusion of fairy tales ending with a **marriage** goes: "I was there and drank mead and wine. It ran down my mustache but did not go into my mouth." Other typical formulas and idioms concern action, situations, and facts. For example, to express beauty, it is said: "The girls are so beautiful as no tale can tell nor pen describe." Typical of the Eastern Slavic heroic tale is a standard episode demonstrating the strength of the hero by describing how he acquires his weapon and horse. The hero throws his iron mace up into the air, and because it gets bent falling down on his knee, the hero needs a new one forged. Looking for a good horse, the hero lays his hand on a mare. If it falls to its knees, it is too weak; the right one takes his hand without moving. Here and in other cases we see parallels to Russian and Ukrainian epic poetry. A number of formulas and sometimes even entire plots are taken over by the fairy tale and adapted to a rural background—for example, in connection with Il'ya Muromets (see SUS 650C*). Standard expressions also are related to the supernatural being **Baba Yaga**: She lives "in a little house turning on chicken legs." The hero or heroine manages to enter the hut by saying, "Little hut, little hut, stand with your back to the woods, and your front to me!" The Baba Yaga moves "in a mortar, goading it on with her pestle and sweeping away her tracks with the broom."

Quite often the hero's name in East Slavic fairy tales is Ivan or derivatives like Ivanko, Ivaško, Janko, and so on. He is characterized by various epithets: Ivan the Bitch's son and Ivan the Mare's son have been supernaturally conceived; Ivan the **Bear's son** has a bear as **father**; Ivan the Fool or Ivan the **Simpleton** is apparently foolish or stupid. Names such as **Prince** Ivan, Ivan the **Peasant**'s son, Ivan the Soldier's son, or Ivan the Merchant's son indicate their social backgrounds. As in the international fairy-tale tradition, we find two groups of heroes, often the youngest of three brothers. On the one hand, there are unpromising heroes like Ivan the Fool, who become strong and handsome in the course of the story.

On the other hand, there are valiant knights (*geroi-bogatyri*) like Ivan the Bitch's son, who are predominantly dragon slayers. The hero's helpers are often females, his wife or fiancée, sometimes endowed with supernatural capacities, and Baba Yaga, who may also help the heroine. Human adversaries are the **king** or the king's sons-in-law, the hero's uncle, and—especially in Ukrainian and Belarusian tales—the *pan*, the Polish landlord. The most frequent supernatural enemy is the dragon with seven, nine, or twelve heads, to whom the king's daughter is about to be sacrificed. Another supernatural antagonist is Kashchei the Deathless (the Immortal), who usually kidnaps the hero's wife and whose life is located outside of his body (for example, it is hidden in an egg, the egg in a hare, and the hare in a box). Unlike Kashschei, Baba Yaga is an ambivalent figure: she may help the hero or try to damage him. Neither she nor Kashschei the Deathless have direct parallels in East Slavic folk beliefs. In contrast, the Rusalka, a female demonic figure, especially in Belarusian and Ukrainian legends, is connected with folk beliefs about "impure" dead persons. **Women** who died by drowning, girls who died before getting married, or children who died unbaptized were said to become a Rusalka. The Rusalka is described as a beautiful young girl in a wedding dress or as an ugly old woman, appearing like a water, forest, or field spirit, and clearly distinct from the romantic literary figure of the Rusalka, who is a water nymph, a beautiful girl with a fish tail in love with a human youth. She became popular due to works by Russian, Ukrainian, and Polish poets such as Pushkin, Vasily A. Zhukovsky, Gogol, Shevchenko, Mickiewicz, and Juliusz Słowacki. Outlaw folklore plays an important part in the narrative traditions of the Ukrainian Carpathians—for example, in tales about the bandits Oleksa Dovbush or Nikolai Shuhai, who became popular heroes (see **Thief, Thieves**).

Western Slavs

The folk traditions of the Western Slavs belong to the Central and Western European narrative area and share a common store of plots and **motifs**. The stock of motifs gleaned in the nineteenth century, when folktale collecting from **oral tradition** first started, fits well into the overall pattern of European narrative culture. The most ancient sources of fairy-tale and **fable** motifs among the Western Slavs are found in old Czech literature—for instance, in the *Chronica Bohemorum* by Cosmas of Prague (early twelfth century), some of them connected with the famous legend of Libuše, the mythical female ancestor of Přemyslid dynasty. Her story inspired German and Czech artists from Hans Sachs, Herder, and the Romantics up to Bedřich Smetana (in the **opera** *Libuše*, 1881). Regional modifications of Latin exempla collections have been known since the thirteenth and fourteenth centuries and their vernacular translations since the fifteenth century, including the ***Gesta Romanorum*** (Czech, mid-fifteenth century; Polish, 1540). Inserted into sermons, these stories conveyed narrative motifs and tale types to a broader public, including the illiterate. From the sixteenth century on, facetiae and anecdotal tales in the tradition of Giovanni Francesco Poggio, Heinrich Bebel, and Johannes Pauli became popular, as did the **chapbook**s *Griselda*, *The Seven Sages*, *Salomon and Markolf*, ***Till Eulenspiegel***, *Melusine*, and *Genovefa*. In the eighteenth century, the French ***contes de fées*** and tales from the ***Arabian Nights*** were popularized.

The most famous and influential collections of Czech folktales were published by the authors Božena Němcová (1845–47) and Karel Jaromír Erben (1865). Whereas Erben tried to create an ideal **variant**, representative of Czech national oral tradition, Němcová cultivated a more subjective novella style and considered folktales part of written national literature. Other important collections are those by Beneš M. Kulda from Moravia (1854, 1872) and Anna Popelková from Eastern Bohemia (1897), followed above all by collections by the folklorist Václav Tille (1902) and Josef Št. Kubín (1908, 1910). After 1945, new material was collected by the folklorists Jaromír Jech (1959), Oldřich Sirovátka (1959), and Antonín Satke (1958). It is an interesting phenomenon that Tille (using the pseudonym Vaclav Rihas), Kubín (in his later years), Sirovátka, and Jech not only published scholarly tale editions but also adapted tales for popular editions and/or created poetic texts based on folklore.

Czech narrative tradition is distinguished more by humor than by mythical or heroic feature. It prefers novelistic and anecdotal subjects to fantasy. In fairy tales, action alternates with descriptions of realistic details, and formulas are less frequent than in East Slavic tradition, except in fairy tales from Moravia, which are close to the Slovakian tales. The standard introductory formula goes, "Once upon a time there was a ..." or, more briefly, "There was a ...." Closing formulas, often in rhymed form, show a greater variety. One typical closing states: "And the ground was made of paper, and I fell through it up to here." Among fairy tales, The Three Stolen Princesses (ATU 301), All Stick Together (ATU 571), and The Youth Who Wanted to Learn What Fear Is (ATU 326) are very common. Typical Czech manifestations of folktale characters with a wide international distribution include that band of companions with extraordinary abilities (ATU 513A, Six Go through the Whole World): the tall one, who is able to extend himself to any length; the fat one, who can blow up his stomach to any volume; and the sharp-sighted one, whose glance can destroy things by igniting them or by making them explode. The hero or heroine's antagonist is sometimes a water spirit, usually an evil character who pulls human beings, especially girls, into the water. Sometimes, however, he serves as a helpful figure and sometimes as a stupid ogre. In Czech legends, novellas, and anecdotes, the Austrian emperor Joseph II appears in the role of the just ruler who, in disguise, mingles unrecognized with the simple people—a testimony to the long-lasting Czech affiliation with Habsburg Austria, which lasted until 1918.

The main initiators of collecting Slovak folktales were Samuel Reuss and his sons, L'udovít Štúr, the organizer of the Slovak freedom movement and cofounder of the Slovak written language, and finally the writer Ján Francisci, who published the first Slovakian collection of folktales in 1845 (under the pseudonym Janko Rimavský). Beginning in the 1840s, manuscripts of folktales collected by various persons were copied by hand and compiled as popular light reading. The main genre that emerges from nearly 10,000 preserved manuscript pages, published by Jiří **Polívka** (1923–31), is the **fairy tale**. The classical Slovak folktale collections, which are reprinted up to the present day, are those edited by Pavol Dobšinský and August Horislav Škultéty in 1858–61 and by Dobšinský alone in 1880–83. Systematic fieldwork was carried out beginning in 1925 by the Slavicist Frank Wollman and his students. Materials collected since the 1950s have been published in popular editions by Gašparíková (1981, 1984/85), Konštantín Palkovič (1988), and others.

In general, Slovak fairy tales, which are related to Ukrainian and Hungarian traditions, are more archaic and vital than those of neighboring Poland and the Czech Republic. According to recent research, the form and the canon of Slovak fairy tales are greatly influenced by the editions of Dobšinský, who had endowed the tales with a decorative style by intensifying the use of elements like threefold repetition or formulas. In contrast to the other West Slavic fairy tales, Slovak tales sometimes have longer introductory formulas. A frequently used introduction begins, "In the seventy-seventh country beyond the Red Sea" and continues in different ways—for instance, with Cockaigne motifs such as "and beyond the glass mountain, where the water ran and the sands poured, where the roofs were covered with sides of bacon and the fences interweaved with sausages." Among the most frequent Slovak fairy tales are The Three Stolen Princesses (ATU 301) with the demonic figure of Loktibrada (a man with a long beard who lives in the underworld) as the hero's antagonist; The Dead Bridegroom Carries off His Bride (ATU 365); and The Maiden Who Seeks Her Brothers (ATU 451). International tale types show variations. For example, in Slovak variants of Three Hairs from the Devil's Beard (ATU 461), the hero does not travel to the **devil** but to the sun or to a dragon; and in most Slovak variants of The Juniper Tree (ATU 720), the slaughtered boy is not resuscitated but remains a bird. Other than in Czech tradition, the ideal ruler is not Joseph II in legends and anecdotes, but the Hungarian King Matthias Corvinus (Slovak territories were under the rule of Hungary or Austria-Hungary from the eleventh century until 1918).

Outlaw folklore is widespread in the entire Carpathian region. Stories about the national hero Jánošík, a historical Slovak bandit (1688–1713), are especially important in Slovak narrative tradition. Jánošík became the incarnation of a noble bandit, like Robin Hood, who robbed the rich and gave to the poor. He has been idealized since the time of the Romantic movement. In socialist times he was viewed as a fighter against feudalism, and nowadays he is exploited commercially in **tourism**. Stories about him have a legendary character combined with elements of the fairy tale: He was nursed for seven years and received marvelous objects—a magic axe, belt, and shirt—from **witch**es or a magician as a reward for his service. The objects make him invisible and invincible; and sometimes he also has companions with marvelous strength.

The Sorbs, the least-populous people among the Western Slavs, have lived under German rule for centuries. As a rural population, the towns in their settlement areas were dominated by German culture. Sorbian folktales were first recorded by Jan A. Smoler (Johann E. Schmaler) and published as an appendix to the famous collection of Sorbian songs (1843) by Smoler and Leopold Haupt. Beginning in the 1860s, students and clergymen collected tales and printed some of them in periodicals. The majority of the collected materials are legends, as are those of German collectors such as Wilibald von Schulenburg (1880, 1882). In 1956, the folklorist Pawoł (Paul) Nedo compiled the scattered Sorbian folktale material and published it in a bilingual Sorbian and German edition.

According to Nedo, animal tales have a prominent place in Sorbian narrative tradition, especially stories about the fox and the **wolf**. Twenty-five tale types are animal tales, forty-nine fairy tales, five religious tales, six novellas, and seven types are about the stupid ogre. Sorbian tale tradition often parallels German and Czech traditions. In fairy tales, the heroes and heroines or their parents are mostly farmhands, servants, **soldier**s, herdsmen, and journeymen, but seldom kings and **princess**es—doubtlessly a reflection of the social situation of the rural Sorbian population. The style of Sorbian fairy tale is extraordinarily terse and concise and is often characterized by repetition of formulations. A further stylistic device is a predilection for diminutives, which, however, are not characteristics of children's language but serve to emphasize characters and things positively. There is a tendency to spin out legends, in particular the popular water spirit legends, so that they become fairy tales. The legendary figure of the wizard Krabat is combined with the story about the apprentice who outdoes his diabolical master (ATU 325, The Magician and His Pupil). This and other stories about Krabat were made popular by the authors Otfried Preußler (1971) and Jurij Brězan (1968, 1976, 1994, 1995).

An interest in Polish folklore was awakened by the European Romantic movement, the Polish poets Mickiewicz, Słowacki and others, but in particular by the loss of national sovereignty in 1795. Collecting folktales became an important patriotic duty. The first collectors, Kazimierz W. Wójcicki (1837), Roman Zmorski (1852), Karól Baliński (1842), and above all Gliński (1853), made folktales popular through their literary adaptations. Intensive collecting in all Polish regions started with Oskar Kolberg (published 1857–90), who had many regional followers. The first linguistic recordings in dialect were made by Lucjan Malinowski (1869), followed later by Friedrich Lorentz from the Kashubian-speaking area (1913/24) and Kazimierz Nitsch (1929). Many collections from the 1960s until the 1980s were compiled by Dorota Simonides.

According to the catalogue of Polish tale types by Julian Krzyżanowski, anecdotes and humorous tales are the most frequent genres in the Polish narrative tradition (564 types, including the tales of the stupid ogre), followed by fairy tales (296), religious tales (94), animal tales (94), and novellas (88). Among the most frequent fairy-tale types are "The Youth Who Wanted to Learn What Fear Is" (ATU 326), The Smith and the Devil (ATU 330), and The Princess on the Glass Mountain (ATU 530). Among religious tales, Robber Madej (ATU 756B) is widespread. Polish fairy tales are characterized by a certain rationalism, while the wonderful and marvelous elements remain in the background. The style is quite laconic and succinct. As in Czech folktales, Polish fairy tales may start with the formula "Once upon a time . . .", while closing formulas vary from short nonsense verses (for example, "The nose has two little holes, and the story has an end") to longer ones (such as, the storyteller pretends that he himself had attended the wedding, but when they fired a salute, they put him by mistake into the gun barrel and shot, which is how he arrived among the audience). Legends often contain fairy-tale elements, for example, the popular stories about the sleeping knights (Krzyżanowski no. 8256); about the great magician Twardowski, who, like Dr. Faust, made a pact with the devil (no. 8251); and about the bandit Janosik, the hero of Slovakian origin, in stories from the Tatra (no. 8252).

Southern Slavs

Southeast Europe, especially the Balkans, is a particularly complex area when it comes to distinguishing the specific ethnic or national features of its folktales. Forming a bridge between Europe and Asia, where the spheres of influence have been changing for centuries between the Ottoman and the Habsburg empires, causing permanent migrations of people, this was a relatively limited area where various ethnic and cultural groups were living together. Beyond the bipolar division between the Latin (Catholic) and the Byzantine (Orthodox) cultural spheres, there are additional cultural zones: an Eastern Alpine region with a Central European character, an Adriatic coastal region with a Roman-Slavic cultural symbiosis, and an Eastern Orthodox region under more intense Turkish-Ottoman and Islamic influence. In the nineteenth century, when folktale collecting started, various minorities were living among the Southern Slavs—for example, Greeks, Turks, Albanians, Pomaks, Vlachs, Roma, and others in Macedonia and Bulgaria. Until the disintegration of Yugoslavia in the 1990s, Serbo-Croatian was the common written language of Croatians, Bosniaks, Serbs, and Montenegrins, which led to a certain intertwining of traditions. Slovenes, Macedonians, and Bulgarians speak different Slavic languages.

Narratives of the traditionally Catholic Slovenes, who in their main areas lived under the rule of the Habsburg dynasty from the fourteenth century until 1918, belong largely to those of Central Europe. Evidence for folktales exists from the sixteenth century onward. Since the late 1840s, folktales have been collected and printed mostly in periodicals. In 1886, a selection was edited by Bogomil Krek, and several regional collections followed. In the second half of the twentieth century, modern scholarly collections from Slovenians in Italy and Hungary were published by Milko **Matičetov** (1973) and others. The most popular edition of Slovenian folktales is the one originally published in 1952 (with many later editions) by Alojzij Bolhar.

The traditions of the Catholic Croatians from northwestern Croatia share common features with the Slovenian and generally the Central European traditions, while those from Dalmatia are part of the Mediterranean culture and those from Bosnia and Herzegovina have Oriental elements. International narrative plots are documented in Croatian religious and secular literature since the fourteenth and the fifteenth centuries. Dalmatia and especially Dubrovnik (Ragusa), with its close contacts to Venice, were important centers of cultural exchange. The tragic love story of Hero and Leander (ATU 666*), for example, localized in Dubrovnik in Giovan Francesco **Straparola**'s version, is already attested in the fifteenth century as a local legend of Dubrovnik. The first collection of Croatian folktales was published by the Slovenian Matija (Kračmanov) Valjavec in 1858, followed by editions of Rikardo F. Plohl Herdvigov (1868), Rudolf Strohal (1886/1901/04), and others. More recent collections are due above all to Maja **Bošković-Stulli** (for example, 1959, 1963).

Serbia, which became part of the Ottoman Imperium in the fifteenth century, and the principality of Montenegro, which was tributary to the Ottoman Empire, both belong to the Eastern Orthodox area. International narrative motifs are documented since the fourteenth century in manuscripts of Serbian and Montenegrin monasteries as well as in translated works of Eastern and Western provenience (for example, *Barlaam and Josaphat* or *Tristan and Isolde*). In 1821, Vuk **Karadžić**, the creator of the modern Serbian written language, published the first Serbian collection of folktales. His enlarged main edition of 1853, nearly 40 percent of which has been collected in Montenegro, became the classical collection. The second most important folktale edition was the work of Veselin Čajkanović (1927). Luka Grđić-Bjelokosić (1902) und Novica Saulić (1921/25/31) also collected in Montenegro. Since 1945, there have been regional collections, for example by Dragutin M. Đordjević from Eastern Serbia.

Before the conquest of Bosnia by the Ottomans (1463) and the conversion of its Slavic inhabitants to Islam, the socioreligious movement of Bogomilism, first arising in Bulgaria, played an important part in Bosnian cultural life. Attestations of this movement, considered as heretical, are found in apocrypha and cosmological legends with dualistic tendencies. In many cases, it is hard to say if folktales collected in Bosnia and Herzegovina are Croatian, Serbian, or Bosniak tales, for the tellers are often unknown and there was an interethnic exchange of repertoires. Many of them were probably told by Muslims or had been influenced by them. Collections include *Bosanske narodne pripovjedke* (*Bosnian Folktales*, 1870), compiled by students of the Catholic seminary in Đakovo, as well as those of Nikola Tordinac (1883) and Kamilo Blagajić (1886). Alija Nametak's edition (1944, 1975) contains exclusively folktales of Bosniaks from Bosnia and Herzegovina.

The interest in the narrative traditions of the Orthodox Slavic Macedonians—belonging in the **Middle Ages** alternately to the Byzantine Empire, to Bulgarian and Serbian states, and from 1371 until 1912 to the Ottoman Empire—first arose during the fight against the dominant Greek influence in church and educational institutions. Some Macedonians considered themselves Bulgarians, as did Kuzman (A. P.) Šapkarev, who published the first folktale collection from Macedonia under the title *Bălgarski narodni prikazki i verovanija* (*Bulgarian Folktales and Beliefs*, 1885). Stefan Verković had already collected folklore materials in the 1850s, and some years later, Marko K. Cepenkov started collecting, publishing most of his important collections in a Bulgarian scholarly periodical (reprinted after 1945 in Macedonian and Bulgarian editions). Tanas Vražinovski collected folktales after 1945 (1977, 1986), including folktales from Macedonian immigrants in Canada (1990).

The rich written narrative traditions of the Bulgarians, having lived in close relationship to the Byzantine culture—the Alexander Romance, for instance, had been translated from Greek sources in the tenth or eleventh century—had been broken up in the late fourteenth century through the Ottoman occupation, which lasted until 1878. Deprived of cultural centers and dominated by Greek clergymen in the higher strata of the Orthodox Church, cultural life in Bulgaria was largely characterized by oral traditions. The first folktales in printed collections were published by G. Ch. N. Lačoglu and Nikola M. Astardžiev (1870), Vasil D. Čolakov (1872), and in the enlarged edition by Šapkarev (1892). Since 1889, nearly all collections appeared in the periodical *Sbornik za narodni umotvorenija, nauka i knizhnina* (*Collection of Folk Poetry, Science and Literature*; since 1923, *Sbornik za narodni umotvorenija i narodopis*) or as special volumes of this periodical (for example, folktales of the Sakar Mountain by Evgenija Miceva, published in 2002). Representative editions were published by Angel Karalijčev and Veličko Vălčev (1963), as well as by Ljubomira Parpulova and Doroteja Dobreva (1982). Interest in the narrative traditions of the Islamic Pomaks in Southern Bulgaria arose only recently.

Southern Slavic oral traditions share a number of common features, parts of which are paralleled in the traditions of non-Slavic neighbors such as Greeks, Turks, Albanians, or Romanians. In the cultural tradition of the Southern Slavs, oral epics played a prominent part, handing down themes and ideologies that for centuries had been relevant to the historic and political consciousness of the society, such the popular cycle about Prince Marko and the cycle of Kosovo. The historic model for Prince Marko was an insignificant vassal of an Ottoman sultan in the fourteenth century who had to fight against Christian armies. In South Slavic tradition, however, he became the incarnation of a fighter against the Turkish invaders and a protector of the Christian faith. As recently as the 1960s, 1,600 songs and 400 legends about "Krali Marko" could be recorded in Bulgaria. The cycle of Kosovo describes the decisive battle on the Kosovo Field (1389), where the Christians were defeated by the Islamic Ottomans. These cycles continue to be relevant in literature and political propaganda up to the present day. The epic songs contain fairy-tale motifs and episodes, such as the hero's departure to win a bride, battles against dragons, confrontations with **fairies**, and the return of the hero. Up to the twentieth century, they were performed mostly by illiterate singers and provided the basis of Milman Parry's and Albert Bates Lord's oral-formulaic theory (see **Oral Theory**). Later historical songs are devoted to the fights of the Haiduks and Uskoks against the Turks, figures oscillating between freedom fighters and common robbers. The freedom-fighter tradition was continued in the songs and legends about partisans in World War II.

In general, fairy tales are introduced with the short formula "Once upon a time" or they get directly to the point. Concluding formulas mostly pretend in various manners that the tellers themselves had attended the wedding party at the happy ending of the story. Macedonian and Bulgarian fairy tales often end with a **moral** expressed in a form close to **proverbs**.

The heroes of fairy tales are **prince**s, in Croatian sometimes counts, but above all poor youngsters, often shepherds. Typical of Serbian, Macedonian, and Bulgarian tales is the social institution of chosen brotherhood (*pobratimstvo*). For example, in a Bulgarian fairy tale, the extraordinary companions become the hero's chosen brothers. The hero's enemies are his older brothers, malevolent kings, and various supernatural beings. Most common are dragons, who sometimes are living in a family, like humans. The cannibalistic lamia, a kind of dragon, often with a dog's head, is known in tales from Croatia to Bulgaria. It is related to the classical dogheads (Greek: *kynokephaloi*) that appear in tales from Slovenia and Northern Croatia as anthropomorphous figures with one eye in their foreheads and goat's legs. Versions about the maiden-killer (ATU 311, Rescue by the Sister; see **Bluebeard**), which have a very special form in Southeast Europe, present a large number of potential supernatural enemies. In Macedonian and Bulgarian variants (Daskalova Perkowski et al. no. *311C), for example, the demonic and cannibalistic antagonist is a vampire, a dragon, a devil, an Arapin (black Arab), Arapin Och, Giant Och, or a dog-headed man. *Och* is the name of a giant, devil, or black Arab who appears when a person utters the sound "och," and it is popular throughout the northern Mediterranean area. The black Arab is a relatively frequent negative figure, well known also in South Slavic songs. In some Macedonian and Bulgarian fairy tales, he has an external soul and kidnaps the hero's wife, like Kashchei the Deathless in East Slavic tales.

Besides the dragon, the most popular supernatural being in South Slavic folklore is the *vila* or *samovila*, often acting in groups. The *viles* are beautiful fairies with long loose **hair** who live in the forests and mountains and love music and dance. They are ambivalent figures. In fairy tales, they sometimes play a negative part: they steal the eyes of an old man or keep watch over a spring; or a *samovila* kills the sister of nine brothers, while another turns her husband into stone and a settlement into a lake. However, they also function as **magic helpers** of the hero, giving him flying horses and wonderful arms and reviving him with the water of life. Sometimes they marry young shepherds but leave them when they break a taboo. It is said that the most beautiful women in the world are descendants of a *vila*.

Common to all Southern Slavs are tales where the three Fates appear. When they predestine the fate of a new child, born to a poor **family**, they are overheard by a wealthy stranger. He learns that the newborn girl will become his wife or, if it is a boy, will marry his daughter (ATU 930A, The Predestined Wife; ATU 930, The Prophecy). All of his counterattacks, including murder, fail: the prediction comes true. In other stories, too, the predictions of the Fates (dying by the bite of a snake, drowning in a well at a fixed time, etc.) cannot be changed by those who have heard them (ATU 934, Tales of the Predestined Death; Daskalova Perkowski et al. no. 934A**).

In the Balkan countries under Ottoman rule, the "Orient" was less an exotic topos than it was in western Europe. Rather, it was a reality of life that expressed itself in narratives. Apart from sharing stories with the Turks, narratives of the entire Balkan region contain Turkish elements, especially as far as the lexicon of the tales is concerned, less in the West than in the East, but most prominently in Bosnia and Herzegovina. Numerous Turkish terms from material, intellectual, and religious culture can be found (for example, terms for persons such as *beg, aga, vezir, hadži, derviš, kadi, paša, sultan,* etc.). The man without a beard, a characteristic negative figure in Southeast European and Eastern Mediterranean folktales, is named Čoso or K'ose by virtue of Turkish influence in Croatian, Serbian, Macedonian, and Bulgarian narratives. Humorous tales about **Nasreddin** Hodža, a widespread figure throughout the Ottoman Empire, became extraordinarily popular in the Balkans. Whereas in Serbian anecdotes, the rogue hero Ero outwits Turkish opponents in particular, and in jokes from Bosnia and Herzegovina, Suljo and Mujo (shortened forms of the proper names Suleyman and Mustafa) discuss all kinds of problems, in Macedonia and Bulgaria, Clever Peter is a counterpart of Nasreddin Hodža. Many anecdotes deal with both of them. Sometimes they collaborate to cheat others and tell lies, and sometimes they act as rivals. Mostly, but not always, the winner is Clever Peter, who has been established as a national hero in Macedonia and Bulgaria. *See also* Albanian Tales; Russian Tales; Soviet Fairy-Tale Films.

Further Readings: Adlard, John. *Nine Magic Pea-Hens and Other Serbian Folk Tales Collected by Vuk Karadžić*. Edinburgh: Floris, 1988; Barag, L. G., et al. *Sravnitel'ny ukazatel syuzhetov: Vostochnoslavyanskaya skazka*. Leningrad: Nauka, 1979; Cameron, Hector (pseudonym Hector MacQuarrie). *Little Yellow Shoes, and Other Bosnian Fairy Stories*. London: Angus & Robertson, 1960; Cooper, David L., ed. *Traditional Slovak Folktales Collected by Pavol Dobšinský*. Armonk, NY: M. E. Sharpe, 2001; Ćurčija-Prodanović, Nada. *Yugoslav Folk-Tales*. 1957. London: Oxford University Press, 1966; Cvetanovska, Danica, and Maja Miškovska. *101 Macedonian Folk Tales*. Skopje: Bigoss, 2003; Daskalova Perkowski, Liliana, et al. *Typenverzeichnis der bulgarischen Volksmärchen*. Edited by Klaus Roth. Helsinki: Academia Scientiarum Fennica, 1995; Erben, Karel J., *Panslavonic Folk-Lore in Four Books*. Translated by W. W. Strickland. New York: B. Westermann, 1930; Fillmore, Parker, ed., *Czech, Moravian and Slovak Fairy Tales*. New York: Hippocrene Books, 1998. Reprint of *Czechoslovac Fairy Tales*. 1918; Gašparíková, Viera. *Katalóg slovenskej l'udovej prózy/Catalogue of Slovak Folk Prose*. 2 volumes. Bratislava: Národopisný ústav SAV, 1991–92; Gašparíková, Viera, and B. N. Putilov. *Geroi ili zboinik? Obraz razboinika v fol'klore Karpatskogo regiona /Heroes or Bandits: Outlaw Traditions in the Carpathian Region*. Budapest: European Folklore Institute, 2002; Krzyżanowski, Julian. *Polska bajka ludowa w układzie systematycznym*. 2 volumes. Wrocław: Zakład Naradowy imienia Ossolińskich Wydawnictwo Polskiej Akademii Nauk, 1962–63; Krstić, Branislav. *Indeks motiva narodnih pesama balkanskih Slovena/Motif Index for the Epic Poetry of the Balkan Slavs*. Edited by Ilija Nikolić. Belgrad: Srpska Akademija nauka i umetnosti, 1984; Kunaver, Dušica, *Slovene Folk Tales*. Ljubljana: Dusica Kunaver, 1999; Kuniczak, Wiesław S., *The Glass Mountain: Twenty-Eight Ancient Polish Folktales and Fables*. New York: Hippocrene Books, 1997; Marshall, Bonnie C. *Tales from the Heart of the Balkans*. Edited by Vasa D. Mihailovich. Englewood, CO: Libraries Unlimited, 2001; Nedo, Paul, et al., eds. *Die gläserne Linde: Westslawische Märchen*. Bautzen: Domowina-Verlag, 1972; Nicoloff, Assen. *Bulgarian Folktales*. Cleveland: Nicoloff, 1979; Oparenko, Christina. *Ukrainian Folk-Tales*. Oxford: Oxford University Press, 1996; Pešková, Renata. *Czech Fairy-Tales*. Prague: Vitalis, 2000; Polívka, Jiří, ed. *Súpis slovenských rozprávok*. 5 volumes. Turčiansky sv. Martin: Matica slovenská, 1923–31; Roth, Klaus, and Gabriele Wolf, eds. *South Slavic Folk Culture: A Bibliography of Literature in English, German, and French on Bosnian-Hercegovinian, Bulgarian, Macedonian, Montenegrin and Serbian Folk Culture*. Columbus: Slavica Publishers, 1994; Tille, Václav. *Soupis českých pohádek*. 2 volumes. Praha: Nákladem České Akademie věd a umění, 1929–37.

Ines Köhler-Zülch

Sleeping Beauty

"Sleeping Beauty" is one of the most popular fairy tales in the world. The general outline of the tale is as follows: A royal couple is celebrating the christening of their only child, a girl. The **fairies** who have been invited to the celebration bestow every kind of blessing upon the child, but a fairy whom the parents have neglected to invite suddenly appears on the scene and curses the child, so that a spindle will bring about her **death** during her adolescence. Another fairy who is present manages to alter the curse, so that the child will now merely fall into a deep and long sleep until a charming **prince** awakens her with a kiss and marries her, resulting in their living happily ever after. All of the predictions made by the fairies come true, so that the princess is indeed awakened by a kiss from a prince, who then marries her.

The tale of Sleeping Beauty is classified under and lends its name to the international **tale type** ATU 410. It is not widely spread in **oral tradition** and most variants are essentially derived from written sources. The tale, however, has been the object of considerable literary and scholarly attention. The first traces of the plot in literature appear in two anonymous works of the fourteenth century, the Catalan **novel** *Frayre de Joy et Sor de Plaser* and the episode of Troylus and Zellandine at the conclusion of the third book of the French romance *Perceforest*. In both works, the fundamental elements of the plot appear in their initial form. A young beauty, named Sor de Plaser in the Catalan novel and Zellandine in *Perceforest*, falls into an enchanted sleep and is shut up in an enchanted tower, where she is found by a youth. In these variants, the youth impregnates her and she gives **birth** well before her awakening and subsequent **marriage** to the youth.

In literary versions of the seventeenth century, after the young beauty has been awakened, a female rival appears. In Giambattista **Basile**'s "Sole, Luna e Talia" ("Sun, Moon, and Talia"), on the day the beauty is born, the palace magicians predict that Talia will face great danger from a flax splinter. In spite of the efforts of her father, the **king**, to prevent any contact likely to cause such a disaster, the girl touches the marvelous distaff of an old woman and falls dead. The king then locks her body away in a castle in the country, where she reclines on a velvet throne. Another king, while pursuing his hunting falcon, discovers the girl and, being unable to wake her, lies with her. He returns home and Talia gives birth to two children, Moon and Sun, who remove the fatal splinter by sucking on their **mother**'s finger. The king returns and maintains clandestine contact with Talia, thus provoking the jealously of his **queen**, who thus attempts to harm Talia and her children. The queen, however, is punished and the king marries Talia.

In the version of Charles **Perrault**, a daughter is born to a hitherto childless royal couple; among the guests at the christening feast are several fairies. An aggrieved fairy, who has not been invited to the feast, arrives and utters a curse whereby a spindle will bring about the death of the child. Among the fairies who have been invited to the christening celebration, only one remains who has not yet uttered her blessing, and she is able to lessen the effect of the curse, so that the child will sink into a profound sleep when the time comes. She does so, the whole palace falling into a sleep with her, and 100 years later is awakened by a kiss from a prince. In this version, the role of jealous rival is allotted to the mother of the prince who wakes her and who likewise keeps secret his contact with her and the children born of their union, Jour and Aurore.

Two centuries later, the Brothers **Grimm** published a version entitled "Dornröschen" ("Brier Rose"). The version they took down from their informant and the version they published in the first edition of their fairy-tale collection in 1812 seem to have been indebted to the earlier version by Perrault, but neither included the birth of the children or the episode involving the jealous mother. The first edition of their collection did include a separate tale entitled "Die Schwiegermutter" ("The Mother-in-Law"), which is more than reminiscent of the final section of Perrrault's tale. "The Mother-in-Law," however, was neither appended to the tale of "Brier Rose" nor retained in future editions of the Grimms' work. Instead, Wilhelm Grimm continued to refine the style of "Brier Rose," without adding the jealous **ogress**, and created the version of the tale that has become canonical.

The appearance of these various plots over the course of several centuries suggest the evolution of preexisting mythological themes and **motifs**. The motif of the long magic sleep also appears in the story of the sleeping Brunhilde in the *Volsunga Saga*. Likewise, there is a clear parallel between fate and **spinning** on the one hand and the *moirai* or *parcae* of the Greco-Roman world on the other.

The versions by Perrault and the Brothers Grimm are undoubtedly responsible for the popularity of the tale, even inspiring versions of the story in **opera** and **dance**. One of the most successful adaptations of the tale is Pyotr Il'ich **Tchaikovsky**'s ballet *Sleeping Beauty*, which premiered in St. Petersburg in 1890 with choreography by Marius Petipa. The imagery and music of Walt **Disney**'s animated version of 1959, although it ultimately springs from the main part of Perrault's version, is equally inspired by Tchaikovsky's work and is perhaps the most familiar of modern versions of the tale.

The passivity of Sleeping Beauty, caused by the eternal magic sleep, which leads her to embody perfect femininity in the form of marriage and maternity, has given rise to considerable discussion, together with psychoanalytic and feminist interpretations. Bruno **Bettelheim** approached the tale from a Freudian point of view, arguing that the story symbolizes the passage from **childhood** via puberty to sexual awareness. For many feminist scholars, Sleeping Beauty is the epitome of the passive female awaiting the arrival of Prince Charming. Revisionist versions of the tale often playfully, but completely, subvert the **myth**. Josef Wittmann's poem "Sleeping Beauty" (1979), for example, is told by a male who rejects his role as a prince. Instead, pressed for time in the workaday world, he has no time for dreams himself and urges the sleeping woman to keep on dreaming. *See also* Feminism; Gender; Initiation; Poetry; Sex, Sexuality.

Further Readings: Bettelheim, Bruno. *The Uses of Enchantment: The Meaning and Importance of Fairy Tales*. New York: Knopf, 1976. 225–36; Haase, Donald. "The Sleeping Script: Memory and Forgetting in Grimms' Romantic Fairy Tale (KHM 50)." *Merveilles et contes* 4 (1990): 167–76; Papachristophorou, Marilena. *Sommeils et veilles dans le conte merveilleux grec*. Helsinki: Suomalainen Tiedeakatemia, 2002. 80–97; Vries Jan de. "Dornröschen." *Fabula* 2 (1959): 110–21; Zipes, Jack. "Fairy Tale as Myth/Myth as Fairy Tale: The Immortality of Sleeping Beauty and Storytelling." *The Brothers Grimm: From Enchanted Forests to the Modern World*. 2nd edition. New York: Palgrave MacMillan, 2002. 207–29.

Marilena Papachristophorou

Smith, Kiki (1954–)

Born in Nuremberg, Germany, and widely recognized as one of the most original artists of her generation, Kiki Smith frequently incorporates fairy-tale **motif**s in her work. Smith's primary media are sculpture and printmaking, but she also works with drawing, painting, writing, and sewing. Revisiting and reinventing fairy tales, Smith creates with her **art** an intensely disarming nostalgia—familiar, unsettling, and new.

From the early 1980s to the present, Smith's work reveals a particular obsession with "**Little Red Riding Hood**." Images from the fairy tale appear again and again in drawings, prints, sculptures, paintings, and paper dolls. In this way, her work incorporates repetition and reproduction, two of contemporary fairy-tale art's major motifs.

In *Kiki Smith: Telling Tales* (2001) and *Kiki Smith: Prints, Books & Things* (2003–4), two major twenty-first century exhibitions of her fairy-tale work, childlike images coexist peacefully with violent content. Common motifs in these shows include girls being eaten, girls gazing at **wolves**, wolves birthing humans, and girls becoming wolves. Formally, it is abstraction that makes the work so beautifully and uniquely read through a fairy-tale lens. Sparse and abstract, Smith's fairy-tale works often evoke the wonder of childhood picture books. Paired with a calm, benevolent portrayal of carnage, this wonder has a dislocating effect. Of fairy tales, Smith modestly has said, "They're all sort of mixed up in my head, and that's what I love. I just know they're active, they're active in me." *See also* Birth; Transformation.

Further Readings: Posner, Helaine, and Smith, Kiki. *Kiki Smith: Telling Tales.* New York: International Center of Photography, 2001; Weitman, Wendy. *Kiki Smith: Prints, Books & Things.* New York: Museum of Modern Art, 2003.

Kate Bernheimer

Snow White

The best-known version of the German fairy tale "Sneewittchen" or "Snow White" was published in the 1857 edition of Jacob and Wilhelm **Grimm**'s *Kinder- und Hausmärchen*

"Snow Drop" illustrated by Mary Sibree in *Alice and Other Fairy Plays for Children* by Kate Freiligrath-Kroeker (London: W. Swan Sonnenschein and Allen, 1880), p. 70. [Courtesy of the Eloise Ramsey Collection of Literature for Young People, University Libraries, Wayne State University]

(*Children's and Household Tales*). The story starts with a **queen** who wishes for a daughter with skin white as snow, lips red as **blood**, and hair black as ebony. After the **birth** of Snow White, her **mother** dies and the king remarries. His new wife has a magic **mirror**, and when this tells her that Snow White is more beautiful than she, she orders a huntsman to kill the girl and cut out her lungs and liver. The hunter lets Snow White escape in the forest and brings the queen the lungs and liver of a young boar instead. Snow White seeks refuge in a house with seven **dwarf**s, where she keeps house for them. Her evil stepmother then attempts three times to kill her: with tight laces, a sharp comb, and a poisoned apple. Each time, Snow White is revived by the dwarfs, but they find her apparently dead after she has eaten the poisoned apple. They see that her beauty does not fade, and display her in a glass coffin. A **prince** that passes by falls in love with Snow White and wants to take her home. When his servants stumble while carrying the coffin, she coughs up the poisoned apple and awakes. The evil stepmother is punished at Snow White and the prince's wedding, when she is forced to dance to **death** in red-hot **shoe**s.

In their annotations, the Brothers Grimm list the Hassenpflug family as their main source for this tale. It was only in the second edition of the *Children's and Household Tales* (published in 1819) that the stepmother was introduced. The first occurrence of the Grimm version of "Snow White" was in a letter that Jacob Grimm sent to his friend Friedrich Carl von Savigny. It is also contained in the Ölenberg manuscript of the *Kinder- und Hausmärchen* from 1810. In these earlier versions, it is not Snow White's stepmother but her own mother who tries to kill her. This has led several psychoanalytic critics, such as J. F. Grant Duff and Bruno **Bettelheim**, to interpret "Snow White" as a story about repressed oedipal feelings (or about Snow White's Electra complex). Their analysis is supported by the fact that the **father**'s role is much bigger in the earlier manuscript version, wherein he comes to fetch Snow White from the seven dwarfs' house. Bettelheim interprets the stepmother as a projection of the young child who cannot accept that his mother may be angry and severe.

"Snow White" was the first fairy tale to be adapted to a full-length animated film by Walt **Disney** in 1937. The tale was shortened substantially: the introduction about Snow White's biological mother was dropped, as were the episodes with the tight laces and the poisoned comb. Disney turned Snow White into a **Cinderella** figure at the beginning of the movie, enhanced the role of the dwarfs and the prince, and changed the ending. In the movie, Snow White is revived when the prince kisses her, and her stepmother dies when she falls from a rock struck by lightning.

Apart from the Grimm version, Steven Swann Jones has counted more than 400 variants of "Snow White" from Europe, Asia Minor, Africa, and (to a lesser extent) the Americas. There are similarities to "La schiavottella" ("The Young Slave") from Giambattista **Basile**'s *Lo cunto de li cunti* (*The Tale of Tales*, 1634–36), as well as to "Richilde" from Johann Karl August **Musäus**'s *Volksmärchen der Deutschen* (*Folktales of the Germans*, 1782–86). Ernst Böklen has made an inventory of all the different ways in which the protagonist is killed (from a poisoned flower to a tight shirt), as well of all the different forms that the seven dwarfs take (bears, monkeys, **thieves**, and old **women**, among others). This variety of **motif**s has been expanded by recent parodies and retellings of the tale: in Fiona French's *Snow White in New York* (1986), for instance, the protagonist seeks refuge with a group of seven jazz musicians, and her stepmother kills her with a poisoned cherry.

Much criticism of "Snow White" has focused on the figure of the evil (step)mother. Shuli Barzilai has a different explanation for the stepmother's anger than jealousy: she sees her as a woman who cannot accept that her child will grow up. Sarah Gilbert and Susan Gubar regard Snow White and her stepmother as two female stereotypes: the angel and the monster. Since these are the only roles available for women in a patriarchal society, Snow White will eventually turn into her stepmother. This is not entirely negative: Gilbert and Gubar consider the queen as an artist, a creative plotter.

The (step)mother is also the focus of many modern fictional reinterpretations of "Snow White." In *White as Snow* (2000), Tanith **Lee** explains the mother's hatred for her daughter because she was raped by the king. In Robert **Coover**'s "The Dead Queen" (1973), Prince Charming discovers that Snow White's stepmother had plotted her own death: bored by his wife, he wishes to kiss the dead queen instead. Other famous retellings for adults include Donald **Barthelme**'s postmodern *Snow White* (1967) and Angela **Carter**'s short story "Snow Child" (1979).

The tale has been used as the basis for a number of young-adult novels. Adèle Geras locates the story in the 1950s in *Pictures of the Night* (1992): Snow White, here called

Belle, flees to Paris to escape her stepmother and eventually marries a doctor. Other authors who have adapted "Snow White" for young readers include Roald **Dahl**, Gregory **Maguire**, Tracy Lynn, Priscilla Galloway, and Wim Hofman. *See also* Animation; Film and Video; *Snow White: A Tale of Terror.*

Further Readings: Barzilai, Shuli. "Reading 'Snow White': The Mother's Story." *Signs* 15 (1990): 515–34; Crago, Hugh. "Who Does Snow White Look At?" *Signal* 45 (1984): 129–45; Gilbert, Sandra M., and Susan Gubar. *The Madwoman in the Attic: The Woman Writer and the Nineteenth-Century Literary Imagination.* New York: Yale University Press, 1979; Grant Duff, J. F. "Schneewittchen: Versuch einer psychoanalytischen Deutung." *Imago* 20 (1934): 95–103; Jones, Steven Swann. *The New Comparative Method: Structural and Symbolic Analysis of the Allomotifs of "Snow White."* Helsinki: Academia Scientiarum Fennica, 1990.

Vanessa Joosen

Snow White: A Tale of Terror (1997)

Directed by Michael Cohn, this live action fairy-tale feature film from 1997 was released directly to cable **television**. It can also be found under the titles *The Grimm Brothers' Snow White* and *Snow White in the Black Forest.* The elaboration of the title appears to be aimed at distinguishing the film from Walt **Disney**'s *Snow White and the Seven Dwarfs,* to which it is a wholehearted antithesis. It is a self-consciously dark and gothic version of the **Snow White** tale that infuses the familiar story with an attempt at period realism, together with an interest in the more unpleasantly Freudian aspects of stepmother/daughter jealousy. The horror elements serve to dramatize psychological conflict with deliberately nasty symbolism, including black magic, sex magic, murder, and madness.

The film's play with realism includes careful cultural placing. German names such as Baron Hoffman and Dr. Gutenberg locate the film specifically in the world of the Brothers **Grimm**. Beautiful period costuming also contributes to the film's visual richness, and the castle and surrounding thick forests have a grittily realistic edge. The film also revisits the traditional seven dwarfs, choosing to refigure them as people marginalized not by their size, but by their low social status and various kinds of physical deformity; their harsh existence in the mines is powerfully contrasted to the privilege of Lily, the Snow White figure, and her **family**. The film's subversive project culminates in the rejection of the attractive but essentially weak **prince** figure in favor of one of the "dwarves" as a partner for Lily.

Snow White benefits enormously from the presence of Sigourney Weaver in the role of Claudia, the stepmother. While she is clearly a wicked **witch,** she is also a tortured and human presence whose anguished investment in her own beauty and in the attention of her husband is very real. She becomes the center of the film, overshadowing the somewhat pale and uninteresting Lily. The film repeatedly takes elements of the original tale and exaggerates them to horrific effect, so that the stepmother's jealousy of Lily leads to her miscarrying her son, and the **mirror** is not simply a reflection of Claudia's beauty, but the seat of her power. Other effective moments include the metamorphosis of the **blood**-on-snow **motif** to a flood of red as Lily's **mother** dies in a carriage accident, and the visual focus on the all-too-real "human" heart that is fed to Lily's **father** as well as her stepmother.

Snow White: A Tale of Terror is generally more preoccupied with the darker psychological underpinnings of the fairy tale than with self-conscious structural play. Nonetheless, it frames Lily's tale very neatly with the blood-on-snow motif that kills her mother, and the film's conclusion amid falling snow. This is reinforced by the oral voice of an old nurse who tells the story of Lily's **birth** almost exactly in the words of the Brothers Grimm. *See also* Film and Video; Freud, Sigmund; Psychological Approaches.

Further Reading: Stephens, John, and Robyn McCallum. "Utopia, Dystopia, and Cultural Controversy in *Ever After* and *The Grimm Brothers' Snow White.*" *Marvels & Tales* 16 (2002): 201–13.

Jessica Tiffin

Sociohistorical Approaches

The sociohistorical approach to folktales and fairy tales focuses on the meaning, production, and reception of a tale within its historical, social, and cultural **context**. As products of sociohistorical circumstances, folktales reflect the conditions, values, religious beliefs, social concerns, **politics**, and ideologies informing the lives of a certain people at a specific time. Although **tale type**s and **motif**s may be spread widely across geographical and cultural borders, suggesting a certain universality, each version of a tale depends on the context in which it was produced, received, and interpreted. Therefore, each version communicates a different message tailored to its audience, sometimes reinforcing and sometimes subverting or questioning social values pertaining to the time and place in which it was conceived.

Lutz **Röhrich**, in his groundbreaking study *Märchen und Wirklichkeit* (1956; translated as *Folktales and Reality*, 1979), suggests that folktales are a reflection of the reality in which they were produced, the characters and the settings being based upon real people and their surrounding culture. In that sense, folktales mirror the stages of socialization of one specific group of people, and each version is representative of its own cultural context. Röhrich differentiates between the past sociohistorical realities represented in folktales, and illustrated for example by **marriage** rituals, and the contemporary sociohistorical reality reflecting the social background and culture of the individual authors, who bring their personal experience to the folktale, coloring it with meaningful decorative elements. In his essay "The Quest of Meaning in Folk Narrative Research" (1988), Röhrich warns, however, about the dangers of interpreting a folktale. Since a tale is subject to many layers of interpretations, it is important to understand their common meaning, conveyed by the core narrative and transcending time and place. To be passed on and remembered, the folktale has to be meaningful to different peoples and traditions. This meaning, common to every version of the same tale, will then be understood in different ways according to the circumstances of each version's production and reception. Therefore, the sociohistorical approach also seeks to explain how a tale is understood, valued, and used by a given audience in a specific social, historical, and cultural context.

The ethnographic historian Robert Darnton, in *The Great Cat Massacre and Other Episodes in French Cultural History* (1984), is also concerned with the meaning expressed in folktales by contemporaries of the French Old Regime and how their vision of the world is represented in the tales. Darnton examines the body of French folktales collected by folklorists since the nineteenth century and tries to understand through comparative studies the French peasant mentality of the Old Regime. Drawing on a large number of texts, both oral and literary, Darnton reconstructs the main concerns of the common people between the fifteenth and eighteenth centuries by asking what similarities and common experiences peasants shared and represented in the tales they produced. He notes, for example, the differences found among versions of the same tales in France and Germany, and he concludes that French culture is characterized by qualities such as humor and domesticity.

Moreover, he identifies throughout the tales produced during that period common motifs such as a lack of **food** and the parental neglect of children, which historians corroborate as historical fact (see **Childhood and Children**). Knowing the background against which these narratives were created, Darnton is able to grasp the reality at the core of tales such as Charles **Perrault**'s "Le petit poucet" ("Little **Thumbling**"), "Le maître chat ou le chat botté" ("The Master Cat, or **Puss in Boots**"), "Cendrillon ou la petite pantoufle de verre" ("**Cinderella**, or The Glass Slipper"), or their oral versions. Far from being allegories, the tales reflect, for Darnton, an image of what the French peasantry experienced in their daily lives. From this perspective, the tales appear to have functioned as accumulated knowledge, giving guidance to the peasants for conducting their lives by showing them the real dangers of encountering strangers, the cruelty of the ruling regime, and the necessity of relying on their own wits to survive.

The German scholar Rudolph **Schenda**, in his numerous studies since 1958, studies the oral and literary tradition of folk stories in the context of their production by examining the role technology might have played in their diffusion. Schenda's main claim is that written materials serve as points of origin for oral retellings. He supports his views with ample material illuminating the way literature was transmitted between the **Middle Ages** and the nineteenth century in Europe through **broadside**s, booklets, **chapbook**s, almanacs, and other forms of popular print, relayed in nonliterate villages by preachers, travelers, and others all over Europe. Following Schenda's lead, Ruth B. Bottigheimer also considers oral folktales in the context of print-based patterns of dissemination to understand their effects on the development of a tale type. In her article of 1993 on the story of the "Lazy Boy," Bottigheimer shows that this tale was disseminated in print and then took on local coloration as it passed into **oral tradition**s around the world.

Sociohistorical studies of French **literary fairy tale**s have shown the complexity of the genre and the misinterpretations that occur when fairy tales are not studied in context. Raymonde Robert, in *Le conte de fées littéraires en france de la fin du XVIIe à la fin du XVIIIe siècle* (*The Literary Fairy Tale in France from the End of Seventeenth to the End of Eighteenth century*, 1982), was the first scholar to undertake extensive research on the social and historical context of the French high society that produced fairy tales. Robert's work laid the foundation for scholars such as Lewis C. Seifert, who, in his *Fairy Tales, Sexuality and Gender in France, 1690–1715* (1996), has brilliantly linked the fashion of fairy tales at Louis XIV's court with the ongoing Quarrel of the Ancients and the Moderns. Patricia Hannon, in *Fabulous Identities: Women's Fairy Tales in Seventeenth-Century France* (1998), takes a more feminist approach to show that **women** predominated in the creation of this literary genre. In an article of 2006, Charlotte Trinquet shows that the Marie-Catherine d'**Aulnoy**'s fairy tale "Finette Cendron" is, despite all of its marvelous elements, a perfect reflection of the world in which it was created. These and other scholars have adopted sociohistorical approaches to understand the French literary fairy tale because of the genre's long history of neglect, due principally to the power that the French Academy has had in both creating and censoring the French literary canon. Charles Perrault had been a member of the French Academy, and for more than two centuries, his little volume of eight fairy tales had hidden the scope of fairy-tale writing in France. To paraphrase Michèle Simonsen, he was the tree hiding the forest (*Le conte populaire français*, 1981). There was, therefore, another history behind the official literary history that needed to be revealed to fully understand the importance of the genre and its implication for the future of fairy tales in Europe.

Working with Italian fairy tales, Nancy L. Canepa, in *From Court to Forest* (1999), has drawn upon the work of Röhrich to show how Giambattista **Basile**'s *Lo cunto de li cunti* (*The Tale of Tales*, 1634–36) reflects contemporary social reality through the recreation of everyday life in seventeenth-century Naples. For example, Canepa draws a parallel between the magical and the scientific world, arguing that mechanisms such as automatons, which were a fad at the time, supplant **magic object**s in a number of tales. As Darnton did for eighteenth-century French peasantry, Canepa uncovers the social and political reality that surrounded Basile and his audience. She also demonstrates how Basile's work reflects popular art forms such as songs and games, customs, values, ideologies, and even the geography of seventeenth-century Naples—that is, the world as it was known to Basile and his readers. Moreover, her research is groundbreaking in the sense that she has successfully identified Basile the creator of the first European collection of literary fairy tales, an honor previously bestowed upon Perrault. Even more important for French scholars, she has established the link between Basile and the work of the French authors of fairy tales in the seventeenth century, especially in terms of the similar sociopolitical contexts in which the tales were written. Her work not only sheds light on Italian the genre in Italy but also enlarges the spectrum in which scholars can understand the French fairy tale in its more complex relationship to the historical and social circumstances of its production.

Jack **Zipes** is the most influential scholar advocating and using sociohistorical approaches in the study of fairy tales. In *Breaking the Magic Spell: Radical Theories of Folk and Fairy Tales* (1979, revised 2002), Zipes emphasizes the importance of learning about the history of folktales and fairy tales within the cultural context of their creation to fully grasp their value and potential. Applying Norbert Elias's concept of the "civilizing process" to fairy-tale studies, Zipes demonstrates that the folktale, especially the literary fairy tale, functioned as an instrument of civilization in the hands of the precapitalist ruling classes of Europe. Zipes's reading of "**Beauty and the Beast**," including the eighteenth-century French versions by Gabrielle-Suzanne Barbot de **Villeneuve** and Jeanne-Marie **Leprince de Beaumont** is instructive. According to Zipes, the tale expresses the political context of the social classes of the epoch and conveys the message that the bourgeoisie should remember its place in society, which would of course be well under the aristocracy. The father is punished because of his **transgression** into aristocratic grounds (the Beast's castle), and the heroine is rewarded because she chooses virtue and inner beauty instead of pride and greed, a common tendency among the enriched bourgeoisie.

Zipes also uses the sociohistorical approach to study the socialization of children through books and movies in the context of the age of multimedia. His book *Sticks and Stones: The Troublesome Success of* **Children's Literature** *from Slovenly Peter to Harry Potter* (2001), as well as much of his other work, deals with the image of the world and the values conveyed to children via books and other cultural texts supposedly created especially for them and their best interests. In pursuing this research, Zipes takes into account not only those texts that reinforce sociocultural norms but also those that present alternatives. In a reading of the animated movie **Shrek** (2001), for instance, he underlines the ability of the **film** to subvert accepted standards and challenge the conventional message of the **Walt Disney Corporation**. Zipes, then, is as much interested in those tales that subvert social norms as he is in those that promulgate them.

Sociohistorical approaches to folktales and fairy tales have been applied in a wide variety of ways. They are all, however, predicated on the claim that the meaning of a particular tale can be understood only within the historical, social, and cultural context of its production and reception. The tradition exemplified by Röhrich, Darnton, Schenda, Robert, Zipes, and others has added significantly to our understanding of folktales and fairy tales and their role in specific societies, and it has led to a fuller appreciation of the general manner in which folktales and fairy tales are generated, disseminated, adapted, revised, and in some cases subverted and reutilized for social and political purposes. This approach has the further advantage of foregrounding how different sociohistorical contexts lead to a variety of interpretations that interact with each other over time and geographical locations. *See also* Anthropological Approaches.

Further Readings: Bottigheimer, Ruth B. "Luckless, Witless, and Filthy-Footed: A Sociocultural Study and Publishing History Analysis of *Lazy Boy*." *Journal of American Folklore* 106 (1993): 259–84; Freudmann, Felix R. "Realism and Magic in Perrault's Fairy Tales." *L'Esprit Créateur* 3 (1963): 116–22; Harth, Erica. *Ideology and Culture in Seventeenth-Century France.* Ithaca: Cornell University Press, 1983; Kamenetsky, Christa. *The Brothers Grimm and their Critics: Folktales and the Quest for Meaning.* Athens: Ohio University Press, 1992; Röhrich, Lutz. *Folktales and Reality.* Translated by Peter Tokofsky. Bloomington: Indiana University Press, 1991; Schenda, Rudolf. "Telling Tales—Spreading Tales: Change in the Communicative Form of a Popular Genre." Translated by Ruth B. Bottigheimer. *Fairy Tales and Society: Illusion, Allusion, and Paradigm.* Edited by Ruth B. Bottigheimer. Philadelphia: University of Pennsylvania Press, 1986. 75–94; Warner, Marina. *From the Beast to the Blonde: On Fairy Tales and Their Tellers.* New York: Farrar, Straus and Giroux, 1994; Zipes, Jack. *Fairy Tales and the Art of Subversion: The Classical Genre for Children and the Process of Civilization.* New York: Wildman Press, 1983; ———, ed. *The Trials and Tribulations of Little Red Riding Hood.* 2nd edition. New York: Routledge, 1993.

Charlotte Trinquet

Soldier

The disadvantaged "everyman" is a favored hero in folktales, and no one fits this category better than a discharged or deserting soldier, especially one whose wounds threaten him with a future of begging. Such soldier-heroes appear in many different **tale type**s (notably types ATU 306, The Danced-Out Shoes; ATU 361, Bear-Skin; and ATU 562, The Spirit in the Blue Light). This last type, exemplified by Jacob and Wilhelm **Grimms**' "Das blaue Licht" ("The Blue Light") and Hans Christian **Andersen**'s "Fyrtøjet" ("The Tinder Box"), is particularly relevant.

Type 562 tales characteristically open describing a wounded and recently discharged soldier. His hopelessness is mitigated when he miraculously acquires a lantern or other item that controls a supernatural helper. The soldier uses this newly found power to gain revenge over the **king**, whom he blames for his misfortune. This he inexplicably does by forcing the king's daughter to do maid service for him each night. With time, the soldier is exposed, captured, and sentenced to die. However, at the last minute, his **magic helper** strikes down the executioner and everyone around him. The king rescues himself by giving the soldier his daughter in **marriage** and ceding to him the kingdom. This tale is thus a fantasy expression of the ultimate mutiny. A soldier takes possession of a **princess**, then forces the king to abdicate in his favor.

Another tale type that features a soldier as hero is ATU 475, The Man as Heater of Hell's Kettle. Aleksandr **Afanas'ev**'s "The Magic Shirt" is typical. In this story, a soldier deserts the army after having been mistreated by an unjust sergeant. Hiding in a forest, he accepts an apprenticeship from a **dragon** and agrees to keep a fire burning under the latter's cauldron. (In most versions, the deserter's employer is the **devil**.) At the end of his service, the deserter discovers that his former sergeant is inside the cauldron he has kept boiling. The dragon devours the stew—sergeant and all—and rewards the soldier with a magic horse and shirt, which ultimately bring him wealth and power. This story thus fulfills a fantasy that in real life an abused soldier could only dream of. He successfully deserts the army, punishes a hated superior, and enriches himself in the process.

Traditionally, military service has been dominated by males, but one group of folktales, a subset of type ATU 884, The Forsaken Fiancée: Service as Menial, depicts a woman disguised as a man performing military service so well that she passes for a male. Representative of this type is "Theodora in the Army" from R. M. Dawkins' *Modern Greek Folktales* (1953). Here, the heroine, to save her father from military service, disguises herself as a man and joins the army, where she successfully serves for three years. A fellow soldier suspects her gender and subjects her to a series of tests, but she passes them all, thus easily proving her "masculinity." In the end, she reveals her true **gender** and marries her companion. *See also* Punishment and Reward; Woman Warrior.

Further Readings: Fink, Gonthier-Louis. "The Fairy Tales of the Grimms' Sergeant of Dragoons J. F. Krause as Reflecting the Needs and Wishes of the Common People." *The Brothers Grimm and Folktale.* Edited by James M. McGlathery. Urbana: University of Illinois Press, 1988. 146–63; Röhrich, Lutz. *Folktales and Reality.* Translated by Peter Tokofsky. Bloomington: Indiana University Press, 1991. 184–98, 202–03.

D. L. Ashliman

Solinas Donghi, Beatrice (1923–)

In 2003, Beatrice Solinas Donghi won the coveted Premio Andersen (Andersen Prize) for lifetime achievement in recognition of her long career as one of the most cherished and innovative Italian authors of tales and **children's literature**. Best known for her modern approach to the traditional folktale in such collections as *Le fiabe incatenate* (*The Linked Fairy Tales*, 1967) and *La gran fiaba intrecciata* (*The Great Interlaced Fairy Tale*, 1972), Solinas Donghi also published **novel**s for adults and children that are laced with folkloric themes and **motif**s.

Born in Serra Riccò, Italy, Solinas Donghi followed in the tradition of nineteenth-century folklorists like Giuseppe **Pitré** when she preserved in text folktales from Genoa and Liguria in *Fiabe a Genova* (*Genovese Folktales*, 1972) and *Fiabe liguri* (*Ligurian Folktales*, 1980).

Solinas Donghi contributed to folklore criticism with the collection of articles *La fiaba come racconto* (*The Fairy Tale as Story*, 1976). In a letter to Solinas Donghi dated June 30, 1969, Italo **Calvino** praised her article "Divagazioni su varie Cenerentola" ("Digressions on Various **Cinderella**s"), which would later be included in *The Fairy Tale as Story*, as a significant contribution to Italian culture, stating that it had been almost a century since anyone had seriously considered comparativistic folklore. For Calvino, Solinas Donghi's study distinguished itself with its plentiful references and intelligent, spirited discourse. *See also* Italian Tales.

Further Reading: "Sei lettere di Italo Calvino a Mario Boselli, Beatrice Solinas Donghi, Goffredo Fofi e Antonio Preti." *Nuova Corrente* 33 (1986): 409–19.

Gina M. Miele

Sorcerer, Sorceress

Sorcerers and sorceresses are figures capable of performing magic using **magic objects** and aids. Sorceresses are generally sympathetic to the protagonist and play supporting roles; sorcerers are often the protagonist's nemesis and propel the tale's narrative.

In the history of magic, clear divisions exist among witchcraft, sorcery, and their practitioners. A **witch**'s power is inherent, a sorceress's learned. Sorcery can be taught and practiced by anyone working with magical aids, such as wands, **mirrors**, and herbs. While both witches and sorceresses might perform black magic (*maleficium*) to harm others, sorcery is usually reserved for beneficent or empowering purposes.

Although the terms are often used interchangeably in modern parlance, witches and sorceresses are distinctly different figures in folktales and fairy tales with separate realms of action. Hans-Jörg Uther's *The Types of International Folktales* (2004) gives only three tale types for "sorceress" (ATU 310, The Maiden in the Tower [Petrosinella, Rapunzel]; ATU 405, Jorinda and Joringel; and ATU 449, Sidi Numan) but a tenfold number for "witch." Uther's index lists only four tale types for "sorcerer." There appears to be an international preference for tales with malevolent magical females.

Unlike witches, their more pervasive counterparts who appear unbidden with evil intent, sorceresses are actually sought out to perform helpful magic, to restore balance to the community, and to advise on matters of the heart. They might be asked to foretell the future, divine the location of lost objects or persons, or effect a healing. Theirs is a learned and studied art, as the frequent mentions of their books of magic suggest. One of the sorceresses' most sought-after skills is their knowledge of herbs' medicinal and magical powers. They often brew or collect the ingredients necessary for love potions, fertility aids, healing ointments, and even salves for reviving the dead. They are generous with their gifts, teaching supplicants spells and **incantation**s or providing magic objects, like mirrors that reveal the true appearance of a bewitched person, a magic flute that revives a dead daughter in Russian and Greek tales, or a magic wand that disenchants a stony friend in Retoromanic and Austrian tales. In the role of their real-life historical counterparts (the "wise women"), fairy-tale sorceresses might be asked to perform countermagic to disenchant others, but their wand may just as easily transform humans into stones or dogs, snakes, mice, or other animals. Sorceresses may themselves be shapeshifters, becoming **cat**s or owls during the day (as in Jacob and Wilhelm **Grimm**s' "Jorinda and Joringel"). They are benevolent advisors: in **Greek tales**, for example, heroes seek the advice of a sorceress on performing some impossible task or finding a lost **family** member. In their nurturing role for the good of the community, sorceresses provide foster care for lost or endangered **children**. Unlike witches, who are always described as ugly, old, and mean, the sorceresses' appearance and **age** remain a mystery, and they fade from the narrative after giving advice and aid.

Sorcerers, in contrast, are almost uniformly portrayed as maleficent and have roles much more like witches. They have no positive magical counterparts and are more pivotal characters in the narrative because they often interact with the hero in battles of wits and one-upsmanship. It is not uncommon for sorcerers to exhibit their powers to impress or intimidate. In some tales, the sorcerer is described as a cannibal or in league with the **devil** (an accusation leveled at real-life sorcerers). Occasionally, they are healers or exorcists, relieving people of demonic possessions, but they rarely dabble in herbal remedies or the healing arts. Sorcerers sometimes give advice on finding missing loved ones; they may foster young maidens while their **father** is having a hard time making ends meet, although they are just as likely to kidnap the children for no apparent reason and to release them unharmed only after some difficult challenge has been met. They play a very limited role in love magic. Like sorceresses, they often possess magical aids (most frequently a magic wand and book of spells, or a sack full of snakes and another filled with bugs), or they may bestow them on others (such as the seven-league boots in tales from Poland). Their book of magic is often their undoing—the most recurrent sorcerer tale internationally is ATU 325, The Magician and His Pupil, in which the sorcerer's apprentice studies the book, soon rivals his master in skill, and finally conquers him in wand-to-wand combat. As shapeshifters, sorcerers fall victim to their own bravado: they execute various **transformation**s when goaded by adversaries, only to be swallowed in their final transformation as a mouse (the most famous example is "**Puss in Boots**"). Almost all of the tales highlight the perils of ego, since the sorcerer is inevitably dispatched or self-destructs in the end.

The question arises as to what extent these images of magical **men** and **women** reflect the historical record on witchcraft, sorcery, and the healing arts. One result of the Christianization of the Greco-Roman and Germanic worlds was that the emphasis on witchcraft and magical arts became associated with diabolical arts and heresy. In the course of the **Middle Ages**, the sorceress was demonized. Traditions from other areas Christianized later are rich with descriptions of positive feminine sorcery—Iceland, for example, has almost no tales with an evil sorceress or witch. National and linguistic borders also play a role. The German Grimms, for example, regularly preferred the identification of all female magicians (good or bad) as witches. In Germany, even geographic descriptions came to be disenchanted and instead bewitched. In 1649, the Brocken (a mountain in eastern Germany that was believed to be the sorceresses' meeting place) had a *Zauber-Teich* (magical pond) and a *Zauber-Brunn* (magical well); by the end of the eighteenth century, these places had been renamed "the witches' well" and "the witches' pond." *See also* Magic Helper.

Further Reading: Michelet, Jules. *The Sorceress: A Study in Middle Age Superstition*. Translated by A. R. Allinson. Paris: Charles Carrington, 1904.

Shawn C. Jarvis

South Asian Tales

The Indian subcontinent is characterized by tremendous diversity—physical-ecological, linguistic, cultural, and religious. The region's cultural geography stretches from the high mountain communities of the Himalayan region (Nepal, Bhutan, Tibeto-Burman areas of Bangladesh, the western Himalayas, Karakorum, and Hindu Kush), to the deserts and riverine or marine coastal, subtropical and tropical, hill country and lowlands of Pakistan and India, and on to Sri Lanka and the Andaman Islands, the whole area host to a wide range of nominal ethnic groups, castes, and so-called tribes. Even the term "tribe" means very different things in regard to social organization: so-called tribal Balochi and Pashtun populations number in the millions and occupy territory spanning the Pakistan-Afghanistan border as extended, flexible semiconfederacies of notionally lineage-based groups, whereas a number of small, linguistically distinct minority populations in India and Bangladesh are also called "tribes." The idea of "caste" in much of the geographic area has its own problematics, but caste membership, where it occurs, in part organizes the distribution of responsibilities for and rights to different **performance** forms or genres among different social groups. As for linguistic diversity, there are well over 100 languages in the region (more than 200 depending how "language" and "dialect" are defined), a minority of which are dominant and expanding their influence through mass media and education, many of which are as yet non-written and a good number now endangered.

Religions of the subcontinent include Hinduism, Islam, Buddhism, Jainism, Zoroastrianism, Christianity, Judaism, "Kafir," and other local animist belief systems, with various ways of approaching the sacred (for example, mystical-devotional, disciplinary-meditative, or instrumental, as in shamanism), both within each religion and among them. Such broad religious diversity ensures indeterminacies of the boundaries of belief (or lack thereof): how (or why, or whether), in defining supernatural events, people distinguish religion (the workings of deities, saints, and their helpers, and interlocutors or technicians of the sacred, such as shamans and priests) versus magic (**sorcerer**s good and bad, **witch**es, ghosts, and even demons, vampires, and jinns as supernaturals to be managed or countered rather than propitiated) versus fantasy, the fanciful or imaginary, not infrequently including figures that belong in others' orthodox belief systems.

A case in point is the *pari*, a category of supernatural in Persian and several South Asian languages, the term being cognate to the English word "**fairy**" and often so translated. In **wonder tale**s in several languages, the *pari*, usually female, is a staple, a beautiful and powerful magical ally of the hero (sometimes of the heroine), and a frequent object of human heroes' romantic quests. In the western Himalayas (Karakorum of northern Pakistan), however, the *pari* are a very real and dangerous presence, a race of beings male and female, appearing much like humans in form but far more powerful, who inhabit the high mountains. They resent human encroachment yet also can be attracted to individual people. They cause at least inconvenient, sometimes physically dangerous possession states in which the *pari* abducts the human object of interest, taking him or her off (in spirit and perhaps also in body) to attend *pari* social events. Maria Marhoffer-Wolf provides a detailed ethnographic documentation of *pari* beliefs and related human experiences and practices, including shamanism, within the Werchik (Burushaski) cultural environment of the Yasin Valley in northern Pakistan. Witnessing a rather violent possession event in the neighboring valley of Ishkoman in 1990, the author of this entry was told by her Muslim host, a schoolmaster who had just used recitation of Qur'anic verses and "blowing" on the victim to exorcise a male *pari* from his fourteen-year-old niece, that the *pari* and the things that they do are acknowledged by verses of the Qur'an which state that God has created any number of beings and things of which humans may be unaware. *Pari* encounter stories in this and adjacent communities took the form of personal experience narratives and local **legend**s attached to living local people, mysterious and fascinating but not fantastical in the sense of wonder tales. One middle-aged man, famous for his prowess as a hunter of ibex, an endangered wild mountain sheep, also suffered from male-pattern baldness, rare in this population. Ibex are revered as a pure species, and considered to be the flocks of the *pari*. The friend who introduced us remarked, laughingly but with a degree of belief, that it was said the *pari* had taken the hunter's hair in revenge because he had killed so many of their goats. He and others who habitually hunted in high mountain meadows and above the treeline reported personal encounters with *pari*. Likewise, in some examples from Inayat-ur-Rahman's *Folktales of Swat* (1968–84), *pari* are not the benign supernaturals they are elsewhere, and tales of exorcism are well represented in the collection.

Pari exorcism or shamanic cooperation with them would hardly pass scrutiny by the Muslim revivalists currently working in the region, however. Loud (sometimes violent) debates, quiet disagreements, and tolerated diversities abound over "orthodox" versus "unorthodox" beliefs and approaches to the supernatural in all its forms, rendering problematic the use of a genre term such as **"folktale"** or "wonder tale," so central to our discussion otherwise, making any truth attribution for narrative subject matter culturally **context**-specific. On the subcontinent, the ostensible "fictional" quality of folktale and fairy tale is extremely porous. One person's wonder tale or **joke** may well be someone else's devotional **parable**, **myth**, or legend.

Such indeterminacies render genre categories applied to "tales" equally unstable, whether they are defined by thematic content, by context (of production or performance and/or of interpretation whether as ritual or entertainment, private and domestic, or public), or by medium and form (spoken with or without illustrations; written text printed or not; or acted out as in **dance**, folk **theater**, including shadow or **puppet theater**, **film**, **television**, etc.). As Ved Prakash Vatuk observes, "Folktales appear in a variety of genres [or performance modes]" (Vatuk, 195), such as sung verse (*bhajan*, which Vatuk translates as "ballad") and folk **opera** (*sang*). The latter exists in performance and also in an interesting vernacular literary form, as printed librettos, transcribed, Vatuk thinks, by literate troupe members from orally composed operas. The librettos contain, besides plot outlines, the texts of key dialogues, featured duets and solos, and some stage directions. Vatuk observes that these librettos are inexpensively printed and sold in bazaars as stories to be read, and from which to learn the songs, for enjoyment by nonactors. To these performance forms can be added sung verse with narrative scroll illustrations (the performers pointing out the relevant illustrations as the scroll and the narrative unfurl) and prose within or without ritual context. R. C. Temple, writing in his *Legends of the Punjab* in 1884, observed that the plot structure of Punjabi folktales and the "bardic poems" he collected was identical, but he went on to argue that the textual conservatism of the bardic poems (regularized by meter and rhyme) supports a more meticulous preservation of detail, such as names of characters and specificity of events, even to the extent of near-verbatim similarity between performances of a given tale by different bards. In contrast, he regarded Punjabi prose folktales negatively, as easily garbled, often poorly preserved derivatives of the bardic poems:

> I hope to show here abundantly that the bardic poem and the folktale are constructed on precisely the same lines as far as the pure story goes, even where the former is fastened on to really historical characters and mixed up with the narrative of *bona fide* historical facts [which Temple evidently values]. The folktale is very often in fact a mere scene, or jumble of scenes, to be found in the poem, where only the marvellous story has been remembered, while the names and surroundings of the actors to whom it is attributed has [*sic*] been forgotten. (Temple, v–vi)

This devolutionary hypothesis, that one genre is a degenerate derivative of another, has not been widely applied in folklorists' narrative research of the last fifty years; rather, the comparative fixity or flexibility of texts in performance, their degrees of specificity and ellipsis, would be treated synchronically as stylistic qualities of their respective genres.

Ritual tales in prose in some cases may be identical to or very similar variants of tales heard in nonritual performance, but they form a necessary part of many common votive rituals, both Hindu and Muslim. The narrative performance within the rite usually provides an origin story for the ritual while affirming its efficacy. Such narratives are called *vrat kathā* in Hindi. Lakshmi Narasamamba, in an essay of 2006, reports that Deccani Urdu-speaking Muslim **women** in East Godavari (south-central India) use a single term, *kahânî*, for both ritual tales and tales told for entertainment. In Afghan (Dari) Persian, tales would be called *naql* ("narrative," as distinct from *afsânah*, "**fantasy** or wonder tale") when they are associated with Muslim votive rituals (*nazr*), even when the same story plot, with largely the same diction, may be told in or out of ritual context. In Muslim context, religious reformers generally discourage such rituals as unorthodox, but they are widely popular, and especially as performed by women. Almost all of the stories in C. A. Kincaid's Marathi-language, Deccani Hindu (south-central Indian) story collection—*Deccan Nursery Tales or Fairy Tales from the South* (1914)—have the key discursive feature of votive narratives, in that major characters in the story must ritually retell how they received help from a benign supernatural, to others who in turn ritually perform the story to still others, so that faith in the supernatural helper is propagated while the tellers stay in the good graces of the supernatural sponsor whether deity or saint. This narrative imperative is thus the oral-performative equivalent of a chain letter. Kincaid, however, does not describe any of these tales in actual ritual performance, but merely casts them as children's stories with a general **moral** or devotional "tag."

One of the most enigmatic of vow-stories, "The Three Nights' Moon"—from Barrett Parker and Ahmad Javid's *Collection of Afghan Legends* (1970)—begins, "People of Afghanistan for many years have recounted that if a person sees the [apparently full] moon for three successive nights he must go to his mother or some other lady and ask her to tell the legend of the three nights' moon" (Parker and Javid, 83). But the Kabul version of the legend that Parker and Javid relate (like a version this author recorded in Herat, Afghanistan, in 1975) does not actually contain any efficacious origin narrative explaining the appearance and effect of the three-night moon, told by a senior or knowledgeable woman: it merely recounts how male protagonists who saw the moon neglected to ask anyone to tell them the legend, and thus suffered. The telling implies that this "coda," the **cautionary tale** of their suffering and rescue, is the tale to be told if one should see the three nights' moon. Normally, votive tales comprise an origin story for the votive ritual, often adding a "coda" story in which protagonists fail to carry out the ritual retelling of the story, suffer badly, and are rescued only when they remember to carry out the narrative rite.

Noting the complexities of South Asian local narrative genre terminology and forms, Susan Wadley has outlined the following three macrocategories of oral or oral/literary narrative that apply widely across the subcontinent (with various local generic and subgeneric names):

1. Tales with named characters, most often **king**s and **queen**s, generally considered to be mythological/legendary and true (*ithihas* or "history" in Hindi). Such tales are told by both **men** and women, with men predominating. They tend to have relatively long, convoluted plots, and frequently also exist in published literary form, in Sanskrit or Persian.

2. Tales with unnamed characters, usually identified by occupation or caste ("Once there was an oil-presser," "Once there was an old thorn-gatherer"), in which **magic object**s or persons and unlikely events nonetheless illustrate key (actual) cultural concepts and social relationships. Such tales tend to be short, and are told by men, women, and children alike. They are not considered historically "true" and are often humorous. Not generally published as popular or elite literature (as is category 1) nor featured in tale collections told by men and collected by men, they are common in collections of women's tales made by colonial-period women.

3. Ritual tales, discussed above, comprise Wadley's third category. Such tales are told from the oral repertoire or read from cheap pamphlets or **chapbook**s purchased in local markets, as part of a

ritual. They mostly have unnamed human protagonists, as in category 2, interacting with well-known supernatural agents (deities or saints). Wadley notes, "Pamphlets containing the tale for a specific ritual, or for all the rituals of a month or year, are commonly found in markets. These are the most widely available and read published folktales, and are the only printed tales found in many homes" (Wadley, 219). (Farther afield, the author of this entry has observed the same type of inexpensive pamphlets or handbooks detailing the procedure for votive rituals, with story texts, newly available in the Tajik Persian and Uzbek languages, offered for purchase on sidewalk bookstalls outside mosques in the former Soviet Central Asia, alongside pamphlet instructions for more orthodox religious practices, such as how to execute daily prayers correctly or how to make the Muslim *hajj* pilgrimage to Mecca. Such pamphlets were not so publicly available during the Soviet period, when orthodox religious practice, including five-times-daily prayer, and forms of popular piety were downplayed or discouraged.)

The indeterminacy and diversity of local categories, based as they are on use as well as form, create problems in the application of international comparative tools and methodologies, as evidenced by the uneasy fit of the Aarne-Thompson **tale-type** index with South Asian and other non-European genres and forms, and by the flattening effects, categorical and interpretive, of structural analysis. Under these circumstances, and because some narrative forms and traditions of South Asia have been closely studied while many others of equally wide distribution remain virtually unresearched, it is easier to discuss some of the ways South Asian oral narrative and its literary relatives have been studied, rather than stipulate how they should be defined. Sadhana Naithani and Leela Prasad offer close, critical analyses of the discourse of colonial-era **collectors'** introductions to and analyses of oral narrative collections as evidence of the collectors' ideologies and pragmatic aims. British colonial administrators advocated folktale collecting as a way of inventorying local customs, beliefs, and attitudes, implicitly or explicitly in support of more effective administrative (or political) control. For example, Temple writes of his collection that "so much prominence has been given to the stories of saints and holy personages, because it is by a careful study of such things that we can hope to grasp the religious and superstitious ideas that dominate the bulk of the Indian population" (Temple, xxvi). Temple also stipulates that the collection of texts is valuable for his peers' language study, and thus in *Legends of the Punjab*, he publishes a voluminous dual-language collection with close attention to the features of the local Punjabi dialect. Missionary collectors likewise saw oral traditional narrative as a window on local worldviews and ideologies, and as a resource for acquiring professionally necessary linguistic competence, thus valuable for the mixed purposes of understanding and preserving (as texts in books) "endangered" culture (but endangered by what, if not by the collectors' professional intention to change the daily behavior and beliefs of its adherents?). With an implicit eye toward missionizing, J. Hinton Knowles writes in *Kashmiri Folk Tales* in 1887, "The vocation of a missionary brings one into close and constant 'touch' with the people, from whom, as I glide along in the boat, or walk by the way, or squat in the hut, or teach in the school, I have learnt many things. My primary object in collecting these tales was to obtain some knowledge of Kashmiri [language] … [M]y secondary object was to ascertain something of the thoughts and ways of the people … I venture to publish the whole collection [of tales] in a book and thus save them from the clutches of oblivion … my contribution towards that increasing stock of Folk-lore which is doing so much to clear away the clouds that envelop most of the practices, ideas, and beliefs which make up the daily life of the natives of our great dependencies, control their feelings, and underlie many of their actions" (Knowles, v, x). Here, one might ask, "Whose 'clouds'?"

Indigenous intellectuals' motivation for documenting oral narrative and other traditional expressive forms—for instance, the poet and fiction writer Rabindranath Tagore, winner of the 1913 Nobel Prize in Literature, who initiated and championed documentation of oral culture by Bengali intellectuals—in the colonial period often more closely resembled the cultural nationalist and politically liberatory goals of the Brothers **Grimm**. They sought to document not superstitious backwardness and simplicity of beliefs that Temple or Knowles deemed to "dominate" or "control" the consciousness of the Indian population, but the aesthetic expressiveness and ethical and emotive power of vernacular culture. Tagore and his literary colleagues also saw indigenous **oral tradition** as a source for literary inspiration, perceiving from their modernizing perspective a productive interface between, or interdependency of, the oral and the written.

A more recent example of a collection making substantially positive claims for ethnic identity-related cultural content is Aisha Ahmad and Roger Boase's *Pashtun Tales from the Pakistan-Afghan Frontier* (2003). They perceive tale logic in general in this collection as specifically to represent *Pashtunwali*, the oral-traditional ethical code claimed as the core principle of Pashtun behavior and identity. The three main action principles of *Pashtunwali* are *badal*, "exchange, reciprocity," which mandates blood revenge but also positive reciprocity in such matters as **marriage** exchange, visits, and other support offered for weddings and condolence calls; *melmastia*, "hospitality, sanctuary," including unconditional physical protection extended to all who come as guests (which even overrides the imperative to avenge prior injuries); and *nanawati*, forgiveness for those who submit to one's authority. Other preoccupations the compilers detect in the collection and identify as major concerns for Pashtuns are by no means unique to them: belief in fate or destiny, anxiety over debt as part of **peasant** life, the vital importance of male heirs, the presumed stupidity or disloyalty of "menial tribes" (non-Pashtun client groups, including barbers, weavers, and certain professional entertainers and craftspeople, who are not bound by *Pashtunwali*), and a polarized attitude toward women, portrayed as categorically either "fickle" (sexually disloyal) or "virtuous."

While Ahmad and Boase suggest a rather monochromatic **gender** ideology operating among Pashtuns, one of the more productive interpretive directions in the study of South Asian narrative and other expressive genres in recent decades has yielded a series of projects to distinguish the dynamics of gender ideology as operating between men and women within their respective communities. A. K. Ramanujan's classic article, "Towards a Counter-System: Women's Tales," avoids setting women's narratives apart from men's but argues that they should be heard as a distinguishable set of voices and claims on par with those of men. Studies by Joyce B. Flueckiger and by Gloria G. Raheja and Ann G. Gold use a genre-systems approach to describe a range of ideological positions or sentiments, distributed across different local genres within communities, revealing resistance or simply alternatives to strictly patriarchal constructions of women's subordinate position.

Exploring both song and tale, Raheja and Gold detect registers of discourse working as a layered system of representation and contestation within different performance contexts. In their interpretation, it is not a question of "either/or" of patriarchal versus antipatriarchal values, but a question of the relative force, the relative salience, and the relative persuasiveness of these discursive forms, in their shifting contexts, traditional and post-traditional, that enables a positive assertion of female identity and **sexuality**, and alternative visions of kinship relations within patriarchy, not hard to find in the women's performance genres they document. They make detailed reference to female consciousness as expressed in traditional female scripts (story, song) that include quite explicit models for female agency, female heroism, and successful female intervention with deities, arguing for "a multiplicity of culturally valued strategies or perspectives for constructing selfhood and moral discourse" (Raheja and Gold, 10).

Margaret A. Mills (1985) for Afghanistan and P. S. Kanaka Durga for southern India both note the greater tendency of women to perform both female-centered and male-centered tales, whereas men concentrate on male-centered stories. Kanaka Durga further attributes women's interest in male-centered tales to women's capacity to imagine their own empowerment as parallel with men's: "The evident interchangeability of gender roles (in terms of **transformation** and transcendence in the performance context of a narrative) is a strategy adopted by narrators (here, invariably women) to claim their due social status" (Kanaka Durga, 88). Devdutt Pattanaik for Hindus and Mills (1985) for Muslims discuss **cross-dressing** as a form of disguise and **trickster** agency.

Kanaka Durga and Kirin Narayan and Urmila Devi Sood, in *Mondays on the Dark Night of the Moon* (1997), acknowledge the role of performers' personal histories (specifically, autobiographical narratives). Kanaka Durga puts it succinctly, "Narrators live in the narratives they tell," while Leela Prasad, in her introduction to *Gender and Story in South India*, revisits the tales of Anna Liberata de Souza as they relate to her personal history, recorded with the tales by Mary Frere in 1868, a "poetic transformation of personal tragedy, that cannot find closure" (Prasad, Bottigheimer, and Handoo, 16). Mary Frere was alone in her time, indeed in her century, in offering an account of her interlocutor's difficult personal history as relevant to her artistry. Narayan, at the specific request of the master storyteller Urmila Devi Sood, did not discuss the parallels between her repertoire and her life history, but remarks, "A repertoire is a choice selection, assembled by chance, by occasions for repeated hearing, by aesthetic predilection, and by themes compelling to the teller. As a selective corpus lodged inside a mind, shared by a sensibility, the tales in a person's repertoire relate to each other, they comment on, disagree with, and extend discussion on interrelated themes" (Narayan, 212).

This observation on an individual's traditional repertoire as formed by aesthetic and critical preference and reflection moves us quite far from the generalizations of Temple and Knowles, quoted above, depicting traditional performers as controlled or dominated by culture in the form of beliefs articulated through traditional narratives. Indeed, the critique of colonial folklorists' notions of collective cultural domination through tradition developed hand in hand with the recovery of ways to discern individual agency and resistance in traditional expressive performance, within an undeniably disempowering social order (whether of caste, class, or patriarchy). Yet assessments of the workings of collective consciousness need not disappear in the face of the study of individual artists: it is through detailed understanding of individuals reflecting on personal circumstances through their narrative performances, and how their performances are received by their audiences in a variety of contexts, that the observer can come to some understanding of the dynamics of story performance in general within a cultural setting, of the more collective possibilities for subversive, resistant, and critical articulations, a "counter-system" in Ramanujan's terms. A tale **motif** such as the lustful stepmother who tries to seduce her stepson and then cries rape when he rejects her, or the closely related "Potiphar's wife" motif, can be shown to be widespread in South Asian tale tradition (Vatuk, 190–221), and also to hold a very personal saliency in the repertoire of an individual who has directly suffered from such acts, as in "Rajamma's" recounting of the persecution and subsequent disappearance of her beloved son (Kanaka Durga, 100–101).

This depiction of only two major historical points or phases in the development of interpretive strategies for the enormously diverse corpus of South Asian tales entails a cavalier segue from the colonial documentary agenda of the nineteenth and early twentieth centuries to very recent gender-based juxtapositions of individual artistic agency with culturally specific discursive resources and constraints. The currents and crosscurrents of the history of tale-telling over the last 200 years are, of course, still richer and more complex. Perhaps in its ellipsis it makes a good story. It would be prudent, though, to avoid constructing only this generation of scholars as heroes of interpretation. Generations to come will no doubt provide trenchant critiques and advances on recent documentary and interpretive strategies. Yet the admission of individual agency and culturally contexted personal histories into our models for the performance and transmission of traditional narratives has done much to illuminate the dynamic artistry of tale performance. This interpretive advance can be well illustrated by the work of tale interpretation in South Asia, though there remains so much to be done. *See also* Benfey, Theodor; Colonialism; Jātaka; *Kathasaritsagara; Panchatantra*; Persian Tales; *Sukasaptati.*

Further Readings: Ahmad, Aisha, and Roger Boase. *Pashtun Tales from the Pakistan-Afghan Frontier.* London: Saqi Books, 2003; Flueckiger, Joyce B. *Gender and Genre in the Folklore of Middle India.* Ithaca, NY: Cornell University Press, 1996; Frere, Mary. *Hindoo Fairy Legends: Old Deccan Days.* 3rd edition. 1881. New York: Dover, 1967; Kanaka Durga, P. S. "Transformation of Gender Roles: Converging Identities in Personal and Poetic Narratives." *Gender and Story in South India.* Edited by Leela Prasad, Ruth B. Bottigheimer, and Lalita Handoo. Albany: SUNY Press, 2006. 87–140; Knowles, J. Hinton. *Kashmiri Folk Tales.* 1887. Islamabad: Lok Virsa, 1981; Marhoffer-Wolf, Maria. *Frauen und Feen: Entwicklung und Wandel einer Beziehung.* Köln: Rüdiger Köppe, 2002; Mills, Margaret A. *Rhetorics and Politics in Afghan Traditional Storytelling.* Philadelphia: University of Pennsylvania Press, 1991; ———. "Sex Role Reversals, Sex Changes and Transvestite Disguise in the Oral Tradition of a Conservative Muslim Community in Afghanistan." *Women's Folklore, Women's Culture.* Edited by Rosan A. Jordan and Susan J. Kalcik. Philadelphia: University of Pennsylvania Press, 1985. 187–213; Naithani, Sadhana. "Prefaced Space: Tales of the Colonial British Collectors of Indian Folklore." *Imagined States: Nationalism, Longing, and Utopia in Oral Cultures.* Edited by Luisa del Giudice and Gerald Porter. Logan: Utah State University Press, 2001. 64–79; Narasamamba, K. V. S. Lakshmi. "Voiced Worlds: Heroines and Healers in Muslim Women's Narratives." *Gender and Story in South India.* Edited by Leela Prasad, Ruth B. Bottigheimer, and Lalita Handoo. Albany: SUNY Press, 2006. 67–86; Narayan, Kirin, with Urmila Devi Sood. *Mondays on the Dark Night of the Moon: Himalayan Foothill Folktales.* New York: Oxford University Press, 1997; Parker, Barrett, and Ahmad Javid. *A Collection of Afghan Legends.* Kabul: Franklin Press, 1970; Pattanaik, Devdutt. *The Man Who Was a Woman and Other Queer Tales.* New York: Harrington Park Press, 2002; Prasad, Leela. "The Authorial Other in Folktale Collections in Colonial India: Tracing Narration and its Dis/Continuities." *Cultural Dynamics* 15.1 (2003): 5–39; Prasad, Leela, Ruth B. Bottigheimer, and Lalita Handoo, eds. *Gender and Story in South India.* Albany: SUNY Press, 2006; Raheja, Gloria G., and Ann G. Gold. *Listen to the Heron's Words: Reimagining Gender and Kinship in North India.* Berkeley: University of California Press, 1994; Ramanujan, A. K. "Towards a Counter-System: Women's Tales." *Gender, Genre and Power in South Asian Expressive Traditions.* Edited by Arjun Appadurai, Frank J. Korom, and Margaret A. Mills. Philadelphia: University of Pennsylvania Press, 1991. 33–55; Temple, R. C. *The Legends of the Punjab.* 1884. Islamabad: Lok Virsa, 1981; Vatuk, Ved Prakash. *Studies in Indian Folk Traditions.* Delhi: Manohar, 1979; Wadley, Susan. "Folktale." *South Asian Folklore: An Encyclopedia.* Edited by Margaret A. Mills, Peter J. Claus, and Sarah Diamond. New York: Routledge, 2003. 218–20.

Margaret A. Mills

Soviet Fairy-Tale Films

The story of Soviet films in the fairy-tale genre can be sketched largely through the work of Ukrainian director Aleksandr Ptushko (1900–1973) and Russian-Irish director Aleksandr

Rou (1906–73). They were not the only filmmakers working with tales, but they were the most consistent. They used mainly indigenous tales, rather than imported; and they worked in ways complementary to each other, Ptushko being drawn to **folktale**s for a general audience, while Rou specialized in **fairy tale**s for **children**. Their films, and others, present tales from literature and **folklore**, as impacted by revolution, war, political edicts, and issues of national identity.

In 1917, when Ptushko and Rou were still young, the Russian Bolshevik party, led by Lenin, seized power in Moscow. This had manifold consequences, the most far-reaching for cinema being that Lenin judged it the most effective medium for creating revolutionary political consciousness and therefore decided to subsidize and control it. Another was the formation of the Union of Soviet Socialist Republics: fifteen conjoined states, dominated by the biggest one (Russia), each having its own film studios.

Among the Soviet films made in Lenin's lifetime, very few used material from folktales or fairy tales. Then, for a decade after his death in 1924, the Communist Party line on the genre maintained that it was bourgeois rubbish (because, for example, it glorified tsars). Writers and filmmakers consequently dared not touch it.

Rehabilitation came in a speech delivered to the 1934 Soviet Writers' Congress by Maksim Gorky, world-famous author, head of the Writer's Union, and an associate of Stalin (winner of the leadership struggle that had followed Lenin's death). Gorky declared that folklore's Ivans and Vasilisas belonged to the people, were acceptable to the party, and could be used by writers within the established Soviet style: didactic socialist realism.

Against this background, Ptushko spent three years writing and directing *Novy Gulliver* (*The New Gulliver*, 1935), which mixed hundreds of puppets with live action to create a Soviet version of Jonathan Swift's eighteenth-century satire. For this, Ptushko gained the title Honored Artist of the Republic and was put in charge of puppet **animation** at Mosfilm.

There his folktale career started with shorts, notably *Skazka o rybake i rybke* (*The Tale of the Fisherman and the Fish*, 1937), based on an old tale retold by revered Russian poet Aleksandr **Pushkin**, the centenary of whose death was marked that year by official celebrations throughout the USSR. When a fisherman catches a fish that promises to grant any **wish** if allowed to live, the fisherman agrees, insisting he wants nothing in return, but is soundly berated by his wife, who makes him go back with increasingly extravagant requests for wealth and power (see **Fisherman and His Wife**). Always the fish obliges, until the wife demands to be made Empress of the Ocean. At that the fish vanishes—along with everything given to the fisherman and his lazy, greedy wife.

Before the decade was over, Ptushko progressed to a full-length tale, *Zolotoi klyuchik* (*The Golden Key*, 1939), based on a recent Soviet reinterpretation, by Aleksei Tolstoy, of Carlo **Collodi**'s *Pinocchio*. It suited Ptushko's skill in blending puppet and human action, for its main character, Buratino, is a little long-nosed wooden boy, carved by the destitute organ-grinder Pappa Carlo. In a traveling show, Buratino comes up against the evil puppet-master Karabas-Barabas, and through a triumph of collective effort steals his golden key, thereby gaining access to a book full of liberating ideas and a ship on which to escape oppressors.

During these prewar years, Rou too began with a fishy folktale. Following the establishment of the child-oriented production house Soyuzdetfil'm Studio (known since 1948 as the Gorky Film Studio), Rou directed a live-action tale that begins like Ptushko's, then diverges. The difference in *Po shchukhemu velenya* (*By the Pike's Command*, 1938, released in the

West as *The Magic Fish*, 1942) is that the fisherman, Yemelya, is young and single—and does want wishes granted. After a series of magical interventions by the fish, he succeeds in transforming the temper, and winning the hand, of a corrupt Tsar's beautiful daughter.

Rou followed this with *Vasilisa prekrasnaya* (*Vasilisa the Beautiful*, 1939), in which a **father** sends his three sons into the world to find brides. Two return with nice young ladies, but the third, Ivan, brings a frog who claims to have been cursed by an evil serpent, Gorynych. Ivan overcomes great obstacles, including the **witch Baba Yaga**, in a character-building quest to turn his frog into his bride.

Then, while World War II raged in Europe but had not reached Moscow, Rou filmed a literary favorite, Pyotr **Ershov**'s nineteenth-century poem *Konyok gorbunok* (*The Little Humpback Horse*, 1941, released in the West in 1943), with a budget that made color possible for the first time. When a young shepherd, Ivan, frees a beautiful white pony, his reward is a humpback horse which makes up for its physical deficiencies by being able to talk (see **Punishment and Reward**). In the service of a lecherous tsar, Ivan is sent to find the fabled **princess** Silver Morning, and with his horse has adventures on land, under the sea, and in the sky. Upon his return he is jailed for taking so long, but the princess rejects the tsar, preferring Ivan and his horse.

The Nazi invasion of Russia and Ukraine in June 1941, and the subsequent 900-day siege of Leningrad, ended this phase of filmmaking, but started another. *Volshebnoe zerno* (*The Magic Seed*, 1941, directed by Fyodor Filippov and Valentin Kadochnikov) was a generic tale, incorporating traditional **motif**s which presented symbolically the clash between Communism and Nazism. A singing blacksmith gives two peasant children, Maryka and Andreika, a seed which, planted in good soil, will spread universal happiness and freedom. However, the children face a powerful enemy, the **ogre** Karamur, who, through his army of ugly Longnoses, plans to keep the world in a state of subjection and exploitation. With help from a resourceful scientist, a magical flute, and a black slave, the children ultimately defeat Karamur and plant the seed.

In the same vein, Rou's *Kashchei bessmertny* (*Kashchey the Immortal*, 1943) used characters from Russian folklore to stand in for Hitler and Stalin. The film begins with the evil **sorcerer** Kashchei sending his barbaric Black Knights to burn and destroy a peaceful Russian village. Having hidden his soul outside his body, Kashchei believes he can never be killed. However, with help from a **peasant**, the mighty bogatyr' (epic hero) Nikita Kozhemyaka flies on a magic carpet to Kashchei's palace, locates his hidden soul, and decapitates him.

A different kind of result stemming from the invasion was that in October 1941, with the German army nearing Moscow, Russian studios were evacuated to distant republics within the Union. A former mentor of Rou's, Yakov Protazanov, traveled to Uzbekistan, where he found inspiration in the statue of a man on a donkey in Bukhara's town square. Weaving together local stories about that man—**Nasreddin**, a lowly, quick-witted Muslim cleric who, seven centuries before, had protected the weak against a venal emir—Protazanov directed *Nasreddin v Bukhare* (*Nasreddin in Bukhara*, 1943). This was well-received not only within the USSR but also in the West (under the title *Adventures in Bokhara*, 1944).

Outside Moscow, the Nazi invasion was repulsed by the Red Army in December 1941, but Leningrad was not relieved until January 1944; and the conflict continued until the summer of 1945. Around 25 million Soviet citizens had died in what was called the Great Patriotic War, and the party now required opinion-formers to convey, without negativity or ambiguity, the message that the sacrifice had been worthwhile. In the 1930s, a Stalinist dictum had claimed that the citizens of the USSR were born to make fairy tales come true; now the idea to be promulgated was that happy-ever-after had arrived.

Before this edict was published, Ptushko scored a success with his puppetless *Kamenny tsvetok* (*The Stone Flower*, 1946). Based on a 1939 literary version, by Pavel Bazhov, of a miners' tale from the Ural Mountains, it discusses the right use of craftsmanship. Beginning as a fireside tale, it goes back fifty years to an apprentice stonemason, Danila, who fashions a beautiful flower out of malachite but rejects it as imperfect. He leaves his fiancée, Katya, and binds himself to an enchantress, the Lady of Copper Mountain, in whose underground workshop he at last sculpts a perfect flower, only to realize that his happiness lies elsewhere: what he truly wants is to love Katya and contribute to the life of the community.

The message in *The Stone Flower* was not up-to-date, but its validation of labor and society averted criticism. It received a Stalin Prize as one of the best fiction films of 1946, was seen by more Soviet citizens than any other film that year, and won the International Prize for Color at the Cannes Film Festival. This led to its immediate release in the West, where it was welcomed as a relief from the heavy nationalistic politics of the USSR's wartime movies (of all genres).

For a while it was unclear how folktale fairy-tale films could adapt to the party's new line, but gradually ways of tackling the issue emerged. Famed writer Evgeni Shvarts, taking a cue from *The Magic Seed*, developed the concept of "modern fairy tales." His idea was to put new life into old tales by such means as mixing and matching elements from any sources, foregrounding science and art as the only true magic, updating characterization, and invoking the power of the natural world.

An early manifestation of this approach was seen in Shvarts's script for *Zolushka* (**Cinderella**, 1947, directed by Nadezhda Kosheverova and Mikhail Shapiro). Charles **Perrault**'s narrative structure is still there, but with variations. Cinderella is now a shy peasant girl, the daughter of a woodcutter; the characters' dialogue and behavior are idiomatic and modern (the prince delights in throwing paper airplanes at people); and Cinderella's **sisters** are plain and silly rather than ugly and vicious.

In this climate, Ptushko made his most overtly didactic folktale film: *Sadko* (1952). Returning to Novgorod after a decade away, Sadko, a minstrel-sailor, is so appalled by the misery caused by the workers' poverty relative to the merchants' wealth that he vows to take a company to find the Bird of Happiness. An underwater princess helps him obtain ships and money. In India, the company thinks it has found the Bird of Happiness, but it turns out to be a phoenix, which lulls people into forgetting their problems rather than overcoming them. Returning home, the company survives a tempest only when Sadko offers his life to the King of the Ocean, before being again saved by the princess. Back in Novgorod, realizing his quest was misconceived, Sadko kisses the soil and proclaims, directly to the camera: "Here is our happiness!"

Again Ptushko won foreign festival awards, but international distributors, at the height of the Cold War, were more circumspect. In the United States, for example, when *Sadko* was released six years later, it was in a truncated, dubbed, **television**-oriented version retitled *The Magic Voyage of Sinbad* (see **Sindbad**).

Stalin died in 1953, to be succeeded by Nikita Khrushchev, who took a more liberal line in some matters. With a relaxation of centralized control making itself felt, several Soviet republics produced folktale films as part of a reassertion of national identity. In Kiev, Sergei Paradzhanov and Yakov Bazalyan shot *Andriesh* (1954), derived from a Ukrainian tale about a young shepherd whose magic flute helps him conquer wizards and demons. Similarly, *Volshebnaya svirel'* (*The Magic Pipe*, 1954, directed by Aleksandr Zarkhi) tells the story of a Belarusian hero, Nesterka, who defended the poor against oppression. At the end of the decade, Azerbaijani folklore inspired *Na dal'nikh beregakh* (*On the Far Shores*, 1959, directed by Alisettar Atakishiev), which depicts the people's fight against a despotic khan who is blocking their water supply.

Meanwhile, Ptushko was continuing his productive decade. For *Il'ya Muromets* (1956), he went back 1,000 years to a medieval bogatyr' celebrated in old Russian **ballad**s. Paralyzed for three decades, Il'ya is told by pilgrims that the Tugars are threatening Kyiv, and given a special herbal potion that cures him. Gaining superhuman strength, he accepts the sword of the legendary national hero Svyatogor, and a tiny horse, Burushka, which can swim and fly as well as run. For the next twenty years, Il'ya, with his brother-in-arms Alyosha Popovich, defends Rus and serves Prince Vladimir, remaining loyal even when falsely imprisoned. Il'ya's wife bears a son, Little Falcon, who is captured by the Tugars, and grows up to be a valiant fighter, not knowing his mother, and thinking himself the son of the Tugar Khan. The film climaxes with a one-on-one battle between father and son, followed by victory over the Tugars through decapitations of their last line of defense—Gorynich, the three-headed, fire-belching **dragon**. Il'ya orders that the khan be not slain summarily but tried in court by the people; he then hands the sword of Svyatogor to Little Falcon, who vows to use it only to keep Rus free.

With *Muromets*, Ptushko became the first Soviet director to use a wide-screen system, employing this enlarged canvas to show vast numbers of horses and riders galloping into battle, or column after column of shackled women and children being forced into captivity. It was popular in the USSR but too specifically Russian to find much favor in the West. (In the United States four years later, it was given the *Sadko* treatment and released as *The Sword and the Dragon*.)

In the same year as *Muromets*, a "modern tale," *Starik Khottabych* (*Old Khottabych*, 1956, directed by Gennady Kazansky), achieved high popularity. Based on a popular 1930s novel updated by author Lazar Lagin, it creates an **Arabian Nights** situation in 1950s Moscow. When Khottabych, a 3,752-year-old wizard imprisoned in a bottle on a riverbed for 1,000 years, is liberated by a Young Pioneer, Vol'ka, he vows to repay him with all the knowledge and magic at his command. However, Vol'ka is not impressed by Khottabych's gifts: on a flying carpet, he gets too cold; presented with a troupe of elephants, camels, and circus performers, he disdains the idea of becoming a "slave owner"; at a soccer match, he gets angry with Khottabych when he moves the goalposts at one end, thereby bringing undeserved shame on the losing team. Above all, Kottabych creates problems for Vol'ka at school, because his contributions are 1,000 years out of date. Against this, Khottabych begins to appreciate such facets of Soviet life as workers' sanatoria (he mistakes one for a wealthy potentate's palace), electric power, jet travel, and ice cream ("better than the highest sultan's sweetest sherbert"). Realizing Vol'ka does not need his magic, Khottabych asks to be taught modern science, and ends the film with the words: "We shall yet see many miracles!" (Indeed, one year later, the USSR sparked off the Space Race with the United States by sending artificial satellites—Sputniks 1 and 2—into orbit.)

Ptushko also was focusing on technology, but of a less complex kind. For *Sampo* (1959, codirector Holger Harrivirta), a joint production with Finland, he drew on the **Kalevala**, a Nordic myth about the origins of the world. A sampo is a mill that produces gold, salt, and grain. Underlying the struggle (the conflict with Louhi the witch) and the special visual effects (a woman walking on waves, a fire-breathing snake-trampling iron horse, and a talking birch tree) is a story that validates labor and community and ends with faith that a better life is coming.

In the same year, Rou returned to the fairy-tale genre. He chose a modern tale with a script by Shvarts, based on his postwar play *Mariya-iskusnitsa (Maria the Skillful,* also known as *The Magic Weaver,* 1959). An ex-**soldier**, on his way home after a war to become a farmer, shares his food with animals, rescues a bear from a snare, and sings, "Never do anything mean! Keep your honor clean!" Meeting little Ivanushka, sad because an evil water-wizard, the self-styled Vodocrut XIII, has abducted his mother, Maria, the soldier asserts he cannot live in peace while children are weeping. Their quest leads to the bottom of a lake filled with traps and dangers; and when, with help from Vodokrut's granddaughter, they find and rescue Maria, she does not recognize her son, having been brainwashed by the underwater mantra: "Freedom or slavery—it is all one."

The focus of the film is on the character of the soldier, presented as a Soviet everyman hero. He engages the viewer's sympathy by introducing himself, directly to the camera, right at the start. Against the malice and magic that drive the submarine world, he stands for patriotism, honor, economic and political analysis, comradeship, and oneness with nature—the virtue that helps him and the children finally rid the world of Vodokrut and his regime.

For *Korolevstvo krivykh zerkal* (*The Kingdom of Crooked Mirrors*, 1963), Rou took the idea of Lewis **Carroll**'s *Through the Looking-Glass and What Alice Found There* (1871) and gave it a Soviet makeover in a contemporary setting. A girl named Olya falls into a **mirror**, gains valuable knowledge about herself by meeting her reflection, Yalo, and returns home determined to change. In a similar playful yet meaningful style, *Skazka o poteryannom vremeni* (*The Tale of Time Lost*, 1963) was a unique example of Ptushko working in Rou's territory. In a variation on *Vice Versa* (1882), the body-swap story by the English novelist F. Anstey, four decrepit, mischievous sorcerers, desperate to regain youthful vitality, persuade four children to change places with them. At first, the children-in-old-bodies are happy at not having to go to school, but soon wish they could get back the good *young* days.

Rou was back on more familiar ground with *Morozko* (*Grandfather Frost*, 1965), the tale of Nasten'ka, whose virtues and good looks are so resented by her cruel stepmother and ugly stepsister that she is sent to the woods to freeze to death. However, Grandfather Frost, moved to compassion, helps her survive, and makes her rich. Meanwhile, in another part of the forest, a handsome young Ivan is undergoing trials and gaining self-knowledge. Under the title *Jack Frost*, this was released in the West a year later.

At the end of the decade, Rou directed two more modern tales, conceived directly for the screen, about life-changing quests. *Ogon', voda i ... mednye truby* (*Through Fire, Water and ... Brass Pipes*, 1968) even takes its name from a Russian proverb about gaining wisdom by going through tribulations. The hero, Vasya, is gathering wood when he meets the girl of his dreams, Alyonushka, only to see her abducted before his very eyes by Kashchei the Immortal. This film was followed by *Varvara-krasa, dlinnaya kosa* (*Beautiful Barbara with Long Plaits*, also known as *Barbara the Fair with the Silken Hair*, 1969). Co-written by Rou, this centers on a tsar, Eremei, who one day, on a stock-taking trip over his kingdom, is trapped by the underwater tsar, Chudo-Yudo. In return for freedom, Eremei promises Chudo-Yudo anything he owns but does not know he owns. Released, Eremei discovers in horror that, far away, his wife has just given **birth** to a son.

Finally, Rou brought back to the screen the witch Baba Yaga, a folktale favorite who had appeared in many previous productions. In *Zolotye Roga* (*The Golden Horns*, 1972), she kidnaps two little girls and turns them into deer. When their **mother** goes on a desperate quest to find them, the Sun, the Moon, and the Wind help her in various ways.

For the last film with which he was associated, *Finist—yasny sokol* (*Finist—Bright Falcon*), Rou served as co-writer only. *Finist* could have been conceived partly as a tribute to Ptushko, who died early in 1973, just after completing *Ruslan i Lyudmila* (based on Pushkin's epic poem about Ruslan's adventures as he battles to find his bride Lyudmilla, abducted by Chernomor on their wedding day). However, Rou himself died later that same year, so the project was picked up by Gennady Kazansky and—with a dedication to Rou, rather than Ptushko—released in 1975. It starts like a sequel to Ptushko's *Muromets*: under attack by the powerful Kartaus, Russians turn to the young warrior Bright Falcon, confident he will protect them. However, Kartaus, skilled in witchcraft as well as military arts, turns Finist into a hideous, hairy beast, using a spell which can be broken only if a beautiful girl falls in love with him. At the climax, Finist defeats Kartaus in a mighty battle. Mixed with the action and magic is a leavening of comedy, music, and dance that characterizes this as ultimately from the school of Rou, not Ptushko.

After the passing of these two Aleksandrs, the last years of Soviet folktale and fairy-tale films featured a strong component of non-Soviet source material, often as the basis for international coproductions and further nationalistic flowerings in some of the republics.

Hans Christian **Andersen** tales figured prominently among the imported material. In *Rusalochka* (*The Little Mermaid*, 1976, directed by Vladimir Bychkov), a coproduction with Bulgaria, Andersen himself was inserted into the narrative as one of the characters; *Printsessa na goroshine* (*The Princess on the Pea*, 1977, directed by Boris Rytsarev) incorporated "The Swineherd" and other Andersen motifs to expand the original two-page story into an eighty-seven-minute film; and *Solovei* (*Nightingale*, 1980, directed by Nadezhda Kosheverova) integrated two stories—"The Emperor's Nightingale" and "The Emperor's New Clothes"—that show autocrats as vain and weak. Another foreign source was the Belgian Maurice **Maeterlinck**, author of a well-known symbolist play that prompted a union unthinkable in earlier decades: the USSR and the United States combined to produce, in Russian studios, a lavish version of *Sinyaya ptitsa* (*The Blue Bird*, 1976, directed by George Cukor), with Elizabeth Taylor as Maternal Love, Jane Fonda as The Night, and Cicely Tyson as The **Cat**.

Among the films based on national folklore was the Uzbek *Semurg* (1972, Chabibullah Faisijew), in which the eponymous magical bird helps a young herdsman, Bunjad, overthrow the destructive wizard Jalmagys. Two years later, the Georgian *Ivane Kotorashvilis ambavi* (*The Legend of Ivan Kotorashvili*, 1974, directed by Nodar Mangadze) presented an eighteenth-century peasant whose patriotism is so strong that he single-handedly defeats a horde of invaders. In the final decade of the Soviet Union, Kazakhstan contributed *Boisya, vrag, devyatogo syna* (*Enemy, Beware the Ninth Son*, 1984, directed by Viktor Pusurmanov and Viktor Chugunov), which brought to the screen the mighty sorcerer Tasbol, who spreads misery and misfortune throughout the land until, as prophesied, he is vanquished by the ninth son of a herdsman.

One of the last Soviet films in the genre, *Spriditis* (1985, directed by Gunars Piesis) came from a Baltic republic showing the same spirit as those in Asia. A coproduction between Riga and Prague, adapted from a 1903 play by the Latvian writer Anna Brigadere, it is about a much-loved hero who has become a symbol of the Latvian nation. The film shows how, because of a nasty stepmother, he travels far, with his spade over his shoulder, determined to find the Land of Happiness. For a while he works with the Mother of Winds and the Mother of Woods; they pay him, but not the fortune he desires. After overcoming a giant and a miser, he is promised half a kingdom and a whole princess if he rids a castle of its **devil**. He succeeds, but the **king** cheats him, so he returns to the place of his birth, having learned that the Land of Happiness is nowhere else than home.

With the breakup of the Soviet Union on December 26, 1991, subsidized production, already dwindling, ended. Films now had to make their own financial way in the world. However, the heroes and heroines of earlier years were not forgotten; they simply switched genres. The ruler served by Il'ya Muromets is *Knyaz' Vladimir* (*Prince Vladimir*, Russia, 2000, directed by Yury Batanin), an animated feature that presents Vladimir's Christianisation of Russia not as myth but as fact-based history. Later, Ily'a's brother-in-arms was the animated hero of *Alyosha Popovich i Tugarin Zmei* (*Alesha Popovich and Tugarin the Serpent*, Russia, 2004, directed by Konstantin Bronzit), an adventure in which Alesha, having failed to save his town from destruction, goes on a redemptive quest with his fiancée, grandmother, long-suffering donkey, and talkative horse. And in the teen comedy *Khottabych* (Russia, 2006, directed by Pyotr Tochilin), the now 3,802-year-old genie has to come to terms with the age of the **Internet**. *See also* DEFA Fairy-Tale Films; Film and Video.

Further Readings: Balina, Marina, Helena Goscilo, and Mark Lipovetsky, eds. *Politicizing Magic: An Anthology of Russian and Soviet Fairy Tales.* Evanston, IL: Northwestern University Press, 2005; Berger, Eberhard, and Joachim Giera, eds. *77 Märchenfilme: Ein Filmführer für jung und alt.* Berlin: Henschel, 1990; Figes, Orlando. *Natasha's Dance: A History of Cultural Russia.* London: Penguin Books, 2002; Leyda, Jan. *Kino: A History of the Russian and Soviet Film.* London: Allen and Unwin, 1960; *Screen for Children.* Special issue of *Soviet Film* (April 1974).

Terry Staples

Spanish Tales

Spanish storytellers have played an important role in shaping folktales from many different sources, giving them the stamp of their culture, and carrying them to the far reaches of the Spanish Empire. Their stories correspond to the **tale type**s that Antti **Aarne** and Stith **Thompson** described in their classification of European folktales. Spanish, English, German, and North American **collectors** have recorded the stories that circulated in **oral tradition** and published them in many collections. Scholars have found numerous parallels between oral folktales and Spanish **novel**s and plays.

One of the earliest sources for written versions of oral folktales is the *Libro de los Gatos* (*Book of Cats*), a manuscript hidden for many years in the Biblioteca Nacional de Madrid. The manuscript contains sixty-six pieces of folklore written down by anonymous authors who used language typical of the period from 1350 to 1400. Scholars have raised questions about the origin of the folktales in this collection since the same stories are found in a Latin manuscript written by the English monk Odo of Cheriton.

One folktale in the *Libro de los Gatos* is the story of "The Two Companions," a **variant** of the tale type that folklorists call The Two Travelers (ATU 613). The story may have circulated in Spanish oral tradition in the late 1300s because of its great antiquity and widespread geographical distribution. According to Stith Thompson, this story probably

"The Tale of the Two Travelers." Drawing by Beatrice Taggart from *The Bear and His Sons: Masculinity in Spanish and Mexican Folktales* by James Taggart. [Copyright © 1997. By permission of the University of Texas Press.]

originated in Asia, appeared in the Middle East, and then entered into European oral tradition. Thompson also noted that it was found in Buddhist, Hindu, Jaina, and Hebrew literature as well as the **Arabian Nights**, Gaimbattista **Basile**'s *Lo cunto de li cunti* (*The Tale of Tales*, 1634–36), and Jacob and Wilhelm **Grimm**'s *Kinder- und Hausmärchen* (*Children's and Household Tales*, 1812–15). It appears in the repertoires of many contemporary storytellers in Spain.

The Two Travelers is usually a story of a good and a bad brother, and in the version that appears in the *Libro de los Gatos*, apes, who may have represented dark-skinned Moors, blind and banish the good brother in the wilderness. In later variants, the Moors drop out of the story, which turns into a **parable** of a rich but envious brother who sends his poor brother into the wilderness. The poor brother reemerges a wealthy man because he foils the plot of demons to cause a plague, hide the water supply of a town, or cause discord in a married couple, and earns a handsome reward. The rich but envious brother goes into the same part of the wilderness, where the demons tear him to pieces.

Spaniards also reworked the ancient story of Jason and Medea, turning it into the folktale of "Blancaflor," or "White Flower," with a happier ending. In the play that Euripides wrote in the fifth century BCE, Jason betrays Medea after she had given him her love, helped him obtain the golden fleece, killed her brother while escaping from her family, and bore him two beautiful sons. Medea kills her sons in response to Jason's treachery. According to Grace Knopp, Spanish storytellers probably adopted this tale from the Romans during their occupation of the Iberian Peninsula and reshaped it by adding the episode of "The Forgotten Fiancée," giving the story a happy ending. In this episode, Blancaflor uses her magic to make her lover remember all that she did for him just as he is about to marry another woman.

Spanish tellers also have shaped the well-known story of "The **Bear's Son**," which has many parallels with the Anglo-Saxon **epic** poem *Beowulf* from the eighth century CE. As a folktale, the story is a metaphor for male socialization and tells how an unruly boy becomes a man after he shows his courage and defeats the **devil**. Versions of this story collected during the last two centuries combine the Christian idea of redemption with Spanish gallantry.

What is known about Spanish folktales comes from their publication in collections that appeared long after the anonymous authors wrote the items of **folklore** contained in the *Libro de los Gatos*. Ralph Boggs identified three major periods in the publication of Spanish folktales. The first period occurred in the mid-1800s, when Fernán Caballero (the pseudonym of Cecilia **Böhl de Faber**) and other Spaniards wrote down stories they had heard from oral storytellers. The second period was in the 1880s, when Spaniards organized folklore societies and published journals containing folktales. The third period was in the 1920s, when Constantino Cabal and Aurelio de Llano Roza de Ampudia published their collections of folktales from Asturias.

These three periods were a time of **nationalism** in Europe, when many looked to the **folk** to find evidence of a national culture. However, Spaniards were also experiencing the end of an empire that stretched at one time from the Americas to the Philippines. The efforts of Spaniards to write down the folktales of the rural storytellers immediately preceded and followed the Generation of '98, a group of writers who tried to find the soul of Spain in the small towns and villages of the Spanish countryside.

Soon after the War of 1898, North Americans of Spanish ancestry took a great interest in Spanish folktales. One of these was Aurelio M. **Espinosa**, who was born in the San Luis Valley of southern Colorado. Espinosa began his scholarly career studying dialectology among the Spanish speakers or Hispanos who lived in the San Luis Valley. In 1910, he became a professor of Romance languages at Stanford University, where he trained a generation of scholars who carried out many important projects on Spanish folktales in Spain and in the Americas. In 1920, he obtained a grant from the American Philosophical Society to travel to Spain, where he collected many folktales in the Castilian-speaking regions of that country. His three-volume collection of folktales, *Cuentos populares españoles* (*Spanish Popular Tales*, 1923–26), was an extremely important source for Ralph Boggs's *Index of Spanish Folktales*, published in 1930.

Espinosa was primarily interested in folktales for their literary value rather than as cultural documents. Therefore, he did not include the names or any other information about the storytellers in his collection. Moreover, he wrote the tales in proper, readable Spanish rather than according to how storytellers actually speak their language. In this respect, Espinosa was like many of the Spaniards who collected and published tales during the three periods of Spanish folktale publishing. Boggs complained that he found few tales of "high scientific value" in those published collections. Exceptions include the collections by Aurelio de Llano Roza de Ampudia.

However, a later generation of Spaniards, who came along after Boggs compiled and published his index, tried to correct this. Marciano Curiel Merchán published *Cuentos extreme-os* (*Tales from the Frontier*, 1944), a collection of folktales from Cáceres and Badajóz; Arcadia de Larrea Palacín published another collection with tales from Cádiz, *Cuentos gaditanos: Cuentos populares de Andalucia* (*Gaditan Tales: Popular Tales of Andalusia*, 1959); and Luis Cortés Vazquez published tales from Leon, Galica, and Salamanca in *Leyenda, cuentos y romances de Sanadria* (*Legends, Tales, and Romances of Sanadria*, 1976) and *Cuentos populares salmantinos* (*Salamancan Popular Tales*, 1979). These collectors provided more information about the storytellers and took pains to represent the spoken language. Consequently, their collections have more value as documents of Spanish culture.

The publication of folktale collections with more information about the storytellers enables scholars to understand more completely how storytellers represent their personal experience in accord with their culture. These later collections were particularly useful in James M. Taggart's *Enchanted Maidens*, a study of the way that men and women in Cáceres tell the same stories differently. Cáceres **women** and men tell many stories that are regional variants of widespread European folktales, but they tell them in particular ways and in accord with their position in their communities and with their ideas about femininity and masculinity. Marciano Curiel Merchán, Arcadio de Larrea Palacín, and Luis Cortés Vázquez, along with earlier collectors such as Aurelio de Llano Roza de Ampudia, provided sufficient information on storytellers to enable one to see if **gender** patterns in one region run through stories from other areas of Castilian-speaking Spain.

The woman's point of view emerges clearly in female versions of "**Snow White**" and "**Cinderella**." Neither of these stories probably originated in Spain, but Spanish women tell them often and give them their own flavor. In the case of "Snow White," women storytellers protect the images of the older woman. They often describe the older woman as unconcerned about her own beauty but promoting her own daughter's at the expense of her stepdaughter. Unlike men, women do not include Snow White's **mother** or stepmother consulting a magic **mirror** to find out if she is the most beautiful woman in the world. Only Spanish men do this, and they play up the rivalry between an older woman and a younger one in accord with their own ideas about sexual competition. The tendency for women to protect the image of the older woman fits a family structure wherein mothers and daughters have close relationships. In many parts of rural Spain, married women prefer to live with or near their mothers.

When telling "Cinderella," Spanish men idealize women by describing the heroine as always beautiful. Women express skepticism about men who fall in love with them for their beauty. In both male and female stories, Cinderella attracts the attention of the prince because she has a star on her forehead, is naturally beautiful, or wears beautiful dresses. As the anthropologist Julian Alfred Pitt-Rivers noted for rural Andalusia, men court women by paying them compliments in the hope of creating the aura of romantic love, called the illusion or *la ilusión* in Spanish. Women represent those compliments as tokens of love the prince gives to Cinderella at the ball. The women narrators express their concern about whether the men really know who they are by adding a long episode in which Cinderella, wearing unflattering clothing, returns the tokens. She places them in the soups or custards she serves to the prince, who is ailing because he longs for the beautiful woman he met at the ball. Cinderella's aim is to have him recognize her in other than beautiful form before she consents to marriage.

The stories of Spanish origin that the colonialists brought to many parts of the Americas enable one to place the Spanish stories in a broader perspective. Some of the particular features of the Spanish stories that emerge when placed next to the Spanish-American stories are related to courtship and marriage. Spanish women are fond of telling stories like "The Clever Maiden," who outwits a thief by cutting off his hand when he tries to enter her house. The women tell many of these stories to encourage maidens to maintain their premarital chastity. This group of stories has had little appeal in those parts of the Americas where women marry at a young age.

A number of authors of classic works of Spanish literature have made use of folktales. Miguel de Cervantes Saavedra included the sketch of one oral tale in his famous *Don Quixote* (1605–15), and Calderón de la Barca, Tirso de Molina, and Alarcón y Moreto used oral folktales in their plays. In nineteenth-century Spain, the **literary fairy tale** emerged. These stories—which ranged from adaptations of oral tales to **wonder tale**s and stories of the supernatural and fantastic—were produced by well-known writers such as Pedro Antonio de Alarcón, Cecilia Böhl de Faber, Gustavo Adolfo **Bécquer**, Luis **Coloma**, Juan Eugenio **Hartzenbusch**, Antonio de **Trueba**, Juan **Valera**, and Benito **Pérez Galdós**. The tradition continued into the twentieth century with fairy-tale writings by Concha **Castroviejo**, Aurora Mateos, Carmen **Martín Gaite**, and others. In the realm of cinema, filmmaker Pedro Almodóvar updated the classic tale of "Sleeping Beauty" in his **film** *Hable con ella* (*Talk to Her*, 2002), a clever and subtle adaptation that critiques contemporary society.

Fairy tales have also moved from literary to oral tradition, such as the story of "**Beauty and the Beast**." Jeanne-Marie **Leprince de Beaumont**'s French version of 1756 has become an important oral story in several Spanish villages in the provinces of Cáceres, Salamanca, and Soria. Spanish storytellers sometimes combine "Beauty and the Beast" with the closely related tale of "**Cupid and Psyche**." Women tend to tell "Beauty and the Beast" in different ways to describe what it means to make the transition to marriage. *See also* Latin American Tales; North American Tales.

Further Readings: Boggs, Ralph. *Index of Spanish Folktales.* Helsinki: Academia Scientiarum Fennica, 1930; Darbord, Bernard. *Libro de los gatos: Édition avec introduction et notes.* Paris: Klincksieck, 1984; Espinosa, Aurelio M. *The Folklore of Spain in the American Southwest: Traditional Spanish Folk Literature in Northern New Mexico and Southern Colorado.* Edited by J. Manuel Espinosa. Norman: University of Oklahoma Press, 1985; Fedorchek, Robert M., trans. *Stories of Enchantment from Nineteenth-Century Spain.* Lewisburg: Bucknell University Press, 2002; Jiménez y Hurtado, M. *Cuentos españoles contenidos en las produccíones dramáticas de Calderón de la Barca, Tirso de Molina, Alarcón y Moreto.* Madrid: Suarez, 1881; Knopp, Grace. "The Motifs of the 'Jason and Medea Myth' in Modern Tradition (A Study of Märchentypus 313)." Dissertation. Stanford University, 1933; Novoa, Adriana. "Whose Talk Is It? Almodóvar and the Fairy Tale in *Talk to Her.*" *Marvels & Tales* 19 (2005): 224–48; Pitt-Rivers, Julian Alfred. *The People of the Sierra.* 1961. Chicago: University of Chicago Press, 1966; Soliño, María Elena. *Women and Children First: Spanish Women Writers and the Fairy Tale Tradition.* Potomac, MD: Scripta Humanistica, 2002; Taggart, James M. *The Bear and His Sons: Masculinity in Spanish and Mexican Folktales.* Austin: University of Texas Press, 1997; ———. *Enchanted Maidens: Gender Relations in Spanish Folktales of Courtship and Marriage.* Princeton, NJ: Princeton University Press, 1990; Thompson, Stith. *The Folktale.* 1946. Berkeley: University of California Press, 1977.

James M. Taggart

Spell. *See* Incantation

Spiegelman, Art (1948–)

An American comic artist and writer well known for his series Maus (1986 and 1991), Art Spiegelman has also produced a number of folktale **adaptation**s as part of his Little Lit series (2000–). Spiegelman's work has ranged over the years from obscure adult comics to serious comic histories to **children's literature**.

While Spiegelman began working in the 1960s and 1970s as a contributor to alternative comic series such as *Real Pulp* and *Young Lust*, his first major exposure came in 1986 with the publication of his first book in the series of Maus, *Maus: A Survivor's Tale.* In this work, Spiegelman adapted his father's experiences in Poland during the period leading up to World War II into a comic-book form. The series was notable partially for Spiegelman's portrayal of humans as anthropomorphic animals, with mice standing in for Jews, **cat**s for Germans, and **pig**s for Poles. Spiegelman drew on the notion of **animal tale**s and used animals as metaphors for human behaviors. The relationship between Nazis and Jews was metaphorically outlined through the relationship between cats and mice. Spiegelman continued this series in 1991 with *Maus: A Survivor's Tale II; And Here My Troubles Began.* This second volume received critical acclaim, and the **graphic novel** collections have remained in print since the early 1990s.

Spiegelman's next foray into work based on **folklore** came in 2000 with *Little Lit: Folklore & Fairy Tale Funnies,* the first volume of his Little Lit series. In this large-format book, Spiegelman and his wife Françoise Mouly gathered a number of comic adaptations of folktales, **fable**s, and fairy tales. Primarily humorous, these adaptations are designed for children and include several different styles of modern folktale adaptation.

Spiegelman's own "Prince Rooster: A Hasidic Parable," Walt Kelly's "The Gingerbread Man," Barbara McClintock's "The Princess and the Pea," Lorenzo Mattotti's "The Two Hunchbacks," and David Mazzucchelli's "The Fisherman and the Sea Princess" are all direct retellings of folktales. William Joyce's "Humpty Trouble," Daniel Clowes's "The Sleeping Beauty," and David Macauly's "Jack and the Beanstalk" all represent adaptations of familiar folkloric material in a humorous context. Joost Swarte's "The Leafless Tree," Kaz's "The Hungry Horse," and Harry Bliss's "The Baker's Daughter" represent modernized adaptations of traditional tales.

In interviews, Spiegelman described this project as an attempt to introduce young people to folklore, which he considers a strong influence on his own work. What is notable about this collection overall are the ways in which Spiegelman's prior work shows through. The stories are illustrated in bizarre and occasionally grotesque ways, which bears strong similarities to Spiegelman's work in the 1980s on the Garbage Pail Kids, a series of humorous collectible stickers, and to his work in independent comics, including the well-known *Raw.* This combination is evident in the artists chosen, half of whom come from independent comics and half from children's **illustration**.

Spiegelman's Little Lit series has continued with two additional volumes. While these subsequent volumes have moved away from the folktale format, they retain some folkloric connections. As the series continues, Spiegelman has indicated interest in publishing more folklore for children. *See also* Cartoons and Comics.

Further Readings: Spiegelman, Art, and Françoise Mouly, eds. *Folklore & Fairy Tale Funnies.* Little Lit. New York: HarperCollins, 2000; Wilner, Arlene Fish. "'Happy, Happy Ever After': Story and History in Art Spiegelman's *Maus.*" *Considering* Maus: *Approaches to Art Spiegelman's "Survivor's Tale" of the Holocaust.* Edited by Deborah R. Geis. Tuscaloosa: University of Alabama Press, 2003. 105–21.

B. Grantham Aldred

Spinning

Preindustrial societies, especially those in colder climates, dedicated substantial labor and material resources into the making of **clothing**. Beginning with sheep shearing and flax harvesting, there was a chain of arduous tasks: washing, carding, spinning, dying, weaving, cutting, and stitching; and, traditionally, these fell largely to **women**. Survivals of this process depicted in folktales suggest that spinning was the most tedious of these tasks.

The importance of spinning among women's household duties is reflected in countless linguistic, mythological, and folkloric sources. In English, the word "distaff" (designating a device for holding the fiber to be spun) has evolved into a synonym for "female," as in the expression "distaff side of the family," meaning one's **mother** and her blood relatives. The Germanic goddess Frigg (Odin's wife) was associated with spinning and is said to have spun the clouds. In Sweden, the constellation Orion's Belt is called *Friggerock* (Frigg's Distaff). Following Scandinavia's conversion to Christianity, it was given a secondary name, Mary's Distaff, a designation also used in Scotland.

In southern Europe, the Greek goddess Athena and her Roman counterpart Minerva were patrons of women's crafts, including spinning. Furthermore, Greek **myth**s about the three Moirae (Fates) turned spinning into a metaphor for human destiny: Clotho spun the thread of life from her distaff; Lachesis drew out the thread and measured it; then finally Atropos cut the thread, determining the manner of one's **death**.

Fittingly, spinning has become a symbol for **storytelling**, with the expression "to spin a yarn" being a synonym for "to tell a story." The connection between spinning and storytelling is beautifully illustrated in the frontispiece to Charles **Perrault**'s pioneering *Histoires ou contes du temps passé* (*Stories or Tales of Times Past*, 1697), with its well-crafted **illustration** of an old woman seated before a fireside while spinning and telling stories to three children at her feet.

Given the importance of female work for the well-being of a **family**, it is natural that numerous folktales evolved describing pragmatic bridal tests used by a suitor to select an efficient and diligent wife. Such tests normally involve practical household skills, most prominently spinning. Tales of type ATU 1451, The Thrifty Girl, offer good examples. "Die Schlickerlinge" ("The Leftovers"), as recorded in **Kinder- und Hausmärchen** (*Children's and Household Tales*, 1812–15) by Jacob and Wilhelm **Grimm**, is characteristic. A man is about to marry a woman unskilled at spinning when he notices another woman wearing a dress made from bits and pieces of flax left over from the bride's wasteful spinning. Impressed with the new woman's skill, he abandons his fiancée and forthwith marries the woman who spins efficiently.

Another bridal test is depicted in tales of type ATU 1453, Key in Flax Reveals Laziness. For example, "The Hidden Key," published in *Swedish Folktales and Legends* (1993) by Lone Thygesen Blecher and George Blecher, tells how a suitor visiting a potential fiancée hides the key to her chest in the unspun flax on her spinning wheel. Three weeks later, he returns and is told that the key cannot be found. Now knowing that the would-be bride spins very little, he quickly turns his **marriage** quest elsewhere.

The widely distributed tale of the type known as The Lazy Spinning Woman (ATU 1405) describes in its various forms different ways that women try to avoid the task of spinning, for which they are at the least censured and possibly severely punished—even disowned. Richard Chase's Appalachian tale "Sam and Sooky," as recorded in his *Grandfather Tales* (1948), is typical of its European forebears. Sam's new wife Sooky did not learn to card and spin as a girl. Now a married woman and attempting these tasks for the first time, she becomes frustrated with the carding combs and the spinning wheel and throws them into the fire. Sam says nothing. Later, Sam goes to work in the woods while Sooky sets out to pick wild berries. Stepping into a briar patch, she accidentally tears off her skirt. Looking down at her uncovered legs, she does not recognize herself; she then runs to Sam and asks him where Sooky is. He answers, "At home," to which she replies, "If Sooky is at home, then I'm not Sooky," and she wanders off, apparently never to return. Thus, the lazy wife not only loses her husband and home, but her very identity as well.

In addition to their entertainment value, the tales discussed thus far function as **cautionary tale**s, warning young women about the dire consequences of failing to be a good household worker. Not all folktales about spinning are negative, portraying only unskilled or lazy spinners and their attendant bad luck. Some tales stress the positive side by showing how diligence can bring good fortune.

One such **didactic tale** about women's domestic labor is "Spindel, Weberschiffchen und Nadel" ("Spindle, Shuttle, and Needle," ATU 585) from the Grimms' collection. In this story, an industrious orphan girl supports herself through spinning, weaving, and sewing. One day, her spindle miraculously dances away, leaving a trail of golden thread, until it comes to the **king**, who is passing through the village searching for a bride. Next, the shuttle escapes, weaving a carpet as it runs; and the needle flies about her room, magically covering everything with beautiful cloth and curtains. Drawn by the thread from the spindle, the king appears at her door and asks the young spinster to marry him. Honoring the **magic object**s that led the king to his bride, he preserves the spindle, shuttle, and needle in the royal treasure chamber. Although not specifically stated, this last act suggests that the new **queen**, now freed from her accustomed tasks, will henceforth have no need for these implements. This story thus offers hope, if only in the realm of **fantasy**, that through diligence and toil any young woman can gain a fairy-tale marriage and freedom from further household duties.

An important function of storytelling is fantasy escape, and a number of folktale types provide for their listeners a vicarious release from the drudgery of spinning by giving their heroines permanent relief from such work. Foremost among these is **tale type** ATU 501, The Three Old Spinning Women. A version from Kentucky, "The Girl That Weren't Ashamed to Her Own Kin," as recorded by Marie Campbell in her *Tales from the Cloud Walking Country* (1958), is typical of its many European counterparts. A woman is scolding her daughter for her inability to spin, weave, and sew. The king overhears the dispute and enquires about the problem. Ashamed to admit the truth, the mother claims that she is chastising the girl for wanting to spin, weave, and sew all the time. Impressed with her purported industry, the king decides at once to take the girl home as a bride for his son, the **prince**. But before the wedding can take place, the bride-to-be must prove herself, and on three successive days she is put into a room with a large quantity of wool to spin, weave, and sew into garments. Three mysterious old women appear and do the work for her. Each has an ugly deformity: respectively a wide thumb, a big foot, and a fat lip; and each asks as her only payment to be invited to the girl's wedding. The work is accomplished, the wedding takes place, and the three women appear. The bride welcomes them, then the prince asks about their deformities, to which they reply that their oversized parts come from spinning, weaving, and sewing. The horrified prince proclaims that his bride will never again have to do such work.

This story thus functions as the ultimate fantasy escape tale. An ordinary girl fails to meet her family's and the community's expectations with respect to spinning, weaving, and sewing, and as a direct result—through the intervention of **magic helper**s and a generous portion of good luck—she ends up with the ultimate fairy-tale reward: marriage to a prince, and all this with the added bonus of her husband's vow that she will be spared these tasks in the future. Such stories follow a formula exactly opposite to the one set by traditional cautionary tales, where the leading character receives direct **punishment** for unacceptable behavior.

Arguably, the best known of all folktales about spinning are those of type ATU 500, The Name of the Supernatural Helper, and most famous of all is the Grimm brothers' version,

"Rumpelstilzchen." Ironically, in this popular tale's first printed version (1812), there is no mention of spinning. The heroine's father boasts that his daughter knows how to "transform straw into gold," with no mention of an implement to be used. Only in the second edition of Grimms' collection (1819) is the act of spinning introduced. Indeed, spinning plays no role in a number of **variant**s of ATU 500 tales, in which the heroine, through various circumstances—most often beyond her control—comes under the power of a sinister being and then frees herself by discovering his or her name. However, help with spinning is central in many such tales, and this is the form most familiar to storytellers today.

Versions of ATU 500 are told throughout Europe, often as **legend**s containing elements that ask for the reader's belief. A common element is the unusual form of the supernatural helper's name, for example, Nägendümer (Germany), Purzinigele (Austria), Silly go Dwt (Wales), Titteli Ture (Sweden), Tom Tit Tot (England), and Whuppity Stoorie (Scotland). An additional shared feature is the role that luck plays in the threatened woman's discovery of the secret name. In virtually all such tales, the name is learned through a chance encounter with the sprite, sometimes by the heroine herself; often by her husband, who reports what he has seen and heard without knowing its significance; and sometimes by a third party. But however the information comes to her, the heroine immediately senses its importance and uses it both effectively and with a flair for drama.

Gaining control over a supernatural being by pronouncing his or her name is a belief shared by many ancient cultures. Other primeval beliefs and customs concerning spinning survived well into the nineteenth century. In an appendix to his *Deutsche Mythologie* (1835; translated as *Teutonic Mythology*, 1883), Jacob Grimm lists more than 1,000 numbered superstitions from northern Europe, including dozens of beliefs regulating spinning. Among other prescriptions, these superstitions promoted child labor, for example: "A person will have good luck if he is wearing a shirt that is made from thread spun by a girl younger than seven years" (no. 115), and: "A shirt spun by a girl between five and seven years old is protection against magic" (no. 656).

Furthermore, a number of superstitions regulated the spinning on certain days, beliefs that are reflected in folktales. Foremost among these was the prohibition against leaving unspun fiber on the wheel over Sundays or religious holidays. Exemplary in this regard is the German legend "Die Frau Holle und die Flachsdiesse" ("**Mother Holle** and the Distaff"), as recorded by August Ey in his *Harzmärchenbuch* (*Harz Fairy-Tale Book*, 1862). Two **sisters**—one industrious and the other lazy—sit spinning the day before Easter. The lazy one quits early, leaving unspun flax on her distaff, and then goes out to amuse herself at the Easter Eve celebration. The industrious sister continues to work until 11:00 P.M., when Frau Holle, carrying a silver distaff like a magic wand, bursts into the room and blesses her. The next morning, the diligent sister discovers that her old wooden spinning wheel has been replaced by a new one of shining gold. The lazy sister finds that, during the night, her flax has been transformed into straw, and her chest is now filled with chopped straw instead of the linen cloth that had been there.

Not all **folklore** encourages relentless spinning. Numerous superstitions prohibit spinning under certain circumstances. For example, in Jacob Grimm's aforementioned collection of superstitions, the belief is recorded that "if a woman spins wool, hemp, or flax within six weeks of her confinement, her child will someday be hanged" (no. 240). This superstition spared a recently delivered woman the task of spinning, not for her own sake but for the protection of her child. In apparent contradiction to the above tale about Mother Holle, many superstitions prohibited spinning on specific days, especially Christian holy days. Numerous cautionary tales warn of the consequences of such sacrilegious labor.

In some instances, these tales derive from pre-Christian times. An excellent example is the story "Friday," collected by Aleksandr **Afanas'ev** and recorded in W. R. S. Ralston's *Russian Folk-Tales* (1873). A woman fails to pay due reverence to Mother Friday, and she spends the day spinning. That night, Mother Friday storms into the woman's room, picks up a handful of dust from the recently spun flax, and pokes it into the sinner's eyes. The next morning, the injured woman promises never again to dishonor Mother Friday, and that night, the latter returns and heals the repentant woman's eyes. The tale's final sentence affirms the **moral** of the story: "It's a great sin to dishonor Mother Friday—combing and spinning flax, forsooth!" The Mother Friday featured in this tale is undoubtedly a survival of a pre-Christian Slavic goddess akin to Venus or Frigg (or possibly Freyja), the Roman and Germanic goddesses who gave their names to the day Friday in western European languages.

Another spinning tale, this one from Germany with apparent heathen roots, is Bernhard Baader's "Spinne nicht in der Nacht vor Fronfasten" ("Do Not Spin in the Night before Ember Day") from his *Neugesammelte Volkssagen aus dem Lande Baden* (*Newly Collected Folk Legends from the Land of Baden*, 1859). At 11:00 P.M. just before an Ember Day (one of three specific fast days at the beginning of each season, formally set apart by Pope Gregory VII in the eleventh century), a woman is still spinning when a mysterious woman bursts into her room. She gives the spinner a dozen spools, demanding that they all be spun full before midnight. The frightened woman runs to her priest for counsel. He advises her to spin three threads around each spool, in the name of the Father, the Son, and the Holy Ghost. This she does, finishing at the strike of twelve. Immediately afterward, the sinister figure returns for the spools, saying, "You did well to follow Black-Coat's advice; otherwise you would have seen what I would have done to you!" With this she departs. *See also* The Kind and the Unkind Girls.

Further Readings: Ashliman, D. L. *The Name of the Helper.* 2006. http://www.pitt.edu/~dash/type0500.html; Bottigheimer, Ruth B. "Spinning and Discontent." *Grimms' Bad Girls and Bold Boys: The Moral and Social Vision of the Tales.* New Haven, CT: Yale University Press, 1987. 112–22; Clodd, Edward. *Tom Tit Tot: An Essay on Savage Philosophy in Folk-Tale.* London: Duckworth and Company, 1898; Tatar, Maria. "Spinning Tales: The Distaff Side." *The Hard Facts of the Grimms' Fairy Tales.* 2nd edition. Princeton, NJ: Princeton University Press, 2003. 106–33; Zipes, Jack. "Rumpelstiltskin and the Decline of Female Productivity." *Fairy Tale as Myth/Myth as Fairy Tale.* Lexington: University Press of Kentucky, 1994. 49–71.

D. L. Ashliman

Splash (1984)

Directed by Ron Howard, *Splash* is a romantic comedy about a **mermaid** and a man. *Splash* was the inaugural release of Touchstone Pictures, The **Walt Disney Company**'s first adult-oriented movie division, and its subject matter originally suggested Touchstone's connection with Disney. Along with Disney's animated *The Little Mermaid* (1989), *Splash* today is invoked as evidence of the corporation's ongoing investment in fairy tales, an interest first demonstrated in Walt **Disney**'s early film adaptations. Yet *Splash* is no more than a loose adaptation of Hans Christian **Andersen**'s "The Little Mermaid," notably eliminating Andersen's emphasis on the costs and consequences of the mermaid's human transformation to create a conventional Hollywood romance.

Splash begins in flashback, with a young boy's encounter with a mermaid. Twenty years later, the drowning Allen Bauer (Tom Hanks) is rescued by the same mermaid (Daryl Hannah). During their initial land encounter, in which the mermaid appears naked but with legs, the two fall in love. The mermaid then tracks Allen to New York where, because her tail appears as legs when dry, she passes as a beautiful, exotic woman who calls herself Madison.

Markedly deviating from Andersen's story, *Splash* minimizes the mermaid's decision to become human to heightens an opposites-attract romance. Madison suffers no pain in her transformation, does not lose her voice but easily learns to speak English, and does not appear to abandon relationships with other merpeople. Instead, most of the film's comic moments and romantic tensions derive from either Madison's otherness, in repeated attempts to hide her tail and conform to the human world, or Allen's ignorance of her identity. Without a human past or even an identity discrete from Allen, Madison adapts to Allen's world rather than he to hers. Allen believes Madison is simply a foreigner who is sexually eager, naïve, emotionally vulnerable, and compliant to his desires. As such, Madison is Allen's perfect woman and one who helps him overcome his ambivalence about **marriage**. When he proposes, she reluctantly accepts, even though to do so would make permanent her transformation. Madison's eventual capture for scientific study causes Allen to question whether he loves her for herself, a common romantic complication. In the final, significant deviation from Andersen's story, one that adheres to mainstream film conventions, Allen overcomes his doubts, rescues Madison, and abandons the human world to join her underwater and live happily ever after.

Interestingly, Howard deleted a key scene that would have established more firmly *Splash's* relationship to Andersen's "The Little Mermaid." That scene, in which an older mermaid warns Madison about loving a human, was deleted from the theatrical release; a clip exists on the DVD of *Splash*. **See also** Adaptation; Film and Video.

Further Reading: White, Susan. "Split Skins: Female Agency and Bodily Mutilation in *The Little Mermaid*." *Film Theory Goes to the Movies*. Edited by Jim Collins, Hilary Radner, and Ava Preacher Collins. New York: Routledge, 1993. 182–95.

D. K. Peterson

Stahl, Caroline (1776–1837)

A German writer who presaged the **Grimm**s' vision of the fairy tale as a social and moral primer, Caroline Stahl published a dozen highly popular children's books. Her *Fabeln, Mährchen und Erzählungen für Kinder* (*Fables, Fairy Tales, and Stories for Children*, 1818) presented tales, poems, and morality plays about the rewards of honesty, selflessness, and good behavior (see **Punishment and Reward**). Writing for upper-class children, she enjoined them to avoid envy, tattling, vanity, careless play, and arrogance toward the lower classes.

The Grimms took a special interest in this collection and deemed eight tales clearly from the **oral tradition**. Citing her collection as one of their sources for a number of their tales, including "Rumpelstiltskin" and "**Hansel and Gretel**," Wilhelm Grimm included Stahl's "Der undankbare Zwerg" ("The Ungrateful **Dwarf**") as "Schneeweißchen und Rosenrot" ("Snow White and Rose Red") in the third edition of the *Kinder- und Hausmärchen* (*Children's and Household Tales*) and in the 1850 Small Edition of that work, which contained a selection of tales especially for children. "Snow White and Rose Red" became one of the most beloved Grimm tales.

In 1823, Stahl published *Mährchen für Kinder* (*Fairy Tales for Children*). She was also a frequent contributor to prominent literary journals, including the *Morgenblatt*, *Abendzeitung*, *Deutsches Unterhaltungsblatt*, and *Gesellschafter*. *See also* German Tales.

Further Readings: Stahl, Caroline. "The Godmothers." *The Queen's Mirror: Fairy Tales by German Women 1780–1900*. Edited and translated by Shawn C. Jarvis and Jeannine Blackwell. Lincoln: University of Nebraska Press, 2001. 133–38; ———. "The Wicked Sisters and the Good One: A Fairy Tale." Translated by Shawn C. Jarvis. *Marvels & Tales* 14 (2000): 159–64.

Shawn C. Jarvis

Stamps

Although modern e-mail communication has reduced the fascination with stamps depicting various colorful subjects, postal services around the world continue to produce commemorative stamps of various types. Serious stamp collectors, and the general public alike, have long delighted in such special stamps, notably those that depict well-known **motifs** from fairy tales and folktales. While these stamps might be aesthetically pleasing and at the same time recall traditional tales, the postal offices are well aware of the pecuniary value of selling sets of such folkloric stamps. There is no doubt that money is to be made by the commercial exploitation of fairy tales or folktales, be that in the form of little figurines, puppets, T-shirts, posters, or those small but enjoyable stamps.

Especially well-known fairy-tale motifs have repeatedly been illustrated on stamps, with folktales being depicted much less frequently. However, the "Pied Piper of Hamelin" with children following the piper appeared on a German stamp in 1977. While the fairy tales of Jacob and Wilhelm **Grimm** have been used on stamps by many national postal services, it should be noted that motifs from Charles **Perrault**'s and Aleksandr **Afanas'ev**'s French and Russian fairy-tale collections or from the *Arabian Nights* also appear. Since the major motifs of national variants of a specific fairy tale might include considerable differences (for example, there is no glass slipper or a pumpkin coach in the German variant of "**Cinderella**"), the stamps from varying countries will have their differences. Also, since folktales are not as internationally known as fairy tales, there will be some stamps that are not easily decipherable for cultural outsiders.

Quite understandably, it has been the German postal service that has been especially committed to issuing fairy-tale stamps. In 1959 (Wilhelm Grimm had died in 1859), one could purchase a stamp depicting the Brothers Grimm, and this was followed during the 1960s by a series of four stamps each illustrating the major motifs of individual fairy tales. Included were "**Little Red Riding Hood**," "**Hansel and Gretel**," "**Snow White**," "The Coin Girl," "The Wolf and the Seven Young Kids," "Cinderella," "**Sleeping Beauty**," "**Mother Holle**," and "The **Frog King**." But these stamps had their special price, for in addition to their normal value of ten to fifty cents, one had to pay between five and twenty-five cents extra to help needy children. This was clearly an innovative and worthwhile attempt to raise money for a good cause. The idea caught on, for in 1985 (Jacob Grimm was born in 1785), the Swiss postal service followed suit with similar stamps, once again using such popular fairy tales as "Little Red Riding Hood," Snow White," Cinderella," and "Hansel and Gretel."

Not to be outdone, the East German postal service issued a set of six Brothers Grimm stamps in the same year. As expected, there was one stamp showing Jacob and Wilhelm Grimm, while the other five stamps illustrated one major motif each from the internationally somewhat less-known fairy tales "The Seven Ravens," "Lucky Hans," "**Puss in Boots**," "The Sweet Porridge," and "The Brave Little **Tailor**." Many other countries have followed suit, notably Bulgaria, the Czech Republic, Denmark, Finland, Hungary, Luxembourg, Poland, Romania, and Russia. Obviously, these affordable stamps were quite a success, and there were many collectors who collected and framed them as a special treasure. In a world that is ever more visually oriented, it is at least to a degree that fairy tales are kept in circulation by way of such appealing **illustration**s on stamps.

Further Reading: Partington, Paul G. *Fairy Tales and Folk Tales on Stamps.* Milwaukee: American Topical Association, 1970.

Wolfgang Mieder

Steig, William (1907–2003)

A critically acclaimed American cartoonist whose work appeared in the *New Yorker* from the 1930s, William Steig did not publish his first children's book until the puzzle book *C D B!* appeared in 1968. Steig went on to write and illustrate more than thirty books for children, including the Caldecott Award-winning *Sylvester and the Magic Pebble* (1969), the Newbury Honor books *Abel's Island* (1976) and *Doctor Desoto* (1982), and the Caldecott Honor book *The Amazing Bone* (1976).

Steig's playful yet dignified **illustration**s and rich prose demonstrate a deep respect for the intelligence of his young readers. While his narratives often rely on the classic patterns found in **myth**s, **fable**s, and fairy tales, they avoid easy **moral**s and one-dimensional characters. Indeed, unlike their classical fairy-tale counterparts, Steig's heroes and heroines question their position in the worlds they inhabit. In *Amos and Boris* (1971), the reciprocal rescue and friendship between Amos, a seafaring mouse on a quest for adventure, and Boris, a kindly whale, transcends its **Aesop**ian plot through the developing complexity of its characters. In his 1990 book *Shrek* (made into a popular movie in 2001), Steig, with touching hilarity, deconstructs fairy-tale conventions of love and beauty by presenting his green **ogre** as a romantic lead who wins the hand of an ugly princess. In many of Steig's tales, the magic of the fairy-tale world is also intensified by the "beauty and mystery" of the natural world. While Pearl, the young **pig** from *The Amazing Bone*, borrows a **witch**'s magic to escape a fox, she is so moved by the spring landscape that "she could almost feel herself turning into a flower." In 1998, Steig lent his own transformative illustrations to wife Jeanne's fractured fairy-tale collection, *A Handful of Beans* (1998). *See also* Children's Literature; *Shrek* and *Shrek II*.

Further Readings: Bottner, Barbara. "William Steig: The Two Legacies." *Lion and the Unicorn* 2.1 (1978): 4–16; Topliss, Iain. *The Comic Worlds of Peter Arno, William Steig, Charles Addams and Saul Steinberg.* Baltimore: Johns Hopkins University Press, 2005.

Barbara Tannert-Smith

Stepmother. *See* Mother

Stevenson, Robert Louis (1850–1894)

The fame of Scottish writer Robert Louis Stevenson rests above all on *Treasure Island* (1883), *A Child's Garden of Verses* (1885), and *Strange Case of Dr. Jekyll and Mr. Hyde*

(1886), books whose celebrity has tended to obscure the range of Stevenson's oeuvre. He took a keen interest in folktales and worked on "a volume of **Märchen**." The latter was published (though not in the format Stevenson wanted) as *Island Nights' Entertainments* (1893), which contained two innovative fairy tales—"The Bottle Imp" and "The Isle of Voices."

Stevenson was born into a famous engineering family in Edinburgh, where he trained unwillingly as an engineer and subsequently as a lawyer. He never earned a living in either of these professions and finally managed to establish himself as a professional writer after the international success of *Dr. Jekyll and Mr. Hyde*. He suffered from lung disease and left Scotland for a variety of locations, including France, Switzerland (where he set his fairy tale "Will o' the Mill," 1878), the United States, and finally the South Pacific. In 1890, he settled on Samoa.

As an amateur anthropologist and a friend of Andrew **Lang**, Stevenson was fascinated by the folktales he encountered both in Scotland and later during his voyages in the Pacific. He was convinced there were analogies between the cultures of the Pacific Islanders and that of the Scottish Highlanders, which had been brutally suppressed after the Jacobite Rising of 1745 (the subject matter of *Kidnapped*, 1886). Stevenson "traded" tales with Pacific islanders to elicit the folktales later included in his posthumously published *In the South Seas* (1898).

Other than passages of pastiche linking tales set in contemporary London and Paris, Stevenson's *New Arabian Nights* (1882) has, despite its title, little to do with the *Arabian Nights*. The latter—known also, of course, as *The Arabian Nights' Entertainments*—is also alluded to in the title of *Island Nights' Entertainments*, originally planned as a "volume of Märchen." Due to the connivance of his publisher and literary agent, this projected collection of fairy tales was in Stevenson's view ruined by the inclusion of a realistic **novella**. The centerpiece of Stevenson's projected collection, "The Bottle Imp," was based on traditional **German tales** of the *Flaschenteufel*, of which there are versions by Johann Jacob Christoffel von Grimmelshausen, Friedrich de la Motte **Fouqué**, and the Brothers **Grimm**. This idea was transposed by Stevenson into contemporary Hawai'i and San Francisco. "The Isle of Voices" derives from a variety of Pacific sources, including oral material and possibly King Kalakaua's *Legends and Myths of Hawaii* (1887). Had Stevenson's "volume of Märchen" eventually come to fruition, it would probably have included "The Waif Woman" (based on William Morris's translation of Icelandic **saga**s) and some stories in a Celtic style that appeared posthumously in the *Fables* appended to *Dr. Jekyll and Mr. Hyde*. *See also* Pacific Island Tales.

Further Readings: Gray, William. "The Incomplete Fairy Tales of Robert Louis Stevenson." *Journal of Stevenson Studies* 2 (2005): 98–109; ———. *Robert Louis Stevenson: A Literary Life*. New York: Palgrave Macmillan, 2004; Stevenson, Robert Louis. *South Sea Tales*. Edited by Roslyn Jolly. Oxford: Oxford University Press, 1996.

William Gray

Storm, Theodor (1817–1888)

Theodor Storm is primarily known as an outstanding representative of German poetic realism, but fairy tales also constitute a prominent if largely neglected part of his literary output. Storm's first fairy tale, "Der kleine Häwelmann" ("The Little Häwelmann," 1849), has remained popular with German children to this day. "Stein und Rose" ("Stone and Rose") followed in 1850 and was reissued in a considerably altered version as "Hinzelmeier" four years later. In 1866, Storm published *Drei Märchen* (*Three Fairy Tales*), a volume of three previously published **literary fairy tale**s including "Die Regentrude" ("The Rainmaiden," 1864), "Bulemanns Haus" ("Bulemann's House," 1865), and "Der Spiegel des Cyprianus" ("The Mirror of Cyprianus," 1865).

Storm was profoundly interested in all forms of **folklore**, mythology, and the occult. Each of his fairy tales exploits some element of mythology to highlight aspects of human behavior. Storm also collected **folktales** himself, along with Theodor Mommsen and Karl Müllenhoff, who published their common efforts in a collection entitled *Sagen, Märchen und Lieder der Herzogthümer Schleswig, Holstein und Lauenburg* (*Legends, Folktales, and Folksongs from the Dukedoms of Schleswig, Holstein, and Lauenburg*, 1845), which was used as a schoolbook in Schleswig Holstein until 1945. *Am Kamin* (*At the Fireside*, 1862) contained eight ghost stories, none of which Storm incorporated into his collected works (1886–89), however. Finally, the early manuscript "Hans Bär" ("Hans Bear") was posthumously discovered among his papers and published in 1930. *See also* German Tales; Ghost Story.

Further Readings: Artiss, David S. "Theodor Storm's Four Märchen: Early Examples of His Prose Technique." *Seminar* 14 (1978): 149–68; Peischl, Margaret T. "Theodor Storm's 'The Rainmaiden': A Creative Process." *Marvels & Tales* 11 (1997): 74–91.

Willi Höfig

Storytelling

The definition crafted in 2000 after much debate by the Board of Directors of the National Storytelling Network, the principal professional storytelling organization in the United States, reads: "Storytelling is the interactive art of using words, vocalizations, and/or physical movement and gesture to reveal the elements and images of a story to a specific live audience." The definition is suggestive in what it excludes as well as what it includes. It does include interactivity, the reciprocal flow of energy between teller, audience, and narrative in the moment of live performance. It thus excludes writing, filmmaking, **television**, video gaming, and other mediating frameworks that interpose between teller and listeners. These later arts, however, grounded as they are upon the genres and principals of storytelling, are ever willing to appropriate the hallowed name of their ancestor for its intimacy and mythic resonance. In its essence, story*telling* as we will use the term here is a live and living art, a process of communication and communion between teller and listeners, shaped by various traditions but mediated as little as possible by distancing technologies.

The difficulty in maintaining a definition of storytelling *as* storytelling and not as a metonymy for something quite different is to be found less in the word or the process it denotes than in the cultural mindset within which the act of definition must be attempted. Walter Ong has pointed out that the assumptions of literacy-based civilization have so permeated our thought processes as to breed unchallenged oxymorons such as "oral literature" (or "literary storytelling"). In *Image, Music, Text*, Roland Barthes has beautifully enumerated how narrative (as opposed to storytelling) can exist in "a prodigious variety of genres, themselves distributed among different substances—as if any material were fit to receive man's stories." Marshall MacLuhan postulated that "environments are invisible"; and the environment of literature- and media-saturated culture has certainly hidden in plain sight our dependence on the technological artifacts of the story-making process. Storytelling, both as concept and as artistic/political movement, would refocus our attention on the process in its unencumbered form.

Historically, storytelling in primarily oral cultures has functioned as an expression of any and all social castes but takes on distinctive characteristics depending on the nature and functions of a particular group. Thus, storytelling of and for elites or ruling castes tends toward what we know as bardic storytelling, its principal genres being **epic**, praise song, and genealogy. Whether Homeric epics, the Irish **legend**s of Cuchulain and the *Tain bo Cuiligne*, or the African Mwindo epic, these stories are generally highly formalized and formulaic, passed on by hereditary professional lineages, and often chanted to the accompaniment of stringed instruments such as the harp, lyre, gusle, rebec, or kora.

Storytelling in occupational groups (warriors, hunters, fishermen, pastoralists, and agriculturists, among others) or religious groups revolves around the hero types and activities of that group, whether the genre be epic, **tall tale**, **wonder tale**, or sacred teaching tale. These show wide variation in form, ranging from ceremonial or ritual tellings resembling those of traditional epic performances to less formal exchanges in coffeehouses, homes, barracks, or courtyards of monasteries or prayer houses.

Storytelling in peasant or servant groups tends toward the wonder tale, as Max **Lüthi**, Jack **Zipes**, and others have shown, to provide imaginative release from the harsh conditions of workaday life. They are often performed as an accompaniment to repetitive menial tasks, such as food storage (picking, canning, drying, and threshing), cloth-weaving, or net-mending, as Appalachian, Hebridean, and Hungarian storytellers have testified. Or they can be just vessels to carry community spirits across the long winter nights. The hero or heroine's journey from outcast wayfarer through magical trials to blessed estate seems designed to lift the laboring heart and mind and to anaesthetize sore fingers. **Animal tale**s are widespread in African, African American, Native American, European, and Asian traditions. Stories in which human and divine traits and conflicts are embodied in animal forms, these tales range in function from simple children's **fable**s and **jest**s to sacred creation **myth**s. **Märchen** and animal tales may thrive in less formal contexts than bardic or ritual tellings; yet there remains something ceremonious about the repetition of traditional stories, whether in ceili houses (the houses where neighbors gather in rural Irish and Scottish communities for music, dancing, and storytelling) or fishing shacks, around a shaman's fire or a child's bed, or, more recently, at library story hours or revival storytelling festivals.

The storytelling process is often imprecisely understood from opposite sides of the orality/literacy divide. Milman Parry and Albert B. Lord reported that the illiterate bards from whom they collected South Slavic epics naturally assumed that their literate interlocutors could perform such feats of **memory** as the singers themselves had just demonstrated, and much more as well, since the educated **folk** had the additional power of literacy. And literate persons often still make the error of assuming that oral traditional storytellers are reciting their stories and verses word for word, as literates would memorize a play or a poem.

Only since we have transited into the epoch of electronic recording and transmitting media has it become possible to examine such notions with any precision, as Parry and Lord were able to in the Balkans in the 1930s and again in the 1950s with their early recording devices. They recognized that oral memory is a process of stitching together performances out of formulaic elements—traditional images, metaphors, stylized action passages, and a range of other syntactic and discursive chunks, arranged with some improvisatory freedom to fit the audience and the occasion. A traditional storyteller learns from hearing these elements repeated in sufficient variety yet stylistic consistency that he or she can make use of their patterns to freely reproduce the community's repertoire of tales, adding their own variations, reflections, and responses to the pressures of the environment. Thus, oral storytelling performances can emerge rather fluidly from the language web of community talk, as Henry H. Glassie beautifully elucidates in the Irish ceili storytelling in *Passing the Time in Ballymemnone* (1982). A particular tale may appear in multiple **variant**s, from different narrators in different settings, yet each variation can be experienced by the group authentically as "the story."

While tellers in bardic or religious orders are often trained to what amounts to professional standards and lineages, and perform a distinct high-status social function, tellers in rural or peasant communities can be equivalently recognized and valued by their own peers. In cultures around the world where orality remains a dominant force of cultural transmission, tellers such as the *seanachies* of rural Ireland recorded by the Irish Folklore Commission, or Jack tale tellers of the Hicks-Harmon-Ward extended family of Beech Mountain, North Carolina, are well known as cultural resources and authorities both within and beyond their immediate communities. Yet, as these redoubts of oral culture are increasingly encroached upon first by literacy and then still more disruptively by electronic culture, the practices and repertoires of traditional storytelling are subject to the twin perils of attrition or revival.

The vanishing subject has been both the lamentation and driving force of folklore scholarship since its inception with Johann Gottfried Herder and Jacob and Wilhelm **Grimm**. When Hector Urquhart, friend and **informant** of the great Scottish folktale collector John Francis Campbell, was a young man in the early nineteenth century, he wrote of the common custom in the Gaelic Highlands of his childhood of gathering to listen to folktales and fairy tales (or *sgeulachd*) as told by itinerant tailors, shoemakers, or other traveling folk. "It was also the custom," he wrote, "when an *aoidh*, or stranger, celebrated for his store of tales, came on a visit to the village, for us, young and old, to make a rush to the house where he passed the night … just as I myself have seen since when a far-famed actor came to the Glasgow theater" (Campbell, 5). Yet Urquhart goes on to report that, after the minister and the schoolmaster came to the village in the 1830s, their disapproval of the practice and their teaching of the written word caused oral storytelling to die away almost completely.

More than a century later, African storyteller Raouf Mama described a similar turn in his native Benin:

> In the space of twelve years—from 1960, when Benin was granted independence, to 1972, the year of the Beninese revolution—storytelling evenings in Beninese homes declined considerably. Today, that time-honored tradition has gone out of existence. Much of the blame for this must be laid on the colonial educational system, which sought to make the Beninese look down on his native tongue, customs and tradition, culture, and folklore. (MacDonald, 9–10)

Similarly, the Appalachian storyteller Ray Hicks, an iconic fixture at the National Storytelling Festival from 1973 to 2000, often said that the doctrinaire ministers of the hardshell Baptist churches drove the traditional wonder tales out of his region of the mountains. "They taught 'em out," he would say. "Said they's wrong." The coming of television to rural areas has had a particularly corrosive impact on the customs of social gathering and listening that are the necessary habitat of extended-form storytelling sessions in the home. These factors and others have driven the transposition of storytelling to more formally constructed contexts, such as libraries, schools, and storytelling revival festivals.

Anthony Wallace placed revivals as one class of revitalization movement, which he defined in general as "the deliberate, organized, conscious effort on the part of members of a society to construct a more satisfying culture" (Wallace, 265). Revival movements celebrate values, customs, and rituals that are thought to have been part of the everyday lives of earlier generations, and whose eclipse is held to symbolize a larger decline in the cultural health of the present. Such movements have long been part of the self-regenerating fabric of cultural life. They tend to emerge in periods when social, political, economic, or technological changes put great stress on cultures and individuals. Though their explicit agenda is to bring back practices belonging to an idealized past, their actual mechanisms are usually homeostatic, and serve to integrate contemporary innovations in context and process by buffering them with traditional imagery and reassuring ritual.

Folk arts in general and storytelling in particular have regularly served as grist for the cultural revival mill. The revival of storytelling in the latter three decades of the twentieth century was part of a pattern that reaches back to include the fairy-tale enthusiasm at the court of Versailles that produced the works of Charles **Perrault**, Marie-Catherine d'**Aulnoy**, and their peers; the Hasidic movement in eighteenth and nineteenth century Judaism, which gave a central sacred role to storytelling and generated both the legends of the Baal Shem Tov and the mystical fairy tales of his great-grandson Nachman of Bratslav; the German Romantic movement, fired by the folkloristic proclamations of Herder and the Brothers Grimm; and the Romantic-nationalist movements that followed the German lead in nearly every country in Europe and the Americas, producing great collections of national and regional folklore and often serving as cultural cover for significant political and social consolidation and change.

In the United States, there was an important if now nearly forgotten revival of storytelling in the 1890s and the first decades of the 1900s that neatly mirrored the storytelling movement at the century's close. It began in the emerging library and public school systems. Library story hours were established in the Carnegie and New York Public Library systems in the 1890s, and the training of children's librarians came to include storytelling as an essential vocational skill (Alvey). The National Story Tellers' League was founded in 1903 by Richard Wyche at a summer school for public-school teachers in Knoxville, Tennessee, to promote storytelling in schools. Manuals and inspirational tracts on storytelling as an art form were published by Sarah Cone Bryant, Marie Shedlock, Wyche, and others, all recommending folktales, fairy tales, and **literary fairy tale**s by the likes of Hans Christian **Andersen**, Oscar **Wilde**, or Howard Pyle, and biblical stories, Arthurian legends, and Greco-Roman myths. Storytelling was regarded as an important resource for settlement schools, which were being established in urban areas to serve the children of burgeoning immigrant populations, as well as in isolated rural areas such as the southern Appalachians.

Both these institutions, libraries and schools, provided secular vocational paths for passionate, idealistic young adults, primarily female. They served an urgent social purpose, namely the socialization of poor children to the cultural norms of the literate middle class. It is suggestive of the implicit agendas of this storytelling movement (and their eventual fulfillment, diversion, or cancellation) that its fervor began to wane in the 1920s in synchrony with laws granting women the vote (1919) and restricting immigration (1924). Yet its accomplishments were to create institutional bases for organized storytelling in the United States and northern Europe—albeit in primarily book-centered, oral interpretive contexts—which were in place and ready to support resurgences of fervor around the art at the end of the century.

In 1973, in a small town on the edge of the Blue Ridge Mountains, a festival was organized that became a focus for such a resurgence. The National Storytelling Festival in Jonesborough, Tennessee, offered safe haven to young women and men fresh from the countercultural movements of the 1960s, hungry for a cultural vehicle that promised reconciliation, social connectedness, and artistic healing. Over the succeeding decades, performers and listeners have been drawn to the festival and others like it around the United States, Canada, and western Europe. Many of the tellers have discovered storytelling independently, sometimes in the earlier contexts of community oral traditions, library work, or teaching, but more often as voyagers from related art forms, such as theatrical impersonation, oral interpretation, performance poetry, mime or New Vaudeville, stand-up comedy, singer/songwriting, or folk music. They came together in Jonesborough and similar sites under a banner of a revival of **oral tradition**; yet, like many a crusade or parade banner, it served to camouflage even as it exalted the diversity of backgrounds and motives beneath it.

At the outset at least, revival storytelling repertoires have been dominated by folktales and fairy tales, often buttressed by Freudian, Jungian, or Campbellian cross-cultural interpretive frameworks (see **Psychological Approaches**). Traditional tellers with distinctive community repertoires of wonder tales, such as Ray Hicks in the United States, Joe McNeil in Canada, and Duncan Williamson in Scotland, have had formative influences on storytelling revival performers and repertoires; and many important younger tellers, such as Diana Wolkstein, the late Jackie Torrence, Laura Simms, and the English teller Ben Hagerty have based their careers at least initially on the telling of folktales (though recent festival repertoires in the United States have been increasingly dominated by personal memoir). In part this renaissance of folktale telling was due to these stories' easy identification with tradition and their naturalness in solo and small group performance; but it may also owe to the fact that the form of the wonder tale as described by Joseph Campbell or Vladimir **Propp** mirrors uncannily the process of a revitalization movement itself.

Wallace described periods of increasing individual or communal stress (separation), followed by a revealed vision of a new way of life (initiation), often based on earlier, forgotten forms and rituals. These revitalizing breakthroughs lead to the creation of organizations, such as the National Story Tellers' League or the National Storytelling Network, to communicate the new path and assimilate it into existing social forms (return). Revival storytellers tend to see themselves as heroes or heroines of their own wonder-tale quests, with storytelling as the magical gift enabling them to vanquish the glass mountain of alienated labor, and to make a meaningful living from their art in order to live "happily ever after." Regardless of the status of the everafter, storytelling as a potential of human expression promises to remain with us for as long as we remain human. *See also* Beech Mountain Jack Tale; Jack Tales.

Further Readings: Alvey, Richard G. "The Historical Development of Organized Storytelling for Children in the United State." Dissertation. University of Pennsylavania, 1974; Barthes, Roland. *Image, Music, Text.* New York: Noonday, 1977; Campbell, J. F., trans. *Popular Tales of the West Highlands: Orally Collected.* New edition. 2 volumes. Edinburgh: Birlinn, 1994; Glassie, Henry. *Passing the Time in Ballymenone.* Bloomington: Indiana University Press, 1982; Lord, Albert M. *The Singer of Tales.* Cambridge, MA: Harvard University Press, 1960; MacDonald, Margaret Read, ed. *Traditional Storytelling Today: An International Sourcebook.* Chicago: Fitzroy Dearborn, 1999; McLuhan, Marshall. *Understanding Media: The Extensions of Man.* New York: McGraw, 1965; Ong, Walter. *Orality and Literacy: The Technologizing of the Word.* London: Routledge, 1982; Pellowski, Anne. *The World of Storytelling.* Expanded and revised edition. Bronx, NY: Wilson, 1990; Sobol, Joseph Daniel. *The Storytellers'*

Journey: An American Revival. Urbana: University of Illinois Press, 1999; Wallace, Anthony F. C. "Revitalization Movements." *American Anthropologist* 58 (1956): 264–81.

Joseph Daniel Sobol

Straparola, Giovan Francesco (c. 1480–1558)

The fame of the Italian writer and poet Giovan Francesco Straparola today rests on his collection of stories *Le piacevoli notti* (*The Pleasant Nights*, 1550–53). Although the most important narrative model for the *Nights* was the **novella** tradition descended from Giovanni **Boccaccio**'s *Decameron* (1349–50), Straparola also embarked in the innovative direction of incorporating **folktale**s and **fairy tale**s into his collection. Almost nothing is known of Straparola's life, except that he was born in Caravaggio in the north of Italy and later moved to Venice.

The **frame narrative** of the *Nights* tells of the arrival in Venice, during Carnival season, of the historical personage Ottaviano Maria Sforza, ex-bishop of Lodi, who together with his widowed daughter Lucrezia Sforza Gonzaga has fled Milan for political reasons. He and his party proceed from Venice by boat to Murano, a nearby island, where they take refuge in a marvelously appointed palace with a garden in full flower, despite the season. It is decided that the remaining nights of Carnival will be spent telling tales, and a group of young ladies and gentlemen is summoned to form the company. It is above all the rather abstractly characterized women who narrate the tales, while the men, among whose ranks are included historical men of letters such as Pietro Bembo and Bernardo Cappello, listen. The seventy-four original tales are divided among thirteen nights; five tales are told each night except the eighth (six tales) and the thirteenth (thirteen tales). Songs and dances precede each night, and the tales end with "enigmas," or **riddle**s, often obscene. There is no well-defined thematic division of the days, as in the *Decameron*, apart from the predominance of **motif**s of magic on the third day. The tales include folktales and fairy tales (approximately fifteen, with several others containing common folkloric motifs); direct translations from Girolamo Morlini's Latin *Novellae* (1520), which itself evidenced interest in the **Aesop**ian beast **fable** (twenty-three tales); novellas with the more traditional Boccaccian themes of trickery or amorous intrigue; and assorted moral **exempla** and tragic and heroic stories.

The experimentation with various narrative genres and modes of representation was not uncommon at the time when Straparola wrote, near the end of the golden age of the European novella. In particular, the attraction to the fairy tale exemplified the general interest in folk traditions present in the late Renaissance, as well as the intuition that the bourgeois protagonist of the novella was no longer the convincing paradigm he had once been. The proliferation of lower-class heroes who inhabit marvelous worlds, marry **princess**es, and are passively aided by magic—instead of using their intelligence and enterprise to actively change the course of events—suggests how fantastic such social betterment perhaps seemed in the "real world" of Straparola's time.

Most of the *Nights'* tales that constitute familiar fairy-tale types are of European and Oriental origin; it is thought that Straparola may have invented several himself. They all had significant influence on the subsequent history of the genre, appearing in later collections such as Giambattista **Basile**'s *Lo cunto de li cunti* (*The Tale of Tales*, 1634–36) and Jacob and Wilhelm **Grimm**s' *Kinder- und Hausmärchen* (*Children's and Household Tales*, 1812–15). They are: tales 1.2, "Cassandrino" (Grimms' "The Master **Thief**"); 1.3, "Pre'

Scarpacifico" (Grimms' "Little Farmer"); 1.4, "Tebaldo and Doralice" (Basile's "The Bear"; Charles **Perrault**'s "Donkey-Skin"; the Grimms' "All Fur"); 2.1, "The Pig King" (Grimms' "Hans My Hedgehog"); 3.1, "Crazy Peter" (Basile's "Peruonto"; Grimms' "Simple Hans"); 3.3, "Biancabella" (elements of Basile's "Penta With the Chopped-Off Hands" and "The Two Little Pizzas"); 3.4, "Fortunio" (elements of the Grimms' "The Nixie in the Pond"); 4.1, "Costanza and Costanzo" (Grimms' "How Six Made Their Way in the World"); 4.3, "Ancilotto" (Grimms' "The Three Little Birds"; Carlo **Gozzi**'s "The Green Bird"); 5.1, "Guerrino" (Grimms' "Iron Hans"); 5.2, "Adamantina" (Basile's "The Goose"; Grimms' "The Golden Goose"); 7.5, "The Three **Brothers**" (Basile's "The Five Sons"; Grimms' "The Four Skillful Brothers"); 8.4, "Master Lattanzio" (Grimms' "The Thief and His Master"); 10.3, "Cesarino di Berni" (Basile's "The Merchant"; Grimms' "The Two Brothers"); and 11.1, "Costantino Fortunato" (Basile's "Cagliuso"; Perrault's "**Puss in Boots**").

These tales effectively combine the realistic and the fantastic to create a flavor quite different from the Grimms' and other better-known tales. We see this, for instance, in "The Pig King." In this tale, Galeotto, the **king** of England, and his wife desperately long for a child. Three **fairies** satisfy their desire, but one of them wishes that the child be born with the skin of a **pig**, which he may shed only after taking three wives. The pig marries, one by one, the three daughters of a poor woman. The first two express their disgust at his filth and the way he fills their wedding beds with excrement (described in meticulous detail), and for this are killed by him. But the third, Meldina, proves accepting of his animal nature, and is rewarded for her love by the sight of her husband shedding his skin to become a beautiful youth, after which he and wife ascend to the throne (see **Punishment and Reward**).

In 1555, the stories from the *Nights* were published in a single volume in which one of the tales was replaced by two new tales, bringing the total to seventy-five. Over the next half-century, Straparola's work became a veritable best seller, with more than twenty editions. In the late sixteenth century, the *Nights* encountered problems with ecclesiastical censors due to the anticlerical thematics and obscenity of some of the tales, and in 1624, it was placed in the Index of Prohibited Books. *See also* Italian Tales.

Further Readings: Bottigheimer, Ruth B. *Fairy Godfather: Straparola, Venice, and the Fairy Tale Tradition.* Philadelphia: University of Pennsylvania Press, 2002; Cottino-Jones, Marga. "Princesses, Kings, and the Fantastic: A Re-Vision of the Language of Representation in the Renaissance." *Italian Quarterly* 37 (2000): 173–84; Pirovano, Donato. Introduction. *Le piacevoli notti.* By Giovan Francesco Straparola. Edited by Donato Pirovano. 2 volumes. Rome: Salerno Editrice, 2000. ix–xlix; Rua, Giuseppe. "Intorno alle *Piacevoli notti* di G.F. Straparola." *Giornale Storico della Letteratura Italiana* 15 (1890): 111–51; 16 (1890): 218–83.

Nancy Canepa

Strindberg, August (1849–1912)

Like many other Nordic playwrights of the late nineteenth century, the Swedish author August Strindberg was strongly influenced by the contemporary beliefs that the most appropriate material for plays was national history and folktales. From an early point, Strindberg read and collected material dealing with Swedish folk life, folk traditions, folk **ballad**s, and folktales. He also read the ancient Icelandic **saga**s and Eddic poems, and all this reading and collecting provided him with **motif**s and models for work throughout his life. Following the example of Henrik Ibsen's *Per Gynt* (1867), one of Strindberg's earliest plays, *Lycko-Pers Resa* (*Lucky*

Per's Journey, 1883), deliberately blends satire and fairy-tale material as it relates a journey taken through the world by a fifteen-year-old who has been given a magic ring by a **fairy**.

The central "folkloristic" period in Strindberg's work can be said to be the very early twentieth century. In 1902–03, he wrote the plays *Kronbruden* (*The Bridal Crown*) and *Svanevit* (*Swanwhite*) and then a collection of fairy tales composed in the style of Hans Christian **Andersen**, *Sagor* (*Fairy Tales*, 1903). *The Bridal Crown*, dealing with a **mother** who drowns a child, contains numerous motifs drawn from Swedish folk **legend**. The symbolist work *Swanwhite*, influenced by Maurice **Maeterlinck**, tells of a **princess** who overcomes the opposition of her evil stepmother and brings her **prince** back to life through the force of love. **See also** Scandinavian Tales; Theater.

Further Reading: Strindberg, August. *Apologia and Two Folk Plays: The Great Highway, The Crownbride, and Swanwhite*. Translated by Walter Johnson. Seattle and London: University of Washington Press, 1981.

Terry Gunnell

Structuralism

Structuralist criticism adapts the principles of twentieth-century linguistics to the study of **folktale** and **fairy tale**. Structuralism (a term introduced by the Russian American linguist Roman Jakobson) explains surface events and phenomena—narratives, rituals, and customs—by seeking structures and patterns below the surface of consciousness. It was the same search for deep structure that drove Karl Marx to devise his explanation of human history, and Sigmund **Freud** to look below the surface of his patients' dreams for their interpretation. Structuralism grew out of the linguistic analyses of the Swiss linguist Ferdinand de Saussure and the formalism applied to folktales by the Russian Vladimir **Propp**; it was given its most comprehensive formulation by the Prague scholars Petr Bogatyrev and Jan Mukařovský. Formalist analyses of narratives by French scholars Denise Paulme and Claude Bremond show its influence. Structuralist study of folktale or fairy tale distinguishes between the story as it is told and the social, political, and artistic systems in which a story resides.

Such separations are characteristic of structuralism. In linguistics, Saussure made a separation between a system of elements, which he called *langue*, and the concrete manifestation of the system, which he called *parole*. To analyze folktales, fairy tales, or **myths**, the structuralist will search for deep structure, focusing not on conscious **storytelling** behavior (as the **performance** method does) but on the unconscious structure of the stories. Structuralism consistently distinguishes between what is observed in **fieldwork** and what the observer makes out of it, just as Freud distinguished between the surface content of a dream and his interpretation of it. At the same time, structuralism has to take into account the interaction between observer and observed, and keep a clear separation between object language (the language of the performance) and metalanguage (the critic's responses and commentaries).

The French anthropologist Claude Lévi-Strauss, author of the four-volume study *Mythologiques* (1964–71), or *Introduction to the Science of Mythology*, acknowledges but also is critical of Propp as a predecessor, and pioneered the structural approach to folk narrative. Taking obscure texts of oral literature found among South American Indians and rendering them readable and understandable, Lévi-Strauss practices a unique form of literary criticism. Some texts that Lévi-Strauss calls myths others would classify as folktales; better definition of genres would be a goal of structuralism, which has treated hardly any fairy tales. In a programmatic essay of 1955, Lévi-Strauss compares the process of uncovering the real structure of a folktale or myth to the problem one would have in reconstructing an orchestral score if someone had perversely printed it all in one line, instead of putting the parts to be played simultaneously by different instruments on the same page. Lévi-Strauss therefore rearranges the elements of the stories he studies to reestablish the significant connections he believes are present in them. Light may be opposed to dark, male opposed to female, or raw food opposed to cooked food. The assumption is that those connections or oppositions can be reduced to a limited number (contrary, contradictory, neutral), and that the limited number of such connections illustrates fundamental operations of the human mind.

An accessible version of structuralist mythology is the essay "Four Winnebago Myths," in which Lévi-Strauss discovers a previously invisible connection between one story and a group of three other stories that are more obviously related. The first myth is the story of two friends, one of them a chief's son, who decide to sacrifice their lives for the welfare of the community. After undergoing a series of ordeals in the underworld, they reach the lodge of Earthmaker, who permits them to become reincarnated and to resume their previous lives among their relatives and friends. In the second myth, a hero is ready to sacrifice his unspent lifespan, not, as in the first myth, for the benefit of the group, but rather for the benefit of only one individual, his beloved wife. Both husband and wife are permitted to live on. The third myth explains how the members of the Medicine Rite, after **death**, undergo several tests in Spiritland (as the protagonists of the other myths did); overcoming these, they gain the right to become reincarnated. The fourth myth tells of the daughter of a tribal chief who falls in love with an orphan, dies of a broken heart, and is then restored to life by the orphan, who however must submit to and overcome certain tests, not in Spiritland but here on earth, in the very lodge in which the young woman died. Lévi-Strauss manages to show a relationship between this last story and the others by relying on ethnographic context to point out that the first three show Winnebago society in its traditional form, while the last one shows it upside down. All four myths are based upon a fundamental opposition: on the one hand, the lives of ordinary people unfolding toward a natural death, followed by immortality in one of the spirit villages; on the other hand, heroic life voluntarily curtailed for the sake of a supplementary life quota, for others as well as for oneself. The author points out in this essay that his structural analysis is not meant to displace the examination of what myths or folktales mean to the people who tell and hear them. But there is a deeper meaning of which they are unaware.

According to Lévi-Strauss, a myth is actually a logical structure whereby a society can resolve symbolically a contradiction it can never resolve in reality, such as life versus death. He often finds in myths some mediating figure that is crucial in overcoming the polar opposition. So, in the fourth Winnebago myth, the two characters are opposed to each other: male and female, low and high on the social scale, a miraculous hunter and a social defective. The girl dies a natural death, and the boy dies socially—that is, he stays alone. But the girl's ghost remains on earth, and the boy finally is unable to live; both become **wolves**, twilight creatures, mediating figures who combine good and evil features. **Trickster**s are often mediating figures.

Principles of Structuralism

1. System: Structuralism insists that all the myths and folktales it treats be thought of and analyzed as a system, in their interrelations to each other. The Oedipus story would not stand alone: it would be connected to other stories, presumably from the same or related peoples.

2. Synchronic study: Linguistic systems, Saussure insisted, are to be studied without reference to their history, that is, *synchronically*. The study of phenomena in their historical dimensions he labeled *diachronic*.

3. Distinction between signified and signifier: For Saussure, the connection between a word (signifier) and what it refers to (signified) is never natural, only arbitrary; meaning is the result of a social construction. Later, poststructuralist writers, misinterpreting Jacques Derrida, extend this arbitrariness to mean that nothing exists but a "free play of signifiers."

4. Relations rather than items: Lévi-Strauss does not treat the characters and incidents of stories as independent entities but instead takes the relations between these characters and incidents as the topic of study. The sun in a myth has no meaning in and of itself; that would be to treat its signification. Rather, the meaning of the sun arises from "the relations of correlation and opposition in which it stands to other mythemes [= elements] within this myth."

5. Search for general laws: Structuralist mythology aims at discovering general laws of folktale creation, which should be valid for all people.

Problems

1. How shall the "system" of folktales be defined? Where does it come from if not history: from ethnicity, language, and canon-formation? Classical folktale scholarship and Romantic nationalism conspired to make a canon of Jacob and Wilhelm **Grimm**'s tales in Germany and Aleksandr **Afanas'ev**'s tales in Russia. A "system" of fairy tales is easier to define: the literary tradition initiated by Marie-Catherine d'**Aulnoy** has sufficiently clear boundaries of language and style to be seen as a system allowing the study of interrelations among its members.

2. Structuralism seems to turn away from the vitality of the individual and the dynamics of the social, subordinating them to an impersonal system, which thereby takes on a superorganic flavor. Critics who argue that Saussure left no freedom for the understanding of language will agree that Lévi-Strauss ignored people's delight in tale performance.

3. Characters, which mean so much to the reader of folktale or fairy tale, and which are a primary category in the criticism of fiction, become, in structuralist criticism, no more than tools.

4. Why should a reader of "**Little Red Riding Hood**" or "**Puss in Boots**" pay more attention to the relations of characters than to the spell cast by their adventures, or

5. Look for general laws behind them?

One answer is that the structuralist occupies a different position from the child who is being read to or the member of an in-group or a foreign culture. Interpretive criticism exists to elucidate, not merely appreciate. Addressing a Western audience, Lévi-Strauss asserts that the justification of structuralism "lies in the unique and most economical coding system to which it can reduce messages of a most disheartening complexity, and which previously appeared to defeat all attempts to decipher them." Another answer is that the structural study of narrative does not turn away from history or **context**; indeed, it invites the integration of the synchronic and the diachronic. "Structure," Lévi-Strauss writes, "has no distinct content; it is content itself, apprehended in a logical organization conceived as property of the real." His myth analyses continually invoke corroborative ethnographic detail.

The most far-reaching elaboration of structuralist analysis of narrative is the work of A. J. Greimas, who effects a synthesis of formalism and structuralism. When he analyzes a short story by Guy de Maupassant, Greimas deliberately introduces not fewer than ten methods of segmenting it, whereas Propp devised only one. Greimas's assumption would be that every fairy tale or folktale is produced by a "narrative grammar," which is distinct from the grammar of the natural language in which the story is told or written. It is because linguistics is scientific and rigorous that it has recommended itself to him. Out of scientific rigor, other scholars have developed a systematic analysis of narrative called narratology.

Particularly useful for stories is Greimas's "semiotic square" (renamed a rectangle by his commentators), which diagrams the relations of the terms underlying literary structures. One obvious relation in folktales is the *contrary* (young/old, rich/poor, grief/joy). There is also the *contradictory* (kind/cruel, freedom/slavery). Between these, there are mediatings like the Winnebago boy and girl who become wolves (before/during/after; likable/indifferent/hateful). In its abstract form, the rectangle states these relations logically:

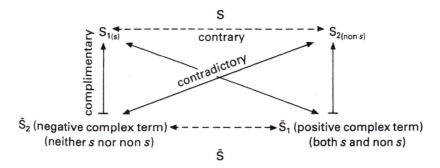

A. J. Greimas's "semiotic square." From Ronald Schleifer, *A. J. Greimas and the Nature of Meaning: Linguistics, Semiotics and Discourse Theory* (Lincoln: University of Nebraska Press, 1987), p. 25. Reproduced with permission of Ronald Schleifer.

The rectangle is not purely logical or formal; it attempts to account for meaning. Take Charles **Perrault**'s "La barbe bleue" ("**Bluebeard**"), for example. **Marriage** to this wife-killer equals death; the contrary to it, the absence of marriage, would be spinsterhood (Sister Anne's plight till the end). The story delivers the wife to a state contradictory to both marriage and death: she inherits her husband's wealth and lives on (equivalent to Propp's final **function**). The fourth term, missing from the story but present to its readers, is "normal" life, fecundity, perhaps with a husband. The semantic rectangle would look like this:

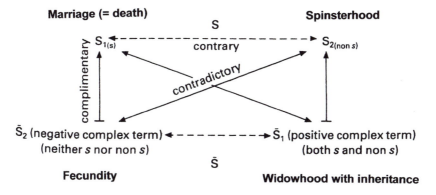

"Bluebeard" and the semiotic square.

Greimas's rectangle functions to replace Perrault's tale in its sociohistorical context, pointing beyond the text to the possibilities and constraints that its historical moment allows. Thus, structuralism is an invitation to study the social and historical context of a narrative as well as its internal form.

Because it addresses narrative systems rather than individual stories, structuralism seldom produces criticisms of single pieces. An outstanding exception is an essay about a Chinook story in which Dell Hymes, a linguistic anthropologist, derives the terms for his structural analysis from within the mythology of the people. The story reveals in its end that Seal has failed to protect her younger brother from being murdered. In a detailed linguistic analysis of the text, Hymes explains the names and titles of the characters; he compares related Northwest Coast tales; he uncovers three strands of imagery; he points to the pathos of the story's ending; and he examines its transmission through a chain of female narrators. His innovative interpretation of a seemingly fragmentary piece argues for a structuralism that understands a given set of words, whether oral or written, as both a synchronic system and part of a diachronic process. This approach assumes that structure is multileveled and that the relation of levels to one another can be established and understood.

The myths treated by Claude Lévi-Strauss in the four volumes of *Mythologiques* treat progressively more complex problems. "Statements in the discourse of myth," he writes, "reproduce the structure of language but only because there is a shift of gear which disengages it from its normal operation: the basic elements of myth function like those of language, but they are from the start more complex in nature." As structuralism has developed, it too has expanded. It treats the more complex problems of folktale and fairy tale: synchronic communication and diachronic change. *See also* Ethnographic Approaches; Linguistic Approaches; Native American Tales.

Further Readings: Greimas, A. J., and François Rastier. "The Interaction of Semiotic Constraints." *Game, Play, Literature*. Edited by Jacques Ehrmann. Boston: Beacon Press, 1968. 86–105; Hymes, Dell. *"In Vain I Tried to Tell You": Essays in Native American Ethnopoetics*. New edition. Lincoln: University of Nebraska Press, 2004; Lévi-Strauss, Claude. "Four Winnebago Myths." *Culture in History: Essays in Honor of Paul Radin*. New York: Columbia University Press, 1960. 351–62; Pace, David. "Beyond Morphology: Lévi-Strauss and the Analysis of Folktales." *Cinderella: A Casebook*. Edited by Alan Dundes. Madison: University of Wisconsin Press, 1988. 245–58; Steiner, Peter, ed. *The Prague School: Selected Writings, 1929–1946*. Austin: University of Texas Press, 1982.

Lee Haring

Sukasaptati

The *Sukasaptati* (*Seventy Tales of a Parrot*) is the Sanskrit prototype of a widely read Oriental collection of tales that by way of its Persian and Turkish versions is generally known in the West as *Tutiname* (*Book of the Parrot*).

The origin of the *Sukasaptati* probably dates back to as early as the tenth century CE. Besides three different Sanskrit redactions, the work exists in **translation**s into several Indian vernacular languages and also into languages such as Tibetan, Malay, and Urdu. A first Persian version, translated early in the fourteenth century, was soon succeeded by the more prominent one prepared by the author Nakhshabi around 1329–30. Shorter versions include those by Persian author Mohammad Qaderi or Turkish author Sari 'Abdallah Efendi, both prepared in the seventeenth century. In the nineteenth century, the collection had even more popular versions, such as various translations into vernacular Arabic or the Persian **chap-book** *Chehel Tuti* (*Forty Parrots*), which was still widely read in the middle of the twentieth century. A version of the work was already known in the early nineteenth century to German poet Johann Wolfgang von **Goethe**.

Similar to other Oriental collections of tales, such as the *Arabian Nights*, all versions of the *Book of the Parrot* with only little variation share a common **frame narrative**. In this frame tale, a young woman during the prolonged absence of her husband is tempted to go out at night to visit her lover. A tame parrot keeps her from going by first arousing her curiosity and then telling her a tale that keeps her spellbound until it is too late to go out. With this stratagem, the parrot prevents the woman from indulging in extramarital relations until her husband returns. In some versions, the woman keeps two parrots. The male parrot, when asked for advice about what to do, in acting as the husband's representative threatens that he will inform her husband; the wife kills this parrot in an outburst of anger. The female parrot, instead, has recourse to the mentioned ruse, usually by advising the woman to do whatever needs to be done, but to be conscious of the consequences of her behavior.

As the frame tale is concerned with the longing for extramarital sexual relations, so are several of the included tales. While tales with happy endings usually rely on the application of a clever ruse, others simply demonstrate a negative example. Many of the tales from a modern point of view have been judged as misogynist since they develop the theme of "wiles of **women**" that has been extremely popular ever since the biblical story of Joseph and Potiphar's wife. Numerous versions of the work, moreover, incorporate various folktales or jocular narratives without an obvious link to the frame tale. The final **moral**, if such a moral is given, normally implies the admonishment either not to behave as foolish or to act as clever as the tale's protagonist.

Further Readings: Clouston, William Alexander. *Flowers from a Persian Garden and Other Papers*. London: David Nutt, 1890. 121–82; Gladwin, Francis. *The Tooti-Nameh or Tales of a Parrot*. London: J. Debrett, 1801.

Ulrich Marzolph

Swan, Anni (1875–1958)

The Finnish storyteller Anni Swan is considered to be one of the most significant authors of **children's literature** in the first half of twentieth century in Finland. Swan's first collection of fairy tales, *Satuja* (*Fairy Tales*, 1901), was followed by several collections of fairy tales published between 1901 and 1933. The first collections are influenced by international folktales and are distinguished by a symbolic language and lyrical descriptions that are romanticized and mythologized. Swan followed the educational tradition of Zacharias **Topelius**, with the distinction that the pedagogical material in her stories was not as significant as in Topelius's work (see **Pedagogy**). Even she regarded fairy tales as a means to develop a child's imagination.

Throughout her work, Swan used the structure and **motif**s of folktales as textual and stylistic elements in her stories. Her later writings evoke, however, a more realistic view of the world. A recurring theme in her books is differences between social classes. Her fairy tales and juvenile books deal with values such as friendliness, tolerance, and morality. Even Swan's classic juvenile novels such as *Tottisalmen perillinen* (*Heir of Tottesund*, 1914), *Iris rukka* (*Poor Iris*, 1916), and *Ollin oppivuodet* (*Olli's Apprentice Years*, 1919) are influenced by folktales, although the morals and motives are more complex and realistic. Swan's books were illustrated by prominent Finnish artists such as Rufolf Koivu, Martta Wendelin, and Venny Soldan-Brofeldt. *See also* Finnish Tales.

Further Readings: Maija, Lehtonen. *Anni Swan*. Porvoo: WSOY, 1958; Nevala, Maria-Liisa, ed. *Suomalaisen naiskirjallisuuden linjoja*. Helsinki: Otava, 1989.

Elina Druker

Swan Maiden

A swan maiden is a beautiful young woman who appears in the form of a swan, and who regains human shape periodically when she lays aside her suit of feathers. To the imaginative mind, the beauty of a swan would suggest something of mysterious or otherworldly qualities, and this easily combined with the ancient idea that animals had some special connections with humans.

The notion that swans might be transformed humans could thus take root in different contexts. One such context must have given rise to this **motif**, which is expressed in a particular narrative. This tale has a young man coming upon a group of swan maidens as they are bathing in a lake or other body of water. They are in human shape, having laid aside their swan suits, and the young man grabs one. The startled maidens hasten to put on their suits, but the one whose garb has been taken has no choice but to follow the young man to his dwelling. She becomes his wife, but some time later—when he is away from home on business—she finds the swan suit, dons it again, and returns to the water.

It is apparent that this simple form of the story is the basic one, and that it originated somewhere in eastern Europe, but it was already spreading far and wide in prehistory. It was so attractive a motif that it could be used to heighten the drama and increase the human interest in a variety of narrative contexts, and so it was borrowed in **myth**s, **folktale**s, and historical **legend**s. In Hindu literature, for instance, swan maidens become celestial beauties; and when a mortal seizes one, he is brought by her into a beautiful otherworld. A mythological context is also given in the plot in the early Irish story "Aislinge Oengusso" ("The Vision of Aonghus"), which has the handsome youth-deity Aonghus searching for the beautiful lady Caer, whom he saw in a dream, and eventually finding her in swan shape by a lake. He himself assumes this shape and flies away with her to his otherworld dwelling in a tumulus. In medieval literary compilations, such as the Arabic *Thousand and One Nights* (see **Arabian Nights**) and the Anglo-French lays of **Marie de France**, the plot is subsumed into complicated stories of how, having lost the lady when she recovers her raiment, a hero must undergo several adventures before he recovers her.

A structure with various narrative strands was in fact the usual context for the swan-maiden plot in the folktales of Europe and Asia—such as those under the general heading of ATU 400, The Man on a Quest for His Lost Wife. For instance, when the swan maiden recovers her suit and leaves the hero, he goes in search of her and is assisted by a variety of helpful creatures and **magic object**s. When he eventually finds her, she may have forgotten him, thus occasioning the necessity for him to jog her memory with some ruse, such as giving to her a cake in which is hidden a ring that she had previously given to him. It is interesting to note how these extended narratives tend to duplicate the motifs by repeating them in reverse order—she recovers her suit, and he recovers her; she presents a ring, and he represents it to regain her.

In its simplest and most direct form, the plot was perpetuated by giving it the function of a genealogical legend, and in this form it thrived in the **folklore** of central and western

Europe. The man who discovered the swan maiden was identified with the historical ancestors of several noble families. Therefore, as the **mother** of this particular ancestor's children, she was herself the ancestress of the **family**. Here the plot usually retains its sad ending, but a wistful and romantic note may be added to the effect that she was often seen to hover near her children, keeping a protective eye on them. As the story was told in coastal areas of Scandinavia and Scotland, she was converted into a seal-woman, who was the ancestress of some local families; and in Ireland, she usually is a **mermaid**.

Since medieval times, in different parts of Europe, the swan-maiden motif has become confused with some other motifs of similar function. Most prevalent was the idea that she placed an injunction on her husband against doing certain things—such as boasting of her, visiting her at certain times, or striking her or otherwise insulting her—and that she left him when he either wittingly or unwittingly broke the injunction. Such motifs originally belonged to a different genre of legend, that concerning the incompatible **marriage** of a mortal to an otherworldly bride, such as the Irish legend of Macha or the French legend of Mélusine.

The swan-maiden motif has long been popular also in another kind of narrative (such as ATU 313, The Magic Flight; and ATU 465, The Man Persecuted Because of His Beautiful Wife). According to this tale, the swan maiden does not leave her mother, but the lover has to perform impossible tasks set by an envious **king** or by the maiden's own tyrannical **father**. She helps him to perform these tasks. Here the plot has become entangled with an even more ancient story, which concerns a young man who falls in love with the beautiful daughter of an **ogre**. The young lady helps her lover to perform nearly impossible tasks and then to elope with her. Among the tasks is to identify her from a number of other women who look exactly like her; and this, along with the basic love theme, would appear to have been what attracted the swan-maiden plot to the context, for that situation is akin to the way in which the young man gets the particular swan maiden from among the others when he seizes her suit of feathers.

A distinctive legend found in some western European literary sources in the **Middle Ages**, that of the swan-children, has no direct connection with the swan-maiden motif. This describes how a girl and her **brother**s are magically transformed into swans by a malicious woman, and how after many sufferings the girl manages to disenchant herself and her brothers and to regain human shape. This legend seems to have developed in the Netherlands before the Middle Ages, and to have spread to France, Britain, and Ireland, where it is now best known as the story of the Children of Lir. *See also* Animal Bride, Animal Groom; Transformation; Undine.

Further Readings: Baring-Gould, S. *Curious Myths of the Middle Ages.* London: Rivingtons, 1872. 471–523, 579–603; Hartland, Edwin Sidney. *The Science of Fairy Tales.* London: Walter Scott, 1891. 255–332; Leavy, Barbara Fass. *In Search of the Swan Maiden: A Narrative on Folklore and Gender.* New York: New York University Press, 1994; Uther, Hans-Jörg. *The Types of International Folktales.* Volume 1. Helsinki: Helsinkin: Academia Scientiarum Fennica, 2004. 194–98, 231–33, 273–74.

Dáithí Ó hÓgáin

T

Tailor

Simple craftsmen such as tailors performed well as everyday heroes (or sometimes villains) in the folktales of preindustrial societies. These were characters with whom storytellers and their listeners easily could identify. Such workers often traveled from house to house and from village to village seeking trade. Thus they themselves were carriers of news, gossip, and stories. Without doubt, such **storytelling** itinerant workers contributed greatly to the image of the tailor prevalent in folktales of many types: simple and naïve but clever and brave. Lacking the resources of wealth, weaponry, and physical strength, they nevertheless prevail against formidable opponents through a combination of fearlessness, good luck, and cunning.

Although tailors appear in folktales of many types, they are especially well represented in the family of stories built around **tale type** ATU 1640, The Brave Tailor, told around the world. These are prime examples of episodic tales, comprising a series of largely interchangeable adventures. Typical is the episode depicting a stone-throwing contest between the tailor and an **ogre**. The ogre throws a stone, which falls back to earth; the tailor (who serendipitously has a bird in his pocket) throws a bird, which disappears into the air.

Although most events traditionally built into ATU 1640 tales are not inherently related to the craft of tailoring, the episode of the Sewing Contest (ATU 1096) does show work-specific details appreciated by anyone familiar with stitching. In these tales (or episodes built into longer stories), the tailor engages the **devil** or an ogre in a sewing contest. The hero chooses a needle with a short thread but gives his opponent a very long thread. It takes the latter so long to pull each stitch tight that the tailor easily wins.

In contrast to the generally positive depiction of tailors in folktales, a shady aspect manifests itself as well. Traditionally, tailors fashioned garments from cloth furnished by their customers. Leftover pieces belonged to the customers, but tailors were often accused of stealing remnants for their own use, and a number of folktale types reflect this suspicion. In ATU 1574, The Tailor's Dream, a dishonest tailor dreams that on Judgment Day, his penance will be to make a flag from all the cloth he has stolen. Chastened, he forgoes further pilfering until given the chance to steal a particularly fine piece of cloth. He justifies himself, claiming that this specific piece would not be needed in the flag. In ATU 1574A, The Stolen Piece of Cloth, a thievish tailor intends to sew a piece of stolen cloth inside his own coat but inadvertently stitches it to the outside, thus revealing his theft.

Finally, tales of type ATU 800, The Tailor in Heaven (found throughout Europe), describe a dishonest tailor who nonetheless talks his way into heaven. From his perch on high, the self-righteous tailor observes an old washerwoman on earth stealing two scarves from the laundry, and he angrily throws a footstool at her. God, incensed at this hypocrisy, expels him from heaven. *See also* Clothing; Thief, Thieves.

Further Readings: Jason, Heda. "The Brave Little Tailor: Carnivalesque Forms in Oral Literature." *Acta Ethnographica Hungarica* 38 (1993): 385–95; Röhrich, Lutz. "The Social Milieu." *Folktales and Reality*. Translated by Peter Tokofsky. Bloomington: Indiana University Press, 1991. 184–98; Senft, Gunter. "What Happened to 'The Fearless Tailor' in Kilivila: A European Fairy-Tale From the South Seas." *Anthropos: International Review of Anthropology and Linguistics* 87 (1992): 407–21.

D. L. Ashliman

Taketori monogatari

One of the best-known **Japanese tales**, *Taketori monogatari* is also known by the names "The Tale of the Bamboo Cutter" and "The Tale of Princess Kaguya." The tale is generally believed to have originated in the tenth century, making it one of the oldest continually circulating Japanese narratives.

The story of the *Taketori monogatari* is one of an old woodcutter who finds a miniature girl in a stalk of bamboo. The bamboo cutter and his wife raise the child, Kaguya, and become wealthy as the girl becomes a beautiful woman. However, when approached by suitors, she refuses them all, placing impossible tasks before them, even rebuffing the emperor. Eventually, it is revealed that Kaguya is not human; she is a **princess** of the moon, to which she is obliged to return. The emperor, saddened by her departure, sends a messenger to the top of Mount Fuji to burn a note to Kaguya. In some versions, the emperor also burns an elixir of immortality on the mountain, thus giving it the name Mount Fuji from *fushi*, the Japanese word for immortality.

The *Taketori monogatari* has been adapted frequently, including several times in Japanese **graphic novel**s and **film**s. Two of the better known examples are the movie *The Castle beyond the Looking Glass* (2002) and the manga *Kaguyahime* (*Princess Kaguya* 1994–). The tale also plays a major part in *Big Bird in Japan* (1991), an American made-for-**television** movie linked to Jim **Henson**'s *Sesame Street*. *See also* Animation; Japanese Popular Culture.

Further Readings: Keene, Donald, trans. "The Tale of the Bamboo Cutter." *Monumenta Nipponica* 11 (1955): 329–55; Kristeva, Tsvetana. "The Pattern of Signification in the *Taketori Monogatari*: The 'Ancestor' of All *Monogatari*." *Japan Forum* 2 (1990): 253–260; *Taketori monogatari*. Japanese Text Initiative. Electronic Text Center, University of Virginia Library. http://etext.lib.virginia.edu/japanese/taketori/AnoTake.html.

B. Grantham Aldred

Tale Type

The term tale "type" denotes a closely related group of different **variant**s of a tale from a literary or **oral tradition** and refers to the narrative structures employed in **folktales**—that is, etiological legends, **animal tale**s, tales of magic, **religious tale**s, **legend**s, realistic tales (**novellas**), **anecdote**s and **joke**s, **tall tale**s, formula tales, **ballad**s, **myth**s, **fable**s, medieval romances, **exempla**, **fabliaux**, and so on. A tale type is not itself a tale but instead merely an ideal construction that is common to and abstracted from different versions of a narrative. In other words, tale types are descriptive inventories, which are arranged according to certain aspects but lack a rigorous theoretical structure. The designation "tale type"—from the Greek *týpos*, meaning shape, form—should be distinguished from the characterizations "type," "typology," or "figure," which always recur in the same form.

Furthermore, a distinction must also be made between the "tale type" and "stereotype." Stereotypes do not take any individual traits into consideration. Instead, they are used to create categories by ascribing particular human qualities to a group and its members. In the context of narratology, they often have a tendency to epic idealization.

The term "tale type," in contrast, is designed purely to describe a literary phenomenon, similarly to "system" or "structure." The term refers to the general or original manifestation of a text, an idea, or a fact. Tale types are theoretical constructs destined to delimit texts from one another. They capture the autonomous narrative threads of folktales. The folktales belonging to a particular tale type contain identical, or at least similar, content and can be traced back historically to the same "genetic" origin. A tale type can be clearly distinguished from a "**motif**" or "detail" as small narrative units, on the one hand, and the theme as the central and abstract idea of a text, on the other. Nevertheless, the notions "tale type" and "motif" may still overlap in some sense; often a single motif is also a tale type, especially in anecdotes and jokes or in formula tales.

Texts that are assigned to the same tale type contain the same stock of microforms and have a parallel narrative structure. Tale type is defined by the American folklorist Stith **Thompson** in his book *The Folktale* (1946) as "a traditional tale that has an independent existence. It may be told as a complete narrative and does not depend for its meaning on any other tale. It may indeed happen to be told with another tale, but the fact that it may appear alone attests to its independence. It may consist of only one motif or of many. Most animal tales and jokes and anecdotes are types of one motif. The ordinary *Märchen* (tales like **Cinderella** or **Snow White**) are types consisting of many of them" (Thompson, 415). With regard to the difference between tale type and motif, Thompson points out that: "A type-index implies that all versions of a type have a genetic relationship; a motif-index makes no such assumption" (Thompson, 416). The designation "tale type" is in competition with other terms such as "**archetype**," "**oicotype**," "subtype," "theme," "variant," or "version." But "tale type" clearly refers to a stable narrative core consisting of components such as motifs that are organized in a specific logical and chronological order. It is not an exception that tale types are characterized either by unusual events or situations or by the way their protagonists interact. Recurrent components can be traced back to "classical" models, such as Cinderella (ATU 510A), the **Dragon**-Slayer (ATU 300), or the myth of Oedipus (ATU 931). Frequently, the different folktales belonging to one tale type display a variety in introductions and endings.

Likewise, there is an affinity between the term "tale type" and the homogeneous book tale. What we are dealing with here is a dominant form of a folktale that prevails against other cognate tales belonging to the same tale type (for example, an **Andersen** tale, a **Grimm** tale, or a **Perrault** tale). In an attempt to classify rapidly expanding collections, late nineteenth-century scholars in Europe increasingly began to explore the wealth of tales stemming from the oral tradition (for example, Johann Georg von Hahn explored **Greek tales**, George Laurence Gomme **English tales**, and Michail Petrov Arnaudov Bulgarian tales). In this way, these texts were made available for the comparative study of folktales. The systematizations were supposed to be the basis for documenting the collections, genres, and the stock of folktales originating from different countries and regions. The aim was to ascertain the extent to which the sources and stylistic traits were connected as well as the degree of interdependency between oral and literary traditions. In addition, the classifications served as scientific tools to promote access to certain folktales or collections. It was Reinhold **Köhler**, Johannes **Bolte**, Jiří **Polívka**, and Emmanuel Cosquin who provided important impulses in this direction. The publication in 1910 of *Verzeichnis der Märchentypen* (*Index of the Types of the Folktale*), a German-language classification compiled by the Finnish folklorist Antti **Aarne**, a student of Kaarle Krohn, was the most influential contemporary contribution to the field from an international perspective. Aarne developed his system on the basis of Finnish, Danish (Sven **Grundtvig**), and German folktales (the Brothers Grimm). Following a numeric system, his catalogue is divided into categories based on the traditional genres of **folkore**: animal tales (nos. 1–299), ordinary tales (nos. 300–1199), and anecdotes and jests (nos. 1200–1999). Moreover, his classification distinguishes between actors and incidents. We are greatly indebted to Stith Thompson for his comprehensive extension and overhaul of Aarne's catalogue. In his revision of the catalogue, Thompson described the tale types more thoroughly and more precisely, incorporated the newly published regional type catalogues, made reference to the various source **archives** of different countries, added secondary sources, and indicated a small selection of literary **adaptation**s. His major work, *The Types of the Folktale* (known as AT, AaTh, or the Aarne-Thompson index), published in English in 1928, was not merely limited to folktales in a narrow sense, as becomes clear from Thompson's preface: "these tales are divided for the purpose of classification into three principal groups: animal tales, regular folk-tales, and humorous tales." In 1961, he revised his tale-type catalogue, extending the coverage of the index and recognizing in his preface that the "work might be called 'The Types of the Folk-Tale of Europe, West Asia, and the Lands Settled by These Peoples'" (Thompson, 7). When one considers the sheer amount of bibliographical material its author had to master, it is hardly surprising that the catalogue also attracted criticism. Experts in the field highlighted the following points that required consideration:

1. A typology of narratives implies an exact, scientific scheme, a situation that does not exist in narrative tradition in the real world.

2. The definitions of genres and the classification according to characters are often neither thematically nor structurally consistent. For example, no distinct genre is represented by AT 850–999, Novelle (Romantic Tales).

3. The concentration of the "Finnish School" on nineteenth-century oral tradition relegated literary sources to a secondary position and often obscured important older forms and occurrences of the tale types.

4. The system encompassed only European narrative tradition, with relevant material from western Asia and European settlements in other regions. Even in Europe, the traditions were documented unevenly. Documentation varied considerably from place to place, and for some countries (for example, Denmark and Russia), no information was provided at all. Evidence from Portugal, and from eastern and southeastern Europe, was often missing. The narrative traditions of small ethnic groups (Basques, Ladini, Fisians, Sorbs, etc.) were not, or not sufficiently, documented.

5. The presentation of separate localized types with only a few variants each unnecessarily obscured both the picture of their place in tradition and the classification system of the catalogue as a whole.

6. References to relevant scholarly literature were often missing.

7. References to variants were usually taken from older collections, not from new ones.

8. The descriptions of the tale types were in many cases too brief, too often imprecise, and too often centered unjustly only on the male characters.
9. The inclusion of so-called irregular types was dubious.
10. Too much of the documentation for the existence of many of the types lay in archival texts that were difficult to access.

In *The Types of International Folktales* (2004)—the new international type catalogue by Hans-Jörg Uther and his editorial staff (Sabine Dinslage, Sigrid Fährmann, Christine Goldberg, and Gudrun Schwibbe)—this criticism is taken into account without forsaking the traditional principles of how the tale types are presented. In this new catalogue—known as the ATU (Aarne-Thompson-Uther) index—the descriptions of the tale types have been completely rewritten and made more precise based on all of the results of research available up to approximately 2003. The essential research cited for each type includes extensive documentation of its international distribution as well as monographic works on that type or the cycle of types to which it belongs. Note has been made of the many types scattered throughout the various sections of the Aarne-Thompson catalogue whose internal properties or structural similarities and affinities with other types had previously been overlooked. The adoption of types or subtypes listed in regional catalogues into the ATU has been limited: many oicotypes have been integrated into widely distributed types with significant regional variations (an oicotypical substratum), rather than as additional types or numbered subtypes.

The concept of "tale type" used here must be understood to be flexible. It is not a constant unit of measurement or a way to refer to lifeless material from the past. Instead, as part of a greater dynamic, it is adaptable and can be integrated into new thematic compositions and media. The background for this model of narrative alteration and innovation is evident in a change of paradigm that took place in recent decades in historical-comparative folktale research. Earlier research had been handicapped by a shortage of necessary information regarding historical and recent narrative material, especially from Europe, in all the genres. In such a system, it was impossible to document all oral and literary forms with a worldwide distribution. The genre-based structure of the earlier Aarne-Thompson catalogue, and the thematic conception that this implied, made this impossible. History has shown that folk narratives from outside of Europe fit its thematically oriented sections only in part and often with difficulty. This is particularly true of myths, **epic**s, legends, and etiological accounts, and also of lesser genres such as anecdotes, jokes, rumors, and genres such as life history, family history, and refugee experiences that have been studied only recently. For these genres, some other system is needed.

Up until the 1960s, folktale scholars generally believed that oral traditions had existed unchanged for centuries and thus provided an important source of evidence for the belief systems of their ancestors. Thus, oral traditions constituted a more important source for national identity than did later written sources. This Romantic-era valuation, which originated during the nineteenth century and continued into the twentieth, a period of intense nationalization in Europe, had a lasting influence on the perceived importance of the documentation of oral tradition. While Aarne had essentially ignored older, literary sources, Thompson sometimes made reference to important literary texts by Giovanni **Boccaccio**, Geoffrey **Chaucer**, Giambattista **Basile**, and Johannes Pauli. However, knowledge of the existence of this literary dissemination played too minor a role when the spread and development of the traditions were assessed. Written sources were, for the most part, undervalued. The oldest written texts, particularly of animal tales, were often dismissed as a subtype or an "irregular" form. Although this kind of oversight reveals deficiencies in the ahistorical treatment of documents, the problem cannot be remedied within the tale-type numbering system. In modern times, the perspective is different, and written sources are valued more highly.

As we now know, many so-called oral narratives have a rich literary history. Some can be traced back to works of literature, in which the fantasy of homo narrans (the storytelling human being) can be seen in new adaptations that are responses to the changes in the function of the tale. This is particularly true, for example, of the fables associated with the name **Aesop** and for similar narratives from Oriental traditions. Other examples of literary genres important for oral tradition include medieval Arabic **jest**s, European exempla and farce, and the fabliaux and novellas of the late **Middle Ages**, all of which entered early modern literature. These narratives are completely different from the numerous **etiologic tale**s of illiterate peoples. Although the definitions of a tale type as a self-sufficient narrative and of a motif as the smallest unit within such a narrative have often been criticized for their imprecision, these are nevertheless useful terms to describe the relationships among a large number of narratives with different functional and formal attributes from a variety of ethnic groups, time periods, and genres. On pragmatic grounds, a clear distinction between motif and type is not possible because the boundaries are not distinct. With this attitude, monographic investigations can distinguish between content and theme and still consider form and function as the properties that determine the narrative's genre.

Some early advocates of narrative classification envisioned an exact system like that of the natural sciences, analogous to biological classification. This vision was later influenced by semantic and structural research. The hope for precision must be seen as a product of the wishful thinking of the time. Nevertheless, narratives must be analyzed not arbitrarily but according to structural considerations. Just as genres of narrative are only intellectual constructs, so, then, is any typology. Broad definitions permit similar themes and plots to be included, so that, in the course of the history of the origins and development of a tradition, its different functions can be discerned. A precise analysis guarantees that variations in narrative tradition will not be reduced to a simple multicultural homogeneity.

The ATU type catalogue is a bibliographic tool that characterizes such diversity, represented by published narratives of different ethnic groups and time periods, with a description of each type followed by references to catalogues, texts, and published research. Paradoxically, a description of a tale type can show its various and changing structural elements but not its meaning or functions. Nor can such a description show the variation in the motifs contained in the individual texts, variation that is essential for understanding the narrative's age, the process of its transmission, and its importance in tradition.

The list of potential sources includes historical works of various degrees of popularity, such as calendars, magazines, and popular books read for educational purposes, language study, or pleasure. In the past, European tradition unjustly dominated the international tale-type catalogue. Where this imbalance continues into the ATU, it is due not to any ethnocentric ideology, but merely reflects the present state of knowledge. For many countries and regions, the systematic classification of narrative tradition has begun only recently.

Existing type catalogues covering the folktales from various regions and countries specifically explore traditional genres such as myths, legends, ballads, and anecdotes. In the early 1960s, special systems were devised for the classification of legends, ballads, and exempla. These have provided a template for subsequent indexes. Other catalogues have concentrated on special fields: for example, mythological legends and legends about **death**. Although the criteria according to which these catalogues are arranged are mainly content-oriented, the important lemmas always refer to the international type catalogue ATU. *See also* Historic-Geographic Method; Nationalism.

Further Readings: Aarne, Antti. *The Types of the Folktale: A Classification and Bibliography.* Translated and enlarged by Stith Thompson. 2nd revision. 1961. Helsinki: Academia Scientiarum Fennica, 1987; Ben-Amos, Dan. *Do We Need Ideal Types (in Folklore)?* Turku: Nordic Institute of Folklore, 1992; *Enzyklopädie des Märchens.* Edited by Kurt Ranke et al. 11 volumes to date. Berlin: Walter de Gruyter, 1977–. (See the entries: "Anordungsprinzip"; "Archetyp"; "Detail"; "Geographisch-historische Methode"; "Motiv"; "Motivkataloge.); Heissig, Walther, and Schott, Rüdiger, eds. *Die heutige Bedeutung oraler Traditionen: Ihre Archivierung, Publikation und Index-Erschließung/The Present-Day Importance of Oral Traditions: Their Preservation, Publication and Indexing.* Opladen: Westdeutscher Verlag, 1998; Jason, Heda. *Motif, Type and Genre: A Manual for Compilation of Indices and a Bibliography of Indices and Indexing.* Helsinki: Academia Scientiarum Fennica, 2000. 24–29; Mullen, Patrick B. "Tale-Type." *Encyclopedia of Folklore and Literature.* Edited by Mary Ellen Brown and Bruce A. Rosenberg. Santa Barbara: ABC-CLIO, 1998. 641–43; Thompson, Stith. "Classifying Folk Narrative." *The Folktale.* 1946. Berkeley: University of California Press, 1977. 413–27; *Tools of the Trade: Reconsidering Type and Motif Indexes.* Special issue of *Journal of Folklore Research* 34.3 (1997); Uther, Hans-Jörg. "Type- and Motif-Indexes, 1980–1995: An Inventory." *Asian Folklore Studies* 55 (1996): 299–317; ———. *The Types of International Folktales: A Classification and Bibliography.* 3 volumes. Helsinki: Academia Scientiarum Fennica, 2004.

Hans-Jörg Uther

Tall Tale

A tall tale is a humorous tale, often based on exaggeration and told as if it were true. Because of its outrageous description of the hero's impressive adventures, it is also known as a "tale of lying" or a "windy." In *The Types of International Folktales*, tall tales are classified under types ATU 1875–1999.

The tall tale has connections to a variety of genres. In a **legend**, the events in a tall tale are described in great detail. Except for its use of humor, the style of the tall tale also resembles the style of the personal narrative. It also can be associated with the **anecdote** and **nonsense tale**, as it uses absurd **motif**s that occur across genres. Tall tales play along the boundary between what is real and what is not. Very often the narrative approaches the incredible events gradually, starting out with realistic descriptions and then moving into the realm of exaggeration. The storyteller might introduce the tall tale as a true tale, so the listeners react as if they believed the fantastic story as well.

Tall tales are typically told by men, especially by the representatives of the traditionally "masculine" professions, and therefore they belong to the tale tradition of hunters, for instance. Tall tales are often first-person narratives or include references to the relatives or acquaintances of the storyteller. Tall tales can be documented as early as the first century CE, when, in one of Plutarch's stories, the incredible claim is made that "words were congealed as soon as spoken" (ATU 1889F, Frozen Words [Music] Thaw).

It is quite usual for the storyteller to turn into a mythical hero who can perform impossible deeds with ease. The American tall-tale hero Paul Bunyan has even risen to the status of national hero. Reflecting the defining role of the hero and his exploits, the term "Münchhausen tale" has been used synonymously with "tall tale." The former designation gained popularity due to the numerous unbelievable stories supposedly told by the historic figure Baron Karl

Friedrich Hieronymus von Münchhausen. The literary versions of these tales were published by Rudolf Erich Raspe in *Baron Münchhausen's Narrative of his Marvellous Travels and Campaigns in Russia* (1785) and by Gottfried August Bürger in *Wunderbare Reisen zu Wasser und zu Lande, Feldzüge und lustige Abenteuer* (*Marvelous Travels by Water and by Land, Compaigns and Humorous Adventures*, 1787), a translation, adaptation, and expansion of Raspe's work. Tale type ATU 1889 (Münchhausen Tales) and its many subtypes consist of a great number of exaggerations and lies of Baron Münchhausen.

Internationally, one of the best-known tall-tale types is ATU 1960, The Great Animal or Great Object, with subtypes that tell, for example, of a tremendous ox or an exceptionally tall tree that reaches the sky. Tall tales also include the story of an incorrigible liar who has no time to lie but, when asked to, answers nonetheless with yet another lie (ATU 1920B, "I Have No Time to Lie").

Tall tales have been widely used in humorous and realistic literature, for example by Mark **Twain**. Because tall tales bear a resemblance to personal narratives, scholars and collectors have recently begun paying them increased attention. This new interest in the relation of tall tales to personal narrative is probably why, despite the popularity of Münchhausen tales in northern and central Europe, the collecting of tall tales became more popular in twentieth-century America. *See also* Jest and Joke; North American Tales.

Further Reading: Brown, Carolyn S. *The Tall Tale in American Folklore and Literature*. Knoxville: University of Tennessee Press, 1987.

Risto Järv

Tang Kristensen, Evald (1843–1929)

Evald Tang Kristensen was a Danish folklorist. Whereas the Romantic-era collections of **folktale**s were based primarily on scholarly **editing** of **informant**s' and vicarious collectors' work, it was Tang Kristensen's greatest contribution that he modernized the method of **collecting** by going directly to the sources of oral tales among the rural proletariat of central Jutland. A rich harvest of folktales, often in versions reflecting the narrative tone of specific informants, was thus gleaned from Tang Kristensen's numerous journeys on foot from 1867 onward, especially in western Jutland, where the folklorist felt particularly at home. Originally a teacher, Tang Kristensen received a state subsidy from 1888 that enabled his complete dedication to collecting folktales, **legend**s, and **ballad**s.

During the first Romantic phase of Danish **folklore** studies, individuals such as Svend **Grundtvig** focused on creating **archives** of the national soul, thus plucking the relics of the **Middle Ages** while showing less interest in the function of **oral tradition**s among the rural peasantry. Tang Kristensen, however, considered systematic methodology a link between the old rural narrators and the modern scientific study of folktales. Like contemporary folklorists, such as Kaarle Krohn and Antii **Aarne** in Finland, Tang Kristensen paved the way for modern research. Because of the focus on the cultural **context** of the folktale, the informants' names were usually recorded and the material published in extensive editions, often rendering a vivid impression of the narrator's voice. *See also* Scandinavian Tales.

Further Reading: Rossel, Sven H., ed. *A History of Danish Literature*. Lincoln: University of Nebraska Press, 1992.

Helene Høyrup

Tawada Yōko (1960–)

Author of short stories, **novels**, **poetry**, and plays, Tawada Yōko frequently employs elements of both Japanese **folktale**s and German **legend**s in her work. Born in Tokyo, Tawada moved to Germany in 1982, shortly after graduating from Waseda University, where she majored in Russian literature. While completing her postgraduate studies in Europe, Tawada began to study the twelfth-century classic *Konjaku monogatari* and **Seki** Keigo's *Nihon mukashibanashi shūsei* (*A Compilation of Japanese Folktales*, 1950–58). The discovery of these **Japanese tales** was a turning point for Tawada, triggering her interest in folktales and fairy tales and inspiring her to write *Inumukoiri* (*The Bridegroom Was a Dog*), which won the 1993 Akutagawa Prize.

The title story, "The Bridegroom Was a Dog," is a radical critique of **animal groom** tales which, as critics have pointed out, also draws on enchanted bride stories, particularly the well-known folktale "Tsuru nyōbō" ("The Crane Wife"). In Tawada's short story, a mysterious doglike man appears without warning and moves into a cram-school teacher's suburban home. The introduction of folktale fragments into a contemporary setting is typical of much of Tawada's work; indeed, she has stated in interviews that she enjoys the interesting and unexpected twists and turns that her writing takes when she blends the contemporary with heterogeneous fragments of traditional tales.

The Bridegroom Was a Dog was Tawada's first collection to appear in English (1998). After a five-year interval, it was followed by another: *Where Europe Begins* (2003)—a translation of *Wo Europa anfängt*, which had been published in Japanese and German in 1991. The first story in the collection, "Nyūyoku" ("The Bath"), is narrated by a woman who wakes up one day covered in scales. As she tells her story, which includes an encounter with a ghost, her narrative is disrupted by "once upon a time" fairy tales that Tawada weaves into the text to draw attention to its textuality. The ten stories in *Where Europe Begins* also include the tale, resembling a **fable**, about a monk who leaps into a pond trying to embrace his own reflection; and the title story, an account of a Japanese woman's journey to Moscow on the Trans-Siberian Railway, which—in its blending of Siberian fairy tales, diary excerpts, letters, and reminiscences—is simultaneously a journey through storytelling.

Tawada's interest in **intertextuality** and the intertextual possibilities of folktales and legends is also evident in the title story of her collection *Futakuchi otoko* (*The Man with Two Mouths*, 1998), which follows a group of Japanese tourists who, on a tour of Lower Saxony, come face-to-face with the infamous medieval jester **Till Eulenspiegel**. In a series of loosely connected vignettes, the tourists are treated to a number of tricks and **jest**s that parallel many of Eulenspiegel's adventures. In "Fuefuki otoko" ("The Pied Piper"), published in the same volume, Tawada divides the **Grimm** brothers' legend "Die Kinder zu Hamelin" ("The Children of Hamelin") into discrete units that she rewrites before systematically cataloguing in the order of the Japanese syllabary.

Tawada's work has continued to be recognized in both Germany and Japan, and in addition to the Akutagawa Prize, she received the Adalbert von **Chamisso** Prize (1996), the Tanizaki Prize (2003), and the Goethe Medal (2005).

Further Reading: Yamade Yūko. "Tawada Yōko and the Rewriting of Japanese Folklore." "Identity, Translation, and Embodiment in Migrant and Minority Women's Writings in Japan, English Canada, and Québec." Dissertation. Université de Montréal, 2002. 45–59.

Marc Sebastian-Jones

Taylor, Edgar (1793–1839)

As the first to translate tales by Jacob and Wilhelm **Grimm** into English, Edgar Taylor contributed to the Grimms' international reception and the fairy tale's popularity in England during the nineteenth century. Taylor and his collaborator, David Jardine, published their translations anonymously in two volumes under the title *German Popular Stories* (1823–26). Taylor avowed that the translations were intended not only to amuse children and adults but also to stimulate interest in England's own folk traditions. Accordingly, *German Popular Stories* included **illustration**s by the artist George **Cruikshank** and annotations offering commentary of a more scholarly nature.

Taylor and Jardine did not introduce the Grimms' tales to English-speaking readers without some distortion. Drawing largely on the 1819 edition of the Grimms' ***Kinder- und Hausmärchen*** (*Children's and Household Tales*), they offered fewer than a third of the stories in the Grimms' collection. Of the fifty-five tales published in *German Popular Stories*, two are composites while four others represent German authors other than the Grimms. Moreover, in adapting the tales for English children and sensibilities, Taylor and Jardine altered some passages significantly.

The success of Taylor's illustrated selection of tales inspired the Grimms to publish a popular edition of their own—called the Small Edition—which first appeared in 1825 and contained a sampling of fifty tales with illustrations by their artist-brother Ludwig Emil **Grimm**. *See also* Children's Literature; Translation.

Further Reading: Sutton, Martin. *The Sin-Complex: A Critical Study of English Versions of the Grimms'* Kinder- und Hausmärchen *in the Nineteenth Century.* Kassel: Brüder Grimm-Gesellschaft, 1996.

Donald Haase

Tchaikovsky, Pyotr Il'ich (1840–1893)

Pyotr Il'ich Tchaikovsky is often referred to as a Russian composer who used western European forms and idioms. Nevertheless, the imprints of Russian folk music, its harmonies and melodies, display a distinctly Russian character. Some critics even tend to name him the successor of Mikhail **Glinka**, the so-called father of Russian music. Born as the second son, in the town of Kamsko-Votkinsk, east of Moscow, Tchaikovsky began piano lessons at the age of five. In 1850, his father, a mining engineer, was appointed director of the St. Petersburg Technological Institute, and the family moved to the capital. In St. Petersburg, Tchaikovsky was accepted at the School of Jurisprudence, where he also was given the opportunity to continue his instruction on the piano. When his mother died of cholera in 1854, he composed a waltz in her memory. After finishing school, Tchaikovsky worked as a government clerk in the Ministry of Justice, and, at the age of nineteen, he began studies in composition at the St. Petersburg Conservatory. He graduated in 1865, after which he was appointed professor of composition and of the history of music. For the next ten years, Tchaikovsky devoted himself entirely to teaching and composing.

Among his first efforts in the genre of **opera** was *Undina* (***Undine***, 1869), based on Vasily Zhukovsky's translation of Friedrich de la Motte **Fouqué**'s Romantic fairy-tale **novella** of a **motif** from German mythology. The St. Petersburg Opera, however, did not include *Undine* in its repertoire. Tchaikovsky, who was disappointed with the judgment, burned almost the whole score, and the opera was never staged. A few remaining fragments later were used in other works. In 1873, Tchaikovsky composed incidental music for Aleksandr Ostrovsky's play *Snegurochka* (*The Snow Maiden*). Well known from Russian fairy tales, Snegurochka is the daughter of Spring and Frost, incapable of falling in love, since her heart would become warm and she would melt. Ostrovsky's drama was eventually made into an opera by Nikolai **Rimsky-Korsakov** in 1882.

The inspiration for Tchaikovsky's opera *Kuznets Vakula* (*The Blacksmith Vakula*) in 1876 came from Nikolai Gogol's hilarious tale "Noch' pered Rozhdestvom" ("The Night before Christmas," 1832), about the blacksmith who wins his bride by flying on the **devil**'s back to get her the slippers of the empress. Despite the humor of the story, the opera was a not well received, partly because of its melancholic mood. Tchaikovsky approved of the public's reaction, blaming himself for the failure. Fond as he was of the music, he revised and renamed the opera. When *Cherevichki* (*The Slippers*) opened at the Bolshoi Theatre in Moscow on December 31, 1887, Tchaikovsky himself conducted.

Ten years earlier, he had launched his first ballet, *Lebedinoe ozero* (*Swan Lake*, 1877). The tragic story emanates from the German **legend** about the **swan maiden**. Odette, a young maiden, has been turned into a swan by the curse of an evil **sorcerer**, but becomes human every night. When she meets a **prince** who is out hunting, they immediately fall in love. Unfortunately, the sorcerer interferes once again, and the lovers are united only in **death**. Variations of the swan-maiden **motif** can also be found in **Russian tales** and folk lyrics.

In 1888, Tchaikovsky was asked by the librettist and director of the Russian Imperial Theaters Ivan Vsevolozhsky to deliver the score for a ballet based upon Charles **Perrault**'s "La belle au bois dormant" ("**Sleeping Beauty**," 1697). It has been claimed that the **Grimm**s' version of the tale was of equal importance for Tchaikovsky's conception. Tchaikovsky's *Sleeping Beauty* (1890) tells the well-known story in three acts. The last act is devoted entirely to the wedding, and among the guests are several fairy-tale characters: **Little Red Riding Hood** dances with the **wolf**, **Puss in Boots** woos the White Cat, while **Cinderella** and her prince dance a waltz. The ballet was staged at the Mariinsky Theatre in St. Petersburg in January 1890 and was met with enthusiasm. Tchaikovsky himself considered it one of his best works. He was less satisfied with *Shchelkunchik* (*The Nutcracker*, 1892), his third ballet, which was based on E. T. A. **Hoffmann**'s epoch-making tale, *Nußknacker und Mausekönig* (*The Nutcracker and the Mouse King*, 1816). The idea for the ballet belonged to the choreographer Marius Petipa, who in fact, had a revised version of the tale by Alexandre Dumas pére in mind. Nevertheless, the basic plot of Hoffmann's tale is preserved in the ballet, which opened successfully in 1892. The critics were positive and expressed their admiration for Tchaikovsky's ability to create a structure out of what they regarded as merely a confusing story.

Two years earlier, in 1890, Tchaikovsky had written the score for a libretto by his brother Modest. The libretto was based on "Pikovaya dama" ("The Queen of Spades"), a short story written by Aleksandr **Pushkin** in 1833. The story can be classified as a fantastic tale since it combines the everyday world with the supernatural, which eventually leads to a mental crisis. Pushkin's original story was modified to make the drama suitable for opera. In the short story, Herman, the gambling officer, is sent to an asylum after his mental breakdown, while his beloved Lisa marries another man. The opera version presents the love story as more genuine, which is shown through the music, described by a critic as a "string of romances." *The Queen of Spades* (1890) was the second of Tchaikovsky's operas based on a text by Pushkin. The first one, *Evgeny Onegin* (*Eugene Onegin*), based on the most famous novel of Russian literature (completed in 1831), had its première as an opera on March 29, 1879. Here, as in several of his symphonies, concerti, and other works, Tchaikovsky's engagement with folk songs and folk music is clearly perceptible. In fact, Tchaikovsky had previously edited a collection of folk songs and their piano arrangements in 1869. Among them is the famous *Burlatskaya* (*The Barge-Haulers' Song*). *See also* Dance; Music.

Further Readings: Abraham, Gerald. *Studies in Russian Music.* Freeport, NY: Books for Libraries Press, 1968; Kearney, Leslie. *Tchaikovsky and His World.* Princeton, NJ: Princeton University Press, 1998; Wiley, Roland John. *Tchaikovsky's Ballets: Swan Lake, Sleeping Beauty, Nutcracker.* Oxford: Clarendon Press; New York: Oxford University Press, 1985.

Janina Orlov

Television

The turn to visual culture that occurred in the late nineteenth and early twentieth centuries with cinema and its moving pictures seemed to intensify in the mid-twentieth century with the development of television. Like **film** in its first decades, television was perceived as a threat to oral and literary culture. Placed inside the home, the television set would be easily accessible and require no particular degree of literacy or interaction. Watching television would be a private, passive experience. These concerns are similar to those that were expressed in the late eighteenth and early nineteenth centuries about the effects that literacy and book production were allegedly having on oral tradition. Jacob and Wilhelm **Grimm**'s *Kinder- und Hausmärchen* (*Children's and Household Tales*, 1812–15) was published in part to document oral folktales before they had completely died out in the wake of print culture.

The threats posed by new technologies are typically overstated. To be sure, Joseph Daniel Sobol, in writing about **storytelling** in this encyclopedia, notes that television does in fact seem to have adversely affected domestic storytelling gatherings in rural communities. In terms of fairy-tale production, however, television has contributed significantly to the dissemination of the fairy tale and solidified its presence in twentieth- and twenty-first-century popular culture. This is not an aesthetic or ideological judgment about the quality or cultural value of television's efforts in the realm of fairy-tale production. Rather, it is simply an observation that television has made frequent use of fairy-tale materials and kept the genre in public consciousness. Walt **Disney**'s animated films may dominate the contemporary fairy-tale canon, but it is noteworthy that already in 1976, a German survey confirmed that television was the primary source of contemporary knowledge about fairy tales. This may speak on the one hand to television's having indeed overshadowed oral and print culture; but, on the other hand, it testifies to television's role in fairy-tale dissemination.

From animated cartoons, situation comedies, and dramatic series, to feature films, made-for-television movies, and so-called reality television, the fairy tale has made its appearance in a variety of televised genres and formats. In its conventional form, television is a commercial medium offering mass entertainment, so it is no surprise that many of television's fairy-tale broadcasts have been familiar, predictable, and consistent with the viewers' expectations. Like cheaply produced picture-book versions of fairy tales, television relies on the fairy tale's readily available plots and popularity. One favorite format, for example, is the fairy-tale musical special, a staple of television in the United States since the 1950s. Typically these specials are simply a vehicle for established stars to provide musical and dance entertainment in the context of a well-known fairy tale. Whether it is Mickey Rooney

Left to right: Bridgette Anderson (Gretel), Joan Collins (The Witch), and Rick Schroder (Hansel) in season 2 of the Showtime TV Series *Faerie Tale Theatre*, 1983. [Showtime/Photofest]

and Fran Allison starring in *Pinocchio* in 1957, Sammy Davis Jr. and Carol Channing in *Alice in Wonderland* in 1985, or Whitney Houston and pop singer Brandy in a live broadcast of **Cinderella** in 1997, most mass-entertainment specials have left no significant mark on the history of the fairy tale. On the other hand, the repeated televised broadcasts of Victor Fleming's 1939 feature-film version of **The Wizard of Oz** became a popular tradition that helped to enrich the American experience of fairy tale.

At its best, television has contributed innovative fairy-tale **adaptation**s that now have cult status or form part of a new and popular fairy-tale canon. This is especially true of **animation**, which might be expected to take greater liberties with classical fairy tales—and thus be more engaging, surprising, and amusingly disrespectful than the usual live-action fare. In the United States, the fairy-tale cartoons of animators such as Walter Lantz, Isadore "Friz" Freleng, and Frederick "Tex" **Avery**, made originally for theatrical release in the 1930s and 1940s, made their way ultimately to television and the home-video market. Characterized by self-reflexivity, irony, comical allusions to social reality, impatience with fairy-tale clichés, and an equally impatient libidinous energy, these witty (and sometimes censored) animated fairy-tale adaptations are the antithesis of Walt **Disney**'s animated features, with their idealization of romantic love. These cartoons are arguably part of an alternative fairy-tale canon, and it is telling that three animated versions of "**Little Red Riding Hood**" have been listed in Jerry Beck's book, *The 50 Greatest Cartoons: As Selected by 1,000 Animation Professionals* (1994)—namely, Avery's *Red Hot Riding Hood* (1943) and *Little Rural Riding Hood* (1949), and Freleng's *Little Red Riding Rabbit* (1944).

American television produced its own canon-busting fairy-tale animations in the early 1960s in the form of Jay Ward's ***Fractured Fairy Tales***, a regular feature on the popular children's programs *Rocky and His Friends* (1959–61) and *The Bullwinkle Show* (1961–64). These irreverent parodies of classic fairy tales delighted in wordplay and mocking the conventions of traditional storytelling, and, like the cartoons of Avery and Freleng, they deflated fairy-tale clichés with irony and allusions to contemporary reality. In his *Fractured Fairy Tales*, Ward not only provided an alternative to Disney's saccharine fairy tales, he also poked fun at Disney himself. In the **Sleeping Beauty** episode, for example, Ward's **Prince** Charming decides not to wake the **princess** from her sleep but to construct a theme park around her.

In Japan, the form of animation known as "anime" has made substantial use of fairy tales, and fairy-tale anime series that originated for Japanese television have had a significant reception on television internationally. While anime may create new fairy-tale and fantasy plots, it also draws heavily on **Japanese tales** and Western fairy tales alike. For example, from 1989 to 1995 the American cable network Nickelodeon ran *Grimm's Fairy Tale Classics*, which was the English-language version of a forty-six-part Japanese television series (1987–88). In their transfer to American television—typically on cable networks—these series have sometimes undergone adaptation and domestication. For instance, the fifty-two-episode Japanese series based on the books of American author L. Frank **Baum**, which was shown in Japan in 1986 and came to American cable television in 1987 under the title *The Wonderful Wizard of Oz*, was edited by HBO into a smaller number of longer movies. The production and reception of anime series provide a particularly interesting case of the intercultural transmission of fairy tales. Whereas American popular culture is notorious for its influence on other cultures, anime demonstrates the impact of **Japanese popular culture** on audiences in the United States. The transaction is particularly rich and interesting due to the fact that Japanese series are frequently adaptations of Western tales. Thus, Western classics originally adapted for Japanese television audiences are transmitted back to Western audiences in a Japanese art form, through the lens of Japanese culture, and in a format adapted for television. The dynamics of this phenomenon and television's role in the transcultural dissemination of fairy tales deserves further investigation.

The criticism of fairy tales that had been sparked by **feminism** and **sociohistorical approaches** during the 1970s and '80s paved the way for significant changes in the fairy tales produced for mass audiences on television. With an eye to creating something new—and socially relevant—HBO's *Happily Ever After: Fairy Tales for Every Child* (1995–98) was a multicultural series for children that set more than three dozen classic tales in new cultural settings. For example, "**Snow White**" takes place in a Native American context, "**Puss in Boots**" in Hawai'i, "The Snow Queen" in an Inuit environment, and "**Beauty and the Beast**" in Africa. Called by some "politically correct," the series reflects the era's efforts to revise classical fairy tales to meet the needs of a diverse society. As its promotional slogan declared: "There are lots of new faces in fairy tale land . . . and the place will never be the same."

In the realm of live-action series, Shelley **Duvall**'s *Faerie Tale Theatre* (1982–87) was an interesting experiment to reimagine well-known tales by bringing multiple perspectives to the series as a whole. This was no homogenized series of tales reflecting Duvall's own vision. Instead, each tale in the series, which originally appeared on the Showtime cable network, featured a well-known director who brought a unique visual style and approach to interpreting the story. Settings were based on the styles of diverse artists and fairy-tale illustrators. Although famous actors were cast in the leading roles, the series was not intended to serve merely as a showcase. In each instance, the re-visioning of the fairy tale was primary. Although the series is of uneven quality, it was a refreshing undertaking and gave audiences—both children and adults—a new way of experiencing well-worn tales.

Perhaps the most innovative anthology series in the United States was Jim **Henson**'s *The Storyteller*, which premiered on the commercial television network NBC in 1988. Working with both puppets and actors, Henson adapted nine fairy tales, mostly from the Brothers

Grimm, using scripts written by renowned author Anthony Minghella. The title of the series refers to Henson's use of a **frame narrative**, in which a storyteller—whose narrative authority is open to question—introduces the tale to the viewing audience. The stories that Henson and Minghella tell may be clever, but they are neither lighthearted nor sentimental, and they deal with themes as sober as **incest**, power, fear, betrayal, and parental rejection.

Serious themes were also taken up by the dramatic television series ***Beauty and the Beast*** (1987–90). Set in contemporary New York City, the show involved the relationship between Catherine, a wealthy but socially committed attorney, and Vincent, a lion-faced man living with the homeless in tunnels below the city. As might be expected from a prime-time dramatic series, the romantic relationship between this beauty and beast dominated, but the series was nonetheless notable for using the fairy tale to deal with America's social problems. During its three-year run on network television, the show struck a chord with viewers and still has a considerable fan base to this day. Its first season was finally released on DVD in 2007.

Most of the examples so far have illustrated how television has adapted entire fairy-tale narratives to the small screen. However, television's role in the dissemination of the fairy tale has also involved its piecemeal use of the genre—that is, its tendency to promote fairy-tale fragmentation. For example, situation comedies based on fairy tales—such as *Bewitched* (1964–72), *I Dream of Jeannie* (1965–70), and *The Charmings* (1987–88)—do not adapt entire stories but rather individual **motif**s and characters. In these examples, the **witch**, the genie in a bottle, and Snow White and Prince Charming are all removed from their fairy-tale texts and contexts and transplanted to the American suburbs. The sitcoms themselves are not really fairy tales or fairy-tale adaptations; they simply include recognizable figures from fairy tales. Such fragmentation occurs often on television. Commercial **advertising** on television relies frequently on the audience's recognition of traditional characters—the figures of Little Red Riding Hood, Sleeping Beauty, Cinderella, the Princess on the Pea, and the **Frog King**, for example. Television dramas, too, invoke fairy tales with discrete allusions. For example, the popular American prime-time series *Desperate Housewives* (in an episode called "Running to Stand Still" in 2004) and *Medium* (in "The Night of the Wolf," aired in 2005) both allude to "Little Red Riding Hood." Even game shows, such as *Jeopardy* and *Wheel of Fortune*, rely on contestants (and home audiences) being able to recognize motifs and characters from classic fairy tales. In postmodern culture, fairy tales may be known less as complete, coherent narratives than as allusion, punch line, and commercial hook, and television both reflects and contributes to this fragmentation of the genre (see **Postmodernism**).

The Cinderella tale and its constituent motifs have always been an important part of American culture, and it is noteworthy that Cinderella is at the heart of certain programs that constitute the latest television phenomenon—so-called reality television. Series such as *Who Wants to Marry a Millionaire?* (2000) and *The Bachelor* (2002–) are based on the idea that a woman can achieve wealth and social status through **marriage** to a "prince charming" who picks her from a group of beautiful women vying for his affection. From the palatial settings and special gowns to the competition among women competing for the same man and the motif of the *Brautschau* (showing of the bride, looking for a bride), these twenty-first century television programs reinforce the conventional fairy tale and the perception of commercial television as a realm of **wish** fulfillment and happily-ever-after endings.

Nonetheless, television's potential for empowering viewers is significant. The viewing choices are greater than ever, not only due to the competition among the traditional commercial networks, cable channels, and satellite providers, but also due to the ability to use television sets in conjunction with videocassette and DVD players. The viewer has more programming choices than ever, as well as the ability to transcend cultural boundaries by acquiring visual texts from around the world. Using television sets in conjunction with home computers is now also a possibility, as is using computer screens and mobile phones to watch materials once available only on stationary television sets or in movie theaters. These same tools give the viewer the ability to manipulate the text and control the way content is presented. As a genre characterized by endless variation and adaptability, the fairy tale would seem to lend itself to reinvention under these circumstances. As technology continues to advance and the visual experience becomes more interactive, it will be interesting to see how the production and reception of the fairy tale changes to take advantage of these new possibilities. *See also* Amano Yoshitaka; DEFA Fairy-Tale Films; Gaiman, Neil; *Once upon a Mattress;* Peter Pan Films.

Further Readings: Dégh, Linda, and Andrew Vázsonyi. "Magic for Sale: Märchen and Legend in TV Advertising." *Fabula* 20 (1979): 47–68; Haase, Donald. "Television and Fairy Tales." *The Oxford Companion to Fairy Tales.* Edited by Jack Zipes. Oxford: Oxford University Press, 2000. 513–18; Jenkins, Henry. "'It's Not a Fairy Tale Any More!' Gender, Genre, *Beauty and the Beast.*" *Textual Poachers: Television Fans and Participatory Culture.* New York: Routledge, 1992. 120–51; Jerrendorf, Marion. "Grimms Märchen in Medien: Aspekte verschiedener Erscheinungsformen in Hörfunk, Fernsehen und Theater." Dissertation. Tübingen, 1985; Preston, Cathy Lynn. "Disrupting the Boundaries of Genre and Gender: Postmodernism and the Fairy Tale." *Fairy Tales and Feminism: New Approaches.* Edited by Donald Haase. Detroit: Wayne State University Press, 2004. 197–212; Schmitt, Christoph. *Adaptionen klassischer Märchen im Kinder- und Familienfernsehen: Eine volkskundlich-filmwissenschaftliche Dokumentation und genrespezifische Analyse der in den achtziger Jahren von den westdeutschen Fernsehanstalten gesendeten Märchenadaptionen mit einer Statistik aller Ausstrahlungen seit 1954.* Frankfurt a.M.: Haag und Herchen, 1993.

Donald Haase

Tenèze, Marie-Louise (?–)

Marie-Louise Tenèze is a French folklorist who collaborated with Paul **Delarue** on the catalogue of French tales *Le conte populaire français: Catalogue raisonné des versions de France et des pays de langue française d'outre-mer* (*The French Folktale: Structured Catalogue of Versions from France and French-Language Countries Overseas,* 4 volumes, 1957–2000). This catalogue adapts the Aarne-Thompson index of **tale type**s to the French and Francophone corpus of tales. After Delarue's death in 1956, Tenèze finished preparing the catalogue's first volume (on supernatural adversaries) for publication. Tenèze published four more volumes of the catalogue: the second (1964) extends the classification to supernatural helpers, objects, and forces; the third (1976) focuses on tales featuring animal characters; the fourth, in two parts (1985–2000), deals with religious tales and French versions of romantic tales.

Affiliated with the Société française d'ethnographie (French Ethnographical Society) and the Centre national de la recherche scientifique (National Scientific Research Organization), Tenèze has published extensively on folk narratives. In her research, she distinguishes between three types of modifications to which oral narratives have historically been subject upon finding their way into print: the first concerns religion (for example, the **devil** and God replace characters such as the **ogre** and **fairy**); the second pertains to psychology (narrative functions fulfilled by living organisms and creatures like plants and animals are assumed by psychological forces such as jealousy and curiosity); the third involves **parody** (when a narrative's symbolic meanings are no longer discernible, some storytellers adapt the tale to a contemporary context by means of satire). Tenèze's book *Les contes merveilleux français: Recherche de leurs organisations narratives* (*French Fairy Tales: An Investigation of Their Narrative Structures*, 2004), was awarded the Grand Prix de l'Imaginaire. *See also* French Tales.

Further Reading: Tenèze, Marie-Louise. "The Devil's Heater: On the 'Contexts' of a Tale." Translated by Brunhilde Biebuyck. *Journal of Folklore Research* 20 (1983): 197–218.

Harold Neemann

Tennyson, Alfred, Lord (1809–1892)

Alfred, Lord Tennyson. [Library of Congress]

The massive body of **poetry** that Alfred, Lord Tennyson produced both before and after his 1850 elevation as England's Poet Laureate evinces his lifelong fascination with fairy tales and Celtic **folklore**. His 1830 volume *Poems Chiefly Lyrical* not only contains "Recollections of the **Arabian Nights**" but also features poems such as "The Kraken," "The Sea-Fairies," and a pairing of "The Merman" and "The **Mermaid**." These verses reflect the impact of Thomas Crofton **Croker**'s *Fairy Legends and Traditions of the South of Ireland* (1825–28), a compendium that introduced Tennyson to the timeless but dangerous underwater world postulated by the Brothers **Grimm**. Croker's collection also allowed Tennyson to connect a female world of sirens, nymphs, and **fairies** to Arthurian romance. His 1832 poem "The Lady of Shalott" opposes the mysteriously "cursed" and reclusive weaver whom peasants regard as a "fairy" to Camelot's masculine Sir Lancelot. This apposition is fully taken up in the twelve-part *Idylls of the King*, the serial poem that Tennyson kept expanding from 1859 to 1885. Guinevere, whom Celtic tradition had linked to fairies, and Nimüe or Vivien, a seductress who enchants the wizard Merlin, now contribute to the erosion of Arthur's chivalric order.

Tennyson also reworked traditional fairy tales: he placed his 1830 retelling of Charles **Perrault**'s "**Sleeping Beauty**" into a longer, framed, verse-narrative he called "The Day-Dream" (1842). And he gave a comic turn to "Jack and the Beanstalk" and "**Bluebeard**" when he cast both poems into hexameters (1874). *See also* Celtic Tales.

Further Reading: Paden, W. D. *Tennyson in Egypt: A Study of the Imagery in His Early Work.* New York: Octagon Books, 1971.

U. C. Knoepflmacher

Terayama Shūji (1935–1983)

Terayama Shūji gained international recognition during the 1970s for his work as a playwright and director of the experimental **theater** group Tenjō Sajiki. He was also a poet, photographer, essayist, filmmaker, and author of almost 100 fairy tales. Born in the remote mountainous prefecture of Aomori in northern Japan, many of Terayama's early works, like *Aomori-ken no semushi otoko* (*The Hunchback of Aomori*, 1967), draw heavily on the **myth**s and folk traditions of the region. *Inugami* (*Inugami: The Dog-God*, 1969) explores spirit possession, while *Jashūmon* (*Heretics*, 1971) reworks the **legend** of *ubasute* (the practice of abandoning elderly—usually female—relatives in the mountains). In other plays, such as *Nuhikun* (*Directions to Servants*, 1978) and *Aohigekō no shiro* (***Bluebeard's Castle***, 1979), Terayama draws less on traditional Japanese **folklore**; however, he continues to revise previous writings and to borrow openly and extensively from **literary fairy tale**s and other disparate sources.

The influence of folktales and fairy tales can be traced throughout Terayama's oeuvre. In addition to his work with the theater group Tenjō Sajiki, he translated Arthur **Rackham**'s ***Mother Goose*** (published in three volumes as *Mazā Gūsu*, 1977–78), created a picture-book version of the ***Arabian Nights*** (published as *Senichiya monogatari* in 1968), and, in 1982, published a collection of fairy-tale parodies, *Boku ga ōkami datta koro: sakasama dōwa shi* (*When I Was a Wolf: Topsy-Turvy Fairy Tales*). Terayama's own innovative but critically neglected fairy tales were collected in 1994–95 as *Terayama Shūji meruhen zenshū* (*The Complete **Märchen** of Terayama Shūji*). *See also* Intertextuality; Parody.

Further Reading: Sorgenfrei, Carol Fisher. *Unspeakable Acts: The Avant-Garde Theatre of Terayama Shūji and Postwar Japan.* Honolulu: University of Hawaii Press, 2005.

Marc Sebastian-Jones

Thackeray, William Makepeace (1811–1863)

William Makepeace Thackeray had a sharp, cynical eye for human folly, most famously seen in his **novel** *Vanity Fair* (1847–48). While most of his work is realist social commentary, he also relentlessly pillories romance **motif**s in his **ballad**s and stories, producing biting parodies that undercut the idealism of the form. The best example of this is his "Fireside **Pantomime**," *The Rose and the Ring* (1855), a fairy-tale narrative (ostensibly aimed at children and the lucrative and sentimental Victorian Christmas market) which offers extended and sophisticated satirical play. *The Rose and the Ring* mimics an oral mode of **storytelling** but is self-consciously excessive in its treatment of fairy-tale figures as comic caricatures, an effect reinforced by the novel's cartoonlike **illustration**s.

Thackeray playfully attacks various aspects of fairy-tale narrative, most strongly the motif of common objects infused with unreasonable magical power (see **Magic Object**). The Rose and Ring of the title bestow the gift of beauty on the possessor, who is adored by all, to the detriment of genuine moral worth and good character. **Prince** Giglio and **Princess** Rosalba eventually overcome the usurpation of their thrones to become a validated couple whose affection transcends the magical augmentation required by their less intelligent, less moral counterparts. The fairy godmother tradition is also ruthlessly attacked: the Fairy Blackstick is a down-to-earth figure whose most successful gift to royal children is to deprive them of royal privilege. Thackeray's purposes are thus entirely moral, and his sense of the magical solutions of fairy tale somewhat condemnatory.

Further Reading: Sorensen, Gail D. "Thackeray's *The Rose and the Ring*: A Novelist's Fairy Tale." *Mythlore* 15 (1989): 37–38, 43.

Jessica Tiffin

Theater

Theater that presents folktales and fairy tales is found in many cultures around the world. The traditions discussed in this entry are arranged geographically and, within each region, chronologically. Only dramatic **performance** that is not viewed as an enactment of sacred **myth** or ritual and that involves either spoken or mimed roles is discussed in this entry.

India

Indian theater began several centuries before the Common Era, although its origins are obscure to current scholars. Traditional forms involve dance, song, and instrumental music as well as acting. Costume and movement are highly stylized. Perhaps the earliest Indian playwright whose works survive is Bhasa (whose dates remain uncertain). Bhasa was known only as a name for centuries, but several Sanskrit plays attributed to him were rediscovered in 1912. Most of them are based on the *Mahabharata*, *Ramayana*, and the *Puranas*. Four are nonscriptural, *Avimaraka* (*Love's Enchanted World*), *Daridracarudatta* (*The Poverty of Carudatta*), *Pratijnayaugandharayanam* (*The Vow of Yaugandharayana*), and *Svapnavasavadatta* (*The Dream of Vasavadatta*), the latter two portraying the legendary King Udayana. The royal world of these plays is filled with daring-do, magic, mistaken identities, and courtly love; consequently, many writers refer to them as "fairy-tale plays."

Another influential ancient writer is Kalidasa, in approximately the fourth century CE. Among his plays are *Malavikagnimitra* (*Malavika and Agnimitra*), *Abhijnanasakuntalam* (*The Recognition of Sakuntala*), and *Vikramorvasiyam* (*Pertaining to Vikrama and Urvasi*),

Dorothy Seacombe plays the Beast in the 1928 pantomime production of *Beauty and the Beast* at the Lyceum Theatre. [Hulton-Deutsch Collection/Corbis]

all of which depict **king**s who fall in love and must endure magical or supernatural opposition before achieving final happiness. Later Sanskrit writers as well as Indian vernacular dramatists drew upon the same romanticized royal life and often the same stories. For instance, the seventh-century King Harsa wrote theatrical pieces for court performance, including *Rathnavali* (the name of a character), which again portrays King Udayana, and *Nagananda* (*Joy of the Serpents*), depicting a **prince**'s efforts to save snakes about to be sacrificed to the deity Garuda. Other important Indian playwrights include King Sudraka (c. fourth century CE), whose *Mrcchakatika* (*The Little Clay Cart*) reworks Bhasa's *Poverty of Carudatta*, and Bhavabhuti (seventh or eighth century CE), whose *Malatimadhava* (*Malati and Madhava*) is another courtly love story involving magic. Over several centuries, Indian theater influenced the course of drama in Southeast Asia, including Thailand, Indonesia, and Cambodia. The subject matter was taken from Hindu **epic**s and mythology, usually arranged to gamelan music.

Today, Indian theater incorporates both a wide variety of native forms usually based on traditional stories and the more "realistic" international theater introduced to India in the nineteenth century. For instance, Hindi playwright Habib Tanvir's *Charandas chor* (*Charandas the Thief*, 1973) adapted a folktale about a generous **thief** who insists upon telling the truth at all times. Other traditional plays are produced in modern **adaptation**s, sometimes in English as well as in Indian languages.

China

Performance arts, such as dance, song, acrobatics, and clowning, are mentioned in Chinese records from the Shāng Dynasty (c. 1500 BCE). Later, dancers in costume, apparently interpreting stories, are mentioned in Confucian literature (c. 500 BCE). When traditional Chinese theater began is not entirely clear. Purely spoken theater did not exist in China until it was imported in the late nineteenth century, since which time it has usually been associated with realism. Fairy-tale themes are far likelier to be portrayed in **puppet theater** and musical theater.

Chinese musical theater is often called "**opera**" in English, although that is inaccurate. For instance, not all of the dialogue is sung, but some is recited as poetry. In some styles, only major characters sing. Although many plays are based upon Chinese history and mythology, others are drawn from folktales and works of fiction, especially classic romances like *Xī Yóu Jì* (*Journey to the West*, originally published in 1592) by **Wú** Chéng'ēn, including the popular character Sūn Wùkōng (Monkey King, also known as Stone Monkey and Aware of Vacuity), and the **legend** of *Baí shé zhuàn* (*White Serpent* by Féng Mènglóng, seventeenth century, as well as several oral versions). Other stories include *Hónglóu mèng* (*Dream of the Red Chamber*, c. 1760–91) by Cáo Xuěqín and Gāo'è and *Sānguó yǎnyì* (*Romance of the Three Kingdoms*, fourteenth century) by Luó Guànzhōng. Like playwrights elsewhere, Chinese authors adapt the stories, changing plots and revising characters as they dramatize so that **variant**s of well-known stories appear; two versions of *White Serpent* may differ in many regards.

There are many local styles of Chinese theater, including "Beijing," popular throughout China and well known internationally, and "Guǎngzhōu," also widespread in China. In all forms, the acting is highly stylized, employing standardized gestures and expressions that can be interpreted easily by the audience, adding a layer of understanding beyond the literal meaning of the dialogue. Makeup is used to suggest character attributes rather than physical appearance. The performance depicts the emotional or psychological essentials of a story, not visual accuracy.

Chinese theater continues to develop. Until the twentieth century, **men** played all of the roles and still do in some productions, although women now appear regularly. During the twentieth century, Chinese scores were sometimes arranged for Western musical instruments. Modern plays are based on traditional stories, such as *Journey to the West* (1987) by Stan Lai, who was born in the United States but is based in Taiwan (offering an example of intercultural production and reception). More recently, *The Monkey King, Real or Fake*, a Shaoxin-style dramatization of part of the same epic, debuted in 2003 with computerized effects and a Western orchestra.

Japan

Japanese theater has taken many forms, and in all of its native traditions, spirits mingle freely with mortals. The oldest such theatrical style is Nō (often written "Noh"), with a body of approximately 250 plays, and its associated art form, Kyōgen (plays performed as comic relief between the five Nō dramas offered in one day). Fairy themes are common. For instance, the Kyōgen *Tamamonomae* (*The Beautiful Fox Witch*) and the Nō play *Sesshōseki* (*The Death Rock*, sometimes attributed to Hiyoshi Yasukiyo) present the same folktale **motif** (B15.7.7.1, Nine-tailed fox). Similarly, a legend about a demon becomes the source of two Nō plays, *Kurozuka* (a name, sometimes called *The Black Tomb*) and *Adachigahara* (*The Goblin of Adachigahara*) by Zeami Motokiyo, and a Kyōgen, *Dōjōji* (*The Temple of Dōjōji*, also called *The Bell of Jealousy*). The two Nō plays were written for rival troupes of actors.

While Nō and Kyōgen have traditionally been perceived as aristocratic, Kabuki has generally had wider appeal (and a larger repertoire). Kabuki was founded by Okuni, a temple dancer, in 1603; however, for most of its history, Kabuki has been performed only by men. Major Kabuki writers include Chikamatsu Monzaemon, Takeda Izumo, and Nishizawa Ippō. Many plays were written collaboratively by multiple writers. Individual Kabuki plays were originally daylong events, but due to competition between theaters, less exciting sequences were dropped and scenes from other plays added. Since audiences already knew the stories by heart, the appeal was the artistry and excitement of the performance rather than the suspense of an unfamiliar story.

Kabuki aims to portray emotion believably, but in the context of magic and the supernatural. Stage machinery and costumes are employed to create the illusion of magic. In particular, transforming living things from one state to another is important in Kabuki. For instance, as in **Japanese tales**, foxes often assume human form. Besides Tamamonomae, examples include Kuzunoha, a vixen who becomes human and bears a child with her husband Abe no Yasuna, and Tadanobu, who becomes human to reclaim a drum made of the skins of his fox parents. Both foxes appear in traditional plays and more recent adaptations.

Unlike Nō, Kabuki has continued to add new plays. For instance, *Fuji musume* (*Wisteria Maiden*, 1826) by Katsui Gempachi dramatizes a painting's coming to life to seek the love of a young man. Kimura Tomiko's *Kurozuka* (1939) retells the old Nō story in a modern Kabuki, with choreography inspired partially by Russian ballet. Similarly, techniques have evolved; for example, in his modern play based on a Chinese **ghost story**, *Gensō to Yōkihi* (*Gensō and Yōkihi*, 1987), performer Bandō Tamasaburō III incorporated acting styles from Beijing theater. Also in the late twentieth century, *musume* Kabuki ("young women's Kabuki") appeared, with **women** taking all of the roles, creating a **gender** reversal of traditional Kabuki.

During the nineteenth century, Kabuki waned in popularity and Nō almost vanished, but after World War II, Japanese theater, including Nō and Kabuki, underwent a rebirth, with master artists being given government stipends to encourage the arts. In addition, many Japanese writers embrace Western-style theater but adapt it to Japanese culture. Many such playwrights have taken inspiration from international sources, such as **Terayama** Shūji, who wrote for the Tenjō Sajiki theatrical troupe in the 1970s, and Kara Jūrō, who uses fairy tale and other fantastic elements in his plays. Betsuyaku Minoru's *Matchi-uri no shōjo* (*The Little Match Girl*, 1967), retells Hans Christian **Andersen**'s tale as the story of a young woman who was lost as a child and dies only after confronting her parents.

The Middle East

Although dance, **storytelling**, and puppetry were common, theater did not exist in most of the Middle East before the nineteenth century. Iran is unusual among Islamic countries in the region for having an ancient theater tradition (which it shares with Armenia). In addition, Turkish tradition features a dance and spoken theater, *ortaoyunu*, which some scholars compare to *commedia dell'arte* in its use of physical humor and stock characters. Similar performances also occur in Iran and Armenia, with more emphasis in those countries upon verbal repartee.

Persian drama is roughly as old as Indian and Greek drama and, based upon linguistic and other evidence, seems to have influenced and been influenced by both. Much of the mime and comedy of ancient Persia was based upon folktales, including stories of magic and supernatural beings. Like Indian theater, the Persian forms continued to evolve into modern times. Turkish records mention performances by Iranian actors in the seventeenth century, and folk theater still presents traditional comedies in both Iran and Armenia.

Purely spoken theater began in the Middle East in the nineteenth century. Its primary use has not been to dramatize fairy tales, but some writers have found folktales a way of appealing to their audience's shared cultural heritage. Among these are the Lebanese theater pioneer Marun al-Naqqash and Egyptians, including the prolific dramatist Tawfiq al-Hakim, who wrote *Shahrazad* (**Sheherazade**, 1934); Mahmud Wasif and Mahmud Taimur (both of whom wrote plays depicting events in the career of **Harun al-Rashid**); and Alfred Faraj in his *Ali Janah al-Tabrizi wa-tabi 'uhu Quffah* (*Ali Janah from Tabriz and Quffah, His Henchman*, 1969). Their sources include folktales and the **Arabian Nights**.

The Americas

In many North American cultures, performance art is largely a matter of dance, song, chant, and storytelling. However, in Central and South America, some performances are more truly folk theater, such as the Quiché farce *Charamiyex* (*The Flute Player*). *Güegüence o macho ratón* (*Honored Elder or the Brave Mouse*) is a Nahuatl and Spanish comedy from Nicaragua dating to the days of the Spanish Empire; its title character is a folk **trickster** who outwits the colonial Spanish governor.

In colonial times and afterward, the theatrical forms of many Native peoples were suppressed by both religious and civil authorities as undermining Christianity; for instance, the folkloric tragedy *Rabinal-Achí* seems to have been last performed in the 1820s. However, many indigenous folktales are still performed in adapted form, particularly at Corpus Christi and Carnival, especially in Brazil and Cuba. Folktale elements of Europe and Africa were also blended with Native traditions, such as the Spanish characters Bato and Gila (comic shepherds), who began to appear in Christmas pageants known as *pastorelas*. Also, street theater not linked to religious occasions, termed *géneros chicos* or *sainetés*, which often dramatize folktales, came to be performed in lands as diverse as Argentina, Cuba, and Mexico. (Plays written specifically in the European tradition are considered below under "Europe and the West.")

Sub-Saharan Africa

Africa is home to many diverse cultures, many of which have multiple performance traditions. Many theatrical forms appear in sub-Saharan Africa, including among such people as the Khomani San, the Malians, and the Mande. In many African traditions, audience participation is often important. In some traditions, as in the Akan people's Anansem (enactments of **Anansi** tales), a narrator interrogates audience and performer alike; in others, a performer drafts audience members to portray supporting characters. In several traditions, audience members initiate interaction with performers directly.

One of the most accessible traditions for non-Africans is the Yoruba alarinjo, about which much has been written in Nigeria and elsewhere. Alarinjo is professional theater (its amateur counterpart is called "apidan"). Performances depict folktales and stories about the supernatural. Alarinjo takes place outdoors, often in a marketplace, with the audience surrounding the performers. As many as fifteen men wearing masks act out the roles while drummers play and a chorus sings. Plays are oral compositions that other theatrical troupes witness and learn, resulting in the development of a common body of plots and themes. Some aspects of performance are dictated by tradition, while at other times, alarinjo actors vary their performances according to the moment, such as offering satiric commentary on local events. Characters are stock and include both Yoruba and foreigners.

Alarinjo and other traditional dramatic forms vied for popularity with local interpretations of Western theater during the nineteenth and early twentieth centuries. After Nigerian independence, writers such as Wole Soyinka, Ola Rotimi, and Femi Osofisan began creating new plays drawing upon both international and African sources, including folktales. At the same time, some African playwrights are adapting foreign fairy tales, such as Zimbabwean Stephen Chifunyise and his associate Robert McLaren in their *The Little Man of Murewa* (2005), an adaptation of Andersen's "Little Claus and Big Claus."

Europe and the West

Although the phrase "Western theater" sometimes suggests stage realism, verisimilar theater dates only to the mid-nineteenth century. Before that, acting, staging, and writing were more stylized.

Classical Theater.   Some of the earliest surviving European plays suggest folktales as source material, including Greek Old Comedy pieces like Aristophanes' *Ornithes* (*The Birds*, 414 BCE) and *Batrachoi* (*The Frogs*, 405 BCE). In these plays, talking animals mock human behavior and magical **transformation**s occur. Men in masks portrayed all of the roles, singing and dancing as well as speaking. Later, the New Comedy also featured folktale elements, such as Menander's *Dyskolos* (*The Bad-Tempered Man*, 316 BCE), in which a young man and his clever slave outwit a cranky old man and marry his daughter, a theme common in *commedia dell'arte* centuries later.

In Rome, comedies often embodied folktale themes and motifs, like the twin **brothers** (Motif K1311.1, Husband's twin brother mistaken by woman for her husband) in *The Menaechmi* (ca. 200 BCE) of Titus Maccius Plautus. Roman mimes were bawdy farcical performances employing speech, dance, and song, and relied upon stock characters like Dosennus, a greedy humpback, and Pappas, a stingy old man.

Medieval and Renaissance Theater.   When Roman stability declined, literary theater languished across the empire. Yet other theatrical arts survived, like mummery, whose relation to Roman mime (as opposed to local traditions) is asserted by some historians and denied by others. Most mummers enacted folktales; some, for instance, portrayed ritual combats which came to be associated with St. George and the Seven Champions of Christendom in England. Across Europe, mummers and other performers offered skits during holidays and festivals. In Russia, for example, wandering minstrels called *skomorokhi* performed skits, told stories, and gave puppet shows.

In Italy, similar skits evolved into the *commedia dell'arte*, an improvisational theater drawing upon folk elements, especially clever servants or young lovers who outwit wealthy old men. A wide range of stock characters, among them Pulcinella (Punch), Arlecchino (Harlequin), Columbina (Columbine), Pantalone (Pantaloon), and il Dottore (the Doctor), appeared in many "scenarios" (dramatic outlines) that would be fleshed out according to the talents of the performers and the mood of the audience. Stories were often earthy, featuring theft or **sexuality** and also **magic object**s and other fairy-tale elements.

Most medieval and early Renaissance literary theater grew around religious occasions. As late as the sixteenth century, *Meistersinger* Hans Sachs of Nuremberg wrote short dramatizations of comic folktales for Shrove Tuesday (*Fastnachtsspiele*); these were similar in plot to *commedia dell'arte* scenarios but did not involve *commedia* characters. Ludovico Ariosto's poem *Orlando Furioso* (c. 1505–16) inspired many skits and plays with its chivlaric setting. Gil Vicente, a Portuguese who wrote in his own language as well as in Spanish, also dramatized humorous folktales.

Seventeenth- and Eighteenth-Century Theater.   In Spain, Guillén de Castro y Belvis wrote of magical and comic themes. Some of his works, translated, became the sources for writers in English and other languages. His *Fuerza de la costumbre* (*Force of Custom*, 1618) is sometimes cited as the source for Francis Beaumont and John Fletcher's *Love's Cure, or the Martial Maid* (1647). Sixteenth-century author Pedro Calderón de la Barca, although more often associated with revenge tragedies, also wrote fairy-tale plays, including *La vida es sueño* (*Life Is a Dream*, c. 1635), dramatizing a king's effort to avoid a prophesied destiny.

In England, several plays presented fairy or folktale themes. The most famous of these are *A Midsummer Night's Dream* (1600) and *The Tempest* (1611) by William **Shakespeare**, but there are many others, such as Thomas Dekker's *Old Fortunatus* (1600), Beaumont and Fletcher's *Philaster, or Love Lies Bleeding* (c. 1609), and *The Birth of Merlin* (attributed to William Rowley, 1662). George Peele dramatized several fairy stories, including the *Old Wives' Tale* (1595). Of debated authorship is *The Maid's Metamorphosis* (1600, based on **Ovid**).

Later in the seventeenth century, many French writers adapted fairy tales as operas or ballets, but some wrote for spoken theater as well. Jean-Baptiste Molière developed the *comédie-ballet*, combining spoken theater with dance, and wrote such works as *Plaisirs de l'île enchantée* (*Pleasures of the Enchanted Isle*, 1664) and *Psyché* (1671). Jean-François Marmontel, better known for his operatic libretti, also wrote *comédies-ballets*. After the publication of the fairy tales of Marie-Catherine d'**Aulnoy** in 1690, sentimental plays meant to suggest innocence and purity were popular, such as Pierre-Claude Nivelle de la Chaussée's "Orientalist" work, *Amour pour amour* (*Love for Love*, 1742).

In Italy, Carlo Goldoni wrote scenarios as well as complete plays involving *commedia dell'arte* characters. He also created comedies of manners reflecting folktale elements. One, *I due gemelli veneziani* (*The Two Venetian Twins*, 1747), was based on Plautus' *Menaechmi*. His late *Le bourru bienfaisant* (*The Beneficent Bear*, 1771) features a *commedia*-like love plot but without *commedia* characters or physical humor. His younger contemporary Carlo **Gozzi** created many fairy-tale plays, such as *Turandot* and *L'amore delle tre melarance* (*Love for Three Oranges*, 1761), often adapted to opera and melodrama. Gozzi's fairy-tale plays exerted a significant influence on theater and other literary forms across Europe well into the nineteenth and even twentieth centuries.

Also evolving from the *commedia dell'arte*, French and English **pantomime** started as silent performance. However, English pantomimes began to feature both speech and song in the eighteenth century. At the same time, plays such as J. Charles Smith's *The Fairies* (1755) and Charles Dibdin the Elder's *Queen Mab* (1769) provided a literary approach to fairies onstage.

Nineteenth-Century Theater. With the birth of the gothic, the supernatural came into vogue. For the most part, early gothic writers ignored **fairies** in preference to ghosts and *revenants*, such as in Charles **Nodier**'s *Le vampire* (1820). However, fairy tales soon appeared, as in Alfred de Musset's *Fantasio* (1834), which critics cite as reflecting the influence of E. T. A. **Hoffmann**, Shakespeare, and others.

Romantic writers in particular embraced fairy tales as an imaginative evocation of emotional and symbolic truth. A common theme of many Romantic plays is the interaction of magical or fairy worlds with the human realm, a fertile source of symbolism for writers. Some, like Denmark's Adam **Oehlenschläger**, wrote "closet dramas" meant to be read as **poetry** rather than staged, although Oehlenschläger's plays were later performed successfully, including *Aladdin* (1805), for which Carl Nielsen composed incidental music in 1919. Another Scandinavian, Swede P. D. A. Atterbom, penned *Lycksalighetens ö* (*The Isle of the Blessed*, or *The Isle of Bliss*, 1824–27). In Germany, Ludwig **Tieck**, a theater director as well as an author, wrote a number of important fairy-tale plays, including *Der Balubart* (**Bluebeard**, 1797), *Der gestiefelte Kater* (**Puss in Boots**, 1797), *Die verkehrte Welt* (*Topsy-Turvey World*, 1799), *Prinz Zerbino* (1799), *Leben und Tod des kleinen Rotkäppchens* (*The Life and Death of **Little Red Riding Hood***, 1800), *Däumling* (**Thumbling**, 1812), and *Fortunat* (1816). Tieck's plays are noted both for their literary and social satire and for playing ironically with traditional theatrical suspension of disbelief. In Austria, Ferdinand Raimund and Johann Nepomuk Nestroy created the genre of *Volksstück* (folk play), musical and comic folk-style plays with fairy-tale plots.

In France, writers such as Charles-Augustin de Bassompierre Sewrin, Nicholas Brazier, Marc-Antoine Désaugiers, Maurice **Maeterlinck**, and the brothers Hippolyte and Théodore Cogniard wrote musical fairy-tale comedies called *folies féeriques*, or simply *féeries*. These works dramatized the fairy-tale plot, unlike English pantomimes, which used it as a framework for a loosely structured display of comedy and acrobatics. Pantomimes of the early nineteenth century employed much stage illusion (especially transformations) and cross-dressed women as "boys" shortly after mid-century.

An influential writer of English fairy theater during the first half of the nineteenth century who drew his inspiration from French *féeries* was James Robinson **Planché**, whose works, somewhat like contemporary German plays, toy with satire and self-referential humor. However, a taste for spectacle developed among the public. As acting styles and staging issues (costume and scenery, for instance) came to be more verisimilar in the early nineteenth century, theater in general grew literal-minded. By mid-century, it was expected that fairies should fly over the stage or ghosts sink into it, and even that landscapes should change in "transformation scenes." Although satirical extravaganzas by William Schwenk Gilbert and Charles Millward continued in Planché's tradition, many audiences favored escapism. French *féeries* also began to incorporate abundant spectacle, while in London, Dionysius

Boucicault's *Babil and Bijou, or the Lost Regalia of Fairyland* (1872) presented a six-hour pageant of music, color, and illusion. It cost so much to produce that it failed financially, but a condensed version was successful.

In much of Europe, fairy tales were being dramatized in an entirely different vein. For instance, in Russia, "lyrical dramas" developed the conflicting worlds symbolically, often taking their plots from fairy tales and folktales. Aleksandr Ostrovsky, who sought to create a theater for commoners rather than primarily for aristocrats, dramatized a tragic Russian folktale in *Snegurochka* (*The Snow Maiden*, 1873). Abraham Goldfaden, often called the "father of Yiddish theater," wrote a musical fairy tale, *Di kishefmakhern* (*The Witch*, 1887). Swede Johan August **Strindberg** depicted realistic psychology, but in a mystical and symbolic stage world. His dreamlike fairy-tale plays helped lead to the development of theatrical expressionism in Scandinavia and Germany. Belgian Maurice Maeterlinck also wrote emotionally evocative symbolic plays, including some with fairy-tale themes, such as *Pelléas et Mélisande* (1892), *Alladine et Palomides* (1894), and *La Princesse Maleine* (1889). *Pelléas et Mélisande* was later adapted as an opera by Claude Debussy in 1902. Gerhart Hauptmann's *Die versunkene Glocke: Ein deutsches Märchendrama* (*The Sunken Bell: A German Fairy-tale Drama*, 1896) depicted a popular "lyric" theme, the interactions of two worlds, elfin and human, contrasted in dreamlike sequences and realistic scenes.

Twentieth- and Twenty-First Century Theater. Both lyrical drama and extravaganza flourished at the beginning of the twentieth century. Aleksandr Blok's "lyrical drama" presenting *commedia* characters in a dreamlike setting, *Balaganchik* (*The Puppet Show*), appeared in 1906. A. Ansky's Yiddish play *Tsvishn tsvey veltn, oder der dibuk* (*The Dybbuk, or Between Two Worlds*, 1920) examined passion and death.

On the other hand, theatrical illusion was still popular, and many productions incorporated tricks borrowed from stage magic. The most lasting such play is Sir James Matthew **Barrie**'s *Peter Pan, or The Boy Who Would Not Grow Up* (1904), which combined a memorable story with convincing effects, such as the levitation harness allowing Nina Boucicault (daughter of Dionysius) to fly as Peter. Barrie wrote directions for some special effects that proved impractical, but many were featured in both the first performance and subsequent productions. Edmond Rostand's *Chantecler* (1910) depended less on effects but still offered stunning sets as background for the comically self-deluded title character.

As the century progressed, fairy tale themes continued to allow writers to examine ideas symbolically. Czech brothers Josef and Karel **Čapek** wrote plays that depict folktale and fairy-tale themes in a "lyric" tradition, such as Karel's *Věc Makropoulos* (*The Makropoulis Case*, 1922). Finnish author Runar Schildt's *Galgamannen: En midvintersaga* (*The Gallows Man: A Midwinter's Tale*, 1937) examined power and compassion via the device of a cursed talisman. Jean Cocteau's *Les chevaliers de la table ronde* (*Knights of the Round Table*, 1937) recast familiar stories as a conflict between illusion and reality.

Jean Giraudoux's retelling of *Ondine* (1939) used the Romantic motif of conflicting worlds to contrast inhuman perfection and human imperfection (see **Undine**). The theme of love rendering an inhuman being human occurred in other plays; for instance, Howard Richardson and William Berney's *Dark of the Moon* (1945) used the device satirically to contrast evil **witch**es with worse mortals. In a different approach to the interaction of worlds, Mary Chase's comedy *Harvey* (1944) humorously suggests that close association with the fairy realm may resemble insanity.

Inspired partially by literary **magical realism**, Argentine Conrado Nalé Roxlo dramatized legends and other traditional stories, while Mexican author Octavio Paz adapted *La hija de Rappaccini* (*Rappaccini's Daughter*, 1956) from Nathaniel **Hawthorne**'s short story. Numerous Latin American playwrights dramatize traditional stories but generally have focused on mythology rather than fairy tales.

Many late twentieth-century plays examine realistic psychology in a fairy-tale setting. Louise Page explored women's roles in ***Beauty and the Beast*** (1986, based on Gabrielle-Suzanne de **Villeneuve**'s version). Stephen Sondheim and James Lapine's ***Into the Woods*** (1986) portrays familiar fairy-tale characters discovering the consequences of their actions. The first act presents the familiar tales; the second shows the unexpected aftermath.

Fairy tales continue to inspire playwrights in the twenty-first century. Australian Marilyn Campbell has attracted critical attention with her adaptations of fairy stories. Leonid Filatov adapted a Russian folktale as a satire, *Pro Fedota-strel'tsa, udalogo molodtsa: Skazka dlya teatra* (*The Tale of Soldier Fedot, the Daring Fellow: A Fairy Tale for Stage Performance*). Irish playwright Martin McDonagh in *The Pillowman* (2003) depicts a police investigation set in an unnamed Eastern European dictatorship where brutal murders seem to be inspired by fairy tales. In New Zealand, Polynesian legends and folktales inspired *Maui—One Man Against the Gods* (2005), by Tanemahuta Gray, Janine Gainsford, Jamie Ogilvie, and Andre Anderson. *Maui* combines traditional Maori storytelling and dance with modern acting. On the other hand, the tradition of escapist extravaganzas continues, for instance with the **Walt Disney Company**'s stage versions of its animated movies.

Children's Theater

A product of the late nineteenth century, children's theater originated as an educational tool to dramatize proper behavior. Earlier, plays were not written or performed specifically for children. Works based on fairy tales, folktales, or myths were created for adults; parents would take children to plays that they judged appropriate. Many plays that became children's favorites, such as *Peter Pan*, L. Frank **Baum**'s Broadway version of *The Wizard of Oz* (1901), and Victor Herbert's *Babes in Toyland* (1903), were created for adults as much as for children.

Fairy-tale plays specifically for children finally came into their own in the early twentieth century. In 1909, Jacinto **Benavente** established a children's theater in Madrid, writing comic and satirical pieces for it that are still popular in Spanish-speaking countries. In the English-speaking world, A. A. Milne's *Toad of Toad Hall* (1929), adapted from Kenneth Grahame's *Wind in the Willows* (1908), and Madge Miller's *The Land of the Dragon* (1946) sought to engage children's imaginations. Charlotte Chorpenning adapted multiple fairy tales to theater through the mid-twentieth century, finding them to have a broad appeal. Belgian Arthur Fauquez adapted medieval tales for his *Le roman de Renart* (***Reynard the Fox***, 1958 in English), with an endearing but unethical hero. Mary Melwood's *The Tingalary Bird* (1964) depicts a mysterious bird that interacts with a psychologically believable elderly couple.

During the 1970s, Moses Goldberg created "participation plays" to draw children into the theatrical experience, such as his *Aladdin* (1973). David Wood began writing children's fairy-tale plays in the 1970s, also relying upon audience involvement. American Suzan Zeder wrote an adaptation of Baum's *Ozma of Oz* (1978), which, like Zeder's other plays, is marked by believable portrayals of emotion. Aurand Harris, the most-produced American children's playwright, did not focus primarily upon fairy tales, but wrote *Robin Goodfellow* (1977, based on Shakespeare's *A Midsummer Night's Dream*) and *The Magician's Nephew* (1984, adapted from on the novel by C. S. **Lewis**). Doreen B. Heard adapted *The Love for Three Oranges* (2001), creating gags modern audiences would understand, but preserving the original plot.

Globally, children's theater has grown in significance. In Veliky Novgorod, Russia, the biennial King-Fairy Tale International Theatre Festival brings together international participants to learn from each other and to perform for both children and adults. In India, Ayeesha Menon's *Punch-a-Tantra* suggests **fable**s still have value for chaotic modern life. In Mexico, the theater troupe el Teatro para Niños en Yucatán adapts familiar tales as children's plays; writers such as Patricio Guzmán in Chile, José Antonio Rial in Venezuela, and Andrès Básalo in Argentina do likewise for local theater groups. Although early children's favorites were composed for adults, more recent children's plays display an understanding of **childhood** thought and perception, yet often intrigue adult audiences with their sophistication. *See also* Cross-Dressing; Dance; Film and Video; Music.

Further Readings: Cavaye, Ronald, Paul Griffith, and Akihiko Senda. *A Guide to the Japanese Stage: From Traditional to Cutting Edge.* New York: Kodansha International, 2004; Green, A. E. "Folk Drama." *The Cambridge Guide to World Theatre.* Edited by Martin Banham. New York: Cambridge University Press, 1988. 352–55; Jarvis, Shawn C. "Drama and Fairy Tales." *The Oxford Companion to Fairy Tales.* Edited by Jack Zipes. New York: Oxford University Press, 2000. 137–41; Jennings, Coleman A. *Theatre for Children: Fifteen Classic Plays.* New York: St. Martin's Press, 2005; Nicholson, David B. "The Fairy Tale in Modern Drama." Dissertation. City University of New York, 1982; Richmond, Farley P., Darius L. Swann, and Phillip B. Zarrilli, eds. *Indian Theatre: Traditions of Performance.* Honolulu: University of Hawaii Press, 1990; Sand, Maurice. *The History of the Harlequinade.* 2 volumes. New York: Benjamin Blom, 1915.

Paul James Buczkowski

Theia Lena. *See* Metaxa-Krontera, Antigone

Therapy. *See* Trauma and Therapy

Thief, Thieves

A thief or robber is by definition someone who steals or furtively takes away someone else's property. Always an outlaw, this character has assumed an important role in folktales and fairy tales throughout the ages. Thieves and outlaws proliferate in medieval **folklore** and abound in the literature of sixteenth- and seventeenth-century Europe, as the well-known "rogue pamphlets," dealing with the lives of vagrants or vagabonds, testify in England.

Medieval Period

In medieval folklore, there are three distinguishable classes of thieves, which in British stories of outlaws can be best exemplified by the following characters: (1) Gamelyn (fourteenth century), known to be the head of an outlaw band, protector of thieves; (2) the Anglo-Saxon earl Hereward the Wake (eleventh century) and the legendary yeoman Robin Hood (fourteenth century or earlier), both heroic gentleman thieves, the first the son of a **princess** and a man of immense strength, the latter born of a princess and a woodsman; and

(3) Eustace the Monk and Fulk Fitzwarin (both c. thirteenth century), whose stories are framed by a magic environment, abounding in references to **witch**es, **devil**s, and monsters.

The tales about these thieves all arose in the midst of domestic unrest. The outlaw represents those alienated and threatened by the dominant power structure. Thus, Gamelyn fights the injustices perpetuated by his brother, the **king**, and his law. Hereward goes against William the Conqueror, who represents Norman occupation and the values of French-speaking rulers. Robin Hood fights the Sheriff of Nottingham, uniting yeoman and dispossessed nobles against church leaders and corrupt members of the upper aristocracy. Only Eustace and Fitzwarin seem to be more ruthless and single-minded thieves. However, both prey on one man—King John (1199–1216)—by robbing his merchants and civil servants.

In the end, almost all of these outlaw heroes seem to achieve their goals, abandon thievery in most cases, and are rewarded. Gamelyn recovers his lands, Hereward escapes his enemies and flees, Robin Hood restores justice, and Fulk Fitzwarin is reconcilled with King John. As far as Eustace the Monk is concerned, the **legend** is ambiguous. While he preys only on his father's murderer, he steals for purely personal gain and protects no one. He is said to have been beheaded in August 24, 1217.

These tales have been collected differently. Gamelyn's story survives in an anonymous English romance entitled *The Tale of Gamelyn* (c. 1350). The deeds of Hereward, also known as Hereward the Outlaw or Hereward the Exile, are recorded in the twelfth-century *Gesta Herewardi* (*Deeds of Hereward*), and some of his legends were incorporated into later legends of Robin Hood. Robin Hood's legend survives in different **ballad**s, plays, and games of the **Middle Ages**, but the first appearance of this outlaw in a surviving manuscript is in William Langland's *Piers Plowman* (1377). The story of Fulk Fitzwarin has also been noted for its parallels to the Robin Hood legend, surviving in a miscellany of works in Latin, French, and English, dating from approximately 1325–40, which are based on a lost late-thirteenth-century verse romance. The French story of Eustace the Monk, a mercenary and a pirate, is compiled in a thirteenth-century vernacular romance entitled *Li Romans de Witasse le Moine* (translated into modern English by Glyn Burgess in *Two Medieval Outlaws: Eustace the Monk and Fouke Fitz Waryn*, 1997).

But there were other medieval literary forms that would celebrate the life of lower-stratum outlaws, associating them with a culture of humor. Such is the case of comic elements in church drama and in animal **epic**s, **fabliaux**, and *Schwänke* (humorous tales, **jest**s). These genres, particularly the fabliaux and the *Schwänke*, will influence the development of the jestbooks, whose protagonist, the jester, is always a merry antihero. A good example is the legendary figure of late medieval-early Renaissance Europe, **Till Eulenspiegel**; another is Unibos, from as early as the end of the tenth century (cf. *Unibos* [*One Ox*], a medieval Latin poem written by a cleric from France, Lorraine, or the Netherlands).

Modernity

At the beginning of modernity, the proliferation of the poor in the growing cities allowed thieves of a different kind to acquire a central role in the stories of the time, which then circulated orally and through pamphlets. In England, the rogue pamphlets, a mixture of fact and fiction, by Gilbert Walker, John Awdeley, Thomas Harman, Robert Greene, and Thomas Dekker, for example, are famous for celebrating the life of criminals. The underground world of London was portrayed in these pamphlets. Some, the "cony-catching pamphlets," dealt more specifically with thieves versed in the art of "cony-catching" or deceiving the public, for example, card and dice players and prostitutes.

The antiheroes of such stories inspired folk songs and ballads and generally contributed to the development of literature, becoming living legends to the present day. Such is the example in English literature of *Moll Flanders* (1722) by Daniel Defoe, inspired by the legendary figure Mary Godson or Mary King, the famous cutpurse (pickpocket); or *Jonathan Wild* (1743) by Henry Fielding, based on the historical character of the same name, who terrorized London in the eighteenth century.

Thieves and Folktale

In the category Realistic Tales, Hans-Jörg Uther's *Types of the International Folktale* (2004) devotes an entire section to "Robbers and Murderers" (ATU types 950–969), which attests to the central role that these outlaws often play as characters in folktales. The thieves, robbers, and highwaymen who populate European folktale collections can reflect both the fear and fascination associated with outlaws. Demonized instead of romanticized, thieves and robbers embody a source of genuine danger. The robbers in **tale type**s such as The Robber Bridegroom (ATU 955) and The Woman among Robbers (ATU 956B) reveal themselves ultimately to be murderers and cannibals whose criminal behavior must be publicly identified and punished. On the other hand, the thief in Jacob and Wilhelm **Grimm**'s "Der Meisterdieb" ("The Master Thief," 1843)—which belongs to the tale type known as Tasks for a Thief (ATU 1525A)—exploits the notion of the thief as popular antihero. In Grimms' tale, a master thief who has overcome his **peasant** origins and made himself wealthy by stealing only from the rich uses his skills to outwit the lord of the castle, his **soldier**s, and the **clergy**. While his audacious success leads to his expulsion from lord's country, there is no doubt that this master thief's trickery, which makes a fool of the powers that be, earns him a heroic status.

Thief and Trickster

In Native American tales, the **trickster** figure (either **Coyote**, Raven, Mink, Bluejay, or Hare) is often portrayed as a thief and a cheat. Although he might steal daylight, fire, water, and the like, he does it for the benefit of humanity. Coyote, for example, usually steals for the sheer pleasure of the trick itself, yet ultimately he is acting on behalf of the human race. Indeed, the theft of fire is the earliest and most typical kind of trickster-hero **myth**. The legend becomes the pattern for a series of tales of theft: of the sun, water, fish, game animals, acorns, and even cereal grains. To steal these vital substances from superior forces hostile to humanity, the trickster has to use his own strength and cunning.

Often **Uncle Remus** tales also depict the famous hero Br'er Rabbit as a thief, usually to convey a **moral**. These tales are very similar not only to stories found in Africa and Brazil but also to European medieval animal epics and **fable**s. Br'er Rabbit and Br'er Tarrypin compete with the jackal or the hare in India, the jackal, the fox, or the tortoise in Africa, the cotia (a species of tortoise) in Brazil, and the fox in European medieval folklore. They use their cunning skills on victims as varied as the lion, the tiger, the **wolf**, the hyena, and the jaguar. Br'er Rabbit and Br'er Tarrypin frequently victimize Br'er Fox, Br'er Wolf, Br'er Bear, or Br'er Possum. *See also* Punishment and Reward; Thief of Bagdad Films.

Further Readings: Bakhtin, Mikhail. *Rabelais and His World*. Translated by Helene Iswolsky. Bloomington: Indiana University Press, 1984; Bright, William. "Nature Culture, and Old Man Coyote." http://

www.ncidc.org/bright/OLD_MAN_COYOTE.doc; Gerber A. "Uncle Remus Traced to the Old World." *Journal of American Folklore* 6 (1893): 245–57; Kinney, Arthur F., ed. *Rogues, Vagabonds, and Sturdy Beggars: A New Gallery of Tudor and Early Stuart Rogue Literature Exposing the Lives, Times, and Cozening Tricks of the Elizabethan Underworld*. Amherst: University of Massachusetts Press, 1990; Knight, Stephen. *Robin Hood: A Complete Study of the Greenwood Outlaw*. Oxford: Blackwell, 1994; Lindahl, Carl, John McNamara, and John Lindow, eds. *Medieval Folklore: An Encyclopedia of Myths, Legends, Tales, Beliefs, and Customs*. 2 volumes. Santa Barbara, CA: ABC-CLIO, 2000; Ricketts, Mac Linscott. "The North American Indian Trickster." *History of Religions* 5 (1966): 327–50.

Ana Raquel Fernandes

Thief of Bagdad Films

The Thief of Bagdad films comprise, besides various minor representatives, the original *Thief of Bagdad* (1924) starring Douglas Fairbanks Sr., its 1940 remake by Alexander Korda, and the animated cartoon feature *Aladdin* (1992) produced by the **Walt Disney Company.**

With his *Thief of Bagdad*, the famous actor Fairbanks created a film classic of truly monumental scope, for which he acted as producer, script writer, and main character. The plot of the 140-minute silent film is a vague **adaptation** of ATU 653A, The Rarest Thing in the World, a tale that is first attested as the tale of "**Prince** Ahmed and the **Fairy** Peri Banu" in the *Arabian Nights*. While the film is labeled an "Arabian Nights Fantasy," it takes place in a fairy-tale Bagdad of huge dimensions, with buildings reminiscent of early skyscrapers and an interior decor dwarfing its characters.

Douglas Fairbanks and Julianne Johnston in the 1924 film *The Thief of Bagdad*. [United Artists/Photofest]

In the lengthy exposition, the main character is introduced as a cunning **thief** who selfishly demonstrates his lack of social morality as a successful way to make a living. When intruding into the palace to steal the royal treasure, he falls mortally in love with the **princess**. To win her, he masks as Prince Ahmed; but his disguise is uncovered, and he is flogged and left to the mercy of a wild ape. Saved by the princess, who has secretly discovered that he is her fated bridegroom, he reforms and sets out to "earn his happiness." As Ahmed experiences various adventures, three other suitors return with the rarest things they have found. The Indian prince has acquired a magic crystal informing the suitors about a serious (induced) illness that has befallen the princess; with the magic flying carpet of the Persian prince, they quickly return to the palace, and the magic healing apple of the Mongol prince cures the princess. When the princess, however, decides not to marry either of them, the Mongol prince has his troops conquer the city. Meanwhile, Ahmed learns about the events, returns on his flying horse, and, with a magic powder, produces a huge army that vanquishes and punishes the evil Mongols. He is happily united with the princess. In the film's spectacular final scene, both fly above the streets of the city toward eternal happiness.

Fairbanks's *Thief of Bagdad* is a typical story of "the American dream," demonstrating that even the poorest and most undeserving character can achieve personal happiness through individual effort and dedication. The film's Oriental ambience is but a fairy-tale cliché. In a similar vein, it is interesting to note that the tale supplying the film's basic plot does not belong to the original *Arabian Nights*. It was introduced into the collection by Antoine **Galland** from the oral **performance** of a gifted Syrian storyteller, and in its present form presumably mirrors Western (and Christian) values and norms.

The second *Thief of Bagdad*, directed by Hungarian Alexander Korda, introduces a number of changes. Korda separates the roles of thief and suitor, and instead of the evil Mongol prince, Korda introduces the stereotypical evil vizier Jafar as the protagonist's opponent. The film begins with a blind beggar telling his tale. He is Prince Ahmad, the justice-loving but thoroughly naïve young grandson of **Harun al-Rashid**, who left the affairs of state to his vizier, realizing only too late that Jafar aimed to usurp his place. The thief character Abu is the "lowest of the lowest," who—according to an old storyteller's wisdom—shall one day bring justice to the oppressed people. Having escaped from prison, Ahmad and Abu reach Basra, where Ahmad falls in love with the princess. When Jafar officially woos the princess, he first secures her **father**'s consent by presenting the toy-loving **king** with a mechanical flying horse. Jafar then magically blinds Ahmad and transforms Abu into a dog, and finally has the king killed by a mechanical statue. Jafar then relocates the princess (who had escaped in men's clothes) and convinces her to break the magic spell binding Ahmad and his friend by letting him embrace her. By conjuring a storm, he separates the friends, and Abu lives through various adventures, some of which are reminiscent of those in the first film adaptation. In the final scene, Abu arrives in Bagdad on a flying carpet just in time to save Ahmad from being beheaded and shoots Jafar as he tries to escape on his mechanical flying horse.

Korda's film profits from the natural beauty of Sabu, a former Indian "elephant boy" who acted his most famous role in Korda's 1942 adaptation of Rudyard Kipling's *Jungle Book* (1894). While Korda's *Thief of Bagdad* consciously acknowledges its predecessor, it is labeled an "Arabian fantasy," and its ethical message has dramatically changed from Fairbanks's movie. Korda's film is a parable of justice, and the thief character is a kind of Robin Hood who unselfishly supports the righteous but feeble ruler against the tyrannical usurper.

Even though overtly an animated cartoon version of the tale "Aladdin and the Wonderful Lamp" from the *Arabian Nights,* Disney's *Aladdin* draws heavily from both earlier versions of the *Thief of Bagdad*. As in the first version, Aladdin is a good-for-nothing boy, and the princess a self-conscious young woman who claims the right to choose her husband herself. While the characters of suitor and thief have again been combined in Aladdin, Abu makes his appearance as Aladdin's pet monkey. The toy-loving king and his vizier, the evil magician Jafar, owe their introduction to the second film version, as does princess Jasmin's pet tiger Rajah. The message of the Disney cartoon is again similar to that of Fairbanks's version, in that a sympathetic underdog in prototypical fulfillment of the "American dream" actively shapes his future and rises from the lowest imaginable position to that of highest power. *See also* Animation; Film and Video; *Popeye the Sailor*; Silent Films and Fairy Tales.

Further Readings: Bernstein, Matthew, and Gaylyn Studlar, eds. *Visions of the East: Orientalism in Film.* New Brunswick, NJ: Rutgers University Press, 1997; Cooperson, Michael. "The Monstrous Births of 'Aladdin.' "*Harvard Middle Eastern and Islamic Review* 1 (1994): 67–86. Reprinted in *The* Arabian Nights *Reader.* Edited by Ulrich Marzoloph. Detroit: Wayne State University Press, 2006. 265–82; Liptay, Fabienne. *Wunderwelten: Märchen im Film.* Remscheid: Gardez!, 2004. 153–79; Marzolph, Ulrich. "Das Aladdin-Syndrom: Zur Phänomenologie des narrativen Orientalismus." *Hören, Sagen, Lesen, Lernen: Bausteine zu einer Geschichte der kommunikativen Kultur.* Edited by Ursula Brunold-Bigler and Hermann Bausinger. Bern: Peter Lang, 1995. 449–62.

Ulrich Marzolph

Thomas, Jean. *See* Ungerer, Tomi

Thompson, Stith (1885–1976)

In American **folktale** scholarship, few individuals were as influential as Stith Thompson. Thompson received his doctorate in English literature from Harvard and went on to teach English and **folklore** at Indiana University, where he helped set up the summer folklore institutes that would become the Department of Folklore. During his career, he made several pivotal contributions to the study of the folktale.

His first contribution, *The Types of the Folktale*—a translation and revision of Antti **Aarne**'s *Verzeichnis der Marchentypen* (1910)—was first published in 1928 and appeared again in 1961 with further revisions. It would become known as the Aarne-Thompson taletype index. Thompson's collection *Tales of the North American Indians*, a survey of tales from throughout North America, was published in 1929.

Thompson's most original contribution to the study of folk literature was his *Motif-Index of Folk-Literature*, first published between 1932 and 1936, in which he presented a broad cross-cultural index of **motif**s. In 1946, Thompson published *The Folktale*, a scholarly volume detailing not only different cultural approaches to folklore but also examining various approaches to folktale scholarship.

A proponent of the **historic-geographic method**, Thompson published one of the best-known studies of this type, *The Star Husband Tale* (1953). In this study, Thompson examined the distribution of a Native American folktale and examined the variations between versions collected from different tribes. *See also* Native American Tales; Tale Type.

Further Readings: Aarne, Antti. *The Types of the Folktale: A Classification and Bibliography.* Translated and enlarged by Stith Thompson. 2nd revision. 1961. Helsinki: Academia Scientiarum Fennica, 1987; Dorson, Richard M. "Stith Thompson (1885–1976)." *Journal of American Folklore* 90 (1977): 2–7; Thompson, Stith. *The Folktale.* 1946. Berkeley: University of California Press, 1977; ———. *Motif-Index of Folk-Literature: A Classification of Narrative Elements in Folktales, Ballads, Myths, Fables, Mediaeval Romances, Exempla, Fabliaux, Jest-Books, and Local Legends.* Revised and enlarged edition. 6 volumes. Bloomington: Indiana University Press, 1955–58.

B. Grantham Aldred

The Thousand and One Nights. See Arabian Nights; Arabian Nights Films

Thumbling, Tom Thumb

Thumbling, or Tom Thumb, is the main character of the international tale type classified as ATU 700. This well-known hero who is no bigger than a thumb has a long history, and in a number of English versions, there exist links to the Arthurian **legend** of the Knights of the Round Table, in which Merlin plays a part in Tom's **birth**. What made him so popular in **folklore** and **chapbook** literature is his ability to fare well despite his miniature size, as in *The History of Tom Thumbe the Little* by Richard Johnson (1621).

Tales that depict this tiny hero typically fall into two categories. The first involves the remarkable activities and **epic**-like adventures of the tiny character, a child who is typically the size of a thumb but can even be as tiny as a millet seed or a grain of rice. Apparently incapable of growing any larger physically, Thumbling nonetheless embarks on what can only be called heroic adventures. His physical stature determines his actions: he can travel in the ear of a horse or on the back of a mouse; he may be born in a cabbage or swallowed by a cow or a fish. Because of his tiny nature, Thumbling is often gobbled up by a creature larger than he, and various episodes of this kind recall the biblical story of Jonah and the whale (see **Bible, Bible Story**). His adventurous spirit and wit see him through these adventures.

The second Thumbling category deals with child abandonment and abuse and therefore has a strikingly modern resonance for the contemporary reader. Tom Thumb and his siblings are abandoned in a forest by their parents. It may be famine and starvation that prompt such a desperate gesture, or the jealousy of a stepmother who wants to get rid of children from a previous **marriage**. In this tale, the little character must protect his **brothers** against the cruelty and cannibalistic instincts of an **ogre** or a **witch** by using his wit and resourcefulness (ATU 327, The Children and the Ogre). His diminutive stature enables him to outsmart evil schemes, and, like David defeating Goliath, Little Thumb can trick mean ogres and witches, save his siblings, and return home. One of the most famous tales using this theme is Charles **Perrault**'s "Le petit poucet" ("Little Thumbling"; ATU 327B, The Brothers and the Ogre). In Perrault's tale, however, the character's miniature size, indicated by his name and in the title, does not play a significant role in the plot. The emphasis in Perrault's version and in this group of tales is not on the size of the character, but on the basic vulnerability of the child in relationship to the ogre or witch. Other well-known stories in this cycle of tales include Giambattista **Basile**'s "Ninnillo e Nennella"; *The History of Little Tom Thumbe*, a chapbook from 1840; and Jacob and Wilhelm **Grimm**'s "**Hansel and Gretel**" (ATU 327A), to name just a few. The story of Tom Thumb and other small heroes and heroines remains an illustration of the triumph of wit over brute force. *See also* Cannibalism.

Further Reading: Zipes, Jack. "From Odysseus to Tom Thumb and Other Cunning Heroes: Speculation about the Entrepreneurial Spirit." *The Brothers Grimm: From Enchanted Forests to the Modern World.* 2nd edition. New York: Palgrave MacMillan, 2002. 91–106.

Claire L. Malarte-Feldman

Thurber, James (1894–1961)

Ohio-born James Thurber produced the bulk of his writing for the *New Yorker* from 1927 until the 1950s, in humorous essays and short stories notable for their despairing, melancholy wit; however, he also wrote **fable**s and fairy tales that display a high degree of self-conscious narrative and linguistic play. He is famous for his minimalist, unlikely **cartoons**, which show a similar interest in the breakdown of accepted form into comic chaos. For Thurber, **fantasy** is a form of escape from unpleasant reality, seen most strikingly in his famous tale "The Secret Life of Walter Mitty" (1941). Escape is usually flawed and impossible in reality; interestingly, however, the trademark ironic cynicism of Thurber's essays and realist writing is muted by the expectations of fairy tale, so that his tales exist in tension with the main body of his work. This contrast centers particularly on his view of **women**, which, while bitingly negative in much of his writing, becomes idealized and conciliatory in the tales.

Thurber's two collections of fables, *Fables for Our Time* (1940) and *Further Fables for Our Time* (1956), are wry, ironic revisions of both fairy tales and fables in the **Aesop** mold, mostly with animal protagonists. They feature revisions such as a revolver-wielding **Little Red Riding Hood** and tend to offer an encapsulated cynicism that relies on a sustained **parody** of Aesop's traditional **moral** or of proverbial wisdom. In these mini-narratives, the magical is too often revealed as a trick or self-deception, rather than being celebrated as it is in Thurber's fairy tales; realism collides with the marvelous, which breaks down under the stress.

Conversely, Thurber's fairy tales are more **utopia**n in thrust. While they are ostensibly aimed at children, their parodic investigation of form and meaning is highly sophisticated. The word games and linguistic play that run through Thurber's writing find a new expression in his tales, most notably in *The White Deer* (1945) and *The Wonderful O* (1957). *The White Deer* and *The Thirteen Clocks* (1950) are his most sustained play with fairy-tale forms, offering variations on the **prince** who is set impossible tasks to win the hand of a **princess**. The familiar narrative patterns of fairy tale in these works suffer the same breakdown and slippage as does language in his other writing, but ultimately confusion and the failure of meaning are safely contained within a metanarrative revealed at the end of the story, one which offers utopian closure and reconciliation.

Thurber's shorter fairy-tale works are more suitable for young readers, particularly the sumptuously illustrated *Many Moons* (1943), which affirms and celebrates the wisdom of the child protagonist against the absurd logic of the adults. "The Great Quillow" (1944) is more complex, its focus once again linguistic; the marauding giant Hunder is ultimately defeated by cunning play with narrative and meaning by the tale's craftsman hero, a true inheritor of the **archetype** of the clever **tailor**. *See also* North American Tales.

Further Readings: Black, Stephen A. *James Thurber: His Masquerades—A Critical Study.* The Hague: Mouton, 1970; Holmes, Charles S. *The Clocks of Columbus: The Literary Career of James Thurber.* London: Secker and Warburg, 1973.

Jessica Tiffin

Tieck, Ludwig (1773–1853)

Ludwig Tieck was one of the first German Romantics to write plays and stories based on traditional **folktale**s, or **märchen**, and to invent tales and poems of his own that he also called märchen. His experiments with the genre became important in the Romantic movement in Germany and in the development of the supernatural tale and **literary fairy tale**.

Tieck, the son of a prosperous rope-maker in Berlin, studied philology and literature, but decided early to become a professional writer and later a theater director. Though he wrote in many different forms and styles, his varied work with fairy tales is perhaps the most significant. In 1797, under the pseudonym Peter Leberecht, he published a volume misleadingly called *Volksmärchen* (*Folktales*), which contained some of his strangest and most individual tales, particularly "Der blonde Eckbert" ("Eckbert the Blond"). An often repeated and varied song in the tale, "Waldeinsamkeit" ("Forest Solitude"), emphasizes Eckbert's growing disassociation and confusion. As he lies dying, he discovers that his wife was his half-sister, and that his two shadowy friends Walther and Hugo, both ultimately his victims, were mysterious emanations of the old woman his wife had betrayed.

In his collection *Romantische Dichtungen* (*Romantic Tales*, 1799), Tieck published "Der getreue Eckart" ("The Faithful Eckart"), based on old German **legend**s and **ballad**s. As in "Eckbert the Blond," the hero of the second part, Tannenhäuser, becomes less and less able to distinguish the borderline between a supernatural world and reality. His doubts lead him to live in the mountains in increasing solitude, where he trusts no one; when he returns to the real world, he murders the beloved woman he believed dead. Other tales like "Der Runenberg" ("Rune Mountain," 1804) and "Die Elfen" ("The **Elves**," 1812) also stress the central character's disintegration in a deeply ambiguous and constantly darkening world.

Tieck's fairy-tale plays, however, often make the tension between real and dramatic space the occasion for lively and amusing **theater**. In plays like *Der gestiefelte Kater* (***Puss in Boots***, 1797), based on Charles **Perrault**'s tale, and *Die verkehrte Welt* (*The Upside-Down World*, 1799; translated as *The Land of Upside Down*, 1978), he constantly alternates simple fairy-tale scenes with critical commentary, sometimes from a represented audience. His playful, ironic destruction of dramatic illusion tests the distinction between fiction and reality, but without the dark overtones of the explorations in his tales.

In 1812–16, Tieck incorporated many of his literary fairy tales and fairy-tale plays into a collection called *Phantasus*. Imitating earlier fictions by Giovanni **Boccaccio** and Pedro Calderón de la Barca, and perhaps by earlier fairy-tale writers such as Giambattista **Basile** and Marie-Catherine d'**Aulnoy**, Tieck has the characters in the outer tale (that is, the **frame narrative**) read and discuss the earlier material. He continued to write literary fairy tales throughout his long career, including the tale "Die Vogelscheuche" ("The Scarecrow," 1835). In 1827–31, Thomas Carlyle translated many of his tales, bringing them to the attention of English-speaking readers. *See also* German Tales.

Further Reading: Scheck, Ulrich. "Tales of Wonder and Terror: Short Prose of the German Romantics." *The Literature of German Romanticism*. Edited by Dennis Mahoney. Rochester, NY: Camden House, 2004. 101–23.

Elizabeth Wanning Harries

Till Eulenspiegel

Till Eulenspiegel is a legendary figure of late medieval and early Renaissance Europe. The earliest-known complete version of the book bearing his name is a printed quarto published by Johannes Grüninger in Strassburg in 1515, followed by an edition in 1519, a slightly rewritten improvement by the same author of the first edition. The author of Eulenspiegel's adventures is thought to be Hermann Bote. In the foreword to the tales, however, the initial "N." appears for the surname of the announced author, who states that he is writing in the year 1500 and that, although he is unfamiliar with written Latin and does not possess adequate expertise for the job, he has been asked to compile a number of tales—witty, well-known stories already in existence—to provide the reader with pleasant entertainment.

Till Eulenspiegel is presented in the book as a famous jester who lives during the fourteenth century and dies in 1350. His name in modern German means "owl glass," "owl **mirror**," "wise mirror," or, metaphorically, "wise reflection." For the audience at the time, the name must have suggested a certain sort of mischievous behavior. The readers, seeing their stupidity and evil reflected in Eulenspiegel's tricks, were to be led—at least such is the implication—to better behavior. At the same time, in Low German the name Eulenspiegel (Ulenspegel) seems also to convey the suggestion to "wipe one's behind."

Eulenspiegel is more than an entertaining **trickster**; he is a mischief-maker, an actor, **thief**, liar, and prankster. He is a vagabond and an adventurer of sorts, well known for his exploits in Germany, Flanders, and Holland. There are also tales set in Rome, Prague, Denmark, and Poland. But most of the protagonist's adventures take place in and around the Hanseatic city of Braunschweig, which is also Eulenspiegel's birthplace according to the editions of 1515 and 1519. This fictional character belongs to the category of the mythical buffoon and rascal, both humorous and vicious, charming and repulsive.

The witticisms found in the adventures of Till Eulenspiegel suggests that the author was familiar with medieval folktales, collections of **fabliaux**, jestbooks, or *Schwankbücher* (see **Jest and Joke**). At least thirty-three tales appear to be taken directly from earlier authors, and many contain echoes, phrases, and aphorisms found in previous texts, jests, stories, and **exempla**. The tales abound in wordplays, puns, popular sayings, and maxims. For the Renaissance audience, the pleasure certainly lay in the overt retelling of popular **anecdote**s.

Eulenspiegel's stories are part of a long, humanist satirical tradition (Martin Luther, Niccolò Machiavelli, Benvenuto Cellini, François Rabelais, and Erasmus). They reveal the author's intention to mock and satirize the pretentiousness of humanity in general. The stories' style combines vulgarity and sensitivity, elegance and poor taste, violence and sympathy, and eloquence and scatology. The book is a critique of religious hypocrisy and other social ills, dishonest **clergy**, officals, and nobles, scholars, tradesmen, farmers, citizens, and politicians, and may be compared with medieval German drama, Geoffrey Chaucer's *Canterbury Tales*, and the tales of Hans Sachs.

Despite having been written in a pre-national Germany, *Till Eulenspiegel* has occupied an important position in German literature. Its protagonist is as famous as King Arthur in England and Roland of *La chanson de Roland* in France. The book, which has been translated worldwide, has had an enormous influence that endures to this day. It goes beyond literature, belonging to the world of **art**, **music**, philosophy, and **dance**. The most famous influence in modern times is Richard Strauss's tone poem *Till Eulenspiegels lustige Streiche* (*Till Eulenspiegel's Merry Pranks*, 1895). *Eulenspiegel*'s impact is also evident in works such as Wilhelm Busch's *Max und Moritz* (1865), adapted for children, and, as some have suggested, in Friedrich Nietzsche's *Also sprach Zarathustra* (*Thus Spoke Zarathustra*, 1883–85). And in addition to Renaissance artists, such as Hans Baldung Grien, Eulenspiegel has figured in the art of Josef Hegenbarth, Alfred Kubin, Frans Masereel, and A. Paul Weber.

The Till Eulenspiegel Museum is located in Schöppenstedt, and the *Eulenspiegel-Jahrbuch* has been published since 1960. Together with the version of Eulenspiegel's adventures by Charles Theodore Henri de Coster (Brussels, 1867) and Erich Kästner's well-known **adaptation** for children of 1938, *Streiche des Till Eulenspiegel* (*Till Eulenspiegel, the Clown*), there is also a 1975 film, *Till Eulenspiegel*, co-written by Christa and Gerhard Wolf, directed by Rainer Simon, and produced by **DEFA** in the German Democratic Republic. *See also* Simpleton.

Further Reading: Oppenheimer, Paul, trans. and ed. *Till Eulenspiegel: His Adventures.* New York: Routledge, 2001.

Ana Raquel Fernandes

Time and Place

Telling Time

Like all folk narratives (and most other stories), **märchen** or **wonder tale**s narrate the
past. While in their storying they create true chunks of a past that never was, they do so in
the present, whereas the future continuously provides new pasts to be expressly narrated. In
the act of performing a tale, which happens in what might be called performance time or
narration time, both telling time and listening time are of equal length and simultaneous,
and narration time can be measured in terms of historical time; on the other hand, the
amount of time narrated in the narrative time of a tale—a day, let us say, or several days or
even several years—is both ahistoric and usually much longer than it takes to narrate it in
historical time, "our" time or narration time. Not all, in fact, sometimes very little narratable
time is actually narrated so that the sum of narrated and un-narrated time which we may
call "recounted" (that is, re-counted) time is much larger than appears at first glance, as the
episodic nature of märchen ignores the interstices between the episodes. For instance, out of
a total of sixteen years of recounted time, only nineteen days may be actually narrated.

Rehearsing the Future

Although the narration of the past is often a successful means by which to cope with the
present and face the future, folklore protagonists are sometimes still ill-prepared to outmaneu-
ver or even come to grips with the monstrous, demonic, or numinous phenomena with which
the designated action requires them to collide. Such confrontations are crucial when chosen
protagonists have been entrusted with a special mission, given a dangerous task to perform,
or are on a questing journey of great risk. They are consequently at their wits' end and do not
know what to do next. One way of dealing with the problem is offered when a helper,
whether a **magic helper** or not, gives good advance advice anticipating in a detailed, verbal
rehearsal the precise scope and nature of salutary future action (as if the future had already
become the past), advice that has to be put into unquestioning practice in complete obedience
to the instructions without the slightest variation when the relevant circumstances arise.

The Past as Time

In spite of its ahistoricity, narrative time is made accessible to the listeners/readers of folktales. It may be removed from the datable, calendar-bound, documentable chronology of history (although there are exceptions) but is structured in its temporality by units familiar to
both teller and listener: a base binary division into day and night and a further organization
through its fundamentally diurnal character—morning, midday, evening, and night. Its overall
beginning and end are signaled by such phrases as "Once upon a time" and "They lived happily ever after," phrases that not only initially ease the story in question out of historical narrative time into ahistorical narrative time but also finally back into historical time again.

These formulaic beginnings and endings are devices that storytellers use to alert their listeners/readers to the fact that what follows or has just been presented is trustworthy only within the expectations normally associated with a wonder tale, for folk-narrative time, in its "otherness," is the time in which apple trees speak, magic is abroad, and the dead return to challenge, help, or warn the living. It is also the time when the frustratingly impenetrable barrier between life and **death** ceases to divide, when the rigidly three-dimensional confined to a personal, individual, and noninterchangeable body finds yearned-for release in spectacular or secret **transformation**, and when the numinous and profane interact with astonishing ease and eagerness.

Suspended Time

In narrative time, time itself can take on a different quality in so far as—under certain circumstances, for instance, within the confines of a hedge of thorns—a beautiful **princess** and her household can be made to sleep for 100 years at the prick of a needle and an old woman's curse. This is not a state of timelessness, however, or disregard of time, as has sometimes been suggested, but rather a case of locally suspended time, while the outside world presumably continues in its accustomed human pattern. In the world of "**Sleeping Beauty**" are glimpses of an extended, extensive present, an irresistible attraction for those who are in no position to stop the "march of time." Similarly, for those humans who deliberately or accidentally enter fairyland, the passage of time may be imperceptibly slowed down, usually in directly relatable proportions to historical time. What seems like ten minutes or hours among the **fairies** may be ten days or ten years in human terms; a single night in fairy time is really 100 years; and a week turns out to have been the passing of seven generations. A night's dance at a wedding in a fairy mound has taken up to 200 years of calendar time; listening to a bird's song has lasted 300 years.

The Past as Place

Introductory, formulaic phrases such as "Once upon a time," "In days of old when wishing still did some good," and the like have conditioned tellers and listeners/readers of folktales to regard the past exclusively in temporal terms, a perspective supported by the linear, episodic nature of the stories' actions. A closer, comparative reading of numerous open formulae and investigations of the story structures reveals very quickly that the past is as much a place as a time. In many instances, one only has to read on to the adverbial phrase that follows immediately on the formulaic "Once upon a time" to become aware of the predominantly spatial dimension of magic tales: "Once upon a time, in a certain part of the wide world"; "Once upon a time, there was an old king, living beyond the beyond"; "A long time ago, in a certain place"; "There was once a wicked king who lived in a large castle which stood on a high hill in a lonely wood"; "There was a famous king in a wild part of the country where strangers seldom came"; and so on. In many examples, the phrase "Beyond the beyond" can be seen as the spatial equivalent of the temporal "Once upon a time," and whereas the latter intimates that narrative time is ahistorical, the former indicates that narrative space is acartographical and therefore unmappable. However, as there is a recounted time with its narrated and unnarrated portions, so there is a recounted space with narrated and unnarrated parts. In fact, there is more narrated, linear space than its temporal equivalent, and the two meet and support each other in one of the main folktale features, the journey—that is, the movement from space to space in time. It is therefore more than justified that the opening formula be expanded to "Once upon a time and place," and perhaps also the closing phrase to "And they lived happily *there* for ever after," allowing the narration of the true encapsulation of our pre-occupation with definite beginnings and endings.

A more detailed scrutiny of opening adverbial phrases of tales shows that, in quite a few of them, there is no overt reference to time at all: "On the edge of a large forest lived a woodcutter and his wife"; "Beyond the beyond, beyond the seven seas, and beyond this farthest shores, there lived a poor Gypsy"; "In a certain village there was a very rich family"; "An old woman and her son lived in a lonely wee house on a hillside"; and so forth. Even if one admits that the word "there" in these sentences can be construed as having not only a temporal but also a spatial quality—that it can encompass the meaning of "then" as well—the overwhelming impression remains that it is space that is narrated rather than time, an observation borne out by the examination of the structure of childhood reminiscences.

Just as the temporal aspects of märchen are made transparent for listeners and readers through the use of familiar components of time such as, first and foremost, the day, but also subdivisions like morning, noon, evening, and night, so the story's landscape thrives, in general, on the inclusion of reference points in its mappable counterparts. The landscaped world of the folktale is therefore not identifiable by what it is but by *where* it is. It is recognizable through the strategic deployment of significant, generic topographic features. This familiar habitat needs no identifying name, or—put somewhat differently—it defies naming because it is not individually pinpointed but is potentially realizable in multiple locations. Even if it has been distanced through forceful horizontal journeys, or, if it is reachable only through vertical descents such as going down a well, through a hidden passage under a bed, or through a hole in the floor, it is not unlike the familiar habitat of home, though it is nevertheless a world of otherness, of evil intentions, of receiving rewards for kindnesses shown, and, of course, of magic waiting to be dispensed. If one is fortunate or deserving enough to return, one is often even better, richer, or more favored than before.

Time and Space in Contemporary Legends

In contrast to the märchen, the contemporary **legend** relies for proof of its veracity or, at least, of its believability, on references to named locations and a specific time frame, the former often in the not-too-distant neighborhood, the latter contemporary with or close to the time of the legend's telling. They are the spatial and temporal props of the common opening phrase: "You may not believe this, but it's true." Believable legends are usually performed or created by a credible teller for a credulous audience. Their protagonists tend to be unidentified or even unidentifiable friends of a friend (FOAF), hence their designations as "foaftales." These "contemporary legends"—a better term than "urban myths" (or "**urban legend**s") since they are neither mythical nor confined to an urban environment—address human anxieties, fear, needs, and wishes and, in so far as their protagonists can be envisaged as a surrogate for the listener, can have therapeutic effects. Thus they are, in that sense, first-person narratives told in the third person. Vague spatial and temporal references and the use of the present tense in their telling ("There is this traveling salesman driving down the road …") diminish their effectiveness and are, therefore, inappropriate. In no other folk-narrative genres are time and space so closely linked.

The Past as Time and Space

Adding the notion of the past as place to the familiar concept of the past as time may not be easy in either perception or practice. Consequently, an opening phrase like "Once upon the time and place" may be considered cumbersome and perhaps even regarded as unnecessary ("Long, long ago and beyond the beyond" may be an acceptable alternative). Be that as it may, the successful performer, whether in the spoken or the written medium, depends to a large extent on an awareness and effective harnessing of these twin characteristics. Their structuring function is an essential feature of any folk narrative, be it a märchen or a contemporary legend. *See also* Fantasy; Magical Realism.

Further Readings: Doležel, Lubomir. "A Scheme of Narrative Time." 1973. *Semiotics of Art: Prague School Contributions.* Edited by L. Matejka and I. R. Titunik. Cambridge, MA: MIT Press, 1976. 209–17; Messerli, Alfred. "Spatial Representation in European Popular Fairy Tales." *Marvels & Tales* 19 (2005): 274–84; Müller, Günther. "Die Bedeutung der Zeit in der Erzählkunst." 1947. *Morphologische Poetik.* Tübingen: Max Niemeyer, 1974. 247–68; Nicolaisen, W. F. H. "Concepts of Time and Space in Irish Folk Tales." *Celtic Folklore and Christianity: Studies in Memory of William W. Heist.* Edited by Patrick K. Ford. Santa Barbara: McNally and Loftin, 1983. 150–58; ———. "The Past as Place: Names, Stories, and the Remembered Self." *Folklore* 102 (1991): 3–15; ———. "Rehearsing the Future in the Folktale." *New York Folklore* 11 (1985): 231–38; ———. "Space in Folk Narrative." *Folklore in Two Continents: Essays in Honor of Linda Dégh.* Edited by N. Burlakoff and C. Lindahl. Bloomington: Trickster Press, 1980. 14–18; ———. "The Structure of Narrated Time in the Folktale." *Le conte: Pourquoi? Comment?* Edited by Geneviève Calame-Griaule, Veronika Görög-Karady, and Michèle Cliche. Paris: Éditions du Centre National de la Recherche Scientifique, 1984. 417–36; ———. "Time in Folk-Narrative." *Folklore Studies in the Twentieth Century.* Edited by Venetia J. Newall. Woodbridge, Sussex: D. S. Brewer, 1978–80. 314–19.

W. F. H. Nicolaisen

Tolkien, J. R. R. (1892–1973)

Although he was born in South Africa, John Ronald Reuel Tolkien grew up in England and is very much a figure of English literature. His identity as an Oxford academic and philologist underpins his highly influential **fantasy** literature, set in the magical world of Middle-earth. In addition to producing critical writing and his famous fantasies *The Hobbit* (1937) and *The Lord of the Rings* (1954–55), Tolkien is the author of numerous works that encompass **poetry**, fantasy, fairy tale, and the mythology and history of Middle-earth. The publication and popularity of *The Lord of the Rings* could be said to have shaped the modern popular genre of fantasy literature.

Tolkien's use of magical narrative is both self-conscious and deeply rooted in the folkloric and literary traditions of western Europe, notably Scandinavian **folklore** and **epic**, Germanic **saga**, and English medieval romance. Other influences include George **MacDonald**, Lord Dunsany, and the fairy-tale collections of Andrew **Lang**. Tolkien's most overt discussion of the operation of fantasy comes in his essay "On Fairy Stories" (an Andrew Lang lecture in 1938, later published in 1947). Despite the title, this does not deal only with fairy tale or folklore, but also with the notion of magical narrative in general and the operation of symbolic storytelling. His discussion is notable for its sense of the **faerie** realm as both beautiful and dangerous and for its particularly acute analysis, and ultimate denial, of the association between children and magical narrative. Another work, "Leaf by Niggle"

(1947), is an allegorical story that explores the nature of the imagination and of artistic creation in terms similar to those of "On Fairy Stories."

Tolkien's first published **novel** was *The Hobbit*, which had its genesis in stories he told to his children; even in written form, the tale retains elements of the oral voice. Although it is clearly **children's literature**, the fantasy world in which it is set is that of Tolkien's elaborately constructed mythology and language, found later in *The Lord of the Rings* and *The Silmarillion* (1977). *The Hobbit* is framed as a classic quest narrative, with a party of heroes and an assisting enchanter in search of a **dragon**'s hoard; elements such as a troll encounter and a **riddle** game are very much those of folklore. It also playfully exaggerates fairy tale's tendency to favor the poor, weak, or downtrodden hero in its construction of Bilbo Baggins, a middle-aged, domestic, and decidedly unheroic figure as its protagonist. The outcome of the quest is subversive of fairy-tale expectation, as the hero's eventual triumph is moral rather than physical, and he does not actually kill the dragon. The ending slides away from a simple adventure quest into a more epic narrative with political and ideological elements, very far removed from the easy resolution of the fairy tale, and foreshadowing its sequel. At the same time, it constitutes an interesting comparison to *Farmer Giles of Ham* (1949), also a dragon-slaying narrative, but one phrased more overtly as a mock medieval romance in which the cheerfully unheroic farmer overcomes the dragon through trickery and common sense.

The sweeping historical, mythological, and linguistic background to Middle-earth emerges more strongly in Tolkien's most famous novel, the three-part *The Lord of the Rings*. Its structure has some similarities to *The Hobbit*, particularly in its focus on an unlikely hobbit hero forced into epic adventure; it is, however, at once a much grander and a much darker picture, the ultimately triumphant renewal of its conclusion undercut by notes of nostalgia and loss. While the story revolves around the discovery and possession of a **magic object**, this is both more powerful and more sinister than those found in fairy tale. Interestingly, Tolkien's novel tends to construct more of a fairy-tale notion of the magical than do many of his successors in the genre. Like the fairy-tale protagonist, his heroes are not themselves inherently magical but are assisted by powerful **magic helper**s and artifacts. Tolkien's **Elves**, particularly, encapsulate many of the folkloric ideas about the faerie realm and its inhuman inhabitants. Ultimately, however, in its interest in history, politics, war, and the hero-**king**, *The Lord of the Rings* owes more to the epic and the romance than it does to the fairy tale.

After Tolkien's death, his son, Christopher Tolkien, edited a large body of fragmentary material, including *The Silmarillion*, Tolkien's epic collection of Middle-earth mythology and history, on which he worked throughout much of his life. This material forms a unique body of synthetic folklore, some of which emerges in *The Lord of the Rings* in the form of songs, poems, and stories, and which lends considerable depth and richness to the world of Middle-earth. The volumes include *Unfinished Tales of Numenor and Middle Earth* (1980) and the ten books known collectively as *The History of Middle-earth* (1983–96). The tone of many of the pieces is mythic rather than folkloric, their elevated language akin to that of the romance. An exception is *The Adventures of Tom Bombadil* (1962), a collection of poetry aimed primarily at children, with singsong rhythms and magical, generally bucolic themes appropriate to their purported genesis among the hobbits.

In addition to the Middle-earth material, Tolkien wrote several shorter works for children, among them *Smith of Wooton Major* (1967), a dreamy, nostalgic tale that deals with interactions between the human world and the distant, enchanted realm of faerie. *Roverandom* (1998) is another in the series of stories told to Tolkien's children, an attractive adventure tale with a dog turned into a toy. Like the *Father Christmas Letters* (1976), this is a whimsical, gently humorous children's fantasy.

Tolkien's importance for fantasy in the twentieth and twenty-first centuries is enormous and is reflected in the mainstream cinema release of Peter Jackson's film trilogy of *The Lord of the Rings*, both confirming and expanding Tolkien's cult following. *See also* Dwarf, Dwarves; English Tales; Film and Video; Myth.

Further Readings: Chance, Jane. *Tolkien and the Invention of Myth: A Reader.* Louisville: University Press of Kentucky, 2004; Shippey, T. A. *The Road to Middle-Earth.* Enlarged edition. London: Harper-Collins, 1993.

Jessica Tiffin

Tolstoy, Lev (1828–1910)

Lev Tolstoy, renowned for his **novel**s, short stories, and philosophical writings, also devoted an important part of his work to educational issues. Having left the social and literary circles of St. Petersburg in 1859, Tolstoy returned to his estate Yasnaya Polyana, where he established two schools for the children of his serfs. He also published twelve issues of *Yasnaya Polyana* (1862–63), a periodical in which he formulated and discussed his pedagogical ideas. Enclosed with the journal, the reader would find folktales and fairy tales, bylinas (folk **epic**s and **ballad**s), **anecdote**s, **fable**s, and **proverbs**. These were later to become the main components of Tolstoy's two primers, *Azbuka* (*The ABC Book*, 1872) and *Novaya Azbuka* (*The New ABC Book*, 1875). They were followed by four volumes of readers based on similar material.

The first book was severely criticized, which led to a thorough revision. For the second version, Tolstoy wrote down more than 100 new fairy tales and stories. These included "Tri medvedya" ("Three Bears"), which was a retelling of "Goldilocks and the Three Bears," and "Nagrada" ("The Reward"), a tale about a smart **peasant** and the wisdom of the tsar originally published in Aleksandr **Afanas'ev**'s collection. "Tsar' i rubashka" ("The Tsar and the Shirt"), a story of Arabian origin, demonstrates that power is no guarantee for happiness and health. In "Mal'chik s pal'chik," Tolstoy retells Charles **Perrault**'s "Le petit poucet" ("Tom Thumb," 1697), although Tolstoy's version also leans heavily on the Russian folktale "Mal'chik s pal'chik i lyudoyed" ("Tom Thumb and the Cannibal"). *See also* Pedagogy; Russian Tales.

Further Readings: Egan, David R., and Melinda A. Egan. *Leo Tolstoy: An Annotated Bibliography of English Language Sources from 1978 to 2003.* Lanham, MD: Scarecrow Press, 2005; Tussing Orwin, Donna, ed. *The Cambridge Companion to Tolstoy.* Cambridge: Cambridge University Press, 2002.

Janina Orlov

Tom Thumb. *See* Thumbling, Tom Thumb

Topelius, Zacharias (1818–1898)

Zacharias Topelius was a Finland-Swedish journalist, historian, and author of **children's literature** who played an essential role in establishing Finnish children's literature and exerted a great influence on Nordic children's literature and fairy-tale aesthetics. A professor of Finnish history at the University of Helsinki, Topelius also had great significance for

Finnish culture and literature and is widely regarded as the founder of Finnish historical literature. His classic historical **novel**, *Fältskärns Berättelser* (*The Surgeon's Stories*, 1851–67), today considered as **young adult fiction**, is set in the Thirty Years' War. Under the influence of Hans Christian **Andersen**, Topelius wrote educational fairy tales in the style of Nordic National Romanticism. He published his first leaflet with fairy tales in 1848. It was illustrated by his wife, Emelie, and included in the four-part collection *Sagor* (*Fairy Tales*, 1847–52). Most of Topelius's novels appeared first in newspapers and were later collected into books. His collected poems, songs, fairy tales, and plays for children were published in an eight-part series *Läsning för barn* (*Reading for Children*, 1865–96). A special selection of this classic collection was published in 1903 with illustrations by prominent artists such as Carl Larsson, Albert Edelfeldt, and Ottilia Adelborg.

Topelius's most popular fairy-tale plays for children include reworkings of "Sleeping Beauty" and "Cinderella." Other famous fairy tales are *Hallonmasken* (*Rasberry Worm*, 1854), *Adalminas Pärla* (*The Pearl of Adalmina*, 1893), and *Walters äventyr* (*Walter's Adventures*, 1855). *Björken och stjärnan* (*The Birch and The Star*, 1870) is one of his most beloved fairy tales and is distinguished by lyrical descriptions of nature in a patriotic and romantic tone. His stories also show the influence of biblical **motif**s, **legend**s, and **Finnish tales**. Folk poetry, especially the **Kalevala**, the Finnish national **epic**, had a very important impact on his works. Many generations of primary schoolchildren read *Boken om vårt land* (*The Book of Our Country*, 1875), an illustrated book depicting Finland's history, geography, and culture. Religious and ethical qualities and Romantic nationalism are also characteristic of Topelius's children's poems and songs. His language is dynamic and detailed, distinguished by playful humor. Oral features are used as textual and stylistic elements in his stories. Topelius regarded fairy tales as a means to develop children's imagination. Although his view of the child is romantic and idealized, his thoughts concerning children's literature are modern and groundbreaking for his time. He disapproved of a moralistic approach to children's literature. Instead, he encouraged artistic expression, playfulness, and fantasy and emphasized the importance of children's self-sufficiency. ***See also*** Finnish Tales; Scandinavian Tales.

Further Readings: Orlov, Janina. "Var glad som sparven kvittrar." *Finlands svenska litteraturhistoria: Åren 1400–1900*. Edited by Johan Wrede. Helsinki: Svenska litteratursällskapet i Finland, 1999. 339–50; Lehtonen, Maija. "Puoli vuosisataa lastenkirjailijana—Zacharias Topelius." *Pieni suuri maailma: Suomalaisen lasten-ja nuortenkirjallisuuden historia*. Edited by Liisi Huhtala et al. Helsinki: Tammi, 2003. 20–31.

Elina Druker

Tourism

Travel is intrinsically connected to narration: processing new and unfamiliar sights and experiences brings forth a need to communicate them in travel diaries, travelogues, and other verbal and visual types of telling about one's journey. The folktale in turn often narrates the wondrous journey of its protagonists. Through opening formulas such as "Once upon a time, in a land far far away," folktale tellers invite listeners to participate themselves in a mental, fictional journey. In addition to this linkage through movement and narration, the folktale appeals to the tourist industry for other reasons as well: Folktales as mentifacts (mentifacts represent the ideas and beliefs of a culture) are—so far—a mostly free and thus ideal resource for all kinds of economic ventures. Hence, they are deployed in the realm of

Photo of "Rapunzel mit Kindern"—"Rapunzel with Children"—from the brochure *Auf den Spuren der Brüder Grimm*. [Copyright © ARGE Deutsche Märchenstraße. Used by permission.]

tourism as (1) metaphoric resources, (2) theming devices for landscapes, and (3) in reified form as actual destinations such as fairy-tale amusement parks or touristic travel routes.

The tale's generic premise is so deeply rooted in cultural **memory** that it can be drawn on for **advertising** just about any form of travel or vacation. A holiday is intended as a time away from everyday life and has been described in ritual terms as a "time out of time," a pilgrimage, or a liminal period. As the "generic" folktale takes place in an alternate universe and has its main protagonists succeed in fulfilling their hopes and **wish**es, praising travel destinations in fairy-tale allusions is a promising prospect from an advertising point of view as much as from a potential tourist's expectations. Whether it is an entire, to Westerners "exotic," country, a city, or even just a hotel or a bedroom, describing them as places "right out of a fairy tale" or as accommodations where one will "feel like a **princess**" will resonate with many readers of travel brochures. It is not only the plot of a folktale or its stock figures that serve as a resource for advertising copy. The long history of folktale **illustration** offers powerful visual memories that can be crafted into the language of tourism.

Folk narratives, like many works of literature, are deeply associated with particular regions, cities, or entire landscapes. While **legend**s are marked through their linkage to specific places and times, tales are associated with certain types of landscape that provide a background for a tale's action. In the store of images from the European tale, for instance, forests figure prominently as sites of confusion and wandering, rescue and assistance, as well as hiding places. Terming forests as "fairy-tale forests" is thus a frequent touristic means to utilize images from the folktale and develop activities especially for families to enjoy in such a landscape. The shared cultural knowledge of what a fairy-tale forest stands for provides a background within which guided walks, fairy-tale **performance**s, or participatory activities resonate with more than the trees, moss, forest paths, and broken sunlight. Other such tale imagery found in tourism involves flower-filled, rolling meadows peopled with **fairies**. Open prairies are occasionally themed, though far less strongly, with **tall tale**s, evident in sales of postcard jackalopes and other creatures. Folktales have also achieved connections to particular landscapes through their history of collection and publication. The **Grimm**s' ***Kinder- und***

Hausmärchen (*Children's and Household Tales*, 1812–15) are strongly associated with central German landscape. Although the tales themselves are international **tale type**s, the place of the printed collection in the German national consciousness fostered the linkage and opened it for touristic use. Since 1975, the Deutsche Märchenstraße (German Fairy-Tale Route) has been guiding motorists from Hanau to Bremen with opportunities to stop at locales associated with specific tale characters—for example, **Sleeping Beauty**'s castle, the **Frog King**'s fountain, or Rapunzel's tower. Similarly, Hans Christian **Andersen**'s character the little mermaid is part and parcel of Copenhagen's image and is used in the city's tourism marketing. The narrative collections of Japanese folklorist **Yanagita** Kunio are said to have had a strong impact on the nature of early domestic tourism in Japan.

Theme parks devoted to the fairy tale take the practice of theming landscapes a step further. A part of the landscape is set aside and outfitted in more- or less-elaborate form with materialized tale figures and **motif**s. Visitors enjoy seeing the representations and identifying the tale source. In some instances, additional amusements (for example, rides and carousels) are added. The first examples of fairy-tale parks can be dated to early twentieth-century Europe, but the breakthrough for this form of leisure came with the opening of Disneyland in 1955. Walt **Disney**'s animated versions of folktales and fairy tales contribute a fair share of the characters, buildings, and crafted landscapes of this environment. Visitors are meant to enter a land of wonder and amusement and experience encounters with all kinds of narrative plots, mediated through space, movement, and film, as well as costumed enactments of narrative characters. In this venue, folktales are truncated and mixed together with source material from very diverse aspects of cultural knowledge (nature exploration and technology, among others). The Disney formula for economic success further contains the merchandising of its animated films. Fairy-tale characters in their Disney shapes and colorations thus also became souvenirs—key chains, plastic figurines, prints on T-shirts and baseball caps, and so forth.

In 2005, UNESCO selected the Grimms' *Children's and Household Tales* to become part of the "Memory of the World." While the wording of the nomination emphasized the universal dimension of the collection, the German state of Hessia and the city of Kassel, where important manuscripts and rare editions are housed, expressed pride in their "ownership" of such a treasure and the hope that this selection would bring benefit to the area. The impact of such "ennobling" measures on the intertwining of folktales, tourism, and monetary gain can at this point only be guessed. *See also* Walt Disney Company.

Further Readings: Bendix, Regina. "On the Road to Fiction: Narrative Reification in Austrian Cultural Tourism." *Ethnologia Europaea* 29 (1999): 29–40; Robinson, Mike, and Hans-Christian Andersen, eds. *Literature and Tourism*. London: Continuum, 2002; Schama, Simon. *Landscape and Memory*. New York: Vintage Books, 1996.

Regina Bendix

Tournier, Michel (1924–)

A major French novelist and essayist, Michel Tournier has often confessed his admiration for the genre of the fairy tale, which inspires both his fiction and his nonfiction. In the essay "Barbe-Bleue ou le secret du conte" ("**Bluebeard** or the Secret of the Tale," 1981), he uses the example of Charles **Perrault**'s famous tale to attempt to show the elusive power of the genre. Fascinated by the figure of the **ogre**, Tournier's second **novel**, *Le Roi des Aulnes*

(*The Ogre*), which won the Prix Goncourt in 1970, presents Abel, a French prisoner of war responsible for kidnapping dozens of young boys for recruitment by the Nazi SS during World War II, as an heir to the ogre in "Le petit poucet" ("Little **Thumbling**").

The **film adaptation**, *The Ogre* (2004), by Volker Schlöndorff, is appropriately presented as a dark fairy tale. In *Gilles et Jeanne* (1983), which tells the story of the notorious Gilles de Rais, the legendary Bluebeard, Tournier establishes a more logical analogy between the child murderer and Perrault's ogre. His subversive use of fairy tales to challenge social conventions is particularly evident in *La fugue du petit Poucet* (*Tom Thumb Runs Away*), first published in 1979, a modern, provocative retelling of Perrault's fairy tale. In this book, Pierre Poucet runs away from his authoritative **father** and is welcomed in the forest by M. Logre, an androgynous, peace-loving, vegetarian hippie, and his seven enchanting daughters. *See also* French Tales.

Further Reading: Roberts, Martin. *Michel Tournier: Bricolage and Cultural Mythology.* Saratoga, CA: ANMA Libri, 1994.

Sandra L. Beckett

Transformation

The **wonder tale** and **fairy tale** are, in essence, transformative narratives on transformations. On the one hand, both their narrative patterns and metatextual variations convey dynamics of change rather than a static framework; on the other, their themes hinge on processes of **initiation** and metamorphosis. Thus, the form and contents of wonder tales concur in conveying a transformational pattern of thought. Of course, the dynamics of oral transmission have to do with this property. In the absence of fixed texts, individual tellers in oral settings—consciously or otherwise—alter the materials they narrate. But while this is more or less true of all **folklore**, the connection between wonder tales and fairy tales and transformations is the essence of this genre, even beyond **oral tradition**. It is with good reason that Anne **Sexton** named her rewriting of fairy tales *Transformations* (1971).

Vladimir **Propp** highlighted the complex nature of the transformative essence of wonder tales. Propp showed that tales draw on a pool of about 150 components, which tale tellers organize into a framework of thirty-one **function**s enacted by seven character types. Propp's framework was meant to be static, for he assumed that each tale component is clear-cut, each function is discrete, and each character is singular. But in all three levels, Propp did acknowledge what he called "transformation or metamorphosis." Indeed, he realized that characters often merge into each other, and that attributive elements as well as functions are subject to "laws of transformation." Hence, Propp brought to attention the dynamic principle of wonder tales.

Other scholars built on this breakthrough in various ways. For example, Claude Lévi-Strauss proposed that among Propp's thirty-one functions, several are reducible to the same function reappearing at different points of the narrative after undergoing one or a number of transformations. And Eleazar Meletinsky, on noting that almost every personage can perform opposite functions, inferred that functional fields are continuous, and that they form a "cyclic structure." Indeed, wonder tales hinge on cyclic transformation between enchantment and disenchantment, which involve metamorphosis—in other words, reversible transition between contrasted aspects of dramatis personae.

But the point that the transformative essence of wonder tales befits the core theme of metamorphosis is only the first aspect of the proposition that wonder tales are transformative narratives on transformations. There is a second aspect to that proposition, visible in Propp's insistent assimilation between metamorphosis and "transformations of tales." In fact, his observation that wonder-tale themes engender each other through "transformation or metamorphosis" implies that the entire store of fairy tales is to be examined as a chain of **variant**s. And, Propp argues, to unfold the overall "picture of transformations" brings out the core theme of wonder tales.

According to Propp, the one "**archetype**" from which all other themes are derived is actually the kidnapping of a **princess** by a **dragon**. This is significant insofar as Propp, in his *Istoricheskie korni volshebnoi skazki* (*Historical Roots of the Wondertale*, 1946), highlights thematic transformations between fighting a dragon, being swallowed by one, entering the realm of the dead (a transition he considers the wonder-tale's axis), and metamorphosis proper. Hence, Propp brings together thematic transformations and character metamorphoses under the paradigmatic dragon image of cyclic **time** forever rewinding itself through periodic **death** and rebirth—the essence of enchantment/disenchantment transitions in wonder tales.

In sum, wonder tales are a transformative genre dealing with metamorphosis according to protean imagery of cyclic time, which dragonlike figures synthesize. In other words, transformations affect tale characters displaying paradoxical traits (for it is their fate to cycle through contrasted aspects of themselves) as well as themes mutating through chains of variants (for each text supposes, and echoes, other versions).

Moreover, the morphing nature of tales entails that transformations endure as long as tellers abide, that is, even beyond oral tradition. Why is this so? Arguably, one reason tales are inherently transformative is that taletellers nearly always incorporate personal interpretation into the materials they pass on. Moreover, this dynamic process of interpretation happens along chains of listeners, then readers, and then academic specialists.

Granted, there is a sizable difference between folk audiences on the one hand, and academic specialists on the other, responding to a given theme. Whereas taletellers come to terms with tales in terms of more tales (which is how new variants crop up), academics engage tales in analytic terms by means of metanarrative discourses (which is how interpretive models arise). But in a realm of narrative transformations, such distinction is only relative. In a review Claude Lévi-Strauss wrote for *Diogène* in 1954, he mentions the "very dangerous game" the mythologist (or folklorist) plays by placing one's intellectual mechanisms in the service of any given narrative scheme, thus allowing it to live on and to operate that same mysterious "alchemy" that afforded it solidity and endurance throughout continents and millenaries. Lévi-Strauss' point is that academic metadiscourses often exude the very essence of folk narratives they mean to reflect upon. In other words, academic interpretations may unwittingly crystallize into idiosyncratic variants of the folkloric themes they engage. Thus, Lévi-Strauss acknowledges his own work on **myth** can be taken as "the myth of mythology." From this viewpoint, interpretation and generation of variants appear as indissoluble aspects of **storytelling** chains reaching up to our time.

In principle, conflation between the metafolkloric level of academic discourse and the narrative-interpretative way of folklore may show in the guise of theoretical studies haunted by the inner logic of themes they engage as well as in the shape of recreated stories relaying reflexive (post)modern discourse. While Lévi-Strauss's point concerns the first case, the second instance is evident, for instance, in the way the Brothers **Grimm** incorporated their scholarly knowledge and interpretations of folklore into the tale versions they rewrote, thus producing hybrid variants. In the same trend, but more radically, Angela **Carter** has rewritten a number of folklore themes in light of her own intellectual pursuits. Interestingly, it has been said that **postmodernism** would not make sense without Carter, and that her relationship with the fairy tale lies at the core of her contemporaneity.

In a striking experiment, Carter dealt with the theme of **Little Red Riding Hood** in a group of mutually echoing short stories, one radio script, and one homonymous screenplay (for Neil Jordan's 1984 film *The Company of Wolves*). By thus retelling one single subject matter in various, mutually reverberating ways, Carter mimicked a live tradition. Since her stories present variations on a common theme, they beg for intertextual readings—like folkloric versions do (see **Intertextuality**). And since Carter's readings of the theme come embedded in multinarrative interplay, rather than being conveyed through analytic discourse, she evades a hard-set interpretation that would close up on itself—as a single text would tend to. In short, Carter's cluster of retellings shows transformation between variants, and it enacts transformation between the oral folklore of yore and contemporary concerns. Moreover, even the briefest examination of the cluster of short stories entitled "The Werewolf," "The Company of Wolves," and "Wolf-Alice"—alongside the radio and the movie scripts called "The Company of Wolves"—brings out thematic transformations concerning **initiation**, **werewolf** metamorphosis, and **blood** symbolism. These themes, of course, hinge on transitions between enchantment and disenchantment, the otherworld and this world. Thus, Carter's transposition of old tales into our time is a good example of multithreaded tale transformations.

Carter's first transformation consists of placing this theme on the seasonal hinge of the year, when the "door" of the winter solstice stands open, notwithstanding the fact that most previous versions situate the story in early summertime. This decision facilitates exploring the underlying werewolf theme. In Carter's terms, wolves may be more than they seem; the worst wolves are hairy on the inside, for their fur is turned inward like a sheepskin jacket. Thus, werewolves are wolves under a human mien. Such dual creatures lack a proper place, and the hinge of the year—when things do not fit together as well as they should—is the proper time for them. Moreover, midwinter is the nighttime of the year, and wolves prowl at night. Indeed, the lupine creatures are like shadows or wraiths. They have passed through the **mirror**, so to speak, and now live on the other side of things. On midwinter, though, they can sink through the open doors of the solstice. In sum, the home of werewolves is nowhere, and on the winter solstice they glide between the two worlds. Therefore, Carter's midwinter setting emphasizes the between-and-betwixt ontology of werewolves in folklore, which she chooses to bring center stage.

The second transformation regards a constant symbol of femininity. References to flower- and berry-picking abound in previous versions. But, of course, midwinter is no season for flowers. Therefore, Carter places a metaphoric flower at center stage. She calls the heroine Rosaleen, and likens her to a "little bud" and a "blossom." Moreover, Carter associates flowers plucked from granny's best rose tree to the bright red shawl granny is knitting for Rosaleen. Thus, by focusing on metaphorical flowers, Carter enhances the traditional link between blooming flowers and a maiden's puberty.

Consider the traditional **color** symbolism she uses. At first, the heroine is like an unbroken egg, a sealed vessel shut tight with a plug of membrane. White is the untainted color of this virginity, while red connotes the upcoming blood crisis. The girl's shawl, made to match her rosy cheeks, is quite a bloody red. It is said to be as red as the blood the girl must spill; the color of poppies, of sacrifices, and of her menses. Overall, the recurring image of red on white denotes the heroine's budding, magic condition, which is also the hinge of life, neither one thing nor the other, neither child nor woman—some magic, in-between thing, an egg that holds its own future within.

The third transformation concerns highlighting the notion that the hinge setting is appropriate regarding the two main characters. Carter emphasizes the strong affinity between the werewolf and the maiden who meet in bed—for both are in transit, so to speak. Throughout, the author insists on the duality of the werewolf, who is in both worlds without being in either, as well as of the maiden, who is in neither life stage but has a foot in each. Hence, by focusing on a hinge and on passages, Carter emphasizes parallelism between the maiden and the werewolf, and initiation and metamorphosis. This amounts to assimilating the morphing heroine to the shape-shifting werewolf. Hence, the maiden "snarls" while painting her mouth red. Also, she understands the notion that some wolves are hairy on the inside in terms of the image of a coat of sheepskin—and she wears precisely one such coat when leaving home for the forest. And, last but not least, the movie script actually has her turn into a wolf.

Carter sustains this pubertal metamorphosis on unimpeachable folkloric grounds. Clearly, the heroine's metamorphosis into a wolf coincides with her initiation into womanhood; otherwise put, she turns into a wolf as she passes on the side of blood. Having gone into the forest in a sheepskin coat, or else dressed in red (according to the version one considers, just like in oral tradition), the heroine meets a werewolf under the guise of a hunter. The hunter naturally stands for the werewolf because both shed blood. In a sense, all **men** are hunters/werewolves insofar as they shed the blood of **women**, as if the latter were prey. Thus, men have "the beast within." But Rosaleen's mother makes it clear that women have a beast of their own to match men's—which, again, suggests equivalence between women and werewolves. One reason for this is that both enact lunar periodicity. It is the heroine's destiny to externalize internal blood, much as it is the fate of werewolves to externalize inner **hair**. Wolf-Alice illustrates the equivalence between blood and hair when she spends hours examining the "new skin" born of her bleeding. If the full moon is indeed the time for both the bleeding of women and the furry condition of werewolves, then feminine menstruation amounts to a furry condition—and the end of bleeding amounts to a renovation of skin. Hence, after Rosaleen eats a juicy red apple, granny remarks she will not stay a young girl much longer, and a snake uncoils itself—as if to confirm the link between blood, skin change, and the moon.

The traditional theme hinges on the relationship between two women through a skin-shifter (werewolves used to be called *versipelles* in Latin), and Carter builds on this pattern. Since she also identifies granny with the werewolf, both granny and the girl fuse with the skin-shifter. And, given equivalence between werewolves and serpents regarding skin shifting, the werewolf identity of both women hints that a rejuvenating change of skin happens between the waning elder and the waxing maiden. Indeed, it is granny who hands the maiden a shawl the color of the blood she must spill when she joins the wolf in bed, there to adopt a wolf's pelt. The heroine eats the apple in granny's garden (whence the red roses also came) before passing under a snake. And the girl, having been the explicit cause of granny's death, prospers thereafter in her house. In short, both women are assimilated to the skin-shifter because the werewolf's skin swapping—likened to the serpent's rejuvenating sloughing—stands for periodic blood and the renovation of womanhood. Thus, the maiden's initiation into full womanhood entails absorbing the older women's blood, which relegates the drained woman to ancestor status. Carter's rewriting of the **Cinderella** theme, in "The Burned Child," exactly reenacts this pattern.

In sum, Angela Carter's retelling of wonder tales conveys her well-known feminist outlook even while providing inklings on traditional symbolism, which her narrative interpretations faithfully preserve and enhance. Carter's tales, like werewolves and pubertal maidens, are poised between two worlds. And, like all wonder tales and fairy tales, their business is transformation; hence, they are both postmodern and tottering with age. This is just another way of saying that wonder tales and fairy tales are transformative narratives on transformations, metamorphosing along chains of listeners, readers, and writers. *See also* Birth; Hybridity, Hybridization.

Further Readings: Carter, Angela. *The Bloody Chamber*. 1979. London: Vintage, 1995; ———. *The Curious Room*. Edited by Mark Bell. London: Vintage, 1997; Meletinsky, Eleazar, et al. "Problems of the Structuralist Analysis of Fairytales." *Soviet Structural Folkloristics*. Edited by Pierre Maranda. The Hague: Mouton, 1974. 73–139; Propp, Vladimir. *Morphology of the Folktale*. Translated by Laurence Scott. Revised and edited by Louis A. Wagner. 2nd edition. 1968. Austin: University of Texas Press, 1996; ———. *Theory and History of Folklore*. Translated Ariadna Y. Martin and Richard P. Martin. Minneapolis: University of Minnesota Press, 1984; Sexton, Anne. *Transformations*. Boston: Mariner Books, 2001; Vaz da Silva, Francisco. *Metamorphosis: The Dynamics of Symbolism in European Fairy Tales*. New York: Peter Lang, 2002.

Francisco Vaz da Silva

Transgression

Narratives of transgression are prompted by one of the main catalysts for folktale action: interdiction (whether as prohibition, command, or cultural practice). Following from and developing Vladimir **Propp**'s identification of transgression as a **function** linked with interdiction near the beginning of a folktale, structuralist analysis has attributed a key role to the concept in discussions of folk narrative. Because transgression is commonly followed by processes of **punishment** and rehabilitation, it generally has a normative function in affirming societal rules and practices, but this is not always so: social change is primarily produced by transgression and the subsequent acceptance of a new mode of behavior. Therefore, transgression can be judged to be either positive or negative.

An interdiction is addressed primarily to the protagonist of the story. This may take the form of a prohibition, such as, "Do not leave the path," "Do not open this door/this box," "Do not attempt to look at me"; or it may be a command, such as, "Take good care of your brothers"; or it may be implicit and oblique, as "I fear for you if you do this" or "This action should not be performed." Thus, the unarticulated interdiction in the tale of **Beauty and the Beast** (ATU 425C)—"The roses should not be picked"—exemplifies a particularly oblique form of interdiction, in that a lesser character transgresses a prohibition that has not been stated (although perhaps is implicit in conventions of hospitality). Furthermore, Beauty's request to her **father**, "Bring me a rose," has positioned him to transgress. Finally, Beauty's transgression of her promise to the Beast that her visit to her father will not extend beyond a week is the catalyst for her avowal of love that transforms the Beast back to human shape. Given the thoroughly positive outcome (as in the version by Jeanne-Marie **Leprince de Beaumont**), the teleology of the tale seems to affirm that such unwitting transgressions can be the instrument of providence.

As this example suggests, transgression is not restricted to a structural function of the role of the principal character but is also constituted by the actions of other characters. Where transgression overtly serves as **exemplum**, the relationship of action and punishment is clear. In Charles **Perrault**'s version of the tale of **Little Red Riding Hood** (ATU 333), for example, the protagonist dies as a consequence of her transgression. Jacob and Wilhelm **Grimm**'s disobedient Little Red Riding Hood also faces **death** when she is devoured by her opponent, the **wolf,** although the hunter's intercession ultimately rescues the little girl, now all the wiser, from the wolf's belly. However, the Grimm version also punishes the wolf ("You old sinner," as the hunter call him) for his transgressions. The protagonist in the tale of **Snow White** (ATU 709) three times breaks the interdiction not to speak with anyone or open the door, and repeatedly comes close to losing her life. The mitigating circumstance is that the transgressions of her stepmother, in her repeated attempts to destroy Snow White, are far more reprehensible and hence lead inevitably to her death by torture. A principal character may also be the victim of transgression, as in the numerous father-daughter **incest** stories falling within the **tale type** ATU 510B (Peau d'Asne). The daughter's need to erase her identity and to lead a fugitive and abjected life functions as a correlative of the transgressive abuse that sets events in motion, although the animal skin in which she disguises herself may also figure in the very **sexuality** that had made her an object of desire. Robin **McKinley**'s novelization of the tale type as *Deerskin* (1993) strips away the indirectness to examine how a woman's destiny can be tied to **gender** roles culturally constructed within a framework of power which privileges **men** over **women**.

The general sense of "transgression" is as a violation of, or going beyond the bounds of, a law, rule, command, or the like. Transgression is physical, cultural, and moral. Contemporary distinctions between purposive transgression, which is socially formative, and ludic transgression, which may be more carnivalesque, are inherent in folktale. In modern critical discourses, however, purposive transgression tends to be treated as a positive concept, denoting rejection of the conservative or the repressive in social, political, and personal life. Since a society cannot change without transgression, transgression must run counter to some "official" code(s). Hence, a contrast may be made between transgressive behavior that has *constructive* outcomes for the self or society, and behavior that has *destructive* outcomes, and therefore upholds traditional behavior.

It is perhaps because of the modern interest in constructive transgression that the folk **ballad** of "Tam Lin" has been retold eleven times in **novel** form since 1985. All modern retellings reproduce the central story schema of a mortal who is taken by **fairies**, meets a young woman at a well, and is reclaimed by her before he can be dispatched as the due paid to hell by the fairies every seven years. An interdiction against visiting the well, which the heroine of the ballad transgresses, encapsulates social interdictions against female sexual agency and premarital sexual activity, and the transgression results in pregnancy. The ballad and some of its retellings have the potential to question the social bases of the interdiction, exposing it as an expression of patriarchal attempts to control female sexuality and, at a deeper level, of the ambivalent attraction/repulsion felt toward "wild" sex and embodied in the Fairy Queen. Thus the heroine, at a crucial moment in her life—the onset of adulthood and hence nubility—is confronted by a socially imposed interdiction (do not go here; do not do this) that contains her sexuality. It may seem folly to disobey the interdiction, but well-being, effective individual agency, and even—for Tam Lin—life itself depend on the action. Folktale form and content are used to examine the importance of free will and choice in human life, while insisting that individuals must take responsibility for the consequences of their actions.

In addition to its function as a significant plot initiator by a principal character, transgression performs other functions within folktale narratives. It characteristically marks a moral boundary separating acceptable from unacceptable behavior, and hence may affirm dominant ideology; but it is also used to disrupt conventional tenets of behavior and the participants' moral responses to those tenets, thereby asserting the inadequacy of the moral schemata used to interpret events. Transgression narratives thus represent attempts to come to terms with or even implement cultural change. *See also* Forbidden Room.

Further Readings: McCallum, Robyn. *Ideologies of Identity in Adolescent Fiction: The Dialogic Construction of Subjectivity.* New York: Garland, 1999; Propp, Vladimir. *Morphology of the Folktale.* Translated by Laurence Scott. Revised and edited by Louis A. Wagner. 2nd edition. 1968. Austin: University of Texas Press, 1996; Stallybrass, Peter, and Allon White. *The Politics and Poetics of Transgression.* London: Methuen, 1986; Wilson, Robert. "Play, Transgression and Carnival: Bakhtin and Derrida on Scriptor Ludens." *Mosaic* 19.1 (1986): 73–89.

John Stephens

Translation

Most commonly, translation refers to the process and product of transferring meaning from one language into another, a necessary but secondary activity whereby, for instance, tales from the **Grimm**s' *Kinder- und Häusmärchen* (*Children's and Household Tales,* 1812–15) became available to English-language readers through Edgar **Taylor** as *German Popular Stories* in 1823. This kind of translation is central to everyday social life and has informed portentous cultural shifts, as seen in the history of the **Bible**'s translation into classical, national, and vernacular languages around the globe.

The utility and promise of translation as a tool of human communication are overwhelmingly evident, but its challenges and pitfalls are equally overwhelming, as the meanings we seek to convey mutate in transit from one language to another. When translation is understood in more general terms as the interpretation of meanings across systems that have different rules or conventions, similar problems arise. Although its negotiations often go undetected, this intersemiotic translation has a significant impact on how social groups and their stories are represented in dominant cultures and media.

Translation has been a focus of philosophical inquiry from classical times into the twenty-first century—from Cicero to Walter Benjamin to Gayatri Chakravorty Spivak—eventually evolving into the academic discipline of translation studies in the 1970s. Considering the practice of translation and its study as framed by history, national politics, unequal social and aesthetic relations, **gender**, institutions, and technological shifts, translation studies is proving to be a significant approach to the study of stories circulating across cultures.

Any time we listen to, read, view, recall, tell, or retell a story, the experience is the product of translation processes ranging from the psycholinguistic—how do we neurologically retain certain narratives?—to the performative—what kinds of ideological and aesthetic choices go into the visual **illustration** of the Beast as lion, panther, or extraterrestrial in the classic fairy tale "**Beauty and the Beast**"?—to the social dynamics of reception—which translations are more popular and why? The translation of folktales and fairy tales across media, languages, genres, and cultures has mattered enormously to the history and reception of these narrative genres.

Linguistic translation has been a driving force in the international reception of folktale and fairy-tale collections. Significant European examples include Italo **Calvino**'s post-World-War-II translations of regional tales from different dialects into Italy's national language; nineteenth-century translations of the Grimms' German tales into other national languages; the 1761 publication in English of Jeanne-Marie **Leprince de Beaumont**'s "La belle et la bête"; and translations of the *Arabian Nights*, starting with Antoine **Galland**'s French rendering in 1704. Scholars have amply shown how these cases illustrate the contributions of translation to the history of folktale and fairy-tale traditions in national contexts, or, in the case of the *Arabian Nights*, to the Western invention of Oriental and Orientalist fairy tales. Such contributions are not always straightforward, however, just as the history of translation often appears to be fortuitous. Translation into a language that functions as a commercial and social lingua franca—as English currently does—can have a wide impact on the international scholarly understanding of any given national tradition, as has occurred with the recent translation of Laura **Gonzenbach**'s nineteenth-century Sicilian tales from German into Italian and then into English. Focusing not only on the faults or merits of individual translations but also on their domesticating or foreignizing strategies of equivalence, studies of fairy-tale classics in translation offer insights into national and gender ideologies as well.

Another form of translation that is motivated by and in turn contributes to the international popularity of folktales and fairy tales is the move from one medium of communication to another as a result of technological advances, cultural shifts, and artistic choices. Examples of such translations across media include how printed collections of fairy tales have resulted from the collection of oral tales, as documented for the Brothers Grimm; from their (presumed) recollection, as with Charles **Perrault**'s *Histoires ou contes du temps passé* (*Stories or Tales of Times Past*, 1697); from their real or imagined **performance**, as in the actual French **salon**s of the late seventeenth century and the fictional world of Giambattista **Basile**'s *Lo cunto de li cunti* (*The Tale of Tales*, 1634–36); and from a combination of all of the above. **Adaptation**s of fairy tales to **film and video** introduce yet another set of dynamics. For example, one clue to the reliance of Walt **Disney**'s *Cinderella* (1950) on Perrault's version is the famous glass slipper. In print, this was possibly the result of a mishearing, the mistranslation of the homonyms *vair* (fur) and *verre* (glass) onto the page. On screen, it translated magic and sparkle most successfully. Understanding the relationship between orality and print as a form of translation has also led some folklorists to advocate "full translation" in the transcription of the oral tales they collect so as to mark on the page nonverbal and performance-centered features of the telling.

Linguistic and cultural translation has also been both a powerful tool and an important effect of what Edward Said called Orientalism and of **colonialism** around the globe. Translations of the *Arabian Nights* into European languages reveal more about the translators' mindset and the concerns of the time than about the Muslim or Eastern manners and customs that they purport to represent, often by moving from a fictional episode to a generalization about the culture in a footnote or introduction. Sadhana Naithani's work has focused on how folktale **collecting** and translating in British India were often literally the product of an administrative colonial enterprise. Paratextual features of folktale collections in print, such as prefaces, notes, and illustrations, also play an important role in the construction of a foreign "culture" where colonized tellers have been translated into nameless informants.

Scholarly work on the translation of fairy-tale classics into non-European languages is another promising area of scholarship.

The translation of a story also involves questions of genre classification and adaptation. Examples of such cultural translation range from sanitized versions of "**Little Red Riding Hood**" in picture books to fairy-tale **jokes**; and cross-culturally, to the ethnocentric translation of **Native American tales** and Oceanian stories as "fairy tales" (see **Pacific Island Tales**). The translation of genre markers such as *conte de fées*, **märchen**, *fiaba*, **fairy tale**, **wonder tale**, or **folktale** is in itself not a simple matter. *See also* Linguistic Approaches.

Further Readings: Asad, Talal. "The Concept of Cultural Translation in British Social Anthropology." *Writing Culture: The Poetics and Politics of Ethnography.* Edited by James Clifford and George E. Marcus. Berkeley: University of California Press, 1986. 141–64; Dollerup, Cay. *Tales and Translation: The Grimm Tales from Pan-Germanic Narratives to Shared International Fairytales.* Amsterdam: John Benjamins, 1999; Haase, Donald. "Framing the Brothers Grimm: Paratexts and Intercultural Transmission in English-Language Editions of the *Kinder- und Hausmärchen.*" *Fabula* 44 (2003): 55–69; ———. "Hypertextual Gutenberg: The Textual and Hypertextual Life of Folktales and Fairy Tales in English-language Popular Print Editions." *Fabula* 47 (2006): 222–30; Heidmann, Ute, and Jean-Michel Adam. "Text Linguistics and Comparative Literature: Towards an Interdisciplinary Approach to Written Tales; Angela Carter's Translation of Perrault." *Language and Verbal Art Revisited: Linguistic Approaches to the Study of Literature.* Edited by Donna R. Miller and Monica Turci. London: Equinox, 2007; Marzolph, Ulrich, ed. *The Arabian Nights in Transnational Perspective.* Detroit: Wayne State University Press, 2007; McCarthy, William Bernard, ed. *Jack in Two Worlds: Contemporary North American Tales and Their Tellers.* Chapel Hill: University of North Carolina Press, 1994; Naithani, Sadhana. "Prefaced Space: Tales of the Colonial British Collectors of Indian Folklore." *Imagined States: Nationalism, Utopia, and Longing in Oral Cultures.* Edited by Luisa Del Giudice and Gerald Porter. Logan: Utah State University Press, 2001. 64–79; Sallis, Eva. *Sheherazade through the Looking Glass: The Metamorphosis of* The Thousand and One Nights. Richmond, Surrey: Curzon, 1999; Schacker, Jennifer. *National Dreams: The Remaking of Fairy Tales in Nineteenth-Century England.* Philadelphia: University of Pennsylvania Press, 2003; Venuti, Lawrence, ed. *The Translation Studies Reader.* London: Routledge, 2000.

Cristina Bacchilega

Trauma and Therapy

The idea that fairy tales have a therapeutic value and the potential to help individuals deal with traumatic events has its modern roots in **psychological approaches** to fairy tales, especially Sigmund **Freud**'s theory of psychoanalysis. This is not to say, however, that therapeutic value of narrative and **storytelling** had not been implicitly recognized before the development of psychoanalytic theory at the end of the nineteenth century. Many important works of literature depict storytelling as a strategy for coping with stressful situations and traumatic events. Perhaps the most famous example—and also the most telling in the context of fairy tales—is the **frame narrative** of the *Arabian Nights*, wherein **Sheherazade** employs storytelling as a means of coping with the traumatic threat of being executed by her husband, Shahriyar. Sheherazade's stories, however, function not simply as a strategy to delay her execution indefinitely but more significantly as a means of bringing about a change in the murderous behavior of Shahriyar, who by the end of 1,001 nights of storytelling has been cured of his madness. The therapeutic value of fairy tales that is implicit in works such as the *Arabian Nights* becomes explicit in the works of Freud, his followers, and other psychologists and writers throughout the twentieth century.

According to Freud, the language of fairy tales, like the language of dreams, works symbolically by giving expression to repressed conflicts, anxieties, wishes, and taboo desires. Interpreted symbolically, fairy tales reveal the workings of the human psyche and identify the inner experiences that influence human behavior. In the context of Freudian psychoanalytic theory, this means that the symbolism of fairy tales can reveal the source of psychological pathologies, both in the culture generally and in the lives of specific individuals. This, in turn, gives the fairy tale a psychotherapeutic value and function. Like the dream, the fairy tale becomes a tool to help the psychoanalyst diagnose the problem and to help the client understand and deal with his or her neuroses.

Starting with this basic premise, psychoanalysts and psychologists have used the fairy tale in various ways. Some of Freud's followers used fairy tales to understand the symbolic language of their patients' dreams, especially to identify and describe the pathology of sexual repression. Freud himself, in the famous case of the **Wolf** Man, pointed out that the symbolism in his patient's dreams, which manifested sexual anxieties that were due to **childhood** trauma, was similar to the symbolism in "**Little Red Riding Hood**" and "The Wolf and the Seven Young Kids." Carl Gustav **Jung**, who had studied with Freud but developed his own branch of analytic psychology, was less inclined to view the symbols of dreams and fairy tales as expressions of individual pathologies. Instead, Jung posited that these symbols were **archetype**s—universal symbolic forms—that are therapeutic because they help individuals find their way to **transformation** and self-realization. Jungian psychoanalyst Hans Dieckmann offered numerous descriptions of his clinical experience with patients, whose therapy was facilitated by a consideration of their favorite childhood fairy tales, which appeared to speak to their own individual needs and issues.

In addition to the clinical use of fairy tales, there has been a flood of self-help books purporting to show how traditional tales can help people solve personal problems and lead happier, more fulfilling lives. Germany and Switzerland in particular have produced numerous books of this sort, including a whole series called *Weisheit im Märchen* (*Wisdom in the Fairy Tale*, 1983–85) and a string of books by Swiss Jungian psychotherapist Verena Kast. For example, in her book *Familienkonflikte im Märchen* (*Family Conflicts in the Fairy Tale*, 1984), Kast focuses on the fairy tale's depiction of familial conflicts and its suggested paths toward resolution and personal growth. It was in the United States, however, that the therapeutic benefit of the fairy tale was first truly popularized. This occurred in the form of Bruno **Bettelheim**'s influential work of 1976—*The Uses of Enchantment: The Meaning and Significance of Fairy Tales*—which made the case to a very wide audience that fairy tales help children deal with the psychological conflicts and existential dilemmas that they experience on an unconscious level. As the German translation of Bettelheim's book states: *Kinder brauchen Märchen*—that is, "children need fairy tales."

The fairy-tale therapies advocated by Bettelheim, the self-help industry, and both Freudian and Jungian psychoanalysis have received a good deal of criticism. Some critics object to the basic premises of psychoanalysis; others fault the advocates' failure to take into account the cultural and political ideologies embedded in fairy tales and the way that societies have used the genre as a tool of socialization—all of which makes its "therapeutic" value suspect.

Whether fairy tales possess a timeless and inherent therapeutic value is debatable. Still, there are autobiographical accounts that demonstrate how individuals have appropriated fairy tales for their own purposes to deal with traumatic events. For example, in *Telling: A Memoir of Rape and Recovery* (1999), Patricia Weaver Francisco uses Hans Christian Andersen's "The

Snow Queen" to structure her memoir and to help tell the story of her journey from trauma to empowerment. In drawing on Andersen's fairy tale to tell her own story, Weaver's *Telling* recalls the research of Elaine J. Lawless on the empowering role of narrative among battered **women**. Author and editor Terri Windling's anthology of tales entitled *The Armless Maiden* (1995) is intended for adult survivors of childhood abuse. In addition, recent research on war and the Holocaust draws on both literary and autobiographical texts to show how children and others traumatized by these events have sometimes turned to fairy tales to cope and work through their traumatic experiences. In these cases, individuals are "interpreting" fairy tales for their own uses—adapting them to their traumatic circumstances and reappropriating them as strategies for coping and emotional survival. *See also* Incest; Sex, Sexuality; Violence.

Further Readings: Clinton, Jerome W. "Madness and Cure in the *Thousand and One Nights*." *Fairy Tales and Society: Illusion, Allusion, and Paradigm*. Edited by Ruth B. Bottigheimer. Philadelphia: University of Pennsylvania Press, 1986. 35–51; Grolnick, Simon A. "Fairy Tales and Psychotherapy." *Fairy Tales and Society: Illusion, Allusion, and Paradigm*. Edited by Ruth B. Bottigheimer. Philadelphia: University of Pennsylvania Press, 1986. 35–51; Haase, Donald. "Children, War, and the Imaginative Space of Fairy Tales." *Lion and the Unicorn* 24 (2000): 360–77; Lawless, Elaine J. *Women Escaping Violence: Empowerment through Narrative*. Columbia: University of Missouri Press, 2001; Windling, Terri, ed. *The Armless Maiden and Other Tales for Childhood's Survivors*. New York: Tor, 1995.

Donald Haase

Trickster

A trickster is one who engages in trickery, deceives, and violates the moral codes of the community. Oral and written tales associated with this pervasive figure are usually humorous, and the tales generally combine both comical and satirical elements. The entertainment value of trickster tales is predicated on not only the trickster's clever actions per se but also on the subversive nature of his trickery. Members of his society derive satisfaction from witnessing the sociopathic trickster violate social norms, often in fact to the benefit of others, which can give him the status of a folk hero. In this way, trickster tales also convey moral lessons within a society.

Worldwide Trickster

The trickster is a mythic figure, both creator and destroyer, associated with traditional culture throughout the world. In Scandinavian mythology, the god Loki, whose adventures are narrated in *Edda* by the Icelander Snorri Sturluson, is portrayed as an ambiguous character who uses his cunning to either help or deceive other gods. For example, he helps Thrym steal Thor's hammer and then travels with Thor, disguised as Freyja's handmaiden, to recover it. He is a trickster who disrupts the order of gods and then often helps to restore it.

In Celtic mythology, Dagdae, from *dago-dévos* (the good god), often identified in early Irish literature with the sun, uses his divine powers to seduce **women** and deceive their husbands. The adventures of this fertility god are narrated in the tenth-century *Wooing of Étaín*. Other important tricksters are linked with cultures as diverse as the Navajo of the southwestern United States and the Ojibwa of northern Minnesota, who have a very special creation **myth**. The Ojibwa hold that earth was created when Winabijou, a legendary trickster, finds himself at the top of a pine tree surrounded by water. After asking a muskrat to retrieve mud from the bottom, Winabijou makes an island which grows to the size of the earth.

The Yoruba in West Africa also have a well-known trickster god. The name of this African *orisha* (deity or spirit) is Eshu-Elegbara. He is the gatekeeper between the realms of man and gods. Despite being the god of communication and spiritual language, Eshu embodies many trickster elements: deceit, humor, lawlessness, and rampant **sexuality**. This Pan-African trickster, who figures in the mythologies of Yoruba cultures found in Nigeria, Benin, Brazil, Cuba, and Haiti, among others, is also connected with the vernacular African American "Signifying Monkey," as described by Henry Louis Gates. Although two separate trickster figures, they are related, since both allow for a reflection on the use of language and its interpretation. Both tricksters articulate the black tradition's theory of its literature.

Moreover, in **African American tales**, figures such as Br'er Rabbit or the crafty slave John deceive their oppressors, Br'er Fox and Old Marster, who embody the leaders of slave-holding societies. These stories, which can be traced back to trickster figures in Africa, particularly the hare, were made popular in the United States by Joel Chandler **Harris** in his collections of **Uncle Remus** tales in the nineteenth century.

Trickster Coyote and Native American Tales

Native American traditional stories are rich in trickster figures such as Frog, Blue Jay, Bear, and **Coyote**. These figures are believed to have existed prior to humans and to have created the world. They are usually known as the First People. And although they have names we associate with animals, plants, and other natural phenomena, they are different. Among the First People, Coyote stands out. He is found in numerous oral American stories (from British Columbia to Guatemala, and from the Pacific Ocean to the Great Plains). The earliest written mentions of Coyote date from the nineteenth century, and Mark **Twain** is one of the first authors to write about this legendary trickster (*Roughing It*, 1872).

It is in western North America (California, the Great Basin, and the Plateau region) that one is more likely to find the prototypical Old Man Coyote, the mythic trickster. In Navajo narratives in particular, and in the mythology of North American Indians in general, the trickster refers not only to the practical joker but also to the transformer and culture-hero (see the studies of Mac Linscott Ricketts and Paul Radin). Coyote appears in various myths performing different roles: the wanderer, the bricoleur, the outlaw, the **thief**, and the cheat. He is often depicted as a glutton and a lecher, incapable of restraining his most basic desires. Coyote stories are often humorous, as Coyote usually finds himself outwitted. Yet the listener or reader laughs not only at Coyote but also with him.

Today, in Native American cultures, Coyote stories still flourish and are used to teach traditional values. Jarold Ramsey, in *Love in an Earthquake* (1973), is among the contemporary scholars and poets who use this legendary figure. Examples of the postmodern trickster may also be found in the novels of Native American and First Nations' writers such as Louise **Erdrich** and Thomas King.

The Female Trickster

Although the trickster starts as an amorphous being, he gradually discovers his own identity, oscillating between female and male, but eventually preferring his masculinity. This gives him a higher degree of autonomy and mobility in the public sphere, allowing him to mock and subvert the existing political, social, and economic structures.

Nevertheless, there are numerous examples of female tricksters worldwide, usually found in private, domestic spaces: parlors, kitchens, and bedrooms (for example, **Sheherazade**). Frequently, female tricksters transgress the boundaries between **men**'s and women's spheres and enter public space. These figures represent women's struggle for autonomy from men.

In Native American culture, one finds examples of female tricksters in the Keresan Coyote Girl and Kochininako—or Yellow Woman—stories. The Yellow Woman is actually a mythic figure who wanders away from her people and goes off with a mountain spirit, asserting herself as an extremely autonomous character. Leslie Marmon **Silko**'s *Storyteller* (1981) incorporates various versions of the Yellow Woman myth.

The Trickster in Medieval Literature

Human tricksters abound in humorous literature, drama, chronicles, **fabliaux**, and romances of the **Middle Ages**. These medieval tricksters often possess great sensual appetites for **food**, sex, and lower bodily functions, taking great interest in scatology.

The fabliaux, popular narratives of incidents that befall ordinary people who are frequently depicted as foolish or ridiculous, present characters given to practicing deceit and who are also often victims of treachery: the cunning wife, the cuckolded husband, the lover, the prostitute, the priest, the knight, the squire, and the *jongleur*. Often the trickster may be identified with the *jongleur* (the stereotypical figure of the itinerant minstrel). He is presented as being able to satisfy all of his needs and desires (food, sex, etc.).

Indeed, the majority of tricksters in medieval tradition are male. However, female tricksters also have a significant presence in the fabliaux, as is the case with Geoffrey **Chaucer**'s "Miller's Tale" and Guérin's "De Bérangier au lonc cul" ("Berangier of the Long Ass," c. 1200). The first concerns a wife, Alison, who surpasses both her husband and two suitors, Nicholas and Absolon, emerging as the master trickster. The latter is the tale of the daughter of a poor aristocrat who marries a rich usurer's son. She exposes his cowardice by disguising herself as a knight and challenging him to fight her or kiss her ass. Eventually he chooses the latter option without finding out her trick.

One notable example of a trickster is **Till Eulenspiegel**, a well-known fictional character belonging to the category of the mythical buffoon and rascal, both humorous and vicious, presented as a famous jester living during the fourteenth century. The multifaceted Eulenspiegel is not simply a humorous jokester, but also a troublemaker, thief, liar, and prankster who figuratively holds up a mirror to his audience, ridiculing them and, ostensibly, prompting them to improve their conduct.

The trickster is thus well represented in lower-class figures. Besides Eulenspiegel, other characters of particular interest in medieval times are: Unibos, from as early as the end of the tenth century (in *Unibos* [*One Ox*], a medieval Latin poem written by a cleric from France, Lorraine, or the Netherlands); Marcolf (in *Dialogus Salomonis et Marcolfi*, c. 1190, a comic dialogue between the trickster Marcolf and the wise King Solomon); and Parson Amis (in *Pfaffe Amis* by Der Stricker in the thirteenth century). *Unibos*, in particular, seems to have been very popular in **oral tradition**, as the well-known folktale "The Rich and the Poor **Peasant**" suggests. Briefly, it is the story of a poor man who deceives a rich one by playing upon his gullibility, either for revenge or fun or both. Here again, the subversive function of the trickster is evident in his turning the tables on the powers that be. ***See also*** Jest and Joke; Moral; Wú Chéng'ēn; Yep, Laurence.

Further Readings: Babcock-Abrahams, B. "'A Tolerated Margin of Mess': The Trickster and His Tales Reconsidered." *Journal of the Folklore Institute* 11.3 (1975): 147–86; Bright, William. *A Coyote Reader.* Berkeley: University of California Press, 1993; Gates, Henry Louis, Jr. *The Signifying Monkey: A Theory of African-American Literary Criticism.* New York: Oxford University Press, 1988; Harrison, Alan. *The Irish Trickster.* Sheffield: The Sheffield Academic Press for the Folklore Society, 1989; Landay, Lori. *Madcaps, Screwballs, and Con Women: The Female Trickster in American Culture.* Philadelphia: University of Pennsylvania Press, 1998; Lindow, John. *Scandinavian Mythology: An Annotated Bibliography.* New York: Garland, 1988; Pelton, Robert D. *The Trickster in West Africa: A Study of Mythic Irony and Sacred Delight.* Berkeley: University of California Press, 1980; Radin, Paul. *The Trickster: A Study in American Indian Mythology.* London: Routledge and Kegan Paul, 1956; Ramsey, Jarold. *Reading the Fire: The Traditional Indian Literatures of America.* Seattle: University of Washington Press, 1999; Ricketts, Mac Linscott. "The Structure and Religious Significance of the Trickster-Transformer-Culture Hero in the Mythology of North American Indians." Dissertation. University of Chicago, 1964; *Trickster's Way.* http://www.trinity.edu/org/tricksters/TrixWay.

Ana Raquel Fernandes

Trnka, Jiří (1912–1969)

Jiří Trnka, Czech illustrator and animated filmmaker, was a youthful protégé of famed puppeteer Josef Skupa. He went on to the Prague School of Arts and Crafts, and in the years following graduation, operated a **puppet theater** for one season, designed for the Czech National Theatre, and illustrated many children's books, including volumes of Czech and Slovak folktales, **literary fairy tale**s, and an edition of **Grimm**'s *Fairy Tales* (1942; English edition, 1961). After World War II, he joined the Czech Film Institute and soon set up a studio for puppet **animation**. His first full-length **film**, *Špalíček* (*The Czech Year*, 1947), included folktale elements, and his second, *Císařův slavík* (*The Emperor's Nightingale*, 1949), still one of his most famous, dramatized the tale by Hans Christian **Andersen**.

His continuous experiments with puppets and film included *Staré pověsti české* (*Old Czech Legends*, 1953) and *Dobrý voják Švejk* (*The Good Soldier Schweik*, 1955). In the mid-1950s, he also returned to **illustration**. His more mature illustration style appears in Andersen's *Fairy Tales* (1955; English edition, 1959), and *The Arabian Nights* (1957; English edition, 1960). In 1959, he released his puppet film masterpiece, *Sen noci svatojánské* (*A Midsummer Night's Dream*). In his films, the puppets seldom speak, the story being conveyed through action enhanced by **music** rather than dialogue. They therefore in some ways carry forward the aesthetic of **silent films**. Though his studio was state-supported, his movies are free of Marxist ideology. Indeed, his last film, *Ruka* (*The Hand*, 1965), is an allegorical attack upon that ideology. The animation studio he established, which today bears his name, continues to make puppet films. *See also* DEFA Fairy-Tale Films; Illustration; Soviet Fairy-Tale Films.

Further Reading: Boček, Jaroslav. *Jiří Trnka: Artist and Puppet Master.* Translated by Till Gottheiner. [Prague:] Artia, 1965.

William Bernard McCarthy

Trueba, Antonio de (1819–1889)

The author of historical novels, short fiction, and poems, Antonio de Trueba played an important role in the preservation of folktales and fairy tales in Spain. Appointed archivist and historian of Biscay in 1862, he spent the greater part of ten years in Bilbao, a seaport on the Bay of Biscay. Like his friend Cecilia **Böhl de Faber**, he became interested in the **oral tradition** and gathered documents pertinent to the history and **folklore** of the entire region. In the preface of *Nuevos cuentos populares* (*More Popular Tales*, 1880), Trueba noted that he and Böhl de Faber "almost simultaneously began to collect and publish tales gleaned from the oral tradition." Like the Brothers **Grimm** and Böhl de Faber, Trueba never intended to transcribe rigorously what he heard and recorded. He wished to preserve traditional tales, but only by giving them an acceptable literary form. So Trueba reshaped the tales he collected to conform to his notion of what constituted good literary judgment, taste, and style.

A number of Trueba's fairy tales are variations of the Grimms' stories, but he attests to their oral provenance, as in the case of "Las aventuras de un sastre" ("The Adventures of a **Tailor**"), which appeard in *Cuentos de varios colores* (*Tales of Several Colors*, 1866). In the preface of that collection, he writes that "The story with the title 'The Adventures of a Tailor' was told to me two years ago by a Biscayan girl, and she said that it had been told to her by her grandmother. When I asked the latter where she came across this tale, she replied that she had heard it as a child." While there are similarities between Trueba's and the Grimms' versions of this tale, there are also notable differences, especially the beginnings and endings. Nonetheless, both the Spanish and the German versions of this tale express basic human truths about honesty and integrity.

Trueba repeatedly stated that his inspiration was the Spanish oral tradition, a point that is emphasized by the subtitle of his 1866 collection *Cuentos de vivos y muertos: Contados por el pueblo y recontados por ...—Tales of the Living and the Dead: Told by the People and Retold by....* A representative tale from this collection is "El yerno del rey" ("The King's Son-in-Law"). In its details, "El yerno del rey" is a near clone of another Grimm tale, "The **Devil** with the Three Golden Hairs": the **king** puts the baby boy in a box and throws it in a river; the boy is found and brought up by a miller and his wife; robbers open the boy's letter to the queen and substitute another; the king requires the boy to fetch three of the devil's **hair**s; and, on his way to hell, the boy is asked three times to solve a conundrum, begging off each time. There are minor differences: Trueba's boy is fifteen, whereas the Grimms' boy is fourteen; Trueba begins with the avariciousness of the king, but the Grimms do not; and, in the devil's abode, Trueba's boy is assisted by the evil one's lady, whereas the Grimms' is assisted by his grandmother. Perhaps the biggest difference is the ending, when Trueba's boy showers gold on both his biological and adoptive parents. Thus, like many fairy tales, the bad (in the person of the king) receive their comeuppance, and the good (in the person of the king's son-in-law) receive their reward, for the king will forever wander in search of gold while his son-in-law, owing to the monarch's absence, will receive his crown.

Trueba contributed a version of the **tale type** Godfather **Death** (ATU 332) with "Tragaldabas" (literally, a voracious eater or glutton), which he published in *Narraciones populares* (*Popular Stories*, 1874). Together with Böhl de Faber's "Juan Holgado y la Muerte" ("Juan Holgado and Death") and Pedro Antonio de Alarcón's "El amigo de la muerte" ("Death's Friend"), "Tragaldabas" forms part of a nineteenth-century Spanish trilogy of pieces that have Death making his supplicants into doctors. Once again, Trueba insists that his muse is the people. In his introduction to the story, he asserts, "I have taken this tale from the mouth of the people, and they, not I, are the author." The story of a gluttonous shepherd named Lesmes, the tale abounds in satire and fun that are good-humored and good-natured. *See also* Collecting, Collectors; Spanish Tales.

Further Readings: Fedorchek, Robert M., trans. *Death and the Doctor.* Lewisburg: Bucknell University Press, 1997; ———, trans. *Stories of Enchantment from Nineteenth-Century Spain.* Lewisburg: Bucknell University Press, 2002.

Robert M. Fedorchek

Tsushima Shūji. *See* Dazai Osamu

Tutuola, Amos (1920–1997)

Amos Tutuola was a Nigerian writer who authored stories or "ghost novels," "episodic romances made out of tales" and "naive quest romances" (Collins) that were adapted from Yoruban folktale tradition and blended with modern **motif**s. Feeling underutilized as an office servant in Lagos, he started writing in the late 1940s. He later earned his living from shopkeeping and running a bakery and chicken farm. The first of Tutuola's nine titles was *The Palm-Wine Drinkard and His Dead Palm-Wine Tapster in the Deads' Town* (1952), which tells of the search of a hedonistic palm-wine boozer for his palm-wine tapster, who fell dead from a tree. The journey to the world of the dead leads the boozer through the wilderness, where he is confronted with weird spirits and curious creatures who subject him to tests that he passes with the help of magic and his wife, whom he married on the way. In the end, this lover of palm wine is told that the tapster's return to the living is impossible. Instead, the boozer is enlightened about life and death and presented a wonderful egg, which he later uses to reconcile heaven and earth, thus saving the world from a devastating drought.

Especially innovative motifs appear in *My Life in the Bush of Ghosts* (1954), which includes ghosts with radio voices and a "Television-Handed Ghostess." Using Stith Thompson's *Motif-Index of Folk-Literature*, Bernth Lindfors has conducted a motif analysis of the **novel** and confirmed that Tutuola employs a high percentage of genuinely new motifs. Tutuola's writing is characteritzed by an apparently ungrammatical Yoruba-English idiom and stylistic naïveté, which caused him to be at first severely criticized in Nigeria and highly lauded by Dylan Thomas and other Western critics. Later, however, he was rehabilitated at home by writers such as Chinua Achebe and Wole Soyinka.

Tutuola's later books follow the sequential and initiatory patterns of his early books, which were best sellers and translated into several European languages. Tutuola was influenced by the Yoruban **novella**s of Daniel Orowole **Fagunwa**'s, and he himself has had an impact on other Nigerian writers and artists (with his feedback into oral **storytelling** still unrecorded). Harold Collins rightly states that "surely one day Amos Tutuola will be recognized as West Africa's first classic in world literature" (Collins, 128). *See also* African Tales.

Further Readings: Belvaude, Catherine E. *Amos Tutuola et l'univers du conte africain.* Paris: L'Harmattan, 1989; Collins, Harold. *Amos Tutuola.* New York: Twayne, 1969; Dussutour-Hammer, Michèle. *Amos Tutuola: Tradition orale et écriture du conte.* Paris: Présence Africaine, 1976; Lindfors, Bernth. "Amos Tutuola: Oral Tradition and the 'Motif-Index.' "*African Textualities: Texts, Pre-Texts, and Contexts of African Literature.* Trenton, NJ: Africa World Press, 1997. 87–108; ———, ed. *Critical Perspectives on Amos Tutuola.* London: Heinemann, 1980.

Thomas Geider

Mark Twain. [Library of Congress]

Twain, Mark (1835–1910)

Mark Twain was a humorist, satirist, author, and reporter who contributed several important, widely acclaimed literary works that portray American folklife. Born in 1835 as Samuel Langhorne Clemens, Twain grew up on the banks of the Mississippi River in Hannibal, Missouri, a locale that would later serve as a source of great inspiration for his writings. Twain's ability to extrapolate the culture, dialect, and **folklore** of the areas that he visited is evident in his writings, which provide a rich sampling of American and European folklife. Twain's works express the contemporary folklife of his time, an era characterized by several major shifts in American culture, including the Civil War, Reconstruction, industrialization, and emancipation.

Twain utilized numerous folktale and fairy-tale themes throughout his career. For example, "The Celebrated Jumping Frog of Calaveras County" is a reinterpretation of a **tall tale** he overheard in a California saloon. In this manner, Twain manipulated traditional folktale formats to suit his personal style. He also published several short stories that were derived from European fairy-tale conventions, such as "Two Little Tales" (1901) and "The Belated Russian Passport" (1902). Many of Twain's writings pay homage to fairy-tale conventions, and he borrowed themes found in the fairy tales of Jacob and Wilhelm **Grimm** and the *Arabian Nights*.

Twain's major fictional works are considered by many to be American literary classics. These include novels such as *The Adventures of Tom Sawyer* (1876), *The Prince and the Pauper* (1882), *The Adventures of Huckleberry Finn* (1884), and *A Connecticut Yankee in King Arthur's Court* (1889). In addition to his contributions as a fiction writer, Twain also penned several nonfiction accounts detailing his experiences traveling across America, such as *Roughing It* (1872) and *Old Times on the Mississippi* (1876), in which he carefully documented his encounters with Native Americans and other common **folk** by observing their customs, **clothing**, stories, and work.

Critics have questioned Twain's status as a folklorist by alleging that he merely incorporated folkloric traditions to enhance the realism of his fiction rather than collect tales in a regimented fashion. For example, in *Huckleberry Finn*, Twain incorporates religious folk beliefs; superstitions and rituals; and symbolism as found in omens, animal signs, ghosts, and **witch**es to accentuate the motivations behind the characters' actions.

Despite these criticisms, Twain's career as a journalist and observer nurtured his skills in transforming his experiences into prose. His childhood along the Mississippi River served as the inspiration for many of his memorable characters and his incorporation of the stories, beliefs, rituals, and customs of the people whom he encountered serve as a reminder of Twain's ability to synthesize folktale and fairy-tale traditions into popular literature. *See also* North American Tales.

Further Readings: Cuff, Roger Penn. "Mark Twain's Use of California Folklore in His Jumping Frog Story." *Journal of American Folklore* 65 (1952): 155–58; West, Victor Royce. *Folklore in the Works of Mark Twain*. Lincoln, NE: n.p., 1930.

Trevor J. Blank

Twins

Most cultures deem multiple **birth**s as special events, although they are not always celebrated as positive occasions. Scriptures and **myth**s present a mixed view of twins. The biblical Jacob and Esau as well as Romulus and Remus from Roman mythology are remembered more as opponents than as brotherly supporters. The Yuma myth "The Good Twin and the Evil Twin," as recorded in *American Indian Myths and Legends* (1984) by Richard Erdoes and Alfonso Ortiz, describes the world's creator Kokomaht as a good twin and an evil twin combined in one entity. On the positive side, the divine twins Castor and Polydeuces (Pollux) of classical mythology are celebrated for their cooperation and complementary skills, as are their Vedic counterparts the Ashvins, divine twin horsemen in the Hindu sacred book *Rigveda*.

Legends from many cultures suggest that in ancient times children of multiple births were threatened with infanticide because such births were believed by some to result from the **mother**s' infidelity. "The Twin Brothers," as recorded by M. I. Ogumefu in *Yoruba Legends* (1929), offers an example from West Africa. This story unfolds at a time when "it was the universal custom to destroy twins immediately at birth, and the mother with them."

Another example comes from the Netherlands in the story "As Many Children as There Are Days in the Year" (ATU 762, Woman with Three Hundred and Sixty-Five Children), recorded by Jacob and Wilhelm **Grimm** in their *Deutsche Sagen* (*German Legends*, 1816–18). A countess claims that a woman with twins has had two lovers, to which the accused woman replies, "Then may you bring to the world as many children as there are days in the year." Shortly afterward, the countess becomes pregnant and does indeed give birth to 365 children.

Tales of type ATU 303, The Twins or Blood-Brothers, end more happily. A Spanish version, "The Castle of No Return," recorded in Stith **Thompson**'s *One Hundred Favorite Folktales* (1968), is exemplary. A woman miraculously gives birth to twin boys. Years later, the older brother leaves home and wins the hand of a **princess** by killing a serpent. Soon afterward, he seeks out a forbidden castle, where he is placed under a spell by a **witch**. His younger brother learns of his danger, finds the castle, and rescues him. Thus, the complementary (even opposite) qualities represented by these two **brothers** result in a happy ending for all.

A female counterpart to this tale is "Lurvehette" ("Tatterhood"; ATU 711, The Beautiful and the Ugly Twin Sisters) from *Norske Folkeeventyr* (*Norwegian Folktales*, 1841–44) by Peter Christen **Asbjørnsen** and Jørgen **Moe**. In this story, twin **sisters** are born under magical circumstances. The firstborn is ugly and aggressive; the younger twin is beautiful and shy. Contrary to fairy-tale expectations, the ugly sister is the real heroine, and through her daring initiatives she overcomes numerous problems and arranges a royal **marriage** for herself and her twin. On her wedding day, the ugly sister miraculously becomes beautiful; thus, the tale has a truly happy ending. *See also* Family; Infertility.

Further Reading: Ashliman, D. L. *Multiple Births in Legend and Folklore.* 2006. http://www.pitt.edu/~dash/manykids.html.

D. L. Ashliman

U

Ubbelohde, Otto (1867–1922)

Best known for illustrating Jacob and Wilhelm **Grimm**'s fairy tales, German artist and illustrator Otto Ubbelohde was raised in Marburg, the son of a university teacher, before receiving training as a portrait and landscape artist in Weimar and Munich. Though his real passion was for painting, his conservative style and failure to fully embrace the art nouveau movement left much of his work in obscurity. Ubbelohde derived his income largely from **illustration** and popular commercial productions, such as postcards, calendars, plates, and picture-carpets. His fairy-tale illustrations are particularly significant for their reference to the Hessian natural landscape and local architecture. A proponent of the *Lebensreform* (life reform) movement, which rejected the excesses of modern industrial capitalism in favor of a return to a simpler, healthier rural lifestyle, he drew inspiration from nature: **Mother Holle** can be seeing shaking her featherbeds over the Rimberg mountain, and the tower in "Rapunzel" is modeled on a house in Amönau, near the artist's longtime home in Goßfelden. Ubbelohde's illustrations have been lauded for their fine sense of movement and animation, an effect he achieved through detailed realism and stark black-and-white lines with minimal shading.

Otto Ubbelohde's illustration of Grimms' "Fitcher's Bird" in *Kinder- und Hausmärchen gesammelt durch die Brüder Grimm* (Leipzig: Turm-Verlag, 1907–9).

Further Readings: Oberfeld, Charlotte. "Auch ein Beitrag zur 'Heimat'-Diskussion: 'Heimatkünstler' Otto Ubbelohde—Illustrator der Grimmschen Märchen." *Sprache und Brauchtum: Bernhard Martin zum 90. Geburtstag.* Edited by Reiner Hildebrandt and Hans Friebertshäuser. Marburg: Elwert, 1980. 414–17; Verweyen, Annemarie. "Das Märchenschloß in alten und neuen Bilderbüchern." *Märchen in Erziehung und Unterricht.* Edited by Ottilie Dinges, Monika Born, and Jürgen Janning. Kassel: Erich Röth-Verlag, 1986. 220–25.

Kristiana Willsey

Uncle Remus

The fictional central character in the **frame narrative**s of Joel Chandler **Harris**'s collections of African American folktales, Uncle Remus is one of the most popular literary creations of the nineteenth century. He is the star of more than a half dozen of Harris's works, including *Uncle Remus: His Songs and Sayings; The Folklore of the Old Plantation* (1880), *Nights with Uncle Remus: Myths and Legends of the Old Plantation* (1883), and *Uncle Remus and His Friends: Old Plantation Stories, Songs, and Ballads, with Sketches of Negro Character* (1892). In each of these, he plays the role of the benevolent black grandfather figure—a friendly former slave who, in thick dialect, conveys story after story to the young children of his Anglo betters. In a style that sometimes resembles that of a minstrel show caricature, he talks, sings, or jokes, presenting an unthreatening face to white readers in a time when African Americans were most definitely perceived as a threat.

At the same time, Uncle Remus also serves as a mouthpiece for Harris's **collecting** activities. Harris spent the better part of his adult life acquiring African American folk narratives and songs from a variety of different, mostly Anglo-American sources and rendering them as accurately as possible in eye dialect (that is, in a written form based on spellings reflecting a nonstandard pronunciation). The publishers of books featuring Uncle Remus tended to categorize them as humor or **children's literature**, but for Harris, they represented first and foremost a scholarly endeavor. *See also* African American Tales; Race and Ethnicity.

Further Reading: Harris, Joel Chandler, and Richard Chase, comp. *The Complete Tales of Uncle Remus.* Boston: Houghton Mifflin, 1955.

Adam Zolkover

Undine

Undine (from *unda*, Latin for "wave") is a German water sprite or nymph. She has many analogues or cousins, from the sirens of Greek mythology and the **mermaid**s common in European songs and tales to Mélusine of French **legend** and the Lorelei of the Rhine River. Some believe these figures were modeled on the genus *sirenae*, large aquatic mammals with fishlike tails (like manatees). Typically they are portrayed as dangerously seductive and untrustworthy. Like the sirens of the *Odyssey*, they lure **men** to their **death**s.

In the first extended literary version of the tale, however, Friedrich de la Motte **Fouqué**'s "Undine" (1811), Undine is sent to the human world to gain a soul. In contrast, Paracelsus—Fouqué's acknowledged source—presented "water women" in his *Liber de Nymphis* (*Book of Nymphs*) simply as seductresses, emphasizing the difficulties of **marriage** between human and immortal. Fouqué introduces Undine as the foster child of an old fisherman and his wife, living on a spit of land between the sea and a mysterious forest; she seems to be simply an extraordinarily beautiful and capricious girl when she meets the knight Huldebrand. Only after their marriage does he learn that she comes from under the sea and will lose the soul she has just gained through marriage and return to the sea if he is ever unfaithful. When she and her husband take his former friend Berthalda to live with them in his castle Ringstetten, her rivalry with the mortal woman, as well as the continual threats of her uncle, the water nix Kühleborn, eventually lead to her disappearance in the river Danube. She returns only after the marriage of Huldbrand and Berthalda, first causing Huldbrand's death, then becoming a spring that runs eternally around his grave.

Fouqué's emphasis on the oppositions of human and supernatural, dry land and water, and socialized male and elemental female became the source for many versions of the story. E. T. A. **Hoffmann** wrote an **opera** *Undine: Zauberoper in drei Akten* (*Undine: A Magic Opera in Three Acts*, 1816) with Fouqué's assistance. Other operas based in part on his story include Albert Lortzing's *Undine* (1845) and Antonín **Dvořák**'s *Rusalka* (1901). Hans Christian **Andersen** emphasized the Romantic search for a soul in his tale "Den lille havfrue" ("The Little Mermaid," 1837). Several ballets came from Fouqué's story, from *Ondine* (1843) by Jules Perrot and Cesare Pugni to Hans Werner Henze's *Undine* (1957). Maurice Ravel used water **motif**s in "Ondine," a movement of his piano piece *Gaspard de la Nuit* (1909). Jean Giradoux's play *Ondine* (1939) was also based on the story. Both Ingeborg Bachmann, in her short story "Undine geht" ("Undine Leaves," 1961), and Jane **Yolen,** in her poem "Undine" (1997), made Undine the narrator of her own tale, questioning the patriarchal paradigms that structure traditional versions. Undine has even become an important character in video games, often as an elemental water spirit. *See also* Swan Maiden.

Further Reading: Lillyman, William J. "Fouqué's 'Undine.' " *Studies in Romanticism* 10 (1971): 94–104.

Elizabeth Wanning Harries

Unfinished Tale

The Types of International Folktales identifies "Unfinished Tales" as a specific **tale type**—ATU 2250—in which the narrator "tells about someone who has found something, but stops just as the tale gets interesting." More generally, however, the term "unfinished tale" encompasses a variety of tale types whose narratives remain intentionally incomplete.

Storytellers everywhere employ trick tales as jokelike ploys to announce that story time is over. These *mock stories* remain unfinished by design and are often rhymed, giving them an affinity to **Mother-Goose** rhymes. An example from England is the nonstory of Jack-a-Nory (ATU 2271, Mock Stories for Children): "I'll tell you a story about Jack-a-Nory, and now my story's begun. I'll tell you another about Jack and his brother, and now my story is done!" This Jack's name was given wide exposure in the popular BBC **television** series *Jackanory* (1965–96) featuring celebrities reading children's tales.

Ironically, one type of unfinished story repeats endlessly (ATU 2300, Endless Tale). One example from many **variant**s told around the world is "An Endless Story" from **Seki** Keigo's *Folktales of Japan* (1963). Innumerable rats aboard a ship decide to drown themselves, and each one is described individually as it cries out *"chu chu"* and jumps overboard.

An unfinished tale with more substance, but still no resolution, is "The Golden Key" (ATU 2260, The Golden Key), the last numbered story in Jacob and Wilhelm **Grimm**'s *Kinder- und Hausmärchen* (*Children's and Household Tales*, 1812–15). Here, a boy finds a golden key and an iron chest, which he proceeds to open. "But," concludes the storyteller, "we must wait until he has finished unlocking it. Then we shall find out what kind of wonderful things there were in the little chest." By closing their collection with this enigmatic tale without an end, the Grimms may be saying that folktales, too, are endless. There is no final word. *See also* Nonsense Tale.

Further Reading: Thompson, Stith. "Formula Tales." *The Folktale.* 1946. Berkeley: University of California Press, 1977. 229–34.

D. L. Ashliman

Ungerer, Tomi (1931–)

Tomi Ungerer (the pseudonym of Jean Thomas) is a prolific writer, illustrator, cartoonist, and graphic artist who has lived on several continents, written in different languages, and presents the dark vision of a satirist for adults and young people alike. From an Alsatian family, he was born in Strasbourg, where his family produced astronomical timepieces. His father died when Ungerer was a boy, and his memoir *Tomi: A Childhood under the Nazis* (1998) describes his childhood experiences as a French-speaking child living under German rule during World War II. This period produced some of his first drawings, and he was later attracted to the sketches in the *New Yorker* and especially Saul Steinberg. Comprising **cartoons**, posters protesting racism and the Vietnam War, and erotica for adults, as well as almost 100 books for children, Ungerer's work is marked by a sardonic twist, turning expectations around and challenging ordinary **storytelling**. In this vein, if he recasts traditional tales such as "**Little Red Riding Hood**" in *A Storybook from Tomi Ungerer* (1974) or writes original fairy tales such as *Zeralda's Ogre* (1967) or *The Three Robbers* (1962), the theme is always upset. The villain frequently is transformed into a hero, such as Red Riding Hood's **wolf**, or the traditional hero becomes the villain. *The Three Robbers*, which begins "Once upon a time," describes a trio of miscreants who begin gathering up orphans, Pied-Piper-like, until the orphans convert them to serving as good parents.

After studying art in France, Ungerer moved to the United States in 1956 and published his first book, *The Mellops Go Flying*, the following year. This turned into a series of five volumes. Soon thereafter, he illustrated the first of Jeff Brown's popular series of Flat Stanley (1964) books. He is known for frequently employing animals as characters and for using simple outlined drawings filled in with dark colors that fill the page, reflecting developments in **advertising** and graphic arts in the 1950s and 1960s. In 1974, Ungerer published *Allumete: A **Fable**, with Due Respect to Hans Christian **Andersen**, the **Grimm** Brothers, and the Honorable Ambroise Bierce*, and in 1990 illustrated *Tomi Ungerer's Heidi* (written by Johanna Spyri). He won the 1998 Hans Christian Andersen Award for Illustration, and since the 1970s has lived with his family in Europe. *See also* Illustration.

Further Readings: Ungerer, Tomi. *The Poster Art of Tomi Ungerer.* Edited by Jack Rennert. New York: Darien House, 1971; ———. *Tomi: A Childhood Under the Nazis.* Lanham, MD: Roberts Rinehart, 1998.

George Bodmer

Urban Legend

A subtype of **legend** that deals with modern situations and contemporary events, the urban legend is currently one of the most widespread folk-narrative forms, whether transmitted by word of mouth, mass media, or the **Internet**. Scholars coined the term "urban legend" in the 1970s to show that stories based on folk beliefs also exist in cities as well as in more rural areas, part of an expansion of the academic concept of **folklore** in both Europe and the United States at that time. Urban legend is also related to rumor, the passing on of unverified or unsecured information in statement form. Some scholars see rumor as incipient legend and legend as elaborated rumor, and so interpret these contemporary communication patterns in similar ways, regardless of whether or not their information is later verified, or whether or not they are believed by the people transmitting them.

Specific urban legends are often about bizarre, unusual, horrific, or humorous events that point to an array of anxiety-producing social and technological issues under discussion in modern times. Stories shared by young adults, like those popularized in horror films such as Jamie Blanks's 1998 *Urban Legend*, deal with initiation from **childhood** to adult status, changing **gender** roles, and questions about moral and ethical choices in a late-capitalist world. "The Roommate's Death," for example, a legend in which a college coed doesn't open her dorm-room door when she hears someone pounding on it and so contributes to her roommate's **death** by not letting her in, raises questions about students' security and responsibilities when the university acting in the place of the parent (in loco parentis) no longer operates as it once did.

Narrative variations of the "foreign objects in **food**" **motif**, whether about rat parts or genetically modified ingredients in Kentucky Fried Chicken or about mice, human fingers, or urine in factory-bottled soft drinks, suggest widespread and often justifiable concern with the current mass production and distribution of "fast food." Yet fast-food legends may also mark social conflict symbolically as well. They may indicate concern about **women** entering the workforce in greater numbers after World War II, no longer cooking meals at home, and therefore leaving **family** members vulnerable to possible contamination in mass-produced food products. Legends about ethnic restaurants serving dogs, cats, or rats in their dishes may also indirectly register fears about recent immigration.

Legends about a Ku Klux Klan-supported secret ingredient in the chicken batter at Church's Chicken and Popeyes Chicken & Biscuits franchises that sterilizes black men may seem plausible to some African Americans, given the history of racial discrimination. Likewise, legends about Ray Kroc, the founder of McDonald's Hamburgers, funding the Church of Satan may seem plausible to some Christian fundamentalists as they consider the dangers of secularism from their perspective. Themes of conspiracy interweave with themes of contamination, highlighting specific "cultural logics" of different groups responding to crises that may be contested by others. The generic opening of many urban legends, "I heard it from a friend of a friend" (FOAF), indicates both the transmission patterns as well as the polemic nature of legend telling, as credible sources are lined up by those arguing to prove their respective points.

Some worldwide urban legends, such as those containing the "organ theft" motif or those about the origin and spread of the AIDS virus, trace international debate on social issues. Travelers from Europe and the United States have been warned about literally "watching their backs" in the urban legend about a business traveler in a foreign country waking up in a hotel room with one kidney missing after picking up a woman at a bar ("The Kidney Heist"). Villagers in Central and South America have feared adoption rings taking their children for use in medical research and organ transplants in the United States as expressed in "Baby Parts" stories about such traffic. The 2002 feature film *Dirty, Pretty Things*, directed by Stephen Frears, brings "first world" and "third world" conflicts together in a London hotel, where immigrant workers sell their kidneys for false passports.

Some scholars have recently questioned the usefulness of the term "urban legend," finding the alternative term "contemporary legend" more accurate, because not all current legends are exclusively urban, as the "organ theft" examples above indicate. *Contemporary Legend*, the journal of the International Society for Contemporary Legend Research (ISCLR), exemplifies this trend. Other scholars note that "urban" or "contemporary" legends may be modern variants of much older legends, so the basic term "legend" suffices. The history of the "The Castrated Child" legend is a case in point. Stories about a young boy castrated by gang members of another ethnic group in a shopping-mall restroom surfaced in the United States, initially in connection with the 1967 Detroit race riots, the race of victim and perpetrators dependent on the ethnicity of the tellers. Researchers have identified comparable stories of atrocities to children mirroring ethnic and religious conflicts throughout history, including those of the medieval "Blood Libel," in which Christians accused Jews of using Christian babies as human sacrifices, and those of second-century CE Rome, in which the same libel was used by patrician Romans against the emerging Christian community. Urban legends, however labeled, will continue to circulate across media and to frame questions for their times. *See also* Anti-Semitism; Race and Ethnicity; Time and Place.

Further Readings: Bausinger, Hermann. *Folk Culture in a World of Technology.* Translated by Elke Dettmer. Bloomington: Indiana University Press, 1990; Bennett, Gillian. *Bodies: Sex, Violence, Disease and Death in Contemporary Legend.* Jackson: University Press of Mississippi, 2005; Brunvand, Jan Harold. *The Truth Never Stands in the Way of a Good Story.* Urbana: University of Illinois Press, 2000; Campion-Vincent, Véronique. *Organ Theft Legends.* Jackson: University Press of Mississippi, 2005; Dégh, Linda. *American Folklore and the Mass Media.* Bloomington: Indiana University Press, 1994; Fine, Gary Alan, and Patricia A. Turner. *Whispers on the Color Line: Rumors and Race in American Culture.* Berkeley: University of California Press, 2001; Fine, Gary Alan, Véronique Campion-Vincent, and Chip Heath, eds. *Rumor Mills: The Social Impact of Rumor and Legend.* New Brunswick, NJ: Aldine Transaction, 2005; Goldstein, Diane. *Once Upon a Virus: AIDS Legends and Vernacular Risk Perception.* Logan: Utah State University Press, 2004; Tucker, Elizabeth. *Campus Legends: A Handbook.* Westport, CT: Greenwood Press, 2005.

Janet L. Langlois

Urform

An urform is the archetypal form of the text or its original from (*Urform* in German). The term has been used mainly by the followers of the **historic-geographic method**, who assumed that it is possible to reconstruct the original form of an oral tale by comparing its available **variant**s across time and space. They presumed that each tale has its single origin at a specific historic time and in a specific geographic area (**monogenesis**), and that the tale begins spreading from there. The goal of the method was to locate the time and place of the tale's origin. To reconstruct the urform, one first had to find all of the existing variants and then derive the kernel of the tale on the basis of these variants.

The urform is an abstract construction, just like any **tale type**. The idea of finding the original form of the text can be seen in the **mythological approaches** of the nineteenth century, but the direct predecessor of this philological approach was the research of Julius Krohn, who concentrated on finding the original form of the songs in the *Kalevala*. This method was developed by his son Kaarle Krohn, who used the term "urform" in his doctoral thesis when analyzing **animal tale**s and found that originally the animal tale classified under ATU 1 (The Theft of Fish) used to feature a bear and a fox (instead of a **wolf** and a fox) and that the tale is actually an **etiologic tale**. Krohn came up with the idea of wavelike **diffusion** of tales and added it to the existing concept that tales spread in a chainlike fashion.

Among the better-known folklorists who tried to find the urform (or the urtext) were Antti **Aarne**, Walter **Anderson**, Kurt **Ranke**, Jan-Öjvind Swahn, and Warren E. Roberts. Albert Wesselski and Carl Wilhelm von Sydow argued against the idea that there was a single urform. Von Sydow stated that each tale has multiple original forms. He did not accept the idea that the original form of a folktale is necessarily the best, most complete, and most logical one, and that once the original form has been located, it should also indicate the tale's home. More recent folktale research (most notably that of Thomas A. Burns) has also found the idea of establishing a single urform questionable since **motif**s and motif clusters are very fluid between different tale types. *See also* Polygenesis.

Further Readings: Burns, Thomas A. "Folkloristics: A Conception of Theory." *Folk Groups and Folklore Genres: A Reader.* Edited by Eliott Oring. 1977. Logan: Utah State University Press 1989. 1–20; Krohn, Kaarle. *Folklore Methodology.* Translated by Roger L. Welsch. Austin: University of Texas Press, 1971.

Risto Järv

Utopia

Folktales and fairy tales often present an alternative view of the world, a vision of a better life. That is their utopian element. Sir Thomas More's *Utopia* (1551), a critique of sixteenth-century social and political life, depicts a place where everything will be different and better. The utopian element in folktales critiques people's everyday lives, building on their sense that "something's missing." Some tales bring back an imagined earlier era of solidarity and social harmony; others point to what is missing in the present, such as **food** or money. Stories of the land of Cockaigne, where food and wine are superabundant (painted by Brueghel), point to undernourishment (ATU 1930, Schlaraffenland). In antiquity, Herodotus told of a **fantasy**land where no one had to work for food, "a meadow in the skirts of their city full of the boiled flesh of all manner of beasts, which the magistrates are careful to store with meat every night, and where whoever likes may come and eat during the day. The people of the land say that the earth itself brings forth the food" (*Histories* 3.17–18). The tale of **Aladdin** is about deprivation and poverty. Stories in which the powerless have power, like The Clever Farmgirl (ATU 875), in which a woman performs seemingly impossible tasks, point to what is missing in the social order. The reversal of **women**'s experienced reality is utopian; **performance** of such a tale may be a moment for imagining the future. Anticipation of the future transpires when the **wonder tale** invites us into an alternative world: there, a youth overcomes a **dragon**, a plant or tree signals that someone at a distance is in mortal danger, **magic object**s and **magic helper**s aid the hero, and people transform into animals and back again.

When tales reassert the existing social order, and the clever woman becomes a faithful wife, they abandon utopia for ideology and justify things as they are. Many **animal tale**s end in hopeless enmity, even when the animals begin as friends. When **Cat** invites Rat to ride on his back across the water and then dumps him (see ATU 58, The Crocodile Carries the Jackal), ideology tells us that the outcome is predictable. **Aesop**'s **fable**s often convey the message that some of us will always be enemies, as when animals of different species invite each other to dine, and the guest cannot eat the food (ATU 60, Fox and Crane Invite Each Other).

Psychologically, utopia begins in fantasy. Giovanni **Boccaccio**'s story about a man duped into thinking that he is invisible plays on fulfilling a **wish** every child has had (*Decameron* 8.3; Motif J2337). **Trickster** tales, being attacks on social rules or property, are obviously fantasies of escape, but they also point out witty ways of coping with authorities who are bigger than the protagonist. The trickster, by breaking society's rules, speaks in favor of those very values, which would survive in the utopian future. The greater the contrast between the world or behavior depicted in a tale and the world in which it is told, the greater its potential for inciting in the listener or reader a moment of utopian vision. *See also* Politics.

Further Readings: Bloch, Ernst. *The Utopian Function of Art and Literature: Selected Essays.* Translated by Jack Zipes and Frank Mecklenburg. Cambridge, MA: MIT Press, 1988; Del Giudice, Luisa. "Mountains of Cheese and Rivers of Wine: Paese di Cuccagna and Other Gastronomic Utopias." *Imagined States: Nationalism, Utopia, and Longing in Oral Cultures.* Edited by Luisa Del Giudice and Gerald Porter. Logan: Utah State University Press, 2001. 11–63.

Lee Haring

V

Valenzuela, Luisa (1938–)

The work of Argentinean novelist, short-story writer, and essayist Luisa Valenzuela is consistently characterized by its subversive and provocative attitude toward patriarchy and censorship. Valenzuela as a feminist is particularly suspicious of discourse that appears to subjugate **women**, such as traditional versions of fairy tales. Using wit and humor, Valenzuela rewrites classical European fairy tales, giving them new life through irony, sociopolitical commentary, and postmodern play.

The collection of short stories *Simetrías* (*Symmetries*, 1998) includes a section with six rewritings of fairy tales whose collective title clearly signals their subversive nature: "Cuentos de Hades" (literally, "Tales from Hades"), puns on "hadas" (**fairies**) and "hades" (Hades). Margaret Jull Costa's skillful **translation** gives the English reader "Firytales." In these rewritings, as Valenzuela explains in her short essay "Ventana de Hadas" ("Fairies' Window"), the author sees herself reincarnating the voices of old women storytellers, who she imagines used to tell these tales before Charles **Perrault** and his successors appropriated them and rendered them cautionary and morally restrictive. The tales rewritten include "**Little Red Riding Hood**," "The **Frog King**," "The Princess on the Pea," "**Sleeping Beauty**," "**Cinderella**," and "**Snow White**." Each of Valenzuela's rewritings operates by pointing out and challenging underlying sexist ideologies or stereotyping and by exposing them to ridicule. This feminist aspect is balanced with a great deal of wit and humor, which is generated by the process of simultaneous recognition and defamiliarization. In Valenzuela's fairy tales, woman is writing her own story in full ironic consciousness of the weight of preexisting versions, a fact highlighted by one of the **prince**s, in whose kingdom all the courtiers play at "Post-Modernism." Valenzuela also incorporates a degree of sociopolitical commentary; in her version of "**Bluebeard**," entitled "La llave" ("The Key"), female curiosity is explicitly linked—via the final dedication—to the calls of the Mothers of the Plaza de Mayo for information on "disappeared" relatives in Argentina's Dirty War of 1976–83, and curiosity is rewarded rather than punished (see **Punishment and Reward**). Conversely, in "Cuarta versión" ("Fourth Version") from the collection *Cambio de armas* (*Other Weapons*, 1985), "**Hansel and Gretel**," "Sleeping Beauty," and "**Beauty and the Beast**" are all referenced as part of the text's complicity in shrinking from the truth of political repression and disappearances into the false reassurance of a world of fairy tales.

"No se detiene el progreso" ("You Can't Stop Progress") wittily reevaluates the figure of the bad fairy at Sleeping Beauty's christening. In Spanish, she is recast as a "Brhada," punning on "bruja" (**witch**) and "hada" (fairy), and in the English translation becomes a "Wairy." Valenzuela's version makes her sensible and sanguine about her age and ugliness. Her supposedly malicious gift to the young **princess** is reinterpreted as intensely practical; not wishing to waste her powers on the girl's external appearance, the Wairy's gesture is one of radical action to ensure that dangerous bobbins are banned and new, improved **spinning** wheels are introduced.

The Sleeping Beauty section is similarly invested with new significance. The implications of her having been oblivious to the world for 100 years are first ironically then surreally developed. Sleeping Beauty is out of touch with the news and has old-fashioned ideas, but— with heavy sarcasm—the narrator suggests that worldly knowledge is not required by a young lady. The bland and docile female figure then awakes—both literally and sexually—to become something sinister, unfamiliar, and threatening by undergoing a vegetal metamorphosis. This unexpected outcome either plays on supposed male subliminal fears of the engulfing female or provides a hyperbolic satire of the view of woman as closer to nature.

"4 Príncipes 4" ("4 Princes 4") consists of a series of sketches in which the princes are given distinctive characters. Príncipe I (Prince I) is revealed as a vain character who destroyed the woman who kissed him, since she witnessed his demeaning metamorphosis from frog back into man. His subsequent regret that there is no one left who can tell his story allows for a new angle on reading this tale. Whereas traditionally both characters were painted as bland stereotypes who predictably marry, here he is disagreeably arrogant and she no longer passive. The woman now has serious textual significance, which the man has erased to protect his own vain image, but paradoxically at irretrievable loss to himself.

The theme of the woman's awakening as something sinister—as seen in "You Can't Stop Progress"—continues in the second sketch, wherein Prince II endlessly practices beneficent waking-kisses on princesses. To his irritation, the young women wake up too much and start expressing their desires. Here, the stereotypical fairy-tale princess as passive and recumbent, there to be beautiful and docilely bedded and wedded, is made ludicrously explicit through the prince's attitude and is simultaneously shattered by the active, liberated women he encounters. Little Red Riding Hood is similarly eroticized and active; her journey through the woods symbolizes gathering experience, which is made explicitly sexual since the narrator links men with ripe fruits; the final scene is one of mutual devouring, where child-woman, grandmother, and **wolf** become one. In Valenzuela's latest contribution to the fairy-tale genre, she invents a new but similarly feisty heroine based on the **myth** of Ariadne, who is called "Otrariana"—which is a wordplay on "another Ariadne" and "otramente," or "otherwise." Set in a castle-state with a dark forest at the margins, the tale invokes many classic mythemes, only to subvert them. The happy ending is that Ariana loses her "vulnerability" and remains friends forever with the forester. *See also* Feminism; Feminist Tales; Postmodernism; Sex, Sexuality.

Further Readings: Boland, Roy C. "Luisa Valenzuela and *Simetrías*: Tales of a Subversive Mother Goose." *Antípodas* 6–7 (1994–95): 229–37; Magnarelli, Sharon. "*Simetrías*: 'Mirror, Mirror on the Wall....'" *World Literature Today* 69.4 (1995): 717–25; Valenzuela, Luisa. *Other Weapons.* Translated by Deborah Bonner. Hanover, NH: Edicones de Norte, 1985; ———. *Symmetries.* Translated by Margaret Jull Costa. London: Serpent's Tail, 1998.

Fiona J. Mackintosh

Valera, Juan (1824–1905)

One of nineteenth-century Spain's most respected authors, Juan Valera wrote **novel**s, short stories, **poetry**, essays, and literary criticism. A career in the diplomatic service took him far and wide, and, conversant in six languages, he early on developed a broad interest in folktales and fairy tales. Knowledgeable about popular genres as cultivated in western Europe and South America, he hoped to publish a collection of **Spanish tales**, modeled on Jacob and Wilhelm **Grimm**'s German collection, that would have dated back to the fourteenth century and Juan Manuel's *Libro del Conde Lucanor* (*The Book of Count Lucanor*, c. 1335). However, the project never came to fruition.

Valera read widely, and came across English translations of folktales told by Japanese nursemaids. In his book titled *De varios colores* (*In Several Colors*, 1898), he writes: "I am so taken with these stories that I cannot resist the temptation of translating a few of them into Spanish." Two of the more celebrated of these tales are "El pescadorcito Urashima" ("Urashima the Fisherman," 1887), about a youth who leaves the Palace of the Dragon and cannot return because he opens a secret box; and "El espejo de Matsuyama" ("Matsuyama's Mirror," 1887), about a **mirror** that transmits a **mother** and daughter's mutual love.

Valera also wrote a number of amusing tales such as "La muñequita" ("The Little Doll") and "La reina madre" ("The **Queen** Mother"), but his fame as an author of fairy tales rests principally on two stories that are gems of nineteenth-century Spanish short fiction: "El pájaro verde" ("The Green Bird," 1860) and "El hechicero" ("The Wizard," 1894). In his dedication of the collection *Cuentos y diálogos* (*Stories and Dialogues*, 1882), Valera states that he heard "The Green Bird" from the mother of the Duke of Rivas, the famous Spanish Romantic playwright and poet. Like the story of the same title by Luis **Coloma**, Valera's fairy tale, which has an Oriental setting, involves a **prince** who transforms into a green bird. Valera's tale also parallels Coloma's story when the young woman who falls in love with it/him must go in search of her prince for their love to be consummated in **marriage**.

"The Wizard" also stems from the Spanish **oral tradition** that Valera sought to preserve. This tale abounds in mysterious settings and events as it relates how a free-spirited girl falls in love with an enigmatic and little-seen poet who dwells in a castle. After the poet disappears, the girl blossoms into a beautiful young woman and later makes a trek, like the **princess** of "The Green Bird," through a forbidding forest and a scary cavern to be reunited with him and seal their love. ***See also*** Spanish Tales.

Further Readings: DeCoster, Cyrus. *Juan Valera.* Boston: Twayne, 1974; Fedorchek, Robert M., trans. *Stories of Enchantment from Nineteenth-Century Spain.* Lewisburg: Bucknell University Press, 2002; Valera, Juan. "The Green Bird." Translated by Robert M. Fedorchek. *Marvels & Tales* 13 (1999): 211–33; ———. "The Queen Mother." Translated by Robert M. Fedorchek. *Marvels & Tales* 17 (2003): 262–268.

Robert M. Fedorchek

Variant

Folklore knows no original or canonic texts, for it thrives in multiple versions of any given item. In the realm of **folktale**s, "variant" designates one of two or more narratives exhibiting usually slight differences. Since each folktale comprises many variants, no particular narrative represents it fully. Neither should it be seen as a single closed text, for variants suppose and reflect one another. Therefore, the task of reconstituting the life history of a folktale (as advocated by the **historic-geographic method**) involves considering many variants. And scholars with an interpretive disposition tend to engage in intertextual readings (see **Intertextuality**).

Beyond **oral tradition**, variation persists in **literary fairy tale**s. Consider two extreme examples: Jacob and Wilhelm **Grimm** conflated variants in composite texts, thus embedding an intertextual approach into newly defined master tales that reentered tradition and have spanned multiple exegeses. Contrariwise, Angela **Carter** chose to recreate mutually echoing variants of folkloric themes, so that her stories prompt intertextual resonances. In both cases, variation and the authors' interpretations go hand in hand and elicit fresh readings. And on the **Internet** and in contemporary cyberspace, intertextual shortcuts (hyperlinks) promote new uses of narrative variation and interpretation. Overall, variation did not die out with oral tradition; rather, new media create ever-fresh variants, as well as new challenges for comprehension. *See also* Tale Type.

Further Readings: Bacchilega, Cristina. "Performing Wonders: Postmodern Revisions of Fairy Tales." *Postmodern Fairy Tales: Gender and Narrative Strategies.* Philadelphia: University of Pennsylvania Press, 1997. 1–25; Dundes, Alan. "Fairy Tales from a Folkloristic Perspective." *Fairy Tales and Society: Illusion, Allusion, and Paradigm.* Edited by Ruth B. Bottingheimer. Philadelphia: University of Pennsylvania Press, 1986. 259–69.

Francisco Vaz da Silva

Verdaguer, Jacint (1845–1902)

Jacint Verdaguer was a writer, clergyman, and Catalan folklorist. Son of a farming family, he studied at a seminary and was ordained into the priesthood in 1870. Between 1877 and 1893, he wrote and published his most important literary works: *Idil·lis i cants místics* (*Idylls and Mystical Songs*, 1879), *Montserrat* (1880), *Cançons de Nadal* (*Christmas Carols*, 1881), *Pàtria* (*Homeland*, 1888), and his two great epic poems *L'Atlàntida* (*Atlantis*, 1877), and *Canigó* (1886). Influenced by the Romantic writers and folklorists Manuel Milà i Fontanals and Marià Aguiló, he collected numerous folkloric materials during his life and used them as a source of inspiration for his poetry.

Two of his folkloric books were published posthumously: *Rondalles* (*Folktales*) in 1905 and *Folk-lore* in 1907. *Rondalles* contains forty-eight narratives, including seventeen folktales, fifteen **legend**s, six **joke**s, three **anecdote**s, four moral examples, two autobiographical tales, and a hagiographic text about Saint John the Baptist. Verdaguer collected some of these narratives during his travels in the Catalan Pyrenees in the summers between 1877 and 1884, while others he collected throughout his life in towns all over Catalonia. In 1992, Andreu Bosch published a critical edition of *Rondalles* that contained eight additional texts, all previously unpublished, which are mainly folktales, legends, and traditions. Among these texts, the Pyrenean legend "Lo ram de Sant Joan" ("Saint John's Flowers"), which Verdaguer included in verse form in song 1 of the poem *Canigó*, is of particular interest. The book *Folk-lore* contains animal mimologisms, traditions, **etiologic tale**s, and **proverbs**. The section on animal mimologisms was published separately in book form in 1933 under the title of *Què diuen els ocells?* (*What Do Birds Say?*).

Over the course of his lifetime, Verdaguer collected 250 songs, many of which Manuel Milà i Fontanals included in *Romancerillo Catalán: Canciones tradicionales* (*Collection of Catalan Ballads: Traditional Songs*, 1882). To mark the centennial of Verdaguer's death, in

2002 the Folklore Research Group of Osona and Salvador Rebés selected seventy-two unpublished songs collected by Verdaguer that are preserved in manuscript form and published them in *Cançons tradicionals catalanes recollides per Jacint Verdaguer* (*Traditional Catalan Songs Collected by Jacint Verdaguer*). Most of these songs are ballads, although some of them are nonnarrative and others satirical. There are also five children's songs.

Verdaguer was the most important poet of the Romantic period in Catalonia. He is considered to be the creator of the modern Catalan literary language, which grew out of a highly balanced use of cultured poetic and linguistic models, and popular ones. Held in high esteem by the intellectuals of his time, Verdaguer was also so widely read among the popular classes that some of his poems have become part of the **oral tradition**. Important composers such as Enric Morera and Manuel de Falla have set many of Verdaguer's poems to **music**, and many have been translated into several languages. In 1943, Verdaguer's *Obres completes* (*Complete Works*) was published, and in 1995, work began on a critical edition, of which five volumes have been published to date. *See also* Collecting, Collectors.

Further Readings: Verdaguer, Jacint. *Obres completes.* 5th edition. Barcelona: Editorial Selecta, 1974; ———. *Obres completes.* Vic: Eumo Editorial/Societat Verdaguer, 1995.

Carme Oriol

Vess, Charles (1951–)

Charles Vess is an American illustrator who is well known for his comic-book **adaptation**s of topics from **folklore**, fairy lore, and fairy tales. Over the years, he has collaborated with the notable fairy-tale adaptors Neil **Gaiman** and Charles **de Lint**, in addition to producing independent illustrations for several works inspired by folklore.

Vess's graphic adaptations of fairy tales began in 1977 with *The Horns of Elfland*. In this volume, Vess presents three folktale-style narratives, two involving villages cursed by **witch**es and one involving a mortal who is kidnapped by fairies. Vess followed this up in 1988 with his *Little Red Riding Hood*, an illustrated adaptation of the popular folktale.

Vess contributed to Neil Gaiman's popular Sandman comic series with adaptations of William **Shakespeare**'s *A Midsummer Night's Dream* and *The Tempest* in 1990 and 1996, respectively. This led to a further collaboration between Gaiman and Vess, first on *Books of Magic* (1993) and then on *Stardust* (1997). In both cases, Vess's artwork drew on traditional fairy beliefs to portray a world of "**faerie**."

In 1995, Vess began his most folkloric project, *The Book of Ballads*. Initially published in semiannual volumes, this work took traditional **ballad**s, many from Francis James Child's collection, and adapted them to a comic-book format. This series included adaptations of "Barbara Allen," "Tam Lin," and "Thomas the Rhymer," among others.

Vess's most recent work in adapting subject matter from folklore and fairy tales are his illustrations for a 2003 reprint of Sir James Matthew **Barrie**'s *Peter Pan* and his increasing collaboration with Charles de Lint on children's stories, beginning in 2003 with *A Circle of Cats*. *See also* Graphic Novel; Illustration.

Further Readings: Sanders, Joe. "Of Storytellers and Stories in Gaiman and Vess's 'A Midsummer Night's Dream.'" *Extrapolation: A Journal of Science Fiction and Fantasy* 45 (2004): 237–48; Vess, Charles, ed. *The Book of Ballads.* New York: Tor Books, 2006.

B. Grantham Aldred

Video. *See* Film and Video

Villeneuve, Gabrielle-Suzanne Barbot de (c. 1695–1755)

Gabrielle-Suzanne Barbot de Villeneuve was the author of *La Belle et la Bête* (1740), the first literary version of **Beauty and the Beast**. Villeneuve's lengthy and complex **novel**, however, was radically transformed just sixteen years later, when Jeanne-Marie **Leprince de Beaumont** excised its most unusual parts and produced the short, didactic children's story that has become the classical tale known today.

Born in Paris as Gabrielle-Suzanne Barbot, she was the child of an aristocratic family from La Rochelle. Married in 1706 to Lieutenant Colonel Jean-Baptiste Gallon de Villeneuve, she soon discovered that her husband was squandering her dowry at the gaming tables; when he died in 1711, her financial situation was precarious. After struggling for more than a decade in the provinces, Villeneuve moved to Paris, where she began her literary career to support herself. She became the companion of the dramatist and royal censor, Prosper Jolyot de Crébillon, with whom she lived until her death.

Villeneuve's first work, a **novella**, appeared in 1734. A series of fairy tales (about a third of her output), published under the titles *La jeune amériquaine, ou Les contes marins* (*The Young American Girl, or the Marine Tales*, 1740–41) and *Les belles solitaires* (*The Beautiful Solitary Women*, 1745) soon followed. Villeneuve's greatest accomplishment is considered to be her novel *La jardinière de Vincennes* (*The Female Gardener of Vincennes*, 1753).

Villeneuve's *La Belle et la Bête* (*Beauty and the Beast*) appeared as the first tale in her collection, *The Young American Girl*; it was later reprinted in the twenty-sixth volume of the forty-one-volume fairy-tale anthology, **Le cabinet des fées** (*The Fairies' Cabinet*, 1785–89). The novel is a mixture of extraordinary descriptions, fairy-tale conventions, innovative dream sequences, and rational argument. The main narrative of the couple's enchanted courtship and **marriage** is followed by the history of the Beast's original **transformation** and the lengthy revelation of Belle's genealogy, which tend to dispel the sense of the marvelous.

In the original edition, the story is told within a **frame narrative**, which is usually removed when the fairy tale is anthologized. Within the frame, the audience of *Beauty and the Beast* is a group of young adults, including a young woman who is about to be married. This accounts for the story's frank references to **sex**, such as the Beast's repeated inquiry to Beauty: "Do you want to sleep with me?" This brutal question suggests Villeneuve's understanding that **women** face the constant threat of rape, even in their marriages. Beauty's ability to defer the event offers a rare example for the time of a woman exercising power in her own behalf. Nonetheless, it is debatable whether the novel, with its overriding emphasis on self-sacrifice, is a truly feminist tale. *See also* Feminist Tales; French Tales.

Further Readings: Cooper, Barbara Rosemarie Latotzky. "Madame de Villeneuve: The Author of 'La Belle et la Bête' and Her Literary Legacy. Dissertation. University of Georgia, 1985; Swain, Virginia E. "Beauty's Chambers: Mixed Styles and Mixed Messages in Villeneuve's *Beauty and the Beast.*" *Marvels & Tales* 19 (2005): 197–223.

Virginia E. Swain

Violence

Popular and folk fictions of all times and places, including fairy tales, have always included violence. The fairy tale is, of course, related to heroic tales, **legend**s, **saga**s, and

myth—all genres that lend themselves more obviously to violent themes. If fairy tales are a means for preliterate societies to pass the time, spread news, and give an artistic formulation to lived experience, it can be no wonder that violence, too, plays a part in them, for violence is very much a part of life. It was only as fairy tales began to be written down in Europe and European-influenced cultures from the seventeenth century onward that they were increasingly perceived to be suitable material for children but not for adults. The proper role of violence then became a topic of debate, as the pedagogic potential of the fairy tale became ever more important. Many writers and recorders of tales felt that violence could no longer be random or unmotivated but rather should fulfill the function of teaching a **moral** to young readers and listeners.

The fairy tale was beginning to be perceived as **children's literature** by the late sixteenth and early seventeenth centuries, when the French writer Charles **Perrault** played his part in producing and popularizing tales of magic and the marvelous based on traditional stories and **motif**s. Perrault's tales, all of which end with one or more morals, engaged a civilizing and moralizing discourse that implied an audience of children. As in contemporary religious writings directed at children or addressed to adults about how to raise children, the common childhood "vices" in fairy tales were curiosity and stubbornness, and these were punished harshly in a growing body of literature that instilled a strong sense of moral duty and respect for authority. However, Perrault's tales still retain the sexual innuendo, sly wit, and levels of violence that define their role as adult entertainment, too.

A watershed was reached with Jacob and Wilhelm **Grimm**'s publication of their *Kinder- und Hausmärchen* (*Children's and Household Tales*, 1812–15). The eventual popularity of this collection changed forever the way the fairy tale was received in the Western world. Believing fairy tales to be the pure products of the common people's wisdom, the Grimms eliminated from their versions anything they felt did not adequately portray this putative purity. This tendency became even more pronounced as Wilhelm Grimm's interest shifted from creating a scholarly collection of ancient folklore for a learned readership to creating a body of tales for the instruction and entertainment of children. References to **sex** and bodily functions were eliminated. While violence was sometimes softened or eliminated, it was retained when it had a didactic or cautionary purpose. Thus, violence tended to occur in Grimms' tales as a fitting (if extremely exaggerated) **punishment** for a crime.

The nineteenth century saw a boom in the production of literature explicitly for children, and almost all of it contained a strong element of moralizing, often by means of very violent imagery. In Heinrich Hoffmann's *Der Struwwelpeter* (*Slovenly Peter*, 1845), a child playing with matches might burn down an entire house, killing himself and other people, or a thumb sucker might have his thumb chopped off. There is a strange contradiction in the attitudes toward children displayed in this tendency. Although children are held to be innocents who should be protected from terrifying stories of unmotivated violence and aggression, there nonetheless persists alongside this romantic idea of childhood innocence the Christian notion of the child as born into sin and requiring strict control if he or she is to become a moral being. Furthermore, although the Grimms and others wished to relate violence to a crime to instill in children a sense that the world is a just place, by relating every violent act to a crime, they paradoxically made the world a very frightening place, indeed, where even peccadilloes are visited by severe and harsh judgment.

The function of violence in literature is a matter of ongoing debate. Maria Tatar noted in her book *Off with Their Heads!*, even in cases where an author clearly intends to frighten children into good behavior, real children often read entirely against the grain, gleefully enjoying the violence for its own sake and identifying not with the punished child in the tale but with the characters who survive unharmed. Children often have a strong sense of poetic justice, wishing to see an evil stepmother punished, for example; but this desire does not always extend to seeing themselves as worthy of such treatment. **Psychological approaches** to fairy tales often see the genre as offering lessons in how to survive, or more accurately, as lessons that one *will* survive, regardless of the hardships one faces. Thus, the nineteenth-century attempt to rationalize violence was misguided: the folk wisdom knew better how to depict the success story of the child or underdog survivor in a harsh world. Violence occurs in fairy tales not to teach a moral, then, but simply because it corresponds to lived reality. The poetic justice brought about when the villain gets his comeuppance in so many fairy tales is frequently more about the success of the hero than about cautioning the reader or audience against the bad behavior that leads to the punishment.

The Grimms have been criticized because of the precise way they bowdlerized their tales, namely that while **witch**es and evil stepmothers very much remain, **father**s who threaten **incest** are notably less evident (Ruth B. Bottigheimer). Jokes at the expense of figures of authority rarely occur. Thus, it is not only the presence of violence but also the contexts in which it is lacking in the Grimms' tales that become problematic. Studies of folktales from other areas show a tradition of subversion in them: lower classes against upper classes, the underdog against the authority figure—in short, the opposite of the kind of tale that purports to teach obedience and docility (Jack **Zipes**; Robert Darnton).

In fact, the folk tradition used violence in a variety of ways, depending on who was telling the tale, and to what audience and in what social context. Like humor, with which violence is often aligned, anyone can be the target. Marginalized groups such as old **women** or Jews are often the butt of the joke or of the violence, but in many **French tales**, for example, so is the powerful figure of the parish priest. It would be impossible to simplify the use of violence in fairy tales to say that it is always subversive or conversely always upholding the status quo. One tale may scapegoat a weak victim; another one may topple a patriarchal figure.

The twentieth and twenty-first centuries have seen contradictory attitudes toward the role of violence in fairy tales. Much ink continues to be spilled on the topic of violence in literature as well as on **television** and in **film**, as parents and educators worry about the effect on young minds. Some psychologists (in particular Bruno **Bettelheim**) have seen in the violence of the fairy tale the opportunity for the child to work out his or her own aggression against his or her parents, whereas Tatar finds in the violence the adults' attempt to control the child. On the one hand, the very vicious punishments still to be found in the Grimms' stories have long been left out of English versions of the tales (for example, the stepsisters of Grimms' **Cinderella** mutilate their own feet to try to make the **shoe** fit, and a dove pecks out their eyes to punish their vanity and selfishness—episodes that are usually missing in English-language versions for children). On the other hand, writers such as Roald **Dahl** and Angela **Carter** have reclaimed violence as suitable material for their fairy-tale revisions. In Dahl's case, one sees the child's somewhat gruesome glee in anything disgusting, and in Carter's work, the psychological veracity of reappropriating the dark side of the psyche. *See also* Anti-Semitism; Cautionary Tale; Childhood and Children; Clergy; Didactic Tale; Mother; Pedagogy; Sisters; Transgression; Trauma and Therapy.

Further Readings: Bottigheimer, Ruth B. *Grimms' Bad Girls and Bold Boys: The Moral and Social Vision of the Tales.* New Haven, CT: Yale University Press, 1987; Darnton, Robert. *The Great Cat Massacre and Other Episodes in French Cultural History.* London: Allen Lane, 1984; Tatar, Maria. "Sex and Violence: The Hard Core of Fairy Tales." *The Hard Facts of the Grimms' Fairy Tales.* 2nd edition. Princeton, NJ: Princeton University Press, 2003. 3–38; ———. *Off with Their Heads! Fairy Tales and the Culture of Childhood.* Princeton, NJ: Princeton University Press, 1992; Zipes, Jack. *Breaking the Magic Spell: Radical Theories of Folk and Fairy Tales.* Revised and expanded edition. Lexington: University of Kentucky Press, 2002.

Laura Martin

Virgin of Guadalupe

Our Lady of Guadalupe, to use her official title, is a manifestation of the Virgin, or mother of Christ, said to have appeared in Mexico in 1531, ten years after the Spanish Conquest. The basilica at Tepeyac, where the miracle is believed to have occurred, has a history traceable to a shrine built in 1555–56. After the War of Independence (1810–21), when troops carried her image into battle, "Guadalupe" became a symbol of Mexican national unity. Today, the basilica, which is three miles north of downtown Mexico City, attracts pilgrims from all parts of Mexico and beyond.

Traditional image of Our Lady of Guadalupe as reproduced on devotional items and souvenir cards.

According to **legend**, a poor Indian named Juan Diego was passing the hill of Tepeyac in December of 1531, when the Virgin, appearing before him, told him to go to the bishop and ask that a church be built in her honor. He was refused, the Virgin sent him again, and he was turned away once more. At this point, Juan Diego's mission was interrupted, as he learned that his uncle was deathly ill and needed him to look for a priest to administer last rites. The Virgin, however, advised Juan Diego not to worry about his uncle. Finally, she allowed him to find fresh roses, which could not have bloomed naturally in the month of December. When he showed these to the bishop—and the Virgin's image suddenly appeared on the poor man's tunic—the bishop was overwhelmed and ordered that the church be built. The uncle, meanwhile, had been miraculously cured.

The legend can be securely dated no earlier than the 1640s. The version that is usually cited was published in 1649 in Nahuatl, the language of the Aztecs, written by the vicar of the shrine at Tepeyac, Luis Laso de la Vega, as he himself states in his introduction; it is evidently an adaptation of the Spanish–language text brought out a year earlier by the Mexican priest Miguel

Sánchez. Since Juan Diego was canonized in the year 2002, the full account, merely summarized here, may now be regarded as a **saint's legend**.

Modern folktale collections reveal that the story of Juan Diego and the Virgin has entered **oral tradition**, though sparingly. A variant in the Tzotzil Maya language of the Chiapas state has been published in Robert Laughlin's *Of Cabbages and Kings: Tales from Zinacantán* (1977). Another is in Stanley Robe's *Mexican Tales and Legends from Veracruz* (1971). Among the general population, faith is tempered with a strain of doubt, well attested in the little book *El mito guadalupano* (1981; *The Myth of the Virgin of Guadalupe*, 1987) by the irreverent cartoonist Rius (Eduardo del Rio); this book was constantly reprinted toward the end of the twentieth century and sold in grocery stores throughout Mexico. *See also* Latin American Tales.

Further Readings: Poole, Stafford. "Guadalupe, Nuestra Señora de." *The Oxford Encyclopedia of Mesoamerican Cultures.* Edited by Davíd Carrasco. Volume 1. New York: Oxford University Press, 2001. 444–46; Sousa, Lisa, Stafford Poole, and James Lockhart. *The Story of Guadalupe: Luis Laso de la Vega's* Huei tlamahuiçoltica *of 1649.* Stanford, CA: Stanford University Press, 1998.

John Bierhorst

Volkov, Aleksandr (1891–1977)

Although he wrote several historical novels, Aleksandr Melent'evich Volkov, a mathematician and professor of metallurgy, is mostly remembered for his **adaptation** into Russian, in 1939, of L. Frank **Baum**'s *The Wonderful Wizard of Oz*. The Russian version—*Volshebnik izumrudnogo goroda* (*The Wizard of the Emerald City*)—met with great success and was reprinted three times before 1941. By 1981, more than 2.5 million copies had been printed in Russian. Volkov's version of Baum's story is a loose **translation**. Chapters have been added or omitted, and the names of characters have been changed. The Tin Woodman, for example, has been upgraded to "Iron." The context and the situations in the Russian version also differ from the American original, especially when it comes to the ideological atmosphere.

Unlike Baum, Volkov confronts his characters with ethical and political questions. They are actually called upon to defend Oz against feudalistic or aristocratic governments and to free the populace. Just like Baum in his own time, Volkov was soon urged by his enthusiastic readers to continue the story. Consequently, he wrote five detached sequels: *Urfin Dzhyuz i ego derevyannye soldaty* (*Urfin Jus and His Wooden Soldiers*, 1963), *Sem' podzemnykh korolei* (*The Seven Underground Kings*, 1964), *Ognenny bog Marranov* (*The Fiery God of the Marrans*, 1968), *Zholty tuman* (*The Yellow Fog*, 1970), and the posthumously published *Taina zabroshennogo zamka* (*The Secret of the Abandoned Castle*), which was released in 1982. The sequels demonstrate Volkov's ability to create captivating adventure stories on his own. *See also* Russian Tales.

Further Readings: Mitrokhina, Xenia. "The Land of Oz in the Land of the Soviets." *Children's Literature Association Quarterly* 21 (1996–97): 183–88; Nesbet, Anne. "In Borrowed Balloons: The Wizard of Oz and the History of Soviet Aviation." *Slavic and East European Journal* 45 (2001): 80–95.

Janina Orlov

W

Walker, Alice (1944–)

American writer and activist Alice (Tallulah-Kate) Walker weaves together patches of southern African American folklife in her **novel**s, short stories, and poems. She writes as a storyteller in the tradition founded during the Harlem Renaissance of the 1920s by African American writer and poet Jean Toomer and by Walker's proclaimed literary ancestor Zora Neale **Hurston**. One of Walker's main themes is the strength of black southern **women** as they managed to retain their spiritual health despite a life of hard work and suffering, and created a universe according to their personal concepts of beauty and aesthetics. In this context, **storytelling** in particular served as a means to pass those ideas on to later generations.

Alice Walker attends the opening performance of *The Color Purple* at the Broadway Theatre in New York City, 2005. [Getty Images]

Walker's characters are ordinary people, the "**folk**," who are rich in love, kindness, and creativity. Their cultural and religious beliefs are skillfully integrated into her stories. In particular, she sheds light on the words of her people, which are usually considered inferior in quality and not given credence as an oral art form. To Walker, Black Vernacular English reflects the experience of African Americans and the preservation of Africanisms. By transferring a primarily oral culture to paper, Walker deconstructs Western standards and legitimizes "folk" language.

Strongly influenced by the traditional slave narrative and works by Sojourner Truth, Harriet Ann Jacobs, and Frederick Douglass, Walker employs folk themes, **oral tradition**s, cultural perceptions, and cultural articulation in her works as social commentary on the racial situation in the United States and the attitudes of her black characters toward themselves.

Besides numerous books of **poetry**, Walker's most notable works include the novels *The Third Life of Grange Copeland* (1970), *Meridian* (1976), *The Color Purple* (1982), *The Temple of My Familiar* (1989), *Possessing* *the Secret of Joy* (1992), and the essay collections *In Search of Our Mother's Gardens: Womanist Prose* (1983) and *The Same River Twice: Honoring the Difficult* (1996). *The Color Purple* won the 1983 Pulitzer Prize for Fiction and the National Book Award, and was adapted into a successful **film** (1985) and a hit Broadway musical (2005). *See also* African American Tales.

Further Readings: Bates, Gerri. *Alice Walker: A Critical Companion.* Westport, CT: Greenwood Press, 2005; Harris, Trudier. "Folklore in the Fiction of Alice Walker: A Perpetuation of Historical and Literary Traditions." *Black American Literature Forum* 11.1 (1977): 3–8.

Juliana Wilth

Walker, Barbara G. (1930–)

Barbara G. Walker is an American scholar and author of feminist literature. Her nonfiction work, including *Woman's Encyclopedia of Myths and Secrets* (1983) and *The Woman's Dictionary of Symbols and Sacred Objects* (1988), has been widely read in New Age circles but criticized for inaccuracy and ideological bias. In *Feminist Fairy Tales* (1996), Walker combines fairy-tale **adaptation**s with rewritten **myth**s and newly invented stories. In the introductions to each of the twenty-eight stories in *Feminist Fairy Tales*, Walker explains her views on the pretext, which are often inspired by feminist and progressive debates or pagan and matriarchal rituals. She reinterprets **"Cinderella"** as a religious allegory about the reemergence of a goddess cult and the defeat of Christianity. In "Barbidol," Walker addresses the capitalist values and aggression promoted by toys such as GI Joe. Yet, some of her own adaptations are quite violent: in "Little White Riding Hood," a tale that promotes ecological values, a girl is almost raped by two hunters—a crime her grandmother avenges by splitting the skull of one of them with a hatchet and feeding his body to **wolves**.

Many of Walker's fairy tales are driven explicitly by ideology and have been criticized for their overt didacticism and lack of humor. Her strategies for rewriting the tales are simple and clear but not unproblematic. Most notably, her positive portrayal of empowered female characters is often at the cost of their male counterparts. *See also* Feminism; Feminist Tales.

Further Reading: Langlois, Janet L. Review of *Feminist Fairy Tales* by Barbara Walker. *Marvels & Tales* 11 (1997): 187–89.

Vanessa Joosen

Walt Disney Company

If any one media expression defined the nature of fairy tale in the late twentieth century, it was the Walt Disney Company. The association between the company and animated fairy-tale **adaptation** began with classics such as ***Snow White*** *and the Seven Dwarfs* (1937) and ***Sleeping Beauty*** (1959) under the leadership of Walt **Disney** himself, but it reached its apotheosis in the extreme commercial success of Disney's animated fairy-tale adaptations in the late 1980s and 1990s—*The Little* ***Mermaid*** (1989), ***Beauty and the Beast*** (1991), ***Aladdin*** (1992), and the beast-**fable** *The Lion King* (1994). These films demonstrate Disney's stranglehold on popular fairy-tale **film** at its strongest point, not only in their technological supremacy but also their canny grasp of consumer desires. In both of these aspects of their production, some notion of the folkloric plays a central part. The fairy-tale and **folklore** forms represent some of Disney's most successful animated films and allow the company to exploit its association with familiar, nostalgic, and culturally desirable material. This carries through into related merchandising, notably in the fairy-tale aspects of Disney's theme parks, which rely on a sense of enchantment, the marvelous, and the otherworldly to promote the notion of losing the everyday self in the unreal. At the same time, fairy-tale elements of the magical and unrealistic encourage the free play of animation technology. Even mainstay Disney characters such as Mickey Mouse and Donald Duck could be seen as contemporized, somewhat debased forms of the wise, talking animal companions of folklore.

The power and importance of Disney as a cultural monolith increased throughout the twentieth century. Apart from its conceptual domination of fairy tale itself, Disney has been synonymous in the contemporary imagination with **animation** in general, as well as with the kind of feel-good family values that carry over into its live-action and distribution arms (among them Touchstone Pictures, Miramax Films, and Buena Vista Motion Pictures Group) and the theme parks and the Disney Channel. Much of the character of the company has its roots in the personality and ideals of Walt Disney himself, which has indelibly stamped the company to an extent that continues powerfully, even long after his death. Despite its notable commercial success and often astute play on consumer desire, the Disney Company in the twenty-first century is in some ways a reactionary presence, adhering to a somewhat outmoded notion of innocence and "family values" and dogged by an inability to change with sufficient speed to meet the demands of contemporary culture. The increasing sexualization of young people and the **violence** and cynicism of much media material render the idealized Disney morality and stereotyping increasingly irrelevant. Disney-animated cinema has thus been overtaken in some senses by more agile cultural producers such as DreamWorks Animation and Pixar Animation Studios, companies more in tune with the contemporary zeitgeist and the ironic stance of much popular culture in a postmodern age (see **Postmodernism**). None of the recent Disney-animated features has approached the success of *Shrek* (2001) or *Finding Nemo* (2003).

By the time Walt Disney died in 1966, the company had already produced some of its most classic fairy-tale and folkloric films, including the groundbreaking *Snow White and the Seven Dwarfs*, *Cinderella* (1950), and *Sleeping Beauty*. The strong imprint of Disney's personality can be seen in the cleanness of image, **family**, and work ethics, and the assumption of a moral high ground that characterize these early works. Their ideological underpinnings conform to a somewhat conservative middle-class morality that strongly reinforces the more reactionary aspects of fairy tale to make problematical assumptions about **gender**, **sexuality**, and culture. Disney fairy tales invariably present a heterosexual ideal in which the white, middle-class nuclear family is celebrated, particularly in the ongoing notion of **marriage** as the only desirable outcome for **women**. In addition, the films are invariably built on fairy tale's utopian dreams of success, the elevation of the underdog to status and wealth after a simplified demonstration of moral worth. Similarly, the fairy-tale encoding of many Disney productions labels the films as safe for children through the nostalgic sense of cultural ownership associated with folkloric forms. This is extended through Disney's characteristic use of children's literary classics as another basis for films, resulting in successful adaptations of such fantasy works as Margery Sharpe's *The Rescuers* (novel, 1959; film, 1977) or Lloyd **Alexander**'s *The Black Cauldron* (novel, 1965; film, 1985).

While identification with familiar forms is central to Disney's animation strategy, it is interesting to trace the gradual foregrounding of consumerist issues, particularly those related to marketing and merchandising, in the company's increasingly sophisticated film-making during the late twentieth century. The fairy-tale trope of the poor protagonist who becomes rich and successful is frequently related to Walt Disney's own life, with an endorsement of a puritan work ethic that reflects his own efforts in establishing the company. Gradually, however, in films from *The Little Mermaid* onward, the notion of hard work rewarded is replaced by an ideology of entitlement to ownership that is firmly rooted in consumerism. Disney characters are frequently established as the rightful owners of cultural artifacts, such as Ariel's collection of above-sea objects, or rightful inheritors, as in Simba's promise from his **father** that some day the land will belong to him; or their identities are caught up with the desire for wealth, as in *Aladdin*. The films thus both advertise and reinforce the notion of Disney merchandise, a significant proportion of the Disney Company's revenue, which operate both as tangible reminders of the fairy-tale universe and as a form of identification with the ultimately privileged heroes of many Disney works. Fairy tale becomes the ideal vehicle for Disney storytelling, not only because of its tendency toward well-defined, simple narratives, but in its ideological embedding of potentially consumerist notions.

Earlier Disney films based on fairy tales offer relatively straightforward adaptations, with the essential story line remaining in place despite embellishment, elaboration, and occasional twisting to fit the Disney formula. The company's appropriation of folklore in *Robin Hood* (1973), on the other hand, makes full use of the somewhat free-form nature of the mythology surrounding this figure to create a central story that is essentially original: its anthropomorphized animal characters both reinforce folkloric stereotypes and allow for witty scripting. A similar principle is followed in *Hercules* (1997), a hodgepodge of semirecognizable ancient Greek mythology. The looser adaptation principle behind this kind of film, while allowing Disney freer rein with plot, also loses the structural simplicity and familiarity that so strengthens the classic fairy-tale narratives; and certainly *Robin Hood* and *Hercules* were not as successful as the more specifically fairy-tale films.

The Little Mermaid signaled a return to the more explicit fairy-tale narratives that made successful early Disney works such as *Snow White* and *Sleeping Beauty*. However, Hans Christian **Andersen**'s tale is more honored in name than in actual execution, and Ariel's story ultimately bears little resemblance to Andersen's tragic fable beyond the central **motif** of a mermaid who wishes to be human. Nonetheless, it sparked the brief renaissance of the full-length fairy-tale feature in Disney animation. *Beauty and the Beast* was even more successful, gaining an Oscar nomination for Best Picture. Its European setting and slightly gothic feel cement notions of folkloric authenticity in their evocation of both French fairy tale and the Brothers **Grimm**, while also tying neatly into the concurrent construction of Euro Disney near Paris. Here, too, the characterization of Belle made a token gesture toward feminist awareness, recouping some of the problematical aspects of Ariel's vapid voicelessness in *The Little Mermaid* and suggesting that Disney is beginning to recognize the dangers of overly reactionary ideologies (see **Feminism**). Ultimately, however, Belle's fate is marriage to a wealthy man.

While *Beauty and the Beast* updates its fairy-tale structures with some contemporary references, even these are somewhat dated: the French and British stereotypes of the animated furniture are early twentieth-century, as are the visual references to Busby Berkeley musicals. *Aladdin* presents the most radical departure from this slightly old-fashioned texture, notably in the character of the Genie, which, as voiced by Robin Williams, exploits the high-speed and extremely current cultural commentary of the stand-up comic. This is an obvious document in Disney's scramble to contemporize its films and most notably exploits the growing tendency for high-profile actors to voice the more important animated characters, providing an occasionally jolting bridge between the idealized realm of fairy tale and the realities of contemporary Hollywood culture. *Aladdin*'s feel is fast, clean, and modern, in contrast to *Beauty and the Beast*'s denser and more nostalgic textures. Its framing is comic, lacking the potentially tragic gothic undertones of *Beauty and the Beast*. *Aladdin*'s narrative employs the familiar motifs of the **Arabian Nights** fairy tale, which has been an accepted part of the Western fairy-tale corpus for several centuries, although Disney's version codes it as attractively exotic in the use of Arabian artistic motifs and Eastern stereotyping in the background characters. The motif of wealth is particularly well developed in this film, with ostentatious display of commodities in such fertile areas as the Cave of Wonders and Aladdin's triumphal entry into the city. Both films retain the traditional Disney **moral**, however: success is about righteous self-discovery and the demonstration of inner worth, a self-conscious development and exaggeration of the moral quest inherent in many fairy tales.

The success of *Beauty and the Beast* and *Aladdin* was followed by that of *The Lion King*, which remains one of the highest-grossing animated films of all time. Like both *Beauty and the Beast* and *Aladdin*, it is constructed around an exoticized non-American culture, here an idealized African savannah teeming with wildlife. The beast-fable format permits the complete elision of actual human inhabitants of the African continent, presenting a *Hamlet*-esque usurpation plot to the essentially tourist gaze of the audience, and lays claim to a simplified notion of African landscape and folklore. *Mulan* (1998) likewise exploits Chinese folklore for its fantasy tale of a **woman warrior**, but the film inevitably returns its apparently empowered heroine to home and marriage despite her success as a hero. Again, stereotype and cultural sampling is rife throughout the film, which produces its "Chinese" flavor largely through highly recognizable Orientalist clichés such as **dragon**s, ancestor veneration, and the Great Wall. The particularly strong cultural character of much folklore and fairy tale thus provides Disney with fertile ground for its characteristic cultural insensitivity, its appropriation of other cultures in a piecemeal and highly exploitative fashion for the purposes of exotic settings and colorful appeal.

From *The Lion King* onward, Disney seems to have moved away from strictly fairy-tale animated films into works that exploit a more generalized notion of the folkloric. For example, animal **transformation** for purposes of moral lessons, a familiar motif from **French tales**, features in *The Emperor's New Groove* (2000) and *Brother Bear* (2003). Both films also enshrine a notion of cultural otherness, respectively that of South America and of Native American shamanism. A more interesting tendency, however, is in films such as *Atlantis: The Lost Empire* (2001) and *Lilo and Stitch* (2002), which explore versions of contemporary rather than historical folklore, the former in the **legend**s of the lost civilization of Atlantis, and the latter in the rather entertaining play with the **urban legend**s of mad scientists, alien intervention, and government cover-ups. This is an edgier, more knowing use of the folkloric than are the more faithful fairy-tale films and resonates better with the Disney flavor of broad comedy. The success, particularly, of *Lilo and Stitch* suggests that this New Age folkloric framing certainly has appeals to modern audiences. A similar awareness can be found in recent Disney offerings such as *Chicken Little* (2005) and in ongoing projects and future releases that deny the idyllic feel of earlier films by combining the classic fairy tale with contemporary life, as in *Enchanted* (2007) and *Rapunzel Unbraided* (working title, 2009).

The most important development in Disney animation over the last few years has been the change from 2-D hand-drawn animation to 3-D computer animation. Hand-drawn craftedness and a rich, painterly feel is synonymous with the Disney studio, which has somewhat resisted the change to the mood and tone of 3-D animation as much as the technology. Disney's profitable distribution deal with Pixar from 1991 has produced animated films that offer an escape from the excessive cleanliness of the Disney image. Pixar offerings are not strictly folkloric, although they are very much fantasy films, mostly focusing on the secret, unsuspected life of objects, or creatures taken for granted by human society: toys, insects, fish, the monster in the cupboard, and even the superhero existence of an insurance officer. The success of Pixar demonstrates the extent to which 2-D animation has lost its hold, precipitating Disney's outright acquisition of the Pixar studio in 1996. Disney's last traditionally hand-animated film was the critically and financially disastrous *Home on the Range* (2004), a beast-fable Western. *Chicken Little* represents the first all-Disney foray into 3-D computer animation. This film demonstrates the extent to which Pixar's success has nudged Disney to move toward the more complex textures and comic speed of the contemporary rather than the nostalgic idyll of the fairy tale that *Brother Bear* tried unsuccessfully to recapture. While *Chicken Little*'s title recalls the classic child's fairy tale, its narrative sets out at a tangent to the familiar story, providing an energetically anthropomorphized animal suburbia that is often wryly satirical. It also utilizes the slightly offbeat urban folklore around alien invasion that was so successful in *Lilo and Stitch*. However, ultimately the potentially subversive or parodic edge to *Chicken Little* is subordinated to the classic Disney emphasis on family, leaving the film's ending somewhat anticlimactic.

While the Disney studios stand for both fairy tale and animated film in the popular imagination, of course the studio and its subsidiaries have a prolific live-action output, again with the emphasis on family viewing. The animated features are most strongly associated with fairy tale, but a thread of the folkloric runs through the output of the live-action studios, most notably in Miramax's fairy tale *Ella Enchanted* (2004). Titles such as *The Princess Diaries* (2001) and *Ice Princess* (2005) also nod to Disney's fairy-tale monopoly. The use of familiar, recognizable symbols in live-action movies echoes that of the fairy-tale films, most successfully in the blockbuster franchise of *Pirates of the Caribbean* (2003, 2006, 2007), which develops the Disney theme-park ride in its play with fantasized pirate romance. Other folkloric output centers on Christmas movies such as *The Santa Clause* (1994) or on animal transformations or talking animals, or, as in *Herbie Fully Loaded* (2005), anthropomorphized cars. In addition, Disney's recent involvement in *The Chronicles of Narnia* (2005, 2008) underlines its long-term association with magical narrative.

The importance of fairy tale as a franchise in the Disney business cannot be overestimated. Canny merchandising has led to the theatrical and DVD rerelease of the early fairy tales, with improved quality, serving to cement in audience minds the irrevocable association between Disney and classic fairy tales. Other successful attempts to cash in on the success of the flagship animated fairy tales include Broadway musicals based on works such as *Beauty and the Beast* and *The Lion King*, both of which have been extremely successful. Disney also exploits fairy-tale output in its ongoing development of DVD or video sequels to its theatrical blockbusters, which, while being cheaply made films of lower technical and script quality, lucratively make use of an established fan base, particularly among children. Thus, while the company's output is prolific and diverse, its core identity depends on the fairy tale for commercial as well as artistic purposes. ***See also*** Children's Literature; Theater; Tourism.

Further Readings: Ayres, Brenda, ed. *The Emperor's Old Groove: Decolonizing Disney's Magic Kingdom.* New York: Peter Lang, 2003; Bell, Elizabeth, Lynda Haas, and Laura Sells, eds. *From Mouse to Mermaid: The Politics of Film, Gender, and Culture.* Bloomington: Indiana University Press, 1995; Brocklebank, Lisa. "Disney's *Mulan*—the 'True' Deconstructed Heroine?" *Marvels & Tales* 14 (2000): 268–83; Giroux, Henry A. *The Mouse that Roared: Disney and the End of Innocence.* Lanham: Rowman and Littlefield, 1999; Ross, Deborah. "Escape from Wonderland: Disney and the Female Imagination." *Marvels & Tales* 18 (2004): 53–66; Zipes, Jack. *Happily Ever After: Fairy Tales, Children and the Culture Industry.* New York: Routledge, 1997.

Jessica Tiffin

Warner, Marina (1946–)

A prolific novelist, critic, and cultural historian, Marina Warner engages extensively with folktale and fairy tale. Warner's writing works through an accumulation of richly detailed layers of historical and cultural evidence, offering a kaleidoscopic perspective on central figures and themes. Her watershed year was 1994, involving as it did the publication of three key works: *From the Beast to the Blonde: On Fairy Tales and Their Tellers*, an extraordinarily wide-ranging account of the fairy tale as a genre rooted in female **storytelling**; *Managing Monsters: Six Myths of Our Time*, the text of Warner's BBC Reith Lectures; and *Wonder Tales*, an edition of original **translation**s of six late seventeenth-century French fairy tales.

More recently, folktales and fairy tales have figured in her study of representations of fear, especially as embodied in masculine form, in *No Go the Bogeyman: Scaring, Lulling, and Making Mock* (1998), and in her 2001 Clarendon Lectures on ideas of identity and metamorphosis, published as *Fantastic Metamorphoses, Other Worlds: Ways of Telling the Self* (2002). Some of Warner's many and varied essays have been collected as *Signs & Wonders: Essays on Literature and Culture* (2003), which includes themed sections devoted to "**Fairies**, **Myth**s, and Magic" and "Reworking the Tale." Fairy-tale influenced fiction includes the **novel** *Indigo* (1992), in part a reworking of William **Shakespeare**'s *The Tempest*, and the story collection, *The Mermaids in the Basement* (1993. *See also* English Tales.

Further Reading: Fraser, Robert. Interview with Marina Warner. *Writing across Worlds: Contemporary Writers Talk.* Ed. Susheila Nasta. London: Routledge, 2004. 364–75.

Stephen Benson

Welty, Eudora (1909–2001)

Mississippi writer Eudora Welty often included fairy-tale, folktale, and mythological elements in her fictional works, set in the rural American south. Welty's cycle of short stories, *The Golden Apples* (1949), relies on components of classical **myth**, while her **novel**, *The Robber Bridegroom* (1942), reworks a Brothers **Grimm** tale of the same name.

Set in New Orleans and along the Natchez Trace during the final days of the American frontier, *The Robber Bridegroom* borrows many elements of the Grimms' story (mysterious bridegroom, talking raven). But its characters and settings possess opposing qualities, including the capacity for both compassion and harm. The robber bridegroom himself is both gentleman and outlaw, and he finds happiness only when he accepts and integrates his two identities—ironically, as a merchant. Other fairy-tale and mythological allusions include a wicked stepmother, a speaking locket that echoes the words of the horse head in "The Goose Girl," and a variation on the **Cupid and Psyche** story.

References to folktale in *The Robber Bridegroom*, meanwhile, emphasize the need for a different kind of personal evolution, a transition from wild to civilized culture reflecting that of young America itself. The outrageous **legend**s and **tall tale**s surrounding characters such as Mike Fink merely underscore a dying way of life. Welty expands these traditional tales into a chronicle of self-awareness and adaptation in a changing time. *See also* North American Tales.

Further Reading: Carson, Barbara Harrell. *Eudora Welty: Two Pictures at Once in Her Frame.* Troy, NY: Whitston, 1992.

Elizabeth Wanning Harries

Werewolf, Wolf, Wolves

References to werewolves, or men-wolves, are as old as written records and come up to the present time. Homer (*Iliad* 10) presents a certain Dolon, "the Crafty," who dons a lupine pelt to (as Euripides explicates in *Rhesus*) become a nocturnal stalking killer. Pliny (*Natural History* 8.34) mentions the ancient Arcadian tradition that one who hangs his **clothing** on an oak tree turns into a wolf and then recovers the same clothes to resume human shape. Both techniques of skin swapping—donning the beast's pelt and stripping human clothes—remain staples of metamorphosis in modern **folklore**.

Werewolfishness was not always stigmatized. For example, Herodotus (*Histories* 4) echoes the rumor that all members of a certain Thracian tribe became wolves once a year; in ancient Rome, youngsters bearing the wolfish name of Luperci had ancient if obscure links to kingship, and they performed end-of-year rites of purification and fertility; Russian Prince Vseslav, the eleventh-century great-grandson of St. Vladimir, is depicted in **epic** tradition as a bloodthirsty werewolf with, however, redeeming resonances; and a seventeenth-century Livonian villager, interrogated by inquisitors, firmly maintained that werewolves fight otherworldly battles for agricultural fertility (Ginzburg, 153).

Nonetheless, the ancient equation between wolves and outlaws prevails. Werewolves are deemed out-of-bounds. Having been born at liminal times (such as solstices) to an impossible position (such as scion of a Catholic priest), or displaying dual features (for example, wrapped in an extra "skin"), werewolves lack a proper position in the human realm. Trapped betwixt and between, werewolves sway between this world and the otherworld without fitting into either. Such a death-in-life condition amounts to the idea that werewolves are persons under a curse—an enchantment, in the parlance of the **wonder tale**. This is not a masculine prerogative, either. Sympathy between werewolves and enchantment shows in ATU 409, The Girl as Wolf, as well as in **legend**s describing how a cursed daughter becomes a wolf for seven years.

That a period lived under the spectral beast's skin should amount to enchantment is noteworthy on two grounds. First, wolves as a species are a staple of metamorphoses because of their constant association with the otherworld. They run in wintertime, as well as in nighttime, supposedly along with roaming specters. Indeed, they present funereal overtones. As British writer Angela **Carter** put it in her radio-play version of "The Company of Wolves," wolves are "like wraiths, like shadows, grey members of a congregation of the damned ... the beasts of blood and darkness" (Carter, 63). Moreover, in wonder tales (chiefly in ATU 425, The Search for the Lost Husband), supernatural bridegrooms under enchantment appear as white wolves, whereas in seasonal rites, green wolves (such as the famous French *loup vert de Jumièges*) represent returning springtime bounty.

Second, the notion that donning the skin of an animal will convert you into that animal's shape is both of the essence of werewolf beliefs and of wonder-tale mechanics. On the one hand, Latin authors called werewolves *versipelles*, "skin-shifters." On the other, to cast or wear a garb toggles tale characters between enchantment and disenchantment. Overall, both werewolf spells and wonder-tale enchantments connote an otherworldly sojourn under a skin, which is tantamount to being inside the beast—thus, among the dead.

Homology between werewolves and tale characters highlights the cyclic fate of both. The latter hide their radiance under a dark cloak and then again display their beauty; likewise, werewolves internalize their human mien under a pelt and then again externalize it. Angela Carter expresses such dynamics of reversal by noting that werewolves are "hairy on the inside" (Carter, 64) and then able to "let their insides come outside" (Carter, 71). That is, internal skin becomes external (and vice versa). Their inner aspect is forever ready to replace the aging envelope, which suggests an analogy between lupine skin-shifters and sloughing snakes. Indeed, the Russian werewolf **prince** mentioned above is the son of a serpent, born in a caul (an extra "skin") and endowed with a power to change skins.

Similarity with serpents fits the notion that bloodthirsty werewolves are both hunters and prey—hunters into prey, as the fate of Homer's Dolon illustrates. Insofar as a change of skin causes renewal, it involves **death**; but, again, this is the sort of death-in-life that wonder tales express as enchantment. In other words, the funereal connotation of werewolves entails renovation because their metamorphoses follow the death-and-rebirth logic of lunar phases. Thus, twelfth-century Gervasium of Tilbury (*Otia imperialia* 3.120) states that lupine metamorphoses accompany moon turnings. And, of course, the lunar dimension remains conspicuous in popular culture.

In sum, as werewolves inherit from wolves a reputation for voraciousness—in both the alimentary and sexual senses—they are accursed figures of death. But, insofar as skin-shifters are lunar figures, they display powers of renovation. Paradoxical to the core, werewolves are accursed epitomes of reinvigoration. Symbolic operators, they embody universal **dragon** imagery in the provincial guise of an elusive, if all-too-familiar, animal.

Although not widely known, "**Little Red Riding Hood**" in **oral tradition** is a werewolf tale. Here, the spectral connotation, voracious reputation, bloodlust, and moon/skins symbolism of werewolves all come into play. This **folktale** successively assimilates old granny in bed, as well as her cannibal granddaughter, to the werewolf. As the tale unfolds in oral tradition, the **blood** and flesh of wolflike granny passes on to the maiden; and the wolfish girl, who incorporates granny and then meets the wolf in bed, ends up figuratively reborn. This scenario of feminine **initiation**, complete with sexual debut, unfolds in terms of **cannibalism** and skin changes. Appropriately, this werewolf tale narrates self-rejuvenation of wolf/granny into wolf/maid through shed blood and garments.

The theme of werewolves has passed into modern life in **film and video**—for example in *Teen Wolf* (directed by Rod Daniel, 1985) and its sequel *Teen Wolf Too* (directed by Christopher Leitch, 1987), the popularity of which demonstrates ongoing fascination with the notion of moon-driven metamorphosis. Undoubtedly, the most sophisticated example is Neil Jordan's film ***The Company of Wolves*** (1982), a fairy-tale-like coming-of-age story based on Angela Carter's werewolf tales. ***See also*** Animal Bride, Animal Groom; Avery, Frederick "Tex"; *Freeway* and *Freeway II*; Sex, Sexuality; Transformation.

Further Readings: Carter, Angela. "The Company of Wolves" [radio play and filmscript versions]. *The Curious Room.* Edited by Mark Bell. London: Vintage, 1997. 61–83, 185–244; Ginzburg, Carlo. *Ecstasies: Deciphering the Witches' Sabbath.* Translated by Raymond Rosenthal. New York: Pantheon Books, 1991; Jakobson, Roman, and Marc Szeftel. "The Vseslav Epos." *Russian Epic Studies.* Edited by Roman Jakobson and Ernest J. Simmons. Philadelphia: American Folklore Society, 1949. 13–86; Rumpf, Marianne. *Ursprung und Entstehung von Warn- und Schreckmärchen.* Helsinki: Academia Scientiarum Fennica, 1955; Vaz da Silva, Francisco. "Iberian Seventh-Born Children, Werewolves, and the Dragon Slayer." *Folklore* 114 (2003): 335–53; Verdier, Yvonne. "Little Red Riding Hood in Oral Tradition." Translated by Joseph Gaughan. *Marvels & Tales* 11 (1997): 101–23.

Francisco Vaz da Silva

Wieland, Christoph Martin (1733–1813)

Christoph Martin Wieland was a German poet, novelist, and essayist. Though considered the leading writer of the German Enlightenment, Wieland often worked with **literary fairy tale**s. His first **novel**, *Der Sieg der Natur über die Schwarmerey, oder Die Abenteuer des Don Sylvio von Rosalva* (*The Victory of Nature over Enthusiasm, or The Adventures of Don Sylvio of Rosalva*, 1764), is based on Miguel de Cervantes Saavedra's *Don Quixote* (1605–15). Like Don Quixote, the hero interprets everything he sees in terms of what he has read—French fairy tales of the 1690s, particularly those by Marie-Catherine d'**Aulnoy**, rather than chivalric romances—leading to a series of ridiculous mistakes and comic encounters. Just as *Don Quixote* includes various versions of the romance, Wieland's hero even tells a fairy tale, "Die Geschichte des Prinzen Biribinker" ("The Story of Prince Biribinker") that both imitates and parodies the **French tales**. *Don Sylvio* is not only a critique of the fairy-tale vogue in late eighteenth-century Germany but also what Jorge Luis **Borges**, speaking of *Don Quixote*, called "a secret, nostalgic farewell."

Wieland also wrote several playful verse narratives that were based in part on fairy-tale material, among them *Idris und Zenide* (1768), *Musarion* (1768), and "Pervonte oder die Wünsche" ("Pervonte or the **Wish**es," 1778–79), a version of a story by Giambattista **Basile**. His collection of Orientalizing prose tales, *Dchinnistan* (1786–87), includes three original ones, as well as several taken from *Le cabinet des fées*, edited by Charles-Joseph, Chevalier de **Mayer** (1785–89). Throughout his long career, Wieland often made casual references to tales by French writers, indicating the popularity of those tales in late eighteenth-century Germany. *See also* German Tales.

Further Reading: Shandley, Robert R. "Time Is Money: Constructing Subjectivity in C. M. Wieland's 'The Philosopher's Stone.'" *Merveilles et contes* 7 (1993): 451–68.

Elizabeth Wanning Harries

Wilde, Oscar (1854–1900)

The Irish playwright, novelist, poet, and writer of fairy tales, Oscar Fingal O'Flahertie Wills Wilde was born in Dublin and from an early age was surrounded by the **Celtic tales** that his parents collected and retold. His father, William Wilde, had published *Irish Popular Superstitions* in 1852, and his mother, Jane Wilde, who wrote Irish nationalist poetry under the pen name of Speranza, produced *Ancient Legends, Mystic Charms, and Superstitions of Ireland* (1887) at around the time Wilde himself turned to writing fairy tales. Educated at Trinity College, Dublin, and at Oxford University, Wilde settled in London in 1879, where

Oscar Wilde. [Library of Congress]

he achieved fame as an aesthete, dandy, and literary personality. His literary career included the creation of a modern **myth** about ageless beauty in his novel *The Picture of Dorian Gray* (1891) and plays of scintillating wit such as *Lady Windermere's Fan* (1892) and *The Importance of Being Earnest* (1895). Wilde's fame became equaled by his notoriety when his final years were engulfed in scandal generated by his trial and two-year imprisonment for homosexual offenses, and he died in obscurity in Paris. It is a poignant irony, often noted, that the hauntingly tragic qualities of Wilde's fairy tales were to foreshadow many of the experiences of his own life.

Published at the start of several very productive years of writing and before he had fully established his literary fame, Wilde's first collection of fairy tales, *The Happy **Prince** and Other Tales*, appeared in 1888, illustrated by Walter **Crane** and George Percy Jacomb Hood. A popular and critical success, the volume contained two of his most enduring and highly regarded tales, "The Happy Prince" and "The Selfish Giant," in addition to three others: "The Nightingale and the Rose," "The Devoted Friend," and "The Remarkable Rocket."

Wilde's second collection, *A House of Pomegranates*, appeared in 1891, illustrated by Charles Ricketts and Charles Shannon. This volume contained four tales: "The Young **King**," "The Birthday of the Infanta," "The Fisherman and His Soul," and "The Star-Child." This second volume is often regarded as a darker collection, which displays a particular concern with socialism and with the role of the artist who does not conform to society's expectations.

Elegant, poetic, **literary fairy tale**s, which were not exclusively intended for children, Wilde's stories showcase his concerns with love, sacrifice, beauty, social inequities, and the role of the artist. Often revealing a sense of sad irony linked to episodes of casual or unthinking cruelty, they contain **moral** messages against selfishness, greed, pomposity, and self-centeredness, and question social hypocrisy and double standards.

Influenced by Hans Christian **Andersen**'s tales, Wilde also was probably inspired toward writing in the genre by stories he told his two sons, his mother's interests in Celtic **folklore**, his wife Constance Lloyd's publishing of fantasies for children, the contemporary wave of interest in fairy tales, and his reading and reviewing of *Fairy and Folk Tales of the Irish Peasantry* (1888), edited and selected by W. B. **Yeats**.

Although less sentimental than Andersen's, Wilde's fairy tales are similarly known for the thread of sadness that runs through them and for their moral content. Most include suffering and self-sacrificial **death** for noble purposes such as the sake of a friend or for love or art, but often this self-sacrifice goes unrewarded, unnoticed, or teaches surviving characters no lessons. In his best-known tales, "The Happy Prince" and "The Selfish Giant," good is rewarded when the protagonists enter paradise, but this is achieved only after death. Some tales appear to subvert Andersen's. "The Nightingale and the Rose" for example, draws on but alters Andersen's "The Nightingale," and "The Star Child" inverts "The Ugly Duckling" by emphasizing the importance of spiritual rather than physical beauty, while "The Fisherman and His Soul" echoes but reverses Andersen's "The Little Mermaid" by showing a man giving up his soul to live in love with a **mermaid**. His soul tempts him back to land and evil deeds, but the fisherman and the mermaid ultimately lie together again in death.

The spiritual and the sensual often merge in Wilde's tales, and many of them have a quality akin to the **parable**. "The Selfish Giant," for example, has an overtly Christian message, and several tales contain Christlike martyr figures, but these are martyrs who suffer but ultimately cannot offer redemption. "The Happy Prince" can be read as a tale of love between **men** and as a story about the sacrificial role of the artist who inevitably suffers while trying to make the world better or nobler. None of the tales has a traditionally "happily ever after" ending and most end with death. Wilde's concerns about inequity between rich and poor weave through many of the tales as does an emphasis on suffering.

The tales have been read as mirroring social divisions in Victorian society but also have been widely seen as biographical, reflecting Wilde's self-expression in distanced form of some of the romantic torments and homosexual relationships in his life. Several have been read as revealing homoerotic bonds between male characters and awareness of Victorian oppression of homosexuality.

Several **adaptation**s of Wilde's tales have been produced, including animated **film** versions of "The Selfish Giant" in 1971, "The Happy Prince" in 1974, and "The Remarkable Rocket" in 1975. "The Happy Prince" also was adapted as a short **opera** using animated models in 1996, and P. Craig Russell has been adapting Wilde's fairy tales into comic book form in several volumes since 1992. *See also* English Tales; Gay and Lesbian Tales.

Further Readings: Edwards, Owen Dudley. "Wilde, Oscar Fingal O'Flahertie Wills (1854–1900)." *Oxford Dictionary of National Biography*. Edited by H. C. G. Matthew and Brian Harrison. Oxford: Oxford University Press, 2004; Ellman, Richard. *Oscar Wilde*. London: Hamish Hamilton, 1988; Goodenough, Elizabeth. "Oscar Wilde, Victorian Fairy Tales, and the Meanings of Atonement." *Lion and the Unicorn* 23 (1999): 336–54; Zipes, Jack. Afterword. *Complete Fairy Tales of Oscar Wilde*. Signet Classic. New York: Penguin, 1990. 205–13; ———. *Fairy Tales and the Art of Subversion: The Classical Genre and the Process of Civilization*. New York: Routledge, 1983.

Adrienne E. Gavin

Willow (1988)

The American **film** *Willow*, directed by Ron Howard and produced by George Lucas, who also conceptualized the story, has a certain affinity with Lucas's *Star Wars* films, with which it shares the format of a basic action-adventure plot that resonates with **myth** and fairy tale. As a **fantasy** film, *Willow* is more directly a genre narrative in the mode of J. R. R. **Tolkien**'s *Lord of the Rings*, although it has a far more ironic stance in its treatment of heroic fantasy. Visually, in its combination of the magical with a gritty realism, it foreshadows some of the treatment Peter Jackson gave *Lord of the Rings* a decade later, not least in its use of New Zealand landscapes.

The world of *Willow* conforms to the standard medieval feudalism of fantasy romance, although there is a satisfyingly fairy-tale ring in the evil Queen Bavmorda and the good **sorceress** Raziel, together with the baby **Princess** Elora Danan, who is fated to destroy the evil **queen**. The film is also concerned on several levels with magical **transformation**; its morphing animals were groundbreaking visual effects for the time. Willow Ufgood, the film's eponymous protagonist, conforms to the classic fairy-tale pattern of the small, unimportant hero whose quest will inevitably succeed, although his progress toward self-knowledge and confidence in wielding magic is more that of the fantasy romance. Likewise, the film's tiny **fairies** and brownies are more Victorian than folkloric, and the hobbit-like nelwyns are very much in the post-Tolkien tradition. *See also* Faerie and Fairy Lore.

Further Reading: *Willow*. Directed by Ron Howard. 1988. DVD. Twentieth Century Fox, 2001.

Jessica Tiffin

Windling, Terri (1958–)

Terri Windling is an American author, artist, and editor of works inspired by fairy tales. Both her edited works and her own fiction have won World Fantasy Awards, demonstrating her importance and competence in shaping fantastic fairy-tale fiction. Windling's work with fairy tales is sensitive and intelligent. Her introductions to edited volumes establish her familiarity with folkloristic scholarship, while her selection of topics reveals a concern for the power structures inherent to fairy tales.

Much of Windling's editorial work has been in partnership with Ellen Datlow. Together they produced *The Year's Best Fantasy and Horror* anthologies (1988–2003), which sometimes included fairy-tale fiction. Most notably, Datlow and Windling coedited a six-volume series of fairy-tale inspired short stories for adults that included *Snow White, Blood Red* (1993), *Black Thorn, White Rose* (1994), *Ruby Slippers, Golden Tears* (1995), *Black Swan, White Raven* (1997), *Silver Birch, Blood Moon* (1999), and *Black Heart, Ivory Bones* (2000). Each volume contains an introduction by Datlow and Windling that celebrates the complexity, sensuality, and **violence** of oral tales that moralistic writers and editors of fairy tales intended for children inevitably tried to suppress. However, Datlow and Windling also have edited collections of retold fairy tales for children ages eight to twelve titled *A Wolf at the Door* (2000) and *Swan Sister* (2003). The editors' introductions to these anthologies make the point that older fairy tales were darker but also brighter, filled with more danger but also with more interesting and more resourceful protagonists.

Windling's solo **editing** work has also been influential in the fairy-tale fiction genre. Her series of **novel**-length fairy tale retellings, The Fairy Tale Series, started in 1986 and contains eight volumes to date. Notable authors who appear in this series include Pamela **Dean**, Charles **de Lint**, Gregory **Frost**, Tanith **Lee**, and Jane **Yolen**. The settings of these novels range from utterly fantastic worlds to familiar urban locations.

Two projects representing Windling's commitment to fairy tales are the Endicott Studio for Mythic Arts and a collection entitled *The Armless Maiden and Other Tales for Childhood's Survivors* (1995). The Endicott Studio, which Windling founded in 1987, was originally a physical studio in Boston and currently survives on the **Internet**. It is an association devoted to the mythic arts, both traditional and contemporary, with roots in **folklore** in general, **myth**, and fairy tale. *The Armless Maiden and Other Tales for Childhood's Survivors* collects fairy-tale prose and **poetry** dealing with child abuse and neglect. In her introduction, afterword, and poetry included in the anthology, Windling connects the dark content of fairy tales to violence against children. Her prose-poem rendition of **tale type** ATU 510B, Peau d'Asne, is notable for its literal interpretation of what is only a hint of **incest** in most folk and literary versions of the tale. Windling also is open to diverse and even divergent readings of fairy tales, especially those that cross genres. Her openness to new readings and her informed opinions on fairy tales reinforce her importance in fairy-tale publishing. *See also* Trauma and Therapy.

Further Readings: Datolow, Ellen, and Terri Windling, eds. *Snow White, Blood Red.* New York: Avon Books, 1993; Windling, Terri, ed. *The Armless Maiden and Other Tales for Childhood's Survivors.* New York: Tor, 1995.

Jeana Jorgensen

Wish

Fairy tales often have a magical being granting characters a wish or a set of three wishes. Usually, those who receive them make foolish choices (Motif J2071, Three wishes misused), so they are curses rather than blessings. In one version known since classical times, a mortal, granted a favor by a deity, wishes to have everything he touches turn to gold. The wish turns unlucky when he finds that even the **food** he tries to swallow also turns to metal, and he prays to have the wish removed (ATU 775, Midas' Short-Sighted Wish).

Another early example comes from the Indian *Panchatantra* (first century BCE–sixth century CE), wherein a tree spirit offers a wish to a weaver who threatens to chop it down. After rejecting his friend's advice to be a **king** and rule wisely, the weaver takes his wife's advice and asks for an extra head and pair of arms, so he can work two looms and earn twice the money. As a result, the horrified villagers kill him as a monster.

An internationally distributed tale (ATU 555) collected by Jacob and Wilhelm **Grimm** as "The **Fisherman and His Wife**" has a similar import. In these versions, ambitious humans are allowed to improve their lot. In the Grimms' version, a couple grows richer and more powerful until the wife oversteps herself by wishing to become like God, whereupon they return to their original poor status. A Chinese tale tells of a mason who wishes to become more powerful than anything. He becomes in turn a sun, a cloud, a wind, and finally a rock, wishing to return to normal only when a fellow mason comes to cut him into building stones.

The now-canonical "three wishes" are first documented in a **bawdy tale** recorded in the *Arabian Nights*. Advised by his wife, a man dissatisfied with his male organ first wishes it too big, then to be rid of it, and finally to bring it back to normal. Many bowdlerized versions (AT 750A, The Three Wishes) circulate: in most, the first wish is for a sausage; angrily, the spouse wishes it on the end of the partner's nose; and the third wish cancels the second.

A modern Indian fairy tale combines this **motif** with the Midas touch story: a couple rescues a holy man and receives three wishes. The husband wishes that whatever he touches turns into a pile of money, while the wife asks that what she touches grow a yard long. When their child walks in, the mother makes his nose grotesquely long while the father causes him to crumble into coins. The third wish cancels the first two and brings the child back to life (Ramanujan).

Ironically, the wish motif most often points out the dangers of being dissatisfied with one's humble lifestyle and suggests that the best wish is to ask that things be exactly as they are. *See also* Utopia.

Further Reading: Ramanujan, A. K. *A Flowering Tree and Other Oral Tales from India.* Edited by Stuart Blackburn and Alan Dundes. Berkeley: University of California Press, 1997.

Bill Ellis

Witch

The term "witch" refers to a person who practices witchcraft. In ordinary usage, "witch" may refer to either **women** or **men**, but in folktales and fairy tales, witches are almost always female. Witches appear in both oral and literary tales, as well as in legends. Many witches are evil or hostile figures, functioning as the key obstacle that a male or female protagonist must overcome before the tale's resolution. Witches generally occupy the role of villain in folktales and fairy tales, though they may also function as donor figures or helpers. When a tale features a supernatural male villain, he is usually identified as a **devil** or ogre rather than as a witch. In fact, Stith **Thompson**'s *Motif-Index of Folk-Literature* lists witches (Motif G200, Witch) as a type of ogre.

In folktales and fairy tales, the figure of the witch is closely related to many other powerful, villainous female characters, including the **mother** or stepmother of the male or female protagonist, or the troll or ogre's mother (**ogress**). These strong but hostile female characters may be explicitly identified as a witch (Motif G205, Witch stepmother; Motif P272.1, Witch foster mother). Folktale witches engage in a range of evil and villainous acts, including cursing

The witch in a scene from Engelbert Humperdinck's opera *Königskinder*. Illustration from photograph in Anna Alice Chapin, *Königskinder: A Fairy Tale Founded on the Fairy Opera* (New York: Harper & Brothers Publishers, 1911).

or enchanting male and female protagonists, cooking and eating children (ATU 327A, **Hansel and Gretel**), and turning the hero into stone (ATU 303, The **Twins** or Blood-**Brothers**). Some encounters with witches in folktales and fairy tales are sexually charged, suggesting the connection between female **sexuality** and female power. Other witches from popular folktale and fairy-tale traditions include the witch who locks Rapunzel in the tower (ATU 310, The Maiden in the Tower) and **Snow White**'s stepmother (ATU 709), who uses a magic **mirror**. Many of Walt **Disney**'s animated fairy-tale **film**s feature witches or **sorceresses** as villains, including Ursula in *The Little **Mermaid*** (1989), the jealous stepmother in *Snow White and the Seven Dwarfs* (1937), and evil Maleficent of *Sleeping Beauty* (1959).

The fairy-tale witch serves a dual role as villain and as (sometimes hostile) donor figure or helper. For example, the donor figure in the tale of **The Kind and the Unkind Girls** (ATU 480) is typically an old woman who is sometimes explicitly identified as a witch. In the introductory sections of many tales, a childless **queen** magically conceives with the assistance of a witch. As discussed by Andreas Johns in *Baba Yaga: The Ambiguous Mother and Witch of the Russian Folktale* (2004), **Baba Yaga** is frequently presented as an ambiguous figure because she alternately fills multiple roles as villain and (sometimes hostile) donor.

Good witches or women with magical powers may function both as donor or helper and as the female protagonist, as in the tale of The Magic Flight (ATU 313). Often the daughter of a demon or a witch, the female protagonist uses a combination of talking objects and **transformation**s to escape with the male protagonist. Although she uses magic, the female protagonist/helper in these tales is usually not explicitly referred to as a witch.

The modern visual image of the "**folklore**" witch, made popular by the film representation of the Wicked Witch of the West in *The Wizard of Oz* (1939), is an old hag with a hooked nose and a mole, wearing a pointed hat and flowing robes, and flying on a broomstick. Visual depictions of witches today have evolved considerably from early modern ones; in twentieth-century images, witches are generally clothed with long, flowing **hair** constrained only by a tall, pointed hat. Early modern representations showed witches as naked women with free-flowing, uncovered hair cavorting with demons. Despite their rather fixed visual representations today, witches in folktales and fairy tales may take many forms (Motif G215.1, Seven-headed witch; Motif G219.2, Witch with beard), even animal (Motif G211, Witch in animal form). In traditional prose narratives, there are many similarities between witches and **fairies**.

In 1965, Ruth Manning-Sanders published *A Book of Witches*, a collection of twelve folktales and fairy tales featuring witches. Sometimes miscategorized as folktales, many traditional narratives that focus on witches properly belong to the **legend** genre. Within traditional European witchcraft legends, the initiation process for becoming a witch involves a woman signing her name in the devil's book and exchanging her soul for witchcraft knowledge. (By contrast, in ATU 361, Bear-Skin, a man exchanges his soul for wealth, but ultimately fulfills his bargain and regains his soul.) This definition of a witch comes from Christian demonological thought and was introduced and popularized primarily through the classic witch-hunter's guide, *Malleus Maleficarum* (*The Witch's Hammer*), by Kramer and Sprenger, first published in the late fifteenth century. Witches in legends may be older, unmarried, lower-status women or newly married, high-status women, such as a clergyman's wife. In 1958, in *The Migratory Legends*, Reidar Th. Christiansen identified eleven migratory legend types featuring witches (ML 3030 to ML 3080). These legend types included ML 3035, The Daughter of the Witch, in which the daughter steals milk from a neighbor's cow; ML 3040, The Witch Making Butter, in which the witch steals cream from neighboring parishes to make butter; and ML 3050, At the Witches' Sabbath, which frequently involves the manipulation of a household item into a form of transportation to the Sabbath. These witchcraft legends typically depict a negative view of women. The witch of legend is devious and poses a direct threat to valuable community resources by stealing milk, butter, or children, or by persuading new brides to sell their souls to the devil in exchange for witchcraft knowledge. ***See also*** Cat; Incantation.

Further Readings: Clark, Stuart. *Thinking with Demons: The Idea of Witchcraft in Early Modern Europe.* New York: Clarendon Press, 1997; Johns, Andreas. *Baba Yaga: The Ambiguous Mother and Witch of the Russian Folktale.* New York: Peter Lang, 2004; Manning-Sanders, Ruth. *A Book of Witches.* London: Methuen, 1965; Newall, Venetia, ed. *The Witch Figure: Folklore Essays by a Group of Scholars in England Honouring the 75th Birthday of Katharine M. Briggs.* London: Routledge, 2004; Pócs, Éva. *Fairies and Witches at the Boundary of South-Eastern and Central Europe.* Helsinki: Academia Scientiarum Fennica, 1989; Scherf, Walter. "Die Hexe im Zaubermärchen." *Hexenwelten: Magie und*

Imagination vom 16.–20. Jahrhundert. Edited by Richard van Dülmen. Frankfurt a.M.: Main: Fischer, 1987. 219–52.

Linda J. Lee

The Wizard of Oz (1939)

The Wizard of Oz, an American movie musical produced and directed by Victor Fleming in 1939, is a highly altered and very sentimental **adaptation** of L. Frank **Baum**'s children's **novel**, *The Wonderful Wizard of Oz*. One feature that most critics remark upon is the transition from monochromatic to full color when Dorothy opens the door of her house and sees Oz for the first time. (The reverse occurs when she awakens from her dream at the end of the film.) The monochromatic portions were originally developed using sepia tones, reminiscent of old photographs, and served to make Dorothy's waking life in Kansas appear less vivid than her dream adventures in Oz. This change was even more striking in 1939, when most audiences had seen little color in motion pictures.

The use of color itself brought several changes to the story. For instance, in the novel, Dorothy wears a blue dress, which the Munchkins take as a sign of respect since blue is their national color, and everything they own or wear is blue. In the movie, Judy Garland, who plays Dorothy, is indeed dressed in blue and white, but there seems to be no particular point since the Munchkins instead wear a circuslike array of bright colors. Another change is in the material of the **witch**'s **shoe**s that Dorothy wears. In the novel, they are silver, and Dorothy dons them to save her own shoes from undue wear. In the movie, the "silver shoes" become the more colorful "ruby slippers," and Dorothy is told they will help protect her.

In general, the visual elements were designed primarily to be striking and colorful rather than to reflect Baum's novel, although the costumes of the main characters, especially the Tin Woodsman, attempted to reproduce the appearance of the characters in William Wallace Denslow's original **illustration**s. Terry, the Cairn terrier who portrayed Toto, was selected partially for her resemblance to the dog in Denslow's drawings. Otherwise, the scenic and costume designers were allowed considerable freedom, and created an art deco Emerald City that really is green (in the book it only appears green because everyone wears green goggles) and a countryside where realistic North American elements like split-rail fences and cornfields merge with the fanciful, such as giant hollyhocks and toucans sitting in apple trees.

The musical was not the first adaptation of Baum's novel. Baum himself had helped adapt it as a Broadway play in 1902, and afterward produced a series of silent movies based on *The Wonderful Wizard of Oz* and other novels from his Oz series. The Broadway play introduced one alteration that appeared in the movie—the magical snowfall that saves Dorothy, Toto, and the Lion from the enchanted poppies. Baum's novel has an army of mice rescue them to repay a debt owed to the Lion, which would have been too difficult to enact on stage. Prior to shooting, the motion picture company, Metro-Goldwyn-Mayer (MGM), contacted Baum's widow Maud to seek her approval for their **adaptation**. She understood that motion pictures made many alterations in adapted stories and gave the writers and director considerable leeway.

The writers revised the script many times before creating the movie as it was filmed. The finished **film** presents a very streamlined version of the story. For instance, the Wizard appears several times in a different frightening form on each occasion. Also, Glinda in the novel is the Witch of the South rather than of the North, while the Witch of the North is a jolly grandmother figure who welcomes Dorothy among the Munchkins. Glinda does not appear in Baum's novel until after the Wizard has departed, and then only after Dorothy and her friends embark on yet another long journey to reach her castle.

Director Fleming sought to avoid having his motion picture seem dated. For example, although he kept the writers' gag of the Wicked Witch of the West skywriting on her broom, he cut a scene in which the characters were dancing a jitterbug in the Haunted Forest. Fleming judged the jitterbug to be a fad but skywriting as a new technology likely to endure. (The jitterbug itself was part of an elaborate pun. As the movie was filmed originally, the Wicked Witch sends an insect to bite the characters and give them the "jitters," making them too nervous to resist the attack of the Flying Monkeys.)

The movie has had both its supporters and detractors since the beginning. Devotees of Baum's novels expressed disappointment at the changes made in the film, in particular that the **fairy** domain of Oz became part of a dream. Some were disappointed that the American "**tall tale**" ethos of Baum's story was replaced with greater sentimentality. Others complained that Garland, then sixteen, looked too mature to portray Dorothy (whose age was changed from six to twelve for the motion picture). One MGM official objected to the scene in which Garland sings "Over the Rainbow" because he felt setting the song in a barnyard was in bad taste.

On the other hand, many critics felt the movie's sense of yearning for home gave it more dramatic appeal than a stricter interpretation of Baum's story might have. The novel has some dark moments that might have proven too intense for the audience (as it was, children screamed as the Wicked Witch's green face filled the screen). At times, for example, the novel features **violence**, chases by wild beasts, and the dangerous crossing of a river. Critics also praised the boldness of the set and costume designs, the inventive camera techniques, and the lavish musical score, including a passage from Modest Mussorgsky's *Night on Bald Mountain* when the characters are trying to escape the Wicked Witch's castle. *See also* North American Tales.

Further Reading: Harmetz, Aljean. *The Making of The Wizard of Oz: Movie Magic and Studio Power in the Prime of MGM—and the Miracle of Production.* Introduced by Margaret Hamilton. New York: Knopf, 1977.

Paul James Buczkowski

Wolf. *See* Werewolf, Wolf, Wolves

Woman Warrior

Literary fantasies that accrue around the figure of the woman warrior reveal much about the tensions underlying **gender** roles and representations in the society that produced them. Saxo Grammaticus (c. 1150–1220) epitomizes the assumption that a woman warrior is socially incongruous: "They put toughness before allure, aimed at conflicts instead of kisses, tasted blood, not lips, sought the clash of arms rather than the arm's embrace, fitted to weapons hands that should have been weaving ... and those they could have appeased with looks they attacked with lances" (Saxo Grammaticus, 212). Wherever the woman warrior has appeared in history or **legend**, she has challenged assumptions about both what it means to be a woman and the idea of the heroic. However, for most of history, she has been perceived as a threat to male

"Brunhilde in full armor" by Charles Keeping in *The Treasure of Siegfried* by E. M. Almedingen (J. B. Lippincott Company, 1964). [Copyright © The Bodley Head Ltd./Random House. Used by permission.]

domination, and legends therefore tend to represent her as an anomaly to be tamed or eradicated. Fantasies about warrior women point to an underlying concern with the boundaries between the sexes, emotionally and socially. Because warfare is commonly perceived as a male activity, antithetical to the reproductive and nurturing roles associated with females, many historical women pursued military careers by crossing gender boundaries and adopting male disguises. **Cross-dressing** in disguise is also attributed to legendary figures, such as the Chinese Hua Mulan, and persists widely in modern **fantasy** literature.

While ancient warrior figures such as the Egyptian Hatshesut and Assyrian Semiramis passed into legend, the most famous women warriors are the Amazons, generally depicted in classical literature as a militant, matriarchal tribe dwelling in Asia Minor. A battle between Greeks and Amazons was a common theme in Greek art. Fascination with the horror and beauty of Amazonian otherness was later encapsulated by the Latin poet Virgil in book 1 of the *Aeneid*, wherein the Amazon Penthesilea is depicted as unnatural: she is insane (*furens*), bare-breasted, and "a girl daring to engage men in battle."

Such ambivalence also characterizes depictions in Celtic legend of **Queen** Medb of Connacht. Medb was an extraordinary warrior who, in the *Táin Bó Cúailnge* (*The Tain*, 8th century), is depicted as blinding enemies by her appearance, running faster than horses, being promiscuous with her favors, and acting ruthless in attaining her desires. Stories of more recent female heroes, such as the title character of American **television**'s *Xena: Warrior Princess* (1995–2001), still draw upon such representations.

Modern tales are also inspired by fantasy versions of the Old Norse Valkyries, originally minor deities who did not engage in battle, but in nineteenth-century art became depicted as beautiful blonde warriors on horseback. The concept underlies the appearance and behavior of the warrior maiden Éowyn in J. R. R. **Tolkien**'s *The Return of the King* (1955): wounded when bravely facing and defeating the Witch-**king** of Angmar at the Battle of Pelennor Fields, her eventual recuperation depends on falling in love, and hence she has similarities with the Valkyrie Brynhildr, a main character in the *Völsunga Saga* (13th century).

Modern popular culture has produced comic book and television heroines such as Wonder Woman. As with earlier legendary figures, Wonder Woman mingled strength and autonomy with physical beauty and susceptibility to the lures of femininity, traits more recently exemplified by the heroine of television's *Buffy the Vampire Slayer* (1997–2003). Likewise, in changing an ancient tale about Confucian filial piety into an affirmation of Western girl-next-door femininity, the **Walt Disney Company**'s animated film *Mulan* (1998) illustrates how stories about women warriors continue to be shaped by cultural ideology. *See also* Clothing; *Pear ta ma 'on maf.*

Further Readings: Brocklebank, Lisa. "Disney's *Mulan*—the 'True' Deconstructed Heroine?" *Marvels & Tales* 14 (2000): 268–83; Saxo Grammaticus. *The History of the Danes.* Translated by Peter Fisher. Edited by Hilda Ellis Davidson. Volume 1. Cambridge: Boydell and Brewer, 1979; Velay-Vallantin, Catherine. *La fille en garçon.* Carcassonne: GARAE/Hésiode, 1992.

John Stephens

Women

Traditional **folklore** scholarship emphasized the role of women as gatekeepers: healers, midwives, matchmakers, and lament singers, implying generic hierarchies based on **gender**. Although folklorists paid lip service to the images and roles traditionally ascribed to women, research on these topics remained limited until the 1970s, when **feminism** gave rise to folklore research that focused new attention on women. Feminist scholars of folklore argued that genre systems are not neutral but are part of a politics of interpretation that give meaning and authority to the categories associated with women, and thus appear to legitimize the way in which women are represented and valued in specific cultures. In the study of folktales and fairy tales, scholars began to reconsider commonly held notions about women and their relationship to these genres, at first focusing critically on the image of women in folktales and fairy tales but ultimately using gender-based perspectives to explore a wider range of important issues.

Representations of Women

As feminist critics pointed out, representations of women in folktales and fairy tales have been based on extreme polarizations and served to perpetuate sexist stereotypes. While heroines who are passive and beautiful have typically belonged to the realm of the good, female characters who are active and strong have usually signaled evil. Ruth B. Bottigheimer's study of "Grimms' bad girls," for instance, has shown how even an activity such as speaking can characterize a female figure as "bad," in contrast to the "good girl," who is silent (or silenced). The oft-studied subgenre of the Innocent Persecuted Heroine—exemplified by fairy tales such as "Rapunzel," "**Sleeping Beauty**," "**Cinderella**," and "The Maiden without Hands"—is a particularly pertinent group of narratives for exploring the image of women. These tales represent the ideal of the passive beauty who silently suffers for her goodness and often ends up entering into **marriage** with a noble man.

The polarization of women as either good or evil is also evident in powerful female agents who have become classic fairy-tale stereotypes. This duality is codified in Stith **Thompson**'s *Motif-Index of Folk-Literature*, where the figure of the "Cruel stepmother" (Motif S31) stands in contrast to the figure of the beneficent "**fairy** godmother" (Motif F311.1), who is described as the "attendant good fairy." These stereotypical female figures sometimes define the poles of persecution and rescue in Cinderella tales, where the innocent young woman is abused by one female and outfitted for the prince's ball by the other.

The **witch** has also defined how the role of women in fairy tales has been understood. Sometimes the role of witch merges with that of cruel stepmother (Motif G205, Witch stepmother; Motif P272.1, Witch foster **mother**). In popular imagination, which has been influenced in particular by fairy-tale **illustration**s and **animation**, the witch has an ugly physical appearance, aligning her in the iconography of the classical fairy tale with the realm of evil. Her affinity for **cannibalism**, as in the case of "**Hansel and Gretel**," also confirms her malevolent nature. The **Baba Yaga** of **Russian tales** and East Slavic lore is another well-known witch with cannibalistic cravings, which appears to underline the identification of female power with evil. However, like witch figures in general, Baba Yaga is actually a highly ambiguous character who can act not only as an adversary but also as a helper—a role that is often overlooked. In fact, identifying stereotypes and generalizing their presence in all folktales and fairy tales threatened to obscure the ambiguity, complexity, and diversity of women characters as much as the biases of traditional folktale scholarship had done.

Scholarship on Women in Folktales and Fairy Tales

Before the introduction of feminist scholarship in the 1970s, scholarly accounts of female representation in folktales showed a demonstrable bias against women. For example, the work of important scholars such as Stith Thompson and Max **Lüthi** dealt in large measure with male protagonists. Even in 1976—in the very midst of the debate about fairy tales inspired by feminism—Bruno **Betteheim**'s popular and influential study, *The Uses of Enchantment: The Meaning and Importance of Fairy Tales*, ignored serious questions about **gender** and insisted that the gender of the protagonist is insignificant for the young readers of fairy tales. The early feminist critique, however, was based on the premise that the biased portrayal of women in folktales and fairy tales was complicit in the socialization process, offering children skewed models of gender norms and behavior that advantaged boys and disadvantaged girls. Folktale scholarship seemed also to be implicated in perpetuating the bias, since it had given inadequate attention to women and questions of gender, and because its tools and methods institutionalized the bias.

One major example of the built-in scholarly bias against women was the system for classifying folktales developed by Antti **Aarne** and Stith Thompson. Feminist folklorists perceived the gendered language used in the Aarne-Thompson index as sexist. The names of tale types referring explicitly to **men** or to women seem to stress the significance of the male's role and diminish the nature of female roles. For instance, whereas AT 400 is labeled The Man on a Quest for His Lost Wife, its counterpart, AT 425, is not called The Woman on a Quest for Her Lost Husband. Instead, it carries the less descriptive, less heroic label: The Search for the Lost Husband—from which the presence of the female has been erased entirely. The assumption implicit in this—that is, that male heroes are the main actors and are therefore more important—has arguably affected the way tales have been assessed and selected for publication. For example, in her *Folktales of Hungary* (1965), Linda **Dégh** explains that she did not generally include **märchen** with female protagonists because these tales were less representative than those featuring male heroes.

The role of **collectors** and **editors** in shaping our understanding of the relationship between women and fairy tales cannot be underestimated. Jacob and Wilhelm **Grimm**, for example, edited and revised the fairy tales collected in their ***Kinder- und Hausmärchen*** (*Children's and Household Tales*, 1812–15), often creating and reinforcing the very images of female characters that came under fire from feminist scholarship. Similarly, the degree to which women-centered tales or stories collected from women storytellers find a place in editions and anthologies depends on the choices made by individual collectors and editors. Research since the 1970s has demonstrated that many of the classic tales that have shaped our view of women in fairy tales were published in collections (frequently from the nineteenth century) that were selected and edited by men, with the consequence that stories about strong girls and women or those told from a female perspective were obscured. In light of these findings, scholars went in quest of woman-centered tales and shifted their focus from women as passive recipients of fairy tales with passive heroines to women as active creators of their own fairy-tale tradition.

Women As Storytellers and Authors

The interest in women as storytellers that emerged from feminist folklore scholarship was important but not pioneering. Russian and Eastern European scholars had already considered the relationship between gender and traditional **storytelling**, most notably in the work of Mark Azadovskii, who examined the psychology and **performance** of a female narrator as early as 1928 in his book *Eine sibirische Märchenerzählerin* (translated in 1974 as *A Siberian Tale Teller*). In the United States, Zora Neale **Hurston** used her ethnographic training to document African American folklore and described the speech styles and verbal skills of African American women in *Mules and Men* (1935). And in *Folktales and Society* (1969), Linda Dégh focused on the narratives of a Hungarian folk community and astutely showed her main informant Zsuzsanna Palko's performance and repertoire, crossing over the boundaries of passive and active bearers of tradition. One of the most important studies in the period after 1970 was Margaret A. Mills's *Rhetorics and Politics in Afghan Traditional Storytelling* (1989). Attuned to the relationship of gender and storytelling, Mills offered the significant finding that men tend to tell stories about men while women tell stories about women and men.

In the past, the paucity of material collected from women was not due solely to the bias of male collectors and editors. Also at work was the fieldworker's limited awareness of spatial organization and gender. Male folklorists typically found their informants in public places. However, because women's spatial experience was confined to domestic space, women were not targeted as the core group of informants. The recent awareness in feminist ethnography, situated around the assumption that the fieldworkers themselves are both a part of the field data and that they even form the data, made scholars reconsider their approaches to and methodologies in their **fieldwork**. In earlier examples of fieldwork, a collector consulted women only when no male informant was available, and this created a secondary role for the female informants. Early fieldworkers did not recognize that in most societies, narrating fairy tales and folktales is a performance by women for women and children. Performances such as these in traditional societies lend themselves especially to the study of socialization, where questions of gender and storytelling intersect in a significant way. Today, many children learn fairy tales through their mothers, grandmothers, and female kin as well as from kindergarten and grade-school teachers.

Collectors, editors, and translators have attempted to correct the neglect of women storytellers and women-centered tales. Numerous editions and anthologies have highlighted tales about women. These include works such as *Schneewittchen hat viele Schwestern: Frauengestalten in europäischen Märchen* (*Snow White Has Many Sisters: Female Characters in*

European Fairy Tales, 1988) by Ines Köhler-Zülch and Christine Shojaei Kawan; *Europäische Frauenmärchen* (*European Tales about Women*, 1996) by Sigrid Früh; and *Fearless Girls, Wise Women, and Beloved Sisters: Heroines in Folktales from around the World* (1998) by Kathleen Ragan—to name just a few. One explicit purpose of these collections is to present fairy-tale heroines who disprove the stereotype of passive women, presenting a richer and more complex alternative to the one-dimensional view of women in fairy tales. Other works have highlighted tales told by women. Hasan El-Shamy, for example, published an important collection of titled *Tales Arab Women Tell and the Behavioral Patterns They Portray* (1999).

The female voice in storytelling has also been rediscovered by literary scholars. Marina **Warner**, in *From the Beast to the Blonde: On Fairy Tales and Their Tellers* (1994), explores the idea of the female voice in storytelling and the neglected tradition of women's fairy tales. In this, she joins scholars such as Lewis C. Seifert, whose work rekindled interest in the important **literary fairy tale**s by French women in the seventeenth and eighteenth centuries, and Jeannine Blackwell and Shawn C. Jarvis, who have helped to recover fairy tales by German women of the eighteenth and nineteenth centuries. Obscured by the canonical tales of Charles **Perrault** and the Brothers Grimm, the female fairy-tale tradition in European literature shows that women have been not only prolific in their production of fairy tales but also engaged very early on with questions of gender and female representation. These tales constitute a vital resource for investigating women's production of fairy tales and rethinking the history of the literary fairy tale.

The same feminist impulses that stimulated scholarly interest in women's tales have also given rise to a host of **feminist tales**. Women writers such as Margaret **Atwood** (Canada), Angela **Carter** (UK), Anne **Sexton** (United States), Carmen **Martín Gaite** (Spain), Ana María **Matute** (Spain), Luisa **Valenzuela** (Argentina), and Suniti **Namjoshi** (India/UK) have variously challenged, questioned, and subverted the classical fairy-tale tradition and the stereotypes associated with it—especially the traditional fairy-tale heroine and her submission to patriarchal expectations. The role of women in fairy tales has also been reevaluated in the realm of popular culture, where the animated **film**s of Walt **Disney** and the **Walt Disney Company** have been so influential. Long the purveyor of the passive-beauty stereotype, Disney made several stabs at projecting a "feminist" heroine in the late twentieth-century—particularly in *Mulan* (1998). In introducing Mulan, the legendary Chinese **woman warrior**, Disney's effort to replace the usual saccharine fairy-tale heroine with a strong, independent, and brave girl is evident. Nonetheless, Disney's animated fairy-tale **adaptation**s—including the classics *Snow White and the Seven Dwarfs* (1937), *Cinderella* (1950), and *Sleeping Beauty* (1959)—remain immensely popular on a global scale and perpetuate what many folklorists and critics consider to be problematic female stereotypes. *See also* The Kind and the Unkind Girls; Mother Goose; Mother Holle; Princess; Queen; Salon; Sisters.

Further Readings: Bacchilega, Cristina. *Postmodern Fairy Tales: Gender and Narrative Strategies*. Philadelphia: University of Pennsylvania Press, 1999; Bacchilega, Cristina, and Steven Swann Jones, eds. *Perspectives on the Innocent Persecuted Heroine in Fairy Tales*. Special issue of *Western Folklore* 52.1 (1993); Bernheimer, Kate, ed. *Mirror, Mirror on the Wall: Women Writers Explore Their Favorite Fairy Tales*. 2nd edition. New York: Anchor, 2002; Bottigheimer, Ruth B. *Grimms' Bad Girls and Bold Boys: The Moral and Social Vision of the Tales*. New Haven, CT: Yale University Press, 1987; Farrer, Claire R., ed. *Women and Folklore: Images and Genres*. Austin: University of Texas Press, 1975; Haase, Donald, ed. *Fairy Tales and Feminism: New Approaches*. Detroit: Wayne State University Press, 2004;

Harries, Elizabeth Wanning. *Twice upon a Time: Women Writers and the History of the Fairy Tale*. Princeton, NJ: Princeton University Press, 2001; Jordan, Rosan A., and Susan Kalcik, eds. *Women's Folklore, Women's Culture*. Philadelphia: University of Pennsylvania Press, 1985. 53–66; Ross, Deborah. "Escape from Wonderland: Disney and the Female Imagination." *Marvels & Tales* 18 (2004): 53–66; Soliño, María Elena. *Women and Children First: Spanish Women Writers and the Fairy Tale Tradition*. Potomac, MD: Scripta Humanistica, 2002; Warner, Marina. *From the Beast to the Blonde: On Fairy Tales and Their Tellers*. New York: Farrar Straus and Giroux, 1994.

Hande Birkalan-Gedik

Wonder Tale

"Wonder tale" is often used interchangeably with the terms "**folktale**," "**fairy tale**," and "**märchen**." Although all four (sub)genres include many of the same **tale type**s, the term "wonder tale" derives from a particular set of historical circumstances and cannot be said to be synonymous with any of these. At its most basic, the wonder tale can be seen as comprising the tale types represented by ATU numbers 300–749 in Hans-Jörg Uther's *The Types of International Folktales* (2004)—that is, the category of folktales referred to as "Tales of Magic." But implicit in the use of the term "wonder tale," like the use of the more inclusive "märchen," is the fundamental imperative of orality—the hallmark of folkloristics and the marker of **authenticity**. Thematically, the fairy tales, or *contes de fées*, of the primarily female writers of the seventeenth- and eighteenth-century French nobility were concerned with aspects of the marvelous—**transformation**s and wonder. However, this was the precise time at which wonders were losing ground in the court. In fact, tales of wonder had shifted from being constitutive of the elite classes in Europe to being seen as that which defined the "**folk**" and were relegated to the margins. Fallen from favor in the courts, however, the marvelous became a marker of authenticity to those folklorists engaged in cobbling together not only a new discipline but new nations. According to this view, the uncontaminated folk, the purveyors of these tales of wonder, were, in their vulgar fascination with the marvelous, the bearers of authenticity. The logic of this conceptualization of the vulgar still underscores much of **folklore** scholarship today and is certainly critical to it historically: into the vulgar were dumped a host of characters—**women**, the old, **peasant**s, illiterates, and children—the stock characters in the folklore about folklore; and these constituted the ideal **informant**s.

Jacob and Wilhelm **Grimm** disparaged the eighteenth-century *Cabinet des fées* (*The Fairies' Cabinet*, 1785–89), the forty-one-volume collection of French fairy tales in which **fairies** are prominent as initiators and arbiters on issues of **gender**, reproduction, and social relations, and gave them scant attention. In comparison to the career of the fairy tale, seen as a literary genre of overworked, affected renditions of more authentic oral versions, the wonder tale was and continues to be privileged among folklorists.

Vladimir **Propp**'s work on the wonder tale (*volshebnaya skazka*) attempted to disassociate the generic requirements from plot and typological constraints, and locate them in structure, history, and ritual. A specifically oral genre defined by an invariable structure, the wonder tale, as defined by Propp, "begins with some harm or villany . . . and develops through the hero's departure from home and encounters with the donor, who provides him with a magic agent that helps the hero find the object of the search. Further along, the tale includes combat with an adversary . . . a return, and a pursuit" (Propp, 102). Propp's insistence that wonder tales be treated not in isolation but in relation to one another, and that they, in fact, constitute a specific genre, is a break from the typological method. However, Propp's database, limited to the 100 **literary fairy tale**s of Aleksandr **Afanas'ev**'s collection, which was itself highly influenced by the organizational methods and ideological premises established by the Grimms, tends to compromise the specific structural paradigm. The structuralist approach to the wonder tale, however, again subsumes the notion of wonder to a rationalizing enterprise.

Tzvetan Todorov, in his examination of the literary genre he calls "the fantastic," attempts to dislodge the marvelous from its rationalist moorings and suggests that the marvelous (the realm of wonder) operates according to different rules, giving it a separate ontological logic. Todorov's approach, which reopens the discussion of the wonder tale in terms of wonders not explained according to the known laws of nature, exposes both the typological and structuralist approaches to the wonder tale as different articulations of a modern, rationalizing enterprise.

Although much of current fairy-tale scholarship in folklore still maintains a mandatory rupture between the oral and the literary and still relies on Richard M. **Dorson**'s fifty-year-old model of folk narrative, which relegates the folktale in general and thus the wonder tale to the realm of pure fiction, there are some scholars, particularly those working in an interdisciplinary mode, who are seeking to expand the notion of the fairy tale and the wonder tale to reincorporate the affective aspect of wonder. In *Why Fairy Tales Stick: The Evolution and Relevance of a Genre*, Jack **Zipes** combines typological and structuralist approaches to the wonder tale and suggests that all contribute "to induce *wonder* and *hope* for change" (Zipes, 50). Differentiating between the literary fairy tale and the oral wonder tale, Zipes asserts, "It is this earthy, sensual, and secular sense of wonder and hope that distinguished the wonder tales from other oral tales such as the **legend**, the fable, the **anecdote**, and the **myth**.... In the oral wonder tale, we are to marvel about the workings of the universe where anything can happen at anytime, and these *fortunate* and *unfortunate* events are never really explained" (Zipes, 50–51).

The term "wonder tale," thus, is extremely protean. It can serve to identify an affect or mood, a structure, or a genre; or it can be used to distinguish oral versions of tales from literary. There is overlap with other designations. When referring to the wonder tale, then, the context of its use is mandatory. *See also* Blood; Childhood and Children; Fantasy; Magical Realism; Oral Tradition; Structuralism.

Further Readings: Propp, Vladimir. *Theory and History of Folklore*. Translated by Ariadna Y. Martin and Richard P. Martin. Minneapolis: University of Minnesota Press, 1984; Todorov, Tzvetan. *The Fantastic: A Structural Approach to a Literary Genre*. Ithaca, NY: Cornell University Press, 1975; Zipes, Jack. *Why Fairy Tales Stick: The Evolution and Relevance of a Genre*. New York: Routledge, 2006.

JoAnn Conrad

Woolf, Virginia (1882–1941)

Readers of English author Virginia Woolf's modernist fictions are often surprised by her investment in fairy tales. Yet she was brought up on the **animal tale**s written by her mother, Julia Duckworth Stephens, and on her "aunt" Anne Thackeray **Ritchie**'s realistic updating of traditional fairy tales. Woolf's personal library included an inscribed copy of Ritchie's *Five Old Friends and a Young **Prince*** (1868), a vindication of five old fairy-tale "friends" that Anne had modernized and given to Julia.

In her **novel** *To the Lighthouse* (1927), fairy tales are associated with the matriarch drawn from Woolf's memories of her **mother**. Drained by her husband's demands, Mrs. Ramsay has "only strength enough to move her finger, in exquisite abandonment to exhaustion, across the page of [the] **Grimm** fairy story" she reads to her son James ("The Window"). Her choice of "the story of the **Fisherman and his Wife**" underscores the infectious paralysis induced by her husband: "'The man's heart grew heavy,' she reads aloud, 'and he would not go.'" Mrs. Ramsay later assures her daughter Cam that "the **fairies** would love" a "horrid" boar's skull she has covered with her shawl in an attempt to create a soothing dreamscape with "bells ringing and birds singing and little goats and antelopes" ("The Window"). This transformative fantasy is cruelly undercut in the novel's last section ("Time Passes"). But it is sustained in "Nurse Lugton's Curtain," a 1924 tale Woolf wrote for a niece. There, antelopes, zebras, giraffes, and other "lovely beasts" float off a blue cloth held by the sleeper who briefly becomes "the great **ogress** . . . called Lugton." *See also* English Tales.

Further Readings: Martin, Ann. *Red Riding Hood and the Wolf in Bed: Modernism's Fairy Tales.* Toronto: University of Toronto Press, 2006; ———. "Sleeping Beauty in a Green Dress: Mrs. Dalloway and Fairy Tale Configurations of Desire." *Virginia Woolf Out of Bounds: Selected Papers from the Tenth Annual Conference on Virginia Woolf.* Edited by Jessica Berman and Jane Goldman. New York: Pace University Press, 2001. 25–31.

U. C. Knoepflmacher

Wossidlo, Richard (1859–1939)

A grammar-school teacher and folklorist, Richard Wossidlo is recognized as one of the fathers and most significant field researchers of German-speaking **folklore** studies. Influenced by the collection of Karl Bartsch—*Sagen, Märchen und Gebräuche aus Meklenburg* (*Legends, Fairy Tales and Customs from Mecklenburg*, 1879–80)—Wossidlo documented the folk culture and folklife of Mecklenburg in northeastern Germany, in particular its oral-narrative and linguistic traditions. Familiar with the Low German language and the life of his fellow countrymen, Wossidlo did not confine himself to editing the material gathered by correspondents but also did his own **fieldwork**. In this way, he overcame the gap between armchair scholars and unschooled **collectors**, such as elementary-school teachers, who collected on behalf of academic **editors**. For decades, folklorists were guided by Wossidlo's method of fieldwork, which he wrote about in his essay of 1906, "Über die Technik des Sammelns volkstümlicher Überlieferungen" ("On the Technique of Collecting Folk Traditions."

Wossidlo worked as a grammar-school teacher of Latin and Greek in Waren/Lake Müritz. Between 1885 and 1939, he traveled to almost every village in Mecklenburg and had more than 5,000 **informant**s tell about their local traditions. Wossidlo's network of correspondents included hundreds of helpers. With the rise of the *Heimatbewegung* (regional movement), he was supported by Low German organizations, and even today in the eyes of Mecklenburgians, Wossidlo stands alongside the writer Fritz Reuter for his role in preserving the region's cultural heritage.

Wossidlo's collection contained approximately one million notes on small pieces of paper, which he categorized into functional groups and **motif**s. His achievement documented folktales, folk songs, proverbs and sayings, regional customs, folk beliefs, folk medicine, and the lives of children, peasants, wage workers, fishermen, craftsmen, and much more.

Wossidlo also aimed to compile a comprehensive dictionary of the eastern Low German dialect and collected material folk culture, thus laying the foundation for the folklore museums of Mecklenburg. When compared to the research of other regions, Wossidlo's collection stands apart because of its unusual breadth, depth, and long period of data collection. The collection's value lies in its having become the central registry of the oral repertoire of Mecklenburg. Even today, it is deemed "authentic" because it is based upon native language and a broad range of socially differentiated informants. In a European context, Wossidlo's corpus may be compared with the collection of the Dane Evald **Tang Kristensen** and the Estonian priest Jakob Hurt.

In 1906, Wossidlo was awarded an honorary doctorate for his multivolume work on the folk traditions of Mecklenburg, *Mecklenburgische Volksüberlieferungen* (4 volumes; *Folk Traditions of Mecklenburg*, 1897–31). The first volume about **riddle**s is regarded as the deepest regional collection of the genre; the second volume represents folklore about animals; and the third and fourth deal with the folklore addressed to (or practiced by) children. From 1900 onward, Wossidlo focused on collecting **legend**s. His plan for an edition of legends envisioned eight volumes, but he could finish only two of them. Although characterized as a *Volksbuch* (a book for the folk) and written in Low German, his legend project is more scholarly than enjoyable because of his morphological method of editing. Instead of reproducing singular, written narratives, Wossidlo presented his material by filling up the structural elements of a **tale type** with multiple **variant**s.

During World War II, Wossidlo edited a collection dealing with the folklore of sailors. In 1952, his estate was brought to Rostock, where it served as basis for the Wossidlo-Forschungsstelle (Wossidlo Research Center), which became, under Wolfgang Steinitz, an Annex of the Institut für deutsche Volkskunde (Institute for German Folklore Studies) of the German Academy of Sciences in Berlin. In the former German Democratic Republic, the socially critical legends of the Wossidlo corpus were selectively published by Gisela Schneidewind as *Herr und Knecht: Antifeudale Sagen aus Mecklenburg* (*Lord and Servant: Antifeudal Legends from Mecklenburg*, 1960). In the Federal Republic of Germany, Gottfried Henßen, the founder of the Zentralarchiv der deutschen Volkserzählung (Central Archives for German Folk Narrative) in Marburg, edited Wossidlo's fairy tales and humorous tales and **anecdote**s, which he had copied in 1937. These were published in 1957 as *Mecklenburger erzählen: Märchen, Schwänke und Schnurren aus der Sammlung Richard Wossidlos* (*Mecklenburg Storytelling: Fairy Tales, Jests, and Humorous Tales from the Collection of Richard Wossidlo*). Siegfried Neumann, a member of the Wossidlo-Forschungsstelle since 1957, published rich source material from Wossidlo's correspondents in *Mecklenburgische Volksmärchen* (*Mecklenburg Folktales*, 1971) and *Volksschwänke aus Mecklenburg* (*Humorous Folktales from Mecklenburg*, 1963). After German unification, Wossidlo's estate became part of the University of Rostock. *See also* Archives; German Tales.

Further Readings: Department of European Ethnology (Wossidlo Arvhive) at the University of Rostock. http://www.phf.uni-rostock.de/ivk/; Schmitt, Christoph. "Universitätseinrichtung mit Landesstellenfunktion: Das Institut für Volkskunde (Wossidlo-Archiv) in Rostock." *Volkskundliche Forschung und Praxis im regionalen Kontext: Eine Präsentation der "Landesstellen" im deutschsprachigen Raum.* Edited by Johannes Moser and Jens Stöcker. Dresden: Thelem, 2005. 111–24; Wossidlo, Richard. "Über die Technik des Sammelns volkstümlicher Überlieferungen." *Zeitschrift des Vereins für Volkskunde* 16 (1906): 1–24.

Christoph Schmitt

Wú Chéng'ēn (c. 1500–1582)

Wú Chéng'ēn was a celebrated Chinese novelist and poet who lived during the Ming dynasty (1368–1644). Born into a poor scholar-merchant family in Jingsu province, Wú showed a deep lifelong interest in marvels and stories of anomalies. He failed the civil service examinations but produced literary works throughout his life, including prose, poetry, and novels.

His most influential work is the 100-chapter **novel** *Xī Yóu Jì* (or *Hsi Yu Chi, Journey to the West*, originally published in 1592), which is based on the popularly circulated oral and written vernacular narratives of an actual seventh-century pilgrimage to India by the Buddhist monk Xuán Zàng (or Tripitaka, 596–664). Reflecting and enriching these folk narratives, Wú recounts the fantastic and mythical journey of Xuán Zàng and his four guardians, namely, Monkey, Pigsy, Sha Monk, and the Dragon Horse. The pilgrims fight demons and experience eighty-one calamities before they reach India and acquire Mahayana Buddhist scriptures.

The journey presents a realm of demons, celestial deities, and religious immortals, arranged hierarchically by using syncretistic Taoist and Buddhist parameters and Confucian moral qualities, such as the degree of self-cultivation toward immorality, karma, and merits possessed by individuals, and the level of insight into truth and enlightenment. Many of the supernatural beings and related stories reflect Chinese mythology, the Taoist pantheon, folk beliefs, and folktales still known today.

The most significant and beloved character created by Wú is the heaven-born Stone Monkey or Sūn Wùkōng (Aware of Vacuity). Subject to no one, Monkey challenges heaven and demands the title "Great Sage, Equal to Heaven." Following the havoc he creates in the celestial palace, Monkey is subdued and trapped under a magic mountain by Buddha and later serves as Xuán Zàng's guardian to accomplish the journey. Scholarly research has focused on tracing the origin of Monkey and related monkey lore in **oral tradition** and historical-religious records. Scholars have also commented on Monkey's **trickster** nature, which is evident in his comical, mischievous, rebellious, and ambivalent behavior. Born outside of the celestial hierarchy, Monkey is confronted by the established power of the central structure but possesses the potentially subversive ability to destabilize the celestial system. When he is subjugated and serves the merit-cultivating journey, Monkey becomes a mediator capable of moving between the realms of the demonic and the divine. His disruptive power becomes an important and constructive force in support of the central structure. Situated in a religious and mythological context, the image of Monkey bears comparison to other trickster tales. *See also* Chinese Tales.

Further Readings: Campany, Rob. "Demons, Gods, and Pilgrims: The Demonology of the Hsi-yu Chi." *Chinese Literature: Essays, Articles, Reviews* 7.1–2 (1985): 95–115; Dudbridge, Glen. *The Hsi-yu Chi: A Study of Antecedents to the Sixteenth-Century Chinese Novel.* Cambridge: Cambridge University Press, 1977; Lai, Whalen. "From Protean Ape to Handsome Saint: The Monkey King." *Asian Folklore Studies* 53 (1994): 29–65; Shahar, Meir. "The Lingyin Si Monkey Disciples and the Origins of Sun Wukong." *Harvard Journal of Asiatic Studies* 52 (1992): 193–224.

Jing Li

Y

Yanagita Kunio (1875–1962)

Born in Hyōgo Prefecture and the sixth son of a physician and scholar, Yanagita Kunio is often described as the founder of **folklore** studies in Japan. After graduating from Tokyo Imperial University in 1900, Yanagita spent almost twenty years working as a bureaucrat in the Ministry of Agriculture and Commerce. He subsequently pursued a career as a journalist until deciding, in the early 1930s, to dedicate himself exclusively to folklore research. In 1934, he gave a series of lectures, published the same year as *Minkandenshōron* (*Theories on Popular Oral Tradition*), in which he introduced British and other European research and outlined a framework for the systematic collection and classification of **folktale**s in Japan. In 1935, Yanagita founded the journal *Minkandenshō* (*Oral Tradition*), which was instrumental in establishing folklore studies as a nationwide discipline in Japan.

Yanagita's engagement with folktales began in 1910 with the publication of *Tōno Monogatari* (*The Legends of Tōno*). In retelling the tales of Tōno, Yanagita wanted to preserve something of Japan's rapidly disappearing premodern culture and **oral tradition**s. He did not do this, however, without feeling compelled to "improve" the stories of his interlocutor, Sasaki Kizen (also known as Sasaki Kyōseki). Reworking and radically altering the tales as he prepared them for publication, Yanagita produced what is now regarded as both a literary masterpiece and a folklore classic.

During his long and distinguished career, Yanagita published a vast number of articles and books including, in 1948, *Nihon mukashibanashi meii* (*An Index of Japanese Folk Tales*). ***See also*** Collecting, Collectors; Japanese Tales; Seki Keigo.

Further Reading: Ivy, Marilyn. "Ghastly Insufficiencies: *Tōno Monogatari* and the Origins of Nativist Ethnology." *Discourses of the Vanishing: Modernity, Phantasm, Japan.* Chicago: University of Chicago Press, 1995. 66–97.

Marc Sebastian-Jones

Yeats, William Butler (1865–1939)

Best known for his Nobel Prize-winning **poetry**, William Butler Yeats had a lifetime association with, and affinity for, the **folklore** of his native Ireland. As a young man, he gained some notoriety for his second collection of poetry, *The Wanderings of Oisin and*

Other Poems (1889), the title composition of which utilized legendary figures of Ireland's pagan past and specifically of the Fenian cycle to examine the burgeoning identity of the modern Irish people. At the same time, in concord with figures like Lady Isabella Augusta Persse **Gregory** and the noted playwright John Millington Synge, Yeats began **collecting** and compiling Irish folktales. He produced a number of works along these lines, including *Fairy and Folktales of the Irish Peasantry* (1888) and his lauded exploration of the repertoire of storyteller Paddy Flynn, *The Celtic Twilight: Men and Women, Ghouls and Faeries* (1893).

His interest in folklore is usually associated with his younger, Romantic period, whereas later in life, he is more strongly linked with modernist figures such as Ezra Pound and T. S. Eliot. Although Yeats published less specifically on the topic of folklore in the second half of his life, he upheld his interest, participating in nationalist activities and maintaining a connection to folklorist Douglas Hyde, founder of the Gaelic League and the first president of Ireland. *See also* Celtic Tales; Nationalism.

Further Reading: Foster, R. F. *W. B. Yeats: A Life*. 2 volumes. London: Oxford University Press, 1996–2003.

Adam Zolkover

Yep, Laurence (1948–)

Laurence Yep, a Chinese American writer of books for young adults and children, has used folktales and Chinese **myth**s to describe the immigrant experience in America. Born and raised in San Francisco, he earned a PhD in English from the State University of New York at Buffalo and is married to the writer Joanne Ryder. Yep has written in a variety of genres, including science fiction, historical fiction, and **fantasy**. The themes and locations of many of his stories are informed by his childhood Chinatown, and he has produced collections of Chinese American immigrants' folk stories, including *The Rainbow People* (1989) and *Tongues of Jade* (1991).

Yep explores the Asian American's use of **folklore** not only to keep rooted in the old country but also to comprehend the new cultural experiences that are encountered; he does this with humor and is especially associated with the **trickster** figure. His books address not only the Asian American reader but all who learn of the difficulties of immigration and the benefits of strong imagination, fantasy, and mythology from their past. Yep often writes in series, such as the nine novels that make up the Golden Mountain Chronicles, which follow a century and a half of American history and seven generations of Chinese Americans. The Dragon series, including *Dragon of the Lost Sea* (1982), *Dragon Steel* (1985), and *Dragon Cauldron* (1991), relates a fantasy of a **princess** seeking her home. **Dragon**s in Yep's writing characterize the imaginative challenge of encountering the new with the magic of the past. *See also* Race and Ethnicity; Young Adult Fiction.

Further Reading: LaFaye, Alexandria. "The 'Double Happiness' of Biculturalism in Chinese American Novels." *Bookbird: A Journal of International Children's Literature* 37.2 (1999): 12–17.

George Bodmer

Yolen, Jane (1939–)

Jane Yolen is an American poet, author, and editor renowned for her innovative work with folktales, fairy tales, and **fantasy**. While many of her stories and **novel**s are marketed as **children's literature** and **young adult fiction**, her fiction and her **poetry** appeal to readers across age groups and in other categories. She has been called the Hans Christian **Andersen** of America, and she has written nearly 300 books, ranging from illustrated children's stories to adult science-fiction novels. Her handling of folktales, fairy tales, and folkloric materials is complex, dynamic, and sensitive.

A graduate of Smith College in 1960, Yolen worked first as an editor before becoming a professional fiction writer in the early 1960s. Though her fiction has won many awards, ranging from the Caldecott Medal and Mythopoeic Fantasy Awards to the World Fantasy Award and Nebula Awards, Yolen is also known for her nonfiction. Among her historical and biographical writing, a fitting example is *The Perfect Wizard* (2004), a biography of Hans Christian Andersen. Another relevant example is *Touch Magic: Fantasy,* **Faerie,** *and Folklore in the Literature of Childhood* (1981), a book of essays exploring the richness and relevance of **folklore** and **storytelling**.

Yolen's numerous interactions with folk narrative can be classified in several ways: oral tales, redacted tales, and **literary fairy tale**s. An example of the first is her edited collection, *Favorite Folktales from Around the World* (1986). The majority of her tales, however, depart substantially from their orally told originals; the next level of distinction depends upon whether an initial tale is still visible underneath the additions. Much of Yolen's fairy-tale-related work—including nonfiction prose, poetry, and tales—is available in the anthology *Once upon a Time She Said* (2005).

The redacted tales Yolen writes often challenge normative assumptions through subtle changes in traditional stories. "Allerleirauh" (1995), for instance, is a revision of ATU 510B (Peau d'Asne) with a pessimistic ending, asserting that this is not a fairy tale—father-daughter **incest** sometimes *does* happen. The critique is implicit within the text rather than presented through the usual happy ending. "Snow in Summer" (2000), a retelling of "**Snow White**" set in the American South, features a protagonist who not only recognizes her disguised stepmother but has the courage to kill her and remain with her seven miner friends rather than marrying. A retelling of an **animal bride** tale, "The White Seal Maid" (1977), gives the captured seal woman agency in that she chooses to remain with her mortal husband for a time to reproduce and repopulate the sea with her offspring. Because Yolen is familiar with folklore scholarship, she sometimes cites the source she is working with or drawing upon for inspiration. For instance, in the essay "The Brothers **Grimm** and Sister Jane" (1993), she explains how three of Grimms' tales have influenced her writing.

Yolen's literary fairy tales, which have the feel of folktales without adhering to any known **tale type**, likewise present new visions and new metaphors of the world, sometimes criticizing oppressive social and power structures. The hunter in "The Hundredth Dove" (1977) is loosely based upon the faithful servant of ATU 440 (**The Frog King** or Iron Henry), yet the hunter's loyalty to a cruel **king** forces the hunter to assess the disastrous consequences of his own actions. Written during the Watergate scandal, this tale is political at its core. A more humorous tale, "Happy Dens or a Day in the Old Wolves' Home" (1984), instead raises the importance of perspective as three (now old) big bad **wolves** recount their misunderstood intentions. *Dream Weaver* (1979) serves as a **frame narrative** for seven other tales, all pastiches that deal with love and loss, healing and despair. Indeed, the frame tale with its blind Dream Weaver begging from a city population deals as much with human nature as the interwoven stories do.

Similar themes occur in Yolen's fairy-tale poetry, which is reflective and multivalent. Some poems, like "Frog **Prince**" (1987) and "Swan/**Princess**" (1995), delve into the layered meanings of a single tale. Other poems, like "Fat Is Not a Fairy Tale" (2000), comically criticize the entire genre (or in this case, the tendency to visualize only skinny fairy-tale heroines). Yolen seems very aware of her place within the grand history of fairy-tale transmission; "Once upon a Time, She Said" (1987), "Ridinghood" (2004), and "**Märchen**" (1994) all locate Yolen within a tradition of tropes, editors, and writers.

Poetry and prose appear congruently in some of Yolen's novels. In the series comprised of *Sister Light, Sister Dark* (1988), *White Jenna* (1989), and *The One-Armed **Queen*** (1998), Yolen tells of an ancient past with matriarchal undertones. She narrates the characters' lives under the heading of "the story" yet also generates folklore and scholarship from the perspectives of the distant future. Hence, **ballad**s, **legend**s, **parable**s, and children's rhymes accompany scholarly articles and letters regarding the little-understood "**gender** wars" and their ramifications for history. Yolen's skill in creating not only a compelling narrative but also the accompanying folklore and scholarship testifies to her deep understanding of narrative folklore.

Another of Yolen's novels deserves mention for its explicit fairy-tale ties. *Briar Rose* (1992) is a dual narrative, retelling "**Sleeping Beauty**" as a Holocaust survivor's experience and relating the survivor's granddaughter's quest to uncover the mystery of her family's past. Yolen's use of the fairy tale as both content and transitional material is fascinating and effective. Interestingly, the book was banned in some areas due to the homosexual character Josef Potoski, who functions as a fairy godmother/father figure in the story.

Yolen's intricate dealings with folktales and fairy tales are at once original and rooted in tradition. Her creative contributions to various literary genres have shaped the face of modern fairy-tale writing. ***See also*** North American Tales.

Further Readings: Hanlon, Tina L. "'To Sleep, Perchance to Dream': Sleeping Beauties and Wide-Awake Plain Janes in the Stories of Jane Yolen." *Children's Literature* 26 (1998): 140–67; Jane Yolen Official Web site. 2000–2005. http://www.janeyolen.com/; Weil, Ellen R. "The Door to Lilith's Cave: Memory and Imagination in Jane Yolen's Holocaust Novels." *Journal of the Fantastic in the Arts* 5 (1993): 90–104; Yolen, Jane. "The Brothers Grimm and Sister Jane." *The Reception of Grimms' Fairy Tales: Responses, Reactions, Revisions.* Edited by Donald Haase. Detroit: Wayne State University Press, 1993. 283–89.

Jeana Jorgensen

Young Adult Fiction

Loosely overlapping with **children's literature**, young adult fiction is a major area for the dissemination and reinterpretation of folktales and fairy tales. Young adult fiction is a flexible category, often intended for readers from the ages of twelve to eighteen years, or more generally the teenage years. It is also a recent category, and often books are repackaged for young adult readers after being marketed in other genres (adult fiction or **fantasy**, for instance). Young adult fiction tends to interact with folktales and fairy tales in significant ways: by retelling individual tales in short story or **novel** form, by combining tale elements and departing in the direction of fantasy, and by expanding on themes that are relevant to adolescent readers.

Direct retellings of folktales and fairy tales for young adults are common, though many of these retellings feature plot twists and attention to **gender** roles and power relations that may seem neglected in earlier versions. Additionally, these retellings tend to focus on teenage protagonists and the changes in their lives, using folktales and fairy tales as tropes to provide parallels for development. Robin **McKinley**'s collection *Door in the Hedge* (1981) and Francesca Lia **Block**'s *The Rose and the Beast: Fairy Tales Retold* (2000) both exemplify the inventive **literary fairy tale**s that modern authors are capable of reimagining. Jane **Yolen**, too, is known for her numerous short stories that rework folktales and fairy tales sensitively and creatively.

There are numerous novel-length retellings of folktales and fairy tales as well. Donna Jo **Napoli** has retold "**Hansel and Gretel**" in *The Magic Circle* (1993); "Rapunzel" in *Zel* (1996); "Rumpelstiltskin" in *Spinners* (1999, coauthored with Richard Tchen); and "**Beauty and the Beast**" in *Beast* (2000). Napoli's retellings are richly descriptive and invoke unusual perspectives. McKinley's novel *Beauty: A Retelling of the Story of Beauty and the Beast* (1978) is another example of a fleshed-out version of a fairy tale. Interestingly, McKinley returned to retell "Beauty and the Beast" twenty years later with her novel *Rose Daughter* (1997). Yolen's *Briar Rose* (1992) is a powerful retelling of "**Sleeping Beauty**" framed by the Holocaust.

Some young adult fiction verges on fantasy yet clearly draws on elements from folktales and fairy tales. Patricia C. Wrede's *Dealing with Dragons* (1990), the first book in the Enchanted Forest Chronicles, is an excellent example of fantasy that uses fairy tales as a point of departure. This book and its sequels, which verge on **parody**, follow the adventures of Cimorene, a willful **princess** who decides to leave royal life to live with the **dragon** Kazul as her librarian and chef. A few steps removed from folktales and fairy tales yet still clearly influenced by them is Brian Jacques's Redwall series (1986–2004), which takes place in fantastic lands inhabited mostly by anthropomorphic small mammals. The plots include quests and **initiation**s, and good and evil are typically clearly delineated as in fairy tales. Patricia A. **McKillip**'s novels incorporate folktale **motif**s; *In the Forests of Serre* (2003) has the feel of Russian folktales, with a **witch** who resembles **Baba Yaga** and a firebird as characters, while *Winter Rose* (1996) mixes fairy lore with fairy-tale elements, specifically "Tam Lin." Lloyd **Alexander**'s work, notably his five-book Chronicles of Prydain series (1964–68) draws on Welsh mythology in addition to folktale motifs regarding quests and magical help. Tamora Pierce's Alanna novels (1983–88), set in fantastic fairy-tale inspired lands, feature a girl who dresses as a boy to become a knight—the kind of **cross-dressing** found in a variety of folktales and fairy tales.

It is possible that folktales and fairy tales are currently seen as an ideal medium for the young adult audience because the tales so often deal with **transformation**s, magical and otherwise, and adolescents are also undergoing changes—physically, socially, and emotionally. Adolescence is often constructed as a liminal category, suspended between **childhood** and adulthood, so it is fitting that issues relevant to teenagers can be worked out in the liminal spaces between fairy tales and fantasy. Also, as Gail de Vos and Anna Altmann point out in *New Tales for Old: Folktales as Literary Fictions for Young Adults* (1999), folktales have a "spongelike hospitality and resilience," along with a simple style that "easily accommodates embellishment" (De Vos and Altmann, 15). In other words, folktales are flexible enough in structure to allow a variety of manipulations, and adolescent concerns are already close enough to be grafted on without major problems.

Domestic abuse figures prominently in many retellings, with responses ranging from the realistic to the fantastic. Terri **Windling**'s writing and editing especially contribute to the literature exploring the overlap between the darker side of fairy tales and adolescent experiences. Windling's edited collection *The Armless Maiden and Other Tales for Childhood's Survivors* (1995) is representative of this endeavor, and it contains her prose poem "Donkeyskin," which literally explores the **incest** motif only hinted at in the folktale. McKinley's novel *Deerskin* (1993), also a retelling of ATU 510B (Peau d'Asne), allows the daughter to escape her **father**'s dark desires *after* they are violently consummated, yet a benevolent magical force enables the daughter not only to heal emotionally but also to develop into a strong person in her own right. Block's *The Rose and the Beast* in particular contains stories that deal with issues of concern to adolescents, such as **sex**, drug use, and **violence**. Block's heroines escape from **Bluebeard** unaided, run away from home and kill the abusive stepfather/**wolf**, and recover from the prick of a (drug-laden) needle with the help of female companionship.

The marketing of folktales, fairy tales, and related fiction under the label of young adult fiction is also interesting because young adult fiction is often stereotyped into genres such as problem-specific stories. Yet, since folktales and fairy tales can be adapted in myriad ways and contain issues that can be emphasized or deemphasized depending on context, they remain formulaically fluid and relevant to old and young audiences alike. *See also* Faerie and Fairy Lore.

Further Readings: De Vos, Gail, and Anna E. Altmann. *New Tales for Old: Folktales as Literary Fictions for Young Adults*. Englewood, CO: Libraries Unlimited, 1999; Huang, Lucia. *American Young Adult Novels and Their European Fairy-Tale Motifs*. New York: Peter Lang, 1999.

Jeana Jorgensen

Z

Zaubermärchen. See Wonder Tale

Zelinsky, Paul O. (1953–)

Paul O. Zelinsky is a contemporary American picture book artist, and an illustrator and reteller of the **Grimm**s' fairy tales. Born in Illinois to a medical illustrator mother, he was educated at the Tyler School of Art. In addition, when he took a class at Yale from American picture book artist Maurice **Sendak**, Zelinsky was encouraged to produce books of his own for young people. His style has ranged from simple line drawings and colorful cartoon-like pictures (in *The Wheels on the Bus* [1990], for instance) to lush **illustration**s based on his extensive research of European painting for his fairy tales. He has often illustrated the works of other writers such as Avi, Beverly Cleary, and Lore Segal.

Some of Zelinsky's works based upon nursery rhymes include *The Wheels on the Bus* and *Knick-Knack Paddywhack!* (2002, a *New York Times* Best Illustrated Books Award). His notable versions of fairy tales include ***Hansel and Gretel***, written by Rika Lesser (1984, a Caldecott Honor Book), and his own adaptations of *Rumpelstiltskin* (1986, a Caldecott Honor Book) and *Rapunzel* (1997), which won the 1998 Caldecott Medal. For these, he painted pictures using Dutch genre painters and Renaissance artists as models. His pictures feature details appropriate to the historical origins of the stories, and his books include short essays concerning his style and the sources of the tales. The results are a detailed, formal, and visually splendid view of these stories. ***See also*** Art.

Further Readings: Peck, Jackie, and Judy Hendershot. "Release from 'Grimm' Captivity: Paul O. Zelinsky Talks about the Making of *Rapunzel*, the 1998 Caldecott Medal Winner." *Reading Teacher* 52 (1999): 570–75; Zelinsky, Paul O. "Artist's Notes on the Creation of *Rapunzel.*" *Journal of Youth Services in Libraries* 11 (1998): 214–17.

George Bodmer

Zipes, Jack (1937–)

Jack Zipes is an American scholar whose sociohistorical approach to fairy tales and **children's literature** has had a significant impact on the course of fairy-tale studies since the late 1970s. His impact has occurred not only through his critical studies of fairy tales but also via his work as an editor and translator. Zipes is the editor of important reference works and anthologies such as *The Oxford Companion to Fairy Tales* (2000), *The Great Fairy Tale Tradition* (2001), and *The Oxford Encyclopedia of Children's Literature* (2006). He is also a prolific translator of fairy tales from the French, German, and Italian traditions. In 1987, he published his acclaimed translation of *The Complete Fairy Tales of the Brothers Grimm*, which includes not only Jacob and Wilhelm **Grimm**'s standard stories but also lesser-known tales from previous editions and from the brothers' annotations and manuscripts. *Beauties, Beasts, and Enchantment* (1989) contains Zipes translations of classic French fairy tales, and *Beautiful Angiola* (2006) makes available the Sicilian folktales and fairy tales collected by Laura **Gonzenbach**. Several of his edited works, such as *The Trials and Tribulations of **Little Red Riding Hood*** (1983) and *Don't Bet on the Prince* (1986), combine fairy-tale criticism with primary texts. As a professor of German studies, Zipes has also published on the Frankfurt School, German theater, twentieth-century German literature, and topics related to Jewish studies.

Especially with his early scholarly works, such as *Breaking the Magic Spell: Radical Theories of Folk and Fairy Tales* (1979) and *Fairy Tales and the Art of Subversion* (1983), Zipes played a crucial role in the development of international fairy-tale criticism, particularly by making recent German theories accessible to an English-reading audience. Zipes's sociohistorical approach to the fairy tale focuses on the relationship between the folktale and the **literary fairy tale**, the Grimm brothers' ideological editing and **contamination** of the fairy tale, and the construction of **gender** and class values in Western culture's most popular tales (see **Feminism**). Much of his research is fueled by his sympathy for socially oppressed groups: Zipes sees the fairy tale as a genre that can provide hope and subversive power to marginalized communities. Because oral tales were partially robbed of their emancipatory, **utopia**n potential when they were appropriated by bourgeois authors and commercial concerns such as the **Walt Disney Company**, Zipes aims to bring about a critical reevaluation of the classical tales and their use in social and cultural contexts. Important sources of inspiration for Zipes's scholarship are the German philosophers Walter Benjamin, Ernst Bloch, and Theodor Adorno.

Since the late 1970s, Zipes has covered a great variety of topics in his fairy-tale research, ranging from works on specific authors (such as Hermann **Hesse**, George **McDonald,** Oscar **Wilde**, and Hans Christian **Andersen**), geographical areas (such as Sicilian tales or the production and reception of fairy tales in the United States), and historical periods (for instance, the Weimar and Victorian eras) to reflections on postmodern fairy-tale rewritings and fantasy literature (by J. R. R. **Tolkien**, J. K. **Rowling**, and others) (see **Postmodernism**). In *Why Fairy Tales Stick: The Evolution and Relevance of a Genre* (2006), Zipes draws on relevance theory and scientific studies of genetics, memetics, linguistics, and evolution to advance a new theory of why certain fairy tales have become so permanently established.

Throughout his career, Zipes has also been involved in children's **theater** and **storytelling** as a way for children in particular to take control of conventional tales instead of being controlled by them. This work has resulted in the acclaimed storytelling program, Neighborhood Bridges, which Zipes directs in collaboration with the Children's Theatre Company of Minneapolis. Zipes's theory and practice of storytelling are documented in his books *Creative Storytelling: Building Community, Changing Lives* (1995) and *Speaking Out: Storytelling and Creative Drama for Children* (2004).

Critics of Zipes's work have addressed the weaknesses in his Marxist approach. Anne Wilson deplored his lack of attention to the humorous and psychological aspects of fairy tales, and points at the speculative nature of some of his theories, for instance when Zipes situates the origin of some feminist aspects of the oral tale in matriarchy. Likewise, coming from a psychoanalytical angle, Paul Nonnekes refuted Zipes's attack on Walt **Disney**. In spite of these critical voices, Zipes remains one of the most influential scholars in fairy-tale studies. His scholarship has been honored with several prizes, including the International Brothers Grimm Award in 1999. *See also* Sociohistorical Approaches.

Further Readings: Bannerman, Kenn. "A Short Interview with Jack Zipes." April 2002. http://www.biting-dogpress.com/zipes/zipes.html; *Jack Zipes and the Sociohistorical Study of Fairy Tales.* Special issue of *Marvels & Tales* 16 (2002): 117–322; Nonnekes, Paul. "The Loving Father in Disney's *Pinocchio*: A Critique of Jack Zipes." *Children's Literature Association Quarterly* 25.2 (2000): 107–15; Wilson, Anne. "The Civilizing Process in Fairy Tales." *Signal* 44 (1984): 81–87.

Vanessa Joosen

Zur Mühlen, Hermynia (1883–1951)

A prolific and versatile author of **novel**s, short stories, radio plays, detective thrillers, and journalistic articles, Hermynia zur Mühlen gained notoriety in the 1920s for her popular socialist **fable**s and fairy tales. Works such as "Die rote Fahne" ("The Red Flag," 1930), "Der Zaun" ("The Fence," 1924), and "Das Schloß der Wahrheit" ("The Castle of Truth," 1924) sought both to model Communist values through allegory and **fantasy**, and to foster a revolutionary spirit within their readership of working-class children. Zur Mühlen also is known as a translator of more than 100 works from French, English, and Russian into German, particularly the novels and plays of Upton Sinclair.

In her popular children's story *Was Peterchen's Freude erzählen* (*What Little Peter's Friends Tell*, 1921), everyday objects speak and reveal the suffering of the laboring class that manufactured them. Zur Mühlen's fables adhere to a relatively consistent model, in which the protagonists overcome a capitalistic regime of economic exploitation through personal initiative and cooperative action. Her other significant works include *Märchen* (*Fairy Tales*, 1922), *Ali, der Teppichweber* (*Ali, the Carpet Weaver*, 1923), and *Es war einmal ... und es wird sein* (*Once There Was ... and There Will Be*, 1930). In 1925, the Daily Worker Publishing Company in Chicago published four of Zur Mühlen's tales, translated into English, in *Fairy Tales for Workers' Children*.

Born in Vienna as Hermine Isabella Maria Folliot de Crenneville-Poutet, Zur Mühlen rejected the Austro-Hungarian nobility to dedicate her life to the socialist cause. Though Zur Mühlen valued the education, cultural awareness, and appreciation of beauty afforded by her aristocratic upbringing, she sought a more meaningful life than that of a privileged countess. In her youth, she traveled widely in Asia and Africa and received an unusually liberal education that refined her sense of social justice.

Her short, unhappy marriage to Baron Victor Zur Mühlen, a German Baltic landowner, ended due to a combination of a lack of intellectual and cultural stimulus and disputes over his treatment of the native farm laborers. After their separation, she spent some time in Switzerland, where she became involved in the Bolshevik movement and joined the German Communist Party in 1919.

Zur Mühlen's Communist politics made her work the target of government scrutiny and censorship: she narrowly escaped charges of literary treason for her 1924 novel *Schupomann*

Karl Müller (*Policeman Karl Müller*) and remained under official police surveillance. Eventually, she and her second husband, Stefan Klein, were forced into exile in Austria, Czechoslovakia, and finally England, where she died. While in Austria, Zur Mühlen published the incisive *Unsere Töchter, die Nazinen* (*Our Daughters, the Nazis*, 1935), immediately banned in Germany for its uncompromising antifascism. After her 1934 split from the KPD (the Communist Party of Germany) over Stalinism's extremes, she found herself unpopular in many arenas.

Despite the success and sociopolitical significance of Zur Mühlen's writings, a general disregard for the interwar period left her largely in obscurity. Her work is only recently being rediscovered through the research of feminist critics, exile scholars, and a renewed interest in the literature of Weimar-era Germany. *See also* Feminism; German Tales.

Further Readings: Altner, Manfred. *Hermynia Zur Mühlen: Eine Biographie.* Bern: Peter Lang, 1997; King, Lynda J. "Hermynia zur Mühlen." *Dictionary of Literary Biography.* Edited by James Hardin. Volume 56. Detroit: Gale Research, 1987. 317–24; Zipes, Jack, ed and trans. *Fairy Tales and Fables from Weimar Days.* Hanover: University Press of New England, 1989.

Kristiana Willsey

BIBLIOGRAPHY AND RESOURCES

Folktale and Fairy-Tale Collections, Editions, Anthologies, and Translations

Abrahams, Roger D., ed. *African American Folktales: Stories from the Black Traditions of the New World.* New York: Pantheon, 1999. Reprint of *Afro-American Folktales*, 1985.

———. *African Folktales: Traditional Stories of the Black World.* New York: Pantheon Books, 1983.

———. *Deep Down in the Jungle: Negro Narrative Folklore from the Streets of Philadelphia.* 1963. Chicago: Aldine, 1974.

Adlard, John. *Nine Magic Pea-Hens and Other Serbian Folk Tales Collected by Vuk Karadžić.* Edinburgh: Floris, 1988.

Aesop's Fables. Translated and edited by Laura Gibbs. Oxford: Oxford University Press, 2002.

Afanas'ev, Aleksandr. *Russian Fairy Tales.* Translated by Norbert Guterman. 1943. New York: Pantheon, 1975.

———. *Russian Secret Tales: Bawdy Tales of Old Russia.* Introduction by G. Legman. New York: Brussel and Brussel, 1966.

———. *Russian Secret Tales: Bawdy Folktales of Old Russia.* 1966. Introduction by G. Legman. New foreword by Alan Dundes. Baltimore: Clearfield, 1998.

Agosin, Marjorie, ed. *Secret Weavers: Stories of the Fantastic by Women of Argentina and Chile.* Fredonia, NY: White Pine Press, 1992.

Ahmad, Aisha, and Roger Boase. *Pashtun Tales from the Pakistan-Afghan Frontier.* London: Saqi Books, 2003.

Alcover, Antoni Maria. *Folk Tales of Mallorca: A Selection from "L'aplec de rondaies mallorquines."* Translated by David Huelin. Palma de Mallorca: Editorial Moll, 1999.

———. *Tales from Majorca.* Translated by John Lynch-Cummins. Palma de Mallorca: Clumba, 1968.

Alpers, Antony. *Legends of the South Sea: The World of the Polynesians Seen through Their Myths and Legends, Poetry and Art.* Christchurch, NZ: Whitcombe & Tombs Ltd., 1970.

Al-Shahi, Ahmed, and F. C. T. Moore, trans. *Wisdom from the Nile: A Collection of Folk-Stories from Northern and Central Sudan.* Oxford: Clarendon Press, 1978.

Amadio, Nadine. *Pacifica: Myth, Magic, and Traditional Wisdom from the South Sea Islands.* Sydney: Angus & Robertson, 1993.

Andersen, Hans Christian. *The Complete Fairy Tales and Stories.* Translated by Erik Christian Haugaard. New York: Doubleday, 1974.

———. *Eighty Fairy Tales.* Translated by R. P. Keigwin. 1976. New York: Pantheon, 1982.

———. *Fairy Tales.* Translated by Tiina Nunnally. Edited by Jackie Wullschlager. New York: Viking, 2004.

———. *H. C. Andersens eventyr: Kritisk udgivet efter de originale eventyrhæfter med varianter.* Edited by Erik Dal, Erling Nielsen, and Flemming Hovmann. 7 volumes. Copenhagen: Reitzel. 1963–90.

———. *The Stories of Hans Christian Andersen.* Translated by Diana Crone Frank and Jeffrey Frank. Boston: Houghton Mifflin, 2003.

Andersen, Johannes Carl. *Myths and Legends of the Polynesians.* 1928. Rutland, VT: C. E. Tuttle Co., 1969.

Appalachian Storyteller: Ray Hicks Series. 5 DVDs. Produced by Luke Barrow. Chip Taylor Communications, n.d.

Apuleius. *Cupid and Psyche.* Edited by E. J. Kenney. Cambridge: Cambridge University Press, 1990.

———. *The Golden Ass.* Translated by P. G. Walsh. New York: Oxford University Press, 1994.

Arnim, Bettina von, and Gisela von Arnim. *The Life of High Countess Gritta von Ratsinourhouse.* Translated by Lisa Ohm. Lincoln: Nebraska University Press, 1999.

Arnim, Gisela von. "The Rose Cloud." Translated by Shawn C. Jarvis. *Marvels & Tales* 11 (1997): 134–59.

Asatchaq, Tukummuq, and Tom Lowenstein. *The Things That Were Said of Them: Shaman Stories and Oral Histories of the Tikiġaq People.* Berkeley: University of California Press, 1992.

Asbjørnsen, Peter Christen, and Jørgen Moe. *East o' the Sun and West o' the Moon: Fifty-Nine Norwegian Folk Tales.* Translated by George Webbe Dasent. 1888. New York: Dover, 1970.

———. *Norwegian Folk Tales.* Translated by Pat Shaw and Carl Norman. 1960. New York: Pantheon, 1982.

———. *Popular Tales from the Norse.* Translated by George Webbe Dasent. London: Routledge, 1900.

Ashliman, D. L. *Voices from the Past: The Cycle of Life in Indo-European Folktales.* 2nd edition. Dubuque: Kendall/Hunt, 1995.

Aston, W. G., trans. *Nihongi: Chronicles of Japan from the Earliest Times to AD 697.* 1896. Tokyo: Tuttle Publishing, 1972.

Auerbach, Nina, and U. C. Knoepflmacher, eds. *Forbidden Journeys: Fairy Tales and Fantasies by Victorian Women Writers.* Chicago: University of Chicago Press, 1992.

Auleear, Dawood, and Lee Haring, trans. and ed. *Indian Folktales from Mauritius.* Chennai, India: National Folklore Support Centre, 2006.

Bailey, James, and Tatyana Ivanova, eds. *An Anthology of Russian Folk Epics.* Translated by James Bailey and Tatyana Ivanova. Armonk, NY: M. E. Sharpe, 1999.

Baissac, Charles. *Sirandann, sanpek: Zistwar en kreol; Baissac's l888 Collection.* Port Louis, Mauritius: Ledikasyon pu Travayer, 1989. English translation of *Le folk-lore de l'île Maurice.* Paris, 1888.

Balina, Marina, Helena Goscilo, and Mark Lipovetsky, eds. *Politicizing Magic: An Anthology of Russian and Soviet Fairy Tales.* Evanston, IL: Northwestern University Press, 2005.

Ballaster, Rosalind. *Fables of the East: Selected Tales, 1662–1785.* Oxford: Oxford University Press, 2005.

Barchilon, Jacques, ed. *Nouveau cabinet des fées.* 1785–89. 18 volumes. Geneva: Slatkine, 1978.

Barchilon, Jacques, and Henry Pettit. *The Authentic Mother Goose Fairy Tales and Nursery Rhymes.* Denver: Alan Swallow, 1960.

Baring-Gould, S. *Curious Myths of the Middle Ages.* London: Rivingtons, 1872.

Bar-Itzhak, Haya, and Aliza Shenhar. *Jewish Moroccan Folk Narratives from Israel.* Detroit: Wayne State University Press, 1993.

Bartsch, Karl. *Sagen, Märchen und Gebräuche aus Meklenburg.* 2 volumes. Vienna, 1879–80.

Bascom, William. *African Dilemma Tales.* The Hague: Mouton, 1975.

———. *African Folktales in the New World.* 1976. Bloomington: Indiana University Press, 1992.

Basile, Giambattista. *Lo cunto de li cunti.* Edited and translated by Michelle Rak. Milan: Garzanti, 1986.

———. *Giambattista Basile's "The Tale of Tales, or Entertainment for Little Ones."* Translated by Nancy L. Canepa. Detroit: Wayne State University Press, 2007.

———. *Das Märchen der Märchen: Das Pentamerone.* Translated by Hanno Helbling et al. Edited by Rudolf Schenda. Munich: Beck, 2000.

———. *The Pentamerone of Giambattista Basile.* Translated and edited by N. M. Penzer. 1932. 2 volumes. Westport, CT: Greenwood Press, 1979.

Basset, René, and Aboubakr Chraïbi, eds. *Mille et un contes: Récits et legendes arabes.* 2 volumes. Paris: José Corti, 2005.

Beaumont, Jeanne Marie, and Claudia Carlson, eds. *The Poets' Grimm: 20th Century Poems from Grimm Fairy Tales.* Ashland, OR: Story Line Press, 2003.

Bechstein, Ludwig. *Beyond Grimm: A Bechstein Sampler.* Translated by Lynn Kohner. Seattle: CUNE, 1997.

———. *Fairy Tales.* Translated by Anthea Bell. London: Abelard-Schuman, 1967.

———. *Märchenbuch: Nach der Ausgabe von 1857, textkritisch revidiert und durch Register erschlossen.* Edited by Hans-Jörg Uther. Munich: Diederichs, 1997.

———. *Neues deutsches Märchenbuch: Nach der Ausgabe von 1856, textkritisch revidiert und durch Register erschlossen*. Edited by Hans-Jörg Uther. Munich: Diederichs, 1997.

———. *Sämtliche Märchen*. Edited by Walter Scherf. Munich: Wissenschaftliche Buckgesellschaft, 1985.

Beck, Brenda E. F., et al., eds. *Folktales of India*. 1987. Chicago: University of Chicago Press, 1999.

Bécquer, Gustavo Adolfo. *Legends and Letters*. Translated by Robert M. Fedorchek. Lewisburg, PA: Bucknell University Press, 1995.

Ben-Amos, Dan, ed., and Dov Noy, consulting ed. *Folktales of the Jews*. 2 volumes to date. Philadelphia: Jewish Publication Society, 2006– .

Benfey, Theodor. *Der Pantschatantra: Fünf Bücher indischer Fabeln, Märchen und Erzählungen*. 2 volumes. Leipzig: F. A. Brockhaus, 1859.

Bennett, Martin. *West African Trickster Tales*. Oxford: Oxford University Press, 1994.

Benwell, Gwen, and Arthur Waugh. *Sea Enchantress: The Tale of the Mermaid and Her Kin*. London: Hutchinson and Co., 1961.

Bermel, Albert, and Ted Emery, trans. and ed. *Five Tales for the Theatre*. Chicago: University of Chicago Press, 1989.

Bester, John, trans. *Once and Forever: The Tales of Kenji Miyazawa*. Tokyo: Kodansha International, 1997.

Bianco, Carla. *The Two Rosetos*. Bloomington: Indiana University Press, 1974.

Bierhorst, John. *Black Rainbow: Legends of the Incas and Myths of Ancient Peru*. New York: Farrar, Straus and Giroux, 1976.

———. *The Dancing Fox: Arctic Folktales*. New York: William Morrow, 1997.

———, trans. *History and Mythology of the Aztecs: The Codex Chimalpopoca*. Tucson: University of Arizona Press, 1992.

———. *Latin American Folktales: Stories from Hispanic and Indian Traditions*. New York: Pantheon, 2002.

———. *The Mythology of North America*. 2nd edition. New York: Oxford University Press, 2002.

———. *The Mythology of South America*. 2nd edition, revised. New York: Oxford University Press, 2002.

———, ed. *The Red Swan: Myths and Tales of the American Indians*. New York: Farrar, Straus and Giroux, 1976.

Blackburn, Stuart. *Moral Fictions: Tamil Folktales from Oral Tradition*. Helsinki: Academia Scientiarum Fennica, 2001.

Blackwell, Jeannine. "German Fairy Tales: A User's Manual; Translations of Six Frames and Fragments by Romantic Women." *Fairy Tales and Feminism: New Approaches*. Edited by Donald Haase. Detroit: Wayne State University Press, 2004. 73–111.

Blanchy, Sophie, and Zaharia Soilihi. *Furukombe et autres contes de Mayotte*. Paris: Éditions Caribéennes, 1991.

Blecher, Lone Thygesen, and George Blecher, trans. and ed. *Swedish Folktales and Legends*. New York: Pantheon, 1993.

Boccaccio, Giovanni. *The Decameron*. Translated by G. H. McWilliam. 1972. Harmdonsworth: Penguin, 1995.

Böhl de Faber, Cecilia. "The Bird of Truth." Translated by Robert M. Fedorchek. *Marvels & Tales* 16 (2002): 73–83.

———. "The Devil's Mother-in-Law." Translated by Robert M. Fedorchek. *Marvels & Tales* 15 (2001): 192–201.

Bontemps, Arna, and Langston Hughes, eds. *The Book of Negro Folklore*. New York: Dodd, Mead, 1958.

Borcherding, Gisela. *Granatapfel und Flügelpferd: Märchen aus Afghanistan*. Kassel: Erich Röth, 1975.

Borges, Jorge Luis. *Borges: Collected Fictions*. Translated by Andrew Hurley. New York: Penguin, 1999.

Bowman, James Cloyd, and Margery Williams Bianco. *Tales from a Finnish Tupa*. From a translation by Aili Kolehmainen. Chicago: A. Whitman, 1964.

Briggs, Katharine M., and Ruth L. Tongue, eds. *Folktales of England*. Chicago: University of Chicago Press, 1965.

Bright, William. *A Coyote Reader*. Berkeley: University of California Press, 1993.

Brunner-Traut, Emma, trans. and ed. *Altägyptische Märchen*. Düsseldorf: Diederichs, 1965.

Budge, Ernest A. Wallis, ed. and trans. *Egyptian Tales and Romances*. London: T. Butterworth, 1931.

Burrison, John A., ed. *Storytellers: Folktales and Legends from the South*. Athens: University of Georgia Press, 1991.

Burton, Sir Richard F., trans. *Vikram and the Vampire, or Tales of Hindu Devilry*. 1870. New York: Dover, 1969.

Bushnaq, Inea, trans. and ed. *Arab Folktales.* New York: Pantheon, 1986.

Caballero, Fernan [Cecilia Böhl de Faber]. *Spanish Fairy Tales.* Translated by J. H. Ingram. New York: A. L. Burt Company, n.d.

Cabrera, Lydia. *Afro-Cuban Tales: Cuentos negros de Cuba.* Translated by Alberto Hernandez-Chiroldes and Lauren Yoder. Lincoln: University of Nebraska Press, 2004.

Calame-Griaule, Geneviève, ed. and trans. *Contes tendres, contes cruels du Sahel nigérien.* Paris: Gallimard, 2002.

Calvino, Italo, ed. *Fiabe.* Torino: Einaudi, 1970.

———. *Italian Folktales.* Translated by George Martin. New York: Pantheon, 1980.

Cameron, Hector [pseud. Hector MacQuarrie]. *Little Yellow Shoes, and Other Bosnian Fairy Stories.* London: Angus & Robertson, 1960.

Campbell, C. G., ed. *Folktales from Iraq.* 1949. Philadelphia: University of Pennsylvania Press, 2005.

Campbell, J. F., trans. *Popular Tales of the West Highlands: Orally Collected.* New edition. 2 volumes. Edinburgh: Birlinn, 1994.

Čapek, Karel. *Nine Fairy Tales: And One More Thrown In for Good Measure.* Translated by Dagmar Herrmann. Evanston: Northwestern University Press, 1990.

Carter, Angela. *The Bloody Chamber.* 1979. London: Vintage, 1995.

———. *Burning Your Boats: The Collected Short Stories.* Harmondsworth: Penguin Books, 1995.

———, ed. *The Old Wives' Fairy Tale Book.* New York: Pantheon, 1990. Reprint of *The Virago Book of Fairy Tales.* London: Virago, 1990.

———, ed. *Strange Things Sometimes Still Happen: Fairy Tales from around the World.* 1993. Boston: Faber, 1994. Reprint of *The Second Virago Book of Fairy Tales.* London: Virago, 1992.

Castroviejo, Concha. *The Garden with Seven Gates.* Translated by Robert M. Fedorchek. Lewisburg, PA: Bucknell University Press, 2004.

Chase, Richard. *The Jack Tales.* Boston: Houghton-Mifflin, 1943.

Choisy, François-Timoléon de, Marie-Jeanne L'Héritier, and Charles Perrault. *The Story of the Marquise-Marquis de Banneville.* Translated by Steven Rendall. New York: Modern Language Association of America, 2004.

Cholakian, Patricia Francis, and Rouben Charles Cholakian, eds. and trans. *The Early French Novella: An Anthology of Fifteenth- and Sixteenth-Century Tales.* Albany: SUNY Press, 1972.

Christiansen, Reidar T., ed. *Folktales of Norway.* Translated by Pat Shaw Iversen. Chicago: University of Chicago Press, 1964.

Claffey, Anne, Linda Kavanaugh, and Sue Russell, eds. *Rapunzel's Revenge: Fairytales for Feminists.* Dublin: Attic, 1985.

Clouston, W. A. *Popular Tales and Fictions: Their Migrations and Transformations.* Edited by Christine Goldberg. Santa Barbara: ABC-CLIO, 2002.

Cole, Joana, ed. *Best-Loved Folktales of the World.* New York: Anchor Books-Doubleday, 1982.

Consiglieri Pedroso, Zophimo. *Portuguese Folktales.* 1882. Translated by Henriqueta Monteiro. New York: B. Blom, 1969.

Contes, devinettes et jeux de mots des Seychelles: Zistwar ek zedmo sesel. Paris: Éditions Akpagnon, 1983.

Cooper, David L., ed. and trans. *Traditional Slovak Folktales Collected by Pavol Dobšinský.* Armonk, NY: M. E. Sharpe, 2001.

Cooper, James Fenimore, trans. *Tricks of Women and Other Albanian Tales.* New York: W. Morrow, 1928.

Cosquin, Emmanuel. *Contes populaires de Lorraine.* 1886. Marseille: LaFitte, 1978.

Cowell, Edward B., ed. *The Jātaka or Stories of the Buddha's Former Births.* Translated from the Pali by various hands. 6 volumes in 3. New Delhi: Munshiram Manoharlal Publishers, 1990.

Coxwell, C. Fillingham. *Siberian and Other Folk-Tales.* London: C. W. Daniel Company, 1925.

Crane, Thomas Frederick. *Italian Popular Tales.* Edited by Jack Zipes. New York: Oxford University Press, 2003.

Creanga, Ion. *Folk Tales from Roumania.* London: Routledge, 1952.

Croker, Thomas Crofton. *Fairy Legends and Traditions of the South of Ireland.* 1825. Edited by Neil C. Hultin and Warren U. Ober. Delmar, NY: Scholars' Facsimiles & Reprints, 1983.

———. *Fairy Legends and Traditions of the South of Ireland.* Edited by Thomas Wright. 1870. Edited by Neil C. Hultin and Warren U. Ober. Ann Arbor: Scholars' Facsimiles & Reprints, 2001.

Crooke, William, and Pandit Ram Gharib Chaube. *Folktales from Northern India.* Edited by Sadhana Naithani. Santa Barbara: ABC-CLIO, 2002.

Crossley-Holland, Kevin, ed. *Folk-Tales of the British Isles.* New York: Pantheon, 1985.

Cuadra Downing, Orlando, ed. *The Adventures of Don Coyote: American Indian Folk Tales*. New York: Exposition Press, 1955.

Ćurčija-Prodanović, Nada. *Yugoslav Folk-Tales*. 1957. London: Oxford University Press, 1966.

Curtin, Jeremiah. *Creation Myths of Primitive America*. Edited by Karl Kroeber. Santa Barbara: ABC-CLIO, 2002.

Cvetanovska, Danica, and Maja Miškovska. *101 Macedonian Folk Tales*. Skopje: Bigoss, 2003.

Dadié, Bernard Binlin. *The Black Cloth: A Collection of African Folktales*. Amherst: University of Massachusetts Press, 1987.

Dance, Daryl Cumber. *Shuckin' and Jivin': Folklore from Contemporary Black Americans*. Bloomington: Indiana University Press, 1978.

Danien, Elin, ed. *Maya Folktales from the Alta Verapaz*. Philadelphia: University Museum Publications, 2005.

Darbord, Bernard. *Libro de los gatos: Édition avec introduction et notes*. Paris: Klincksieck, 1984.

Datlow, Ellen, and Terri Windling, eds. *Black Heart, Ivory Bones*. New York: Avon, 2000.

———, eds. *Black Swan, White Raven*. New York: Avon, 1997.

———, eds. *Black Thorn, White Rose*. New York: William Morrow, 1994.

———, eds. *Ruby Slippers, Golden Tears*. New York: William Morrow, 1995.

———, eds. *Silver Birch, Blood Moon*. New York: Avon, 1999.

———, eds. *Snow White, Blood Red*. New York: Avon Books, 1993.

David, Alfred, and Mary Elizabeth Meek, eds. *The Twelve Dancing Princesses and Other Fairy Tales*. Bloomington: Indiana University Press, 1974.

Davidson, Sarah, and Eleanor Phelps, eds. "Folk Tales from New Goa, India." *Journal of American Folklore* 50 (1937): 1–51.

Dawkins, Richard M., ed. and trans. *Forty-Five Stories from the Dodekanese*. Cambridge: Cambridge University Press, 1950.

———, trans. *Modern Greek Folktales*. 1953. Westport, CT: Greenwood Press, 1974.

Dazai Osamu. *Crackling Mountain and Other Stories*. Translated by James O'Brien. Rutland, VT: Tuttle, 1989.

Dégh, Linda, ed. *Folktales of Hungary*. Translated by Judit Halasz. Chicago: University of Chicago Press, 1965.

Delarue, Paul. *The Borzoi Book of French Folk Tales*. Translated by Austin E. Fife. New York: Alfred A. Knopf, 1956.

Delarue, Paul, and Marie-Louise Tenèze, eds. *Le conte populaire français: Catalogue raisonné des versions de France et des pays de langue française d'outre-mer*. 4 volumes. Paris: Editions Maisonneuve et Larose, 1957–2000.

Die digitale Bibliothek der deutschen Märchen und Sagen. Digitale Bibliothek, special volume. Frankfurt a.M.: Zweitausendeins, 2004.

Dimock, Edward C. *The Thief of Love: Bengali Tales from Court and Village*. Chicago: University Chicago Press, 1963.

Diop, Birago. *Tales of Amadou Koumba*. Translated by Dorothy S. Blair. London: Oxford University Press, 1966.

Donati, Cesarina. *Tre racconti proibiti di Trancoso*. Rome: Bulzoni, 1983.

Donoghue, Emma. *Kissing the Witch: Old Tales in New Skins*. New York: Cotler/HarperCollins, 1997.

Dorson, Richard M. *American Negro Folktales*. Greenwich, CT: Fawcett, 1967.

———, ed. *Folktales Told around the World*. Chicago: University of Chicago Press, 1975.

Dracott, Alice E. *Folk Tales from Simla*. 1906. New York: Hippocrene Books, 1998.

Duffy, Carol Ann. *New Selected Poems*. London: Picador, 2004.

Dundas, Marjorie, ed. *Riddling Tales from around the World*. Jackson: University Press of Mississippi, 2002.

Eberhard, Wolfram, ed. and trans. *Folktales of China*. Chicago: University of Chicago Press, 1965. Revised reprint of *Chinese Fairy Tales and Folk Tales*. 1937.

Edgerton, Franklin, ed. and trans. *The Panchatantra Reconstructed*. 2 volumes. New Haven: American Oriental Society, 1924.

El-Shamy, Hasan M., ed. and trans. *Folktales of Egypt*. Chicago: University of Chicago Press, 1980.

———, ed. and trans. *Tales Arab Women Tell and the Behavioral Patterns They Portray*. Bloomington: Indiana University Press, 1999.

Elsie, Robert, trans. *Albanian Folktales and Legends*. 2nd edition. Peja: Dukagjini, 2001.

Epstein, Steven Jay, ed. *Lao Folktales*. Seattle: University of Washington Press, 2006.

Equilbecq, François-Victor. *Contes populaire d'Afrique occidentale: Précédés d'un essai sur la littérature merveilleuse des noirs*. New edition. Paris: G.-P. Maisonneuve et Larose, 1972.

Erben, Karel J., *Panslavonic Folk-Lore in Four Books*. Translated by W. W. Strickland. New York: B. Westermann, 1930.

Erdoes, Richard, and Alfonso Ortiz, eds. *American Indian Myths and Legends*. New York: Pantheon, 1984.

Fabiola. *The Twelve Marvellous Tales*. Translated by John P. Fitzgibbon. Illustrated by Tayina. Madrid: Ediciones Sinople, 1961.

Faurot, Jeannette. *Asian Pacific Folktales and Legends*. New York: Simon, 1995.

Fedorchek, Robert M., trans. *Death and the Doctor*. Lewisburg, PA: Bucknell University Press, 1997.

———, trans. *Stories of Enchantment from Nineteenth-Century Spain*. Lewisburg, PA: Bucknell University Press, 2002.

Felmy, Sabine. *Märchen und Sagen aus Hunza*. Köln: Diederichs, 1986.

Fillmore, Parker, ed. *Czech, Moravian and Slovak Fairy Tales*. New York: Hippocrene Books, 1998. Reprint of *Czechoslovac Fairy Tales*. 1918.

Flood, Bo, Beret E. Strong, and William Flood. *Pacific Island Legends: Tales from Micronesia, Melanesia, Polynesia, and Australia*. Honolulu, HI: Bess Press, 1999.

Fowke, Edith, comp. and trans. *Folktales of French Canada*. Toronto: NC Press, 1979.

———, coll. *Legends Told in Canada*. Toronto: Royal Ontario Museum, 1994.

———. *Tales Told in Canada*. Toronto: Doubleday Canada, 1986.

Frere, Mary. *Hindoo Fairy Legends: Old Deccan Days*. 3rd edition. 1881. New York: Dover, 1967.

———. *Old Deccan Days, or Hindoo Fairy Legends*. Edited by Kirin Narayan. Santa Barbara: ABC-CLIO, 2002.

Früh, Sigrid, ed. *Europäische Frauenmärchen*. Frankfurt a.M.: Fischer, 1996. Expanded edition of *Die Frau, die auszog, ihren Mann zu erlösen*. Frankfurt a.M.: Fischer, 1985.

Galley, Micheline, ed. *Le figuier magique et autres contes algériens dits par Aouda*. Paris: Librarie Orientaliste Paul Geuthner, 2003.

Gernant, Karen, trans. *Imagining Women: Fujian Folk Tales*. New York: Interlink Books, 1995.

Ghosh, Oroon, trans. *The Dance of Shiva and Other Tales from India*. New York: Signet, 1965.

Gittins, Anne. *Tales from the South Pacific Islands*. Owings Mills, MD: Stemmer House Publishers, 1977.

Gladwin, Francis. *The Tooti-Nameh or Tales of a Parrot*. London: J. Debrett, 1801.

Glassie, Henry. *Irish Folk History: Tales from the North*. 1982. Philadelphia: University of Pennsylvania Press, 1998.

———. *Irish Folktales*. New York: Pantheon, 1987.

Gonzenbach, Laura. *Beautiful Angiola: The Lost Sicilian Folk and Fairy Tales of Laura Gonzenbach*. Translated and edited by Jack Zipes. New York: Routledge, 2006.

Gordon, Marguerite, ed. *Nelson Mandela's Favorite African Folktales*. New York: Norton, 2002.

Gossen, Gary H., ed. and trans. *Four Creations: An Epic Story of the Chiapas Mayas*. Norman: University of Oklahoma Press, 2002.

Gouge, Earnest. *Totkv Mocvse/New Fire: Creek Folktales*. Edited by Jack B. Martin, Margaret McKane Mauldin, and Juanita McGirt. Norman: University of Oklahoma Press, 2004.

Green, Thomas A., ed. *The Greenwood Library of American Folktales*. 4 volumes. Westport, CT: Greenwood Press, 2006.

Gregory, Lady. *Visions and Beliefs in the West of Ireland*. New York: Oxford University Press, 1970.

Griffis, William Elliot. *Dutch Fairy Tales for Young Folks*. New York: Thomas Y. Crowell Co., 1919.

Grimm, Jacob, *Deutsche Mythologie*. 2nd edition. Göttingen: Dieterische Buchhandlung, 1844.

———. *Teutonic Mythology*. Translated by James Steven Stallybrass. 1880–88. 4 volumes. New York: Routledge, 1999.

Grimm, Jacob and Wilhelm. *Die älteste Märchensammlung der Brüder Grimm: Synopse der handschriftlichen Urfasung von 1810 und der Erstdrucke von 1812*. Edited by Heinz Rölleke. Cologny-Genève: Fondation Martin Bodmer, 1975.

———. *The Complete Fairy Tales of the Brothers Grimm*. Translated by Jack Zipes. 3rd expanded edition. New York: Bantam, 2003.

———. *The Complete Grimm's Fairy Tales*. Translated by Margaret Hunt. Revised and corrected translation by James Stern. 1944. New York: Pantheon, 1972.

———. *The German Legends of the Brothers Grimm*. Edited and translated by Donald Ward. 2 volumes. Philadelphia: Institute for the Study of Human Issues, 1981.

———. *The Grimms' German Folktales*. Translated by Francis P. Magoun, Jr., and Alexander

Krappe. 1960. Carbondale: Southern Illinois University Press, 1980.

———. *Grimm's Household Tales.* Translated by Margaret Hunt. 2 volumes. 1884. Detroit: Singing Tree Press, 1968.

———. *Grimms' Other Tales: A New Selection by Wilhelm Hansen.* Translated and edited by Ruth Michaelis-Jena and Arthur Ratcliff. 1956. Edinburgh: Canongate, 1984.

———. *Grimms' Tales for Young and Old: The Complete Stories.* Translated by Ralph Manheim. Garden City: Anchor/Doubleday, 1977.

———. *Kinder- und Hausmärchen: Nach der Großen Ausgabe von 1857, textkritisch revidiert, kommentiert und durch Register erschlossen.* Edited by Hans-Jörg Uther. 4 volumes. Munich: Diederichs, 1996.

———. *Kinder- und Hausmärchen: Nach der 2. vermehrten und verbesserten Auflage von 1819.* Edited by Heinz Rölleke. 2 volumes. Cologne: Diederichs, 1982.

———. *Kinder- und Hausmärchen der Brüder Grimm: Ausgabe letzter Hand.* Edited by Heinz Rölleke. 3 volumes. Stuttgart: Reclam, 1980.

———. *Kinder- und Hausmärchen gesammelt durch die Brüder Grimm: Kleine Ausgabe von 1858.* Edited by Heinz Rölleke. Frankfurt a.M.: Insel, 1985.

———. *Kinder- und Hausmärchen gesammelt durch die Brüder Grimm: Vergrößerter Nachdruck der zweibändigen Erstausgabe von 1812 and 1815.* Edited by Heinz Rölleke and Ulrike Marquardt. 2 volumes and supplemental volume. Göttingen: Vandenhoeck & Ruprecht, 1986.

———. *Kinder- und Hausmärchen gesammelt durch die Brüder Grimm: Vollständige Ausgabe auf der Grundlage der dritten Auflage (1837).* Edited by Heinz Rölleke. Frankfurt a.M.: Deutscher Klassiker Verlag, 1985.

———. *Märchen aus dem Nachlaß der Brüder Grimm.* Edited by Heinz Rölleke. 3rd revised edition. Bonn: Bouvier, 1983.

———. *New Tales from Grimm.* Translated by Ruth Michaelis-Jena and Arthur Ratcliff. Edinburgh: W. and R. Chambers, 1960.

———. *Selected Tales.* Translated by David Luke, Gilbert McKay, and Philip Schofield. Middlesex: Penguin, 1982.

———. *Selected Tales.* Translated by Joyce Crick. Oxford: Oxford University Press, 2005.

———. *Unbekannte Märchen von Wilhelm und Jacob Grimm: Synopse von Einzeldrucken Grimmscher Märchen und deren endgültige Fassung in den KHM.* Edited by Heinz Rölleke. Köln: Diederichs, 1987.

———. *Die wahren Märchen der Brüder Grimm.* Edited by Heinz Rölleke. Frankfurt a.M.: Fischer, 1989.

Grimm, Wilhelm. *Kleinere Schriften.* 4 volumes. Edited by Gustav Hinrichs. Volumes 1–3. Berlin: Dümmler, 1881–83. Volume 4. Gütersloh: Bertelsmann, 1887.

Gyesi-Appiah, L. *Ananse Stories Retold: Some Common Traditional Tales.* Portsmouth, NH: Heinemann, 1997.

Ha, Tae Hung. *Folk Tales of Old Korea.* 1959. Seoul: Yonsei University Press, 1970.

Haddawy, Husain, trans. *The Arabian Nights.* 1990. New York: Norton, 1995.

———, trans. *The Arabian Nights II.* 1995. New York: Norton, 1996.

Hallett, Martin, and Barbara Karasek, eds. *Folk and Fairy Tales.* 2nd edition. Peterborough, Ontario: Broadview Press, 1996.

Hamilton, Virginia. *Her Stories: African American Folktales, Fairy Tales, and True Tales.* New York: Blue Sky/Scholastic, 1995.

Han, Suzanne Crowder. *Korean Folk and Fairy Tales.* Elizabeth, NJ: Hollym, 1991.

Haney, Jack V., ed. *The Complete Russian Folktale.* 7 volumes. Armonk, NY: M. E. Sharpe, 1999–2006.

Harf-Lancer, Laurence, ed. *Lais de Marie de France.* Paris: Librairie Générale Française, 1990.

Haring, Lee, ed. *Indian Ocean Folktales: Madagascar, Comoros, Mauritius, Réunion, Seychelles.* Chennai, India: National Folklore Support Centre, 2002.

Harris, Joel Chandler. *Uncle Remus: His Songs and His Sayings; The Folk-Lore of the Old Plantation.* New York: D. Appleton, 1880.

Harris, Joel Chandler, and Richard Chase, comp. *The Complete Tales of Uncle Remus.* Boston: Houghton Mifflin, 1955.

Hartland, Edwin Sidney, ed. *English Fairy and Folk Tales.* London: Walter Scott, 1890.

Hauff, Wilhelm. *Fairy Tales.* Translated by Jean Rosemary Edwards. London: P. Hamlyn, 1961.

———. *Tales.* Translated by S. Mendel. 1890. Freeport, NY: Books for Libraries Press, 1970.

Hay, Sara Henderson. *Story Hour*. Fayetteville: University of Arkansas Press, 1982.

Hearn, Lafcadio. *Kwaidan: Stories and Studies of Strange Things*. Tokyo: Tuttle Publishing, 2005.

Hearn, Michael Patrick, ed. *The Victorian Fairy Tale Book*. New York: Pantheon, 1988.

Hearne, Betsy, ed. *Beauties and Beasts*. Phoenix, AZ: Oryx Press, 1993.

Henderson, Helena, ed. *The Maiden Who Rose from the Sea and Other Finnish Folktales*. Enfield Lock: Hisarlik Press, 1992.

Hermes, Eberhard, ed. and trans. *The "Disciplina clericalis" of Petrus Alfonsi*. Berkeley: University of California Press, 1977.

Hesse, Hermann. *The Fairy Tales of Hermann Hesse*. Translated by Jack Zipes. New York: Bantam, 1995.

Heston, Wilma, and Mumtaz Nasir. *The Bazaar of the Storytellers*. Islamabad: Lok Virsa, n.d.

Hoffmann, E. T. A. *The Tales of Hoffmann*. Translated by Michael Bullock. New York: Frederick Ungar, 1963.

———. *Three Märchen of E. T. A. Hoffmann*. Translated by Charles Passage. Columbia: University of South Carolina Press, 1971.

Hoogasian-Villa, Susie, ed. *100 Armenian Tales and Their Folkloristic Relevance*. Detroit: Wayne State University Press, 1966.

Hurston, Zora Neale. *Every Tongue Got to Confess: Negro Folk-Tales from the Gulf States*. New York: Harper, 2001.

———. *Go Gator and Muddy the Water: Writings by Zora Neale Hurston from the Federal Writers' Project*. Ed. Pamela Bordelon. New York: Norton, 1999.

Inayat-ur-Rahman. *Folktales of Swat*. Part 1. Rome: IsMEO, 1968. Part 2. Peshawar: Khyber Printers, 1984.

Irving, Thomas Ballantine, ed. and trans. *Kalilah and Dimnah: An English Version of Bidpai's Fables Based upon Ancient Arabic and Spanish Manuscripts*. Newark, DE: Juan de la Cuesta, 1980.

Jacobs, Joseph. *English Fairy Tales and More English Fairy Tales*. Edited by Donald Haase. Santa Barbara: ABC-CLIO, 2002.

Jarvis, Shawn C., and Jeannine Blackwell, eds. and trans. *The Queen's Mirror: Fairy Tales by German Women, 1780–1900*. Lincoln: University of Nebraska Press, 2001.

Jasmin, Nadine, ed. *Madame d'Aulnoy: Contes des fées, suivis des Contes nouveaux ou Les fées à la mode*. Paris: Champion, 2004.

Kaltz, Barbara, ed. *Jeanne Marie Le Prince de Beaumont: Contes et autres écrits*. Oxford: Voltaire Foundation, 2000.

Keene, Donald, trans. "The Tale of the Bamboo Cutter." *Monumenta Nipponica* 11 (1955): 329–55.

Kelin, Daniel A., II, ed. *Marshall Islands Legends and Stories*. Honolulu: Bess Press, 2003.

Kennerly, Karen, ed. *Hesitant Wolf and Scrupulous Fox: Fables Selected from World Literature*. New York: Schocken, 1973.

Kharmawphlang, Desmond L., ed. *Narratives of North-East India*. Volume 1. Shillong, Meghalaya: Profra Publications (North Eastern Hill University), 2002.

Kim, So-Un. *The Story Bag: A Collection of Korean Folk Tales*. Translated by Setsu Higashi. Rutland, VT: Charles E. Tuttle, 1955.

Kincaid, C. A. *Deccan Nursery Tales or Fairy Tales from the South*. 1914. Detroit: Grand River Books, 1971.

Kingscote, G. A., and Pandit Natesa Sastri. *Tales of the Sun, or Folklore of Southern India*. 1890. New Delhi: Asian Educational Services, 1991.

Klymasz, Robert Bogdan. *Folk Narrative among Ukrainian-Canadians in Western Canada*. Ottawa: Canadian Centre for Folk Culture Studies, National Museum of Man, 1973.

Knowles, J. Hinton. *Kashmiri Folk Tales*. 1887. Islamabad: Lok Virsa, 1981.

Koén-Sarano, Matilda, ed. *King Solomon and the Golden Fish: Tales from the Sephardic Tradition*. Translated by Reginetta Haboucha. Detroit: Wayne State University Press, 2004.

Köhler-Zülch, Ines, and Christine Shojaei Kawan. *Schneewittchen hat viele Schwestern: Frauengestalten in europïschen Märchen. Beispiele und Kommentar*. Gütersloh: Gütersloher Verlagshaus Gerd Mohn, 1988.

Kunaver, Dušica. *Slovene Folk Tales*. Ljubljana: Dusica Kunaver, 1999.

Kuniczak, Wiesław S. *The Glass Mountain: Twenty-Eight Ancient Polish Folktales and Fables*. New York: Hippocrene Books, 1997.

Kvideland, Reimund, and Henning K. Sehmsdorf, eds. *All the World's Reward: Folktales Told by Five Scandinavian Storytellers*. Seattle: University of Washington Press, 1999.

———, eds. *Scandinavian Folk Belief and Legend*. Minneapolis: University of Minnesota Press, 1988.

Lang, Andrew, ed. *The Arabian Nights' Entertainments*. 1898. New York: Dover, 1969.

———, ed. *The Blue Fairy Book*. 1889. New York: Dover, 1965.

———, ed. *The Brown Fairy Book*. 1904. New York: Dover, 1965.

———, ed. *The Crimson Fairy Book*. 1903. New York: Dover, 1967.

———, ed. *The Green Fairy Book*. 1892. New York: Dover, 1965.

———, ed. *The Grey Fairy Book*. 1900. New York: Dover, 1967.

———, ed. *The Lilac Fairy Book*. 1910. New York: Dover, 1968.

———, ed. *The Olive Fairy Book*. 1907. New York: Dover, 1995.

———, ed. *The Orange Fairy Book*. 1906. New York: Dover, 1968.

———, ed. *The Pink Fairy Book*. 1897. New York: Dover, 1967.

———, ed. *The Red Fairy Book*. 1890. New York: Dover, 1966.

———, ed. *The Violet Fairy Tale Book*. 1901. New York: Dover, 1966.

———, ed. *The Yellow Fairy Book*. 1894. New York: Dover, 1966.

Lano, Michael, and Robert Viking O'Brien. "The Bride, the Spirit, and the Warrior: A Folktale from the Solomon Islands." *Marvels & Tales* 13 (1999): 69–77.

Laude-Cirtautas, Ilse. *Märchen der Usbeken*. Köln: Diederichs, 1984.

Lee, Tanith. *Red as Blood or Tales from the Sisters Grimmer*. New York: Daws, 1983.

Lemirre, Elisabeth, ed. *Le cabinet des fées*. 4 volumes. Arles: Picquier, 1994.

Lindahl, Carl, ed. *American Folktales from the Collections of the Library of Congress*. 2 volumes. Armonk, NY: M. E. Sharpe, 2004.

Loorits, Oskar, ed. *Estnische Volkserzählungen*. Berlin: de Gruyter, 1959.

Lorimer, D. L. R. *Folk Tales of Hunza*. 1934. Islamabad: Lok Virsa, 1981.

Lorimer, D. L. R., and E. S. Lorimer. *Persian Tales: Written Down for the First Time in the Original Kermani and Bakhtiari*. London: MacMillan, 1919.

Lox, Harlinda, trans. and ed. *Flämische Märchen*. München: Eugen Diederichs, 1999.

Lurie, Alison, ed. *Clever Gretchen and Other Forgotten Folktales*. New York: Crowell, 1980.

———, ed. *The Oxford Book of Modern Fairy Tales*. New York: Oxford University Press, 1993.

Malato, Enrico, ed. and introd. *Posilicheata*. By Pompeo Sarnelli. Rome: Gabriele e Mariateresa Benincasa, 1986.

Marie de France. *Fables*. Edited and translated by Harriet Spiegel. Toronto: University of Toronto Press, 1987.

Marshall, Bonnie C. *Tales from the Heart of the Balkans*. Edited by Vasa D. Mihailovich. Englewood, CO: Libraries Unlimited, 2001.

Marzolph, Ulrich, ed. *Feen-Mährchen: Zur Unterhaltung für Freunde und Freundinnen der Feenwelt; textkritischer Nachdruck der anonymen Ausgabe Braunschweig 1801*. Hildesheim: Olms, 2000.

———, ed. *Nasreddin Hodscha: 666 wahre Geschichten*. 1996. Munich: Beck, 2002.

Marzolph, Ulrich, and Ingrid Tomkowiak, eds. *Grimms Märchen international: Zehn der bekanntesten Grimmschen Märchen und ihre europäischen und außereuropäischen Verwandten*. 2 volumes. Paderborn: F. Schöningh, 1996.

Maspero, Gaston C., ed. *Popular Stories of Ancient Egypt*. Edited by Hasan El-Shamy. 2002. Oxford: Oxford University Press, 2004.

Massignon, Genevieve, ed. *Folktales of France*. Translated by Jacqueline Hyland. Chicago: University of Chicago Press, 1968.

Mathias, Elizabeth, and Richard Raspa. *Italian Folktales in America*. Detroit: Wayne State University Press, 1988.

Mattina, Anthony. *The Golden Woman: The Colville Narrative of Peter J. Seymour*. Tucson: University of Arizona Press, 1985.

Mayer, Charles-Joseph de, ed. *Cabinet des fées, ou collection choisie de contes des fées et autres contes merveilleux*. 41 volumes. Amsterdam and Paris, 1785–89.

Mayer, Fanny Hagin, trans. and ed. *Ancient Tales in Modern Japan: An Anthology of Japanese Folk Tales*. Bloomington: Indiana University Press, 1985.

Megas, Georgios A., ed. *Folktales of Greece*. Translated by Helen Colaclides. Chicago: University of Chicago Press, 1970.

Meyer, Maurits de. *Vlaamse Sprookjes*. 1951. Antwerp: Standaard Uitgeverij, 1995.

Mieder, Wolfgang, ed. *Disenchantments: An Anthology of Modern Fairy Tale Poetry*. Hanover, NH: University Press of New England, 1985.

———, ed. *Grimmige Märchen: Prosatexte von Ilse Aichinger bis Martin Walser*. Frankfurt a.M.: R. G. Fischer, 1986.

————, ed. *Grimms Märchen—modern: Prosa, Gedichte, Karikaturen.* Stuttgart: Philipp Reclam, 1979.

————, ed. *Mädchen, pfeif auf den Prinzen! Märchengedichte von Günter Grass bis Sarah Kirsch.* Köln: Eugen Diederichs, 1983.

Minard, Rosemary, ed. *Womenfolk and Fairy Tales.* Boston: Houghton, 1975.

Mitchnik, Helen. *Egyptian and Sudanese Folk-Tales.* Oxford: Oxford University Press, 1978.

Muhawi, Ibrahim, and Sharif Kanaana. *Speak Bird, Speak Again: Palestinian Folktales.* Berkley: University of California Press, 1989.

Musäus, Johann Karl August. *Volksmärchen der Deutschen.* Munich: Winkler, 1976.

Namjoshi, Suniti. *Feminist Fables. Saint Suniti and the Dragon.* 1981; 1994. New Delhi: Penguin, 1995.

Narayan, Kirin, with Urmila Devi Sood. *Mondays on the Dark Night of the Moon: Himalayan Foothill Folktales.* New York: Oxford University Press, 1997.

Narayana. *Animal Fables of India: Narayana's Hitopadesha or Friendly Counsel.* Translated by Francis G. Hutchins. West Franklin, NH: Amarta Press, 1985.

Naubert, Benedikte. *Neue Volksmärchen der Deutschen.* Edited by Marianne Henn, Paola Mayer, and Anita Runge. 4 volumes. Göttingen: Wallstein, 2001.

Nedo, Paul, et al., eds. *Die gläserne Linde: Westslawische Märchen.* Bautzen: Domowina-Verlag, 1972.

Nicoloff, Assen. *Bulgarian Folktales.* Cleveland: Nicoloff, 1979.

Norman, Howard A., ed. *Northern Tales: Traditional Stories of Eskimo and Indian Peoples.* New York: Pantheon, 1990.

Noy, Dov, and Dan Ben-Amos, eds. *The Folktales of Israel.* Translated by Gene Baharav. Chicago: University of Chicago Press, 1963.

Oparenko, Christina. *Ukrainian Folk-Tales.* Oxford: Oxford University Press, 1996.

Opie, Iona and Peter. *The Classic Fairy Tales.* Oxford: Oxford University Press, 1974.

Oppenheimer, Paul, trans. and ed. *Till Eulenspiegel: His Adventures.* New York: Routledge, 2001.

Orbell, Margaret, trans. *Traditional Maori Stories.* 1992. Auckland: Reed New Zealand, 1997.

O'Sullivan, Sean, ed. and trans. *Folktales of Ireland.* Chicago: University of Chicago Press, 1966.

Päär, Piret, and Anne Türnpu, comps. *Estonian Folktales: The Heavenly Wedding.* Tallinn: Varrak, 2005.

Parai, Raphael, trans. and ed. *Arab Folktales from Palestine and Israel.* Detroit: Wayne State University Press, 1998.

Paredes, Américo, ed. and trans. *Folktales of Mexico.* Chicago: University of Chicago Press, 1970.

Parker, Barrett, and Ahmad Javid. *A Collection of Afghan Legends.* Kabul: Franklin Press, 1970.

Parsons, Elsie Clews. *Folk-Lore of the Sea Islands, South Carolina.* Memoirs of The American Folk-Lore Society 16. Cambridge: American Folk-Lore Society, 1923.

Patard, Geneviève, ed. *Madame de Murat: Contes.* Paris: Honoré Champion, 2006.

Pattanaik, Devdutt. *The Man Who Was a Woman and Other Queer Tales.* New York: Harrington Park Press, 2002.

Peñalosa, Fernando. *Tales and Legends of the Q'anjob'al Maya.* Rancho Palos Verdes, CA: Yax Te' Foundation, 1999.

Penzer, N. M., ed. *The Ocean of Story, Being C. H. Tawney's Translation of Somadeva's Kathā Sarit Sāgara.* 10 volumes. 1924–28. Delhi: Motilal Banarsidass, 1968.

Perdue, Charles L., Jr., ed. *Outwitting the Devil: Jack Tales from Wise County, Virginia.* Santa Fe, NM: Ancient City Press, 1987.

Perrault, Charles. *Contes.* Edited by François Flahaut. Paris: Le Livre de Poche, 1987.

————. *Contes.* Edited by Gilbert Rouger. Paris: Garnier, 1967.

————. *Contes.* Edited by Jean-Pierre Collinet. Paris: Folio, 1981.

————. *The Fairy Tales of Charles Perrault.* Translated by Angela Carter. New York: Bard/Avon, 1979.

————. *Perrault's Complete Fairy Tales.* Translated by A. E. Johnson et al. New York: Dodd, Mead, 1961.

Pešková, Renata. *Czech Fairy-Tales.* Prague: Vitalis, 2000.

Phelps, Ethel Johnston, ed. *The Maid of the North: Feminist Folk Tales from around the World.* New York: Holt, 1981.

————. *Tatterhood and Other Tales.* Old Westbury, NY: Feminist, 1978.

Philip, Neil, ed. *The Penguin Book of English Folktales.* London: Penguin Books, 1992.

Picard, Barbara Leonie. *French Legends, Tales, and Fairy Stories.* London: Oxford University Press, 1955.

———. *Tales of Ancient Persia: Retold from the Shah-Name of Firdausi.* Oxford: Oxford University Press, 1993.

Pino-Saavedra, Yolando, comp. *Folktales of Chile.* Translated by Rockwell Gray. Chicago: University of Chicago Press, 1967.

Poggio Bracciolini, Gian Francesco. *The Facetiae of Poggio.* Paris: Liseux, 1879.

———. *The Facetiae of Poggio and Other Medieval Story-Tellers.* Edited and translated by Edward Storer. London: Routledge, 1928.

Polívka, Jiří, ed. *Súpis slovenských rozprávok.* 5 volumes. Turčiansky sv. Martin: Matica slovenská, 1923–31.

Posey, Alexander. *Chinnubbie and the Owl: Muscogee (Creek) Stories, Orations, and Oral Traditions.* Edited by Matthew Wynn Sivils. Lincoln: University of Nebraska Press, 2005.

Pourrat, Henri. *French Folktales from the Collection of Henri Pourrat.* Edited by C. G. Bjurström. Translated by Royall Tyler. New York: Pantheon, 1989.

Pú Sōnglíng. *Strange Stories from a Chinese Studio.* Translated by Herbert A. Giles. 2 volumes. London, 1880.

———. *Strange Tales from a Chinese Studio.* Translated by John Minford. London: Penguin, 2006.

Ragan, Kathleen, ed. *Fearless Girls, Wise Women, and Beloved Sisters: Heroines in Folktales from around the World.* New York: Norton, 1998.

Ramanujan, A. K. *A Flowering Tree and Other Oral Tales from India.* Berkeley: University of California Press, 1997.

———, ed. *Folktales from India: A Selection of Oral Tales from Twenty-Two Languages.* New York: Pantheon, 1991.

Randolph, Vance. *Pissing in the Snow and Other Ozark Folktales.* 1976. Chicago: University of Illinois Press, 1986.

Ranke, Kurt, ed. *Folktales of Germany.* Translated by Lotte Baumann. Chicago: University of Chicago Press, 1965.

Rausmaa, Pirkko-Liisa, and Ingrid Schellbach-Kopra, eds. *Finnische Volksmärchen.* München: Diederichs, 1993.

Ray and Rosa Hicks: The Last of the Old-Time Storytellers. DVD. Produced by Charles & Jane Hadley. 2000.

Reed, A. W. *Fairy Tales from the Pacific Islands.* Sydney: Reed, 1969.

———. *Myths and Legends of Polynesia.* Wellington: Reed, 1974.

Renel, Charles. *Contes de Madagascar.* 3 volumes. Paris: Ernest Leroux. 1910–30.

Rink, Hinrich. *Tales and Traditions of the Eskimo, with a Sketch of Their Habits, Religion, Language and Other Peculiarities.* 1875. New York: AMS Press, 1975.

Riordan, James. *Korean Folk-Tales.* Oxford: Oxford University Press, 1994.

Robert, Raymonde, ed. *Contes: Mademoiselle Lhériter, Mademoiselle Bernard, Mademoiselle de La Force, Madame Durand, and Madame d'Auneuil.* Paris: Champion, 2005.

Roberts, Moss, trans. and ed. *Chinese Fairy Tales and Fantasies.* New York: Pantheon, 1979.

Ryder, Arthur, trans. *The Panchatantra.* Chicago: University of Chicago Press, 1925.

Ryder, Frank G., and Robert M. Browning, eds. *German Literary Fairy Tales.* New York: Continuum, 1983.

Schami, Rafik. "The Magic Lamp." Translated by Alfred L. Cobbs. *Marvels & Tales* 16 (2002): 84–99.

Scheub, Harold. *The African Storyteller: Stories from African Oral Traditions.* Dubuque: Kendall Hunt Publishing, 1990.

———. *African Tales.* Madison: University of Wisconsin Press, 2005.

———, ed. *The World and the Word: Tales and Observations from the Xhosa Oral Tradition.* Madison: University of Wisconsin Press, 1992.

Schimmel, Annemarie, ed. and trans. *Märchen aus Pakistan: Aus dem Sindhi übersetzt.* Düsseldorf: Diederichs, 1980.

Schoolcraft, Henry Rowe. *Algic Researches: Indian Tales and Legends.* 1839. Baltimore: Clearfield, 1992.

Scott, Bill, ed. *Lies, Flies and Strange Big Fish: Tall Tales from the Bush.* St. Leonards, New South Wales: Allen & Unwin, 2000.

———. *Pelicans and Chihuahuas and Other Urban Legends.* St. Lucia, Queensland: University of Queensland Press, 1996.

Seki Keigo, ed. *Folktales of Japan.* Translated by Robert J. Adams. Chicago: University of Chicago Press, 1963.

Sexton, Anne. *Transformations.* Boston: Houghton Mifflin Company, 1971.

Shealy, Daniel, ed. *Louisa May Alcott's Fairy Tales and Fantasy Stories.* Knoxville: University of Tennessee Press, 1992.

Siddiqui, Ashraf, and Marilyn Lerch. *Pakistani Folk Tales.* New York: Hippocrene, 1998.

Simpson, Jacqueline. *Icelandic Folktales and Legends*. Berkeley: University of California Press, 1972.

———, trans. and ed. *Scandinavian Folktales*. London: Penguin, 1988.

Simpson, William Kelly, ed. *The Literature of Ancient Egypt: An Anthology of Stories, Instructions, and Poetry*. New Haven: Yale University Press, 1972.

Somadeva. *Tales from the Kathā-Sarit-Sāgara*. Translated by Arshia Sattar. New York: Penguin Books, 1994.

Spiegelman, Art, and Françoise Mouly, eds. *Folklore & Fairy Tale Funnies*. Little Lit. New York: HarperCollins, 2000.

Stahl, Caroline. "The Wicked Sisters and the Good One: A Fairy Tale." Translated by Shawn C. Jarvis. *Marvels & Tales* 14 (2000): 159–64.

Starck, Astrid, trans. and ed. *Un beau livre d'histoires/Eyn shön Mayse bukh: Fac-similé de l'editio princeps de Bâle (1602)*. 2 volumes. Basel: Schwabe, 2004.

Stevenson, Robert Louis. *South Sea Tales*. Edited by Roslyn Jolly. Oxford: Oxford University Press, 1996.

Stewart, Tony K., trans. *Fabulous Females and Peerless Pirs: Tales of Mad Adventure in Old Bengal*. New York: Oxford University Press, 2004.

Straparola, Giovan Francesco. *The Facetious Nights of Giovanni Francesco Straparola da Caravaggio*. Translated by W. G. Waters. 4 volumes. London: Society of Bibliophiles, 1898. http://www.surlalunefairytales.com/facetiousnights/index.html.

———. *Le piacevoli notti*. Edited by Donato Pirovano. 2 volumes. Rome: Salerno Editrice, 2000.

———. *Le piacevoli notti*. Edited by Pastore Stocchi. Rome-Bari: Laterza, 1975.

Sveinsson, Einar Ólafur. *The Folk-Stories of Iceland*. London: University College London, 2003.

Swan, Charles, trans., and Wynnard Hooper, ed. *Gesta Romanorum, or Entertaining Moral Stories*. 1876. New York: Dover Publications, 1959.

Swann, Brian, ed. *Coming to Light: Contemporary Translations of the Native Literatures of North America*. New York: Random House, 1994.

———, ed. *Voices from Four Directions: Contemporary Translations of the Native Literatures of North America*. Lincoln: University of Nebraska Press, 2004.

Swynnerton, Charles. *Folk Tales from the Upper Indus*. Islamabad: Lok Virsa, 1978. Reprint of *Indian Nights' Entertainment or, Folk-Tales from the Upper Indus*. 1892.

———. *Romantic Tales from the Panjâb with Indian Nights' Entertainment*. 1908. New Delhi: Asian Educational Services, 2004.

Taketori monogatari. Japanese Text Initiative. Electronic Text Center, University of Virginia Library. http://etext.lib.virginia.edu/japanese/taketori/AnoTake.html.

Tatar, Maria, ed. *The Annotated Brothers Grimm*. New York: Norton, 2004.

———, ed. *The Annotated Classic Fairy Tales*. New York: Norton, 2002.

———, ed. *The Classic Fairy Tales*. New York: Norton, 1999.

Taylor, Archer, ed. *English Riddles from Oral Tradition*. Berkeley: University of California Press, 1951.

Temple, Richard Carnac. *The Legends of the Punjab*. 1884. Islamabad: Lok Virsa, 1981.

———. *The Legends of the Punjab*. 3 volumes. 1883–85. Patiala: Punjabi University Press, 1962.

Thompson, Stith, ed. *One Hundred Favorite Folktales*. 1968. Bloomington: Indiana University Press, 1974.

———. *Tales of the North American Indians*. Cambridge: Harvard University Press, 1929.

Tille, Václav. *Soupis českých pohádek*. 2 volumes. Praha: Nákladem České Akademie věd a umění, 1929–37.

Tukaj, Mustafa. *Faith and Fairies: Tales Based on Albanian Legends and Ballads*. Edited by Joanne M. Ayers. Shkodra: Skodrinon, 2002.

Tutuola, Amos. *Yoruba Folktales*. Ibadan: Ibadan University Press, 1986.

Tyler, Royall, trans. and ed. *Japanese Tales*. New York: Pantheon, 1987.

Ueda Akinari. *Ugetsu monogatari: Tales of Moonlight and Rain*. Translated by Leon Zolbrod. Tokyo: Charles E. Tuttle Company, 1974.

Ury, Marian. *Tales of Times Now Past: 62 Stories from a Medieval Japanese Collection*. Berkeley: University of California Press, 1985.

Uther, Hans-Jörg, ed. *Deutsche Märchen und Sagen*. Digitale Bibliothek 80. CD-ROM. Berlin: Directmedia Publishing, 2003.

———, ed. *Europäische Märchen und Sagen*. Digitale Bibliothek 110. CD-ROM. Berlin: Directmedia Publishing, 2004.

Vaidya, Karunakar. *Folk Legends of Nepal*. Kathmandu: Ratna Pustak Bhandar, 1980.

Valenzuela, Luisa. *Other Weapons*. Translated by Deborah Bonner. Hanover, NH: Edicones de Norte, 1985.

———. *Simetrías*. Buenos Aires: Sudamericana, 1993.

———. *Symmetries*. Translated by Margaret Jull Costa. London: Serpent's Tail, 1998.

Valera, Juan. "The Green Bird." Translated by Robert M. Fedorchek. *Marvels & Tales* 13 (1999): 211–33.

———. "The Queen Mother." Translated by Robert M. Fedorchek. *Marvels & Tales* 17 (2003): 262–68.

van Buitenen, J. A. B., trans. *Tales of Ancient India*. Chicago: University of Chicago Press, 1959.

Verdaguer, Jacint. *Obres completes*. 5th edition. Barcelona: Editorial Selecta, 1974.

———. *Obres completes*. Vic: Eumo Editorial/ Societat Verdaguer, 1995.

Visnu Sarma. *The Pancatantra*. Translated by Chandra Rajan. New Delhi: Penguin Books India, 1993.

Walker, Warren S., and Ahmet E. Uysal, eds. *Tales Alive in Turkey*. Cambridge: Harvard University Press, 1966.

Warner, Marina, ed. *Wonder Tales*. 1994. New York: Frarrar, Straus and Giroux, 1996.

Waters, Donald, ed. *Strange Ways and Sweet Dreams: Afro-American Folklore from the Hampton Institute*. Boston: G. K. Hall, 1983.

Weinreich, Beatrice., ed. *Yiddish Folk Tales*. Translated by Leonard Wolf. New York: Pantheon, 1989.

Wesselski, Albert. *Märchen des Mittelalters*. Berlin: H. Stubenrauch, 1925.

Wheeler, Post. *Albanian Wonder Tales*. London: Lovat Dickson, 1936.

Wilbert, Johannes, and Karin Simoneau, series eds. The Folk Literature of South American Indians. 24 volumes. Los Angeles: UCLA Latin American Center, 1970–92.

Wilde, Oscar. *Complete Fairy Tales of Oscar Wilde*. Edited by Jack Zipes. New York: Penguin, 1990.

Windling, Terri, ed. *The Armless Maiden and Other Tales for Childhood's Survivors*. New York: Tor, 1995.

Wolterbeek, Marc. *Comic Tales of the Middle Ages: An Anthology and Commentary*. Westport, CT: Greenwood Press, 1991.

Yashinsky, Dan, ed. *At the Edge: A Book of Canadian Stories*. Charlottetown, Prince Edward Island: Ragweed, 1998.

Yeats, William Butler. *Fairy and Folk Tales of Ireland*. 1892. New York: Macmillan, 1973.

Yolen, Jane, ed. *Favorite Folktales from around the World*. New York: Pantheon, 1988.

Yolen, Jane, and Heidi E. Y. Stemple, eds. *Mirror, Mirror: Forty Folktales for Mothers and Daughters to Share*. New York: Viking, 2000.

Zall, P. M., ed. *A Hundred Merry Tales and Other English Jestbooks of the Fifteenth and Sixteenth Centuries*. Lincoln: University of Nebraska Press, 1963.

Zipes, Jack, ed. *Beauties, Beasts and Enchantments: Classic French Fairy Tales*. New York: New American Library, 1989.

———, ed. *Don't Bet on the Prince: Contemporary Feminist Fairy Tales in North America and England*. New York: Methuen, 1986.

———, ed and trans. *Fairy Tales and Fables from Weimar Days*. Hanover: University Press of New England, 1989.

———, ed. *The Great Fairy Tale Tradition: From Straparola and Basile to the Brothers Grimm*. New York: Norton, 2001.

———, ed. *The Outspoken Princess and the Gentle Knight: A Treasury of Modern Fairy Tales*. New York: Bantam, 1994.

———, ed. *Spells of Enchantment: The Wondrous Fairy Tales of Western Culture*. New York: Viking, 1991.

———, ed. *The Trials and Tribulations of Little Red Riding Hood*. 2nd edition. New York: Routledge, 1993.

———, ed. *The Trials and Tribulations of Little Red Riding Hood: Versions of the Tale in Sociocultural Context*. South Hadley, MA: Bergin and Garvey, 1983.

———, ed. *Victorian Fairy Tales: The Revolt of the Fairies and Elves*. New York: Methuen, 1987.

Zŏng In-Sŏb, ed. and trans. *Folk Tales from Korea*. 1952. Elizabeth, NJ: Hollym, 1982.

Folktale and Fairy-Tale Studies and Related Scholarship

Aarne, Antti. *The Types of the Folktale: A Classification and Bibliography*. Translated and enlarged by Stith Thompson. 2nd revision. 1961. Helsinki: Academia Scientiarum Fennica, 1987.

Abrahams, Roger D. *Deep Down in the Jungle: Negro Narrative Folklore from the Streets of Philadelphia*. 1963. Chicago: Aldine, 1974.

———. "Phantoms of Romantic Nationalism in Folkloristics." *Journal of American Folklore* 106 (1993): 3–37.

Abrahams, Roger D., and Alan Dundes. "Riddles." *Folklore and Folklife: An Introduction.* Edited by Richard M. Dorson. Chicago: University of Chicago Press, 1972. 130–43.

Accardo, Giovanni. "Le avventure della fantasia: I libri per bambini e per ragazzi di Luigi Malerba." *Studi novecenteschi* 23 (1996): 403–16.

Ahmed, Leila. *Edward W. Lane: A Study of His Life and Works and of British Ideas of the Middle East in the Nineteenth Century.* London: Longman, 1978.

Ajadi, Gabriel Ajiboye. "A Critical Introduction for and an Annotated Translation of D. O. Fagunwa's 'Igbó Olódùmarè (The Forest of God).'" Dissertation. Ball State University, 1985.

Alcover, Antoni Maria. "Com he fet mon Aplech de Rondayes Mallorquines." *Zeitschrift für romanische Philologie* 51 (1931): 94–111.

Ali, Muhsin Jassim. *Scheherazade in England: A Study of Nineteenth-Century English Criticism of the Arabian Nights.* Boulder, CO: Three Continents, 1981.

Allan, Robin. *Walt Disney and Europe: European Influences on the Animated Feature Films of Walt Disney.* London: John Libby, 1999.

Allison, Alida, ed. *Russell Hoban/Forty Years: Essays on His Writings for Children.* New York: Garland, 2000.

Alonso Montero, Xesús. "Antonio Machado y Alvarez ('Demófilo') e a cultura popular galega." *Senara: Revista de Filoloxia* 1 (1979): 127–50.

Altman, Charles. "Two Types of Opposition and the Structure of Latin Saints' Lives." *Medievalia et Humanistica* 6 (1975): 1–11.

Altner, Manfred. *Hermynia Zur Mühlen: Eine Biographie.* Bern: Peter Lang, 1997.

Alvey, Richard G. "The Historical Development of Organized Storytelling for Children in the United States." Dissertation. University of Pennsylavania, 1974.

Amin, Magda. "Stories, Stories, Stories: Rafik Schami's *Erzähler der Nacht.*" *Alif: Journal of Comparative Poetics* 20 (2000): 211–33.

Amodio, Mark C. *Writing the Oral Tradition: Oral Poetics and Literate Culture in Medieval England.* Notre Dame, IN: University of Notre Dame Press, 2004.

Anatol, Giselle Liza, ed. *Reading Harry Potter: Critical Essays.* Westport, CT: Praeger Publishers, 2003.

Andersen, Jens. *Hans Christian Andersen: A New Life.* Translated by Tiina Nunnally. Woodstock, NY: Overlook Press, 2005.

Anderson, Christopher L., and Lynne Vespe Sheay. "Ana María Matute's *Primera memoria*: A Fairy Tale Gone Awry." *Revista Canadiense de estudios Hispánicos* 14 (1989): 1–14.

Anderson, Graham. *Fairytale in the Ancient World.* New York: Routledge, 2000.

———. *Greek and Roman Folklore: A Handbook.* Westport, CT: Greenwood Press, 2006.

Andriès, Lise, and Geneviève Bollème. *La bibliothèque bleue: Littérature de colportage.* Paris: Robert Laffont, 2003.

Angelopoulou, Anna, and Aigli Brouskou. *Catalogue raisonné des contes grecs: Types AT 700–749.* Paris: Maisonneuve et Larose, 1995.

Anghelescu, Mircea. *Introducere în opera lui Petre Ispirescu.* Bucharest: Editura Minerva, 1987.

Anttonen, Pertti. *Tradition Through Modernity: Postmodernism and the Nation-State in Folklore Scholarship.* Helsinki: Finnish Literature Society, 2005.

Aoki Michiko Yamaguchi. *Izumo fūdoki.* Tokyo: Sophia University, 1971.

Apo, Satu. "Lönnrot's Voice in the *Kalevala.*" *Dynamics of Tradition: Perspectives on Oral Poetry and Folk Belief.* Edited by Lotte Tarkka. Helskinki: Finnish Literature Society, 2003. 266–76.

———. *The Narrative World of Finnish Fairy Tales: Structure, Allegory, and Evaluation in Southwest Finnish Folktales.* Helsinki: Academia Scientiarum Fennica, 1995.

———. "A Singing Scribe or a Nationalist Author? The Making of the Kalevala as Described by Elias Lönnrot." *FF Network* 25 (December 2003): 3–12.

Apo, Satu, Aili Nenola, and Laura Stark-Arola, eds. *Gender and Folklore: Perspectives on Finnish and Karelian Culture.* Helsinki: Finnish Literature Society, 1998.

Appadurai, Arjun, Frank J. Korom, and Margaret A. Mills, eds. *Gender, Genre and Power in South Asian Expressive Traditions.* Philadelphia: University of Pennsylvania Press, 1991.

Aprile, Renato. *Indice delle fiabe popolari italiane di magia.* 1 volume to date. Firenze: Leo S. Olschki, 2000– .

Ariès, Philippe. *Centuries of Childhood*. Translated by Robert Baldick. New York: Random House, 1962.

Aristodemo, Dina, and Pieter de Meijer. "Le fiabe popolari fra cultura regionale e cultura nazionale." *Belfagor* 34 (1979): 711–16.

Artiss, David S. "Theodor Storm's Four Märchen: Early Examples of His Prose Technique." *Seminar* 14 (1978): 149–68.

Asad, Talal. "The Concept of Cultural Translation in British Social Anthropology." *Writing Culture: The Poetics and Politics of Ethnography*. Edited by James Clifford and George E. Marcus. Berkeley: University of California Press, 1986. 141–64.

Ashliman, D. L. *Aging and Death in Folklore*. 2006. http://www.pitt.edu/~dash/aging.html.

———. *Censorship in Folklore*. 2006. http://www.pitt.edu/~dash/censor.html.

———. *Fairy Lore: A Handbook*. Westport, CT: Greenwood Press, 2005.

———. *Folk and Fairy Tales: A Handbook*. Westport, CT: Greenwood Press, 2004.

———. *A Guide to Folktales in the English Language: Based on the Aarne-Thompson Classification System*. Westport, CT: Greenwood Press, 1987.

———. "Hermann Hesse's Fairy Tales and Their Analogs in Folklore." *Wegbereiter der Moderne*. Edited by Helmut Koopmann and Clark Muenzer. Tübingen: Niemeyer, 1990. 88–113.

———. *Incest in Indo-European Folktales*. 1997. http://www.pitt.edu/~dash/incest.html.

———. *Multiple Births in Legend and Folklore*. 2006. http://www.pitt.edu/~dash/manykids.html.

———. *The Name of the Helper*. 2006. http://www.pitt.edu/~dash/type0500.html.

———. "Symbolic Sex-Role Reversals in the Grimms' Fairy Tales." *Forms of the Fantastic: Selected Essays from the Third International Conference on the Fantastic in Film and Literature*. Edited by Jan Hokenson and Howard Pearce. Westport, CT: Greenwood, 1986. 192–98.

Ashton, John. *Chap-Books of the Eighteenth Century*. 1882. New York: B. Blom, 1966.

Asor Rosa, Alberto. "Le avventure di Pinocchio: Storia di un burattino." *Letteratura italiana: Le opere III; Dall'Ottocento al Novecento*. Edited by Alberto Asor Rosa. Turin: Einaudi, 1995. 879–950.

Attar, Samar, and Gerhard Fischer. "Promiscuity, Emancipation, Submission: The Civilizing Process and the Establishment of a Female Role Model in the Frame-Story of 1,001 Nights." *Arab Studies Quarterly* 13.3–4 (1991): 1–18.

Attebery, Brian. *The Fantasy Tradition in American Literature: From Irving to Le Guin*. Bloomington: Indiana University Press, 1980.

———. "Gender, Fantasy, and the Authority of Tradition." *Journal of the Fantastic in the Arts* 7 (1996): 51–60.

Avery, Gillian. "Written for Children: Two Eighteenth-Century English Fairy Tales." *Marvels & Tales* 16 (2002): 143–55.

Avery, Gillian, and Julia Briggs, eds. *Children and Their Books: A Celebration of the Work of Iona and Peter Opie*. Milton Keynes: The Open University Press, 1990.

Ayres, Brenda, ed. *The Emperor's Old Groove: Decolonizing Disney's Magic Kingdom*. New York: Peter Lang, 2003.

Azadovskii, Mark. *A Siberian Tale Teller*. Translated by James R. Dow. Austin: University of Texas, 1974.

Azarnoff, Pat. *Health, Illness, and Disability: A Guide to Books for Children and Young Adults*. New York: Bowker, 1983.

Azzolina, David S. *Tale Type and Motif-Indexes: An Annotated Bibliography*. New York: Garland Publishing, 1987.

Baader, Renate. *Dames de lettres: Autorinnen des preziösen, hocharistokratischen und "modernen" Salons (1649–1698)*. Stuttgart: Metzler, 1986.

Babcock-Abrahams, Barbara. "'A Tolerated Margin of Mess': The Trickster and His Tales Reconsidered." *Journal of the Folklore Institute* 11.3 (1975): 147–86.

Bacchilega, Cristina. "Calvino's Journey: Modern Transformations of Folktale, Story, and Myth." *Journal of Folklore Research* 26 (1989): 81–98.

———. "Folktales, Fictions and Meta-Fictions: Their Interaction in Robert Coover's *Pricksongs and Descants*." *New York Folklore* 6.3–4 (1980): 171–84.

———. *Postmodern Fairy Tales: Gender and Narrative Strategies*. Philadelphia: University of Pennsylvania Press, 1997.

———. "Reflections on Recent English-Language Fairy-Tale Fiction by Women." *Fabula* 47 (2006): 201–10.

Bacchilega, Cristina, and Steven Swann Jones, eds. *Perspectives on the Innocent Persecuted Heroine in Fairy Tales*. Special issue of *Western Folklore* 52.1 (1993).

Baer, Florence E. *Sources and Analogues of the Uncle Remus Tales.* Helsinki: Academia Scientiarum Fennica, 1980.

Bagnall, Norma. "An American Hero in Welsh Fantasy: The Mabinogion, Alan Garner and Lloyd Alexander." *New Welsh Review* 2.4 (1990): 26–29.

Bakhtin, M. M. "The Problem of Speech Genres." *Speech Genres and Other Late Essays.* Edited by Caryl Emerson and Michael Holquist. Austin: University of Texas Press, 1986. 60–102.

Balló, Jordi, and Xavier Pérez. "La ascensión por el amor: La Cenicienta." *La semilla inmortal: Los argumentos universales en el cine.* Barcelona: Anagrama, 1997. 193–207.

Bamgbose, Ayo. *The Novels of D. O. Fagunwa.* Benin City: Ethiope, 1974.

Banerjee, Debjani. "Nationalist and Feminist Identities: Moments of Confrontation and Complicity in Post-Colonial Fiction and Film." Dissertation. State University of New York, Stony Brook, 1995.

Banfield, Stephen. *Sondheim's Broadway Musicals.* Ann Arbor: University of Michigan Press, 1993.

Bannerman, Kenn. "A Short Interview with Jack Zipes." April 2002. http://www.bitingdogpress.com/zipes/zipes.html.

Barag, L. G., et al. *Sravnitel'ny ukazatel syuzhetov: Vostochnoslavyanskaya skazka.* Leningrad: Nauka, 1979.

Barber, C. L. *Shakespeare's Festive Comedy: A Study of Dramatic Form and Its Relation to Social Custom.* Princeton, NJ: Princeton University Press, 1959.

Barchilon, Jacques. *Le conte merveilleux français de 1690 à 1790: Cent ans de féerie et de poésie ignorées de l'histoire littéraire.* Paris: Champion, 1975.

Barchilon, Jacques, and Peter Flinders. *Charles Perrault.* Boston: Twayne, 1981.

Barker, Adele Marie. *The Mother Syndrome in the Russian Folk Imagination.* Columbus: Slavica, 1986.

Bârlea, Ovidiu. *Istoria folcloristicii românești.* București: Editura Enciclopedică, 1974.

Barr, Allan. "Disarming Intruders: Alien Women in *Liaozhai Zhiyi.*" *Harvard Journal of Asiatic Studies* 49 (1989): 501–17.

Barr, John. *Illustrated Children's Books.* London: The British Library, 1986.

Barthes, Roland. *Image, Music, Text.* New York: Noonday, 1977.

Bartis, Peter. *Folklife Sourcebook: A Directory of Folklife Resources in the United States.* 3rd edition, revised and expanded. Washington, D.C.: American Folklife Center, Library of Congress, 1997. http://www.loc.gov/folklife/source/index.html.

Bartlett, F. C. "Some Experiments on the Reproduction of Folk Stories." 1920. *The Study of Folklore.* Edited by Alan Dundes. Englewood Cliffs, NJ: Prentice-Hall, 1965. 243–58.

Barzilai, Shuli. "The Blubeard Syndrome in Atwood's Lady Oracle: Fear and Femininity." *Marvels & Tales* 19 (2005): 249–73.

———. "'Grandmother, what a dreadfully big mouth you have!' Lacan's Parables of the Maternal Object." *Lacan and the Matter of Origins.* Stanford, CA: Stanford University Press, 1999. 199–226.

———. "Reading 'Snow White': The Mother's Story." *Signs* 15 (1990): 515–34.

Bascom, William. "The Four Functions of Folklore." *Journal of American Folklore* 67 (1954): 333–49.

———. "Verbal Art." *Journal of American Folklore* 68 (1955): 245–52.

Başgöz, İlhan, and Pertev N. Boratav. *I, Hoca Nasreddin, Never Shall I Die.* Bloomington: Indiana University Press, 1998.

Bastian, Ulrike. *Die "Kinder- und Hausmärchen" der Brüder Grimm in der literaturpädagogischen Diskussion des 19. und 20. Jahrhunderts.* Frankfurt a.M.: Haag und Herchen, 1981.

Bates, Gerri. *Alice Walker: A Critical Companion.* Westport, CT: Greenwood Press, 2005.

Baughman, Ernest. *Type and Motif-Index of the Folktales of England and North America.* The Hague: Mouton, 1966.

Bauman, Richard, ed. *Folklore, Cultural Performances, and Popular Entertainments: A Communications-Centered Handbook.* New York: Oxford University Press, 1992.

———. *Story Performance and Event.* 1986. Cambridge: Cambridge University Press, 1992.

———. *Verbal Art as Performance.* Prospect Heights, IL: Waveland Press, 1977.

Bausinger, Hermann. *Folk Culture in a World of Technology.* Translated by Elke Dettmer. Bloomington: Indiana University Press, 1990.

———. "Zur Kontextforschung in der Folklorewissenschaft der Vereinigten Staaten von Amerika." *Jahrbuch für Volksliedforschung* 26 (1981): 11–14.

Bechtolsheim, Barbara von. "Die Brüder Grimm neu schreiben: Zeitgenössische Märchengedichte amerikanischer Frauen." Dissertation. Stanford University, 1987.

Becker, Richarda. *Die weibliche Initiation im ostslawischen Zaubermärchen.* Berlin: Otto Harrassowitz, 1990.

Beckett, Sandra L. *Recycling Red Riding Hood.* New York: Routledge, 2002.

Belcher, Stephen. "The Framed Tale and the Oral Tradition: A Reconsideration." *Fabula* 35 (1994): 1–19.

———. "Parallel Tracks? The Seven Sages, the Arabian Nights, and Their Arrival in Europe." *South Asian Review* 19.16 (1995): 11–23.

Bell, Elizabeth, Lynda Haas, and Laura Sells, eds. *From Mouse to Mermaid: The Politics of Film, Gender, and Culture.* Bloomington: Indiana University Press, 1995.

Bell-Villada, Gene H., ed. *Conversations with García Márquez.* Jackson: University Press of Mississippi, 2005.

Belvaude, Catherine E. *Amos Tutuola et l'univers du conte africain.* Paris: L'Harmattan, 1989.

Ben-Amos, Dan. "Context in Context." *Western Folklore* 52 (1993): 209–26.

———. *Do We Need Ideal Types (in Folklore)?* Turku: Nordic Institute of Folklore, 1992.

———, ed. *Folklore Genres.* Austin: University of Texas Press, 1976.

———. "Toward a Definition of Folklore in Context." *Journal of American Folklore* 84 (1971): 3–15.

Ben-Amos, Dan, and Kenneth S. Goldstein, eds. *Folklore: Performance and Communication.* The Hague: Mouton, 1975.

Bendix, Regina. "Folk Narrative, Opera and the Expression of Cultural Identity." *Fabula* 31 (1990): 297–303.

———. *In Search of Authenticity: The Formation of Folklore Studies.* Madison: University of Wisconsin Press, 1997.

———. "On the Road to Fiction: Narrative Reification in Austrian Cultural Tourism." *Ethnologia Europaea* 29 (1999): 29–40.

Bendix, Regina, and Rosemary Lévy Zumwalt, eds. *Folklore Interpreted: Essays in Honor of Alan Dundes.* New York: Garland Publishing, 1995.

Bennett, Gillian. *Bodies: Sex, Violence, Disease and Death in Contemporary Legend.* Jackson: University Press of Mississippi, 2005.

Benson, Larry D., and Theodore M. Anderson. *The Literary Context of Chaucer's Fabliaux: Texts and Translations.* New York: Bobbs-Merrill, 1971.

Benson, Stephen. *Cycles of Influence: Fiction, Folktale, Theory.* Detroit: Wayne State University Press, 2003.

———. "'Something's missing': Towards a Listening Space for Fairy-Tale Opera." *New Comparison* 31 (2001): 112–29.

———. "Stories of Love and Death: Reading and Writing the Fairy Tale Romance." *Image and Power: Women in Fiction in the Twentieth Century.* Edited by Darah Sceats and Gail Cunningham. London: Longman, 1996: 103–13.

Berger, Dorothea. "Die Volksmärchen der Deutschen von Musäus, ein Meisterwerk der Rokokodichtung." *PMLA* 69 (1954): 1200–12.

Berger, Eberhard, and Joachim Giera, eds. *77 Marchenfilme: Ein Filmführer für jung und alt.* Berlin: Henschel, 1990.

Bergstrand, Ulla, and Maria Nikolajeva. *Läckergommarnas kungarike: Om matens roll i barnlitteraturen.* Stockholm: Centre for the Study of Childhood Culture, 1999.

Berlioz, Jacques, Claude Bremond, and Catherine Velay-Vallantin. *Formes médiévales du conte merveilleux.* Paris: Éditions Stock, 1989.

Berndt, Ronald M., and Catherine H. Berndt. *The Speaking Land: Myth and Story in Aboriginal Australia.* Ringwood, Victoria: Penguin Books, 1989.

Bernheimer, Kate, ed. *Brothers and Beasts: An Anthology of Men on Fairy Tales.* Detroit: Wayne State University Press, 2007.

———, ed. *Mirror, Mirror on the Wall: Women Writers Explore Their Favorite Fairy Tales.* 2nd edition. New York: Anchor, 2002.

———. "This Rapturous Form." *Marvels & Tales* 20 (2006): 67–83.

Bernstein, Matthew, and Gaylyn Studlar, eds. *Visions of the East: Orientalism in Film.* New Brunswick, NJ: Rutgers University Press, 1997.

Berry, Thomas. "Aleksei Alekseevich Perovsky (Antonii Pogorel'sky)." *Russian Literature in the Age of Pushkin and Gogol: Prose.* Edited by Chrisine Rydel. Detroit: Gale, 1999. 256–63.

Bethea, David M., ed. *The Pushkin Handbook.* Madison: University of Wisconsin Press, 2005.

Bettelheim, Bruno. *The Uses of Enchantment: The Meaning and Importance of Fairy Tales.* New York: Alfred A. Knopf, 1976.

Beyer, Harald, and Edvard Beyer. *Norsk litteratur historie*. Oslo: H. Aschehoug, 1978.

Bierhorst, John. *The Mythology of Mexico and Central America*. 2nd revised edition. New York: Oxford University Press, 2002.

———. *The Mythology of North America*. New York: Morrow, 1985.

———. *The Mythology of South America*. 2nd revised edition. New York: Oxford University Press, 2002.

Bilbija, Ksenija. "In Whose Own Image? Ana María Shua's Gendered Poetics of Fairy Tales." *El rio de los sueños: Aproximaciones criticas a la obra de Ana María Shua*. Edited by Rhonda Dahl Buchanan. Washington, DC: Organization of American States, 2001. 205–18.

Birberick, Anne L. "Rewriting Curiosity: The Psyche Myth in Apuleius, La Fontaine, and d'Aulnoy." *Strategic Rewriting*. Edited by David Lee Rubin. Charlottesville, VA: Rookwood, 2002. 134–48.

Birkalan, Hande. "Nachrichten: Pertev Naili Boratav (1907–1998)." *Fabula* 45 (2004): 113–17.

———. "Pertev Naili Boratav and His Contributions to Turkish Folklore." MA thesis. Indiana University, 1995.

———. "Pertev Naili Boratav, Turkish Politics, and the University Events." *Turkish Studies Association Bulletin* 25.1 (2001): 39–60.

Birkhan, Helmut, et al., eds. *Motif Index of German Secular Narratives from the Beginning to 1400*. 2 volumes. Berlin: Walter de Gruyter, 2005.

Birkhäuser-Oeri, Sibylle. *The Mother: Archetypal Image in Fairy Tales*. Translated by Michael Mitchell. Toronto: Inner City Books, 1988.

Birkin, Andrew. *J. M. Barrie and the Lost Boys*. 1979. New Haven: Yale University Press, 2003.

Black, Stephen A. *James Thurber: His Masquerades—A Critical Study*. The Hague: Mouton, 1970.

Blackham, H. J. *The Fable as Literature*. London: Athlone Press, 1985.

Blackwell, Jeannine. "Fractured Fairy Tales: German Women Authors and the Grimm Tradition." *Germanic Review* 62 (1987): 162–74.

———. "Laying the Rod to Rest: Narrative Strategies in Gisela and Bettina von Arnim's Fairy-Tale Novel *Gritta*." *Marvels & Tales* 11 (1997): 24–47.

———. "The Many Names of Rumpelstiltskin: Recent Research on the Grimms' *Kinder- und Haus-Märchen*." *German Quarterly* 63 (1990): 107–12.

Blair, Walter. "The Funny Fondled Fairytale Frog." *Studies in American Humor* 1 (1982): 17–23.

Blamires, David. "The Meaning of Disfigurement in Wilhelm Hauff's 'Dwarf Nose.'" *Children's Literature in Education* 33 (2002): 297–307.

Bloch, Ernst. *The Utopian Function of Art and Literature: Selected Essays*. Translated by Jack Zipes and Frank Mecklenburg. Cambridge: MIT Press, 1988.

Bloom, Harold, ed. *Gabriel García Márquez*. Philadelphia: Chelsea House, 1992.

———. *Jorge Luis Borges*. Broomhall, PA.: Chelsea House, 2002.

Bluhm, Lothar. *Die Brüder Grimm und der Beginn der Deutschen Philologie: Eine Studie zu Kommunikation und Wissenschaftsbildung*. Hildesheim: Weidmann, 1997.

———. *Grimm-Philologie: Beiträge zur Märchenforschung und Wissenschaftsgeschichte*. Hildesheim: Olms-Weidmann, 1995.

———. "A New Debate about 'Old Marie'? Critical Observations on the Attempt to Remythologize Grimms' Fairy Tales from a Sociohistorical Perspective." Translated by Deborah Lokai Bischof. *Marvels & Tales* 14 (2000): 287–311.

Bluhm, Lothar, and Heinz Rölleke. "Redensarten des Volks, auf die ich immer horche": *Märchen–Sprichwort–Redensart; Zur volkspoetischen Ausgestaltung der "Kinder- und Hausmärchen" durch die Brüder Grimm*. Stuttgart: Hirzel, 1997.

Blumenthal, Eileen. *Puppetry: A World History*. New York: Harry N. Abrams, 2005.

Bly, Robert. *Iron John: A Book about Men*. New York: Vintage Books, 1990.

Boas, Franz. *Race, Language, and Culture*. Chicago: University of Chicago Press, 1940.

Boček, Jaroslav. *Jiří Trnka: Artist and Puppet Master*. Translated by Till Gottheiner. [Prague:] Artia, 1965.

Bochman, Victor. "The Jews and 'The Arabian Nights.'" *The Israel Review of Arts and Letters* 103 (1996): 39–47.

Bode, Andreas. "Humor in the Lyrical Stories for Children of Samuel Marshak and Korney Chukovsky." Translated by Martha Baker. *Lion and the Unicorn* 13.2 (1989): 34–55.

Boggs, Ralph. *Index of Spanish Folktales*. Helsinki: Adademia Scientiarum Fennica, 1930.

Böhm-Korff, Regina. *Deutung und Bedeutung von "Hänsel und Gretel."* Frankfurt a.M.: Peter Lang, 1991.

Boivin, Aurélien. *Le conte fantastique québécois au XIXe siècle*. Montréal: Fides, 2004.

Boland, Roy C. "Luisa Valenzuela and *Simetrías*: Tales of a Subversive Mother Goose." *Antípodas* 6–7 (1994–95): 229–37.

Bolte, Johannes, and Georg Polívka. *Anmerkungen zu den Kinder- und Hausmärchen der Brüder Grimm*. 5 volumes. 1913–32. Hildesheim: Olms, 1963.

Bond, Barbara. "Postmodern Mannerism: An Examination of Robert Coover's *Pinocchio in Venice*." *Critique* 45 (2004): 273–92.

Børdahl, Vibeke, ed. *The Eternal Storyteller: Oral Literature in Modern China*. Richmond, Surrey: Curzon Press, 1999.

Borum, Poul. *Danish Literature*. Copenhagen: Det Danske Selskap, 1979.

Bosisio, Paolo. *Fiabe teatrali*. Rome: Bulzoni, 1984.

Bottigheimer, Ruth B. "'Beauty and the Beast': Marriage and Money—Motif and Motivation." *Midwestern Folklore* 15.2 (1989): 79–88.

———. *Fairy Godfather: Straparola, Venice, and the Fairy Tale Tradition*. Philadelphia: University of Pennsylvania Press, 2002.

———, ed. *Fairy Tales and Society: Illusion, Allusion, and Paradigm*. Philadelphia: University of Pennsylvania Press, 1986.

———. "Fairy Tales, Folk Narrative Research and History." *Social History* 14.3 (1989): 343–57.

———. *Grimms' Bad Girls and Bold Boys: The Moral and Social Vision of the Tales*. New Haven, CT: Yale University Press, 1987.

———. "Iconographic Continuity in Illustrations of 'The Goose Girl.'" *Children's Literature* 13 (1985): 49–71.

———. "Luckless, Witless, and Filthy-Footed: A Sociocultural Study and Publishing History Analysis of *Lazy Boy*." *Journal of American Folklore* 106 (1993): 259–84.

———. "Ludwig Bechstein's Fairy Tales: Nineteenth Century Bestsellers and Bürgerlichkeit." *Internationales Archiv für Sozialgeschichte der deutschen Literatur* 15.2 (1990): 55–88.

———. "Motif, Meaning, and Editorial Change in Grimms' Tales: One Plot, Three Tales, and Three Different Stories. *D'un conte … à l'autre: La variabilité dans la littérature orale/ From One Tale … to the Other: Variability in Oral Literature*. Ed. Veronika Görög-Karady. Paris: Éditions du Centre National de la Recherche Scientifique, 1990. 541–52.

———. "Rudolf Schenda and Folk Narrative." *Europeœa* 3.1 (1997): 123–32.

———. "Silenced Women in the Grimms' Tales: The 'Fit' Between Fairy Tales and Society in Their Historical Context." *Fairy Tales and Society: Illusion, Allusion, and Paradigm*. Edited by Ruth B. Bottigheimer. Philadelphia: University of Pennsylvania Press, 1986. 115–31.

Bottner, Barbara. "William Steig: The Two Legacies." *Lion and the Unicorn* 2.1 (1978): 4–16.

Bowman, Marion. "Vernacular Religion and Nature: The 'Bible of the Folk' Tradition in Newfoundland." *Folklore* 114.3 (2003): 285–95.

Boyer, L. Bryce, Ruth M. Boyer, and Stephen M. Sonnenberg, eds. *The Psychoanalytic Study of Society: Essays in Honor of Alan Dundes*. Hillsdale, NJ: The Analytic Press, 1993.

Brackert, Helmut, ed. *Und wenn sie nicht gestorben sind …: Perspektiven auf das Märchen*. Frankfurt a.M.: Suhrkamp, 1980.

Bradbrook, Bohuslava R. *Karel Čapek: In Pursuit of Truth, Tolerance, and Trust*. Brighton: Sussex Academic Press, 1998.

Brady, Philip, Timothy McFarland, and John J. White, eds. *Günter Grass's "Der Butt": Sexual Politics and the Male Myth of History*. Oxford: Clarendon Press, 1990.

Bray, Dorothy Ann. *A List of Motifs in the Lives of Early Irish Saints*. Helsinki: Academia Scientiarum Fennica, 1992.

Brednich, Rolf W. "Methoden der Erzählforschung." *Methoden der Volkskunde: Positionen, Quellen, Arbeitsweisen der Europäischen Ethnologie*. Edited by Silke Göttsch and Albrecht Lehmann. Berlin: Dietrich Reimer Verlag, 2001. 57–77.

———. *Volkserzählungen und Volksglaube von den Schicksalsfrauen*. Helsinki: Academia Scientiarum Fennica, 1964.

———. *www.worldwidewitz.com: Humor im Cyberspace*. Freiburg im Breisgau: Herder, 2005.

Bredsdorff, Elias. *Hans Christian Andersen: The Story of His Life and Work, 1805–75*. New York: Farrar, Straus and Giroux, 1994.

Bremond, Claude, Jacques Le Goff, and Jean-Claude Schmitt. *L'exemplum*. Turnhout: Brepols, 1982.

Breteque, François de la. "Les contes de Georges Méliès." *Contes et légendes à l'écran*. Special issue of *CinémAction* 116 (2005): 62–71.

Bridgwater, Patrick. *Kafka, Gothic and Fairytale*. Amsterdam: Rodopi, 2003.

Briggs, Katharine M. *The Anatomy of Puck: An Examination of Fairy Beliefs among Shakespeare's Contemporaries and Successors.* London: Routledge, 1959.

———. *A Dictionary of British Folk-Tales in the English Language: Incorporating the F. J. Norton Collection.* 4 volumes. London: Routledge and Kegan Paul, 1970–71.

———. *A Dictionary of Fairies: Hobgoblins, Brownies, Bogies, and other Supernatural Creatures.* Harmondsworth: Penguin, 1977.

———. *An Encyclopedia of Fairies: Hobgoblins, Brownies, Bogies, and Other Supernatural Creatures.* New York: Pantheon, 1976.

———. *The Fairies in English Tradition and Literature.* Chicago: University of Chicago Press, 1967.

———. *Nine Lives: Cats in Folklore.* London: Routledge & Kegan Paul, 1980.

Brocklebank, Lisa. "Disney's *Mulan*—the 'True' Deconstructed Heroine?" *Marvels & Tales* 14 (2000): 268–83.

Bronzini, Giovanni Battista. *La letteratura popolare italiana dell'Otto-Novecento: Profilo storico-geografico.* [Novara]: Istituto geografico De Agostini; [Florence]: Le Monnier, 1994.

Brown, Carolyn S. *The Tall Tale in American Folklore and Literature.* Knoxville: University of Tennessee Press, 1987.

Brown, Eric C. "The Influence of Queen Victoria on England's Literary Fairy Tale." *Marvels & Tales* 13 (1999): 31–51.

Brown, Joan Lipman. *Secrets from the Back Room: The Fiction of Carmen Martín Gaite.* University, MS: Romance Monographs, 1987.

Brown, Mary Ellen, and Bruce A. Rosenberg, eds. *Encyclopedia of Folklore and Literature.* Santa Barbara: ABC-CLIO, 1998.

Brown, Penny. "Gustave Doré's Magical Realism: The *Nouveaux contes de fée*s of the Comtesse de Ségur." *Modern Language Review* 95 (2000): 964–77.

Bruford, Alan. *Gaelic Folk-Tales and Mediaeval Romances: A Study of the Early Modern Irish "Romantic Tales" and Their Oral Derivatives.* Dublin: The Folklore of Ireland Society, 1969.

Brunvand, Erik. "The Heroic Hacker: Legends of the Computer Age." *The Truth Never Stands in the Way of a Good Story.* Urbana: University of Illinois Press, 2000. 170–98.

Brunvand, Jan Harold. *Encyclopedia of Urban Legends.* New York: W. W. Norton, 2002.

———. *The Study of American Folklore: An Introduction.* New York: Norton, 1968.

———. *The Truth Never Stands in the Way of a Good Story.* Urbana: University of Illinois Press, 2000.

Bryan, William Frank, ed. *Sources and Analogues of Chaucer's Canterbury Tales.* Chicago: University of Chicago Press, 1941.

Bryant, Jen. "A Conversation with Donna Jo Napoli, Eileen and Jerry Spinelli." *Image: A Journal of the Arts and Religion* 28 (2000): 79–92.

Buchanan, Rhonda Dahl. "Literature's Rebellious Genre: The Short Short Story in Ana María Shua's *Casa de geishas.*" *Revista Interamericana de Bibliografía* 46.1–4 (1996): 179–92.

Buczkowski, Paul. "J. R. Planché, Frederick Robson, and the Fairy Extravaganza." *Marvels & Tales* 15 (2001): 42–65.

Buijnsters, P. J., and Leontine Buijnsters-Smets. *Lust en leerling: Geschiedenis van het Nederlandse kinderboek in de negentiende eeuw.* Zwolle: Waande, 2001.

Burne, Glenn S. "Andrew Lang's *The Blue Fairy Book*: Changing the Course of History." *Touchstones: Reflections on the Best in Children's Literature.* Volume 2. West Lafayette: Children's Literature Association, 1987. 140–50.

Burns, Thomas A. "Folkloristics: A Conception of Theory." *Folk Groups and Folklore Genres: A Reader.* Edited by Eliott Oring. 1977. Logan: Utah State University Press 1989. 1–20.

Butler, Andrew M., Edward James, and Farah Mendlesohn. *Terry Pratchett: Guilty of Literature.* Reading: The Science Fiction Foundation, 2000.

Butler, Charles. *Four British Fantasists: Place and Culture in the Children's Fantasies of Penelope Lively, Alan Garner, Diana Wynne Jones, and Susan Cooper.* Lanham, MD: Children's Literature Association and The Scarecrow Press, 2006.

Bynum, Brant. *Romantic Imagination in the Works of Gustavo Adolfo Bécquer.* Chapel Hill: University of North Carolina Press, 1994.

Calame-Griaule, Geneviève. "Les chemins de l'autre monde: Contes initiatiques africains." *Cahiers de Littérature Orale* 39–40 (1996): 29–59.

———. *Des cauris au marché: Essais sur des contes africains.* Paris: Société des Africanistes, 1987.

———. "The Father's Bowl: Analysis of a Dogon Version of AT 480." *Research in African Literatures* 15.2 (1984): 168–84.

Calame-Griaule, Geneviève, Veronika Görög-Karady, and Michèle Chiche, eds. *Le conte: Pourquoi? Comment?* Paris: Éditions du Centre National de la Recherche Scientifique, 1984.

Callan, Richard. *Miguel Angel Asturias.* New York: Twayne, 1970.

Camayd-Freixas, Erik. "Magical Realism as Primitivism: An Alternate Verisimilitude." *Romance Languages Annual* 9 (1998): 414–23.

Campany, Rob. "Demons, Gods, and Pilgrims: The Demonology of the Hsi-yu Chi." *Chinese Literature: Essays, Articles, Reviews* 7.1–2 (1985): 95–115.

Campion-Vincent, Véronique. *Organ Theft Legends.* Jackson: University Press of Mississippi, 2005.

Canepa, Nancy. *From Court to Forest: Giambattista Basile's* Lo cunto de li cunti *and the Birth of the Literary Fairy Tale.* Detroit: Wayne State University Press, 1999.

———, ed. *Out of the Woods: The Origins of the Literary Fairy Tale in Italy and France.* Detroit: Wayne State University Press, 1997.

Canton, Katia. *The Fairytale Revisited: A Survey of the Evolution of the Tales, from Classical Literary Interpretations to Innovative Contemporary Dance-Theater Productions.* New York: Peter Lang, 1994.

Capasso, Ruth Carver. "Traduction libre: Science in *Les Contes d'une Grand-mère.*" *George Sand Studies* 16 (1997): 57–68.

Caporello-Szykman, Corradina. *The Boccaccian Novella: Creation and Waning of a Genre.* Bern: Lang, 1990.

Caracciolo, Peter L., ed. *The Arabian Nights in English Literature: Studies in the Reception of* The Thousand and One Nights *into British Culture.* New York: St. Martin's, 1988.

Cardigos, Isabel. *Catalogue of Portuguese Folktales.* Helsinki: Academia Scientiarum Fennica, 2006.

———. *In and Out of Enchantment: Blood Symbolism and Gender in Portuguese Fairytales.* Helsinki: Academia Scientiarum Fennica, 1996.

———. "The Wearing and Shedding of Enchanted Shoes." *Estudos de literatura oral* 5 (1999): 219–28.

Carsch, Henry. "Fairy Tales and Socialization: The Fairy in Grimms' Tales." *Personality and Social Life.* Edited by Robert Endleman. New York: Random House, 1967, 238–55.

———. "The Role of the Devil in Grimms' Tales: An Exploration of the Content and Function of Popular Tales." *Social Research* 35 (1968): 466–99.

———. "Witchcraft and Spirit Possession in Grimm's Fairy Tales." *Journal of Popular Culture* 2 (1969): 627–48.

Carson, Barbara Harrell. *Eudora Welty: Two Pictures at Once in Her Frame.* Troy, NY: Whitston, 1992.

Carter, James Bucky. "Princes, Beasts, or Royal Pains: Men and Masculinity in the Revisionist Fairy Tales of Mary E. Wilkins Freeman." *Marvels & Tales* 20 (2006): 30–46.

Carter-Sigglow, Janet. *Making Her Way with Thunder: A Reappraisal of Zora Neale Hurston's Narrative Art.* New York: Peter Lang, 1994.

Castaldo, Annalisa. "'No More Yielding Than a Dream': The Construction of Shakespeare in *The Sandman.*" *College Literature* 31.4 (2004): 94–110.

Castro, Rafaela G. *Chicano Folklore: A Guide to the Folktales, Traditions, Rituals, and Religious Practices of Mexican Americans.* New York: Oxford University Press, 2001.

Cavicchioli, Sonia. *The Tale of Cupid and Psyche: An Illustrated History.* New York: Braziller, 2002.

Cejpek, Jiri. "Iranian Folk-Literature." *History of Iranian Literature.* Edited by Jan Rypka. Dordrecht: D. Reidel, 1968. 607–709.

Cesaresco, Evelyn Martinengo. "Giuseppe Pitrè." *Folklore* 27 (1916): 314–16.

Chainani, Soman. "Sadeian Tragedy: The Politics of Content Revision in Angela Carter's 'Snow Child.'" *Marvels & Tales* 17 (2003): 212–35.

Chalupa, Cynthia. "Re-Imagining the Fantastic: E. T. A. Hoffmann's 'The Story of the Lost Reflection.'" *Marvels & Tales* 20 (2006): 11–29.

Chamberlain, Basil Hall. *The Kojiki: Records of Ancient Matters.* Tokyo: Tuttle Publishing, 2005.

Chan, Leo Tak-hung. "Text and Talk: Classical Literary Tales in Traditional China and the Context of Casual Oral Storytelling." *Asian Folklore Studies* 56 (1997): 33–63.

Chance, Jane. *Tolkien and the Invention of Myth: A Reader.* Louisville: University Press of Kentucky, 2004.

Chang, Chun-shu, and Shelley Hsueh-Lun Chang. *Redefining History: Ghosts, Spirits, and Human Society in P'u Sung-Ling's World, 1640–1715.* Ann Arbor: University of Michigan Press, 1999.

Chatelain, Héli. *Folk-Tales of Angola*. Boston, 1894.

Chauvin, Victor. *Bibliographie des ouvrages arabes ou relatifs aux Arabes: Publiés dans l'Europe chrétienne de 1810 à 1885*. 12 volumes. Liége: Imprimerie H. Vaillant-Carmanne, 1892–1922.

Chavkin, Allan, ed. *The Chippewa Landscape of Louise Erdrich*. Tuscaloosa: University of Alabama Press, 1999.

Chraïbi, Aboubakr. "Galland's 'Ali Baba' and Other Arabic Versions." *Marvels & Tales* 18 (2004): 159–69.

———, ed. *Les mille et une nuits en partage*. Paris: Sinbad, 2004.

Christiansen, Reidar Thoralf. *The Migratory Legends: A Proposed List of Types with a Systematic Catalogue of the Norwegian Variants*. 1958. Helsinki: Academia Scientiarum Fennica, 1992.

Christie, Ian, and Andrew Moor, eds. *The Cinema of Michael Powell: International Perspectives on an English Film-Maker*. London: BFI Publishing, 2005.

Cianciolo, Patricia. *Illustrations in Children's Books*. Dubuque: Wm. C. Browne, 1970.

Cirese, Alberto M. "Folklore in Italy: A Historical and Systematic Profile and Bibliography." *Journal of the Folklore Institute* 11 (1974): 7–79.

———. "Paragrafi su Vittorio Imbriani demopsicologo." *Problemi: Periodico Quadrimestrale di Cultura* 80 (1987): 228–57.

Clancy, Particia A. "Mme Leprince de Beaumont: Founder of Children's Literature in France." *Australian Journal of French Studies* 16.2 (1979): 281–87.

Clapham, John. "The Operas of Antonín Dvořák." *Proceedings of the Royal Musical Association* 84 (1957–58): 55–69.

Clark, Stuart. *Thinking with Demons: The Idea of Witchcraft in Early Modern Europe*. New York: Clarendon Press, 1997.

Claudel, C. "Golden Hair." *Southern Folklore Quarterly* 5 (1941): 257–63.

Claus, Peter J., and Frank J. Korom. *Folkloristics and Indian Folklore*. Udupi, India: Regional Resources Centre for Folk Performing Arts, 1991.

Claus, Peter J., Sarah Diamond, and Margaret Ann Mills, eds. *South Asian Folklore: An Encyclopedia: Afghanistan, Bangladesh, India, Nepal, Pakistan, Sri Lanka*. New York: Routledge, 2003.

Clausen-Stolzenburg, Maren. *Märchen und mittelalterliche Literaturtradition*. Heidelberg: Universitätsverlag Carl Winter, 1995.

Clements, Robert J., and Jospeh Gibaldi. *Anatomy of the Novella: The European Tale Collection from Boccaccio and Chaucer to Cervantes*. New York: New York University Press, 1977.

Clements, William, ed. *The Greenwood Encyclopedia of World Folklore and Folklife*. Westport, CT: Greenwood, 2005.

Clinton, Jerome W. "Madness and Cure in the *Thousand and One Nights*." *Fairy Tales and Society: Illusion, Allusion and Paradigm*. Edited by Ruth B. Bottigheimer. Philadelphia: University of Pennsylvania Press, 1986. 35–51.

Clodd, Edward. "The Philosophy of Rumpelstiltskin." *Folk-Lore Journal* 7 (1889): 135–63.

———. *Tom Tit Tot: An Essay on Savage Philosophy in Folk-Tale*. London: Duckworth and Company, 1898.

Clouston, William Alexander. *Flowers from a Persian Garden and Other Papers*. London: David Nutt, 1890. 121–82.

Cocchiara, Giuseppe. *The History of Folklore in Europe*. Translated by John N. McDaniel. Philadelphia: Institute for the Study of Human Issues, 1981.

———. *Pitrè la Sicilia e il folklore*. Messina: Casa Editrice G. Anna, 1951.

———. *Popolo e letteratura in Italia*. Turin: Einaudi, 1959.

———. *Storia degli studi delle tradizioni popolari in Italia*. Palermo: G. B. Palumbo Editore, 1947.

Cocteau, Jean. *Beauty and the Beast: Diary of a Film*. Translated by Ronald Duncan. New York: Dover, 1972.

Coldwell, Paul. "Paula Rego—Printmaker." *The Saatchi Gallery*. http://www.saatchi-gallery.co.uk/artists/paula_rego_about.htm.

Colligan-Taylor, Karen. "Miyazawa Kenji: The Seeds of a Land Ethic." *The Emergence of Environmental Literature in Japan*. New York: Garland, 1990. 34–68.

Collins, Harold. *Amos Tutuola*. New York: Twayne, 1969.

Conger, Bill, Jan Susian, and Maria Tatar. *Pixerina Witcherina*. Normal: University Galleries of Illinois State University, 2002.

Conrad, JoAnn. "Docile Bodies of (Im)Material Girls: The Fairy-Tale Construction of Jon Benet

Ramsey and Princess Diana." *Marvels & Tales* 13 (1999): 125–69.

———. "Polyphemus and Tepegöz Revisited: A Comparison of the Tales of the Blinding of the One-Eyed Ogre in Western and Turkish Traditions." *Fabula* 40 (1999): 278–97.

Cooks, Leda M., Mark P. Orbe, and Carol S. Bruess. "The Fairy Tale Theme in Popular Culture: A Semiotic Analysis of *Pretty Woman*." *Women's Studies in Communication* 16.2 (1993): 86–104.

Coomaraswamy, Ananda. "On the Loathly Bride." *Speculum* 20 (1945): 391–404.

Coombs, Felicity, and Suzanne Gemmell, eds. *Piano Lessons: Approaches to the Piano*. London: John Libbey, 1999.

Cooper, Barbara Rosemarie Latotzky. "Madame de Villeneuve: The Author of 'La Belle et la Bête' and Her Literary Legacy. Dissertation. University of Georgia, 1985.

Cooperson, Michael. "The Monstrous Births of 'Aladdin.'" *Harvard Middle Eastern and Islamic Review* 1 (1994): 67–86. Reprinted in *The* Arabian Nights *Reader*. Edited by Ulrich Marzolph. Detroit: Wayne State University Press, 2006. 265–82.

Corballis, Richard, and Simon Garrett. *Introducing Witi Ihimaera*. Auckland: Longman Paul, 1984.

Corten, Irina H. "Evgenii L'vovich Shvarts: A Selected Bibliography." *Russian Literature Triquarterly* 16 (1979): 333–39.

———. "Evgenii Shvarts as an Adapter of Hans Christian Andersen and Charles Perrault." *Russian Review* 37 (1978): 51–67.

———. "Evgeny Lvovich Shvarts: A Biographical Sketch." *Russian Literature Triquarterly* 16 (1979): 222–43.

Cortez, Maria Teresa. "Die Emanzipation der Frau und Grimms Märchen: Portugiesische Fassungen des 19. Jahrhunderts." *A germanística portuguesa em tempo de debate*. Special issue of *Runa: Revista portuguese de estudos Germanísticos* 25.2 (1996): 603–12.

Cosquin, Emmanuel. "Le conte de la chaudière bouillante et la feinte maladresse dans l'Inde et hors de l'Inde." *Études folkloriques: Recherches sur la migrations des contes populaires et leur point de départ*. Paris: E. Champion, 1922. 349–99.

———. *Études folkloriques: Recherches sur la migrations des contes populaires et leur point de départ*. Paris: E. Champion, 1922.

Cottino-Jones, Marga. "Princesses, Kings, and the Fantastic: A Re-Vision of the Language of Representation in the Renaissance." *Italian Quarterly* 37 (2000): 173–84.

Coupe, Laurence. *Myth: The New Critical Idiom*. London: Routledge, 1997.

Cox, Marian Roalfe. *Cinderella: Three Hundred and Forty-Five Variants of Cinderella, Catskin, and Cap o' Rushes*. London: The Folk-lore Society, 1893.

Crafton, Donald. *Before Mickey: The Animated Film, 1898–1928*. Chicago: University of Chicago Press, 1993.

Crago, Hugh. "Who Does Snow White Look At?" *Signal* 45 (1984): 129–45.

Crawford, Robert, and Anne Varty, eds. *Liz Lochhead's Voices*. Edinburgh: Edinburgh University Press, 1993.

Creeser, Rosemary. "Cocteau for Kids: Rediscovering *The Singing Ringing Tree*." *Cinema and the Realms of Enchantment: Lectures, Seminars and Essays by Marina Warner and Others*. Edited by Duncan Petrie. London: British Film Institute, 1993. 111–24.

Croft, Janet Brennan, ed. *Tolkien on Film: Essays on Peter Jackson's The Lord of the Rings*. Altadena, CA: Mythopoeic, 2004.

Cuff, Roger Penn. "Mark Twain's Use of California Folklore in His Jumping Frog Story." *Journal of American Folklore* 65 (1952): 155–58.

Cullen, Bonnie. "For Whom the Shoe Fits: *Cinderella* in the Hands of Victorian Illustrators and Writers." *Lion and the Unicorn* 27.1 (2003): 57–82.

Culley, Jonathon. "Roald Dahl—'It's About Children and It's for Children'—But Is It Suitable?" *Children's Literature in Education* 22 (1991): 59–73.

Curry, Mark, ed. *Metafiction*. London: Longman, 1995.

Cypress, Sandra M. *La Malinche in Mexican Literature: From History to Myth*. Austin: University of Texas Press, 1991.

Dadié, Bernard Bilin. "Le conte, élément de solidarité et d'universalité." *Présence Africaine* 27–28 (1959): 69–80.

———. "Folklore and Literature." Translated by C. L. Patterson. *The Proceedings of the First International Congress of Africanists, Accra, 11th–18th December 1962*. Edited by Lalage Brown and Michael Crowder. Evanston: Northwestern University Press, 1964. 199–219.

———. "Le rôle de la légende dans la culture populaire des noirs d'Afrique." *Présence Africaine* 14–15 (1957): 165–74.

Dal, Erik. *Danske H. C. Andersen-illustrationer, 1835–1975*. Copenhagen: Forening for Boghaandværk, 1975.

Daniels, Morna. *Victorian Book Illustration*. London: The British Library, 1988.

Darnton, Robert. *The Great Cat Massacre and Other Episodes in French Cultural History*. New York: Basic Books, 1984.

Dashwood, Julia. "The Metamorphoses of a Fairy-Tale: Quillard, D'Annunzio and The Girl With Cut-Off Hands." *Romancing Decay: Ideas of Decadence in European Culture*. Edited by Michael St. John, 1999. 118–27.

Daskalova Perkowski, Liliana, et al. *Typenverzeichnis der bulgarischen Volksmärchen*. Edited by Klaus Roth. Helsinki: Academia Scientiarum Fennica, 1995.

Davenport, Tom. "Some Personal Notes on Adapting Folk-Fairy Tales to Film." *Children's Literature* 9 (1981): 107–15.

Davidson, H. R. Ellis. *Katharine Briggs: Story-Teller*. Cambridge: Lutterworth Press, 1986.

Davidson, Hilda Ellis, and Anna Chaudhri, ed. *A Companion to the Fairy Tale*. Cambridge: D. S. Brewer, 2003.

Davies, Mererid Puw. *The Tale of Bluebeard in German Literature from the Eighteenth Century to the Present*. Oxford: Oxford University Press, 2001.

De Vos, Gail, and Anna E. Altmann. *New Tales for Old: Folktales as Literary Fictions for Young Adults*. Englewood, CO: Libraries Unlimited, 1999.

———. *Tales, Then and Now: More Folktales as Literary Fictions for Young Adults*. Englewood, CO: Libraries Unlimited, 2001.

DeCoster, Cyrus. *Juan Valera*. Boston: Twayne, 1974.

Décote, Georges. *L'itinéraire de Jacques Cazotte, 1719–1792: De la fiction littéraire au mysticisme politique*. Genève: Droz, 1984.

Defrance, Anne. *Les contes de fées et les nouvelles de Madame d'Aulnoy*. Geneva: Droz, 1998.

Defrance, Anne, and Jean-François Perrin, eds. *Le conte en ses paroles: La figuration de l'oralité dans le conte merveilleux du Classicisme aux Lumières*. Paris: Édition Desjonquères, 2007.

Dégh, Linda. *American Folklore and the Mass Media*. Bloomington: Indiana University Press. 1994.

———. "Collecting Legends Today: Welcome to the Bewildering Maze of the Internet." *Europäische Ethnologie und Folklore im internationalen Kontext: Festschrift für Leander Petzoldt zum 65. Geburtstag*. Edited by Ingo Schneider. Frankfurt a.M.: Peter Lang, 1999. 55–66.

———. *Folktales and Society: Story-Telling in a Hungarian Peasant Community*. Translated by Emily M. Schossberger. Expanded edition. Bloomington: Indiana University Press, 1989.

———. *Legend and Belief: Dialectics of a Genre*. Bloomington: Indiana University Press, 2001.

———. "The Memorate and Protomemorate" *Journal of American Folklore* 87 (1974): 225–39.

Dégh, Linda, and Andrew Vázsonyi. "The Hypothesis of Multi-Conduit Transmission in Folklore." *Folklore: Performance and Communication*. Edited by Dan Ben-Amos and Kenneth S. Goldstein. The Hague: Mouton, 1975. 207–54.

———. "Magic for Sale: Märchen and Legend in TV Advertising." *Fabula* 20 (1979): 47–68.

deGraff, Amy. "From Glass Slipper to Glass Ceiling: 'Cinderella' and the Endurance of a Fairy Tale." *Merveilles et contes* 10 (1996): 69–85.

Dekker, Ton, Jurjen Van Der Kooi, and Theo Meder. *Van Aladdin tot Zwaan kleef aan: lexicon van sprookjes*. Nijmegen: SUN, 1997.

Del Giudice, Luisa. "Mountains of Cheese and Rivers of Wine: Paese di Cuccagna and Other Gastronomic Utopias." *Imagined States: Nationalism, Utopia, and Longing in Oral Cultures*. Edited by Luisa Del Giudice and Gerald Porter. Logan: Utah State University Press, 2001. 11–63.

Delacampagne, Ariane and Christian. *Here Be Dragons: A Fantastic Bestiary*. Translated by Ariane Delacampagne. Princeton, NJ: Princeton University Press, 2003.

Delarue, Paul. "Les contes de Perrault et la tradition populaire." *Bulletin folklorique d'Île-de-France* 12 (1951): 195–201.

DeMarcus, Cynthia Lynn. "Reawakening Sleeping Beauty: Fairy-Tale Revision and the Mid-Victorian Metaphysical Crisis." Dissertation. Louisiana State University, 1999.

Demisch, Heinz. *Ludwig Richter, 1803–1884: Eine Revision*. Berlin: Mann, 2003.

Demurova, Nina. "Toward a Definition of *Alice*'s Genre: The Folktale and Fairy-Tale Connections." *Lewis Carroll: A Celebration; Essays on the Occasion of the 150th Anniversary of the Birth of Charles Lutwidge Dodgson*. Edited by Edward Guiliano. New York: Potter, 1982. 75–88.

Denecke, Ludwig. *Jacob Grimm und sein Bruder Wilhelm*. Stuttgart: Metzler, 1971.

Denman, Hugh, ed. *Isaac Bashevis Singer: His Work and His World*. Leiden: Brill, 2002.

Di Giovanni, Norman Thomas. *The Lesson of the Master: On Borges and His Work*. New York: Continuum, 2003.

Días, José A. *Jacinto Benavente and His Theatre*. Long Island City: Las Americas Publishing, 1972.

Didier, Béatrice. "George Sand et les structures du conte populaire." *George Sand*. Edited by Simone Vierne. Paris: CDU/SEDES, 1983. 101–14.

Dieckmann, H. "Fairy-Tales in Psychotherapy." *The Journal of Analytical Psychology* 42.2 (1997): 253–68.

Diederichs, Ulf. *Who's Who im Märchen*. München: Deutscher Taschenbuch Verlag, 1995.

Dollerup, Cay. *Tales and Translation: The Grimm Tales from Pan-Germanic Narratives to Shared International Fairytales*. Amsterdam: John Benjamins, 1999.

Donati, Cesarina. *Tre racconti proibiti di Trancoso*. Rome: Bulzoni, 1983.

Doonan, Jane. "Drawing Out Ideas: A Second Decade of the Work of Anthony Browne." *Lion and the Unicorn* 23 (1998) 1: 30–56.

———. "The Object Lesson: Picture Books of Anthony Browne." *Word and Image* 2 (1986): 159–72.

Dorson, Richard M. *America in Legend: Folklore from the Colonial Period to the Present*. New York: Pantheon Books, 1973.

———. *The British Folklorists: A History*. Chicago: University of Chicago Press, 1968.

———. "The Eclipse of Solar Mythology." *Journal of American Folklore* 68 (1955): 393–416.

———. *Folklore and Fakelore: Essays Toward a Discipline of Folk Studies*. Cambridge: Harvard University Press, 1976.

———. "Stith Thompson (1885–1976)." *Journal of American Folklore* 90 (1977): 2–7.

Dorst, John D. "Neck-Riddle as a Dialogue of Genres." *Journal of American Folklore* 96 (1983): 413–33.

Dow, James R. *German Folklore: A Handbook*. Westport, CT: Greenwood Press, 2006.

Dow, James R., and Hannjost Lixfeld, trans. and eds. *German Volkskunde: A Decade of Theoretical Confrontation, Debate, and Reorientation (1967–1977)*. Bloomington: Indiana University Press, 1986.

Drazen, Patrick. "Flying with Ghibli: The Animation of Hayao Miyazaki and Company." *Anime Explosion: The What? Why? & Wow! of Japanese Animation*. Berkeley: Stone Bridge Press, 2003. 253–79.

Duchêne, Roger. *La Fontaine*. Paris: Fayard, 1990.

Dudbridge, Glen. *The Hsi-yu Chi: A Study of Antecedents to the Sixteenth-Century Chinese Novel*. Cambridge: Cambridge University Press, 1977.

Duffy, John-Charles. "Gay-Related Themes in the Fairy Tales of Oscar Wilde." *Victorian Literature and Culture* 29.2 (2001): 327–49.

Duggan, Anne E. "Feminine Genealogy, Matriarchy, and Utopia in the Fairy Tale of Marie-Catherine d'Aulnoy." *Neophilologus* 82 (1998): 199–208.

———. "Nature and Culture in the Fairy Tale of Marie-Catherine d'Aulnoy." *Marvels & Tales* 15 (2001): 149–67.

———. *Salonnières, Fairies, and Furies: The Politics of Gender and Cultural Change in Absolutist France*. Delaware: Delaware University Press, 2005.

Dunbar, Janet. *J. M. Barrie: The Man behind the Image*. London: Collins, 1970.

Dundes, Alan. "Advertising and Folklore." *New York Folklore Quarterly* 19 (1963): 143–51.

———. "The Anthropologist and the Comparative Method." *Journal of Folklore Research* 23 (1986): 125–46.

———, ed. *The Blood Libel Legend: A Casebook in Anti-Semitic Folklore*. Madison: University of Wisconsin Press, 1991.

———. "Bruno Bettelheim's Uses of Enchantment and Abuses of Scholarship." *Journal of American Folklore* 104 (1991): 74–83.

———, ed. *Cinderella: A Folklore Casebook*. Madison: University of Wisconsin Press, 1982.

———. "The Fabrication of Faklore." *Folklore Matters*. Knoxville: University of Tennessee Press, 1989. 40–56.

———. "Fairy Tales from a Folkloristic Perspective." *Fairy Tales and Society: Illusion, Allusion, and Paradigm*. Edited by Ruth B. Bottigheimer. Philadelphia: University of Pennsylvania Press, 1986. 259–69.

———, ed. *Folklore: Critical Concepts in Literary and Cultural Studies*. New York: Routledge, 2004.

———. "From Etic to Emic Units in the Structural Study of Folktales." *Journal of American Folklore* 75 (1962): 95–105.

————, ed. *Little Red Riding Hood: A Casebook.* Madison: University of Wisconsin Press, 1989.

————. *The Morphology of North American Indian Folktales.* 1964. Helsinki: Academia Scientiarum Fennica, 1980.

————. "The Motif-Index and the Tale Type Index: A Critique." *Journal of Folklore Research* 34 (1997): 195–202.

————. "The Psychoanalytic Study of Folklore." *Annals of Scholarship* 3 (1985): 1–42.

————. "The Psychoanalytic Study of the Grimms' Tales: 'The Maiden without Hands' (AT 706)." *Folklore Matters.* Knoxville: University of Tennessee Press, 1989. 112–50.

————, ed. *Sacred Narrative: Readings in the Theory of Myth.* Berkeley: University of California Press, 1984.

————. *The Study of Folklore.* Englewood Cliffs: Prentice Hall, 1965.

————. "The Symbolic Equivalence of Allomotifs: Towards a Method of Analyzing Folktales." *Le conte: Pourquoi? Comment?* Edited by Geneviève Calame-Griaule, Veronika Görög-Karady, and Michèle Chiche. Paris: Éditions du Centre National de la Recherche Scientifique, 1984. 187–97.

————. "Texture, Text, and Context." *Southern Folklore Quarterly,* 28 (1964): 251–265.

————. "'To Love My Father All': A Psychoanalytic Study of the Folktale Source of *King Lear.*" *Interpreting Folklore.* Bloomington: Indiana University Press, 1980. 211–22.

————. "Who Are the Folk?" *Interpreting Folklore.* Bloomington: Indiana University Press, 1980. 1–19.

Dundes, Alan, Lord Raglan, and Otto Rank. *In Quest of the Hero.* Princeton: Princeton University Press, 1990.

Dussutour-Hammer, Michèle. *Amos Tutuola: Tradition orale et écriture du conte.* Paris: Présence Africaine, 1976.

Earthman, Elise. "Instructions for Survival—Or Plans for Disaster? Young Adult Novels with Mythological Themes." *He Said, She Says: An RSVP to the Male Text.* Edited by Mica Howe and Sarah Appleton Aguiar. Madison, NJ: Fairleigh Dickinson University Press, 2001. 161–75.

Eastman, Mary Huse. *Index to Fairy Tales, Myths, and Legends.* 2 volumes. Boston: Faxon, 1937–1952. Continued by Norma Ireland, *Index to Fairy Tales;* and Joseph W. Sprug, *Index to Fairy Tales.*

Edebiri, Unionmwam, ed. *Bernard Dadié: Hommages et Études.* Ivry-sur-Seine: Nouvelles du Sud, 1992.

Edemariam, Aida. "Riches of a Double Life." *The Guardian* October 4, 2003. http://books.guardian.co.uk/review/story/0,12084,1054206,00.html.

Edmonson, Munro S. *Lore: An Introduction to the Science of Folklore and Literature.* New York: Holt, Rinehart and Winston, 1971.

Edmunds, Catherine J. "Pushkin and Gogol' as Sources for the Librettos of the Fantastic Fairy Tale Operas of Rimskij-Korsakov." Dissertation. Harvard University, 1985.

Edström, Vivi. *Astrid Lindgren: A Critical Study.* Translated by Eivor Cormack. Stockholm: Rabén & Sjögren, 2000.

————. *Selma Lagerlöf: Livets vågspel.* Stockholm: Natur og Kultur, 2002.

Egan, Rodney K. *Laurence Housman.* Stroud: Catalpa, 1983.

Egonu, Iheanachor. "The Nature and Scope of Traditional Folk Literature." *Présence Africaine* 144 (1987): 109–17.

Eimermacher, Karl. "Aspekte des literarischen Märchens in Russland." *Beiträge zur russischen Volksdichtung.* Edited by Klaus-Dieter Seemann. Wiesbaden: Harrassowitz, 1987. 92–111.

Ellis, Bill. "Legend/AntiLegend: Humor as an Integral Part of the Contemporary Legend Process." *Rumor Mills: The Social Impact of Rumor and Legend.* Edited by Gary Alan Fine, Veronique Campion-Vincent, and Chip Heath. New Brunswick: Aldine Transaction 2005. 123–40.

Ellis, John M. *One Fairy Story Too Many: The Brothers Grimm and Their Tales.* Chicago: University of Chicago Press, 1983.

El-Shamy, Hasan M. *Brother and Sister, Type 872*: A Cognitive Behavioristic Analysis of a Middle Eastern Oikotype.* Bloomington: Folklore Publications Group, Indiana University, 1979.

————. *Folk Traditions of the Arab World: A Guide to Motif Classification.* 2 volumes. Bloomington: Indiana University Press, 1995.

————. "Siblings in *Alf laylah wa-layla.*" *Marvels & Tales* 18 (2004): 170–86.

————. *Types of the Folktale in the Arab World: A Demographically Oriented Approach.* Bloomington: Indiana University Press, 2004.

Elsie, Robert. *A Dictionary of Albanian Religion, Mythology and Folk Culture.* New York: New York University Press, 2001.

Emenanjo, E. 'Nolue. "The Anecdote as an Oral Genre: The Case in Igbo." *Folklore* 95.2 (1984): 171–76.

Enderwitz, Susanne. "Shahrazâd Is One of Us: Practical Narrative, Theoretical Discussion, and Feminist Discourse." *Marvels & Tales* 18 (2004): 187–200.

Engen, Rodney K. *Walter Crane as a Book Illustrator*. London: Academy Editions, 1975.

Enzyklopädie des Märchens: Handwörterbuch zur historischen und vergleichenden Erzählforschung. Edited by Kurt Ranke et al. 11 volumes. to date. Berlin: Walter de Gruyter, 1977–.

Erb, Cynthia. "Another World or the World of an Other? The Space of Romance in Recent Versions of 'Beauty and the Beast.'" *Cinema Journal* 34.4 (1995): 50–70.

Erickson, John D. *Nommo: African Fiction in French South of the Sahara*. York, SC: French Literature Publications, 1979. 35–90.

Escarpit, Denise. *Histoire d'un conte: Le chat botté en France et en Angleterre*. 2 volumes. Paris: Didier Erudition, 1985.

Espinosa, Aurelio M. *The Folklore of Spain in the American Southwest: Traditional Spanish Folk Literature in Northern New Mexico and Southern Colorado*. Edited by J. Manuel Espinosa. Norman: University of Oklahoma Press, 1985.

Estés, Clarissa Pinkola. *Women Who Run with the Wolves: Myths and Stories of the Wild Women Archetype*. New York: Ballantine, 1997.

Evenson, Brian. *Understanding Robert Coover*. Columbia: University of South Carolina Press, 2003.

Ezra, Elizabeth. *Georges Méliès: The Birth of the Auteur*. Manchester: Manchester University Press, 2000.

Fabreus, Karin. *Sagan, myten och modernismen i Pär Lagerkvists Tidigaste prosa och Onda Sagor*. Stockholm: Stockholm Studies in History of Literature XLV, 2002.

Faris, Wendy B. *Ordinary Enchantments: Magical Realism and the Remystification of Narrative*. Nashville: Vanderbilt University Press, 2004.

Farrer, Claire R., ed. *Women and Folklore: Images and Genres*. Austin: University of Texas Press, 1975.

Feaver, William. *When We Were Young: Two Centuries of Children's Book Illustrations*. London: Thames and Hudson, 1977.

Felsenstein, Frank. *Anti-Semitic Stereotypes: A Paradigm of Otherness in English Popular Culture, 1660–1830*. Baltimore: Johns Hopkins University Press, 1995.

Fernández Olmos, Margarite. "Constructing Heroines: Rosario Ferré's *cuentos infantiles* and Feminine Instruments of Change." *Lion and the Unicorn* 10 (1986): 83–94.

Fernández Rodríguez, Carolina. *La bella durmiente a través de la historia*. Oviedo: University of Oviedo, 1998.

———. "The Deconstruction of the Male-Rescuer Archetype in Contemporary Feminist Revisions of 'Sleeping Beauty.'" *Marvels & Tales* 16 (2002): 51–70.

Feuerstein, Georg. *Holy Madness*. New York: Penguin Books, 1992). 3–53.

Fialkove, Larissa, and Maria N. Yelenevskaya. "Ghosts in the Cyber World: An Analysis of Folklore Sites on the Internet." *Fabula* 42 (2001): 64–89.

Fine, Elizabeth C. *The Folklore Text: From Performance to Print*. 1984. Bloomington: Indiana University Press, 1994.

Fine, Gary Alan. "Joseph Jacobs: A Sociological Folklorist." *Folklore* 98 (1987): 183–93.

———. *Manufacturing Tales: Sex and Money in Contemporary Legends*. Knoxville: University of Tennessee Press, 1992.

Fine, Gary Alan, Véronique Campion-Vincent, and Chip Heath, eds. *Rumor Mills: The Social Impact of Rumor and Legend*. New Brunswick, NJ: Aldine Transaction, 2005.

Fine, Gary F., and Julie Ford. "Magic Settings: The Reflection of Middle-Class Life in 'Beauty and the Beast.'" *Midwestern Folklore* 15 (1989): 89–97.

Finnegan, Ruth. *Oral Literature in Africa*. London: Oxford University Press, 1970.

Flanagan, John T. "Grim Stories: Folklore in Cartoons." *Midwestern Journal of Language and Folklore* 1 (1975): 20–26.

Flueckiger, Joyce B. *Gender and Genre in the Folklore of Middle India*. Ithaca: Cornell University Press, 1996.

Flynn, Gerard. *Luis Coloma*. Boston: Twayne, 1987.

Flynn, Richard. *Randall Jarrell and the Lost World of Childhood*. Athens: University of Georgia Press. 1990.

Foley, John Miles. "Epic as Genre." *The Cambridge Companion to Homer*. Edited by Robert Fowler. Cambridge: Cambridge University Press. 2004. 171–87.

———. *How to Read an Oral Poem*. Urbana: University of Illinois Press, 2002. eCompanion at http://www.oraltradition.org/hrop.

———. *Immanent Art: From Structure to Meaning in Traditional Oral Epic*. Bloomington: Indiana University Press, 1991.

———. "Oral Tradition and the Internet: Navigating Pathways." *FF Network* 30 (June 2006): 12–19.

———. *The Theory of Oral Composition*. Bloomington: Indiana University Press, 1988.

———. *Traditional Oral Epic:* The Odyssey, Beowulf, *and the Serbo-Croatian Return Song*. Berkeley: University of California Press, 1990.

Fortin, Jutta. "Brides of the Fantastic: Gautier's 'Le Pied de momie' and Hoffmann's 'Der Sandmann.'" *Comparative Literature Studies* 41 (2004): 257–75.

Foust, R. E. "Monstrous Image: Theory of Fantasy Antagonists." *Genre* 13 (1980): 441–53.

Fowke, Edith. *Canadian Folklore*. Toronto: Oxford University Press, 1988.

Fowler, James. "The Golden Harp: Mary de Morgan's Centrality in Victorian Fairy-Tale Literature." *Children's Literature* 33 (2005): 224–36.

Francillon, Roger. "Une théorie du folklore à la fin du XVIIème siècle: Mlle L'Héritier." *Hören, Sagen, Lesen, Lernen: Bausteine zu einer Geschichte der kommunikativen Kultur*. Edited by Ursula Brunold-Bigler and Hermann Bausinger. Bern: Peter Lang, 1995. 205–17.

Franken, Christien. *A. S. Byatt: Art, Authorship, Creativity*. Houndmills: Palgrave, 2001.

Franz, Kurt, ed. *Volksliteratur im neuen Kontext: Märchen, Sage, Legende, Schwank; mit einer Bibliographie lieferbarer Ausgaben*. Baltmannsweiler: Schneider Verlag Hohengehren, 2004.

Franz, Marie-Louise von. *Archetypal Patterns in Fairy Tales*. Toronto: Inner City Books, 1997.

———. *The Feminine in Fairy Tales*. Boston: Shambhala, 1993.

———. *The Interpretation of Fairy Tales*. Revised edition. Boston: Shambhala, 1996.

———. *Shadow and Evil in Fairytales*. Dallas: Spring, 1974.

Fraser, Robert. Interview with Marina Warner. *Writing across Worlds: Contemporary Writers Talk*. Edited by Susheila Nasta. London: Routledge, 2004. 364–75.

———. *Man, God, and Immortality*. London: Macmillan, 1927.

Frazer, James G. *Myths of the Origins of Fire*. London: Macmillan, 1930.

Frazer, John. *Artificially Arranged Scenes: The Films of Georges Méliès*. Boston: G. K. Hall, 1979.

Freud, Sigmund. "The Occurrence in Dreams of Material from Fairy Tales." *The Standard Edition of the Complete Psychological Works of Sigmund Freud*. Translated by James Strachey. Volume 12. London: Hogarth Press, 1958. 279–87.

———. "Symbolism in Dreams." *International Folkloristics: Classic Contributions by the Founders of Folklore*. Edited by Alan Dundes. Lanham: Rowman & Littlefield Publishers, 1999. 177–95.

———. "The Theme of the Three Caskets." *Standard Edition of the Complete Psychological Works*. Translated by James Strachey. Volume 12. London: Hogarth Press, 1958. 291–301.

Freudenberg, Rachel. "Illustrating Childhood—'Hansel and Gretel.'" *Marvels & Tales* 12 (1998): 263–318.

Freudmann, Felix R. "Realism and Magic in Perrault's Fairy Tales." *L'Esprit Créateur* 3 (1963): 116–22.

Friedl, Erika, Lois Beck, and Nikki Keddie. "Women in Contemporary Persian Folktales." *Women in the Muslim World*. Edited by Beck and Keddie. Cambridge: Harvard University Press, 1978. 629–50.

Frontczak, Susan Marie. "An Oral Tradition Perspective on Fairy Tales." *Merveilles et contes* 9 (1995): 237–46.

Gág, Wanda. *Growing Pains: Diaries and Drawings for the Years 1908–1917*. New York: Coward, McCann, 1940.

Galinsky, G. Karl. *Ovid's Metamorphoses: An Introduction to the Basic Aspects*. Berkeley: University of California Press, 1975.

Garry, Jane, and Hasan El-Shamy, eds. *Archetypes and Motifs in Folklore and Literature*. Armonk, NY: M. E. Sharpe, 2005.

Gašparíková, Viera. *Katalóg slovenskej l'udovej prózy/Catalogue of Slovak Folk Prose*. 2 volumes. Bratislava: Národopisný ústav SAV, 1991–92.

Gašparíková, Viera, and B. N. Putilov. *Geroi ili zboinik? Obraz razboinika v fol'klore Karpatskogo regiona/Heroes or Bandits: Outlaw Traditions in the Carpathian Region*. Budapest: European Folklore Institute, 2002.

Gatto, Giuseppe. *La fiaba di tradizione orale.* Milan: Edizioni Universitarie di Lettere Economia Diritto, 2006.

Geider, Thomas. *Die Figur des Oger in der traditionellen Literatur und Lebenswelt der Pokomo in Ost-Kenya.* 2 volumes. Cologne: Koeppe, 1990.

Genardière, Claude de la. *Encore un conte? Le Petit Chaperon Rouge à l'usage des adultes.* Nancy: Presses Universitaires de Nancy, 1993.

Gennep, Arnold van. *The Rites of Passage.* Translated by Monika B. Vizedom and Gabrielle L. Caffee. London: Routledge & Kegan Paul, 1960.

Gentile, Giovanni. *Giuseppe Pitrè.* Florence: G. C. Sansoni, 1940.

George, Andrew, trans. *The Epic of Gilgamesh: The Babylonian Epic Poem and Other Texts in Akkadian and Sumerian.* Middlesex: Penguin, 1999.

George, Diana Hume. *Oedipus Anne: The Poetry of Anne Sexton.* Urbana: University of Illinois Press, 1987.

Georges, Robert. "Towards an Understanding of Storytelling Events." *Journal of American Folklore* 82 (1969): 313–28.

Gerhardt, Mia I. *The Art of Story-Telling: A Literary Study of the Thousand and One Nights.* Leiden: Brill, 1963.

Gerstner, Hermann. *Brüder Grimm in Selbstzeugnissen und Bilddokumenten.* 1973. Reinbek bei Hamburg: Rowohlt, 1983.

Ghazoul, Ferial J. *Nocturnal Poetics: The Arabian Nights in Comparative Context.* Cairo: American University in Cairo Press, 1996.

Gilbert, Sandra M., and Susan Gubar. *The Madwoman in the Attic: The Woman Writer and the Nineteenth-Century Literary Imagination.* New York: Yale University Press, 1979.

Gilet, Peter. *Vladimir Propp and the Universal Folktale: Recommissioning and Old Paradigm—Story as Initiation.* Bern: Peter Lang, 1998.

Gilmour, Simon J. "Die Figur des Zwerges in den *Kinder- und Hausmärchen* der Brüder Grimm." *Fabula* 34 (1993): 9–23.

Ginschel, Gudrun. *Der junge Jacob Grimm, 1805–1819.* 2nd expanded edition. Berlin: Akademie-Verlag, 1989.

Ginzburg, Carlo. *Ecstasies: Deciphering the Witches' Sabbath.* Translated by Raymond Rosenthal. New York: Pantheon Books, 1991.

Giroux, Henry A. *The Mouse that Roared: Disney and the End of Innocence.* Lanham: Rowman and Littlefield, 1999.

Gjertson, Donald E. "The Early Chinese Buddhist Miracle Tale: A Preliminary Survey." *Journal of the American Oriental Society* 101 (1981): 287–301.

Glassie, Henry. *Passing the Time in Ballymenone.* Bloomington: Indiana University Press, 1982.

———. *The Stars of Ballymenone.* Bloomington: Indiana University Press, 2006.

Glazer, Mark. "Women Personages as Helpers in Turkish Folktales." *Studies in Turkish Folklore in Honor of Pertev N. Boratav.* Edited by Ilhan Basgoz and Glazer. Bloomington: Maccallum, 1978. 98–109.

Glenn, Kathleen M. "Text and Countertext in Rosario Ferré's 'Sleeping Beauty.'" *Studies in Short Fiction* 33 (1996): 207–18.

Goehr, Lydia. "Radical Modernism and the Failure of Style: Philosophical Reflections on Maeterlinck-Debussy's *Pelléas et Mélisande.*" *Representations* 74 (Spring 2001): 55–82.

Goldberg, Christine. "The Blind Girl: A Misplaced Folktale." *Western Folklore* 55 (1996): 187–209.

———. "The Composition of 'Jack and the Beanstalk.'" *Marvels & Tales* 15 (2001): 11–26.

———. "'The Dwarf and the Giant' (AT 327B) in Africa and Middle East." *Journal of American Folklore* 116 (2003): 339–50.

———. "Gretel's Duck: The Escape from the Ogre in AaTh 327." *Fabula* 41 (2000): 42–51.

———. *The Tale of the Three Oranges.* Helsinki: Academia Scientiarum Fennica, 1997.

Goldenstern, Joyce. "Connections That Open Up: Coordination and Causality in Folktales." *Marvels & Tales* 15 (2001): 27–41.

Goldstein, Diane. *Once Upon a Virus: AIDS Legends and Vernacular Risk Perception.* Logan: Utah State University Press, 2004.

Goldthwait, John. *Natural History of Make-Believe: Guide to the Principal Works of Britain, Europe and America.* New York: Oxford University Press, 1996.

Gollnick, James. *Love and the Soul: Psychological Interpretations of the Eros and Psyche Myth.* Waterloo, Ontario: Wilfrid Laurier University Press, 1992.

Golynets, Sergei. *Ivan Bilibin.* Translated by Glenys Ann Kozlov. New York: H. N. Abrams, 1982.

Goodenough, Elizabeth. "Oscar Wilde, Victorian Fairy Tales, and the Meanings of Atonement." *Lion and the Unicorn* 23 (1999): 336–54.

Gorfain, Phyllis. "Riddles and Tragic Structure in *Macbeth.*" *Misssissippi Folklore Register* 10 (1976): 187–209.

Görög-Karady, Veronika. *Littérature orale d'Afrique noire: Bibliographie analytique.* Paris: Maisonneuve, 1981.

———, ed. *D'un conte ... à l'autre: La variabilité dans la littérature orale/From One Tale ... to the Other: Variability in Oral Literature.* Paris: Éditions du Centre National de la Recherche Scientifique, 1990.

Gould, Joan. *Spinning Straw into Gold: What Fairy Tales Reveal about the Transformations in a Woman's Life.* New York: Random House, 2006.

Graf, Klaus. "Thesen zur Verabschiedung des Begriffs der 'historischen Sage.'" *Fabula* 29 (1988): 21–47.

Grandinetti, Fred M. *An Illustrated History of E. C. Segar's Character in Print, Radio, Television and Film Appearances, 1929–1993.* Jefferson, NC: McFarland and Company, 1994.

Grant Duff, J. F. "Schneewittchen: Versuch einer psychoanalytischen Deutung." *Imago* 20 (1934): 95–103.

Grätz, Manfred. *Das Märchen in der deutschen Aufklärung: Vom Feenmärchen zum Volksmärchen.* Suttgart: Metzler, 1988.

Graulich, Michel. *Myths of Ancient Mexico.* Translated by Bernard R. Ortiz de Montellano and Thelma Ortiz de Montellano. Norman: University of Oklahoma Press, 1997.

Gray, William. "The Incomplete Fairy Tales of Robert Louis Stevenson." *Journal of Stevenson Studies* 2 (2005): 98–109.

Green, Roger Lancelyn. *Andrew Lang: A Critical Biography.* Leicester: E. Ward, 1946.

Greenburg, Harvey Roy. "Rescrewed: *Pretty Woman*'s Co-Opted Feminism." *Journal of Popular Film and Television* 19.1 (1991): 9–13.

Greenlee, Jessica. "No Longer Divided: Wholeness in *Winter Rose.*" *Extrapolation: A Journal of Science Fiction and Fantasy* 42 (2001): 75–86.

Grima, Benedicte. *The Performance of Emotion among Paxtun Women: "The Misfortunes Which Have Befallen Me."* Austin: University of Texas Press, 1992.

Grise, Catherine M. *Cognitive Spaces and Patterns of Deceit in La Fontaine's Contes.* Charlottesville: Rockwood Press, 1998.

Griswold, Jerome. *The Children's Books of Randall Jarrell.* Athens: University of Georgia Press, 1988.

Griswold, Jerry. *The Meanings of "Beauty and the Beast": A Handbook.* Peterborough, Ontario: Broadview Press, 2004.

Grullon, Carmen Amantina. "Once There Was a Writer: The Narrative of Gabriel García Márquez and the Fairy Tale: A Comparative Study." Dissertation. University of Connecticut, 1994.

Gruner, Elizabeth Rose. "Cinderella, Marie Antoinette, and Sara: Roles and Role Models in *A Little Princess.*" *Lion and the Unicorn* 22 (1998): 163–87.

———. "Saving 'Cinderella': History and Story in *Ashpet* and *Ever After.*" *Children's Literature* 31 (2003): 142–54.

Gudin, Christine. "'J'utilise les contes comme un minerai avec lequel j'essaie de faire des bijoux': Entretien avec Michel Ocelot." *Contes et légendes à l'écran.* Special issue of *CinémAction* 116 (2005): 267–74.

Guenther, Mathias. "The Bushman Trickster: Protagonist, Divinity, and Agent of Creativity." *Marvels & Tales* 16 (2002): 13–28.

Guiscafrè, Jaume. "Una bibliografia de les edicions i les traduccions de les rondalles de mossèn Alcover." *Randa* 38 (1996): 151–221.

Gunzberg, Lynn. "Ruralism, Folklore, and Grazia Deledda's Novels." *Modern Lanaguage Studies* 13.3 (1983): 112–22.

Gupta, Suman. *Re-Reading Harry Potter.* New York: Houndmills: Palgrave Macmillan, 2003.

Haase, Donald. "American Germanists and Research on Folklore and Fairy Tales from 1970 to the Present." *German Studies in the United States: A Historical Handbook.* Edited by Peter Uwe Hohendahl. New York: Modern Language Association, 2003. 294–98.

———. "The *Arabian Nights,* Visual Culture, and Early German Cinema." *The* Arabian Nights *in Transnational Perspective.* Edited by Ulrich Marzolph. Detroit: Wayne State University Press, 2007. 245–60.

———. "A Bibliography of Publications by Jack Zipes on Fairy Tales, Fantasy and Children's Literature." *Marvels & Tales* 16 (2002): 132–39.

———. "Children, War, and the Imaginative Space of Fairy Tales." *Lion and the Unicorn* 24 (2000): 360–77.

———, ed. *Fairy Tales and Feminism: New Approaches.* Detroit: Wayne State University Press, 2004.

———. "Framing the Brothers Grimm: Paratexts and Intercultural Transmission in English-Language Editions of the *Kinder- und Hausmärchen*." *Fabula* 44 (2003): 55–69.

———. "German Fairy Tales and America's Culture Wars: From Grimms' *Kinder- und Hausmärchen* to William Bennett's *Book of Virtues*." *German Politics and Society* 13.3 (1995): 17–25.

———. "Gold into Straw: Fairy Tale Movies for Children and the Culture Industry." *Lion and the Unicorn* 12.2 (1988): 193–207.

———. "Hypertextual Gutenberg: The Textual and Hypertextual Life of Folktales and Fairy Tales in English-Language Popular Print Editions." *Fabula* 47 (2006): 222–30.

———. "Is Seeing Believing? Proverbs and the Film Adaptation of a Fairy Tale." *Proverbium* 7 (1990): 89–104.

———. "Overcoming the Present: Children and the Fairy Tale in Exile, War, and the Holocaust." *Mit den Augen eines Kindes: Children in the Holocaust, Children in Exile, and Children under Fascism*. Edited by Viktoria Hertling. Amsterdam: Rodopi, 1998. 86–99.

———. "The Politics of the Exile Fairy Tale." *Wider den Faschismus: Exilliteratur als Geschichte*. Edited by Susan Cocalis and Sigrid Bauschinger. Tübingen: Francke, 1993. 63–75.

———, ed. *The Reception of Grimms' Fairy Tales: Responses, Reactions, Revisions*. Detroit: Wayne State University Press, 1993.

———. "Re-Viewing the Grimm Corpus: Grimm Scholarship in an Era of Celebration." *Monatshefte* 91.1 (1999): 121–31.

———. "The Sleeping Script: Memory and Forgetting in Grimms' Romantic Fairy Tale (KHM 50)." *Merveilles et contes* 4 (1990): 167–76.

———. "Yours, Mine, or Ours? Perrault, the Brothers Grimm, and the Ownership of Fairy Tales." *Once Upon a Folktale: Capturing the Folklore Process with Children*. Edited by Gloria Blatt. New York: Teachers College Press, 1993. 63–77.

Hains, Maryellen. "Beauty and the Beast: 20th Century Romance?" *Merveilles et contes* 3 (1989): 75–83.

Hall, Alaric Timothy Peter. "The Meanings of *Elf* and Elves in Medieval England." Dissertation. University of Glasgow, 2005. http://www.alarichall.org.uk/phd.php.

Hamilton, James. *Arthur Rackham: A Life with Illustration*. London: Pavilion, 1990.

Hammar, Stina. *Solägget: Fantasi och verklighet i Elsa Beskows konst*. Stockholm: Albert Bonniers Förlag, 2002.

Hancock, Cecily, "The 'Me All Face' Story: European Literary Background of an American Comic Indian Anecdote." *Journal of American Folklore* 76 (1963): 340–42.

Hand, Joachim Neidhardt. *Ludwig Richter*. Vienna: A. Schroll, 1969.

Hand, Wayland D. "The Curing of Blindness in Folktales." *Volksüberlieferung: Festschrift Kurt Ranke*. Edited by Fritz Harkort, Karel C. Peeters, and Robert Wildhaber. Göttingen: Schwartz, 1968. 81–87.

Hanlon, Tina L. "'To Sleep, Perchance to Dream': Sleeping Beauties and Wide-Awake Plain Janes in the Stories of Jane Yolen." *Children's Literature* 26 (1998): 140–67.

Hannon, Patricia. *Fabulous Identities: Women's Fairy Tales in Seventeenth-Century France*. Amsterdam: Rodopi, 1998.

———. "Feminine Voice and Motivated Text: Madame d'Aulnoy and the Chevalier de Mailly." *Merveilles et contes* 2 (1988): 13–24.

Hansen, Terrence Leslie. *The Types of the Folktale in Cuba, Puerto Rico, the Dominican Republic, and Spanish South America*. Berkeley: University of California Press, 1957.

Hansen, William. *Ariadne's Thread: A Guide to International Tales Found in Classical Literature*. Ithaca: Cornell University Press, 2002.

———. "Homer and the Folktale." *A New Companion to Homer*. Edited by Ian Morris and Barry Powell. Leiden: Brill, 1997. 442–62.

———. "The Seer and the Computer: On *Philogelos* and Modern Jokes." *Classical Bulletin* 77 (2001): 87–102.

Happ, Alfred. *Lotte Reiniger, 1899–1981: Schöpferin einer neuen Silhouettenkunst*. Tübingen: Kulturamt, 2004.

Harget, James M. "Monkey Madness in China." *Merveilles et contes* 10 (1996): 310–14.

Haring, Lee. "Framing in Oral Narrative." *Marvels & Tales* 18 (2004): 229–45.

———. *Malagasy Tale Index*. Helsinki: Suomalainen Tiedeakatemia, 1982.

Harmetz, Aljean. *The Making of The Wizard of Oz: Movie Magic and Studio Power in the Prime of MGM—and the Miracle of Production*. Introduction by Margaret Hamilton. New York: Alfred A, Knopf, 1977.

Harries, Elizabeth Wanning. *Twice upon a Time: Women Writers and the History of the Fairy Tale.* Princeton, NJ: Princeton University Press, 2001.

———. "The Violence of the Lambs." *Marvels & Tales* 19 (2005): 54–66.

Harris, Trudier. "Folklore in the Fiction of Alice Walker: A Perpetuation of Historical and Literary Traditions." *Black American Literature Forum* 11.1 (1977): 3–8.

Harrison, Alan. *The Irish Trickster.* Sheffield: The Sheffield Academic Press for the Folklore Society, 1989.

Harth, Erica. *Ideology and Culture in Seventeenth-Century France.* Ithaca: Cornell University Press, 1983.

Hartland, E. Sidney. "The Forbidden Chamber." *Folk-Lore Journal* 3 (1885): 193–242.

———. *The Science of Fairy Tales.* London: Walter Scott, 1891.

Harwell Celenza, Anna. *Hans Christian Andersen and Music: The Nightingale Revealed.* Aldershot: Ashgate, 2005.

Hasan-Rokem, Galit. *Proverbs in Israeli Folk Narratives: A Structural Semantic Analysis.* Helsinki: Academia Scientiarum Fennica, 1982.

———. "Reflections on da Silva's Study of Holbek's Interpretation of Fairy-Tales." *Cultural Analysis* 1 (2000): 13–14. http://ist-socrates.berkeley.edu/~caforum/volume1/vol1_article1.html#response2.

Hasan-Rokem, Galit, and Alan Dundes. *The Wandering Jew: Essays in the Interpretation of a Christian Legend.* Bloomington: Indiana University Press, 1986.

Haut, Mavis. *The Hidden Library of Tanith Lee: Themes and Subtexts from Dionysos to the Immortal Gene.* Jefferson: McFarland & Company, 2001.

Hautala, Jouko. *Finnish Folklore Research, 1828–1919.* Helsinki: Societas Scientarum Fennica, 1969.

Hearne, Betsy. *Beauty and the Beast: Visions and Revisions of an Old Tale.* Chicago: University of Chicago Press, 1989.

Heidel, Alexander. *The Gilgamesh Epic and Old Testament Parallels: A Translation and Interpretation of the Gilgamesh Epic and Related Babylonian and Assyrian Documents.* 2nd edition. Chicago: University of Chicago Press, 1949.

Heilman, Elizabeth E., ed. *Harry Potter's World: Multidisciplinary Critical Perspectives.* New York: Routledge, 2003.

Heissig, Walther, and Schott, Rüdiger, eds. *Die heutige Bedeutung oraler Traditionen: Ihre Archivierung, Publikation und Index-Erschließung/The Present-Day Importance of Oral Traditions: Their Preservation, Publication and Indexing.* Opladen: Westdeutscher Verlag, 1998.

Heldmann, Georg. *Märchen und Mythos in der Antike? Versuch einer Standortbestimmung.* Munich: K. G. Saur, 2000.

Henein, Eglal. "Male and Female Ugliness through the Ages." *Merveilles et contes* 3 (1989): 45–56.

Hennig, Dieter, and Bernhard Lauer, eds. *200 Jahre Brüder Grimm: Dokumente ihres Lebens und Wirkens.* 3 volumes. Kassel: Weber & Weidemeyer, 1985.

Henry, Richard, and Deborah F. Rossen-Knill. "*The Princess Bride* and the Parodic Impulse: The Seduction of Cinderella." *Humor: International Journal of Humor Research* 11 (1998): 43–63.

Hereniko, Vilsoni, and Rob Wilson, eds. *Inside Out: Literature, Cultural Politics, and Identity in the New Pacific.* Lanham, MD: Rowman and Littlefield, 1999.

Herles, Helmut. "Sprichwort und Märchenmotiv in der Werbung." *Zeitschrift für Volkskunde* 62 (1966): 67–80.

Herman, L. "Good Enough Fairy Tales for Resolving Sexual Abuse Trauma." *The Arts in Psychotherapy* 24.5 (1997): 439–45.

Hermansson, Casie. *Reading Feminist Intertextuality through Bluebeard Stories.* Lewiston, NY: Edwin Mellen, 2001.

Herrera-Sobek, María. *Chicano Folklore: A Handbook.* Westport, CT: Greenwood Press, 2006.

Heuscher, Julius. *A Psychiatric Study of Myths and Fairy Tales.* Springfield: Thomas, 1974.

Heyden, Franz. "Grimm oder Bechstein? Zur Kritik der Bechsteinschen Märchen." *Jugendschriften-Warte* 6 (1908): 13–15; 8 (1908): 22–24.

Hildebrandt, Alexandra. *Die Poesie des Fremden: Neue Einblicke in Adalbert von Chamissos "Peter Schlemihls wundersame Geschichte."* Eschborn: Klotz, 1998.

Hill, Lynda Marion Hill. *Social Rituals and the Verbal Art of Zora Neale.* Washington, D.C.: Howard University Press, 1996.

Hines, John. *The Fabliau in English.* London: Longman, 1993.

Hintz, Suzanne. *Rosario Ferré: A Search for Identity.* New York: Peter Lang, 1995.

Hirsch, Marianne. *The Mother/Daughter Plot: Narrative, Psychoanalysis, Feminism*. Bloomington: Indiana University Press, 1989.

"History and Scope of the E[nzyklopädie des] M[ärchens]." *Enzyklopädie des Märchens*. http://wwwuser.gwdg.de/~enzmaer/vorstellung-engl.html.

Hixon, Martha P. "Tam Lin, Fair Janet, and the Sexual Revolution: Traditional Ballads, Fairy Tales, and Twentieth-Century Children's Literature." *Marvels & Tales* 18 (2004): 67–92.

Hock, Ronald F., J. Bradley Chance, and Judith Perkins. *Ancient Fiction and Early Christian Narrative*. Atlanta: Scholars Press, 1998.

Hodne, Ørnulf. *The Types of the Norwegian Folktale*. Oslo: Universitetsforlaget, 1984.

Hoffman, Kathryn A. "Of Monkey Girls and a Hog-Faced Gentlewoman: Marvel in Fairy Tales, Fairgrounds and Cabinets of Curiosities." *Marvels & Tales* 19 (2005): 67–85.

Holbek, Bengt. "The Language of Fairy Tales." *Nordic Folklore: Recent Studies*. Edited by Reimund Kvideland and Henning Sehmsdorf. Bloomington: Indiana University Press, 1989. 40–62.

———. *Interpretation of Fairy Tales: Danish Folklore in a European Perspective*. 1987. Helsinki: Academia Scientiarum Fennica, 1998.

———. "Variation and Tale Type." *D'un conte ... à l'autre: La variabilité dans la littérature orale/From One tale ... to the Other: Variability in Oral Literature*. Edited by Veronika Görög-Karady. Paris: Éditions du Centre National de la Recherche Scientifique, 1990. 471–85.

Holden, Lynn. *Forms of Deformity*. Sheffield: Sheffield Academic Press, 1991.

Holland, Peter. "The Play of Eros: Paradoxes of Gender in English Pantomime." *New Theatre Quarterly* 13 (1997): 195–204.

Hollis, Susan Tower. *The Ancient Egyptian "Tale of Two Brothers": The Oldest Fairy Tale in the World*. Norman: University of Oklahoma Press, 1990.

Hollis, Susan Tower, Linda Pershing, and M. Jane Young, eds. *Feminist Theory and the Study of Folklore*. Urbana: University of Illinois Press, 1993.

Holliss, Richard, and Brian Sibley. *Walt Disney's "Snow White and the Seven Dwarfs" and the Making of the Classic Film*. New York: Simon, 1987.

Holmgren, Virginia C. *Cats in Fact and Folklore*. New York: Howell, 1996.

Holzberg, Niklas. *The Ancient Fable: An Introduction*. Translated by Christine Jackson-Holzberg. Bloomington: Indiana University Press, 2002.

Honko, Lauri. "The Formation of Ecotypes." *Folklore on Two Continents:Essays in Honor of Linda Dégh*. Edited by N. Burlakoff and C. Lindahl. Bloomington: Trickster Press, 1980. 280–85.

———, ed. *The Kalevala and the World's Traditional Epics*. Helsinki: Finnish Literature Society, 2002.

———. "Memorates and the Study of Folk Belief." 1965. *Nordic Folklore: Recent Studies*. Edited by Reimund Kvideland and Henning K. Sehmsdorf. Bloomington: Indiana University Press, 1989. 100–09.

———, ed. *Religion, Myth, and Folklore in the World's Epics: The Kalevala and Its Predecessors*. Berlin: Mouton de Gruyter, 1990.

———. *Textualising the Siri Epic*. Helsinki: Suomalainen Tiedeakatemia, 1998.

———, ed. *Textualization of Oral Epics*. Berlin: Mouton de Gruyter, 2000.

———, ed. *Thick Corpus, Organic Variation and Textuality in Oral Tradition*. Helsinki: Finnish Literature Society, 2000.

Hooker, Jessica. "The Hen Who Sang: Swordbearing Women in Eastern European Fairytales." *Folklore* 101 (1990): 178–84.

Hopkinson, Nalo. "Essay: Dark Ink; Science Fiction Writers of Colour." 1998. *Nalo Hopkinson*. 2006. http://nalohopkinson.com/author_nalo_hopkinson/writing/on_writing/dark_ink/essay_dark_ink.html.

Horcasitas, Fernando, and Douglas Butterworth. "La Llorona." *Tlalocan* 4 (1963): 177–209.

Horn, Katalin. "Grimmsche Märchen als Quellen für Metaphern und Vergleiche in der Sprache der Werbung, des Journalismus und der Literatur." *Muttersprache* 91 (1981): 106–15.

———. "Heilserwartung im Märchen und ihre Spiegelung in einer Auswahl moderner Lyrik." *Neophilologus* 73 (1989): 108–18.

———. "Märchenmotive und gezeichneter Witz: Einige Möglichkeiten der Adaption." *Österreichische Zeitschrift für Volkskunde* 37 (1983): 209–37.

Hösle, Johannes. "Volkslied, Märchen und moderne Lyrik." *Akzente* 7 (1960): 570–577.

Hoyle, Karen Nelson. *Wanda Gág*. New York: Twayne, 1994.

Huang, Lucia. *American Young Adult Novels and Their European Fairy-Tale Motifs.* New York: Peter Lang, 1999.

Huang Mei. *Transforming the Cinderella Dream: From Frances Burney to Charlotte Brontë.* New Brunswick, NJ: Rutgers University Press, 1990.

Hubert, Judd D. "From Folklore to Hyperbole in the French Fairy Tale." *Merveilles et contes* 10 (1996): 185–206.

Hudson, Derek. *Arthur Rackham: His Life and Work.* London: Heinemann, 1960.

Huhtala, Liisi, Karl Grünn, Ismo Loivamaa, and Maria Laukka, eds. *Pieni suuri maailma: suomalaisen lasten- ja nuortenkirjallisuuden historia.* Helsinki: Tammi, 2003.

Hult, Marte Hvam. *Framing a National Narrative: The Legend Collections of Peter Christen Asbjørnsen.* Detroit: Wayne State University Press, 2003.

Hume, Kathryn. *Fantasy and Mimesis: Responses to Reality in Western Literature.* New York: Methuen, 1984.

Hundley, Clarence Carroll, Jr. "Fairy Tale Elements in the Short Fiction of Nathaniel Hawthorne." Dissertation. University of North Carolina at Greensboro, 1994.

Hunt, Peter, and Millicent Lenz. *Alternative Worlds in Fantasy Fiction.* London: Continuum, 2001.

Hürlimann, Bettina. *Picture-Book World: Modern Picture-Books for Children from Twenty-Four Countries.* Translated and edited by Brian W. Alderson. London: Oxford University Press, 1968.

Husain, Shahrukh. *Handsome Heroines: Women as Men in Folklore.* New York: Anchor Books, 1996.

Hutcheon, Linda. *Narcissistic Narrative: The Metafictional Paradox.* New York: Methuen, 1984.

Hymes, Dell. *"In Vain I Tried to Tell You": Essays in Native American Ethnopoetics.* New edition. Lincoln: University of Nebraska Press, 2004.

Igoil, Iyortange. "Songs in Tiv Folktales: A Study of Music and Culture Dynamics of a Nigerian Community." *Nigeria Magazine* 151 (1984): 69–72.

Ikeda, Hiroko. *A Type and Motif Index of Japanese Folk-Literature.* Helsinki: Suomalainen Tiedeakatemia, 1971.

Iliffe, Barrie. "Eventyr and the Fairy Tales in Delius." *Frederick Delius: Music, Art and Literature.* Ed. Lionel Carley. Aldershot: Ashgate, 1997. 273–89.

Immel, Andrea, and Jan Susina, eds. *Considering the Kunstmärchen: The History and Development of Literary Fairy Tales.* Special issue of *Marvels & Tales* 17 (2003): 1–187.

Immel, Andrea, Donald Haase, and Anne Duggan, eds. *"Hidden, but not forgotten": Hans Christian Andersen's Legacy in the Twentieth Century.* Special issue of *Marvels & Tales* 20 (2006): 137–290.

Iranzo, Carmen. *Juan Eugenio Hartzenbusch.* Boston: Twayne, 1978.

Ireland, Norma. *Index to Fairy Tales, 1949–1972: Including Folklore, Legends, and Myths in Collections.* Westwood: Faxon, 1973. Continuation of Mary Use Eastman, *Index to Fairy Tales*; see also Joseph W. Sprug, *Index to Fairy Tales.*

Irwin, Robert. *The Arabian Nights: A Companion.* 1994. London: I. B. Tauris, 2004.

———. "Political Thought in *The Thousand and One Nights.*" *Marvels & Tales* 18 (2004): 246–57.

———. "*A Thousand and One Nights* at the Movies." *New Perspectives on Arabian Nights: Ideological Variations and Narrative Horizons.* Edited by Wen-chin Ouyang and Geert Jan van Gelder. New York: Routledge, 2005. 91–10.

Ivanits, Linda. J. *Russian Folk Belief.* Armonk, NY: M. E. Sharpe, 1989.

Ivy, Marilyn. "Ghastly Insufficiences: *Tōno Monogatari* and the Origins of Nativist Ethnology." *Discourses of the Vanishing: Modernity, Phantasm, Japan.* Chicago: University of Chicago Press, 1995. 66–97.

Iwerks, Leslie, and John Kenworthy. *The Hand behind the Mouse: An Intimate Biography of the Man Walt Disney Called "The Greatest Animator in the World."* New York: Disney Editions, 2001.

Jaago, Tiiu. "Friedrich Reinhold Kreutzwald and the Cultural Bridge." *Studies in Estonian Folkloristics and Ethnology: A Reader and Reflexive History.* Edited by Kristin Kuutma and Tiiu Jaago. Tartu: Tartu University Press, 2005. 19–64.

Jaaksoo, Andres. *A Guide to Estonian Children's Literature '85.* Tallinn: Eesti Raamat, 1985.

Jack Tales Issue. Special issue of *North Carolina Folklore Journal* 26.2 (September 1978): 51–143.

Jack Zipes and the Sociohistorical Study of Fairy Tales. Special issue of *Marvels & Tales* 16 (2002): 117–322.

Jackson, Bruce. *Fieldwork.* Urbana: University of Illinois Press, 1987.

———, ed. *The Negro and His Folklore in Nine-teenth-Century Periodicals*. Austin: American Folklore Society and University of Texas Press, 1967.

Jackson, Kenneth Hurlstone. *The International Tale and Early Welsh Tradition*. Cardiff: University of Wales Press, 1961.

Jackson, Rosemary. *Fantasy: The Literature of Subversion*. London: Methuen, 1981.

Jacobs, Connie A. *The Novels of Louise Erdrich: Stories of Her People*. New York: Peter Lang, 2001.

Jacobs, Karen. "From 'Spy-Glass' to 'Horizon': Tracking the Anthropological Gaze in Zora Neal Hurston." *NOVEL: A Forum on Fiction* 30 (1997): 329–60.

Jacobs, Melville. *The Content and Style of an Oral Literature: Clackamas Chinook Myths and Tales*. Chicago: University of Chicago Press, 1959.

Jäder, Karl and Astrid. *Jenny Nyström—den folk-kära*. Stockholm: Gummessons, 1975.

Jahn, Gary R. "Petr Pavlovich Ershov." *Russian Literature in the Age of Pushkin and Gogol: Poetry and Drama*. Edited by Christine A. Rydel. Detroit: Thomson Gale, 1999. 67–70.

Jain, Jasbir. "Innocent Eréndira: The Reversal of a Fairy Tale." *García Márquez and Latin America*. Edited by Alok Bhalla. New York: Envoy Press, 1987, 101–08.

Jakobson, Roman, and Marc Szeftel. "The Vseslav Epos." *Russian Epic Studies*. Edited by Roman Jakobson and Ernest J. Simmons. Philadelphia: American Folklore Society, 1949. 13–86.

Järv, Risto. "The Gender of the Heroes, Story-tellers, and Collectors of Estonian Fairy Tales." *Folklore: Electronic Journal of Folklore* 29 (August 2005): 45–60. http://www.folklore.ee/folklore/vol29/gender.pdf.

Jarvis, Shawn C. "Trivial Pursuit? Women Deconstructing the Grimmian Model in the *Kaffeterkreis*." *The Reception of Grimms' Fairy Tales: Essays on Responses, Reactions, and Revisions*. Edited by Donald Haase. Detroit: Wayne State University Press, 1993. 102–26.

———. "The Vanished Woman of Great Influence: Benedikte Naubert's Legacy and German Women's Fairy Tales." *In the Shadow of Olympus: German Women Writers Around 1800*. Edited by Katherine R. Goodman and Edith Waldstein. Albany: SUNY Press, 1992. 191–209.

Jasmin, Nadine. *Naissance du conte féminin: Les contes de fées de Madame d'Aulnoy*. Paris: Champion, 2002.

Jason, Heda. "The Brave Little Tailor: Carnival-esque Forms in Oral Literature." *Acta Ethnographica Hungarica* 38 (1993): 385–95.

———. *Motif, Type and Genre: A Manual for Compilation of Indices and a Bibliography of Indices and Indexing*. Helsinki: Academia Scientiarum Fennica, 2000.

———. *Types of Indic Oral Tales*. Helsinki: Academia Scientiarum Fennica, 1989.

———. *Whom Does God Favor, the Wicked or the Righteous? The Reward-and-Punishment Fairy Tale*. Helsinki: Academia Scientiarum Fennica, 1988.

Jatoi, Iqbal Ali. *Bibliography of Folk Literature*. Islamabad: Lok Virsa, 1980.

Jenkins, Henry. "'It's Not a Fairy Tale Any More!' Gender, Genre, *Beauty and the Beast*." *Textual Poachers: Television Fans and Participatory Culture*. New York: Routledge, 1992. 120–51.

Jerrendorf, Marion. "Grimms Märchen in Medien: Aspekte verschiedener Erscheinungsformen in Hörfunk, Fernsehen und Theater." Dissertation. Tübingen, 1985.

Jiménez y Hurtado, M. *Cuentos españoles contenidos en las producciónes dramáticas de Calderón de la Barca, Tirso de Molina, Alarcón y Moreto*. Madrid: Suarez, 1881.

Jobling, Ian. "The Psychological Foundations of the Hero-Ogre Story: A Cross-Cultural Study." *Human Nature* 12 (2001): 247–72.

Johns, Andreas. *Baba Yaga: The Ambiguous Mother and Witch of the Russian Folktale*. New York: Peter Lang, 2004.

———. "Slavic Creation Narratives: The Sacred and the Comic." *Fabula* 46 (2005): 257–90.

Johnson, T. W. "Far Eastern Fox Lore." *Asian Folklore Studies* 33.1 (1974): 35–68.

Jolles, Andre. *Einfache Formen: Legende, Sage, Mythe, Rätsel, Spruch, Kasus, Memorabile, Märchen, Witz*. 1929. Tübingen: Max Niemeyer, 1982.

Jomand-Baudry, Régine, and Jean-François Perrin, eds. *Le Conte merveilleux au XVIIIe siècle: Une poétique expérimentale*. Paris: Éditions Kimé, 2002.

Jónas Kristjánsson. *Eddas and Sagas: Iceland's Medieval Literature*. Translated by Peter Foote. Reykjavík: Hið íslenska bókmenntafélag, 1988.

Jones, Steven Swann. *The Fairy Tale: The Magic Mirror of Imagination*. New York: Twayne, 1995.

———. "Folklore in Henry James's Fiction: Turning of the Screw." *Western Folklore* 60 (2001): 1–24.

———. "Joking Transformations of Popular Fairy Tales: A Comparative Analysis of Five Jokes and Their Fairy Tale Sources." *Western Folklore* 44 (1985): 97–114.

———. *The New Comparative Method: Structural and Symbolic Analysis of the Allomotifs of "Snow White."* Helsinki: Academia Scientiarum Fennica, 1990.

———. "Structural and Thematic Applications of the Comparative Method: A Case Study of the 'Kind and Unkind Girls.'" *Journal of Folklore Research* 23 (1986): 147–61.

Joosen, Vanessa. "Fairy-Tale Retellings between Art and Pedagogy." *Children's Literature in Education* 36.2 (2005): 129–39.

Jordan, Rosan A., and Susan Kalcik, eds. *Women's Folklore, Women's Culture.* Philadelphia: University of Pennsylvania Press, 1985.

Jung, Carl Gustav. *The Archetypes and the Collective Unconscious.* Translated by R. F. C. Hull. Edited by Sir Herbert Read et al. 2nd edition. Volume 9.1. New York: Princeton University Press, 1990.

———. *Memories, Dreams, Reflections.* New York: Pantheon, 1961.

———. "The Phenomenology of the Spirit in Fairytales." *The Archetypes and the Collective Unconscious.* Translated by R. F. C. Hull. Edited by Sir Herbert Read et al. 2nd edition. Volume 9.1. New York: Princeton University Press, 1990. 207–54.

Jurich, Marilyn. *Scheherezade's Sisters: Trickster Heroines and Their Stories in World Literature.* Westport, CT: Greenwood, 1998.

Justyna Deszcz. *Rushdie in Wonderland: Fairytaleness in Salman Rushdie's Fiction.* Frankfurt a.M.: Peter Lang, 2004.

Kaiste, Jaana. *Das eigensinnige Kind: Schrecken in pädagogischen Warnmärchen der Aufklärung und der Romantik.* Uppsala: Uppsala Universitet, 2005.

Kaliambou, Maria. *Heimat—Glaube—Familie: Wertevermittlung in griechischen Popularmärchen (1870–1970).* Neuried: Ars Una, 2006.

Kamenetsky, Christa. *The Brothers Grimm and Their Critics: Folktales and the Quest for Meaning.* Athens: Ohio University Press, 1992.

———. "Folklore as a Political Tool in Nazi Germany." *Journal of American Folklore* 85 (1972): 221–35.

———. "Folktale and Ideology in the Third Reich." *Journal of American Folklore* 90 (1977): 168–78.

Kanaka Durga, P. S. "Transformation of Gender Roles: Converging Identities in Personal and Poetic Narratives." *Gender and Story in South India.* Edited by Leela Prasad, Ruth B. Bottigheimer, and Lalita Handoo. Albany: SUNY Press, 2006. 87–140.

Kane, Mohamadou. *Les contes d'Amadou Coumba: Du conte traditionnel au conte moderne d'expression française.* Dakar: Université de Dakar, 1968.

Kao, Karl S. Y. "Domains of Moral Discourse: Self, History, and Fantasy in *Fengshen yanyi.*" *Chinese Literature: Essays, Articles, Reviews* 24 (December 2002): 75–97.

Karlinger, Felix. *Geschichte des Märchens im deutschen Sprachraum.* Darmstadt: Wissenschaftliche Buchgesellschaft, 1988.

Kawan, Christine Shojaei. "A Masochism Promising Supreme Conquests: Simone de Beauvoir's Reflections on Fairy Tales and Children's Literature." *Marvels & Tales* 16 (2002): 29–48.

Kellner, Beate. *Grimms Mythen: Studien zum Mythosbegriff und seiner Anwendung in Jacob Grimms Deutscher Mythologie.* Frankfurt a.M.: Lang, 1994.

Kelly, Karol. "A Modern Cinderella." *Journal of American Culture* 17.1 (1994): 87–92.

Keown, Michele. "Purifying the Abject Body: Satire and Scatology in Epeli Hau'ofa's *Kisses in the Nederends.*" *Postcolonial Pacific Writing.* London: Routledge, 2005. 61–83.

Kerbelyte, Bronislava. *The Types of Folk Legends: The Structural-Semantic Classification of Lithuanian Aetiological, Mythological, and Historical Legends.* Saint Petersburg: Evropeyskiy Dom, 2001.

Ketilsson, Eli. *Troll i Norge.* Oslo: J. M. Stenersens Forlag, 1989.

Khemir, Nacer. "A Wanderer Seeking the Words of Love in Impossible Cities: Nacer Khemir." Interview by Khemais Khayati. Introduction and translated by Maggie Awadalla. *Alif* 15 (1995): 251–59.

Kiell, Norman. *Food and Drink in Literature: A Selectively Annotated Bibliography.* Lanham, MD: Scarecrow, 1995.

Kirby, David K. "The Princess and the Frog: The Modern American Short Story as Fairy Tale." *Minnesota Review* 4 (1973): 145–49.

Kirsten Bystrup. *De tegner for børn: Portrætter af 12 danske bønebogsillustratorer.* Copenhagen: DBC, 1994.

Kleeman, Faye Yuan. "Sexual Politics and Sexual Poetics in Kurahashi Yumiko's *Cruel Fairy Tales for Adults*." *Literary Studies East and West* 12 (1996): 150–58.

Klibbe, Lawrence. *Fernán Caballero*. New York: Twayne, 1973.

Klipple, May Augusta. *African Folktales with Foreign Analogues*. New York: Garland Press, 1992.

Klotz, Volker. *Das europäische Kunstmärchen*. Stuttgart: Metzler: 1985.

Knight, Chris. *Decoding Fairy Tales*. London: Lionel Sims/Radical Anthropology Group, 2004. http://www.radicalanthropologygroup.org/pub_-decoding_fairytales.pdf.

———. "On the Dragon Wings of Time." *Maidens, Snakes and Dragon*. Edited by Chris Knight, Isabel Cardigos, and José Gabriel Pereira Bastos. London: Center for the Study of Imagination in Literature, 1991. 7–50.

Knoepflmacher, U. C. "Introduction: Literary Fairy Tales and the Value of Impurity." *Marvels & Tales* 17 (2003): 26–29.

———. "Of Babylands and Babylons: E. Nesbit and the Reclamation of the Fairy Tale." *Tulsa Studies in Women's Literature* 6 (1987): 299–325.

———. *Ventures into Childland: Victorians, Fairy Tales, and Femininity*. Chicago: Chicago University Press, 1998.

Knopp, Grace. "The Motifs of the 'Jason and Medea Myth' in Modern Tradition (A Study of Märchentypus 313)." Dissertation. Stanford University, 1933.

Koch, John T., and John Carey. *The Celtic Heroic Age*. Andover: Celtic Studies Publications, 1995.

Köhler, Reinhold. *Aufsätze über Märchen und Volkslieder: Aus seinem handschriftlichen Nachlaß*. Edited by Johannes Bolte and Erich Schmidt. Berlin: Weidmannsche Buchhandlung, 1894.

———. *Kleinere Schriften*. Edited by Johannes Bolte. 3 volumes. Weimar: Emil Felber, 1898–1900.

Köhler-Zülch, Ines. "Der Diskurs über den Ton: Zur Präsentation von Märchen und Sagen in Sammlungen des 19. Jahrhunderts." *Homo narrans: Studien zur populären Erzählkultur; Festschrift für Siegfried Neumann zum 65. Geburtstag*. Edited by Christoph Schmitt. Münster: Waxmann, 1999. 25–50.

Köhler-Zülch, Ines, and Isabel Cardigos, eds. *Gender*. Special issue of *Estudos de Literatura Oral* 5 (1999): 1–238.

Kolbenschlag, Madonna. *Kiss Sleeping Beauty Good-bye: Breaking the Spell of Feminine Myths and Models*. New York: Doubleday, 1979.

Komins, Benton Jay. "Western Culture and the Ambiguous Legacies of the Pig." *CLCWeb: Comparative Literature and Culture: A WWWeb Journal* 3.4 (December 2001). http://clcweb journal.lib.purdue.edu/clcweb01-4/komins3-01.html.

König, Ingelore, Dieter Wiedemann, and Lothar Wolf, eds. *Zwischen Marx und Muck: DEFA-Filme für Kinder*. Berlin: Henschel, 1996.

Korom, Frank J. *South Asian Folklore: A Handbook*. Westport, CT: Greenwood Press, 2006.

———. *Village of Painters: Narrative Scrolls from West Bengal*. Santa Fe: Museum of New Mexico Press, 2006.

Koschmann, Victor, ed. *International Perspectives on Yanagita Kunio and Japanese Folklore Studies*. Ithaca, NY: Cornell University East Asia Program, 1985.

Kosok, Heinz. "Thomas Crofton Croker's *Fairy Legends*: A Revaluation." *ABEI Journal: The Brazilian Journal of Irish Studies* 3 (June 2001): 63–76.

Kossmann, Maarten. *A Study of Eastern Moroccan Fairy Tales*. Helsinki: Suomalainen Tiedeakatemia, 2000.

Koszinowski, Ingrid, and Vera Leuschner, eds. *Ludwig Emil Grimm 1790–1863: Maler, Zeichner, Radierer*. Volume 2 of *200 Jahre Brüder Grimm*. Kassel: Weber und Weidemeyer, 1985.

Kovacs, Katherine Singer. "Georges Méliès and the 'Féerie.'" *Cinema Journal* 16.1 (Autumn 1976): 1–13.

Kravchenko, Maria. *The World of the Russian Fairy Tale*. Berne: Peter Lang, 1987.

Kristeva, Tsvetana. "The Pattern of Signification in the *Taketori Monogatari*: The 'Ancestor' of All *Monogatari*." *Japan Forum* 2 (1990): 253–60.

Krohn, Kaarle. *Folklore Methodology*. Translated by Roger L. Welsch. Austin: University of Texas Press, 1971.

Krstić, Branislav. *Indeks motiva narodnih pesama balkanskih Slovena/Motif Index for the Epic Poetry of the Balkan Slavs*. Edited by Ilija Nikolić. Belgrad: Srpska Akademija nauka i umetnosti, 1984.

Krzyżanowski, Julian. *Polska bajka ludowa w układzie systematycznym*. 2 volumes. Wrocław: Zakład Naradowy imienia Ossolińskich Wydawnictwo Polskiej Akademii Nauk, 1962–63.

Kudszus, W. G. *Terrors of Childhood in Grimms' Fairy Tales*. New York: Peter Lang, 2005.

Kushner, Tony. *The Art of Maurice Sendak: 1980 to the Present*. New York: Harry N. Abrams, 2003.

La Harpe, Jacqueline de. "La 'Muse et Grâce' de Voltaire. (Le conte de fées en France vers 1750)." *PMLA* 54 (1939): 454–66.

Labriola, Patrick. "Ludwig Tieck and Nathaniel Hawthorne: The Fairy Tale and the Popular Legend." *Journal of Popular Culture* 38.2 (2004): 325–32.

Lacourcière, Luc. *Le conte populaire français en Amérique du Nord*. Québec: Les Archives de Folklore, Université Laval, 1959.

Lacy, Lyn Ellen. *Art and Design in Children's Picture Books: An Analysis of Caldecott Award-Winning Illustrations*. Chicago: American Library Association, 1986.

LaFaye, Alexandria. "The 'Double Happiness' of Biculturalism in Chinese American Novels." *Bookbird: A Journal of International Children's Literature* 37.2 (1999): 12–17.

Lai, Whalen. "From Protean Ape to Handsome Saint: The Monkey King." *Asian Folklore Studies* 53 (1994): 29–65.

Laiblin, Wilhelm, ed. *Märchenforschung und Tiefenpsychologie*. 5th expanded edition. Darmstadt: Primus, 1995.

Lampart, Fabian. "The Turn to History and the *Volk*: Brentano, Arnim, and the Grimm Brothers." *The Literature of German Romanticism*. Edited by Dennis Mahoney. Rochester, NY: Camden House, 2004. 168–89.

Landay, Lori. *Madcaps, Screwballs, and Con Women: The Female Trickster in American Culture*. Philadelphia: University of Pennsylvania Press, 1998.

Lanes, Selma. *The Art of Maurice Sendak*. New York: Harry N. Abrams, 1980.

Lang, Andrew. "Cinderella and the Diffusion of Tales." *Folk-Lore* 4 (1893): 413–33.

Larzul, Sylvette. *Les traductions françaises des Mille et une nuits: Étude des versions Galland, Trébutien et Mardrus*. Paris: L'Harmattan, 1996.

Lasch, Christopher. *Women and the Common Life: Love, Marriage, and Feminism*. Edited by Elisabeth Lasch-Quinn. New York: Norton, 1997.

Lau, Kimberly J. "Structure, Society, and Symbolism: Toward a Holistic Interpretation of Fairy Tales." *Western Folklore* 55 (1996): 233–43.

Lauer, Bernhard, ed. *Russische Marchen und Sagen*. Kassel: Brüder Grimm-Museum, 1991.

Le Guin, Ursula K., and Susan Wood. *The Language of the Night: Essays on Fantasy and Science Fiction*. New York: Putman, 1979.

Le Marchand, Bérénice Virginie. "Reframing the Early French Fairy Tale: A Selected Bibliography." *Marvels & Tales* 19 (2005): 86–122.

Le Men, Ségolène. "Mother Goose Illustrated: From Perrault to Doré." *Poetics Today* 13.1 (1992): 17–39.

Leach, Maria, and Jerome Fried, ed. *Funk and Wagnalls Standard Dictionary of Folklore, Mythology and Legend*. 2 volumes. New York: Funk and Wagnalls, 1949–50.

Leavy, Barbara Fass. *In Search of the Swan Maiden: A Narrative on Folklore and Gender*. New York: New York University Press, 1994.

Leblans, Anne. "*Kinder- und Hausmärchen:* The Creation of Male Wombs as a Means of Protection against the Fear of Engulfment." *Subversive Sublimities: Undercurrents of the German Enlightenment*. Edited by Eitel Timm. Columbia, SC: Camden House, 1992. 86–97.

Lefanu, Sarah. "Robots and Romance: The Science Fiction and Fantasy of Tanith Lee." *Sweet Dreams: Sexuality, Gender and Science Fiction*. Edited by Susannah Radstone. London: Lawrence & Wishart, 1988. 121–36.

Lehtonen, Maija. "Puoli vuosisataa lastenkirjailijana—Zacharias Topelius." *Pieni suuri maailma: Suomalaisen lasten- ja nuortenkirjallisuuden historia*. Edited by Liisi Huhtala et al. Helsinki: Tammi, 2003. 20–31.

Lehtonen, Maija, and Marita Rajalin, eds. *Barnboken i Finland förr och nu*. Stockholm: Rabén & Sjögren, 1984.

Leinweber, David Walter. "Witchcraft and Lamiae in 'The Golden Ass.'" *Folklore* 105 (1994): 77–82.

Levi, Antonia. *Samurai from Outer Space: Understanding Japanese Animation*. Chicago: Open Court, 1996.

Lévi-Strauss, Claude. "Four Winnebago Myths." *Culture in History: Essays in Honor of Paul Radin*. New York: Columbia University Press, 1960. 351–62.

———. *The Raw and the Cooked: Introduction to a Science of Mythology*. Translated by John and Doreen Weightman. 1969. Chicago: University of Chicago Press, 1983.

———. *The Story of Lynx*. Chicago: University of Chicago Press, 1995.

Levorato, Alessandra. *Language and Gender in the Fairy Tale Tradition: A Linguistic Analysis of Old and New Story-Telling*. London: Palgrave Macmillan, 2003.

Lewis, Franklin. D. *Rumi: Past and Present, East and West; The Life, Teaching and Poetry of Jalâl al-Din Rumi*. Oxford: Oneworld, 2000.

Lewis, Philip. *Seeing through the Mother Goose Tales: Visual Turns in the Writings of Charles Perrault*. Stanford, CA: Stanford University Press, 1996.

Leyda, Jan. *Kino: A History of the Russian and Soviet Film*. London: Allen and Unwin, 1960.

Lieberman, Marcia R. "'Some Day My Prince Will Come': Female Acculturation through the Fairy Tale." *College English* 34 (1972): 383–95.

Lillyman, William J. "Fouqué's 'Undine.'" *Studies in Romanticism* 10 (1971): 94–104.

Lindahl, Carl, ed. *Perspectives on the Jack Tales and Other North American Märchen*. Bloomington: The Folklore Institute, Indiana University, 2001.

Lindahl, Carl, John McNamara, and John Lindow, eds. *Medieval Folklore: An Encyclopedia of Myths, Legends, Tales, Beliefs, and Customs*. 2 volumes. Santa Barbara: ABC-CLIO, 2000.

Lindfors, Bernth. "Amos Tutuola: Oral Tradition and the 'Motif-Index.'" *African Textualities: Texts, Pre-Texts, and Contexts of African Literature*. Trenton, NJ: Africa World Press, 1997. 87–108.

———, ed. *Critical Perspectives on Amos Tutuola*. London: Heinemann, 1980.

Lindholm, Stig. *Med penseln som trollspö*. Stockholm: CKM: Föreningen Jenny Nyströms Vänner, 2004.

Lindow, John. *Handbook of Norse Mythology*. Santa Barbara: ABC-CLIO, 2001.

———. "Response to Francisco Vaz da Silva, 'Bengt Holbek and the Study of Meanings in Fairy Tales.'" *Cultural Analysis* 1 (2000): 11–12. http://ist-socrates.berkeley.edu/~caforum/volume1/vol1_article1.html#response1.

Lindström, Carina. *Sökande, spegling, metamorfos: Tre vägar genom Maria Gripes skuggserie*. Stockholm/Stehag: Symposion Graduale, 1994.

Liptay, Fabienne: *Wunderwelten: Märchen im Film*. Remscheid: Gardez, 2004.

Liú, Shŏuhuá, ed. *Zhōngguó Mínjiān Gùshì Lèixíng Yánjiū*. Wuhan: Huazhong Normal University, 2002.

Lloyd, Timothy. *The Archive of Folk Culture: The National Collection of American and World Folklore*. Washington, D.C.: American Folklife Center, Library of Congress, 1992.

Loivamaa, Ismo, ed. *Kotimaisia lasten- ja nuortenkirjailijoita*. 2nd edition. Helsinki: BTJ Kirjastopalvelu, 1996.

Loorits, Oskar. "Some Notes on the Repertoire of the Estonian Folk-Tale." 1937. *Studies in Estonian Folkloristics and Ethnology: A Reader and Reflexive History*. Edited by Kristin Kuutma and Tiiu Jaago. Tartu: Tartu University Press, 2005. 217–39.

López Austin, Alfredo. *Tamoanchan, Tlalocan: Places of Mist*. Niwot: University Press of Colorado, 1997.

Lord, Albert B. *The Singer of Tales*. Revised edition. Edited by Stephen Mitchell and Gregory Nagy. Cambridge: Harvard University Press, 2000.

Lorenz, Bernd. "Notizen zu Zwölf und Dreihundert im Märchen: Ausdruck bedeutungsvoller Größe und abgegrenzter Bereiche." *Fabula* 27 (1986): 42–45.

Lovell-Smith, Rose. "Dundes' Allomotifs and Female Audiences: A Reading of Perrault's *Les Fées*." *Fabula* 37 (1996): 241–47.

Ludwig Bechstein: Dichter, Sammler, Forscher: Festschrift zum 200. Geburtstag. Edited by Hennebergisches Museum Kloster Veßra. 2 volumes. Meiningen-Münnerstadt: Kloster Veßra, 2001.

Ludwig, Coy L. *Maxfield Parrish*. New York: Watson-Guptill, 1973.

Ludwig, Ralph, ed. *Écrire la "parole de nuit": La nouvelle littérature antillaise*. Paris: Gallimard, 1994.

Lundell, Torborg. *Fairy Tale Mothers*. New York: Lang, 1990.

———. "Gender-Related Biases in the Type and Motif Indexes of Aarne and Thompson." *Fairy Tales and Society: Illusion, Allusion, and Paradigm*. Edited by Ruth B. Bottigheimer. Philadelphia: University of Pennsylvania Press, 1986. 149–63.

Lurie, Alison. *Boys and Girls Forever: Children's Classics from Cinderella to Harry Potter*. New York: Penguin, 2003.

Lüthi, Max. "Aspects of the *Märchen* and the Legend." *Folklore Genres*. Edited by Dan Ben-Amos. Austin: University of Texas Press, 1976. 17–33.

———. *The European Folktale: Form and Nature.* Translated by John D. Niles. Philadelphia: Institute for the Study of Human Issues, 1982.

———. *The Fairytale as Art Form and Portrait of Man.* Translated by Jon Erickson. Bloomington: Indiana University Press, 1984.

———. "Gebrechliche und Behinderte im Volksmärchen." *Volksliteratur und Hochliteratur.* Bern: Francke, 1970. 48–62.

———. *Märchen.* 9th expanded edition. Edited by Heinz Rölleke. Stuttgart: Metzler, 1996.

———. *Once upon a Time: On the Nature of Fairy Tales.* Translated by Lee Chadeayne and Paul Gottwald. 1970. Bloomington: Indiana University Press, 1976.

———. *Volksliteratur und Hochliteratur.* Bern: Francke, 1970.

Lyons, M. C. *The Arabian Epic: Heroic and Oral Story-Telling.* 3 volumes. Cambridge: Cambridge University Press, 1995.

Lyons, Phyllis I. *The Saga of Dazai Osamu: A Critical Study with Translations.* Stanford: Stanford University Press, 1985.

Mabee, Barbara. "Reception of Fairy Tale Motifs in Texts by Twentieth-Century German Women Writers." *FEMSPEC* 1.2 (2000): 16–29.

MacDonald, Margaret Read. *The Storyteller's Sourcebook. A Subject, Title, and Motif Index to Folklore Collections for Children.* Detroit: Neal-Schuman Publishers in Association with Gale Research, 1982.

———, ed. *Traditional Storytelling Today: An International Sourcebook.* Chicago: Fitzroy Dearborn, 1999.

MacKay, Carol Hanbery. *Creative Negativity: Four Victorian Exemplars of the Female Quest.* Stanford: Stanford University Press, 2001.

Mackintosh, Fiona. "Babes in the *Bosque:* Fairy Tales in Twentieth-Century Argentine Women's Writing." *Fairy Tales and Feminism: New Approaches.* Edited by Donald Haase. Detroit: Wayne State University Press, 2004. 149–67.

MacMath, Russ. "Recasting Cinderella: How Pictures Tell the Tale." *Bookbird* 32.4 (1994): 29–34.

MacNamara, Matthew. "Some Oral Narrative Forms in *Lettres de mon moulin.*" *Modern Language Review* 67 (1972): 291–99.

MacNeil, Joe Neil. *Tales until Dawn: The World of a Cape Breton Gaelic Story-Teller.* Translated and edited by John Shaw. Kingston: McGill-Queen's University Press, 1987.

Magnanini, Suzanne. "Foils and Fakes: The Hydra in Giambattista Basile's Dragon-Slayer Tale, 'Lo mercante.'" *Marvels & Tales* 19 (2005): 167–96.

Magnarelli, Sharon. "*Simetrías:* 'Mirror, Mirror on the Wall....'" *World Literature Today* 69.4 (1995): 717–25.

Mahdi, Muhsin. *The Thousand and One Nights (Alf Layla wa-Layla) from the Earliest Known Sources.* 3 volumes. Leiden: Brill, 1984–94.

Maija, Lehtonen. *Anni Swan.* Porvoo: WSOY, 1958.

Mainil, Jean. *Madame d'Aulnoy et le rire des fées: Essai sur la subversion féerique et le merveilleux comique sous l'Ancien Régime.* Paris: Kimé, 2001.

Mair, Victor. *Painting and Performance: Chinese Picture Recitation and Its Indian Genesis.* Honolulu: University of Hawaii Press, 1988.

Makin, Michael, and Jindřich Toman, eds. *On Karel Čapek: A Michigan Slavic Colloquium.* Ann Arbor: Michigan Slavic Publications, 1992.

Malan, Dan. *Gustave Doré: Adrift on Dreams of Splendor.* St. Louis, MO: Malan Classical Enterprises, 1995.

Malarte, Claire-Lise. *Perrault à travers la critique depuis 1960: Bibliographie annotée.* Paris: Papers on French Seventeenth Century Literature, 1989.

Malarte-Feldman, Claire-Lise. "The Challenges of Translating Perrault's Contes into English." *Marvels & Tales* 13 (1999): 184–97.

———. "The French Fairy-Tale Conspiracy." *Lion and the Unicorn* 12.2 (1988): 112–20.

Mandrou, Robert. *De la culture populaire aux XVIIe et XVIIIe siècles.* Paris: Stock, 1964.

Manley, Kathleen E. B. "Atwood's Reconstruction of Folktales: *The Handmaid's Tale* and 'Bluebeard's Egg.'" *Approaches to Teaching Atwood's* The Handmaid's Tale *and Other Works.* Edited by Sharon R. Wilson, Thomas B. Friedman, and Shannon Hengen. New York: Modern Language Association, 1996. 135–39.

Manlove, C. N. *Modern Fantasy: Five Studies.* Cambridge: Cambridge University Press, 1975.

Manlove, Colin. *The Chronicles of Narnia: The Patterning of a Fantastic World.* Woodbridge, CT: Twayne, 1993.

Manna, Anthony L. "The Americanization of the Brothers Grimm: Or, Tom Davenport's Film Adaptation of German Folktales." *Children's Literature Association Quarterly* 13 (1988): 142–45.

Manning-Sanders, Ruth. *A Book of Witches.* London: Methuen, 1965.

Marchalonis, Shirley. "Medieval Symbols and the *Gesta Romanorum*." *Chaucer Review* 8 (1974): 311–19.

Marchese, Giuseppe. *Capuana poeta della vita*. Palermo: Ando, 1964.

Marhoffer-Wolf, Maria. *Frauen und Feen: Entwicklung und Wandel einer Beziehung*. Köln: Rüdiger Köppe, 2002.

Marin, Louis. "*Puss-in-Boots*: Power of Signs—Signs of Power." *Diacritics* 7 (1977): 54–63.

Marin, Louis. *Food for Thought*. Translated by Mette Hjort. Baltimore: Johns Hopkins University Press, 1989.

Marrow, Sherilyn. "When Silver Hands Tarnish Images: A Fairy Tale Analysis from the Disability Perspective." *The Image of the Hero in Literature, Media, and Society*. Edited by Will Wright and Steven Kaplan. Pueblo, CO: Colorado State University, 2004. 353–56.

Martin, Ann. *Red Riding Hood and the Wolf in Bed: Modernism's Fairy Tales*. Toronto: University of Toronto Press, 2006.

———. "Sleeping Beauty in a Green Dress: Mrs. Dalloway and Fairy Tale Configurations of Desire." *Virginia Woolf Out of Bounds: Selected Papers from the Tenth Annual Conference on Virginia Woolf*. Edited by Jessica Berman and Jane Goldman. New York: Pace University Press, 2001. 25–31.

Martin, Laura. *Benedikte Nauberts Neue Volksmärchen der Deutschen: Strukturen des Wandels*. Würzburg: Königshausen und Neumann, 2006.

———. "The Rübezahl Legend in Benedikte Naubert and Johann Karl August Musäus." *Marvels & Tales* 17 (2003): 197–211.

Martin, Richard. "Epic as Genre." *A Companion to Ancient Epic*. Ed. John Miles Foley. Oxford: Blackwell Publishing. 2005. 9–19.

Marzolph, Ulrich. "Adab in Transition: Creative Compilation in Nineteenth Century Print Tradition." *Israel Oriental Studies* 19 (1999): 161–72.

———. "Das Aladdin-Syndrom: Zur Phänomenologie des narrativen Orientalismus." *Hören, Sagen, Lesen, Lernen: Bausteine zu einer Geschichte der kommunikativen Kultur*. Edited by Ursula Brunold-Bigler and Hermann Bausinger. Bern: Peter Lang, 1995. 449–62.

———, ed. *The Arabian Nights in Transnational Perspective*. Detroit: Wayne State University Press, 2007.

———, ed. *The Arabian Nights Reader*. Detroit: Wayne State University Press, 2005.

———. "Mollâ Nasroddîn in Persia." *Iranian Studies* 28.3–4 (1995): 157–74.

———. "Popular Narratives in Galâloddin Rumi's Masnavi." *The Arabist* 12–14 (1995): 275–87.

———. *Typologie des persischen Volksmärchens*. Beirut: Deutsche Morgenländische Gesellschaft, 1984.

Marzolph, Ulrich, and Richard van Leeuwen, eds. *The Arabian Nights Encyclopedia*. 2 volumes. Santa Barbara: ABC-CLIO, 2004.

Max, Frank Rainer. *Der "Wald der Welt": Das Werk Fouqués*. Bonn: Bouvier, 1980.

May, Jill P. *Lloyd Alexander*. Boston: Twayne, 1991.

———. "Walt Disney's Interpretation of Children's Literature." *Language Arts* 58.4 (April 1981): 463–72.

Mayer, David. *Harlequin in His Element: The English Pantomime, 1806–1836*. Cambridge: Harvard University Press, 1969.

Mayer, Fanny Hagin, trans. and ed. *The Yanagita Kunio Guide to the Japanese Folk Tale*. Bloomington: Indiana University Press, 1986.

Mazenauer, Beat, and Severin Perrig. *Wie Dornröschen seine Unschuld gewann: Archäologie der Märchen*. Leipzig: Kiepenheuer, 1995.

Mazhar-ul-Islam. *A History of Folktale Collections in India and Pakistan*. Dhaka: Bengali Academy, 1970.

McCallum, Robyn. *Ideologies of Identity in Adolescent Fiction: The Dialogic Construction of Subjectivity*. New York: Garland, 1999.

McCarthy, William Bernard, ed. *Jack in Two Worlds: Contemporary North American Tales and Their Tellers*. Chapel Hill: University of North Carolina Press, 1994.

McClatchy, J. D., ed. *Anne Sexton: The Artist and Her Critics*. Bloomington: Indiana University Press, 1978.

McClellan, Catharine. *The Girl Who Married the Bear: A Masterpiece of Indian Oral Tradition*. Ottawa: National Museums of Canada, 1970.

McGillis, Roderick. "'Ages All': Readers, Texts, and Intertexts in *The Stinky Cheese Man and Other Fairly Stupid Tales*." *Transcending Boundaries: Writing for a Dual Audience of Children and Adults*. Edited by Sandra L. Beckett. New York: Garland, 1999. 111–26.

McGilvray, D. B. "Sexual Power and Fertility in Sri Lanka." *Ethnography of Fertility and Birth*. Edited by Carol P. MacCormack. 2nd edition. Prospect Heights, IL: Waveland Press, 1994. 62–72.

McGlathery James M., ed. *The Brothers Grimm and Folktale*. Urbana: University of Illinois Press, 1988.

———. *E. T. A. Hoffmann*. New York: Twayne, 1997.

———. *Fairy Tale Romance: The Grimms, Basile, and Perrault*. Urbana: University of Illinois Press, 1991.

———. *Grimm's Fairy Tales. A History of Criticism on a Popular Classic*. Columbia: Camden, 1993.

———. "Magic and Desire in Eichendorff's *Das Marmorbild*." *German Life and Letters* 42.3 (1989): 257–68.

McLeod, Glenda K. "Writer of Fantasy: Madame d'Aulnoy." *Women Writers of the Seventeenth Century*. Athens: University of Georgia Press, 1989. 91–99.

McLuhan, Marshall. *Understanding Media: The Extensions of Man*. New York: McGraw, 1965

McMahan, Alison. *The Films of Tim Burton: Animating Live Action in Contemporary Hollywood*. New York: Continuum, 2005.

McNeely, Nancy C. "Women's Quest for Identity: Folklore and Fairy-Tale Archetypes in Shakesearean Comedy and Romance." Dissertation. Southern Illinois University, Carbondale, 1997.

Méchoulan, Eric. "The Embodiment of Culture: Fairy Tales of the Body in the 17th and 18th Centuries." *Romanic Review* 83 (1992): 427–36.

Meder, Theodoor. "Nederlandse sprookjes in de negentiende en twintigste eeuw." *Tot volle wasdom*. Edited by Berry Dongelmans et al. Den Haag: Biblion, 2000. 31–46.

———. "Viruspaniek: E-mail-lore van Good Times tot Polleke den Hacker." 2001. http://www.meertens.nl/medewerkers/theo.meder/viruspaniek.html.

Mederer, Hanns-Peter. *Stoffe aus Mythen: Ludwig Bechstein als Kulturhistoriker, Novellist und Romanautor*. Wiesbaden: Deutscher Universitäts-Verlag, 2002.

Megas, Georgios A. "Some Oral Greek Parallels to Aesop's Fables." *Humaniora: Essays in Literature—Folklore—Bibliography Honoring Archer Taylor on His Seventieth Birthday*. Edited by Wayland D. Hand and Gustave O. Arlt. Locust Valley, NY: J. J. Augustin, 1960: 195–207

———. *Das Märchen von Amor und Psyche in der griechischen Volksüberlieferung*. Athens: Academy of Athens Publications, 1971.

Meletinsky, Eleazar. *The Poetics of Myth*. Translated by Guy Lanoue and Aleksandre Sadetsky. 1998. New York: Routledge, 2000.

Meletinsky, Eleazar, et al. "Problems of the Structural Analysis of Fairytales." *Soviet Structural Folkloristics*. Edited by Pierre Maranda. The Hague: Mouton, 1974. 73–139.

Mellett, Kerry Eileen. "Infertility and the Therapeutic Use of Fairytales." Dissertation. California Institute of Integral Studies, 2001.

Mendlesohn, Farah. *Diana Wynne Jones: Children's Literature and the Fantastic Tradition*. New York: Routledge, 2005.

Menninghaus, Winfried. *In Praise of Nonsense: Kant and Bluebeard*. Translated by Henry Pickford. Stanford, CA: Stanford University Press, 1999.

Meraklis, Michael G. *Studien zum griechischen Märchen*. Translated and edited by Walter Puchner. Vienna: Selbstverlag des Osterreichischen Museums für Volkskunde, 1992.

Merritt, Russell, and J. B. Kaufman. *Walt in Wonderland: The Silent Films of Walt Disney*. 1991. Baltimore: Johns Hopkins University Press, 1993.

Messerli, Alfred. "Cheap Prints and Visual Medias." *Europeæa* 3.1 (1997): 133–40.

———. "Spatial Representation in European Popular Fairy Tales." *Marvels & Tales* 19 (2005): 274–84.

Metcalf, Eva-Maria. *Astrid Lindgren*. New York: Twayne, 1995.

Mews, Siegfried, ed. *"The Fisherman and His Wife": Günter Grass's "The Flounder" in Critical Perspective*. New York: AMS Press, 1983.

Meyer, Maurits de. *Les contes populaires de la Flandre: Aperçu général de l'étude du conte populaire en Flandre et catalogue de toutes les variantes flamandes de contes populaires, d'après le catalogue des contes types par A. Aarne*. Helsinki: Suomalainen Tiedeakatemia, 1921.

Michelet, Jules. *The Sorceress: A Study in Middle Age Superstition*. Translated by A. R. Allinson. Paris: Charles Carrington, 1904.

Mieder, Wolfgang. "Aphoristische Schwundstufen des Märchens." *Dona Folcloristica: Festgabe für Lutz Röhrich*. Edited by Leander Petzoldt and Stefaan Top. Frankfurt a.M.: Peter Lang, 1990. 159–71.

———. *Die Brüder Grimm und das Sprichwort*. Bern: Peter Lang, 1986.

———. "Fairy-Tale Allusions in Modern German Aphorisms." *The Reception of Grimms' Fairy Tales: Responses, Reactions, Revisions*. Edited by Donald Haase. Detroit: Wayne State University Press, 1993. 149–66.

———, ed. *Festschrift for Alan Dundes on the Occasion of His Sixtieth Birthday on September 8, 1994*. Burlington, VT: The University of Vermont, 1994. Special issue of *Proverbium: Yearbook of International Proverb Scholarship* 11 (1994).

———. *Hänsel und Gretel: Das Märchen in Kunst, Musik, Literatur, Medien und Karikaturen*. Vienna: Praesens, 2007.

———. "Modern Anglo-American Variants of The Frog Prince (AT 440)." *New York Folklore* 6 (1980): 111–35.

———. "Proverbs in Nazi Germany: The Promulgation of Anti-Semitism and Stereotypes through Folklore." *Journal of American Folklore* 95 (1982): 435–64.

———. *Der Rattenfänger von Hameln: Die Sage in Literatur, Medien und Karikaturen*. Wien: Edition Praesens, 2002.

———. "Sprichwörtliche Schwundstufen des Märchens." *Proverbium* 3 (1986): 257–271.

———. "Survival Forms of 'Little Red Riding Hood' in Modern Society." *International Folklore Review* 2 (1982): 23–40.

———. "'To Pay the Piper' and the Legend of 'The Pied Piper of Hamelin.'" *Proverbium* 2 (1985): 263–70.

———. *Tradition and Innovation in Folk Literature*. Hanover, NH: University Press of New England, 1987.

———. "Wilhelm Grimm's Proverbial Additions in the Fairy Tales." *The Brothers Grimm and Folktale*. Edited by James McGlathery. Urbana: University of Illinois Press, 1988. 112–32.

Mikkelsen, Nina. *Virginia Hamilton*. New York: Twayne, 1994.

Mikolchak, Maria. "Misogyny in Alexander Pushkin: Rescuing the Russian Fairy Tale." *Misogynism in Literature: Any Place, Any Time*. Edited by Britta Zangen. Frankfurt a.M.: Peter Lang, 2004. 99–110.

Miller, Lucien. "Southern Silk Route Tales: Hospitality, Cannibalism and the Other." *Merveilles et contes* 9 (1995): 137–69.

Mills, Margaret A. "Of the Dust and Wind: Folktale Translation and Notes." *Everyday Life in the Muslim Middle East*. Edited by Evelyn Early and Donna Lee Bowen. Bloomington: Indiana University Press, 1993. 47–56.

———. *Rhetorics and Politics in Afghan Traditional Storytelling*. Philadelphia: University of Pennsylvania Press, 1991.

———. "Sex Role Reversals, Sex Changes and Transvestite Disguise in the Oral Tradition of a Conservative Muslim Community in Afghanistan." *Women's Folklore, Women's Culture*. Edited by Rosan A. Jordan and Susan J. Kalcik. Philadelphia: University of Pennsylvania Press, 1985. 187–213.

———. "Women's Tricks: Subordination and Subversion in Afghan Folktales." *Thick Corpus, Organic Variation and Textuality in Oral Tradition*. Edited by Lauri Honko. Helsinki: Finnish Literature Society, 2002. 453–487.

Mills, Margaret A., Peter J. Claus, and Sarah Diamond, eds., *South Asian Folklore: An Encyclopedia*. New York: Routledge, 2003.

Milner, Max. *Le diable dans la littérature française de Cazotte à Baudelaire, 1772–1861*. Paris: J. Corti, 1960.

Miner, Madonne. "No Matter What They Say, It's All About Money." *Journal of Popular Film and Television* 20.1 (1992): 8–14.

Mines, Diane, and Sarah Lamb, eds. *Everyday Life in South Asia*. Bloomington: Indiana University Press, 2002.

Minghella, Anthony. *Jim Henson's "The Storyteller."* New York: Alfred A. Knopf, 1991.

Minton, John. *"Big 'Fraid and Little 'Fraid": An Afro-American Folktale*. Helsinki: Academia Scientiarum Fennica, 1993.

Minton, John, and David Evans. *"The Coon in the Box": A Global Folktale in African-American Tradition*. Helsinki: Academia Scientiarum Fennica, 2001.

Mintz, Thomas. "The Meaning of the Rose in 'Beauty and the Beast.'" *Psychoanalytic Review* 56 (1969–70): 615–20.

Mitchell, Sally. *Dinah Mulock Craik*. Boston: Twayne, 1983.

Mitrokhina, Xenia. "The Land of Oz in the Land of the Soviets." *Children's Literature Association Quarterly* 21 (1996–97): 183–88.

Molan, Peter D. "Sindbad the Sailor: A Commentary on the Ethics of Violence." *Journal of the American Oriental Society* 98 (1978): 237–47.

Mommsen, Katharina. *Goethe und 1001 Nacht*. Berlin: Akademie-Verlag, 1960.

Monk, Craig. *Parody as an Interpretive Response to Grimms' "Kinder- und Hausmärchen."* Dunedin: University of Otago, 1998.

Morgan, Peter. "The Fairy-Tale as Radical Perspective: Enlightenment as Barrier and Bridge to Civic Values in Goethe's *Märchen.*" *Orbis Litterarum* 40 (1985): 222–43.

Morris, Gary. "Goosing Mother Goose." *Bright Lights Film Journal* 22 (September 1998). http://www.brightlightsfilm.com/22/texaverytales. html.

Morris-Keitel, Helen G. "The Audience Should Be King: Bettina Brentano von Arnim's 'Tale of the Lucky Purse.'" *Marvels & Tales* 11 (1997): 48–60.

Moser, Dietz-Rüdiger. "Theorie- und Methodenprobleme der Märchenforschung." *Ethnologia Bavarica* 10 (1981): 47–64.

Moser-Rath, Elfriede. "Austrian Märchen." *Folklore* 63 (1952): 79–90.

———. *"Lustige Gesellschaft": Schwank und Witz des 17. und 18. Jahrhunderts in kultur- und sozialgeschichtlichem Kontext.* Stuttgart: Metzler, 1984.

Moss, Anita. "Mothers, Monsters, and Morals in Victorian Fairy Tales." *Lion and the Unicorn* 12.2 (1988): 47–60.

Mueller, Gerhard O. W. "The Criminological Significance of the Grimms' Fairy Tales." *Fairy Tales and Society: Illusion, Allusion, and Paradigm.* Edited by Ruth B. Bottigheimer. Philadelphia: University of Pennsylvania Press, 1986. 217–27.

Muhammad, Ghulam. *Festivals and Folklore of Gilgit.* 1905. Islamabad: Lok Virsa, 1980.

Muhawi, Ibrahim. "Gender and Disguise in the Arabic *Cinderella*: A Study in the Cultural Dynamics of Representation." *Fabula* 42 (2001): 263–83.

Muñoz, Willy O. "Luisa Valenzuela y la subversión normativa en los cuentos de hadas: 'Si esto es la vida, yo soy Caperucita Roja.'" *La palabra en vilo: Narrativa de Luisa Valenzuela.* Edited by Gwendolyn Díaz and María Inés Lagos. Chile: Santiago, 1996. 221–46.

Murayama, Isamitsu: *Poesie–Natur–Kinder: Die Brüder Grimm und ihre Idee einer "natürlichen Bildung" in den "Kinder- und Hausmärchen."* Heidelberg: Winter, 2005.

Murphy, G. Ronald. *The Owl, the Raven, and the Dove: The Religious Meaning of the Grimms' Magic Fairy Tales.* Oxford: Oxford University Press, 2000.

Murray, Janet H. *Hamlet on the Holodeck: The Future of Narrative in Cyberspace.* 1997. Cambridge: MIT Press, 1998.

Mylius, Johan de. *H. C. Andersens liv: Dag for dag.* Copenhagen: Aschehoug, 1998. In English at http://www.andersen.sdu.dk/liv/tidstavle/vis_e.html.

———. *Hr. Digter Andersen.* Copenhagen: Gad, 1995.

Mylius, Johan de, Aage Jørgensen, and Viggo Hjørnager Pedersen, eds. *Hans Christian Andersen: A Poet in Time.* Odense: Odense University Press, 1999.

Naithani, Sadhana. *In Quest of Indian Folktales: Pandit Ram Gharib Chaube and William Crooke.* Bloomington: Indiana University Press, 2006.

———. "Prefaced Space: Tales of the Colonial British Collectors of Indian Folklore." *Imagined States: Nationalism, Longing, and Utopia in Oral Cultures.* Edited by Luisa del Giudice and Gerald Porter. Logan: Utah State University Press, 2001. 64–79.

———. "The Teacher and the Taught: Structure and Meaning in the *Arabian Nights* and the *Panchatantra.*" *Marvels & Tales* 18 (2004): 272–85.

Narasamamba, K. V. S. Lakshmi. "Voiced Worlds: Heroines and Healers in Muslim Women's Narratives." *Gender and Story in South India.* Edited by Leela Prasad, Ruth B. Bottigheimer, and Lalita Handoo. Albany: SUNY Press, 2006. 67–86.

Narayan, Kirin. *Storytellers, Saints and Scoundrels: Folk Narrative in Hindu Religious Teaching.* Philadelphia: University of Pennsylvania Press, 1989.

Narváez, Peter, ed. *The Good People: New Fairylore Essays.* New York: Garland, 1991.

Natov, Roni. "The Dwarf inside Us: A Reading of 'Rumpelstiltskin.'" *Lion and the Unicorn* 1.2 (1977): 71–76.

Neemann, Harold. *Piercing the Magic Veil: Toward a Theory of the Conte.* Tübingen: Narr, 1999.

Nelson, Alondra. "'Making the Impossible Possible.' Interview with Nalo Hopkinson." *Social Text* 20.2 (2002): 97–113.

Nesbet, Anne. "In Borrowed Balloons: *The Wizard of Oz* and the History of Soviet Aviation." *Slavic and East European Journal* 45 (2001): 80–95

Neuburg, Victor E. *Popular Literature: A History and Guide from the Beginning of Printing to the Year 1897.* Harmondsworth: Penguin Books, 1977.

Neuhaus, Stefan. *Märchen*. Tübingen: A. Francke, 2005.

Nevala, Maria-Liisa, ed. *"Sain roolin johon en mahdu": Suomalaisen naiskirjallisuuden linjoja*. Helsinki: Otava, 1989.

———, ed. *Suomalaisen naiskirjallisuuden linjoja*. Helsinki: Otava, 1989.

Newall, Venetia. "Folklore and Male Homosexuality." *Folklore* 97 (1986): 123–47.

———, ed. *The Witch Figure: Folklore Essays by a Group of Scholars in England Honoring the 75th Birthday of Katharine M. Briggs*. London: Routledge, 2004.

Nicholson, David B. "The Fairy Tale in Modern Drama." Dissertation. City University of New York, 1982.

Nicholson, Henry B. *Topiltzin Quetzalcoatl: The Once and Future Lord of the Toltecs*. Boulder: University Press of Colorado, 2001.

Nicolaisen, W. F. H. "Concepts of Time and Space in Irish Folk Tales." *Celtic Folklore and Christianity: Studies in Memory of William W. Heist*. Edited by Patrick K. Ford. Santa Barbara: McNally and Loftin, 1983. 150–58.

———. "The Past as Place: Names, Stories, and the Remembered Self." *Folklore* 102 (1991): 3–15.

———. "Rehearsing the Future in the Folktale." *New York Folklore* 11 (1985): 231–38.

———. "Space in Folk Narrative." *Folklore in Two Continents: Essays in Honor of Linda Dégh*. Edited by N. Burlakoff and C. Lindahl. Bloomington: Trickster Press, 1980. 14–18.

———. "The Structure of Narrated Time in the Folktale." *Le conte: Pourquoi? Comment?* Edited by Geneviève Calame-Griaule, Veronika Görög-Karady, and Michèle Cliche. Paris: Editions du Centre National de la Recherche Scientifique, 1984. 417–36.

———. "Time in Folk-Narrative." *Folklore Studies in the Twentieth Century*. Edited by Venetia J. Newall. Woodbridge, Sussex: D. S. Brewer, 1978–80. 314–19.

Niggemeyer, Hermann. "Das wissenschaftliche Schrifttum von Leo Frobenius." [Bibliography.] *Paideuma* 4 (1950): 377–418.

Nikolajeva, Maria. "Fairy Tale and Fantasy: From Archaic to Postmodern." *Marvels & Tales* 17 (2003): 138–56.

———. "Fairy Tales in Society's Service." *Marvels & Tales* 16 (2002): 171–87.

———. *From Mythic to Linear: Time in Children's Literature*. Lanham, MD: Scarecrow, 2000.

———. *The Magic Code: The Use of Magical Patterns in Fantasy for Children*. Stockholm: Almqvist & Wiksell International, 1988.

Nodelman, Perry, ed. *Fairy Tales, Fables, Myths, Legends and Poetry*. Volume 2 of *Touchstones: Reflections on the Best in Children's Literature*. West Lafayette, IN: Children's Literature Association, 1987.

Nodelman, Perry, and Mavis Reimer. *The Pleasures of Children's Literature*. 3rd edition. Boston: Allyn and Bacon, 2003.

Noiville, Florence. *Isaac B. Singer: A Life*. Translated by Catherine Temerson. New York: Farrar, Straus & Giroux, 2006.

Nøjgaard, Morten, et al., eds. *The Telling of Stories: Approaches to a Traditional Craft; a Symposium*. Odense: Odense University Press, 1990.

Nonnekes, Paul. "The Loving Father in Disney's *Pinocchio*: A Critique of Jack Zipes." *Children's Literature Association Quarterly* 25.2 (2000): 107–15.

Nordlinder, Eva. *Sekelskiftets svenska konstsaga och sagodiktaren Helena Nyblom*. Stockholm: Bonniers Junior Förlag, 1991.

Novoa, Adriana. "Whose Talk Is It? Almodóvar and the Fairy Tale in *Talk to Her*." *Marvels & Tales* 19 (2005): 224–48.

Oberfeld, Charlotte. "Auch ein Beitrag zur 'Heimat'-Diskussion: 'Heimatkünstler' Otto Ubbelohde—Illustrator der Grimmschen Märchen." *Sprache und Brauchtum: Bernhard Martin zum 90. Geburtstag*. Edited by Reiner Hildebrandt and Hans Friebertshäuser Marburg: Elwert, 1980. 414–17.

O'Brien, John. "Harlequin Britain: Eighteenth-Century Pantomime and the Cultural Location of Entertainment(s)." *Theatre Journal* 50.4 (1998): 489–510.

Odber de Baubeta, Patricia Anne. "The Fairy-Tale Intertext in Iberian and Latin American Women's Writing." *Fairy Tales and Feminism: New Approaches*. Edited by Donald Haase. Detroit: Wayne State University Press, 2004. 129–47.

———."Fairy Tale Motifs in Advertising." *Estudos de Literatura Oral* 3 (1997): 35–60; 4 (1999): 23–53.

O'Flaherty, Wendy Doniger. *Other Peoples' Myths*. New York: Macmillan, 1988.

Ó hÓgáin, Dáithí. *The Hero in Irish Folk History*. Dublin: Gill & Macmillan, 1985. 216–70.

———. *The Lore of Ireland*. Cord: The Collins Press, 2006.

Ofek, Galia. "'Tie Her Up by the Hair': Dickens's Retelling of the Medusa and Rapunzel Myths." *Dickens Quarterly* 20 (2003): 184–99.

Ogilvy, J. D. A. "*Mimi, Scurrae, Histriones:* Entertainers of the Early Middle Ages." *Speculum* 38 (1963): 603–19.

Ojinmah, Umelo R. *Witi Ihimaera: A Changing Vision.* Dunedin: University of Otago Press, 1993.

Olrik, Axel. *Principles for Oral Narrative Research.* Translated by Kirsten Wolf. Bloomington: Indiana University Press, 1992.

Ong, Walter. *Orality and Literacy: The Technologizing of the Word.* London: Routledge, 1982.

Orbell, Margaret. *A Concise Encyclopedia of Maori Myth and Legend.* Christchurch: Canterbury University Press, 1998.

———. *The Illustrated Encyclopedia of Maori Myth and Legend.* 1995. Christchurch: Canterbury University Press, 1999.

Orenstein, Catherine. *Little Red Riding Hood Uncloaked: Sex, Morality, and the Evolution of a Fairy Tale.* New York: Basic Books, 2002.

Orieux, Jean. *La Fontaine, ou La vie est un conte.* Paris: Flammarion, 1976.

Oring, Elliot. *Folk Groups and Folklore Genres: An Introduction.* Logan: Utah State University Press, 1986.

———. "Folk Narrative." *Folk Groups and Folklore Genres: An Introduction.* Edited by Elliott Oring. Logan: Utah State University Press, 1986. 121–45.

Oriol, Carme. "Revision of Amades' Classification of the Catalan Folktales." *Fabula* 31 (1990): 304–12.

Orlov, Janina. "Var glad som sparven kvittrar." *Finlands svenska litteraturhistoria: Åren 1400–1900.* Edited by Johan Wrede. Helsinki: Svenska litteratursällskapet i Finland, 1999. 339–50.

Osmond, Andrew. "Nausicaa and the Fantasy of Hayao Miyazaki." *Foundation: The International Review of Science Fiction* 72 (Spring 1998): 57–80.

Osorio, Ruby. *Story of a Girl (Who Awakes Far, Far Away).* St. Louis: Contemporary Art Museum of St. Louis, 2005.

Ostby, Leif. *Theodor Kittelsen.* Oslo: Dreyers Forlag, 1976.

Ostriker, Alicia. "The Thieves of Language: Women Poets and Revisionist Mythmaking." *Signs* 8 (1982): 68–90.

O'Sullivan, Emer. "Rose Blanche, Rosa Weiss, Rosa Blanca: A Comparative View of a Controversial Picture Book." *Lion and the Unicorn* 29 (2005): 152–70.

Ouyang, Wen-chin, and Geert Jan van Gelder, eds. *New Perspectives on Arabian Nights: Ideological Variations and Narrative Horizons.* New York: Routledge, 2005.

Ovenden, Graham, and John Davis. *The Illustrators of Alice in Wonderland and Through the Looking Glass.* London: Academy Editions, 1979.

Owen, Hilary. "Fairies and Witches in Hélia Correia." *Women, Literature, and Culture in the Portuguese-Speaking World.* Edited by Cláudia Pazos Alonso and Glória Fernandes. Lewiston, NY: Edwin Mellen Press, 1996. 85–104.

———. "Hélia Correia's *Montedemo:* The Tale of an (Un)becoming Virgin." *Portuguese Women's Writing, 1972 to 1986: Reincarnations of a Revolution.* Lewiston, NY: Edwin Mellen Press, 2000. 57–72.

Pace, David. "Beyond Morphology: Lévi-Strauss and the Analysis of Folktales." *Cinderella: A Casebook.* Edited by Alan Dundes. Madison: University of Wisconsin Press, 1988. 245–58.

Pagliano, Jean-Pierre. *Paul Grimault.* Paris: Dreamland, 1996.

Papachristophorou, Marilena. "The *Arabian Nights* in Greece: A Comparative Survey of Greek Oral Tradition." *Fabula* 45 (2004): 311–29.

———. *Sommeils et veilles dans le conte merveilleux grec.* Helsinki: Suomalainen Tiedeakatemia, 2002.

Paradiz, Valerie. *Clever Maids: The Secret History of the Grimm Fairy Tales.* New York: Basic Books, 2005.

Parsons, Linda T. "Ella Evolving: Cinderella Stories and the Construction of Gender- Appropriate Behavior." *Children's Literature in Education* 35 (2004): 135–54.

Partington, Paul G. *Fairy Tales and Folk Tales on Stamps.* Milwaukee: American Topical Association, 1970.

Patterson, Annabel M. *Fables of Power: Aesopian Writing and Political History.* Durham, NC: Duke University Press, 1991.

Pattison, Walter T. *Benito Pérez Galdós.* Boston: Twayne, 1975.

Pearce, C. "Story as Play Space: Narrative in Games." *Game On: The History and Culture of Video Games.* Ed. Laurence King. London: Laurence King Publishing, 2002. 112–19.

Peary, Gerald. "Little Red Ridinghood." *Sight and Sound* 57 (Summer 1988): 150.

Peck, Jackie, and Judy Hendershot. "Release from 'Grimm' Captivity: Paul O. Zelinsky Talks about the Making of *Rapunzel*, the 1998 Caldecott Medal Winner." *Reading Teacher* 52 (1999): 570–75.

Peischl, Margaret T. "Theodor Storm's 'The Rainmaiden': A Creative Process." *Marvels & Tales* 11 (1997): 74–91.

Pellowski, Anne. *The World of Storytelling.* Expanded and revised edition. Bronx, NY: Wilson, 1990.

Pelton, Robert D. *The Trickster in West Africa: A Study of Mythic Irony and Sacred Delight.* Berkeley: University of California Press, 1980.

Peñalosa, Fernando. *The Mayan Folktale: An Introduction.* Rancho Palos Verdes, CA: Yax Te' Press, 1996.

Peñuelas, Marcelino C. *Jacinto Benavente.* Translated by Kay Engler. New York: Twayne, 1968.

Peppin, Brigid, and Lucy Micklethwait. *Dictionary of British Book Illustrators: The Twentieth Century.* London: Murray, 1983.

Perella, Nicolas J. Introduction. *The Adventures of Pinocchio: Story of a Puppet.* By Carlo Collodi. Translated by Nicolas J. Perella. Berkeley: University of California Press, 1986. 1–69.

Pérez, Janet. "Once upon a Time: Post-War Spanish Women Writers and the Fairy-Tale." *Hers Ancient and Modern: Women's Writing in Spain and Brazil.* Edited by Catherine Davies and Jane Whetnall. Manchester: University of Manchester, Department of Spanish and Portuguese, 1997. 57–71.

Perrin, Jean-François. "L'invention d'un genre littéraire au XVIIIe siècle: Le conte oriental." *Féeries* 2 (2004–05): 9–27.

Perrot, Jean. "An English Promenade." *Bookbird* 38 (2000) 3: 11–16.

———, ed. *Tricentenaire Charles Perrault: Les grands contes du XVIIe siècle et leur fortune littéraire.* Paris: In-Press Editions, 1998.

Peters, Maureen. *Jean Ingelow: Victorian Poetess.* Totowa, NJ: Rowman and Littlefield, 1972.

Petrie, Duncan. "But What If Beauty Is a Beast? Doubles, Transformations and Fairy Tale Motifs in *Batman Returns*." *Cinema and the Realms of Enchantment: Lectures, Seminars and Essays by Marina Warner and Others.* Edited by Duncan Petrie. London: British Film Institute, 1993. 98–110.

———, ed. *Cinema and the Realms of Enchantment: Lectures, Sermons, and Essays by Marina Warner and Others.* London: British Film Institute, 1993.

Petrini, Mario. *La fiaba di magia nella letteratura italiana.* Udine: Del Bianco, 1983.

Peyroutet, Jean-Luc. *Pierre Gripari et ses contes pour enfants.* Paris: Girandoles, 1994.

Philip, Neil, ed. *The Cinderella Story: The Origins and Variations of the Story Known as "Cinderella."* London: Penguin, 1989.

———. *A Fine Anger: A Critical Introduction to the Work of Alan Garner.* London: Collins, 1981.

Phillpotts, Beatrice. *Mermaids.* New York: Ballantine, 1980.

Picone, Michelangelo, and Alfred Messerli, eds. *Giovan Battista Basile e l'invenzione della fiaba.* Ravenna: Longo Editore, 2004.

Pilinovsky, Helen. "Interstitial Arts: An Interview with Delia Sherman." *Journal of the Fantastic in the Arts* 15 (2004): 248–50.

Pinault, David. *Story-Telling Techniques in the Arabian Nights.* Leiden: Brill, 1992.

Pitt-Rivers, Julian Alfred. *The People of the Sierra.* 1961. Chicago: University of Chicago Press, 1966.

Piva, Franco. "A la récherche de Catherine Bernard." *Oeuvres de Catherine Bernard, I.* Fasano: Schena, 1993. 15–47.

Pócs, Éva. *Fairies and Witches at the Boundary of South-Eastern and Central Europe.* Helsinki: Academia Scientiarum Fennica, 1989.

Poesio, Carla, and Pino Boero. "Gianni Rodari: An Appreciation." *Phaedrus* (1981): 20–21.

Posner, Helaine, and Smith, Kiki. *Kiki Smith: Telling Tales.* New York: International Center of Photography, 2001.

Prahlad, Anand, ed. *The Greenwood Encyclopedia of African American Folklore.* 3 volumes. Westport, CT: Greenwood Publishing Group, 2006.

Prasad, Leela. "The Authorial Other in Folktale Collections in Colonial India: Tracing Narration and its Dis/Continuities." *Cultural Dynamics* 15.1 (2003): 5–39.

Prasad, Leela, Ruth B. Bottigheimer, and Lalita Handoo, eds. *Gender and Story in South India.* Albany: SUNY Press, 2006.

Preston, Cathy Lynn. "'Cinderella' as a Dirty Joke: Gender, Multivocality, and the Polysemic Text." *Western Folklore* 53 (1994): 27–49.

———. "Disrupting the Boundaries of Genre and Gender: Postmodernism and the Fairy Tale." *Fairy Tales and Feminism: New Approaches.*

Edited by Donald Haase. Detroit: Wayne State University Press, 2004. 197–212.

Preston, Cathy Lynn, and Michael J. Preston. *The Other Print Tradition: Essays on Chapbooks, Broadsides, and Related Ephemera*. Garland: New York, 1995.

Prickett, Stephen. *Victorian Fantasy*. Bloomington: Indiana University Press, 1979.

Prieto, René. *Miguel Angel Asturias's Archaeology of Return*. Cambridge: Cambridge University Press, 1993.

Pritchett, Frances. *Marvelous Encounters: Folk Romance in Urdu and Hindi*. Delhi: Manohar, 1985.

———. *The Romance Tradition in Urdu*. New York: Columbia University Press, 1991.

Propp, Vladimir. *Morphology of the Folktale*. Translated by Laurence Scott. Revised and edited by Louis A. Wagner. 2nd edition. 1968. Austin: University of Texas Press, 1996.

———. *Theory and History of Folklore*. Translated by Ariadna Y. Martin and Richard P. Martin. Minneapolis: University of Minnesota Press, 1984.

Puchner, Walter. "Der unveröffentlichte Zettelkasten eines Katalogs der griechischen Märchentypen nach dem System von Aarne-Thompson von Georgios A. Megas." *Die heutige Bedeutung oraler Traditionen: Ihre Archivierung, Publikation und Index-Erschliessung*. Edited by Walther Heissig and Rüdiger Schott. Opladen: Westdeutscher Verlag, 1998. 87–105.

Puhvel, Jaan. *Comparative Mythology*. Baltimore: Johns Hopkins University Press, 1987.

Pupier, Pierre. *Henri Pourrat et la grande question*. Paris: Sang de la terre, 1999.

Purkiss, Diane. *At the Bottom of the Garden: A Dark History of Fairies, Hobgoblins, and Other Troublesome Things*. New York: New York University Press, 2000.

Quiñones Keber, Eloise. *Codex Telleriano-Remensis: Ritual, Divination, and History in a Pictorial Aztec Manuscript*. Austin: University of Texas Press, 1995.

Rabell, Carmen. *Rewriting the Italian Novella in Counter-Reformation Spain*. Woodbridge: Tamesis, 2003.

Rabkin, Eric S. *The Fantastic in Literature*. Princeton, NJ: Princeton University Press, 1976.

Radin, Paul. *The Trickster: A Study in American Indian Mythology*. London: Routledge and Kegan Paul, 1956.

Raeper, William, ed. *The Gold Thread: Essays on George MacDonald*. Edinburgh: Edinburgh University Press, 1990.

Raheja, Gloria G., and Ann G. Gold. *Listen to the Heron's Words: Reimagining Gender and Kinship in North India*. Berkeley: University of California Press, 1994.

Rahn, Suzanne. *Rediscoveries in Children's Literature*. New York: Garland, 1995. 39–50.

———. *The Wizard of Oz: Shaping an Imaginary World*. New York: Twayne, 1998.

Rak, Michele. *Logica della fiaba: Fate, orchi, gioco, corte, fortuna, viaggio, capriccio, metamorfosi, corpo*. Milan: Mondadori, 2005.

Ralph, Phyllis C. "Transformations: Fairy Tales, Adolescence, and the Novel of Female Development in Victorian Fiction." Dissertation. University of Kansas, 1985.

Ramanujan, A. K. "Towards a Counter-System: Women's Tales." *Gender, Genre and Power in South Asian Expressive Traditions*. Edited by Arjun Appadurai, Frank J. Korom, and Margaret A. Mills. Philadelphia: University of Pennsylvania Press, 1991. 33–55.

Rank, Otto, ed. *Myth of the Birth of the Hero and Other Writings*. Ed. Philip Freund. New York: Vintage Books, 1964. 12–96.

Ranke, Kurt. "Einfache Formen." *Journal of the Folklore Institute* 4 (1967): 17–31.

Rappoport, Philippa Ellen. "Doll Folktales of the East Slavs: Invocations of Women from the Boundary of Space and Time." Dissertation. University of Virginia, 1998.

Rasmussen, Knud. *Report of the Fifth Thule Expedition, 1921–24*. Vol. 7, no. 1; vol. 7, nos. 2–3; vol. 8, nos. 1–2; vol. 9; vol. 10, no. 2; vol. 10, no. 3. 1929–52. New York: AMS Press, 1976.

Raynard, Sophie. *La seconde préciosité: Floraison des conteuses de 1690 à 1756*. Tübingen: Gunter Narr, 2002.

Redies, Sünje. "Return with New Complexities: Robert Coover's *Briar Rose*." *Marvels & Tales* 18 (2004): 9–27.

Rees, Alwyn, and Brinley Rees. *Celtic Heritage*. London: Thames & Hudson, 1961.

Rees-Jones, Deryn. *Carol Ann Duffy*. Plymouth: Northcote House, 1999.

Rego, Paula. Interview with Marina Warner. BBC Four. October 21, 1988. http://www.bbc.co.uk/bbcfour/audiointerviews/profilepages/regop1.shtml.

Reichertz, Ronald. *The Making of the Alice Books: Lewis Carroll's Uses of Earlier Children's*

Literature. Montreal: McGill-Queen's University Press, 1997.

Reimer, Mavis. "Making Princesses, Re-Making *A Little Princess.*" *Voices of the Other: Children's Literature and the Post-Colonial Context.* Edited by Roderick McGillis. New York: Garland, 1999. 111–34.

Reinhard, John R. "The Literary Background of the Chantefable." *Speculum* 1 (1926): 157–69.

Revel, Jacques, and Jean-Claude Schmitt, eds. *L'ogre historien: Autour de Jacques Le Goff.* Paris: Gallimard, 1998. 303–33.

Richards, Jeffrey. *Swordsmen of the Screen: From Douglas Fairbanks to Michael York.* London: Routledge, 1977.

Richman, Paula, ed. *Many Râmâyanas: The Diversity of a Narrative Tradition in South Asia.* Berkeley: University of California Press, 1991.

Richter, Dieter, and Johannes Merkel. *Märchen, Phantasie und soziales Lernen.* Berlin: Basis, 1974.

Ricketts, Mac Linscott, "The North American Indian Trickster." *History of Religions* 5 (1966): 327–50.

———. "The Structure and Religious Significance of the Trickster-Transformer-Culture Hero in the Mythology of North American Indians." Dissertation. University of Chicago, 1964.

Riga, Frank P. "Mortals Call Their History Fable: Narnia and the Use of Fairy Tale." *Children's Literature Association Quarterly* 14 (1989): 26–30.

Riley, Michael O. *Oz and Beyond: The Fantasy World of L. Frank Baum.* Lawrence: University Press of Kansas, 1997.

Riordan, James. "Russian Fairy Tales and Their Collectors." *A Companion to the Fairy Tale.* Edited by Hilda Ellis Davidson and Anna Chaudhri. Cambridge: Brewer, 2003: 217–25.

Ritz, Hans. *Die Geschichte vom Rotkäppchen: Ursprünge, Analysen, Parodien eines Märchens.* 14th expanded edition. Kassel: Muriverlag, 2006.

Robe, Stanley L. *Index of Mexican Folktales.* Berkeley: University of California Press, 1973.

Robert, Marthe. *Origins of the Novel.* Trans. Sacha Rabinovitch. Bloomington: Indiana University Press, 1980.

Robert, Raymonde. *Le conte de fées littéraire en France de la fin du XVIIe à la fin du XVIIIe siècle.* 1982. Paris: Champion, 2002.

———. *Contes parodiques et licencieux du 18e siècle.* Nancy: Presses Universitaires de Nancy, 1987.

Roberts, Martin. *Michel Tournier:* Bricolage *and Cultural Mythology.* Saratoga, CA: ANMA Libri, 1994.

Roberts, Warren E. *The Tale of the Kind and the Unkind Girls: Aa-Th 480 and Related Titles.* 1958. Detroit: Wayne State University Press, 1994.

Robertson, Robin. "A Guide to the Writings of Marie-Louise von Franz." *Psychological Perspectives* 38 (Winter 1998–99): 61–85.

Robinson, David. *Georges Méliès: Father of Film Fantasy.* London: British Film Institute/Museum of the Moving Image, 1993.

Robinson, David Michael. "The Abominable Madame de Murat." *Journal of Homosexuality* 41 (2001): 53–67.

Robinson, Mike, and Hans-Christian Andersen, eds. *Literature and Tourism.* London: Continuum, 2002.

Robinson, Orrin W. "Rhymes and Reasons in the Grimms' Kinder- und Hausmärchen." *German Quarterly* 77 (2004): 47–58.

Robinson, William Andrew. "The End of Happily Ever After: Variations on the Cinderella Theme in Musicals, 1960–1987." Dissertation. Bowling Green State University, 1991.

Rochelle, Warren G. *Communities of the Heart: The Rhetoric of Myth in the Fiction of Ursula K. Le Guin.* Liverpool: Liverpool University Press, 2001.

Rodari, Gianni. *The Grammar of Fantasy: An Introduction to the Art of Inventing Stories.* Translated by Jack Zipes. New York: Teachers and Writers Collaborative, 1996.

———. "Le vecchie fiabe sono da buttar via? Pro e contro il gatto con gli stivali." *Il Giornale dei Genitori* December 1971: 11.

Röder, Birgit. *A Study of the Major Novellas of E. T. A. Hoffmann.* Rochester, NY: Camden House, 2003.

Rodríguez-Mangual, Edna M. *Lydia Cabrera and the Construction of an Afro-Cuban Cultural Identity.* Chapel Hill: University of North Carolina Press, 2004.

Roemer, Danielle M., and Cristina Bacchilega, eds. *Angela Carter and the Fairy Tale.* Detroit: Wayne State University Press, 2001.

Rohde, Erwin. *Der griechische Roman und seine Vorläufer.* New York: Georg Olms Verlag, 1974.

Rohdie, Sam. *The Passion of Pier Paolo Pasolini.* Bloomington: Indiana University Press, 1995.

Róheim, Géza. *Fire in the Dragon and Other Psychoanalytic Essays on Folklore.* Edited byAlan Dundes. Princeton, NJ: Princeton University Press, 1992.

Röhrich, Lutz. "Folklore and Advertising." *Folklore Studies in the Twentieth Century: Proceedings of the Centenary Conference of the Folklore Society.* Edited by Venetia J. Newall. Totowa, NJ: Rowman and Littlefield, 1980. 114–15.

———. *Folktales and Reality.* Translated by Peter Tokofsky. Bloomington: Indiana University Press, 1991.

———. "Der Froschkönig und seine Wandlungen." *Fabula* 20 (1979): 170–192.

———. "German Devil Tales and Devil Legends." *Journal of the Folklore Institute* 7.1 (1970): 21–35.

———. "The Quest of Meaning in Folk Narrative Research." *The Brothers Grimm and Folktale.* Edited by James M. McGlathery. Urbana: University of Illinois Press, 1988. 1–15.

———. "Sprichwörtliche Redensarten aus Volkserzählungen." *Ergebnisse der Sprichwörterforschung.* Edited by Wolfgang Mieder. Bern: Peter Lang, 1978. 87–107.

———. *Wage es, den Frosch zu küssen! Das Grimmsche Märchen Nummer Eins in seinen Wandlungen.* Köln: Eugen Diederichs, 1987.

———. "Wandlungen des Märchens in den modernen Bildmedien: Comics und Cartoons." *Märchen in unserer Zeit.* Edited by Hans-Jörg Uther. München: Eugen Diederichs, 1990. 11–26.

———. *Der Witz: Figuren, Formen, Funktionen.* Stuttgart: Metzler, 1977.

Rölleke, Heinz. "Die Brüder Grimm als Bühnenfigur." *Euphorion* 1 (2002): 101–16.

———. *Die Märchen der Brüder Grimm: Eine Einführung.* Munich: Artemis, 1985.

———. *Die Märchen der Brüder Grimm: Quellen und Studien. Gesammelte Aufsätze.* 2nd edition. Trier: Wissenschaftlicher Verlag Trier, 2004.

———. *"Nebeninschriften": Brüder Grimm, Arnim und Brentano, Droste-Hülshoff: Literarhistorische Studien.* Bonn: Bouvier, 1980.

———. "Nochmals zu den Zahlen Zwölf und Dreihundert im Märchen." *Fabula* 28 (1987): 106–09.

———. "Von dem Fischer un syner Fru: Die älteste schriftliche Überlieferung." *Fabula* 14 (1973): 112–23.

———. *Der wahre Butt: Die wundersamen Wandlungen des Märchens vom Fischer und seiner Frau.* Düsseldorf: Diederichs, 1978.

———. *"Wo das Wünschen noch geholfen hat": Gesammelte Aufsätze zu den "Kinder- und Hausmärchen" der Brüder Grimm.* Bonn: Bouvier, 1985.

Rooth, Anna Birgitta. *The Cinderella Cycle.* 1951. New York: Arno Press, 1980.

———. *The Raven and the Carcass: An Investigation of a Motif in the Deluge Myth in Europe, Asia and North America.* Helsinki: Academia Scientiarum Fennica, 1962.

Roper, Jonathan, ed. *Charms and Charming in Europe.* London: Palgrave, 2004.

———. *English Verbal Charms.* Helsinki: Academia Scientiarum Fennica, 2005.

Rose, Ellen Cronan. "Through the Looking Glass: When Women Tell Fairy Tales." *The Voyage In: Fictions of Female Development.* Edited by Elizabeth Abel, Marianne Hirsch, and Langland Elizabeth. Hanover, NH: University Press of New England, 1983. 209–27.

Rose, Jacqueline. *The Case of Peter Pan or, The Impossibility of Children's Fiction.* Revised edition. London: Macmillan, 1994.

Rosenberg, Bruce A. *Folklore and Literature: Rival Siblings.* Knoxville: University of Tennessee Press, 1991.

Rosenberg, Teya, Martha Hixon, Sharon Scapple, and Donna White, eds. *Diana Wynne Jones: An Exciting and Exacting Wisdom.* New York: Peter Lang, 2002.

Rosenvinge, Teresa, and Benjamín Prado. *Carmen Laforet Díaz.* Barcelona: Ediciones Omega, 2004.

Ross, Deborah. "Escape from Wonderland: Disney and the Female Imagination." *Marvels & Tales* 18 (2004): 53–66.

Rossel, Sven Hakon, ed. *Hans Christian Andersen: Danish Writer and Citizen of the World.* Amsterdam: Rodopi, 1996.

Röth, Diether, and Walter Kahn, eds. *Märchen und Märchenforschung in Europa: Ein Handbuch.* Frankfurt a.M.: Haag und Herchen, 1993.

Roth, Klaus, and Gabriele Wolf, eds. *South Slavic Folk Culture: A Bibliography of Literature in English, German, and French on Bosnian-Hercegovinian, Bulgarian, Macedonian, Montenegrin and Serbian Folk Culture.* Columbus: Slavica Publishers, 1994.

Rotunda, Dominic Peter. *Motif-Index of the Italian Novella in Prose.* 1942. Bloomington, Indiana University, 1964.

Rowe, Karen. "'Fairy-born and human-bred': Jane Eyre's Education in Romance." *The Voyage In.*

Edited by Elizabeth Abel, Marianne Hirsch, and Elizabeth Langland. Hanover: University Press of New England. 1983. 69–89.

Rowland, Anthony, and Michelis Angelica, eds. *The Poetry of Carol Ann Duffy: "Choosing tough words."* Manchester: Manchester University Press, 2003.

Rowland, Herbert. *More Than Meets the Eye: Hans Christian Andersen and Nineteenth-Century American Criticism.* Madison: Fairleigh Dickinson University Press, 2006.

Rua, Giuseppe. "Intorno alle *Piacevoli notti* di G.F. Straparola." *Giornale Storico della Letteratura Italiana* 15 (1890): 111–51; 16 (1890): 218–83.

Rubini, Luise. "Bio-Bibliographical Notes." *Europeœa* 3.1 (1997): 141–55.

———. *Fiabe e mercanti in Sicilia: La raccolta di Laura Gonzenbach, la comunità di lingua tedesca a Messina nell'Ottocento.* Florence: Olschki, 1998.

Rumble, Patrick. *Allegories of Contamination: Pier Paolo Pasolini's Trilogy of Life.* Toronto: University of Toronto Press, 1996.

Rumpf, Marianne. *Ursprung und Entstehung von Warn- und Schreckmärchen.* Helsinki: Academia Scientiarum Fennica, 1955.

Russel, David L. "Young Adult Fairy Tales for the New Age: Francesca Lia Block's *The Rose and the Beast.*" *Children's Literature in Education* 33.2 (2002): 107–15.

Russell, Jeffrey Burton. *Lucifer: The Devil in the Middle Ages.* Ithaca: Cornell University Press, 1984.

Rutledge, Amelia A. "Robin McKinley's Deerskin: Challenging Narcissisms." *Marvels & Tales* 15 (2001): 168–82.

Sadan, Joseph. "Jacques Cazotte, His Her Xaïloun, and Hamîda the Kaslân: A Unique Feature of Cazotte's 'Continuation' of the *Arabian Nights* and a Newly Discovered Arabic Source That Inspired His Novel on Xaïloun." *Marvels & Tales* 18 (2004): 286–99.

Sadoul, Georges. *Georges Méliès.* Paris: Seghers, 1961.

Sakaki Atsuko. "(Re)Canonizing Kurahashi Yumiko: Toward Alternative Perspectives for 'Modern' 'Japanese' 'Literature.'" *Oe and Beyond: Fiction in Contemporary Japan.* Edited by Stephen Snyder and Philip Gabriel. Honolulu: University of Hawaii Press, 1999. 153–76.

Sale, Roger. *Fairy Tales and After: From Snow White to E. B. White.* Cambridge: Cambridge University Press, 1978.

Sallis, Eva. *Sheherazade through the Looking Glass: The Metamorphosis of* The Thousand and One Nights. Richmond, Surrey: Curzon, 1999.

Sammons, Martha C. *"A Better Country": The Worlds of Religious Fantasy and Science Fiction.* Westport, CT: Greenwood, 1988.

Sanchez, Victoria. "A. S. Byatt's *Possession*: A Fairytale Romance." *Southern Folklore* 52.1 (1995): 33–52.

Sanders, Joe. "Of Storytellers and Stories in Gaiman and Vess's 'A Midsummer Night's Dream.'" *Extrapolation: A Journal of Science Fiction and Fantasy* 45 (2004): 237–48.

Sargent-Baur, Barbara Nelson, and Robert Francis Cook. *Aucassin et Nicolette: A Critical Bibliography.* London: Grant and Cutler, 1981.

Sawin, Patricia. *Listening for a Life: A Dialogic Ethnography of Bessie Eldreth through Her Songs and Stories.* Logan: Utah State University Press, 2004.

Sawyer, Ruth. "Wee Meg Barnileg and the Fairies." *The Way of the Story Teller.* Revised edition. 1962. London: George G. Harrap, 1990. 205–16.

Schacker, Jennifer. *National Dreams: The Remaking of Fairy Tales in Nineteenth-Century England.* Philadelphia: University of Pennsylvania Press, 2003.

———. "Otherness and Otherworldliness: Edward W. Lane's Ethnographic Treatment of the *Arabian Nights.*" *Journal of American Folklore* 113 (2000): 164–84.

Schama, Simon. *Landscape and Memory.* New York: Vintage Books, 1996.

Schechter, Harold. "The Bloody Chamber: Terror Films, Fairy Tales, and Taboo." *Forbidden Fruits: Taboos and Tabooism in Culture.* Edited by Ray B. Browne. Bowling Green: Bowling Green State University Popular Press, 1984. 67–82.

Schechtman, Jacqueline. *The Stepmother in Fairy Tales: Bereavement and the Feminine Shadow.* Boston: Sigo, 1991.

Scheck, Ulrich. "Tales of Wonder and Terror: Short Prose of the German Romantics." *The Literature of German Romanticism.* Edited by Dennis Mahoney. Rochester, NY: Camden House, 2004. 101–23.

Schenda, Rudolf. *Die Lesestoffe der kleinen Leute: Studien zur populären Literatur im 19. u. 20. Jh.* Munich: Beck, 1976.

————. "Telling Tales—Spreading Tales: Change in the Communicative Forms of a Popular Genre." Translated by Ruth B. Bottigheimer. *Fairy Tales and Society: Illusion, Allusion, and Paradigm*. Edited by Ruth B. Bottigheimer. Philadelphia: University of Pennsylvania Press, 1986. 75–94.

————. *Volk ohne Buch: Studien zur Sozialgeschichte der populären Lesestoffe, 1770–1910*. Frankfurt a.M.: V. Klostermann, 1970.

————. *Von Mund zu Ohr: Bausteine zu einer Kulturgeschichte volkstümlichen Erzählens in Europa*. Göttingen: Vandenhoeck & Ruprecht, 1993.

Scherf, Walter. *Die Herausforderung des Dämons: Form und Funktion grausiger Kindermärchen; eine volkskundliche und tiefenpsychologische Darstellung der Struktur, Motivik und Rezeption von 27 untereinander verwandten Erzähltypen*. München: K. G. Saur, 1987.

————. "Die Hexe im Zaubermärchen." *Hexenwelten: Magie und Imagination vom 16.-20. Jahrhundert*. Edited by Richard van Dülmen. Frankfurt a.M.: Fischer, 1987. 219–52.

————. *Lexikon der Zaubermärchen*. Stuttgart: Kröner, 1982.

————. *Das Märchenlexikon*. 2 volumes. Munich: Beck, 1995.

————. *Das Märchenlexikon*. Digitale Bibliothek 90. CD-ROM. Berlin: Directmedia Publishing, 2003.

Scheub, Harold. *The Tongue Is Fire: South African Storytellers and Apartheid*. Madison: University of Wisconsin Press, 1996.

Schickel, Richard. *The Disney Version: The Life, Times, Art, and Commerce of Walt Disney*. 1968. New York: Simon and Schuster, 1985.

Schimmel, Annemarie. *The Triumphal Sun: A Study of the Works of Jalâloddin Rumi*. 2nd edition. London: East-West Publications, 1980.

Schmidt-Knaebel, Susanne. "Ludwig Bechstein als Märchenautor: Die vier Anthologien im Überblick." *LiLi: Zeitschrift für Literaturwissenschaft und Linguistik* 33.130 (2003): 137–60.

Schmitt, Christoph. *Adaptionen klassischer Märchen im Kinder- und Familienfernsehen: Eine volkskundlich-filmwissenschaftliche Dokumentation und genrespezifische Analyse der in den achtziger Jahren von den westdeutschen Fernsehanstalten gesendeten Märchenadaptionen mit einer Statistik aller Ausstrahlungen seit 1954*. Frankfurt a.M.: Haag und Herchen, 1993.

Schneider, Ingo. "Erzählen im Internet: Aspekte kommunikativer Kultur im Zeitalter des Computers." *Fabula* 37 (1996): 8–27.

Schodt, Fredrik L. *Dreamland Japan: Writings on Modern Manga*. Berkeley: Stone Bridge Press, 1996.

Scholes, Robert. *Fabulation and Metafiction*. Urbana: University of Illinois Press, 1979.

Schott, Rüdiger. "Project of Comparative Analysis of Motifs and Themes in African Tales." *Asian Folklore Studies* 49 (1990): 140–42.

Schrempp, Gregory. "The Re-Education of Friedrich Max Müller: Intellectual Appropriation and Epistemological Antinomy in Mid-Victorian Evolutionary Thought." *Man* ns 18 (1983): 90–110.

Schrempp, Gregory, and Hansen, William, eds. *Myth: A New Symposium*. Bloomington: Indiana University Press, 2002.

Schullerus, Adolf. *Verzeichnes der rumänischer Märchen und Märchenvarianten nach dem System der Märchentypen Antti Aarnes zusammengestellt*. Helsinki: Academia Scientiarum Fennica, 1928.

Schwarcz, Joseph H. *Ways of the Illustrator: Visual Communication in Children's Literature*. Chicago: American Library Association, 1982.

Scott, Carole. "Magical Dress: Clothing and Transformation in Folk Tales." *Children's Literature Association Quarterly* 21 (1996–97): 151–57.

Scott, Keith. *The Moose that Roared: The Story of Jay Ward, Bill Scott, a Flying Squirrel, and a Talking Moose*. New York: St. Martin's Press, 2000.

Seago, Karen. "Transculturations: Making 'Sleeping Beauty': The Translation of a Grimm Märchen into an English Fairy Tale in the Nineteenth Century." Dissertation. London University, 1998.

Seaman, Gerald R. *Nikolai Andreevich Rimsky-Korsakov: A Guide to Research*. New York: Garland, 1988.

Seán, Allan, and John Sandford, eds. *DEFA: East German Cinema, 1946–1992*. New York: Berghahn, 1999.

Sebeok, Thomas E., ed. *Myth: A Symposium*. 1965. Bloomington: Indiana University Press, 1971.

Segal, Robert Allan, ed. *Anthropology, Folklore, and Myth*. New York: Garland, 1996.

Seifert, Lewis C. *Fairy Tales, Sexuality, and Gender in France, 1690–1715: Nostalgic Utopias*. Cambridge: Cambridge University Press, 1996.

———. "Orality, History, and 'Creoleness' in Patrick Chamoiseau's *Creole Folktales.*" *Marvels & Tales* 16 (2002): 214–30.

———. "The Rhetoric of 'invraisemblance': *Les Enchantements de l'éloquence.*" *Cahier du Dix-Septième* 3.1 (1989): 121–39.

Seki Keigo. "Types of Japanese Folktales." *Asian Folklore Studies* 35 (1966): 1–220.

Selby, Emily F., and Deborah P. Dixon. "Between Worlds: Considering Celtic Feminine Identities in *The Secret of Roan Inish.*" *Gender, Place and Culture: A Journal of Feminist Geography* 5.1 (1998): 5–28.

Seljamaa, Elo-Hanna. "Walter Anderson: A Scientist beyond Historic and Geographic Borders." *Studies in Estonian Folkloristics and Ethnology. A Reader and Reflexive History.* Edited by Kristin Kuutma and Tiiu Jaago. Tartu: Tartu University Press, 2005. 153–68.

Sellers, Susan. *Myth and Fairy Tale in Contemporary Women's Fiction.* New York: Palgrave, 2001.

Sendak, Maurice. *Caldecott & Co.: Notes on Books & Pictures.* New York: Farrar, Straus, and Giroux, 1988.

Senft, Gunter. "What Happened to 'The Fearless Tailor' in Kilivila: A European Fairy-Tale From the South Seas." *Anthropos: International Review of Anthropology and Linguistics* 87 (1992): 407–21.

Senn, Doris. "Le piacevoli notti (1550/53) von Giovan Francesco Straparola, ihre italienischen Editionen und die spanische Übersetzung Honesto y agradable entretenimiento de damas y galanes (1569/81) von Francisco Truchado." *Fabula* 34 (1993): 45–65.

Sennewald, Jens E. *Das Buch, das wir sind: Zur Poetik der Kinder- und Hausmärchen, gesammelt durch die Brüder Grimm.* Würzburg: Königshausen & Neumann, 2004.

Sermain, Jean-Paul. *Le conte de fées du classicisme aux lumières.* Paris: Desjonquères, 2005.

Shahar, Meir. "The Lingyin Si Monkey Disciples and the Origins of Sun Wukong." *Harvard Journal of Asiatic Studies* 52 (1992): 193–224.

Shandley, Robert R. "Time Is Money: Constructing Subjectivity in C. M. Wieland's 'The Philosopher's Stone.'" *Merveilles et contes* 7 (1993): 451–68.

Shaner, Mary E. "Joseph Jacobs." *Writers for Children: Critical Studies of Major Authors since the Seventeenth Century.* Edited by Jane Bingham. New York: Scribners, 1987. 309–16.

Shavit, Zohar. "The Concept of Childhood and Children's Folktales: Test Case—'Little Red Riding Hood.'" *Little Red Riding Hood: A Casebook.* Edited by Alan Dundes. Madison: University of Wisconsin Press, 1989. 129–58.

Sheets, Robin Ann. "Pornography, Fairy Tales, and Feminism: Angela Carter's "The Bloody Chamber.'" *Journal of the History of Sexuality* 1 (1991): 633–57.

Shinn, Thelma J. "The Fable of Reality: Mythoptics in John Crowley's *Little, Big.*" *Extrapolation: A Journal of Science Fiction and Fantasy* 31 (1990): 5–14.

Shippey, T. A. *The Road to Middle-Earth.* Enlarged edition. London: HarperCollins, 1993.

Siegmund, Wolfdietrich, ed. *Antiker Mythos in unseren Märchen.* Kassel: Erich Röth-Verlag, 1984.

Siikala, Anna-Leena and Jukka Siikala. *Return to Culture: Oral Tradition and Society in the Southern Cook Islands.* Helsinki: Suomalainen Tiedeakatemia, 2005.

Silko, Leslie Marmon. "Language and Literature from a Pueblo Indian's Perspective." *English Literature: Opening Up the Canon.* Edited by Leslie A. Fiedler and Houston A. Baker. Baltimore: Johns Hopkins University Press, 1979. 54–72.

Silver, Carole G. *Strange and Secret Peoples: Fairies and Victorian Consciousness.* New York: Oxford University Press, 1999.

Silverberg, Robert. *The Golden Dream: Seekers of El Dorado.* 1967. Athens: Ohio University Press, 1996.

Simeone, William. "Italian Folklore Scholars." *Journal of American Folklore* 74 (1961): 344–53.

Simonsen, Michèle. *Le conte populaire français.* Paris: Presses Universitaires de France, 1981.

Simpson, Robin Smith. "Fairy-Tale Representations of Social Realities: Madame d'Aulnoy's *Contes des fées* (1697–98)." Dissertation. Duke University, 1996.

Sircar, Sanjay. "The Generic Decorum of the Burlesque Kunstmärchen: E. Nesbit's 'The Magician's Heart.'" *Folklore* 110 (1999): 75–91.

Sironval, Margaret. *Album Mille et une nuits.* Paris: Gallimard, 2005.

Skord, Virginia. *Tales of Tears and Laughter: Short Fiction of Medieval Japan.* Honolulu: University of Hawaii Press, 1991.

Smith, Albert Brewster. *Théophile Gautier and the Fantastic.* University, MS: Romance Monographs, 1977.

Smith, Edwin, and Andrew Dale. *The Ila-Speaking Peoples of Northern Rhodesia.* 2 volumes. London: Macmillan, 1920.

Smith, Grace Partridge. "The Plight of the Folktale in the Comics." *Southern Folklore Quarterly* 16 (1952): 124–27.

Smith, Greg, and Sarah Hyde, eds. *Walter Crane, 1845–1915: Artist, Designer, and Socialist.* London: University of Manchester, 1989.

Snyder, Louis L. "Cultural Nationalism: The Grimm Brothers' Fairy Tales." *Roots of German Nationalism.* Bloomington: Indiana University Press, 1978. 35–54.

Sobol, Joseph Daniel. *The Storytellers' Journey: An American Revival.* Urbana: University of Illinois Press, 1999.

Soliño, María Elena. *Women and Children First: Spanish Women Writers and the Fairy* Tale Tradition. Potomac, MD: Scripta Humanistica, 2002.

Solms, Wilhelm, and Susan Tebbutt. "On the Demonising of Jews and Gypsies in Fairy Tales." *Sinti and Roma: Gypsies in German-Speaking Society and Literature.* Edited by Susan Tebutt. New York: Berghahn, 1998. 91–106.

Solomon, Charles. *Enchanted Drawings: The History of Animation.* Revised edition. New York: Wings Books, 1994.

Sorensen, Gail D. "Thackeray's *The Rose and the Ring*: A Novelist's Fairy Tale." *Mythlore* 15 (1989): 37–38, 43.

Sorgenfrei, Carol Fisher. *Unspeakable Acts: The Avant-Garde Theatre of Terayama Shūji and Postwar Japan.* Honolulu: University of Hawaii Press, 2005.

Soriano, Marc. *Les contes de Perrault: Culture savante et traditions populaires.* 1968. Paris: Gallimard, 1977.

Soto, Sara. *Magia e historia en los "Cuentos negros," "Por qué" y "Ayapá" de Lydia Cabrera.* Miami: Ediciones Universal, 1988.

Sparing, Margarethe Wilma. "The Family." *The Perception of Reality in the Volksmärchen of Schleswig-Holstein: A Study in Interpersonal Relationships and World View.* New York: University Press of America, 1984. 50–106.

Speaight, George. *Punch & Judy: A History.* Boston: Publishers Plays, Inc., 1970.

Spentzou, Efrossini. *Readers and Writers in Ovid's "Heroides": Transgressions of Genre and Gender.* Oxford: Oxford University Press, 2003.

Sprug, Joseph W. *Index to Fairy Tales, 1987–1992: Including 310 Collections of Fairy Tales, Folktales, Myths, and Legends with Significant Pre-1987 Titles Not Previously Indexed.* Metuchen: Scarecrow, 1994. Continuation of Mary Huse Eastman, *Index to Fairy Tales;* and Norma Ireland, *Index to Fairy Tales.*

Stahl, Sandra Dolby. *Literary Folkloristics and the Personal Narrative.* Bloomington: Indiana University Press, 1989.

Stallybrass, Peter, and Allon White. *The Politics and Poetics of Transgression.* London: Methuen, 1986.

Stanton, Joseph. *The Important Books: Children's Picture Books as Art and Literature.* Lanham, MD: Scarecrow Press, 2005.

Stedman, Allison. "D'Aulnoy's Histoire d'Hypolite, comte de Duglas (1690): A Fairy-Tale Manifesto." *Marvels & Tales* 19 (2005): 32–53.

Steinisch, Sabine. "Subversive Fabulations: The Twofold Pull in Suniti Namjoshi's Feminist Fables." *Engendering Realism and Postmodernism.* Edited by Beate Neumeier. Amsterdam: Rodopi, 2001. 265–77.

Stephens, John, and Robyn McCallum. *Retelling Stories, Framing Culture: Traditional Story and Metanarratives in Children's Literature.* New York: Garland, 1998.

———. "Utopia, Dystopia, and Cultural Controversy in *Ever After* and *The Grimm Brothers' Snow White*." *Marvels & Tales* 16 (2002): 201–13.

Stewart, Susan. *Nonsense: Aspects of Intertextuality in Folklore and Literature.* Baltimore: Johns Hopkins University Press, 1980.

———. "Notes on Distressed Genres." *Journal of American Folklore* 104 (1991): 5–31.

Stiffler, Muriel W. *The German Ghost Story as Genre.* New York: Peter Lang, 1993.

Stites, Richard. "The Domestic Muse: Music at Home in the Twilight of Serfdom." *Intersections and Transportations: Russian Music, Literature, and Society.* Edited by Andrew Baruch Wachtel. Evanston, IL: Northwestern University Press, 1998. 187–205.

Stitt, Michael J. *Beowulf and the Bear's Son: Epic, Saga, and Fairytale in Northern Germanic Tradition.* New York: Garland, 1992.

Stoddart, S. F. "'Happily … Ever …' NEVER: The Antithetical Romance of *Into the Woods*." *Reading Stephen Sondheim: A Collection of*

Critical Essays. Edited by Sandor Goodhart. New York: Garland, 2000. 209–20.

Stone, Harry. *Dickens and the Invisible World: Fairy Tales, Fantasy, and Novel-Making.* Bloomington: Indiana University Press, 1979.

———. "Dickens, Cruikshank, and Fairy Tales." *George Cruikshank: A Revaluation.* Edited by Robert L. Patten. Princeton, NJ: Princeton University Library, 1974. 213–47.

Stone, Kay. *Burning Brightly: New Light on Old Tales Today.* Peterborough: Broadview, 1998.

———. "Fairy Tales for Adults: Walt Disney's Americanization of the Märchen." *Folklore on Two Continents: Essays in Honor of Linda Dégh.* Edited by Nikolai Burlakoff and Carl Lindahl. Bloomington: Trickster Press, 1980. 40–48.

———. *The Golden Woman: Dreaming as Art.* Winnipeg: Shillingford, 2004.

———. "Things Walt Disney Never Told Us." *Journal of American Folklore* 88 (1975): 42–50. Reprinted in *Women and Folklore.* Edited by Claire R. Farrer. Austin: University of Texas Press, 1975. 42–50.

Storer, Mary Elizabeth. *Un épisode littéraire de la fin du XVIIe siècle: La mode des contes de fées (1685–1700).* 1928. Geneva: Slatkine, 1972.

Strayer, Janet. "Trapped in the Mirror: Psychosocial Reflections on Mid-Life and the Queen in *Snow White.*" *Human Development* 39 (1996): 155–72.

Strindberg, August. *Apologia and Two Folk Plays: The Great Highway, The Crownbride, and Swanwhite.* Translated by Walter Johnson. Seattle and London: University of Washington Press, 1981.

Strömstedt, Margareta. *Astrid Lindgren: En levnadsteckning.* 2nd edition. Stockholm: Rabén & Sjögren, 1999.

Subramani. "An Interview with Epeli Hau'ofa." *Inside Out: Literature, Cultural Politics, and Identity in the New Pacific.* Edited by Vilsoni Hereniko and Rob Wilson. Lanham, MD: Rowman and Littlefield, 1999. 39–53.

———. *South Pacific Literature: From Myth to Fabulation.* Suva, Fiji: Institute of Pacific Studies, University of the South Pacific, 1985.

Suschitzky, Anya. "*Ariane et Barbe-Bleue*: Dukas, the Light and the Well." *Cambridge Opera Journal* 9.2 (1997): 133–61.

Susina, Jan. "The Rebirth of the Postmodern Flâneur: Notes on the Postmodern Landscape of Francesca Lia Block's *Weetzie Bat.*" *Marvels & Tales* 16 (2002): 188–200.

Sutton, Martin. *The Sin-Complex: A Critical Study of English Versions of the Grimms'* Kinder- und Hausmärchen *in the Nineteenth Century.* Kassel: Brüder Grimm-Gesellschaft, 1996.

Swahn, Jan-Öjvind. *The Tale of Cupid and Psyche (Aarne-Thompson 425 & 428).* Lund: CWK Gleerup, 1955.

Swain, Virginia E. "Beauty's Chambers: Mixed Styles and Mixed Messages in Villeneuve's Beauty and the Beast." *Marvels & Tales* 19 (2005): 197–223.

Swann, Brian, ed. *On the Translation of Native American Literatures.* Washington: Smithsonian Institution Press, 1992.

Swanwick, Michael. "Singular Interviews: Gregory Frost." *New York Review of Science Fiction* 17.11 (2005): 19.

Swinfen, Ann. *In Defence of Fantasy: A Study of the Genre in English and American Literature since 1945.* London: Rutledge & Kegan Paul, 1984.

Sydow, Carl Wilhelm von. "Geography and Folktale Oikotypes." *Selected Papers on Folklore.* Copenhagen: Rosenkilde & Bagger, 1948. 44–59.

———. *Selected Papers on Folklore: Published on the Occasion of His 70th Birthday.* Copenhagen: Rosenkilde & Bagger, 1948.

Szczepaniak, Monika. *Männer in Blau: Blaubart-Bilder in der deutschspachigen Literatur.* Köln: Böhlau, 2005.

Szumsky, Brian E. "The House That Jack Built: Empire and Ideology in Nineteenth-Century British Versions of 'Jack and the Beanstalk.'" *Marvels & Tales* 13 (1999): 11–30.

Szwed, John F., and Roger D. Abrahams. *Afro-American Folk Culture: An Annotated Bibliography.* New York: Basic Books, 1978.

Taboulay, Camille. *Le cinéma enchanté de Jacques Demy.* Paris: Cahiers du cinéma, 1996.

Taggart, James M. *The Bear and His Sons: Masculinity in Spanish and Mexican Folktales.* Austin: University of Texas Press, 1997.

———. *Enchanted Maidens: Gender Relations in Spanish Folktales of Courtship and Marriage.* Princeton, NJ: Princeton University Press, 1990.

———. *Nahuat Myth and Social Structure.* 1983. Austin: University of Texas Press, 1997.

Tal, Eve. "Deconstructing the Peach: *James and the Giant Peach* as Post-Modern Fairy Tale." *Journal of the Fantastic in the Arts* 14 (2003): 265–76.

Tari, Lujza. "Musical Instruments and Music in Hungarian Folk Tales." *Artes Populares* 16–17 (1995): 767–83.

Taruskin, Richard. "From Fairy Tale to Opera in Four Moves (not so simple)." *Opera and the Enlightenment*. Edited by Thomas Bauman and Marita Petzoldt McClymonds. Cambridge: Cambridge University Press, 1995. 299–307.

———. "Glinka's Ambiguous Legacy and the Birth Pangs of Russian Opera." *19th Century Music* 1.2 (1977): 142–62.

Tatar, Maria. "Fairy Tales in the Age of Terror: What Terry Gilliam Helps to Remind Us about an Ancient Genre." *Slate* 9 September 22, 2005. http://www.slate.com/id/2126727/.

———. *The Hard Fact of the Grimms' Fairy Tales*. 2nd edition. Princeton, NJ: Princeton University Press, 2003.

———. *Off with Their Heads! Fairy Tales and the Culture of Childhood*. Princeton, NJ: Princeton University Press, 1992.

———. *Secrets beyond the Door: The Story of Bluebeard and his Wives*. Princeton, NJ: Princeton University Press, 2004.

Teaiwa, Teresia. "Reading Gauguin's *Noa Noa* with Hau'ofa's *Kisses in the Nederends*: Militourism, Feminism and the Polynesian Body." *Inside Out: Literature, Cultural Politics, and Identity in the New Pacific*. Edited by Vilsoni Hereniko and Rob Wilson. Lanham, MD: Rowman and Littlefield, 1999. 249–63.

Tedlock, Dennis. *Finding the Center: Narrative Poetry of the Zuñi Indians*. New York: Dial Press, 1972.

———. *The Spoken Word and the Work of Interpretation*. Philadelphia: University of Pennsylvania Press, 1983.

Tegethoff, Ernst. *Studien zum Märchentypus von Amor und Psyche*. Bonn: K. Schroeder, 1922.

Tenèze, Marie-Louise. "A la mémoire de Paul Delarue." *Arts et Traditions Populaires* 6 (1958): 289–307.

———. *Les contes merveilleux français: Recherche de leurs organisations narratives*. Paris: Éditions Maisonneuve et Larose, 2004.

———. "The Devil's Heater: On the 'Contexts' of a Tale." Translated by Brunhilde Biebuyck. *Journal of Folklore Research* 20 (1983): 197–218.

Terryberry, Karl J. *Gender Instruction in the Tales for Children by Mary E. Wilkins Freeman*. Lewiston, NY: Edwin Mellen Press, 2002.

Thiel, Anne. "From Woman to Woman: Benedikte Naubert's 'Der kurze Mantel.'" *Harmony in Discord: German Women Writers in the Eighteenth and Nineteenth Centuries*. Edited by Laura Martin. Berne: Lang, 2002. 125–44.

Thomas, Gerald. "Meaning in Narrative: A Franco-Newfoundland Version of AaTh 480 (*The Spinning Women by the Spring*) and AaTh 510 (*Cinderella* and *Cap O' Rushes*)." *Fabula* 44 (2003): 117–36.

Thomas, Hayley S. "Undermining a Grimm Tale: A Feminist Reading of 'The Worn-Out Dancing Shoes' (KHM 133)." *Marvels & Tales* 13 (1999): 170–83.

Thomas, Susanne Sara. "'Cinderella' and the Phallic Foot: The Symbolic Significance of the Tale's Slipper Motif." *Southern Folklore* 52 (1995): 19–31.

Thompson, Ewa M. *Understanding Russia: The Holy Fool in Russian Culture*. New York: University Press of America, 1987.

Thompson, Stith. *The Folktale*. 1946. Berkeley: University of California Press, 1977.

———. *Motif-Index of Folk-Literature: A Classification of Narrative Elements in Folktales, Ballads, Myths, Fables, Mediaeval Romances, Exempla, Fabliaux, Jest-Books, and Local Legends*. Revised and enlarged edition. 6 volumes. Bloomington: Indiana University Press, 1955–58. CD-ROM. 1993.

———. "Myth and Folktales." *Myth: A Symposium*. Edited by Thomas E. Sebeok. 1965. Bloomington: Indiana University Press, 1971. 169–80.

———. *Narrative Motif-Analysis as Folklore Method*. Helsinki: Suomalainen Teideakatemia, 1955.

Thompson, Stith, and Warren Roberts. *Types of Indic Oral Tales*. Helsinki: Academia Scientiarum Fennica, 1991.

Thomson, David. *The People of the Sea: A Journey in Search of the Seal Legend*. Washington: Counterpoint, 2000.

Thum, Maureen. "Misreading the Cross-Writer: The Case of Wilhelm Hauff's 'Dwarf Long Nose.'" *Children's Literature* 25 (1997): 1–23.

Thury, Eva M., and Margaret K. Devinney. *Introduction to Mythology: Contemporary Approaches to Classical and World Myths*. New York: Oxford University Press, 2005.

Tiffin, Jessica. "Ice, Glass, Snow: Fairy Tale as Art and Metafiction in the Writings of A. S. Byatt." *Marvels & Tales* 20 (2006): 47–66.

———. "Marvellous Geometry: Narrative and Metafiction in Modern Fairy Tale." Dissertation. University of Cape Town, 2003.

Ting, Nai-tung. *The Cinderella Cycle in China and Indo-China*. Helsinki: Academia Scientiarum Fennica, 1974.

———. *A Type Index of Chinese Folktales: In the Oral Tradition and Major Works of Non-Religious Classical Literature*. Helsinki: Academia Scientiarum Fennica, 1978.

Tismar, Jens. *Kunstmärchen*. 2nd revised expanded edition. Stuttgart: Metzler, 1983.

Todd, Richard. *Writers and Their Work: A. S. Byatt*. Plymouth: Northcote House, 1997.

Todorov, Tzvetan. *The Fantastic: A Structural Approach to a Literary Genre*. Translated by Richard Howard. Ithaca: Cornell University Press, 1975.

Toelken, Barre. "The Folk Performance." *The Dynamics of Folklore*. Revised and expanded edition. Logan: Utah State University Press, 1996. 117–56.

———. "The Yellowman Tapes, 1966–1997." *Journal of American Folklore* 111 (1998): 381–91.

Toijer-Nilsson, Ying. *Skuggornas förtrogna: Om Maria Gripe*. Stockholm: Albert Bonniers Förlag, 2000.

Tolkien, J. R. R. "On Fairy Stories." 1938. *Tree and Leaf*. London: Allen & Unwin, 1968. 11–70.

Tools of the Trade: Reconsidering Type and Motif Indexes. Special issue of *Journal of Folklore Research* 34.3 (1997).

Topliss, Iain. *The Comic Worlds of Peter Arno, William Steig, Charles Addams and Saul Steinberg*. Baltimore: Johns Hopkins University Press, 2005.

Trachtenberg, Stanley. *Understanding Donald Barthelme*. Columbia, SC: University of South Carolina Press, 1990.

Trilling, Lionel. *Sincerity and Authenticity*. London: Oxford University Press, 1972.

Trinquet, Charlotte. "Le Petit Chaperon Rouge et les divers chemins qu'elle emprunte." *Studies in Modern and Classical Languages and Literatures* 6 (2004): 80–89.

———. "Voix clandestines dans les Contes de fées: L'exemple de *Finette Cendron* de Madame d'Aulnoy." *Cahiers du dix-septième* 10.2 (2006): 65–82.

Tubach, Frederic C. *Index Exemplorum: A Handbook of Medieval Religious Tales*. Helsinki: Suomalainen Tiedeakatemia, 1969.

Tucker, Elizabeth. *Campus Legends: A Handbook*. Westport, CT: Greenwood Press, 2005.

Tucker, Holly. *Pregnant Fictions: Childbirth and the Fairy Tale in Early-Modern France*. Detroit: Wayne State University Press, 2003.

———, ed. *Reframing the Early French Fairy Tale*. Spec. issue of *Marvels & Tales* 19 (2005): 1–156.

Tucker, Holly, and Melanie R. Siemens, trans. "Perrault's Preface to *Griselda* and Murat's 'To Modern Fairies.'" *Marvels & Tales* 19 (2005): 125–30.

Tucker, Nicholas. *Darkness Visible: Inside the World of Philip Pullman*. London: Wizard Books, 2003.

———. "Dr. Bettelheim and Enchantment." *Signal* 43 (1984): 33–41.

Tully, Carol Lisa. *Creating a National Identity: A Comparative Study of German and Spanish Romanticism with Particular Refrerence to the Märchen of Ludwig Tieck, the Brothers Grimm, and Clemens Brentano, and the costumbrismo of Blanco White, Estébanez Calderón, and López Soler*. Stuttgart: Heinz, 1997.

Turner, Victor W. "Betwixt and Between: The Liminal Period in *Rites de Passage*." *The Forest of Symbols*. Ithaca: Cornell University Press, 1977. 93–111.

———. "Social Dramas and Stories about Them." *On Narrative*. Edited by W. J. T. Mitchell. Chicago: University of Chicago Press, 1981. 137–64.

Ungerer, Tomi. *The Poster Art of Tomi Ungerer*. Edited by Jack Rennert. New York: Darien House, 1971.

Urton, Gary. *Inca Myths*. Austin: University of Texas Press, 1999.

Uther, Hans-Jörg. *Behinderte in populären Erzählungen*. Berlin: Walter de Gruyter, 1981.

———. "Bibliographie zur Erzählforschung." *Deutsche Märchen und Sagen*. Digitale Bibliothek 80. CD-ROM. Berlin: Directmedia Publishing, 2003.

———. "Die Brüder Grimm als Sammler von Märchen und Sagen." *Kultur und Politik: Die Grimms*. Edited by Bernd Heidenreich and Ewald Grothe. Frankfurt a.M.: Societätsverlag, 2003. 67–107.

———. "Fairy Tales as a Forerunner of European Children's Literature: Cross-Border Fairy Tale Materials and Fairy Tale Motifs." *Narodna umjetnost* 38.1 (2001): 121–33.

———. "Ludwig Bechstein und seine Märchen." *Palmblätter* 9 (2001): 29–53.

———, ed. *Märchen in unserer Zeit: Zu Erscheingungsformen eines populären Erzählgenres.* Munich: Diederichs, 1990.

———. "Type- and Motif-Indexes, 1980–1995: An Inventory." *Asian Folklore Studies* 55 (1996): 299–317.

———. *The Types of International Folktales: A Classification and Bibliography.* 3 volumes. Helsinki: Academia Scientiarum Fennica, 2004.

Uther, Hans-Jörg, et al., eds. *Katalog zur Volkserzählung: Spezialbestände des Seminars für Volkskunde und der Enzyklopädie des Märchens, Göttingen, des Instituts für europäische Ethnologie, Marburg, und des Instituts für Volkskunde, Freiburg im Breisgau.* 2 volumes. München: Saur, 1987.

Valière, Michel. *Le conte populaire: Approche socio-anthropologique.* Paris: Armand Colin, 2006.

Valk, Ülo. "Authorship and Textuality: The *Kalevipoeg* as Epic Landscape." *Kalevala and the World's Traditional Epics.* Edited by Lauri Honko. Helsinki: Finnish Literature Society, 2002. 407–19.

———. *The Black Gentleman: Manifestations of the Devil in Estonian Folk Religion.* Helsinki: Academia Scientiarum Fennica, 2001.

Vambe, Maurice Taonezvi. *African Oral Story-Telling Tradition and the Zimbabwean Novel in English.* Pretoria: Unisa Press, 2004.

van der Kooi, Jurjen. "Das Zaubermärchen im niederländischen (einschließlich flämischen) und westfriesischen Sprachberreich." *Märchen und Märchenforschung in Europa:Ein Handbuch.* Edited by Dieter Röth and Walter Kahn. Frankfurt am Main: Haag und Herchen, 1993. 156–69.

van Suntum, Lisa Rainwater. "Jostein Gaarder." *Twentieth Century Norwegian Writers.* Edited by Tanya Tresher. Detroit: Gale, 2004. 102–110.

Vandergrift, Kay E. Censorship of Mother Goose and Her Followers. 2006. http://eclipse.rutgers.edu/goose/censorship1.aspx.

Varty, Kenneth, ed. *Reynard the Fox: Social Engagement and Cultural Metamorphoses in the Beast Epic from the Middle Ages to the Present.* New York: Berghahn Books, 2000.

Västrik, Ergo-Hart. "Oskar Loorits: Byzantine Cultural Relations and Practical Application of Folklore Archives." *Studies in Estonian Folkloristics and Ethnology: A Reader and Reflexive History.* Edited by Kristin Kuutma and Tiiu Jaago. Tartu: Tartu University Press, 2005. 203–15.

Vatuk, Ved Prakash. *Studies in Indian Folk Traditions.* Delhi: Manohar, 1979.

Vaz da Silva, Francisco. "Bengt Holbek and the Study of Meanings in Fairy Tales." *Cultural Analysis* 1 (2000): 3–14. http://ist-socrates.berkeley.edu/~caforum/volume1/pdf/silva.pdf.

———. "Complex Entities in the Universe of Fairy Tales." *Marvels & Tales* 14 (2000): 219–43.

———. "Iberian Seventh-Born Children, Werewolves, and the Dragon Slayer." *Folklore* 114 (2003): 335–53.

———. *Metamorphosis: The Dynamics of Symbolism in European Fairy Tales.* New York: Peter Lang, 2002.

Velay-Vallantin, Catherine. *La fille en garçon.* Carcassonne: GARAE/Hésiode, 1992.

———. *L'histoire des contes.* Paris: Fayard, 1992.

———. "Le miroir des contes: Perrault dans les *Bibliothèques bleues.*" *Les usages de l'imprimé.* Edited by Roger Chartier. Paris: Fayard, 1987. 129–85.

Vellenga, Carolyn. "Rapunzel's Desire: A Reading of Mlle de La Force." *Merveilles et contes* 6 (1992): 59–73.

Venugopal, Saraswati. "The Role of Gender in Tale-Telling Events." *Gender and Story in South India.* Edited by Leela Prasad, Ruth B. Bottigheimer, and Lalita Handoo. Albany: SUNY Press, 2006. 55–66.

Verdier, Yvonne. "Little Red Riding Hood in Oral Tradition." Translated by Joseph Gaughan. *Marvels & Tales* 11 (1997): 101–23.

Verweyen, Annemarie. "Das Märchenschloß in alten und neuen Bilderbüchern." *Märchen in Erziehung und Unterricht.* Edited by Ottilie Dinges, Monika Born, and Jürgen Janning. Kassel: Erich Röth-Verlag, 1986. 220–25.

Vevaina, Coomi S. "An Interview with Suniti Namjoshi." *ARIEL: A Review of International English Literature* 29.1 (1998): 195–201.

Vijayasree, C. *Suniti Namjoshi: The Artful Transgressor.* New Delhi: Rawat Publications, 2001.

Vodoz, Jules. *La fée aux miettes: Essai sur le rôle du subconscient dans l'oeuvre de Charles Nodier.* Paris: Honoré Champion, 1925.

Vries Jan de. "Dornröschen." *Fabula* 2 (1959): 110–21.

Wadley, Susan. "Folktale." *South Asian Folklore: An Encyclopedia.* Edited by Margaret A. Mills, Peter J. Claus, and Sarah Diamond. New York: Routledge, 2003. 218–20.

Walker, Nancy A. *The Disobedient Writer: Women and the Narrative Tradition.* Austin: University of Texas Press, 1995.

Wallace, Anthony F. C. "Revitalization Movements." *American Anthropologist* 58 (1956): 264–81.

Walsh, Elizabeth. "The King in Disguise." *Folklore* 86 (1975): 3–24.

Walsh, Michael G. "Grimms' *Kinder- und Hausmärchen* in Postmodern Contexts." Dissertation. Wayne State University, 2001.

Wan, Pin Pin. "Investiture of the Gods (Fengshen Yanyi): Sources, Narrative Structure, and Mythical Significance." Dissertation. University of Washington, 1987.

Ward, Donald. "The German Connection: The Brothers Grimm and the Study of 'Oral' Literature." *Western Folklore* 53.1 (1994): 1–26.

Wardetzky, Kristin. *Märchen—Lesarten von Kindern: Eine empirische Studie.* Berlin: Lang, 1992.

———. "The Structure and Interpretation of Fairy Tales Composed by Children." Translated by Ruth B. Bottigheimer. *Journal of American Folklore* 103 (1990): 157–76.

Warner, Marina. *The Absent Mother, or Women against Women in the 'Old Wives' Tale.* Hilversum [Netherlands]: Verloren, 1991.

———. *Fantastic Metamorphoses, Other Worlds: Ways of Telling the Self.* Oxford: Oxford University Press, 2002.

———. "Fee Fie Fo Fum: The Child in the Jaws of the Story." *Cannibalism and the Colonial World.* Edited by Francis Barker, Peter Hulme, and Margaret Iversen. Cambridge: Cambridge University Press, 1997. 158–82.

———. *From the Beast to the Blonde: On Fairy Tales and Their Tellers.* New York: Farrar, Straus and Giroux, 1994.

———. *Six Myths of Our Time: Little Angels, Little Monsters, Beautiful Beasts, and More.* New York: Vintage, 1995.

Wasko, Janet. *Understanding Disney: The Manufacture of Fantasy.* Cambridge: Polity, 2001.

Wasserziehr, Gabriela. *Los cuentos de hadas para adultos: Una lectura simbólica de los cuentos de hadas recopilados por J. y W. Grimm.* 2nd revised and expanded edition. Madrid: Endymion, 1997.

Waters, Donald, ed. *Strange Ways and Sweet Dreams: Afro-American Folklore from the Hampton Institute.* Boston: G. K. Hall, 1983.

Watts, Steven. *The Magic Kingdom: Walt Disney and the American Way of Life.* Boston: Houghton Mifflin, 1997.

Waugh, Patricia. *Metafiction: The Theory and Practice of Self-Conscious Fiction.* London: Routledge, 1984.

Weber, Eugen. "Fairies and Hard Facts: The Reality of Folktales." *Journal of the History of Ideas* 43 (1981): 93–113.

Weil, Ellen R. "The Door to Lilith's Cave: Memory and Imagination in Jane Yolen's Holocaust Novels." *Journal of the Fantastic in the Arts* 5 (1993): 90–104.

Weinstein, Amy. *Once upon a Time: Illustrations from Fairytales, Fables, Primers, Pop-Ups, and Other Children's Books.* New York: Princeton Architectural Press, 2005.

Weitman, Wendy, and Kiki Smith. *Kiki Smith: Prints, Books & Things.* New York: Museum of Modern Art, 2003.

Welch, Marcelle Maistre. "L'Éros féminin dans les contes de fées de Mlle de La Force." *Papers on French Seventeenth-Century Literature* 60 (1991): 217–23.

Wells, Paul. *Understanding Animation.* New York: Routledge, 1998.

Welsford, Enid. *The Fool: His Social and Literary History.* Gloucester: Peter Smith, 1966.

West, Victor Royce. *Folklore in the Works of Mark Twain.* Lincoln, NE: n.p., 1930.

Westin, Boel. *Familjen i dalen: Tove Janssons muminvärld.* Stockholm: Bonnier, 1988.

Westwood, Jennifer, and Jacqueline Simpson. *The Lore of the Land: A Guide to England's Legends.* London: Penguin Books, 2005.

Whalley, Joyce Irene, and Tessa Rose Chester. *A History of Children's Book Illustration.* London: John Murray, 1988.

White, Colin. *Edmund Dulac.* New York: Scribner, 1976.

White, Susan. "Split Skins: Female Agency and Bodily Mutilation in *The Little Mermaid.*" *Film Theory Goes to the Movies.* Edited by Jim Collins, Hilary Radner, and Ava Preacher Collins. New York: Routledge, 1993. 182–95.

Whited, Lana A., ed. *The Ivory Tower and Harry Potter: Perspectives on a Literary Phenomenon.* Columbia: University of Missouri Press, 2002.

Wiebe, Karl. *This Is Not a Hoax: Urban Legends on the Internet.* Baltimore: PublishAmerica, 2003.

Wiley, Roland John. *Tchaikovsky's Ballets: Swan Lake, Sleeping Beauty, Nutcracker*. Oxford: Clarendon Press; New York: Oxford University Press, 1985.

Wilner, Arlene Fish. "'Happy, Happy Ever After': Story and History in Art Spiegelman's *Maus*." *Considering* Maus: *Approaches to Art Spiegelman's "Survivor's Tale" of the Holocaust*. Edited by Deborah R. Geis. Tuscaloosa: University of Alabama Press, 2003. 105–21.

Wilson, Anne. "The Civilizing Process in Fairy Tales." *Signal* 44 (1984): 81–87.

Wilson, Robert. "Play, Transgression and Carnival: Bakhtin and Derrida on Scriptor Ludens" *Mosaic* 19.1 (1986): 73–89.

Wilson, S. W. A. "Herder, Folklore, and Romantic Nationalism." *Journal of Popular Culture* 6 (1973): 819–35.

Wilson, Sharon Rose. *Margaret Atwood's Fairy-Tale Sexual Politics*. Jackson: University Press of Mississippi, 1993.

Winner, Thomas G. *The Oral Art and Literature of the Kazakhs of Russian Central Asia*. Durham: Duke University Press, 1958.

Wogan-Browne, Jocelyn. *Saints Lives and Women's Literary Culture*. New York: Oxford University Press, 2001.

Wolffheim, Elsbeth. "Demontage der tradierten Märchen-Ideologie." *Jugend und Buch* 26.1 (1977): 25–30.

Wood, Juliette. "Filming Fairies: Popular Film, Audience Response and Meaning in Contemporary Fairy Lore." *Folklore* 117 (2006): 279–96.

Wood, Naomi. "Creating the Sensual Child: Paterian Aesthetics, Pederasty, and Oscar Wilde's Fairy Tales." *Marvels & Tales* 16 (2002): 156–70.

Woodward, Charles L. *Ancestral Voice: Conversations with N. Scott Momaday*. Lincoln: University of Nebraska Press, 1989.

Wührl, Paul-Wolfgang. *Das deutsche Kunstmärchen: Geschichte, Botschaft und Erzählstrukturen*. Heidelberg: Quelle und Meyer, 1984.

Wullschlager, Jackie. *Hans Christian Andersen: The Life of a Storyteller*. New York: Alfred A. Knopf, 2001.

Wunderlich, Richard, and Thomas J. Morrissey. *Pinocchio Goes Postmodern: Perils of a Puppet in the United States*. New York: Routledge, 2002.

Wynchank, Anny. "Transition from an Oral to a Written Literature in Francophone West Africa." *African Studies* 44.2 (1985): 189–95.

Yamade Yūko. "Tawada Yōko and the Rewriting of Japanese Folklore." "Identity, Translation, and Embodiment in Migrant and Minority Women's Writings in Japan, English Canada, and Québec." Dissertation. Université de Montréal, 2002. 45–59.

Yamanaka, Yuriko, Tetsuo Nishio, and Robert Irwin, eds. *Arabian Nights and Orientalism: Perspectives from East and West*. New York: I. B. Tauris, 2005.

Yang, Lihui, and Deming An. *Handbook of Chinese Mythology*. Santa Barbara: ABC-CLIO, 2005.

Yassif, Eli. *The Hebrew Folktale: History, Genre, Meaning*. Translated by Jacqueline S. Teitelbaum. Bloomington: Indiana University Press, 1999.

Yolen, Jane. *Touch Magic: Fantasy, Faerie, and Folklore in Literature of Childhood*. New York: Philomel, 1981.

Zagni, Patrizia. *Rodari*. Florence: La Nuova Italia, 1975.

Zamora, Lois Parkinson, and Wendy B. Faris, eds. *Magical Realism: Theory, History, Community*. Durham, NC: Duke University Press, 1995.

Zelinsky, Paul O. "Artist's Notes on the Creation of *Rapunzel*." *Journal of Youth Services in Libraries* 11 (1998): 214–17.

Ziel, Wulfhild. *Der russische Volksbilderbogen in Bild und Text: Ein kultur- und kunsthistorisches Intermedium*. Frankfurt a.M.: Peter Lang, 1996.

Ziolkowski, Jan M. *Fairy Tales from Before Fairy Tales: The Medieval Latin Past of Wonderful Lies*. Ann Arbor: University of Michigan Press, 2007.

Zipes, Jack. *Breaking the Magic Spell: Radical Theories of Folk and Fairy Tales*. Revised and expanded edition. Lexington: University Press of Kentucky, 2002.

———. *The Brothers Grimm: From Enchanted Forests to the Modern World*. 2nd edition. New York: Palgrave MacMillan, 2002.

———. *Creative Storytelling: Building Community, Changing Lives*. New York: Routledge, 1995.

———, ed. "Cross Cultural Connections and the Contamination of the Classical Fairy Tale." *The Great Fairy Tale Tradition: From Straparola and Basile to the Brothers Grimm*. Edited by Jack Zipes. New York: Norton, 2001. 845–69.

———. *Fairy Tale as Myth/Myth as Fairy Tale*. Lexington: University Press of Kentucky, 1994.

———. *Fairy Tales and the Art of Subversion: The Classical Genre for Children and the Process of Civilization.* New York: Wildman Press, 1983.

———. *Hans Christian Andersen: The Misunderstood Storyteller.* New York: Routledge, 2005.

———. *Happily Ever After: Fairy Tales, Children, and the Culture Industry.* New York: Routledge, 1997.

———. "Introduction: Towards a Definition of the Literary Fairy Tale." *The Oxford Companion to Fairy Tale.* Edited by Jack Zipes. Oxford: Oxford University Press, 2000. xv–xxxii.

———, ed. *The Oxford Companion to Fairy Tales.* London: Oxford University Press, 2000.

———. *Speaking Out: Storytelling and Creative Drama for Children.* New York: Routledge, 2004.

———. *Sticks and Stones: The Troublesome Success of Children's Literature from Slovenly Peter to Harry Potter.* New York: Routledge, 2002.

———. *When Dreams Came True: Classical Fairy Tales and Their Tradition.* New York: Routledge, 1999.

———. *Why Fairy Tales Stick: The Evolution and Relevance of a Genre.* New York: Routledge, 2006.

Zucker, Carole. "Sweetest Tongue Has Sharpest Tooth: The Dangers of Dreaming in Neil Jordan's *The Company of Wolves.*" *Literature Film Quarterly* 28 (2000): 66–71.

Zumwalt, Rosemary Lévy. *American Folklore Scholarship: A Dialogue of Dissent.* Bloomington: Indiana University Press, 1988.

———. "A Historical Glossary of Critical Approaches." *Teaching Oral Traditions.* Edited by John Miles Foley. New York: Modern Language Association, 1998. 75–94.

Journals and Serial Publications

Brüder Grimm-Gedenken.

Cabinet des Fées: A Fairy Tale Journal. (http://www.cabinet-des-fees.com/).

Children's Literature. (http://chla.wikispaces.com/Childrens+Literature).

Children's Literature Association Quarterly. (http://chla.wikispaces.com/ChLAQ).

Cultural Analysis: An Interdisciplinary Forum on Folklore and Popular Culture. (http://ist-socrates.berkeley.edu/~caforum/editorial.html).

Ethnologie Française: Revue Trimestrielle de la Société d'Ethnologie Française. (http://www.culture.gouv.fr/sef/revue/ac_revue.htm).

Etnolog: Bulletin of the Slovene Ethnographic Museum. (http://www.etno-muzej.si/eng_etnolog_index.php).

Estudos de Literatura Oral. (http://www.fchs.ualg.pt/ceao/ingles/inc/journal.html).

Fabula: Zeitschrift für Erzählforschung/Journal of Folktale Studies/Revue d'Etudes sur le Conte Populaire. (http://www.degruyter.de/rs/274_5341_DEU_h.htm).

Fairy Tale Review. (http://www.fairytalereview.com/).

Féeries. (http://w3.u-grenoble3.fr/lire/feeries/index.html).

FF Network. (http://www.folklorefellows.fi/netw/network.html).

Folklore: An Electronic Journal of Folklore. (http://www.folklore.ee/folklore/).

Folklore: English Monthly Devoted to the Cause of Indian Folklore Society.

Folklore Forum. (https://www.indiana.edu/~folkpub/forum/).

Folklorica: Journal of the Slavic and East European Folklore Association. (http://www.arts.ualberta.ca/SEEFA/archive.HTM)

Jahrbuch der Brüder Grimm-Gesellschaft. (http://www.grimms.de/contenido/cms/front_content.php)

Journal of American Folklore. (http://www.afsnet.org/publications/jaf.cfm).

Journal of Folklore Research. (http://www.indiana.edu/~jofr/).

Journal of Mythic Arts: An Online Journal for the Exploration of Myth, Folklore, and Fairy Tales, and Their Use in Contemporary Arts. (http://www.endicott-studio.com/PastIssues3.html).

Journal of the Fantastic in the Arts. (http://www.indiana.edu/~jofr/).

Journal of the Folklore Institute.

The Lion and the Unicorn: A Critical Journal of Children's Literature.

Märchenspiegel: Zeitschrift für internationale Märchenforschung und Märchenpflege. (http://www.maerchen-stiftung.de/).

Marvels & Tales: Journal of Fairy-Tale Studies (previously *Merveilles et contes* [1987-96]). (http://www.langlab.wayne.edu/marvelshome/marvels_tales.html).

Merveilles et contes (since 1997 *Marvels & Tales: Journal of Fairy-Tale Studies*).

Mythlore: A Journal of J. R. R. Tolkien, C. S. Lewis, Charles Williams, and the Genres of

Myth and Fantasy. (http://www.mythsoc.org/publications/mythlore/).

Narodna umjetnost: Croatian Journal of Ethnology and Folklore Research. (http://www.ief.hr/en/narodnaumjetnost/).

Oral Tradition: An Interdisciplinary Academic Journal. (http://journal.oraltradition.org/).

Phaedrus: An International Annual of Children's Literature Research.

Storytelling, Self, Society: An Interdisciplinary Journal of Storytelling Studies.

Trickster's Way. (http://www.trinity.edu/org/tricksters/TrixWay).

Western Folklore. (http://www.westernfolklore.org/WesternFolklore.htm).

Zeitschrift für Volkskunde. (http://www.kultur.uni-hamburg.de/dgv/).

Selected Web Sites

Aesopica: Aesop's Fables in English, Latin & Greek. Laura Gibbs. (http://www.mythfolklore.net/aesopica/). Extensive resource for online versions of Aesop's fables. Includes an index of all fables and a word-search feature for the entire electronic corpus.

The American Folklife Center at the Library of Congress. (http://www.loc.gov/folklife/). Rich and authoritative site of the American Folklife Center at the U.S. Library of Congress. Information on the Archive of Folk Culture, online finding aids, and online access to selected digitized collections and presentations.

American Folklore Society. (http://afsnet.org/). Web site of the American Folklore Society includes information on annual conferences, publications, and diverse information about the nature, study, and practice of folklore.

Andrew Lang's Fairy Books. (http://www.mythfolklore.net/andrewlang/). Electronic versions of Andrew Lang's influential series of colored fairy-tale books.

L'association canadienne d'ethnologie et de folklore (ACEF)/Folklore Studies Association of Canada (FSAC). (http://www.celat.ulaval.ca/acef/). The Web site of this professional organization of folklorists includes information about annual meetings and publications, announcements of events and calls for papers, and links to archives of folklore and ethnology.

Center for Studies in Oral Tradition. University of Missouri, Columbia. (http://www.oraltradition.org). Site of the Center for Studies in Oral Tradition, directed by John Miles Foley. Includes news and articles, an extensive searchable bibliography on oral-formulaic theory, information about the journal *Oral Tradition*, and eCompanions to *Oral Tradition*.

Centro de Estudos Ataíde Oliveira. University of the Algarve. (http://www.fchs.ualg.pt/ceao/ingles/inc/who%20are%20we.html). Information about the resources, research, publications, and archives of Portuguese folktales at the Centre of Studies Ataíde Oliveira, founded by Isabel Cardigos and J. J. Dias Marques. In English at http://www.fchs.ualg.pt/ceao/ingles/inc/folkes.htm.

Charles Perrault's Mother Goose Tales. D. L. Ashliman. University of Pittsburgh. (http://www.pitt.edu/~dash/perrault.html). Electronic versions in English of Charles Perrault's prose tales and in English and French of his verse tales. Links to related sites.

Children's Literature Association. (http://chla.wikispaces.com/). The Web site of this professional organization has information about activities, publications, awards, calls for papers, grants, graduate programs in children's literature studies, and an index to the contents of its annual publication, *Children's Literature*.

The Cinderella Bibliography. Russel Peck. University of Rochester. (http://www.lib.rochester.edu/camelot/cinder/cinintr.htm). A rich and useful listing of materials related to "Cinderella" and "Beauty and the Beast." Includes not only references to literary texts and scholarship but also to a wide variety of other materials, including illustrations and art, music and dance, television and film, games, dolls, and other forms of material culture. The database is effectively organized by categories.

The Cinderella Project. University of Southern Mississippi. (http://www.usm.edu/english/fairytales/cinderella/cinderella.html). A text and image archives of one dozen English versions of "Cinderella" from the eighteenth to the twentieth centuries. The texts are from the de Grummond Children's Literature Research Collection at the University of Southern Mississippi.

Cotsen Children's Library. Princeton University. (http://ccl.princeton.edu/). The Web site of the Cotsen Children's Library at Princeton University, which has extensive holdings related to the fairy tale and sponsors academic conferences on related topics, such as the history of the literary fairy tale and the stories of Hans Christian Andersen. In addition to offering information about the Cotsen's holdings, activities, and possibilities for research, the Web site also provides access to some conference proceedings and publications and its Virtual Children's Book Exhibits.

Davenport Films & From the Brothers Grimm. Davenport Films. (http://www.davenportfilms. com). The Web site of Davenport Films includes information about From the Brothers Grimm, its live-action series of classic folktales and fairy tales, as well as resources for teachers.

Decameron Web. Michael Papio, Michael and Massimo Riva. Brown University. (http://www. brown.edu/Departments/Italian_Studies/dweb/ dweb.shtml). "A growing hypermedia archive of materials dedicated to Boccaccio's masterpiece," encompassing texts, background materials and information, a bibliography, discussion of themes and motifs, and resources for teachers, and a site and text search feature.

DEFA Film Library. University of Massachusetts Amherst. (http://www.umass.edu/defa/). Information about the DEFA Film Library at the University of Massachusetts in Amherst, including the numerous fairy-tale films produced by the DEFA film studio in the German Democratic Republic.

Department of European Ethnology/Wossidlo Archive. University of Rostock. (http://www.phf. uni-rostock.de/ivk/). The Web site of the Wossidlo Archive of folklore at the University of Rostock. English version of site available.

Deutsche Gesellschaft für Volkskunde. (http://www. kultur.uni-hamburg.de/dgv/). The Web site of the Deutsche Gesellschaft für Volkskunde (German Folklore Society). Information regarding conferences, calls for papers, publications, and other announcements.

The Endicott Studio: An Interdisciplinary Organization Dedicated to the Creation and Support of Mythic Art. Terri Windling et al. (http:// www.endicott-studio.com/). This Web site offers perspectives on the fairy tale as a mythic art by various artists, creative writers, and scholars. Access to the organization's online *Journal of Mythic Arts.*

Enzyklopädie des Märchens. (http://wwwuser.gwdg.de/~enzmaer/). The Web site of the German-language *Enzyklopädie des Märchens*, the most comprehensive reference work on folk-narrative research. Includes information about the history and scope of the project, as well as sample articles, list of tale types, and index search feature. English version of the site available.

Estonian Folklore. Estonian Literary Museum. (http://en.folklore.ee/). Information about the study of folkore in Estonia, including useful links to institutions, publications, activities, and the the Estonian Folklore Archives of the Estonian Literary Museum. Access to searchable digitized databases in English, German, and Estonian. English version of the site available.

Europäische Märchengesellschaft. (http://www. maerchen-emg.de/). Web site of the European Fairy-Tale Society, an organization of storytellers and scholars that promotes storytelling and appreciation of the folktale and fairy tale. Site includes information about the organization's activities, annual conference, and publications.

Fairy Tales. A. Waller Hastings. Northern State University. (http://www.northern.edu/hastingw/ fairytale.htm). Related to a course taught at Northern State University, this Web site provides information about concepts and terms, individual collectors and authors, and specific tales. Also includes for students a useful (albeit dated) annotated bibliography of fairy-tale collections, rewritings, and criticism.

Finnish Literature Society. (http://www.finlit.fi/ index.php?lang=eng). Web site of the Finnish Literature Society, an academic and cultural organization promoting research on Finnish oral tradition and Finnish language and literature. Site includes information about the society's folklore archives, awards, grants, activities, and publications. English version of the site available.

Folklinks: Folk and Fairy Tale Sites. D. L. Ashliman. University of Pittsburgh. (http://www.pitt.edu/ ~dash/folklinks.html). Impressive, international list of links to Web sites relevant to the study of folktales and fairy tales.

Folklore and Mythology: Electronic Texts. D. L. Ashliman. University of Pittsburgh. (http://www.pitt. edu/~dash/folktexts.html). Excellent, clearly organized, and reliable source of electronic texts (in English) for the study of folklore and mythology.

Folklore Fellows. Finnish Academy of Science and Letters, University of Helsinki. (http://www. folklorefellows.fi). Web site of the Folklore Fellows, including a catalogue of publications from the series Folklore Fellows Communications

(FFC), information concerning the FF Summer School, and online access to *FF Network*.

The Folklore Society. (http://www.folklore-society.com/). Web site of the Folklore Society of London, with information about conferences, calls for papers, publications, and awards, and access for members to the journal *Folklore*.

Frobenius-Institute. Johann Wolfgang Goethe University. (http://www.frobenius-institut.de/index_en.htm.). Web site of the Frobenius-Institute, originally founded to focus ethnological, historic, and prehistoric research on Africa, but now having a broader, more global agenda. The site offers information about the institute's archives—including its archives of African myths and fairy tales—collections, library, and its journal, *Paideuma: Mitteilungen zur Kulturkunde*. English version of the site available.

The Geoffrey Chaucer Web site Homepage. L. D. Benson. Harvard University. (http://www.courses.fas.harvard.edu/~chaucer/). Excellent site for accessing reliable information, bibliographies, and texts and translations for the study of Geoffrey Chaucer and *The Canterbury Tales*.

Grimm Brothers' Home Page. D. L. Ashliman. University of Pittsburgh. (http://www.pitt.edu/~dash/grimm.html). Authoritative site for information about Jacob and Wilhelm Grimm and their work.

H. C. Andersen. Det Koneglige Bibliotek. (http://www2.kb.dk/elib/lit/dan/andersen/). Access to electronic versions of Hans Christian's Andersen's works in Danish through the Royal Library of Denmark.

Hans Christian Andersen. Odense City Museums. (http://www.museum.odense.dk/h_c_andersen.aspx). Online access to digitized collections of portraits of Andersen and his artwork (drawings, papercuts, and picture books) and manuscripts, in addition to other interesting artifacts and information. English version of the site available.

The Hans Christian Andersen Center. Institute of Literature, Media, and Cultural Studies, University of Southern Denmark. (http://www.andersen.sdu.dk). Authoritative Web site for the study of Hans Christian Andersen. Includes texts by and about Andersen, a gallery of illustrations, a timeline of his life and works, a bibliography, a complete and searchable online index of Anderson's literary works, and other features. English version of the site available.

The Hayao Miyazaki Web. Team Ghiblink. (http://www.nausicaa.net). A fan Web site with extensive coverage of the animated films of Miyazaki Hayao.

Il était une fois ... Les contes de fées. Bibliothèque nationale de France. (http://expositions.bnf.fr/contes/). Originally based on an exhibition at the Bibliothèque nationale de France, this site is illustrated with images and offers diverse information about the history of the fairy tale, fairytale authors, editors, illustrators, and approaches to the fairy tale.

International Research Society for Children's Literature. (http://www.irscl.ac.uk/). Web site of the International Research Society for Children's Literature maintains information about conferences and calls for papers, grants, and the organization's archives. Includes an extensive list of journals in the field of children's literature, with links to the journals' Web sites.

International Society for Folk Narrative Research. (http://www.ut.ee/isfnr/). The Web site of this international organization includes information about its congresses and online access to its substantive newsletter.

The Jack and the Beanstalk and Jack the Giant-Killer Project. University of Southern Mississippi. (http://www.usm.edu/english/fairytales/jack/jackhome.html). A text and image archives of English versions of "Jack and the Beanstalk" and "Jack and the Giant-Killer" from the eighteenth to the twentieth centuries. The texts are from the de Grummond Children's Literature Research Collection at the University of Southern Mississippi.

The Lewis Carroll Home Page. Lewis Carroll Society of North America. (http://www.lewiscarroll.org/carroll.html). A wide-ranging site devoted to works by and about Lewis Carroll, with links to texts, photographs, teaching aids, etc.

The Little Red Riding Hood Project. University of Southern Mississippi. (http://www.usm.edu/english/fairytales/lrrh/lrrhhome.htm). A text and image archives of sixteen English-language versions of "Little Red Riding Hood" from the eighteenth to the twentieth centuries. The texts are from the de Grummond Children's Literature Research Collection at the University of Southern Mississippi.

Märchen-Stiftung Walter Kahn. (http://www.maerchen-stiftung.de/). The Web site of the Märchen-Stiftung Walter Kahn—the Walter

Kahn Fairy-Tale Foundation—an organization committed to the promotion of storytelling and fairy-tale studies. Site includes information about the organization's activities, publications, awards, and its journal, *Märchenspiegel: Zeitschrift für internationale Märchenforschung und Märchenpflege.*

Museum of the Brothers Grimm. Brüder Grimm-Gesellschaft. (http://www.grimms.de/). The Web site of the Museum of the Brothers Grimm and its archives, located in Kassel, Germany. Site includes authoritative information about the Grimms and their multifaceted work in addition to news about the museum's exhibitions and publications of the Brüder Grimm-Gesellschaft (Brothers Grimm Society).

Neighborhood Bridges at the Children's Theatre Company [Minneapolis, MN]. (http://www.neighborhoodbridges.org/). Web site devoted to Neighborhood Bridges, the creative storytelling and drama project based on the book *Creative Storytelling* (1999) by fairy-tale scholar Jack Zipes and developed in cooperation Peter Brosius at the Children's Theatre Company of Minneapolis, MN.

Norske folkeeventyr. Part of *Projekt Runeberg.* Linköping University. (http://runeberg.org/folkeven/). Electronic texts of the Norwegian folktales from the collection of Peter Christen Asbjørnsen and Jørgen Moe.

The Peter & Iona Opie Collection of Folklore and Related Topics. Lilly Library, Indiana University. (http://www.indiana.edu/~liblilly/shorttitle/opie.html). A catalogue of the folklore collection (including folktales and fairy tales) housed in the Peter & Iona Opie Collection at Indiana University.

Ray and Orville Hicks, Storytellers of North Carolina. Part of *Applit: Resources for Readers and Teachers of Appalachian Literature for Children and Young Adults.* Tina L. Hanlon. Ferrum College. (http://www.ferrum.edu/applit/bibs/hicks.htm). Extensive information about audio, video, print, and online resources pertinent to the storytelling of Ray and Orville Hicks (see **Beech Mountain Jack Tales**) and to Appalachian folktales in general.

Sagen.at: Datenbank zur europäischen Ethnologie. Wolfgang Morscher. (http://www.sagen.at/). Electronic collections of folk narratives (legends, fairy tales, etc.). International in scope. Also includes full electronic texts of selected books and articles and other resources and documentation.

Snow White. Kay E. Vandergrift. Rutgers University. (http://www.scils.rutgers.edu/~kvander/snowwhite.html). Web site devoted to "Snow White," encompassing texts, illustrations, teaching ideas, media adaptations, criticism, bibliography, and links to other resources.

Société d'ethnologie française. (http://www.culture.gouv.fr/sef/). Homepage of the Society of French Ethnology.

Society for Storytelling. (http://www.sfs.org.uk/). Web site of a broadly based organization for contemporary storytellers.

SurLaLune Fairy Tales. Heidi Anne Heiner. (http://www.surlalunefairytales.com/). Well-conceived site offering a variety of useful features, especially for students: extensive selections of annotated texts, illustrations, essays, and links. Generous selections of full-text books in the public domain, such as Marian Roalfe Cox's *Cinderella: Three Hundred and Forty-Five Variants* (1893) and Margaret Hunt's 1884 translation of the Grimms' tales (including annotations).

Uysal-Walker Archive of Turkish Oral Narrative. Southwest Collection/Special Collections Library, Texas Tech University. (http://aton.ttu.edu/). An important online archives of Turkish oral narratives. English translations of texts and some audio versions available.

Western States Folklore Society. (http://www.westernfolklore.org/index.htm). Homepage of the Western States Folklore Society, which publishes the journal *Western Folklore.*

INDEX

Page numbers in **bold** indicate entries in the encyclopedia.

ABOUT THE CONTRIBUTORS

Volume Editor

Donald Haase is professor of German at Wayne State University in Detroit. He is the editor of *The Reception of Grimms' Fairy Tales: Responses, Reactions, Revisions* (1993), *English Fairy Tales and More English Fairy Tales* (2002), and *Fairy Tales and Feminism: New Approaches* (2004). He edits *Marvels & Tales: Journal of Fairy-Tale Studies* and the Series in Fairy-Tale Studies.

Editorial Assistants

Helen J. Callow is a graduate student of archival studies at the University of British Columbia. Her scholarly interests include the role of women in the Victorian era and the counterculture of the nineteenth century.

Juliana Wilth is a doctoral student in German at Wayne State University. Her research interests include Berlin and postwar German literature and culture. Her dissertation focuses on the *Wende*-experience by young East Germans and its reverberations in recent literary works.

Advisory Board

Cristina Bacchilega is professor of English at the University of Hawai'i-Mānoa. The review editor of *Marvels & Tales*, she authored *Postmodern Fairy Tales: Gender and Narrative Strategies* (1997) and *Legendary Hawai'i and the Politics of Place: Tradition, Translation, and Tourism* (2007), and coedited *Angela Carter and the Fairy Tale* (2001).

John Bierhorst is the author or editor of more than thirty books on the lore of North, South, and Central America, including bilingual editions of sixteenth-century Nahuatl manuscripts and a Nahuatl-English dictionary. He has held fellowships and research grants from the National Endowment for the Arts and the National Endowment for the Humanities. His books have been translated into Spanish, Italian, Polish, and German.

Anne E. Duggan is associate professor of French at Wayne State University. She has written extensively on the fairy tale and salon culture and is the author of *Salonnières, Furies, and Fairies: The Politics of Gender and Cultural Change in Absolutist France* (2005).

Thomas Geider holds a PhD from the University of Cologne and teaches African linguistics at Johann Wolfgang Goethe-University in Frankfurt, Germany. He has done extensive field research on oral literature in Kenya and Nigeria and has published widely on African folktales as well as on Swahili literature. He is coeditor of the *Swahili Forum*.

Ulrich Marzolph is professor of Islamic studies at the Georg-August-University in Göttingen, Germany, and a senior member of the editorial committee of the *Enzyklopädie des Märchens*. He has published widely on the narrative culture of the Islamic Near and Middle East, most recently *The Arabian Nights Reader* (2006) and *The Arabian Nights in Transnational Perspective* (2007).

Sadhana Naithani is assistant professor at the Centre of German Studies at Jawaharlal Nehru University in New Delhi, India. She is the editor of *Folktales from Northern India* (2002) and author of *In Quest of Indian Folktales: Pandit Ram Gharib Chaube and William Crooke* (2006).

Maria Nikolajeva is a professor of comparative literature at Stockholm University. She is the author and editor of several books, among them *From Mythic to Linear: Time in Children's Literature* (2002). She served as one of the senior editors for *The Oxford Encyclopedia of Children's Literature* and received the International Grimm Award in 2005.

Terri Windling, a writer, artist, and folklorist, has published more than forty books, including a six-volume series of fairy-tale adaptations (1993–99) and *The Wood Wife* (1997). She has won seven World Fantasy Awards, the Bram Stoker Award, and the Mythopoeic Award. She is the founder of the Endicott Studio for Mythic Arts, and the cofounder of Endicott West, an arts retreat in Arizona.

Jan M. Ziolkowski is Arthur Kingsley Porter Professor of Medieval Latin and chair of the Department of the Classics at Harvard University. He has focused his research on medieval literature, especially in Latin; on the classical tradition; and on the influence of folktales on literature in the Middle Ages.

Jack Zipes is professor of German and comparative literature at the University of Minnesota. He has published numerous books and essays on folktales and fairy tales and children's literature. His most recent publication is *Why Fairy Tales Stick: The Evolution and Relevance of a Genre* (2006).

Contributors

Roger D. Abrahams is Hum Rosen Professor of Folklore and Folklife, Emeritus, at the University of Pennsylvania. He has written many books and articles on African American folklore, including his first book, *Deep Down in the Jungle* (1964), and his later study of cornshucking in the American South, *Singing the Master* (1993). His most recent book, written with John Szwed, Nicholas Spitzer, and Robert Farris Thompson, is *Blues for New Orleans* (2006).

B. Grantham Aldred is a doctoral student in folklore and American studies at Indiana University. He studies primarily American folk religion, folklore and identity, and collective storytelling performance.

Satu Apo is professor of folklore studies at Helsinki University in Finland. She has edited the anthologies *Gender and Folklore* (1998, with Aili Nenola and Laura Stark-Arola) and *Topelius elää–Topelius lever* (2005, with Märtha Norrback). She received the Kalevala Award of the Finnish Academy of Sciences and Letters in 1987 and the Elias Lönnrot Award of the Finnish Literature Society in 1988.

D. L. Ashliman, an emeritus professor at the University of Pittsburgh, taught folklore, mythology, German, and comparative literature at that institution for thirty-three years. He also served as guest professor at the University of Augsburg in Germany. His recent publications include two volumes in the *Folklore Handbooks* series of Greenwood Press: *Folk and Fairy Tales* (2004) and *Fairy Lore* (2005).

Cristina Bacchilega is professor of English at the University of Hawai'i-Mānoa. The review editor of *Marvels & Tales*, she authored *Postmodern Fairy Tales: Gender and Narrative Strategies* (1997) and *Legendary Hawai'i and the Politics of Place: Tradition, Translation, and Tourism* (2007), and coedited *Angela Carter and the Fairy Tale* (2001).

Haya Bar-Itzhak is academic head of the Israel Folktale Archives and chair of the folklore division of the Department of Hebrew and Comparative Literature at the University of Haifa. Among other books, she is author of *Jewish Poland—Legends of Origin: Ethnopoetics and Legendary Chronicles* (2001) and coauthor of *Jewish Moroccan Folk Narratives from Israel* (1993).

Shuli Barzilai teaches in the Department of English at the Hebrew University of Jerusalem. She is the author of *Lacan and the Matter of Origins* (1999) and coeditor of *Rereading Texts /Rethinking Critical Presuppositions* (1997). Her fields of special interest include folklore and fairy-tale studies, literary theory, psychoanalytic criticism, and contemporary women writers.

Joanna Beall is a former faculty associate in the Department of Writing Seminars at Johns Hopkins University. She is currently at work on *Tales from a Barren Country: Infertility Stories from around the World*.

Sandra L. Beckett is a professor in the Department of Modern Languages, Literatures and Cultures at Brock University (Canada). She has published extensively on folktales and fairy tales in children's literature and crossover literature. She is the author of *Recycling Red Riding Hood* (2002).

Stephen Belcher has a doctorate in comparative literature from Brown University. He has taught at the University of Nouakchott in Mauritania, the Pennsylvania State University, and the University of Kankan in Guinea. He is the author of *Epic Traditions of Africa* (1999) and *African Myths of Origin* (2005), as well as essays on the medieval frame-tale tradition.

Regina Bendix received her PhD in 1987 from Indiana University and left her position as associate professor of Anthropology at the University of Pennsylvania in 2001 for a professorship at the Institute for Cultural Anthropology/European Ethnology at the Georg-August-

University in Göttingen, Germany. She works on the history of the discipline, narrative, tourism, and the anthropology of the senses.

Stephen Benson is lecturer in contemporary British literature at the University of East Anglia. He has published essays on the folktale, narrative theory, and contemporary fiction, and is the author of *Cycles of Influence: Fiction, Folktale, Theory* (2003).

Kate Bernheimer is assistant professor of English at the University of Alabama. Author of the novels *The Complete Tales of Ketzia Gold* (2001) and *The Complete Tales of Merry Gold* (2006), she also edited *Mirror, Mirror on the Wall: Women Writers Explore Their Favorite Fairy Tales* (1998) and *Brothers and Beasts: An Anthology of Men on Fairy Tales* (2007).

Candace Beutell Gardner, an alumna of the University of Michigan (BA, MA) and Wayne State University (PhD), wrote her dissertation "Infinite Optimism: Friedrich J. Bertuch's Pioneering Translation (1775–77) of Cervantes's *Don Quixote*" (2006), a discussion of the novel's first complete translation from the original Spanish into German.

John Bierhorst is the author or editor of more than thirty books on the lore of North, South, and Central America, including bilingual editions of sixteenth-century Nahuatl manuscripts and a Nahuatl-English dictionary. He has held fellowships and research grants from the National Endowment for the Arts and the National Endowment for the Humanities. His books have been translated into Spanish, Italian, Polish, and German.

Hande Birkalan-Gedik is associate professor of folklore at the Department of Anthropology at Yeditepe University in Istanbul. She has written on folktales, narrative, and gender. She is the editor of *Anthropology from the Past to the Future* (2005). As the recipient of a grant from the Deutsche Forschungsgemeinschaft, she is revising *Typen türkischer Volksmärchen* and will work at the *Enyzklopädie des Märchens*.

Trevor J. Blank is a graduate student in the Department of Folklore and Ethnomusicology at Indiana University, where he serves as president of the Folklore Student Association and Web editor for *Folklore Forum*. His research interests include vernacular architecture, folk art, food, urban legends, and religious folk beliefs.

George Bodmer is a professor of English at Indiana University Northwest, where he teaches children's literature and writes on contemporary illustration and typography.

Ruth B. Bottigheimer has published *Fairy Tales and Society: Illusion, Allusion, and Paradigm* (1986), *Grimms' Bad Girls and Bold Boys: The Moral and Social Vision of the Tales* (1987), *The Bible for Children from the Age of Gutenberg to the Present* (1996), and *Fairy Godfather: Straparola, Venice, and the Fairy Tale Tradition* (2002).

Paul James Buczkowski is a lecturer in English and literature at Eastern Michigan University. He has published on folklore and fiction, including "J. R. Planché, Frederick Robson, and the Fairy Extravaganza" (2001) in *Marvels & Tales*.

Helen J. Callow is a graduate student of archival studies at the University of British Columbia. Her scholarly interests include the place of women in the Victorian era and the counterculture of the nineteenth century.

Nancy Canepa is associate professor of Italian at Dartmouth College. Her scholarly interests include the literary fairy tale and Italian literature and culture of the seventeenth century. She is the author of *From Court to Forest: Giambattista Basile's* Lo cunto de li cunti *and the Birth of the Literary Fairy Tale* (1999) as well as the translator of Basile's *Lo cunto de li cunti* (*The Tale of Tales*, 2007).

Katia Canton is a professor in the School of Communication Arts and the Museum of Contemporary Art at the University of São Paulo. She is the author of *The Fairy Tales Revisited: A Survey of the Evolution of the Tales, from Classical Literary Interpretations to Innovative Contemporary Dance Theater Productions* (1994).

Isabel Cardigos is cofounder of the Centro de Estudos Ataíde Oliveira at the University of the Algarve, which created and developed the archive of Portuguese folktales. Her books include *In and Out of Enchantment: Blood Symbolism and Gender in Portuguese Folktales* (1996) and *Catalogue of Portuguese Folktales* (2006). She is also cofounder and codirector, with J. J. Dias Marques, of the journal *Estudos de Literatura Oral*.

James Bucky Carter is a doctoral student at the University of Virginia. His work has been published in *Marvels & Tales*, *ImageTexT*, and the *International Journal of Comic Art*. He is a contributor to and the general editor of *Page by Page, Panel by Panel: Building Literacy Connections with Graphic Novels* (2007).

Cynthia Chalupa is associate professor of German at West Virginia University. Her literary research interests span the twentieth and twenty-first centuries. She has written about the mirror in the works of Rainer Maria Rilke, Georg Trakl, Ilse Aichinger, and E. T.A. Hoffmann, and on the link between the mirror and self-portraiture. She is currently working on a project concerning the theme of decadence in turn-of-the-millennium German texts.

Aboubakr Chraïbi is Maître de Conférences in Medieval Arabic Literature at the Institut National des Langues et Civilisations Orientales (INALCO) in Paris, France. He works on the *Thousand and One Nights* and on narratology. His recent publications include *Mille et une nuits en partage* (2004) and "Texts of the Arabian Nights and Ideological Variations" (2005).

William M. Clements teaches in the Department of English and Philosophy at Arkansas State University. His books include *Sourcebook in Arkansas Folklore* (1992), *Native American Verbal Art: Texts and Contexts* (1996), and *Oratory in Native North America* (2002). His essays have appeared in such journals as *Southern Quarterly*, *Journal of American Folklore*, *Arkansas Review*, and *South Atlantic Quarterly*.

Alfred L. Cobbs is associate professor of German at Wayne State University, Detroit. He has published on Günter Grass, Franz Kafka, Wilhelm Hauff, German-American literary relations, and German migrants' literature. He is the author of *Migrants' Literature in Postwar Germany: Trying to Find a Place to Fit In* (2007).

JoAnn Conrad is a lecturer at the University of California, Berkeley. Her research and teaching focus on narrative theory and genres, on the fairy tale, and on gender and representations of gender in tales. She has published extensively in *Marvels & Tales*, *Fabula*, the *Enzyklopädie des Märchens*, and the *Journal of American Folklore*.

Nicolae Constantinescu, PhD, is professor of folklore and head of the Department of Ethnology and Folklore at the University of Bucharest, Romania. He is currently teaching folk literature, including traditional and contemporary folk narratives. He is the author of several books in Romanian (*Lectura textului folclroic*, 1986) and in English (*Romanian Folk-Culture: An Introduction*, 1999).

James I. Deutsch is program curator for the Smithsonian Center for Folklife and Cultural Heritage. He also teaches classes on American film at George Washington University, and has taught classes on film and folklore at universities in Armenia, Belarus, Bulgaria, Germany, Kyrgyzstan, Norway, Poland, and Turkey.

Elina Druker is a doctoral student and teacher at the Department of Literature and History of Ideas at Stockholm University. She is currently writing a thesis on Nordic picture book aesthetics of the 1950s.

Anne E. Duggan is associate professor of French at Wayne State University. She has written extensively on the fairy tale and salon culture and is the author of *Salonnières, Furies, and Fairies: The Politics of Gender and Cultural Change in Absolutist France* (2005).

Bill Ellis is professor of English and American studies at Pennsylvania State University in Hazleton. He has written extensively on contemporary legends and religious beliefs, and his books include *Raising the Devil* (1999) and *Aliens, Ghosts, and Cults* (2000). He is working on the use of Western märchen in Japanese anime.

Hasan El-Shamy is a fellow of the American Folklore Society, and professor of folklore, Middle Eastern languages, and cultures, and African studies at Indiana University in Bloomington. He is the author of several books, including *A Motif Index of The Thousand and One Nights* (2006), *Types of the Folktale in the Arab World: A Demographically Oriented Tale-Type Index* (2004), and *Tales Arab Women Tell and the Behavioral Patterns They Portray* (1999).

Robert Elsie is a leading specialist in Albanian studies. He has written more than forty books, mostly on Albanian literature, history, and culture, and is the author of *Historical Dictionary of Albania* (2004) and *Albanian Literature: A Short History* (2005).

Charlotte Eubanks is assistant professor of comparative literature and Japanese at Pennsylvania State University. She has published articles on the fantastic in contemporary Japanese fiction and on folklore in the Meiji period. She is currently working on a study of gender and performance in premodern Buddhist explanatory tales.

Robert M. Fedorchek is professor emeritus of modern languages and literatures at Fairfield University in Connecticuit. He has published twelve books of translations of nineteenth-century Spanish literature, and his translations of Spanish short stories and fairy tales have appeared in *Connecticut Review* and *Marvels & Tales*.

Ana Raquel Fernandes earned a degree in modern languages and literatures at Lisbon University, where she was also awarded a MA in comparative literature. She is a researcher at the Centre for Comparative Studies in Lisbon, and is preparing a PhD on British contemporary literature. Since 2004, she has been a visiting student at Warwick University and has lectured in the Department of Hispanic Studies at the University of Birmingham.

Carolina Fernández-Rodríguez is assistant professor of English literature at the University of Oviedo in Spain. Her research has focused on the study of feminist revisions of fairy tales by contemporary women writers, a topic on which she has published a number of articles and three books. In 1996, her work *Las nuevas hijas de Eva. Re/escrituras feministas del cuento de Barbazul* was given the VII Research Award "Victoria Kent" by the University of Málaga.

Víctor Figueroa is assistant professor of Spanish at Wayne State University. His research focuses on Caribbean literature from a multilingual, pan-Caribbean perspective.

James Fowler, professor of English at the University of Central Arkansas, edits the poetry journal *SLANT*. He has published articles on Dante Alighieri, Lewis Carroll, Robert Browning, Virginia Woolf, Robert Frost, and Elizabeth Bishop, among others. His poems, stories, and personal essays have appeared in such journals as *The Classical Outlook, Zone 3*, and *Karamu*.

Adrienne E. Gavin is a reader in English at Canterbury Christ Church University, where she teaches a range of courses in children's literature and Victorian literature. She is author of *Dark Horse: A Life of Anna Sewell* (2004) and coeditor of *Mystery in Children's Literature: From the Rational to the Supernatural* (2001).

Thomas Geider holds a PhD from the University of Cologne and teaches African linguistics at Johann Wolfgang Goethe-University in Frankfurt, Germany. He has done extensive field research on oral literature in Kenya and Nigeria and has widely published on African folktales as well as on Swahili literature. He is coeditor of the *Swahili Forum*.

Howard Giskin is professor of English at Appalachian State University in Boone, North Carolina. He is interested in Asian and Latin American literature, and has published articles on Argentinean writer Jorge Luis Borges, edited *Chinese Folktales* (1997), and coedited *An Introduction to Chinese Culture through the Family* (2001).

Christine Goldberg, the author of *Turandot's Sisters: A Study of the Folktale AT 851* (1993) and *The Tale of the Three Oranges* (1997), is a specialist in comparative folktale research. She is a regular contributor to the *Enzyklopädie des Märchens* and was on the editorial staff of *The Types of International Folktales* (2004).

William Gray is a reader in literary history and hermeneutics at Chichester University in England. He has published books on C. S. Lewis (1998) and Robert Louis Stevenson (2004) and articles on Goethe, George MacDonald, and Philip Pullman. He is currently writing a book on fantasy fiction from E. T. A. Hoffmann to Philip Pullman.

Terry Gunnell is associate professor of folkloristics at the University of Iceland. He has written on folk legends, festivals, performance, and drama, and is the author of *The Origins of Drama in Scandinavia* (1995).

Donald Haase is professor of German at Wayne State University. He is the editor of *The Reception of Grimms' Fairy Tales: Responses, Reactions, Revisions* (1993), *English Fairy Tales and More English Fairy Tales* (2002), and *Fairy Tales and Feminism: New Approaches* (2004). He edits *Marvels & Tales: Journal of Fairy-Tale Studies* and the Series in Fairy-Tale Studies.

Jack V. Haney was professor of Slavic Languages and literatures at the University of Washington in Seattle until his retirement. He received BA degrees from the University of Washington and Oxford University and his doctorate from Oxford University, where he was a Rhodes Scholar. He is the author of books and articles on medieval Russian literature and the *Complete Russian Folktale*, published in seven volumes, 1999–2006.

Tina L. Hanlon is associate professor of English at Ferrum College and the Hollins University graduate program in Children's Literature. She is coeditor of *Crosscurrents of Children's Literature: An Anthology of Texts and Criticism* (2007) and directs the Web site *AppLit: Resources for Readers and Teachers of Appalachian Literature for Children and Young Adults*.

Patricia Hannon has taught at Catholic University and Sarah Lawrence College. She has published extensively on seventeenth-century French fairy tales.

William Hansen is professor emeritus of classical studies and folklore at Indiana University, Bloomington. His interests include mythology, folktales, and ancient popular literature. Among his books are *Classical Mythology: A Guide to the Mythic World of the Greeks and Romans* (2005), *Ariadne's Thread: A Guide to International Tales Found in Classical Literature* (2002), *Anthology of Ancient Greek Popular Literature* (1998), and *Phlegon of Tralles' Book of Marvels* (1996).

Lee Haring is professor emeritus of English at Brooklyn College of the City University of New York. For thirty years, he conducted research into the oral literatures of the islands of the Indian Ocean, which resulted in numerous articles and the books *Verbal Arts in Madagascar* (1992), *Indian Ocean Folktales* (2002), and *Indian Folktales from Mauritius* (2006).

Elizabeth Wanning Harries teaches English and comparative literature at Smith College, where she is Shedd Professor of Modern Languages. Her recent work on literary fairy tales includes *Twice upon a Time: Women Writers and the History of the Fairy Tale* (2001), as well as articles on redemptive violence and on A. S. Byatt.

Lauri Harvilahti, PhD, is director of the Folklore Archives of the Finnish Literature Society in Helsinki, Finland. He specializes in epics, ethocultural poetics, ethnic identity, and methods of archiving oral poetry.

Lori Schroeder Haslem is associate professor of English at Knox College in Galesburg, Illinois. She has written about culturally based representations of the female body in Shakespeare and in other early modern English literature.

Lisabeth Hock is assistant professor of German at Wayne State University. Her publications on Bettina von Arnim include the monograph *Replicas of a Female Prometheus: The Textual Personae of Bettina von Arnim* (2001). She is currently working on a project about women and melancholy in the nineteenth century.

Willi Höfig, PhD, is a retired librarian living in Niebuell, Germany. He has contributed numerous articles to various German folklore journals and to the *Enzyclopädie des Märchens*. As an author and editor, he has worked in the fields of cultural anthropology and librarianship. In this moment, he is preparing a publication on the history of the fairy-tale film.

Olga Holownia is a PhD student at Warsaw University in Poland. She is currently working on a dissertation about the poetry of Carol Ann Duffy.

Helene Høyrup is associate professor of literary studies, the sociology of literature, and children's culture at the Department of Cultural and Media Studies at the Royal School of Library and Information Science in Denmark. She has published chapters and articles on Scandinavian literature and children's literature in Denmark and internationally.

Marte Hult is an independent scholar who has taught Norwegian and folklore courses at the University of Minnesota and St. Olaf College. She is the author of *Framing a National Narrative: The Legend Collections of Peter Christen Asbjørnsen* (2003) and recently completed a new translation of Hans Christian Andersen stories.

Risto Järv is senior researcher at the University of Tartu in Estonia. He has concentrated on different aspects of fairy tales: the correlation of the gender of storytellers and of the tales' heroes, the use of proper names in fairy tales, as well as the intermingling of the oral tradition with that of the literary fairy tale.

Shawn C. Jarvis is professor of German at St. Cloud State University. Her publications have focused on the fairy tales of German women writers, including Benedikte Naubert and Gisela von Arnim. She is the coeditor and translator of the anthology *The Queen's Mirror: Fairy Tales of German Women, 1780–1900* (2001).

Christine A. Jones is assistant professor of French at the University of Utah. She is the author of several articles on seventeenth-century French fairy tales. Her current work considers the principle of frivolity in French fairy tales and other seventeenth-century arts, such as porcelain, to demonstrate how these arts market smallness and prettiness as valid aesthetic categories.

Vanessa Joosen is completing a PhD at the University of Antwerp in Belgium. She has been granted a from the FWO (National Fund for Scientific Research) scholarship and is researching the interaction between fairy-tale retellings and criticism from 1970 to 2005. With Katrien Vloeberghs, she edited *Changing Concepts of Childhood and Children's Literature* (2006).

Jeana Jorgensen is a doctoral student in folklore at Indiana University. Her research interests involve gender and power in fairy tales, the intersection of folk narratives with popular culture, gender studies, and body art.

Caroline Jumel is assistant professor of French literature at Oakland University in Rochester, Michigan. She has written and presented many papers about George Sand and on French women's literature from various centuries.

Maria Kaliambou, a lector in Modern Greek at Yale University, received her PhD in folklore studies/European ethnology from the University of Munich. She was a postdoctoral research fellow at the University Lille 3 and at Princeton University. In 2006, she received the Lutz-Röhrich-Preis from the Märchen-Stiftung Walter Kahn for her book *Heimat– Glaube–Familie: Wertevermittlung in griechischen Popularmärchen (1870–1970)*.

U. C. Knoepflmacher is Paton Foundation Professor of Ancient and Modern Literature at Princeton University. He has edited or coedited ten collections on Victorian subjects, written more than 100 scholarly articles, and authored six books, among them *Ventures into Child-land: Victorians, Fairy Tales, and Femininity* (1998).

R. Seth C. Knox is an assistant professor of German at Adrian College in Michigan. He received his PhD from Wayne State University and is the author of *Weimar Germany between Two Worlds* (2006).

Ines Köhler-Zülch studied Slavic, Germanic, and Romance languages and literature and wrote her PhD dissertation on the Bulgarian Alexander romance. A long-time member of the editorial staff of the *Enzyklopädie des Märchens* in Göttingen, she is now one of its editors. Her scholarship centers on historical and comparative folk narrative research, especially on southeast European and German traditions, issues of gender, problems of minorities, and the history of folk narrative research.

Janet L. Langlois is associate professor of English (folklore studies) at Wayne State University. She has written extensively on rumors and legends and has most recently coedited a special issue of the *Journal of American Folklore* on emerging legends in contemporary society (2005).

Kimberly J. Lau teaches in the American Studies Department at the University of California in Santa Cruz. She is author of *New Age Capitalism: Making Money East of Eden* (2000) and is currently completing a discursive ethnography of Sisters in Shape, a black women's health and fitness project based in Philadelphia. She has also published and taught on fairy tales and is working on a project that brings feminist psychoanalytic theory to bear on questions of the fairy tale's enduring popularity.

Linda J. Lee is a PhD student in folklore and folklife at the University of Pennsylvania, and she holds an MA in folklore from the University of California, Berkeley. Her research interests include gender issues in folklore and folkloristics, women's popular fiction and folklore, and Italian popular traditions.

Jing Li is assistant professor of Chinese in the Asian Studies Department at Gettysburg College. She received her MA in Chinese folk literature from Beijing University in 1997 and her PhD in folklore and folklife from the University of Pennsylvania in 2004. She has published articles and book chapters on the rise of Chinese folklore and nationalism, Chinese myths, and ethnic tourism, gender, and ethnicity in southwest China.

Paul Lyons is professor of English and chair of graduate studies at the University of Hawai'i-Mānoa, where his research and teaching interests include United States-Pacific cultural exchange, a subject explored in his book, *American Pacificism: Oceania in the U.S. Imagination* (2006).

Fiona J. Mackintosh is a lecturer in Hispanic studies at the University of Edinburgh in Scotland. Her research interests are focused around twentieth-century Latin American women's writing, and she is the author of *Childhood in the Works of Silvina Ocampo and Alejandra Pizarnik* (2003).

Mary Magoulick is associate professor of English and interdisciplinary studies at Georgia College & State University in Milledgeville. She has written primarily on Native American folklore and literature, women's studies, and popular culture. She received a Fulbright Award to teach in Croatia in the spring of 2006.

Claire L. Malarte-Feldman is professor of French at the University of New Hampshire in Durham. She has written extensively on French seventeenth-century literary fairy tales. Her current research interests lie in the field of French children's literature, particularly contemporary rewrites and illustrations of French literary tales and folktales.

Heather Maring is assistant professor in English at Arizona State University. Her publications include an article on the medieval English dream-vision *Pearl* (*Journal of the Midwest Modern Language Association*, 2005) and "Oral Traditional Approaches to Old English Verse" (*Oral Tradition*, 2003). She is currently researching the parallels between oral tradition and ritual performance in medieval English verse.

Laura Martin is senior lecturer (associate professor) of Comparative Literature at the University of Glasgow. She has written extensively on German and American novella of the nineteenth century, and has recently published on the German writer of märchen Benedikte Naubert, *Benedikte Nauberts Neue Volksmärchen der Deutschen: Strukturen des Wandels* (2006).

Ulrich Marzolph is professor of Islamic Studies at the Georg-August-University in Göttingen, Germany, and a senior member of the editorial committee of the *Enzyklopädie des Märchens*. He has published widely on the narrative culture of the Islamic Near and Middle East, most recently *The Arabian Nights Reader* (2006) and *The Arabian Nights in Transnational Perspective* (2007).

William Bernard McCarthy, editor of *Jack in Two Worlds* (1994), is emeritus professor of English at Pennsylvania State University, and taught on the DuBois campus. His articles on folktales, ballads, and oral theory have appeared in a number of journals. He is currently editing an anthology of American folktales.

Thomas McGowan is professor of English at Appalachian State University. Past editor of the *North Carolina Folklore Journal*, he studies oral narrative and material culture in North Carolina's Blue Ridge Mountains. In 2003, he received the University of North Carolina Board of Governors' Award for Excellence in Teaching.

Theo Meder is working as a senior researcher at the Meertens Institute in Amsterdam. He runs a small documentation and research department (DOC Volksverhaal) that specializes in Dutch folktales and narrative culture and also manages the Dutch Folktale Database (http://www.verhalenbank.nl). His publications range from fairy tales, legends, and jokes to crop circle- and PhotoShop-lore.

Wolfgang Mieder is professor of German and folklore at the University of Vermont. He is the author of numerous books, including *Disenchantments: An Anthology of Modern Fairy Tale Poetry* (1985), *Tradition and Innovation in Folk Literature* (1987), *Proverbs Are Never Out of Season* (1993), *The Politics of Proverbs* (1997), *The Proverbial Abraham Lincoln* (2000), and *Proverbs: A Handbook* (2004). He is also the founding editor of *Proverbium: Yearbook of International Proverb Scholarship* (since 1984).

Gina M. Miele, assistant professor of Italian and director of the Coccia Institute for the Italian Experience in America at Montclair State University, specializes in nineteenth- and twentieth-century Italian folktales and is at work on her first novel, *Portrait of an Immigrant as a Young Woman*.

Margaret A. Mills is a professor in the Department of Near Eastern Languages and Cultures at Ohio State University and a leading specialist in the popular culture of the Persian and Farsi-speaking world. Her book *Rhetorics and Politics in Afghan Traditional Storytelling* won the 1993 Chicago Folklore Prize for best academic work in folklore. She is the author and/or coeditor of additional books and numerous other publications.

Sadhana Naithani is assistant professor at the Centre of German Studies at Jawaharlal Nehru University in New Delhi, India. She is the editor of *Folktales from Northern India* (2002) and the author of *In Quest of Indian Folktales: Pandit Ram Gharib Chaube and William Crooke* (2006).

Harold Neemann is associate professor of French at the University of Wyoming. Specializing in seventeenth-century French narrative discourse and the history of ideas, he is the author of *Piercing the Magic Veil: Toward a Theory of the 'Conte'* (1999). His recent research focus has been on travel narratives written by seventeenth-century French women.

W. F. H. Nicolaisen is currently an honorary professor of English in the University of Aberdeen. Among other positions, he has been the president of the Folklore Society (Britain) and the American Folklore Society, which in 2002 honored him with its first Lifelong Achievement Award. In addition to some book-length publications, he has published more than 700 articles and reviews, among them several articles on aspects of time and space in folk narrative.

Maria Nikolajeva is a professor of comparative literature at Stockholm University. She is the author and editor of several books, among them *From Mythic to Linear: Time in Children's Literature* (2002). She served as one of the senior editors for *The Oxford Encyclopedia of Children's Literature* and received the International Grimm Award in 2005.

Dáithí Ó hÓgáin is an Irish writer and folklorist, and formerly associate professor at University College in Dublin. In addition to books of poetry and short stories in Irish, he has edited volumes of folklore and traditional literature and has written widely on cultural history and oral narrative. He drafted the UNESCO policy on the preservation of traditional lore in 1987. His best-known works in English are *The Hero in Irish Folk History* (1985), *Fionn Mac Cumhaill* (1988), *The Sacred Isle* (1999), *The Celts* (2002), and *The Lore of Ireland* (2006). His collected poetry in English was published under the title *Footsteps from Another World* (2001).

Carme Oriol lectures in the Department of Catalan Studies of the Rovira i Virgili University in Tarragona. Her publications include *El cançoner nadalenc català al Principat de Catalunya (1853–1951)* (1995), *Estudi del folklore andorrà en el seu context* (1997), *Introducció a l'Etnopoètica: Teoria i formes del folklore en la cultura catalana* (2002), and *Índex tipològic de la rondalla catalana* (2003, with Josep M. Pujol), as well as numerous articles.

Janina Orlov holds a PhD in Russian literature and language from Åbo Akademi University in Finland. She is senior lecturer of children's literature and literary history at Mälardalen Universiy and Stockholm University in Sweden. She has guest-lectured in many countries and published several articles and reviews on children's literary history, Finnish-Swedish literature, and Finnish literature, as well as on Russian literature.

Nicolay Ostrau received his MA in German from Wayne State University and is a doctoral student at the University of North Carolina at Chapel Hill. His research interests are fairy tale and children's literature, Romanticism, and cultural studies.

Toshio Ozawa, formerly professor of German studies at Tsukuba University, is the head of the Ozawa Folktale Institute Tokyo. He has written on Japanese folktales, conducted comparative research, and translated important works of Max Lüthi into Japanese. In 1992, he established the Märchen Academy Japan, and in 1999 he founded the quarterly journal *Children and Folktales*. In 2007, he received the European Fairy-Tale Prize.

Marilena Papachristophorou is a researcher at the Hellenic Folklore Research Center at the Academy of Athens. She specializes in the oral tradition of Greece, with particular emphasis on folktales, storytelling in modern societies, and fieldwork research. Her major publications include *Sommeils et veilles dans le conte merveilleux grec* (2002) and *Laiki Philologia* (2002).

Fernando Peñalosa is professor emeritus of sociology at California State University, Long Beach, and is currently researching the history of Yosemite National Park.

D. K. Peterson is an instructor of English at North Dakota State University, where she teaches contemporary American literature and culture. Her primary research areas are animation and Disney and inform her examination of animated fairy-tale adaptations. Her work has been published in film and media studies.

Helen Pilinovsky is finishing her dissertation, titled "Fantastic Émigrés: Translation and Acculturation of the Fairy Tale in a Literary Diaspora," at Columbia University. She has written extensively on fairy tales and Victorian literature, and is the cofounder and academic editor of *Cabinet des Fées*.

Andrew E. Porter is a lecturer in classics at the University of Wisconsin-Milwaukee. He has presented papers on various Homeric subjects, and has a particular interest in Homer, Hesiod, and the Homeric hymns (story patterns, characterization, and metonymy). His past work has included research with Rainer Friedrich on "Iliad 9" and with Allison Trites on the Gospel of Luke.

Mojca Ramšak is assistant professor, research fellow, and director of the Center for Biographic Research in Ljubljana, Slovenia. She is the author of two books in Slovene: *Portrait of the Voices: Research of Life-Stories in Ethnology on the Case of Carinthian Slovenes* (2003) and *Sacrifice of the Truth: The Spell of Slippery Discreet Indiscretions* (2006).

Jennifer Schacker is associate professor of English and theater studies at the University of Guelph. Her first book, *National Dreams: The Remaking of Fairy Tales in Nineteenth-Century England* (2003), received the 2006 Mythopoeic Scholarship Award in Myth and Fantasy Studies. Her current research, supported by a grant from the Social Science and Humanities Research Council of Canada, concerns sexual and sartorial transgression in British fairy-tale pantomime.

Christoph Schmitt studied European ethnology at the University of Marburg and received his PhD in 1992. He wrote his dissertation on the adaptation of fairy tales in television programs. He has contributed to the *Enzyklopädie des Märchens* and since 1999 has served as the head of the Institut für Volkskunde (Wossidlo-Archiv) at the University of Rostock. His research centers on ethnological and narratological studies of documents in Mecklenburg-Vorpommern, on European storytelling culture, and on media studies.

Marc Sebastian-Jones is assistant professor of English at Takushoku University, Tokyo. He studied English at the Polytechnic of North London and Japanese at the University of Sheffield. His most recent publications include articles on Japanese junior high school English textbooks and on postmodern music.

Lewis C. Seifert is associate professor of French studies at Brown University. He is the author of *Fairy Tales, Sexuality, and Gender in France, 1690–1715: Nostalgic Utopias* (1996) and of numerous articles on seventeenth-century French literature and culture. His current research concerns the intersection between fairy-tale studies and sexuality studies.

Christine Shojaei Kawan is a member of the editorial staff of the *Enzyklopädie des Märchens* and of the folklore journal *Fabula*. She has published numerous articles, especially on fairy tales and literary themes. With Ines Köhler-Zülch, she has coedited an anthology on women in folktales, *Schneewittchen hat viele Schwestern* (1988).

Carole G. Silver, professor of English at Yeshiva University's Stern College, has written widely on Victorian literature, art, and folklore. Her work includes books and articles on William Morris and Pre-Raphaelitism. Recent publications, especially *Strange and Secret Peoples* (1999), have centered on the Victorian fairy fascination. She is currently editing a volume of *The Fairy Tales of Southern Africa*.

Jacqueline Simpson is a committee member of the Folklore Society of London and has written extensively on English and Scandinavian folklore. She is particularly interested in local and migratory legends. She is the coauthor, with Jennifer Westwood, of *The Lore of the Land: A Guide to England's Legends* (2005).

Joseph Daniel Sobol is a professor in the Department of Curriculum and Instruction at East Tennessee State University, where he directs the graduate program in storytelling. He is author of *The Storytellers' Journey: An American Revival* (1999) and *The House Between Earth and Sky: Harvesting New American Folktales* (2005). He is cofounder and coeditor of *Storytelling, Self, Society: An Interdisciplinary Journal of Storytelling Studies*.

Louise Speed received her MA in English from Wayne State University, where she works with international programs. She has published on film and postmodernism.

Terry Staples, a former researcher/programmer at the United Kingdom's National Film Theatre in London, teaches film, literature, and drama within further education. He has researched and written widely about children both on the screen and in front of it, and is the author of *All Pals Together: The Story of Children's Cinema* (1997).

Mary Beth Stein is associate professor of German at the George Washington University, where she teaches courses on German literature and the fairy tale. She received her PhD in folklore from Indiana University and has published on folklore and folk narrative in *Fabula*, the *Journal of the Folklore Institute*, and *Western Folklore*.

John Stephens is professor of English at Macquarie University, where his main research is on children's literature. His publications include *Language and Ideology in Children's*

Fiction (1992), *Retelling Stories, Framing Culture* (with Robyn McCallum 1998), and approximately 100 articles. His current research involves children's literature and "new world orders" since the end of the Cold War.

Virginia E. Swain is professor of French at Dartmouth College. She has written on eighteenth-century French authors, including Villeneuve, Diderot, and Rousseau, and recently published *Grotesque Figures: Baudelaire, Rousseau, and the Aesthetics of Modernity* (2004). She is currently translating essays and diaries by women of the French Resistance.

James M. Taggart is the Lewis Audenreid Professor of History and Archaeology at Franklin and Marshall College, Lancaster, Pennsylvania. He has written on the folktales of Spain, Mexico, and the Hispanic Southwest. He is the author of *Nahuat Myth and Social Structure* (1983), *Enchanted Maidens* (1990), and *Remembering Victoria: A Tragic Nahuat Love Story* (2007).

Barbara Tannert-Smith is assistant professor of English at Knox College in Galesburg, Illinois, where she teaches fiction writing and children's literature.

Maria Tatar is the John L. Loeb Professor of Germanic Languages and Literatures at Harvard University and Dean for the Humanities. She is the author of *Classic Fairy Tales* (1999), *The Annotated Brothers Grimm* (2004), and *The Hard Facts of the Grimms' Fairy Tales* (2nd edition, 2004).

Jessica Tiffin is a lecturer in the Department of English at the University of Cape Town. Her research interests include postmodern fairy tale, science fiction and fantasy, gothic romance, and Internet culture. Her book, *Marvellous Geometry: Genre and Metafiction in Modern Fairy Tale*, is in progress.

Charlotte Trinquet received her PhD from the Department of Romance Languages at University of North Carolina at Chapel Hill in 2001. She works in early modern French literary fairy tales and French and Italian intertextuality in fairy tales. She has published articles on Marie-Catherine d'Aulnoy's and Charles Perrault's fairy tales.

Holly Tucker is associate professor of French and associate director of the Center for Medicine, Health, and Society at Vanderbilt University. She is the author of *Pregnant Fictions: Childbirth and the Fairy Tale in Early-Modern France* (2003) as well as other studies of the intersection between early medicine and literature.

Hans-Jörg Uther is professor of German literature at the University of Duisburg-Essen and a senior member of the editorial staff of the *Enzyklopädie des Märchens* in Göttingen. He has written extensively on folktales and legends, published critical editions of the Brothers Grimm, and is the editor of the new international tale-type index (2004). He was awarded the Premio Pitrè in 1993 and the Europäischer Märchenpreis in 2005.

Ülo Valk is professor of Estonian and Comparative Folklore at the University of Tartu in Estonia. His publications include articles on legends, mythology, and belief and the book *The Black Gentleman: Manifestations of the Devil in Estonian Folk Religion* (2001).

Francisco Vaz da Silva teaches anthropology and folklore in Lisbon, Portugal. He has written extensively on symbolic folklore and oral fairy tales for professional journals in Europe and America. His publications include a forthcoming seven-volume *Library of European Fairy Tales* (in Portuguese) and *Metamorphosis* (2002).

Reina Whaitiri is from Aotearoa/New Zealand and is assistant professor of Pacific and Maori Literature at the University of Hawai'i at Mānoa. She has coedited two anthologies, *Homeland—New Writing from America, the Pacific, and Asia* (1997) and *Whetu Moana—Contemporary Polynesian Poems in English* (2003).

Kristiana Willsey is a graduate student at Indiana University's Department of Folklore and Ethnomusicology, and has a bachelor's degree in linguistic anthropology from Scripps College. Her research interests include personal narrative, oral history, ethnopoetics and oral performance theory, the nature of textuality, literary feminist fairy tales, and nationalist folklore.

Juliana Wilth is a doctoral student in the Department of German and Slavic Studies at Wayne State University. Her research interests include Berlin and postwar German literature and culture. Her dissertation focuses on the *Wende*-experience by young East Germans and its reverberations in recent literary works.

Jan M. Ziolkowski is Arthur Kingsley Porter Professor of Medieval Latin and chair of the Department of the Classics at Harvard University. He has focused his research on medieval literature, especially in Latin; on the classical tradition; and on the influence of folktales on literature in the Middle Ages.

Adam Zolkover is a graduate student in folklore at Indiana University in Bloomington. His research interests include the history of folklore, folk narrative, and African American folklore. He has previously served as the online editor for *Folklore Forum* and is currently the Modern Language Association's Folklore Bibliography Project coordinator at Indiana University.

ABOUT THE EDITOR

DONALD HAASE is professor of German at Wayne State University. His previous books include *Fairy Tales and Feminism: New Approaches* (2004) and *The Reception of Grimms' Fairy Tales: Responses, Reactions, Revisions* (1993). He is the editor of *Marvels & Tales: Journal of Fairy-Tale Studies*, and his work has appeared in such publications as *Fabula, The Lion and the Unicorn*, and *Proverbium*.